W9-BNH-348

THE WORLD AND THE PARISH

The World and the Parish

Volume Two

UNIVERSITY OF NEBRASKA PRESS · LINCOLN

Selected and edited
with a commentary by
WILLIAM M. CURTIN

WILLA CATHER'S ARTICLES AND REVIEWS, 1893–1902

One of the few really helpful words I ever heard from an older writer, I had from Sarah Orne Jewett when she said to me: "Of course, one day you will write about your own country. In the meantime, get all you can. One must know the world so well before one can know the parish."

WILLA CATHER

International Standard Book Number 0–8032–0706–9
Library of Congress Catalog Card Number 65–10548

Manufactured in the United States of America

Contents

CONTENTS

PART TWO: THE CITY

THE *HOME MONTHLY* · 305

Articles . 308

Reviews . 333

THE MUSICAL WORLD (II) · 375

THE STAR SYSTEM (III) · 420

THE THEATRE (III) · 465

BOOKS AND AUTHORS (IV) · 693

PART THREE: THE WORLD

THE *LIBRARY* · 753

WASHINGTON CORRESPONDENT · 792

GUEST EDITOR OF THE *COURIER* · 836

THE *GAZETTE* · 863

Chronologies appear opposite the first text page of each of the three parts.

Part II

THE CITY

❈ ❈ ❈

Continued from Volume I

Chronology for Part II

1896

July	Willa Cather begins editorial duties on the *Home Monthly* in Pittsburgh.
Fall	Begins contributing play reviews to the *Pittsburg Leader*.
December 6	Begins sending her column "The Passing Show" to the *Journal*.

1897

May 30	Discontinues "The Passing Show" in the *Journal*.
July	While in Red Cloud on vacation, Cather resigns from the *Home Monthly*, but continues to contribute "Old Books and New" column under name of "Helen Delay."
August	Accepts job on *Pittsburg Leader*.
September	Back in Pittsburgh working on the *Leader* telegraph desk and writing play reviews.
October	Begins contributing to *Leader* "Books and Magazines" column. Begins sending "The Passing Show" to the *Courier* on October 23.

1898

February	Spends a week in New York reviewing for the New York *Sun*. Final "Old Books and New" column in the *Home Monthly*.
May 1–15	In Washington, D.C. visiting her cousin Howard Gore.
August	Vacationing in Red Cloud, the Black Hills, and Wyoming.
September	Returns to Pittsburgh. Ill with grippe and goes to stay with the Canfield family in Columbus, Ohio, returning to Pittsburgh in October.
December	Resumes "The Passing Show" in the *Courier*—first column since April 30.

1899

January—December	Continues to work for the *Leader* and to send "The Passing Show" to the *Courier*. Some time during this year meets Isabelle McClung.*
August	In Red Cloud on vacation.
October	Back in Pittsburgh.

1900

March	On March 13 last signed play review in *Leader*. On March 24 first signed contribution in the *Library*.
April	Story, "Eric Hermannson's Soul," in *Cosmopolitan*.
May	On May 12 last "Passing Show" column in the *Courier*.

*The year of this meeting, previously believed to be 1901, was independently ascertained by Bernice Slote and James Woodress, to whom I am indebted for the information.

The Urban Scene

(January 10, 1897—March 18, 1899)

When Willa Cather transferred "The Passing Show" from the Journal *to the* Courier *in the fall of 1897, the editor announced that her contributions would be "in the nature of interviews with distinguished men and women who visit Pittsburgh and criticism—appreciative—of the arts, manners, morals and Women's Clubs of Pittsburgh"* (Courier, *October 23, 1897). But of course "The Passing Show" was much more than that. "The column lived up to its name," E. K. Brown wrote "and if it is not quite a diary of Willa Cather's activities in the East, it permits us to follow her to play and opera, to art gallery and horse show; whatever seized her interest—the latest book, the latest literary gossip, the life of Pittsburgh's Bohemia—was grist to her productive and lively mills."*[1]

Pittsburgh in the late nineties was a city of more than a quarter of a million people, the center of an industrial complex, and its great men were such tycoons as Andrew Carnegie and Henry C. Frick (iron and steel), Andrew Mellon (aluminum and banking), George Westinghouse (air brakes and electricity), and H. J. Heinz (food processing). It could hardly have been more unlike Lincoln, let alone Red Cloud, but Willa Cather seems to have had little difficulty in adjusting to the new atmosphere. Her letters to Lincoln friends in the 1896–1898 period frequently express satisfaction with the fullness of her social life (stressing—perhaps even overstressing—that it is conventional rather than bohemian) and tell of paying calls, of theatres, concerts, parties, and excursions—for example, a picnic excursion with the Press Club.[2] *Among her friends were the Gerwigs—she had known George Gerwig during University days in Lincoln; the George Seibels, whom she met in connection with her work on the* Home Monthly; *the actress Lizzie Hudson Collier; the Edwin Hatfield Andersons—he was the chief*

1. Brown, *Willa Cather*, p. 88.

2. See especially Willa Cather to Mariel Gere, August 4 and 10, 1896; April 25, 1897; n.d. [September 19, 1897]; January 10, 1898; March 7, 1898. In a letter to Will Owen Jones written from Red Cloud, August 31, 1897, she admitted that she overdid her social life in Pittsburgh, but said she had been flattered by the many attentions paid to her.

librarian of the Carnegie Institute Library; and May Willard, who was the children's librarian there. The Canfield family had moved to Columbus, Ohio, in 1895, when James Canfield became president of Ohio State University, and Dorothy Canfield visited Willa Cather on more than one occasion. Add to this list the many people whom she met in the course of her professional activities, and it is clear that the circle of her acquaintances was wide and varied; indeed, it ranged from Christopher Magee (1848–1901), political boss of Pittsburgh,[3] *to matrons in the city's many women's clubs.*

Rather surprisingly, in view of the sentiments she had expressed earlier,[4] *Willa Cather was active at least to some degree in these clubs. Soon after her arrival in 1896 she was taken by Mrs. Gerwig to a tea for the City Federation of women's clubs, and the subject for discussion was Carlyle. Called on for impromptu remarks, Willa Cather stunned the ladies by reeling off her old essay on Carlyle—her first published work—and became the heroine of the occasion.*[5] *While there may be no causal connection, still a year later, in her* Courier *column for November 6, 1897, she admitted belonging to six clubs.*

The following chapter, which is largely comprised of social comment on the Pittsburgh scene and of interviews with distinguished visitors, projects Cather's sense of involvement in a larger world than the "town and gown" world of Lincoln. Though she probably never thought of Pittsburgh as home, she could enter imaginatively into the homecoming of three of its sons—Charles Stanley Reinhart, a painter; Ethelbert Nevin, musical prodigy and composer; and Lieutenant F. W. Jenkins, a young naval officer—and the significance she gives to each of these homecomings is a measure of Willa Cather's understanding of the society of Pittsburgh in the late nineties.

Presbyteria and Bohemia

In a 1900 article Willa Cather wrote that "perhaps no other city in the United States has given a more prominent place to its clergy, either in pulpit or social life, than has Pittsburgh."[6] *Since more than half the congregations in the city were Presbyterian,*[7] *the mores of this denomination*

3. In a letter to Will Owen Jones, January 15, 1897, Willa Cather told of two talks with Magee when she applied for a job on one of his papers (the *Times* and the *News*).

4. See the second selection in "Town and Gown," The Local Scene (II), above.

5. Willa Cather to Mariel Gere, August 4, 1896. For the Carlyle essay, see *KA*, pp. 421–425.

6. "Out of Their Pulpits," *Library*, April 14, 1900, p. 7. In the same paragraph Cather speaks of Pittsburgh's "subservience to the most rigid of blue laws."

7. Baldwin, *Pittsburgh: The Story of a City*, p. 251.

did a good deal to set the tone of at least one stratum of Pittsburgh life. Elizabeth Moorhead, a friend of Willa Cather in her Pittsburgh years, has described the Presbyterianism of that day and place: "[It] offered little encouragement to any sort of artistic activity. Physical comfort was admissible, yes—the good Presbyterian was by no means an ascetic—but duty was the law of life. Aesthetic impulses too often led to a dangerous laxity. The Scotch-Irish, so-called, had brought to Western Pennsylvania their stern Calvinistic doctrine and rule of conduct, not at all incompatible with a materialism which had been fostered no doubt by the struggle for survival. They meant to get on in the world."[8] *A representative "good Presbyterian" was Henry Clay Frick (1849–1919), chairman and manager of the Carnegie Steel Company, who broke the notorious 1892 strike at the steel mills at Homestead, near Pittsburgh, by using Pinkerton men and the state militia. Cather's comments on Frick and his milieu were, of course, intended for Lincoln readers, not for publication in Pittsburgh.*

I suppose all Lincoln readers of that naughty but mighty clever paper, *Town Topics*, know all about Mr. H. C. Frick's little theatrical supper and the breeze it made here. It was this way. Mr. Frick gave a little supper to the Childs boys [Frick's brothers-in-law] who are going abroad. He had his little supper at the Duquesne Club—everything "swell" here is called either "Duquesne" or "Carnegie"—clubs, theatres, parks, lakes, hotels, everything that is big and expensive. During the course of the supper Mr. Frick got the fair and fascinating Anna Held to come over from the theatre and sing to his friends for a consideration of five hundred dollars. At first all went well, but after the champagne had been flowing freely Anna began to sing her seductive little gem, "O, Won't You Come and Play with Me?" and the crowd got so frightfully merry that mademoiselle's manager had to pick her up bodily and take her to her hotel. Now all Pittsburgh is divided into two parts. Presbyteria and Bohemia, and the former is much the larger and more influential kingdom of the two. So

8. Elizabeth Moorhead, *These Two Were Here: Louise Homer and Willa Cather* (Pittsburgh: University of Pittsburgh Press, 1950), p. 19. Cf. Willa Cather's description of a Pittsburgh businessman, Marshall McKann, in "A Gold Slipper": "He had no rooted dislike for pretty women; he didn't even deny that gay girls had their place in the world, but they ought to be kept in their place. He was born a Presbyterian, just as he was born a McKann. . . . His religion was not very spiritual, certainly, but it was substantial and concrete, made up of good, hard convictions and opinions. It had something to do with citizenship, with whom one ought to marry, with the coal business (in which his own name was powerful), with the Republican party, and with all majorities and established precedents." *Youth and the Bright Medusa*, p. 131–132.

Mr. Frick's little escapade didn't go down very well. No one thought much about the Childs boys, but Mr. Frick is a gentleman well along in years, who is a pillar in the church and directs the manifold interests of the Carnegie Steel Company, and writes didactic articles on "How to Succeed in Life" for the *Youth's Companion*, and people were surprised at him. He is the same Mr. Frick, by the way, who made all that sensation about being shot at years ago just after the Homestead strike. He wasn't shot at all, as everyone here knows, but his would-be assassin is doing time in the pen just the same.[9]

Journal, January 10, 1897, p. 13.

The good Presbyterians of Pittsburgh have had a great deal to trouble their souls of late. Last week it was Mr. Frick's little supper at the Duquesne Club, and now it is Frederic Archer's Sunday organ recitals.[10] Mr. Archer is, of course, the leading musician of Pittsburgh. As an organist he is without a peer in America, and as a conductor and composer he is almost equally noted. For over a year he has been giving free organ recitals at the Carnegie Music Hall on Friday afternoons and Saturday evenings. On Saturday night the hall was always crowded, but this is too busy a place to get a large audience on Friday afternoon. The public petitioned the board of trustees to allow Mr. Archer to give his recitals on Sunday afternoons instead of Friday. It was done, and since then hundreds of people have been turned away at the door every Sunday afternoon, and the crowd begins pouring into the hall an hour before the first number is played. The audience is made up almost entirely of musical people. There is a large German element here, the so-called "Pennsylvania Dutch," who are not nearly so black as they are painted, and who for the most part represent about all the culture there is in Pittsburgh. Most of these people are engaged in humble occupations, but if it were not for them bookstores and concert halls would be wholly superfluous things in Pittsburgh. Sunday is the only day of leisure they have, and they go in crowds whereever there is good music to be heard. The Carnegie is full of them every Sunday afternoon, and their proud enjoyment of the music is something refreshing to see.

Now the Presbyterian church of Pittsburgh objects to enjoyment of all kinds, particularly aesthetic enjoyment. It was slow to become aroused to the awful iniquity of playing Mozart and Wagner and Beethoven on

9. Alexander Berkman, an anarchist, was convicted of shooting and stabbing Frick.
10. See the introduction to The Musical Scene (II).

Sunday, but when it is aroused it is an awful force. It is now holding mass meetings in Pittsburgh and mass meetings in Allegheny and petitioning the board of trustees and denouncing Archer, the flesh and the devil. At one of these mass meetings Rev. Harvey Henderson, one of the leading divines, said: "First, it is well settled among Anglo-Saxon nations that neither amusements nor labor should be carried on on the Sabbath. These recitals are to entertain, to amuse, not to educate. Music is a means of expressing human emotion, human feelings; also a means of arousing human emotions and human feelings. It is not an educating force. It fits in any place. It is found in churches, and also in places near the gates of hell. It has no moral quality."

Ah, "a means of arousing human emotion," that is the seat of the trouble. There is nothing on the earth that a Pittsburgh Presbyterian fears and hates as he does the "human emotion." He has no particular objection to greed or ignorance or selfishness or any other undemonstrative sin, but emotion is his synonym for wrong. Perhaps that system of repression is one reason why his people go hear Anna Held and give suppers at the Duquesne Club.

Of course, Archer plays only classical music, very much the same sort of program that Mr. Hagenow's excellent string quartette used to give at the Universalist Church, and which really did so much toward musical culture in Lincoln.[11] But that makes no difference. The Pittsburgh Presbyterian is not a discriminating gentleman, and he cannot be made to see that there is any difference between a sonata of Beethoven's and "Rastus on Parade," or between Julia Marlowe and a couchee-couchee dancer. He is suspicious of any public gathering except a funeral. The fate of Mr. Archer's organ recitals has not yet been decided. But the Dark Ages are slowly disappearing even from Pittsburgh, and it is probable that people will go down to the Carnegie on Sunday afternoon and drink in the depraving melodies of Bach and Schumann and Haydn for years to come. As for Mr. Archer, however, that great artist's attitude is one of indifferent scorn. When a committee of ministers called on him to inform him that "ethically an organ recital on the Sabbath was just as depraving as a minstrel show," he smiled and behaved like the courteous gentleman that he is. For, after all, as he said, "Why waste rhetoric upon men who are spiritually deaf? I am a musician, not a reformer. If they don't want music, I can keep still. There are other cities."

Journal, January 17, 1897, p. 13.

11. See "Too Much Mendelssohn," The Musical World (I), above.

This is the great and glorious week of the horse show, the town has literally blossomed in orange and red and is full of "horsey" women. You can spot them wherever you meet them by their loud neckties and diamond scarf pins and yellow gloves. There are horsewomen from all over the world, from England and the south of France and from all over These States as Walt Whitman put it, and there is one glorious Russian who is almost as big and dark and dangerous looking as the charger she rides.

Of course there is no reason in the world why Pittsburgh should have a horse show, but New York has one and that is pretext enough. We spend our time down here trying to fancy that we live in Gotham. Really, I think I never saw anything funnier than the opening night of that show. The big hall of the riding school was gorgeously decorated in orange and red and the palms and magnolia trees and cut roses were so thick that the whole thing looked as overdone as Pittsburgh festivities usually do. The boxes were adorned like booths at a charity fair and the occupants were in battle array and had come to do execution. There was the Carnegie box and the Magee box and the Darlington box[12] and all the rest of them, seventy in all, and all filled with Gainsborough hats and white gloves and "swallow tails" and "Prince Alberts" and "Tuxedos" and silk hats of the latest shapes and neckties that cried aloud unto heaven. The boxes were so sprinkled with diamonds that from the front the view was quite dazzling. The gallery was packed with all the people in Allegheny who could dress and wear jewels if they might not have boxes. I never knew the presence of diamonds to become so oppressive, they cast a glitter over the whole affair that was not exactly one of elegance. The riders, men and women, were loafing about the judges' stand, surrounded by a crowd of grooms. The men made very stunning figures and the women were most of them dressed about like Isadore Rush when she appeared in Reed's play *The Politician* at the Funke a few years ago.[13] Most everyone had her silk hat tilted at an angle and gestured with her whip a great deal. The big Russian woman who was all in black with crimson at her throat stood rather apart from the rest of them and bit impatiently at her whip handle which was studded with diamonds—probably so as not to be conspicuous.

Every old coachman and stable boy in Pittsburgh had been arrayed in blue coats and white breeches and yellow-topped boots for the august

12. Frederick Darlington (1867–1943), former Westinghouse executive, at this time with the United Electric and Power Company.

13. Cather had reviewed Roland Reed in *The Politician*, *Courier*, September 5, 1895, p. 8; *KA*, 277–278. She also had reviewed him in *The Wrong Mr. Wright*, possibly her first review for the *Leader*, September 22, 1896, p. 9.

occasion and stood about helplessly, a sorry conglomeration of all sizes and types and nationalities. Some of them wore beards and some of them wore moustaches and all of them looked nervous. Now it was almost eight o'clock and the young "bloods" of the town had not yet appeared, that is, not the most blooded of the bloods. Presently they arrived in "tuxedos" and chrysanthemums and yellow gloves. Well, they didn't do a thing but hustle the grooms out and hunt up a barber and have every one of them shaved clean in the dressing rooms! You see this is the first horse show they have ever conducted and they forgot a few things. Presently those poor grooms came back looking cold and blue and more nervous than ever, and the Russian brunette saw what it all meant and threw back her head and laughed and thought some thoughts to herself.

Anon the "bloods" were settled in their boxes and had their glasses out and the gates opened and six tandems trotted out on the tan bark. Then the fun began, or rather it didn't begin. You see most of these people had never really been to a horse show before, they had only read about them in the New York *Sunday World*, and they didn't at all know how to act. They had kept all the dressmakers and tailors in the town busy for a month, and now they were out to be [a] credit to their town and to their great and glorious state. They had an awful sense of responsibility and a vague notion that this great function must be taken seriously—something like a grand opera. Yes, they had their grand opera airs on; they bore their gorgeous apparel and sat in those boxes as rigid as if they had been frozen. I didn't see a smile or hear an animated conversation the whole evening. They didn't stroll about to each other's boxes, they didn't go down to visit the stalls, they didn't do any of those things which people are supposed to do at horse shows. As someone remarked, "I should think just from looking at pictures in *Harper's Weekly* they'd know enough to walk at a horse show!" But they didn't. They sat glued to their chairs, bolt upright, rigid and impassive, just as they sit in their dear Presbyterian churches when they are hearing about that hot old time to come. At the other end of the hall the orchestra droned away at slow waltzes and dead marches and as the driving was perfectly noiseless no other sound broke the stillness but the sizzle and gutter of the arc lights. Sometimes for a half hour at a stretch this appalling stillness would weigh down upon us, until it seemed as if one was at some sort of military funeral. Even when the magnificent Russian jumped hurdles the applause was quite correct and formal as at an opera, though you could see people's eyes glitter with excitement. There is no getting away from a Presbyterian environment, no getting around it, or behind it, or above it. It is ever present, even at horse shows.

Of course the most sensible beings present were down in the horse stalls. They were not Presbyterians, nor were they covered with diamonds, and everything they did was in good taste. But I know as little about horses as most of the people who were present.

Courier, October 23, 1897, p. 8.

Charles Stanley Reinhart

This article on the artist Charles Stanley Reinhart (1844–1896) is a precursor of Willa Cather's 1905 story "The Sculptor's Funeral."[14] *Reinhart gained an international reputation, first as an illustrator for* Harper's Monthly *(1870–1871), then as a painter. His famous large painting "Washed Ashore" was exhibited at the Paris Salon of 1887 and at the Chicago Columbian Exposition in 1893. He was represented by a single work at the dedication of the Carnegie Museum in 1895, but Cather might have seen three of his drawings at the Chicago Art Institute in the summer of 1896. In the* Home Monthly, *October 1896, she included an article on Reinhart by Lawrence Brinton.*

I went out yesterday to the cemetery on the Allegheny River to see the stone erected by his family to Charles Stanley Reinhart lifted into place. It was just a little over a year ago that I went to his funeral. Since I have come to know the town that man's life and work seem as wonderful as a fairy tale. I have heard the story of his life over and over from Gustave Leiser, an artist here who went to Munich to study with Reinhart and who never wearies of talking of him. Anyone who has not lived here can not realize how incongruous, how little short of miserable it is for an artist to come out of Pittsburgh. Why, we only see the sun, who is the father of art, about sixty days out of the year. It is easy enough to understand why lads born in some cities of the world should love art, or even lads in the villages where life is left to form itself. But Charles Stanley Reinhart was born in a purely commercial town, a town of great industries and almost incalculable national resources, then the head of the great river traffic down the Ohio and Mississippi to New Orleans, the center of the rich oil regions, a town red the year around with the light of mighty furnaces, where crude iron is torn from the heart of the earth and forged into steel and sent to all the

14. Bennett, "Willa Cather in Pittsburgh," pp. 70–71. The story was first published in *McClure's* in January 1905, and first collected in *The Troll Garden; CSF*, 173–185.

seaports of the world. A town in which the war for wealth is waged to the uttermost, in which money is omnipotent and success is measured only by decimal points. It passes understanding, almost, that from such a city such a man should come. But Our Lady of Art has strange caprices and she selects her votaries from no one nation or among no one people. She gave to this lad from a smoky manufacturing town what she has denied to many an eager aspirant in older and foreign cities of the world, and quickened in him that one delicate fiber, which hides somewhere in the brain and controls our sense of beauty until Reinhart's was as sensible to form as the eye to light. Leiser has told me how he and "Stars" used to stand together on the old Twenty-Second Street bridge watching the glare of the iron furnaces along the Monongahela at night and the heights of Mount Washington studded with lights until it looked like a great honeycomb of fire. How they used to watch the river steamers bound for New Orleans and dream of lands with fair skies, where the sun shone always and where art was more than a name.

Then came the long weary struggle of his young manhood, his apprenticeship in a railroad office and a shipping office, the indignation of his family and his friends when he threw up an excellent position to go to Munich to study art. For art was considered as something frivolous, entirely beneath a brilliant young man of good family; a trivial thing, like play-acting, possibly immoral, certainly not remunerative. But the "madness of art" had bitten the boy deeply. If art does not often claim a man, when she does, she claims him irrevocably, for life and death.

Of his heroic labors in Germany and Paris, the unremitting toil by which he made up for the neglected years of his youth, I will not attempt to tell, it takes my friend Leiser to do that. As to what he did, you all admired his work in Harper's publications for years. You all saw his picture "Washed Ashore" at the fair in Chicago and felt in it that same mysterious charm of the vast sea spaces which haunts Pierre Loti's novels.

And yet he was so strangely loyal to the country of his youth. Yes, loyal even to grimy Pittsburgh. If Reinhart had been born in Venice when the wings of the lion still ruled the Mediterranean he might have painted doges and madonnas. But he was born in an unlovely age and in a most unlovely city, and a man can not escape the environment of youth; he can only realize its values unseen of other men. This man was born among American laborers, and they were his theme all his life. He knew the dignity of labor—and the tragedy of it. He drew the common man at all forms of trial and recreation; the mechanic, the tradesman, the soldier, the sailor, the politician. Mr. Gibson might be styled the artist of the Four Hundred, but Reinhart was the artist of the people. He was loyal, as all great souls must be, to the form of life he knew, to the people whose suffering he had shared.

Well, last summer they brought him home again, this man who had pursued Art's fleeting shadow unto the ends of the earth, brought him home to art-less Pittsburgh to keep his long watch beside the Allegheny. And no one here knew or cared. The daily papers had a paragraph or two about him. A number of artists and literary men and several great editors came down from New York with his body, but his death was not even known in Pittsburgh. "Reinhart dead? Oh, yes; his brother is a fellow of some means I guess.[15] Stanley never amounted to much." I heard that a hundred times.

There were not a hundred people at his funeral. Scarcely anyone here knows that he is dead or that he even lived. Yet he was the one man from all those thousands who went out and made a world-wide name, who left great works behind him and a tangible memory in the minds of men. Now even from his grave one can see the red light of the furnaces, those innumerable never resting furnaces that melt down the very lives and souls of men into iron. I never knew the emptiness of fame until I went to that great man's funeral. I never knew how entirely one must live and die alone until that day when they brought Stanley Reinhart home.

Courier, October 23, 1897, p. 9.

Will H. Low and Bouguereau

The prize Willa Cather mentions below was to be awarded at the second annual Founder's Day competition of the Carnegie Institute Art Galleries. Among the more prominent of the judges were Winslow Homer (1836–1910), who had won first prize at the inaugural competition with his painting "The Wreckers"; William M. Chase (1849–1916), president of the Society of American Artists; John La Farge (1835–1910), landscape and figure painter; Will H. Low (1853–1932), Willa Cather's guide through the gallery; and Frank Benson, whose work she had admired at the Haydon Art Club exhibition in Lincoln (see The Local Scene [I]). The other judges were Edwin Lord Weeks (1849–1903), painter of oriental subjects; Frank Duveneck (1848–1919), influential Cincinnati art teacher and painter;

15. His brother Joseph was a railroad and financial expert, subsequently president of the St. Louis and Santa Fe Railroad.

Cecelia Beaux (1863–1942), who won the bronze medal at the inaugural competition; Edmund C. Tarbell (1862–1939), an American impressionist; and John M. Swan (1847–1910), British painter and sculptor. The French painter Adolphe W. Bouguereau (1825–1905), who is also discussed, had six canvases in the Carnegie Institute collection.

Last week I called Pittsburgh an artless city. Heavens! If we haven't had "art" thrust upon us from all quarters this week. You see an international committee of artists—or as one newspaper put it—"a committee of international artists," has been here judging the pictures from all over the world that are to be exhibited at the Carnegie gallery next month and deciding which shall have Carnegie's five-thousand-dollar prize. Of course the awards will not be announced yet, that comes off November third, when Andrew Carnegie—you see I put Andrew first—and President McKinley, who owes Andrew half a million dollars worth of votes and knows it, and all the rest of the push will be here.

The committee is made up of the following gentlemen: Winslow Homer, of Scarborough, Me.; E. C. Tarbell, of Boston; William M. Chase, of New York; Will H. Low, of New York; Miss Cecelia Beaux, Edwin Lord Weeks, of Paris; John M. Swan, of London; John La Farge, of New York; Frank Duveneck, of Covington, Ky., and Frank W. Benson, of Salem, Mass.

I was lucky enough to be invited to a dinner given for these gentlemen, and I basely bribed the hostess to ask Mr. Low to take me to dinner. Not because he was Will H. Low, but because he was Robert Louis Stevenson's dearest and nearest friend, the man to whom *The Wrecker* was dedicated. In the words of an immortal poet he

> Talked of many things;
> Of seas and ships and sealing wax,
> Of cabbages and kings.

That is not quoted correctly, and I know someone in Lincoln who will catch me up on it, but never mind. . . .

I will not attempt to speak of the other artists of that august assemblage. Edwin Lord Weeks' accent alone would deserve a column, and Cecelia Beaux's dinner gown deserves a whole *Courier*. She paints such pretty clothes, I wonder why she wears such awful ones.

The next day Mr. Low smuggled me into the gallery where the public —and particularly that part of the public which follows my occupation—

are not yet admitted. I wanted to speak with him about the only picture of Bouguereau's I admire, the picture of a little peasant girl which was bought and brought to Pittsburgh years ago. He said, "O yes, I remember well. Bouguereau asked me if I had seen anything of his *bonne enfant* the last time I was in Paris. O yes, it's good—too good to be repeated, by him at least. He did that years ago when he was a young fellow and poor enough to be sincere."

That was all I wanted to know. I should like to own that picture, but you would never know it was a Bouguereau. I never saw anything else of his at all like it. It is just a little brown peasant girl sitting on a hillside, with her clothing stained with the juice of the vintage and a basket of grapes in her lap. She has nothing of the flashing, unnatural perfection of the Bouguereau women, nothing of that gleaming skin, that virginal, sexless flesh tint that has made him famous and hateful. On the contrary, she is brown, quite brown, and even a little dirty. She is not of the half world of Paris, but a child of the soil, very near to the earth. Her little bare feet are in the wet grass and her toes are curled under a little from the chill of the dew. Her coarse little hands are crossed in her lap, and her eyes are looking wistfully into the distance; sadly, almost as if she looked into the years to come and saw the shameful success that awaited the man who created her. For she was done long ago, before Bouguereau began to paint for gambling halls and barkeepers and Americans.

I wonder if sometimes, as he sits in his magnificent studio in Paris, with its miles and miles of gleaming canvases, its hundreds of white limbs and perfect curves, he does not sicken of the hateful tint that has made him what he is, and close his eyes for a moment and long for this little brown peasant girl, painted by a hopeful boy in the days of the long ago, before he was successful and rich and famous—and despised, and I wonder if he does not almost yearn to be that honest boy again.

Hélas, hélas, les jours d'autrefois!

Courier, October 30, 1897, p. 3.

Philistines on the March

*The Brooklyn woman who opposed the placing of a statue of Heine in Prospect Park was Elizabeth Grannis (1840–1926), president of the National Christian League for Promotion of Purity. Two years earlier Willa Cather had written about the opposition to a Heine statue (*Journal, *December 15, 1895;* KA, *p. 204). The poem used as an epigraph was her own translation.*

The Errand

Arise, arise, my trusty page;
  Saddle your horse, then spring
Upon his back and speed away
  To the palace of the king.
There seek some stable boy or groom,
  And ask of him, "I pray,
Tell me which daughter of the king
  Becomes a bride today?"

And if he says, "The dark-haired one,"
  Bring me the news with speed,
But if he says, "The light-haired one,"
  You need not urge your steed,
But leisurely retrace your way
  In silence, till you see
The rope-walk. Buy a good, stout cord
  And fetch it home to me.

From the German of Heine

The Germans here are rabid at the petition of the Brooklyn women to prevent the erection of a statue of Heine in Prospect Park. But the Germans are prone to take everything too seriously—even Heine. Heine himself would scarcely have taken this affair seriously. He might, indeed, have written a satirical couplet or two and made the Brooklyn dames immortal by way of a generous revenge. It does not matter at all whether Brooklyn has a statue of Heine or not. People who read Heine need no reminder of him, and people who do not read him would never be any the wiser for one. The Brooklyn ladies say that "Prospect Park reflects the smile of God" and that Heine was a depraved man and a poet and his image would seriously interfere with the lofty suggestions of their park. That is all right, let the Brooklyn people have what they want. They want a new fountain and they want it upon the statue of some *littérateur* whose influence would not be harmful to youth. Very well, this is a free country. Let them have a John [Josiah] Gilbert Holland fountain, or an E. P. Roe fountain, or a Ruth Ashmore fountain;[16] who cares? It is thoroughly foolish and useless to dash one's foot against a stone or to attempt to correct the taste of the Philistine.

16. Josiah Gilbert Holland (1819–1881), co-founder of *Scribner's Monthly*, and a sentimental and didactic poet; E. P. Roe (1838–1888), author of religious novels. For Ruth Ashmore, see note 9, The Star System (III), above.

Just a little while before he died Heine wrote, "Alas! the irony of God weighs heavily upon me. The great author of the universe, the Aristophanes of the heavens, wishes to show the petty, earthly, so-called German Aristophanes how immeasurably he excels me in humor and in colossal wit. . . . [*Author's ellipsis.*] But I venture to most submissively offer the suggestion that the sport which the master has inflicted upon his poor pupil is rather too long drawn out."[17]

Yet it seems that the Lord has not had his little joke out with Heine. And on whatever Stygian shore that restless and glowing spirit wanders, be sure he appreciates the jest. One can almost hear the echo of that old Mephistophelian laughter from the Rue d'Amsterdam.

I myself do not think he was the proper sort of person to build a statue to in a Brooklyn park. What, the man who had himself carried to the Louvre and lifting with his finger one paralytic eyelid before the Venus de Milo, wept and complained that her lost arms were pressing the feeble life from him; this man in Brooklyn? Perish the thought! Arise, Elizabeth Grannis, and glut your ire!

> Alas! What are all these destinies thus driven
> pell-mell? Whither go they? Why are they so?
> He who knows that, sees all the shadow.
> He is alone. His name is God.
>
> Victor Hugo

Brooklyn is not the only place where they are solicitous of the welfare of "youth." Youth is commanding general attention in Pennsylvania just now. *Les Misérables* has just been thrown out of the high school library of Philadelphia as an unfitting work for youthful minds. As someone has remarked, "After a while they will leave us nothing but Rabelais and the Bible." The affair has been discussed pro and con by all the newspapers in the state and the result is that more copies of the book have been sold in Pennsylvania in the last three weeks than of any other work of fiction, Marie Corelli's latest not excluded. It has been a Hugo renaissance. Every shopgirl and floorwalker carries a *Les Misérables* on the streetcars. If Victor Hugo were alive and had an American press agent I should know it was a deep laid plot. As it is I have my suspicion that the Philadelphia school board is made up of publishers.

I can remember a time when I would have taken this very seriously and wailed to the extent of several columns and refused to be comforted.

17. From the "Confessions." See *Prose Writings of Heinrich Heine*, pp. 325–326.

But what is the use of invective? The thing did good all around; it made a good story for the newspapers, is a magnificent slam on Philadelphia, showed up a few long-eared officials in their proper shaggy coats, and induced thousands of people to read a great classic.

If one took things hard in a land where Heine fountains are forbidden, and *Les Misérables* thrown out of the libraries, and Lillian Russell considered a great artist and Cuban maidens rescued by enterprising journalists, there would be nothing left to one but suicide or insanity.[18]

Courier, November 6, 1897, p. 2.

The President in Pittsburgh

President William McKinley arrived in Pittsburgh on November 3, 1897, to award the prizes at the Founder's Day exhibition of the Carnegie Institute Art Galleries (see "Will H. Low and Bouguereau," above). That evening Giuseppe Campanari (1855–1927), baritone of the Metropolitan Opera, sang at a concert with the Pittsburgh Symphony Orchestra under the direction of Frederic Archer. As an epigraph for the column Cather quoted from poem XXII of Housman's Shropshire Lad, *which begins: "The street sounds to the soldier's tread, / And out we troop to see...."*

The air was full of music and the streets were full of soldiers. There were soldiers everywhere, for it was Pittsburgh's great day, the day when the McKinleys tarried here.

The President reached Pittsburgh at 11:15 a.m. The approach of the special train was signaled to Battery B, and the guns, which were placed high upon the bluff over the river, began firing the presidential salute. Then the cheering began and it lasted until the President stepped upon the platform at Union Station, and then it was not cheering any more, but the roar of a hurricane, all the noise twenty thousand throats could send into the frosty air.

It is really a great occasion when a big city relaxes itself, when business is suspended in a town where business is paramount, and all the diversified

18. An allusion to the rescue from prison of Evangelina Cisneros, niece of the President of the Cuban revolutionaries, by a reporter for Hearst's New York *Journal*. Much of the remainder of this column concerned the case. Cather wrote that she was "rather interested in poor Evangelina Cisneros, though perhaps that is because one of the six clubs I belong to is at present discussing the 'Working Girl Problem in Spain.'" She went on to compare Cisneros to Anna Held, Bob Fitzsimmons, and Yvette Guilbert, who "all appeal to the same vulgar passion, all are ranked alike as features of the show which must divert that mighty mob from itself and relieve the ennui of a great city."

and antagonistic interests of half a million people are for the moment forgotten and a common enthusiasm makes men akin indeed. The town literally went mad; to be gay was the business of life. The streetcars on Fifth Avenue were stopped, the stores were deserted, everything shut down but the iron mills and I doubt if the advent of the Messiah would stop those.

The parade was a great sight, seen from the balcony built in front of the *Leader* office on Fifth Avenue. The 14th regiment came swinging up the hill like old veterans—they served in the big Homestead strike and know the smell of powder—and the regimental band was playing "El Capitan" as though the day of joy had come. Down the hillside as far as you could see they were coming, regiment after regiment. The sky was almost as blue as a western sky—almost—and where the sunlight came here and there between the tall skyscrapers it cast broad bands of gold over that interminable line of men, making their muskets glitter like silver. At last the President's carriage came surrounded by detectives—but he didn't need them. He was in the arms of his people, so to speak. There wasn't a bluecoat out of all those hundreds who wouldn't have stood up and been shot at all day for him. And as he came from those thronged streets there went up a cry that will always echo in one's ears. It was so gigantic, this elephantine glee of the multitude, this transcendent passion of patriotism before which everything else is dwarfed and pale. It was like a mighty Wagnerian chorus.

Mrs. McKinley was met at the depot by Mrs. Robert Pitcairn, wife of the superintendent of the Pennsylvania railroad, and driven directly to their residence, Cairncarque, where, in the afternoon, Mrs. Pitcairn gave a luncheon to her friends in honor of her guest. Never before was I present at anything so truly gorgeous. It was one of those rare things that are not overdone and yet leave nothing to be wished for. The floral decorations were from New York and Sherry of New York did the catering. Everything moved on velvet wheels. Outside the house the grounds and streets were packed with people under the charge of a score of policemen but inside there were just guests enough to fill the rooms comfortably. The parlors were simply lined with chrysanthemums of that magnificent pink variety which was named after Mrs. Robert Pitcairn. The dining rooms were in green palms and ferns, no flowers visible except the gorgeous American beauties on the tables. But the staircase was the *chef d'oeuvre*. It is some twelve feet wide with a big curve toward the top. The white and gold chrysanthemums were so thick upon it as to only leave room for people to descend two abreast. I should hate to have had to count the thousands of blossoms on that stairway. Presently two boys in livery descended to make sure that the way was clear. Then the orchestra began playing the waltz song from Gounod's *Roméo et Juliette* very softly, and Mrs. McKinley came down the staircase on Mrs. Pitcairn's arm, between the serried ranks of chrysanthemums under the soft light that fell through the stained glass windows. . . .

In the evening of this eventful day the Pittsburgh orchestra opened its season at the Carnegie Music Hall with Campanari as soloist. Of course the house was gorgeous, even before the boxes were filled. The dress circle on that occasion extended from the gallery to the footlights. There was not a sack coat in the house, not a woman who was not a triumph of costume. Pittsburgh audiences are not ordinarily what a New Yorker would call "smart." Perhaps the people are too careless to think dressing worth while, perhaps they are too rich to think it necessary, perhaps they are too lazy to think of it at all. But when they really consider it incumbent upon them, they can accomplish it.

The President set a good example to the nation by appearing at the concert on time. Promptly at eight o'clock he entered his box at the upper righthand side. The orchestra rose to their feet, playing the national hymn, the audience rising after them like one man, and there was not a heart in that multitude which did not beat to that music.

Of course no one was in a concert frame of mind. The cannon smoke had not wholly cleared from the air and the same Fourth of July spirit that had exulted in the streets in the morning was there, ineffectually disguised in a dress coat and opera hat. No one listened to the first number; Beethoven's Symphony in C major. It would have taken something more penetrating than that weakest and most immature symphony of the symphonic master to have caught the attention of that restless crowd. On the whole, considering the occasion, the number was not a fortunate selection. During the andante movement, Governor and Mrs. Hastings, attended by Mr. and Mrs. George Westinghouse, Jr., entered their box on the upper left side.[19]

And here I must digress upon the famous Mrs. George Westinghouse, Jr.—never forget the Jr. Everyone knows that George Westinghouse is the foremost manufacturer of electrical apparatus in America, employing

19. Daniel Hastings, governor of Pennsylvania (1895–1899); George Westinghouse (1846–1914), inventor of the Westinghouse air brake and organizer of the Westinghouse Electric Company.

hundreds of men—who, by the way, are called the Westinghouse slaves—and is a mighty man. Nicola Tesla himself went to work under him. But Mrs. George, when he married her, was not exactly a reputable person—she now looks like a circus rider well along on the downgrade. Now, although money is potent, Presbyterian Pittsburgh still draws the line on a few things, and it drew a large black one on Mrs. George Westinghouse, "Jr." Her servant-girl physiognomy did not help her out either, and she wears an artificial complexion and had her hair—well, treated with "sea baths," as they say in Lincoln. I really never encountered such an extraordinary person in reputable society. Once upon a time some generous woman did invite her to a reception, and Mrs. George took a boy in buttons along to hold up her train and entered the drawing room like a princess of the blood when princesses did such things. One of the guests, a really fine woman, was overcome by the situation and laughed. Mrs. George made a face at her and flounced back into her carriage and went away in tears. After that she shook the smoke of Pittsburgh out of her peroxide tresses and dwells haughtily apart at Lenox, Mass. Their magnificent residence here is called "Solitude," and very fittingly so, for she only deigns to visit her liege lord once every few years on state occasions. She came back last winter to entertain Count Hilkoff, the Russian minister of transportation, and this winter she came back with the McKinleys and left with them. Where or how the McKinleys picked her up, I don't know.

Well, back to the concert. The second number was Campanari's solo, "Vision Fugitive," from Massenet's *Hérodiade*.[20] I had not heard it before, but it was like all Massenet's music, full of that ever present sensuous spirituality of his, like Rossetti's verses, hinting of the warfare between the flesh and the spirit and giving the victory quite frankly and joyously to the flesh, as Massenet always does, but full of vague, delicious yearning. And ah, how he sang it! That little Italian is a man of fire. The applause was tremendous; Mrs. Westinghouse, who doesn't know Massenet from Marmalade, leading. As an encore he sang the Toreador's song, from *Carmen*. And I tell you, for the moment, that little Italian peasant was greater than all the great men before him. Yet after hearing the Signor in opera, I always half regret to hear him in the colder and less individual work of a concert singer. A dress suit is a wet blanket with him; he is freer in a plumed hat with a sword slung to his side. . . .

20. This was the aria sung by Clement Sebastian when he tried out Lucy Gayheart as an accompanist. See *Lucy Gayheart* (New York: Alfred A. Knopf, Inc., 1935), p. 35. See also "Massenet's *Eve*," The Musical World (II), above. Cather had heard Campanari as Ford in Verdi's *Falstaff*; see The Musical World (I), above.

The program closed with Tchaikovsky's glorious overture "1812" played even better than I heard the Boston Symphony Orchestra do it last spring, and with the chimes that Theodore Thomas always uses in its production, loaned by him for this occasion. Such a day could not have been closed more fittingly than by that marvellous expression of the transcendent passion of patriotism that celebrated the downfall of Napoleon's dreams of universal empire and the glorious triumph of Russia and the Greek church. The triumph of the new Russia, that sleeping Titan of the Steppes for the first time awakened, "up-thrust, out-staggering on the world." And it seemed that the bells booming from the Church of the Redeemer in Moscow were ringing the triumph of patriotism clear across the Atlantic.

Courier, November 27, 1897, pp. 2–3.

Nansen: "that unmistakable Norse accent"

Although he failed to reach the North Pole, the Norwegian Arctic explorer Fridtjof Nansen (1861–1930) in his 1893–1896 expedition went farther north than any man up to that time. Willa Cather's account of his illustrated lecture, which appeared in the Leader, *December 1, 1897, was incorporated in her "Passing Show" column, given below. For additional comment on Arctic expeditions, see "Hunting the North Pole," Washington Correspondent, below.*

In "entertaining" Fridtjof Nansen the Writers Club outdid itself. It has, indeed, favored Dr. Watson ["Ian Maclaren"] and [Francis] Hopkinson Smith and Anthony Hope Hawkins and suchlike with supper and smokers and receptions, according to their several deserts. But Nansen is almost as much of a hero as Bob Fitzsimmons, and for him, only a state banquet was fitting. Besides it is the proper thing to banquet Nansen; the Prince of Wales started the fashion and far be it from loyal Americans to disregard such a precedent. They do say, too, that these continued banquets are using him up worse than the Pole, and he quite pines for solitude and icebergs and raw bears' meat and "Boreal climes of the Pole," where reporters and indigestion are not.

This particular banquet was given in the dining hall of the Hotel Henry,—the only other really first-class hotel here is called The Lincoln, by the way. The orchestra fiddled and tooted in a clump of palms and the tables were decorated with La France roses and maidenhair ferns. I will spare you the menu. All the elite were there, for this was no mere humble man of letters whom we were "entertaining." Even the mayor of the city came and made a toast and quoted Shakespeare and ate with his knife. They say that Chris Magee[21] "runs" the mayor and has taught him all he knows about politics. I must say I wish he would teach him table manners.

The toastmaster of the occasion was Mr. Samuel Haraden Church, who is always trotted out on such occasions.[22] Now a word of this gentleman. He is a rather interesting personage. It seems that he used to work for the great and only Carnegie, and Carnegie, the founder of concert halls, art galleries and libraries, took a notion that it would be a worthy and benevolent thing to manufacture a novelist; so he educated Mr. Church and sent him abroad and awaited developments. In the course of time Mr. Church wrote a biography of Oliver Cromwell, which I have not read and consequently can say nothing about. This year a reputable house has published his historical novel, *John Marmaduke*, a story of Cromwell's time, in which one of the characters remarks that he was "raised in Ireland," and in which the fair heroine is called "Miss Catherine" throughout. In a very casual reading I found some two hundred or more of the grossest anachronisms. Andrew Carnegie may control the iron market of the world, but he and all his millions can't make a novelist. That is one of the little perquisites that the Lord reserves for himself.

Well, this celebrated Mr. Samuel Haraden Church began his toast to Nansen with a quotation from *Lucile*,[23] one of the worst he could have selected, too.

> Not a truth has to art or to science been given,
> But brows have ached for it and souls toiled and striven;
> And many have striven, and many have failed,
> And many died, slain by the truth they assailed.

Could anything have been more heart-rending? Poor Nansen! who has all Browning at his tongue's end, and claims even to have read *Prince*

21. See note 3, above. In her letter to Will Owen Jones, Cather also described Magee as the majority stockholder of a traction company and a multimillionaire.

22. Samuel Haraden Church (1858–1943), a railroad executive, subsequently president of the Carnegie Institute. Cather reviewed his *Oliver Cromwell: A History* (1894) in the *Leader*, June 10, 1899, p. 5.

23. For *Lucile*, see note 25, The Star System (II), above. *Prince Hohenstiel-Schwangau* 1870), alluded to in the next paragraph, was a long dramatic monologue by Robert Browning.

Hohenstiel-Schwangau, it only remains to hope that he had never heard of *Lucile* and its odium. The rest of Mr. Church's toast, however, was rather better. . . . Dr. Nansen's reply was as simple and modest as his lecture. . . .

I do not suppose the immense crowd of people who went to the Carnegie Music Hall that night cared particularly for the scientific results of his explorations as they cared to see the man himself, the man who has cut in two the distance between the unknown and the known, who has known the "most disastrous chances of moving accident by flood and field."

For centuries the North Pole has been a standing challenge to adventurous blood. It has been to modern knighthood that. The man who pushes his way into the icebound mystery of the Polar Sea further than any man before him has done is a world hero. That is a kind of achievement which, like military achievement, is comprehensible to every man. To appreciate it requires no knowledge of science or feeling for art, no technical discriminations as in the case of an artistic masterpiece or a scientific discovery. It bespeaks the primitive virtues of hardihood, the power of the strong arm, which strikes an answering chord in the breast alike of the savant and the savage. After all, there is nothing quite like it, that power of the strong arm. It is the glory of Caesar and Napoleon. Nansen may be honored by a few universities because of his scientific discoveries, but to the people at large he is a hero because he reached the eighty-sixth parallel. Much of this talk about the scientific value of such explorations is all nonsense, invented out of consideration for the feelings of the Philistine, who can never accept the poet or the painter, or the actor as such, but must measure them by a material standard. It is in the same spirit that we make practical excuses for art to our stolid friends. Nansen never turned the prow of the *Fram* northward for practical purposes. He said so plainly in his peroration. He went because he was possessed of an old unrest, the Odysseus fever; because there sang in his blood that siren voice that is forever wooing us away from the life of hotels and theatres and electric lights, whispering to us of a larger liberty, of meeting Nature once more breast to breast, coping with her hand to hand, of a life that would be life indeed. Perhaps, too, in this man there awoke the unstained blood of Viking voyagers, centuries dead. . . .

In appearance Fridtjof Nansen is very much like hundreds of well set-up Norsemen you will find the world over. They were always such wanderers, those Norsemen. They have not changed much since the days when Eric the Bold turned his warship toward Iceland. You will find

Nansen's kind within a hundred miles of Lincoln. They are scattered all over those vast midland plains populated by the peasantry of Europe. I have passed some of my days among them. He has the prominent cheek bone, fair ruddy skin, and yellow hair of his people. The commanding features of his face are his masterful mouth, high forehead, and his eyes that are as deep and blue as the water between the ice fissures. His hair stands up all over his head, scorning the sedative influence of the brush, just like that of hundreds of Norwegians down in Webster County, and he has the powerful shoulders of a big Norseman I used to watch stack straw out on the Divide last summer.[24]

He spoke English well, but with considerable hesitation and with that unmistakable Norse accent, so like that of a dozen Eric Ericsons and Olaf Olesons I know that for a moment a desperate homesickness came over me and I bethought me of an old waltz tune that the Norsemen used to play at their dances.

He has, too, their old tricks of telling the most startling things in the most naively calm and phlegmatic manner. I imagine that the people who went to hear thrilling description and bloodcurdling word pictures went away disappointed. After the practitioners of yellow journalism have ransacked the dictionary to find adjectives glaring enough to paint his adventures, it was almost incredible that the man who had actually done all these things should speak of them with such epic simplicity. A committeeman making his official report could not have been more terse and direct. I have heard gentlemen describe a fishing trip much more dramatically. There was something in his terseness and economy of verbiage that recalled the *Commentaries* of Caesar. When he expanded at all it was on the beauties of the polar night or something quite as impersonal. His own deeds of daring he mentioned casually. His terrible swim in the Arctic waters after the drifting boats, which was the greatest feat of personal endurance in all that voyage, he mentioned; but he described the killing of his two faithful dogs as the most trying ordeal he had to face in those three years. "I could not verra well kill my own dog. I kill Yohansen's an' Yohansen he kill mine." Can't you just hear Eric Ericson say it?

Months of marching over ice hummocks in frozen clothing, dragging heavy sledges, he described as "verra hard work." I don't believe the man has a superlative adjective in his vocabulary. He seems better acquainted

24. The Divide, in Webster County, Nebraska, north of Red Cloud, was the plateau between the Little Blue and Republican rivers where the Charles Cather family first lived after coming to Nebraska. It was the scene of many of Willa Cather's novels and stories, including "On the Divide" (published in the *Overland Monthly*, January 1896), in which the central figure was a Norwegian settler, Canute Canuteson. See *CSF*, pp. 493–504.

with big deeds than big words. A hero is a fine thing, but a modest hero is almost too good to be true. . . .

Dr. Nansen said, in a conversation at the hotel before the lecture, that he had read a great deal of Browning during that voyage. I suppose it was in the desperation of a Polar night that he read *Prince Hohenstiel-Schwangau*. Heaven knows it would take nothing less to take most of us through the *Prince!*

His peroration was almost pathetically earnest. He made a plea for those glorious follies of adventure without which the health and virility dies out of a nation. He urged that money and material things were not all of life—sad heresy to utter in Pittsburgh. And, like every poet, every painter, every actor, he humbly apologized to the Philistine for being great. The old apology that only Whistler refuses to make. He quoted some lines from Tennyson's "Ulysses" that must seem to carry a special meaning from one of the world's wanderers to its last:

> One equal temper of heroic hearts,
> Made weak by time and fate, but strong in will
> To strive, to seek, to find and not to yield.

As he quoted the same poem in his toast, he must have a particular weakness for it. . . .

Courier, December 18, 1897, pp. 4–5.

The Perils of Journalism

In a review of Robin Hood, *Willa Cather commented pleasantly on the performance of Jessie Bartlett Davis (1861–1905), but did happen to mention that the lady was no longer in her first youth (see p.386). In the* Journal, *January 17, 1897, Cather reprinted the "caustic letter" the* Leader *received from Miss Davis, with the comment: "Poor Jessie, it was the reference to her age that hurt! And on second thought it was rather unnecessary to mention that. But if she wants to pass as thirty-four [Miss Davis had stated this was her age] she should keep her big blonde son at home and not let him go about playing in college football teams. Notice she says thirty-four: how some women do dread those fatal figures, thirty-five." Some months later, writing of Victor Herbert's light opera* The Serenade, *Cather told the story again for* Courier *readers.*

The Bostonians have been with us again in their new opera, *The Serenade*, by Victor Herbert. The opera is a sad disappointment after one has heard Herbert's *Wizard of the Nile*. I expected him to go on doing that sort of thing and even better. But *The Serenade* is just the ordinary, tuneless American light opera, with the ordinary meaningless orchestration. The only pretty air in it is the serenade, which all the cast sing continuously. . . .

Jessie Bartlett Davis is as infectiously happy as ever. In the first act she appears in skirts and seems rather a chunky, ordinary little woman who is, alas! no longer young. But presently she toddles out in the costume of a Spanish lad and, in spite of certain obvious physical disadvantages, Richard is himself again. Yes, when her coats are properly made she looks younger, prettier, even more slender in trousers.

I had a funny little experience last year with Jessie. It fell to my lot to call upon her and humbly petition her to sing for the Press Club benefit. She was exceedingly cordial and made me the recipient of numerous touching personal confidences which she evidently expected me to "print" and which, not being a press agent, I did not. Well, that night I heard her in *Robin Hood* and said some things in my notice of her performance of which she did not approve and she waxed wroth and wrote an indignant letter to the papers saying she would not sing at the benefit because of my notice and indited a flaming epistle at me in which she called me a "wolf in sheep's clothing"—a sad reflection on my dressmaker. And sing she would not, and I had only the comforting knowledge that I had told the truth—which is not always as comforting as it might be. Yet if I had published all her personal confidences to the town she would probably have been pleased. Such are the inexplicable caprices of prima donnas!

But in spite of our tiff I was mighty glad to see Jessie toddle out upon the stage the other night. She does seem to enjoy it all so, the prancing and capering and warbling, that she charms you into mirth yourself. After half a dozen encores in the last act someone in the gallery howled "Promise Me!" and all that big, enthusiastic audience caught fire and bawled "Promise Me, O Promise Me!" She stepped laughingly to the front again and asked, "What shall I promise you?" and the house applauded and the gallery yelled, "You know." And, standing there in the costume of a Spanish lad, she sang it, that doughty ditty which refuses to grow old. And really as you listened you forgot that the hand organs play it, and that the chambermaid carols it morn and eve in the flat overhead, and when she says "O, let me sit beside you in your eyes" you would sit beside her any old place—even if she had called you a wolf. May the years touch her ever so lightly, and may that smile be as joyous as the springtime always.

Courier, December 4, 1897, p. 2.

On February 1, 1898, the Leader *reported that Adelaide Mould (1881–1923), the daughter of the comic opera star Marion Manola (1866–1914), had run away from the touring company of her mother and Jack Mason (1859–1919). In a departure from her normal journalistic duties, Willa Cather succeeded in interviewing Miss Mould, scoring a national scoop. But, as she related in "The Passing Show," she was not very happy about it.*

This is a long story. I don't write it because I am proud of it, but I know a few maidens about Lincoln who have inclinations toward journalism, and this may serve to dampen their ardor. Then it's rather a relief to confess one's despicable conduct sometimes. Of course you have all heard how Adelaide Mould, Marion Manola's daughter, ran away from her mother's company when it disbanded in Savannah and came north with the manager, eloped with him, the papers had it, landed at New York and came to her father's home in Pittsburgh as soon as he telegraphed her a remittance. Her father, Henry S. Mould, was in Chicago at the time of her arrival here and the girl went to his home and locked herself up. The newspaper men of the town were wild. Here was a quarry worthwhile, "good hunting," as they call it. A runaway actress who was said to be engaged to Mr. Burrows, Speaker [Thomas B.] Reed's nephew, and Mark Eustis, David B. Hill's[25] private secretary, who had eloped with a third man, and who was said to have caused her mother furious jealousy because of her fondness for John Mason, and who, with all this, was only seventeen, locked up alone in a house out on Presbyterian Marchand Street. All day long the oldest and best-trained reporters of the town went out, and not one succeeded in even seeing past the dragon housekeeper at the door. Our men came back discouraged. The other papers had given the thing up and so must we. About four o'clock in the afternoon the managing editor came up to my desk. "I know it is not customary to send the editorial force out on assignments, but the men have failed dead on this Manola business, and I somehow can't give it up. None of the New York reporters got at her, and an interview would mean scooping the country, New York and Philadelphia papers please copy, you know. If you could try it, it would be a great personal favor."

I don't like that sort of business. Since I have been here I have not written any theatrical interviews. You can't do it with any shade of

25. Thomas Brackett Reed (1839–1902), Republican congressman from Maine, 1876–1899, Speaker of the House, 1889–1891. David Bennet Hill (1843–1910), former governor of New York, U.S. senator, 1891–1897.

self-respect. It means trading in personalities. But this was an unusual case, and I felt I rather owed a trial at it to the chief. Then, of course, the prospect of such a "scoop" was alluring. The men rather threw out a challenge and I took it up.

Then I began to prepare for my campaign. I had met Marion Manola several times last year when she was here in vaudeville, and I decided I would strain that point just about all it would stand. I hied me to a florist's and got a few dozen white narcissus and put my card in the box, writing on it that I hoped she would accept them with best wishes from one who had met and admired her mother, and sent them out to her address. I had another point in my favor; I had known slightly a family out in East End with whom Miss Mould and her father used to board. I went out there and found the reporters had overlooked them altogether. The lady of the house was greatly stirred up over the affair; declared that the father was an exquisite who lived beyond his means, a Beau Brummell who cared for nothing but himself and the fit of his coat, the mother an unmentionable person but that the child was as true as gold and that the Lord must have been crazy when he put her with those dreadful people.

Her calling Miss Mould "the child" made me nervous. One may be very young at seventeen, or one may be very old. I was prepared to go to see a woman of the world and to see her by fair means or foul, and she would work me for all I was worth and I would return the compliment, and we would both be amused and each despise the other and that would be an end of it. But I had not come out to pounce upon a child and wheedle out her secrets. I didn't like the look things were putting on.

I arrived at the house about 6:30 and handed the dragon my card, and awaited the coming freeze-out. It was dark in the vestibule and I could not see well, but I knew that someone little and young with a voice like a child's ran up to me and caught my hand and cried, "O, it was so good of you to come! and the flowers almost made me cry, they were the first things that have come to me for so long! You care for my mother, don't you?"

Here was a situation, sending poisoned candies to a child. When we got into the light, I felt guilty of infanticide. Why, she was a child, this giddy adventuress, this runaway actress, this heroine of triple love affairs, a little girl whose mother didn't love her, and I was an older girl who had come there to lay a trap for her. Haughtiness, insolence, would have been easy [compared] to this. How did she look? O, like any other girl who is beautiful. She was slender and carried her head well; her hair was brown with a reddish tinge in it, her mouth just Manola's fine mouth over again, her brow highly arched, her eyes big and dark and deeply set, and much, much too sad for so young a face. Marion Manola herself must have had much that same girlish charm years ago when she first left a church choir out in Cleveland and went to study under Marchesi, before the struggles of her life began and their fires burnt out all that was best in her.

It was no trouble to get her to talk. Ever since her flight from Savannah three weeks before she had been practically a prisoner, besieged by reporters. Since she ran away she had not seen any of her own sex. At seventeen a girl must talk. We went up to her room and she began pouring out such a torrent of girlish confidences that I seized my one chance for decency and as gently as I could stated my business. I hope I shall never have to go through such a moment again. The best I could say was that I would write the truth, and only the truth, and that I would flatly contradict the countless lies that had been told of her. She didn't freeze, she just got a little whiter and looked dazed and said faintly: "O, I didn't understand. I thought you were a friend of mother's." I could only say, "I'm a friend of yours, my dear, and if you'll trust me I'll try to prove it."

She looked at me for a few moments and said simply: "I'll have to trust you, there is no one else. Father may come in a few days, and it may be weeks. You see nobody wants me very much and there doesn't exactly seem to be any place in the world for me."

Never mind what I did then. I must have assured [reassured?] her for she began again. It was the saddest little story I ever heard, and the most hopeless. It came out bit by bit, incident by incident, as a child tells things. I simply could not stop her. She was feverish and her eyes were red with crying.

She had only been out of the convent a year. There she took vocal lessons from a Sister Agatha and sang in the choir. She spoke wistfully of it, that safe-sheltered existence with its routine and calm monotony, among those quiet, serene sisters, so far from the tempestuous emotions that blast and kill, and "that unrest which men miscall delight." And from that she was transplanted at sixteen to the comic opera stage under the tender care of Marion Manola and Jack Mason! Truly the Lord can make delightful stories when he chooses, and as Heine says, "How immeasurably he exceeds us in his humor and colossal wit."[26]

"You see," said the child, "I had only known my mother in my vacation before. She is different when she is playing and with Mr. Mason. I didn't know what it would be like when I went with them."

26. See note 17, above.

Mason, it seems, had always borne a grudge against the child because of her mother's affection for her, and had hated her because she recalled a part of Manola's past in which he had no share. What love the child got from her mother she got by stealth, and I imagine it was not very much she ever got. When they went South business was bad. Mason grew more dissipated than ever and his temper did not improve. Finally, the night before the company disbanded, Mason quarrelled so violently with his wife about the girl that she fell ill and Adelaide had to sing her part. The girl was really as ill as her mother and fainted in the last act of the piece. That night the child made her decision. She had just money enough to reach New York, and next day, while Mason was drunk and her mother in hysterics, she ran away.

"You see mother's life was hard enough anyway, and as long as I was there I seemed to come between her and the only thing she really cares for. He was cruel to her on my account and I couldn't stand it. I couldn't stand, either, to see him wreck all her life along with him. No company will ever get along under his management. Mother could get good engagements away from him, but she won't leave him. I had a sort of hope when I ran away that if she saw it must be me or him, if she saw she must give one of us up, she might break away from him. But she never will. A woman ought to give a great deal for her husband I suppose, but I don't think she ought to give everything—the things that matter more than life, I mean. At any rate I can't help respecting the way they feel towards each other—it doesn't happen often, I believe, that people really care for so long. But you see it leaves me no place. I seem quite crowded out. I am not necessary to mother and he is. My own father doesn't know me very well and I am a great burden to him. They don't teach one how to do things at the convent, I can't do anything but sing a little. I don't know what will happen next. Nothing very good, I am afraid."

I suggested the two gentlemen to whom she was said to be engaged. But that's the part of the story that will never be told by me. I didn't see much encouragement in it for the present so I suggested the stage. The words seemed to produce an actual nausea of the soul in her. She threw out her hands with a gesture of unspeakable disgust, "I'd rather scrub floors for a living. Why, that's an awful life!" Poor little girl, her initiation into stage life had not been a pleasant one and she seemed to have no faith in anything or anybody who had ever been on the other side of the footlights, and for a moment I was glad she hadn't, I didn't want to see that fragile little face blurred by that cruelest of all lives that gradually wears the fine lines from the fairest faces. It recalled that unpleasant and masterly book of Henry James' about, *What Maisie Knew* to think what things those big, sad eyes had already seen, and the girl is only seventeen; just the age when she ought to be finding out how gay life is and that all women are good and all men kind, and that sorrow is a thing only written about in books. O the pity of it! But at any rate it is a very good and a very sweet little girl who has come back to Pittsburgh. There are some natures that the dark side of life can only sadden—never corrupt. But I am inclined to think with the landlady that God was absent-minded when he gave a girl like this one to Marion Manola.

It is not a pleasant thing to go out with a little girl's tears still wet on your handkerchief to write a sensational story about her. In a book the reporter would go in to the managing editor and say with pallid lips, "There is no story!" and get cashiered. But in the rocky old world that is, things don't happen that way. A man had been hired to take my place at the editorial desk, and the men were waiting for my copy. With the grim consolation that I could never feel meaner I wrote the story and I did the best I could for her—which was bad enough—and tried to forget that I had stumbled upon a child's confidence and betrayed it.[27]

Well, we "scooped" New York, which is the end and aim of every paper in the provinces, and the eastern papers copied the yarn and the old newspaper men of the town came around and shook hands, and I made the counting room fork out greenbacks enough to keep that little girl in flowers and Huylers [candy] for many a long day. But if anyone has got a bad conscience to trade, mine is in the market at a low figure. I wouldn't figure in another slaughter of the innocent to "scoop" the earth.

All great infatuations have had their victims from the days of Lancelot and Elaine. They are primarily selfish and they damn the innocent with the guilty. Often enough their shadow falls across a life into which the sunlight should be just coming. It is the old inexorable law the justice of which we cannot understand. Grand passions are the most expensive things in life; so costly that two lives cannot pay for one, there must always be others who pay in blood and tears for a delight that is not theirs. And this

27. In the unsigned story, "Miss Mould Talks," *Leader*, February 6, 1898, p. 5, Willa Cather wrote: "Even reporters sometimes have consciences—rudimentary ones, at least—and the tired look in the child's eyes forbade further questioning. The thought of what tragedies those eyes had looked upon suggested that most unpleasant book of Henry James', *What Maisie Knew*." When Adelaide Mould was married two years later, the *Leader* reprinted some paragraphs from the interview (January 28, 1900, p. 2).

poor little girl seems destined to her share for one of the most notable and lasting infatuations in the annals of the stage.

It was only three years ago that Marion Manola, from the prolonged use of narcotic drugs and financial embarrassment, went temporarily insane. Her creditors had her arrested and took her costumes for debt. She got up out of a sick bed to go to the courtroom. She was acquitted, but her cottage at Winthrop was taken to satisfy the claim. The strain and worry of the courtroom were too much for the little woman who had helped the world smile for so long. Her malady developed where her talent had—on the stage. Her illness first manifested itself by her forgetting her lines and looking hopelessly at Mason for her cue. In a little while she forgot the *Mikado* altogether. She gave up her home and money, but she never gave up Jack Mason; she forgot the parts she had been singing for twelve years, but she never forgot him. It was very pitiful to hear her plead in her illness, "Don't let them take the dress I wore my first night, Jack!" In time she rallied again—for him. The strength of that infatuation held even then. Since then disaster has followed disaster, always finding them together and caring only for that. Even her daughter reverences the sincerity of it. Alone, Marion Manola might have had a brilliant career. Jack Mason spoke truly enough three years ago when a friend from England remarked that he had had no luck since he met Manola, and he replied: "Don't say that, it's she, poor girl, who has never had a lucky day since she met me."

She had given up everything under heaven for him—and now she has given up her child.

Jack Mason's people are still living up on Beacon Street in Boston; among the wealthiest, most cultured and exclusive people. His mother shudders at his name. Marion Manola's daughter is here alone, grateful for the sympathy of a stranger. If people could pay for their follies themselves, life would not be so utterly hard.

Courier, February 19, 1898, pp. 2–3.

Ethelbert Nevin: Return of Narcissus

The homecoming of Ethelbert Nevin (1862–1901) was very different from that of Charles Stanley Reinhart (see above). Nevin was the brother of Theodore W. and Joseph T. Nevin, who had inherited ownership of the Pittsburgh Leader *from their father. The young composer played his first concert in Pittsburgh in 1886, and gave another there in 1893. Most of his time was spent in Europe and Africa, inspiration for many of his songs and compositions. Willa Cather came to know Nevin very well.*[28] *(See "An Evening at Vineacre," The Musical World [III], below.) At the concert reported below, Nevin was assisted by two of his students, Genevieve Weaver and Francis Rogers (1870–1951).*

For thou art fair, dear boy, and at thy birth
Nature and fortune joined to make thee great.
[*King John*, III, i, 57]

Last week was one of some moment in Pittsburgh, for it was the week of Ethelbert Nevin's homecoming. There is nothing quite so inspiringly festive as that night-before-Christmas air of expectancy which a big town puts on to welcome one of its great ones home. Like everyone else I had known Nevin's songs ever since I was old enough to differentiate sounds at all. "O, That We Two Were Maying!," "Little Boy Blue," "There, Little Girl, Don't Cry," "The Mill Song," "Goodnight, Goodnight, Beloved," "When All the Land Was White," "La Vase Brise," who is there who does not know them? I had also known vaguely that he was an American, though that seemed rather impossible. But to associate him with Pittsburgh had never occurred to me, and when I discovered that he was the younger brother of the proprietors of my own paper, then I decided that in life it is the unexpected which happens and the impossible which is true.

It was with considerable smothered excitement that I went to hear him at his first recital at the Carnegie Hall. I had been reading about him all winter, and I was rather afraid the actual article might not come up to all that had been written and said of him. When the stage door at last opened, his two pupils who had come down with him to sing his songs came first, and then there stepped, or rather sprang, upon the stage a youth scarcely five feet three in height, with the slender, sloping shoulders and shapely hips of a girl, and that was Nevin! Barely two-and-thirty in fact, with the face of a boy of twenty. I have never seen a face that mirrored every shade of thought, every fleeting mood so quickly and vividly, and I have never seen a face so exuberantly gloriously young. The shepherd boys who piped in the Vale of Tempe centuries agone might have looked like that, or Virgil's Menalcas, when he left his flock beneath the spreading

28. In a letter of January 10, 1898, to Mariel Gere, Willa Cather tells of going to a dinner for Nevin and of an afternoon when he escorted her while she did some shopping and presented her with a mammoth bunch of violets.

beech tree and came joyous to the contest of song. It is not that his face is comely, far from it; it is the youth and joy of him, the lyric soul that shines through. . . .

He did not turn to his piano at once, he stood like a happy boy pleased at the warmth of his reception, smiling and bowing to old friends in the audience. And in truth that audience was almost a family affair. There were strange people seated here and there in that "select" company; the minister in whose choir this great man had sung when he was a boy, the old man to whose apple orchard he had made clandestine nocturnal visits, the butcher of whose big dog he used to be afraid, the old lady who once tied up his leg for him when he tore it on a locust thorn, the teachers and instructors who had pronounced him a dunce and painted dark pictures of his future because he could not learn the multiplication table, they were all there. . . .

[After playing the accompaniments for seven of his songs] the Boy at the piano sprang up and shook hands with his pupils and dashed out for a glass of water for Miss Weaver and was so generally juvenile and so informal that you half expected him to begin to chat with his audience. Finally this *enfant terrible* was sufficiently calmed to go back to his instrument. The moment he touched the keys one of those swift changes swept over his face and he was another being. It was a tragic face now, but it was the tragedy of youth, like that in de Musset's verses. He played his "Melody"; I don't know what "opus." At any rate it was the same thing that was in his face, tender, hopeless, infinitely sad, the poetic melancholy of the immortally young, of those who always suffer sharply as youth suffers.

The audience simply demanded "Narcissus," as an encore, "Narcissus," which he particularly abominates as being the most puerile of all his early works, and whose popularity is a curse which has followed him around the world. "The only apology I can offer for writing the thing," he said to me next day, "is that I have suffered tenfold more by it than anyone else can have done."

The roses kept going up over the footlights until they were stacked half as high as the piano and the applause did not cease, and so with a disdainful shrug and a sigh he sat down and, contemptuously enough, he played it.

Next Mr. Rogers sang his "Summer Day," and "Vielle Chanson," and that raft song, "On the Allegheny," that Nevin wrote one spring day in his boyhood. You see it's this way: all winter long the raftsman is up in the timber country cutting hemlocks, living in a log camp, sleeping in a shack, working all day long in frozen boots, shut out from the world by the snow-covered mountains. In the spring, when the ice goes out and the ground goes soft and the spring impulse is in the earth and the spring longing in the blood, then the raftsman's work is done and on his strong raft he goes back to the girl who is waiting down the river.

Ahoy, my raft goes down
  To you, to you!
And O, your lover brown
  Is true, is true!

O, the exultant expectancy of it! The very air feels like that of the resistless spring in the mountains, when the sap stains the bark of the maples and the scent of the pines is in all the land, the big rafts come booming down on the swollen currents of the Allegheny. It is an old poem that nature repeats every year among the mountains, but only one heart heard it and only one boy knew, and he was a very sad little boy who could not learn geometry and who wore the dunce cap of his school. Perhaps it was the dunce cap that saved him for the world, kept the ardent soul in him untrammeled and fresh, alert for raft songs while the other boys were thinking about the price of lumber. It has been the helmet of Hermes before, that dunce cap, and has hidden many a genius until his time was ripe.

The next number on the programme was Nevin's "May in Tuscany" (*Maggio in Toscana*), . . . the latest and best thing he has published. Heavens, how the man has grown since the days of "Narcissus!" . . .[29]

A little of [Nevin's] history. He comes of a good stock. The Sewickley Valley is full of Nevins, bankers, merchants, editors, all men who have made their mark and all big fellows who could carry this frolicsome youth about like a baby. They call him "The Boy." He sang from the time he could talk and played from the time he could reach the keyboard. In school he was preternaturally stupid, out of school he was as happy as a young animal. He had no sisters, so he was a girl-boy. He wrote music when he was thirteen. When he was fifteen he went to Boston and

29. Here Willa Cather gave Vance Thompson's interpretation of "May in Tuscany"—"which Nevin gave me as the best comment on it." She does not attempt to give her own impressions, because "my friend Toby Rex has always accused me of too great a tendency to interpret musical compositions into literal pictures, and of caring more for the picture than for the composition in itself." For Vance Thompson, see note 19, The Musical World (III), below.

Benjamin J. Lang[30] told him he had genius. His father sent him abroad to study under Böhme. When he felt the boy was losing his head he called him home. It was time to take life seriously; a Nevin could not waste his life over the piano. Then followed those three miserable years at the Western University of Pennsylvania: years of failure and irksome duties and hope deferred. But it was during those months of yearning that he wrote "One Spring Morning," "A Love Song," "O, That We Two Were Maying," and "Doris." The songs were on everyone's lips and his father yielded. The boy went abroad again to study under Von Bülow. His history since that time belongs to musical biographies.

His homecoming was a bit droll, the descent of this irrepressible youth with his wife and two children and his dogs and an Italian valet upon this solid, substantial, well-reputed family. It was a little like Magda's homecoming. It was there I met him. The first hour was taken up with talks of his life abroad; of his home in Florence, his concerts in Paris, Berlin, Vienna; of the scores of unpublished compositions, some of which will be brought out this year; of his summer up among the Tuscan hills when he shipped a grand piano up to Montepiano and wrote most of *Maggio in Tuscana* in the donkey stable he used for a music room; of all that free and glorious life of production and art. And he who told me of these triumphs, of these ecstasies of creation was a smiling boy perched upon the arm of a leather reading chair.

Finally I asked him what it felt like to be a child of genius in Pittsburgh.

"O those were great old days, except for the failure at school. I never come back without feeling the chagrin of them anew. I picked up language quick enough abroad, but here it was hopeless. I have caught up a little in history and literature of late years, but it's all superficial. In reality I know very little. But as to the old days. The greatest pleasure in them was singing. I had a voice then. Eight of my uncles, the big fellows, you know, formed an octette and they used to go around the little towns giving concerts for charity and they starred me. O yes, I was a star when I was eight and used to be billed in big letters from Altoona to Morgantown. O the bliss of seeing my name on the bills! the letters were never big enough. I was as careful of my throat as a budding tenor. They used to

30. Benjamin J. Lang (1837–1909), pianist and conductor of the Apollo Club of Boston and of the Handel and Haydn Society. In the next sentence: Franz Magnus Böhme (1828–1898), teacher at Hock Conservatory, Frankfort. In the next-to-last sentence of the paragraph: Hans Von Bülow (1830–1894), famed German conductor, pianist, and teacher.

stand me on a table on the stage and sing my accompaniment. And the applause! No prima donna's heart ever beat faster. Ah, there is nothing like it now! I was a convenient prima donna, for I could sing either contralto or soprano and my repertoire included all the plaintive ditties you ever heard. I can feel it all now."

The sprightly youth sprang from the arm of the chair and catching up a newspaper crumpled it up like a fan and holding it modestly in front of him, struck the apologetic prima donna attitude and dolefully warbled forth "But A-A-Alice where art thou?"

A laugh, and the newspaper was sent whirring across the room, and the youth threw himself at full length in the armchair.

"Well, it never occurred to me that I couldn't go on singing Marguerite forever, or that I shouldn't grow up to be a full-fledged prima donna. When I was thirteen my voice changed. Changed? O feeble word! it evaporated, went completely, leaving me only the sorry squeal with which I have just honored you. I was inconsolable. My means of musical expression was gone. I was a sad crybaby of a boy, and I used to weep for hours. And then I wrote that serenade, you know, 'Good Night, Good Night, Beloved.'"

Yes, good friends, he wrote it when he was thirteen, that tender, adolescent melody which Romeo might have sung to Juliet. It was the morning song of genius, the song in which he wooed Our High Lady of Art:

Thine eyes are stars of morning,
Thy lips are blood-red flowers!

Is it any wonder that even that most haughty Lady was not cold to such youth and rapture, that she smiled and came?

As I was trying to make him understand that even in the Far West, which he seemed to regard with a shiver, much as the Ancients regarded Britain, his songs were known and had brought joy into the lives of men, I incidentally told him of how I used to sing a little boy[31] to sleep with his "Little Boy Blue" when the summer stars were peeping, and how the laddie cried for it when I was gone. Perhaps I spoke sadly without meaning to, for there are lakes and rivers and many a league of frozen prairie between me and that little boy now. Very quietly and gravely he rose and went to the piano. Without a word of reply he sang it through softly in the twilight.

31. A reference to her youngest brother, John Esten Cather—Jack, who was born in 1892.

And there I shall leave Ethelbert Nevin. I can tell you nothing more characteristic of him as an artist and a man than that simple action. Someone he had never seen before, would never see again, was sad for a moment; and he knew and cared. That is the essential essence of his genius; that exquisite sensitiveness, that fine susceptibility to the moods of others, to every external thing. That is why he can interpret a poet's song better than the poet himself; that is why he can put the glory and melancholy of a Tuscan summer into sound; that is the all divining intuition.

The man is but two-and-thirty; before him is the vast unachieved, the infinite unconquered. He may never write symphonies; he may never contribute anything of vital importance to the literature of the piano. But as long as the heart in him beats, it will sing. He is merely a troubadour. Since Goring Thomas' death—and nothing will ever compensate the world for that untimely tragedy—we have had no man so thoroughly possessed of lyric inspiration. Before him there is song—song—song. Perhaps fifty glorious singing years. But I cannot realize that he is a great man. I shall always see him as I saw him last, bowing his goodnight, this joyous troubadour with the smile of a boy and the slender shoulders of a girl; "until we meet again."

It was Harlequin, Harlequin, Harlequin,
Son of the Rainbow, he!

Courier, February 5, 1898, pp. 3–4.

Women's Worlds

The two following selections are taken from Willa Cather's Leader *column, "Books and Magazines" (see Books and Authors [III], below). The first reviews the second volume of the* Woman's Bible, *edited under the direction of Elizabeth Cady Stanton (1815–1902), first president of the National Woman Suffrage Association, which she founded with Susan B. Anthony. The second considers a work of distinctly different character:* Here & There & Everywhere: Reminiscences *(1898) by Mrs. Mary Elizabeth Wilson Sherwood (1826–1903). An occasional poet and story writer, Mrs. Sherwood frequently contributed to newspapers and periodicals (under the initials "M.E.W.S."), but was best known for her books on social life and etiquette.*

Woman's Bible, edited by Elizabeth Cady Stanton and her compeers, forms a valuable contribution to the humorous literature of the day. Now that Mark Twain has devoted himself to serious literature, and Mrs.

Stanton has become a humorist, nothing in the line of literary versatility can startle the world.

In the preface to this second volume of their great effort, the ladies have taken the opportunity to answer the remarks of "carping critics" on the first volume. In replying to Mr. T. DeWitt Talmage's[32] jeers at her great work, Mrs. Stanton says:

> There's nothing so becomes a man
> As modest stillness and humility.

This is strange advice to offer so wordy and self-assured a gentleman. Surely Mrs. Stanton would not spoil so unique a character as Dr. Talmage.

Theologians have not ceased to marvel at the temerity of these estimable ladies, who, without scholarship, without linguistic attainments, without theological training, not even able to read the Bible in the original tongues, set themselves upon a task which has baffled the ripest scholarship and most profound learning. They have thrown out parts of the Bible which do not suit them, quite without internal or external evidence to support their position. Other passages, no better supported by the canons of higher criticism, are retained as authentic, seemingly because their sentiment meets with the approval of the editors.

The only aim of these ladies seems to have been to take each female character in the Bible, no matter what the role she plays, and prove that she was a ministering angel unjustly and cruelly misplaced upon a sphere peopled with shocking men, and that although she might temporarily be subjugated by these monsters, she would eventually soar back to Paradise in all her pristine purity, leaving man to go his own grovelling way to the gates Infernal. Ruth, Deborah, Bath-sheba and Esther are each taken up and idealized and romanced about and fondled and wept over, much as Juliet and Rosalind are in Mrs. Jamison's book on the *Girlhood of Shakespeare's Heroines.*[33] Most of the remarks about these Hebrew ladies are entirely without actual foundation and frequently irrelevant. Again and again Mrs. Stanton avows that their Semitic heroines would have led worthy and blameless lives had there been no Semitic heroes. This is probably pertinent, but the same defense could certainly be advanced for the heroes.

In commenting upon the episode of Uriah's death, Mrs. Stanton says: "When the king first recalled Uriah from the field, Uriah went not to his own house as he suspected foul play having heard that Bath-sheba often

32. Thomas DeWitt Talmage (1832–1902), editor of the *Christian Herald.*

33. Cecelia Viets Jamison (1837–1909), author of children's books.

appeared at court. Both the king and Bath-sheba urged him to go to his own house; but he went not. Bath-sheba had been to him all that was pure and beautiful in woman, and he could not endure even the suspicion of guilt in her. He understood the king's plans and probably welcomed death, as without Bath-sheba's love life had no joy for him." Such improvisation is absurd. There is no proof whatever that Uriah was a milksop.

In commenting upon the Queen of Sheba's visit to Solomon the editor remarks: "As the Queen of Sheba did not have seven hundred husbands, she had time for travel and the observation of the great world outside of her domain." Some commentaries of very considerable renown have advanced a theory as to the purpose of the queen's visit, which would indicate that it would have been rather better had she had enough domestic duties to have kept her at home.

Naturally the editors consider Solomon an objectionable person, but his views irritate them not as much as the logic of Paul. Over Paul the good ladies become simply distraught with rage. Christ himself does not entirely escape their withering criticism: "Mary Magdalene is, in many respects, the tenderest and most loving character in the New Testament. Her love for Christ did not die with His death. She waited at the sepulchre; she hastened in the early morning to His tomb; and yet the only comfort Christ gave to this true and loving soul lies in these strangely cold and heartless words: 'Touch me not.'"

Most original of all the novel ideas which Mrs. Stanton presents is her interpretation of the famous parable of the ten virgins. She insists that the allegory has nothing to do with the faithful and the second coming of Christ, but that the five wise virgins represent the new woman and the five foolish—well, the other kind. She argues as follows:

"It fairly describes the two classes which help to make up society in general. The one who, like the foolish virgins, have never learned the first important duty of cultivating their own individual powers, using the talents given to them, and keeping their own lamps trimmed and burning. The idea of being a helpmeet to somebody else has been so sedulously drilled into most women that an individual life, aim, purpose and ambition are never taken into consideration. . . .

"The wise virgins are they who keep their lamps trimmed, who burn oil in their vessels for their own use, who have improved every advantage for their education, secured a healthy, happy, complete development, and entered all the profitable avenues of labor, for self-support.

"These are the women who today are close upon the heels of man in the whole realm of thought, in art, in science, in literature, and in government. With telescopic vision they explore the starry firmament, and bring back the history of the planetary world. With chart and compass they pilot ships across the mighty deep."

Fie! fie! Mrs. Stanton, you must have been reading the New York *Journal*, and found that Kathrine Clemmons has been granted a pilot's certificate to sail Howard Gould's yacht.[34]

Leader, April 8, 1898, p. 11.

Mrs. Sherwood's name has so long been in conspicuous prominence in society journals that she scarcely needs an introduction to the public. The present volume of three hundred pages is devoted to reminiscence of her eventful life and her personal acquaintance with "notables" both at home and abroad. These "notables" range from Washington Irving and N. P. Willis to the Empress Eugénie and Mme. Sarah Bernhardt, and her impressions of these personages will doubtless be of interest to Mrs. Sherwood's "many friends, both in New York and on the continent"; to quote the society journals. The lady's impressions of Rome and Venice, etc., are no less engaging, as one always wonders just what a "leader of society" sees in the various Meccas of Art. Mrs. Sherwood, like most ladies of her set, has her little coterie of artistic acquaintances, and does not scorn to affectionately patronize them. The attitude of "society" toward "art" is always interesting and not infrequently amusing. Anyone who can afford to buy pictures is likely to speak with perfect candor and enviable confidence about paintings and painters, persons who have dined with literary lions are not apt to be conservative or unduly modest in their judgment of the art of letters, and ladies who have bidden an actress to their receptions see no reason why they should not be competent critics of the drama. The fact is, all of these little arts are rather specialities in themselves, trivial as they seem, and even a superficial understanding of them requires quite as much study as the "art of entertaining perfectly" or the science of etiquette. That in her eventful life Mrs. Sherwood has not found leisure to give them this study is painfully evident. . . .

34. Howard Gould (1867–1938) played the hero, Rudolf Rassendyll, in *The Prisoner of Zenda*. Of Kathrine Clemmons, who had played the lead in *A Lady of Venice* in 1894, Odell wrote: "If Mrs. Leslie Carter could emerge into stardom, why might not Kathrine Clemmons, known in the news, but not in the theatre? . . . Well, there are some things that can't be done, and one of them was making a successful star out of Miss Clemmons." *Annals of the New York Stage*, XV, 594.

The most refreshing part of Mrs. Sherwood's lengthy book is her chapter on the literature of the day. In speaking of Mr. J. M. Barrie's *Little Minister* she says: "Here we have a list of Rembrandt paintings; nothing is better, nothing sweeter. Here is a classic. Some critic of Milton said that his Adam entered Eden by way of England," etc. Surely a lady of Mrs. Sherwood's boasted acquaintance with French literature should know that it was Taine who made the above remark. Of Stanley J. Weyman, she says: "He is a benefactor of the human race and a favorite of society." Mr. Weyman may congratulate himself, as that is a combination of virtues seldom achieved. Of Kipling she says that he is "sometimes as grand as a forest of orchids." Somehow orchids fail to suggest the creator of Terence Mulvaney.

"Novels of society," says the lady, "are the novels which society loves. *Marcella* is queen of them all, and *Sir George Tressady*, too, which is only *Marcella* continued. Here a lady speaks." Alas! too true. But is Sir George, too, to be styled a queen? We are also told that Mrs. [Humphry] Ward "knows society, therefore she is invaluable." Of George Meredith the good lady says, "Who reads George Meredith, and for what reason, must ever remain a mystery—unless people like what they cannot understand and in their secret souls despise." In apology for Mrs. Sherwood we can only say that no taste could be so catholic as to include both N. P. Willis and George Meredith. On Marion Crawford the good lady expands, "Marion Crawford is a firm favorite in the boudoirs, and it is a hopeful sign of the times that he is. No one can wish for a better friend for a young woman's mind than this delightful writer." There, Mr. Crawford, your doom is written for you, a doom you have most richly deserved. To Willis is given the care of the external female head, but to you and to Ruth Ashmore the interior is trustfully consigned.

Mrs. Sherwood tells us that "the dreadful *Jude the Obscure*, the flippery [flippant?], vicious tales of refined or coarse cruelty, are no longer countenanced by the best society; and that term means a great deal." Indeed it does. Mrs. Sherwood's reminiscences have demonstrated how much it means, and are a better travesty on the world in which she moves than the scoffing Clyde Fitch has ever written. Going further the lady says: "The *Quo Vadis* and other historical novels by great minds came into being, and fashion stood up straighter and breathed deeper." In spite of the vague grammatical structure of the sentence, we are glad to know of the salutary effect of *Quo Vadis?* upon fashion. . . . We are next told that "It would be impossible at a fashionable dinner party to speak of a character or an episode in one of Henry James' novels that everyone at the table would not know as well whom you mean as if you spoke of Becky Sharp or Mr. Micawber. Society adores Henry James. His last three novels are without doubt his best and most permanent successes, not alone for their consummate merit as literary works, but for their attractive houses, pretty women, and general atmosphere of what is most delightful. These make him the popular favorite in the home of the luxurious."

What Maisie Knew, for instance, is full of the "general atmosphere of what is most delightful!" If it is indeed upon "attractive houses" that Mr. James must base his claims to immortality, the author of *The Tragic Muse* and *The Princess Casamassima* had better study without delay the *Ladies' Home Journal*'s "Interior of a Hundred Homes" and thus make his calling and election sure. "A popular favorite in the home of the luxurious!" O, Mr. James, this after all that we had hoped from you!

Leader, May 6, 1898, p. 9.

Willa Cather could be scathing about militant feminists and society scribblers, but she admired true professionals like Johnstone Bennett (1870–1906), comedienne and male impersonator. The following selection from "The Passing Show" was headed "The Player's Rubáiyát."

Dear John: A bird that's not too old or new,
And lots of chilly fizz to drink, and you
In some gay corner of Martini's place,
Say, wouldn't that be bliss enough for two?

Though some there are who talk of "art" and that,
And some there be would sit where Bernhardt sat,
Ah! let us blow our cash and dodge our duns,
And let the critic murmur through his hat.

For some who wore the laurel on their brow,
And talked of "consecration"—well, I trow
They lie asleep in some sequestered spot,
And Della Fox is burning money now.
—From Johnstone Bennett's Autograph Album

She has been with us again, jovial, natty Johnnie Bennett, a hail-fellow-well-met, and the trimmest tailor-made New Woman of them all. She is another one who has learned how to cheat time: her cheeks are just as ruddy and her big gray eyes as frank and frolicsome and boyish as they were in the days of *Jane*, eight or nine years ago. While she was here she had an abcess on her toe, an unromantic affliction, but a very painful one, and every night she would force her swollen foot into her russet boots, half fainting with pain, and five minutes later would be skipping about the stage of the Bijou Theatre as gay as a schoolboy on his holiday. For downright grit, just give me these professional women. I have seen Lizzie Hudson Collier faint dead away in the wings where she stood waiting for her cue, and then go on and dance radiantly beautiful at an embassy ball, and Olga Nethersole leave the doctor's hands to go on for the first act of *Camille*, and Annie Russell chatter beside the chilly fireside of a drawing-room "set" when her throat was full of bronchitis. Death is the only excuse which the stage manager will accept, and then he is inclined to grumble because the funeral was not postponed until the end of the season.

Courier, February 4, 1899, p. 3.

Lieutenant Jenkins: "Townsman of a stiller town"

On February 15, 1898, the battleship Maine, *sent to Havana on a goodwill tour, was blown up in the harbor with the loss of two hundred and sixty-six lives. Among the dead was Lieutenant Frank W. Jenkins of Pittsburgh. His homecoming late in March heightened the tension that led President McKinley to send an ultimatum to Spain and Congress to declare that a state of war existed as of April 21.*

The day you won your town the race
We cheered you through the market place;
Man and boy stood cheering by
While we bore you shoulder high.

Now, the way all runners come,
Shoulder high we bring you home,
And set you at your portal down
Townsman of a stiller town.

A. E. Housman[35]

35. Cather was obviously quoting from memory the first two stanzas of poem XIX, "To an Athlete Dying Young," in *The Shropshire Lad*, p. 26. Correctly the stanzas read:

The time you won your town the race
We chaired you through the market-place;
Man and boy stood cheering by
And Home we brought you shoulder high.

To-day, the road all runners come,
Shoulder-high we bring you home,
And set you at your threshold down,
Townsman of a stiller town.

I suppose no military funeral since Sherman's has equalled in solemnity that which awaited the body of Lieutenant F. W. Jenkins here when it was sent home from Havana. No city in the country felt the horrors of the *Maine* disaster more keenly than Pittsburgh. Lieutenant Jenkins was born here, had always lived here and enjoyed that universal popularity which only a military officer can know in a big provincial town. All the morning of that fateful fifteenth of February when the news of the disaster first reached us, the dead man's brother sat at my elbow waiting for the message of the clicking wires. Two weeks later an old, broken-hearted woman, dressed in black, came in leaning on his arm to thank the telegraph department for the interest it had taken in her son. She did not say much, she was not melodramatic; but when she left, there was not a dry eye in the office. I doubt if such a scene had occurred since the War of the Rebellion. I sat at my desk thinking with astonishment of the days when I used to laugh at the "patriotic bathos" of *The Ensign*[36] and similar military and naval dramas. The most tawdry of them would move me now.

As the long search for Jenkins' body continued I grew to feel an almost personal interest in it, and when one of our reporters went down to Cincinnati to meet the body I almost wanted to go too. When the casket arrived it was placed in the Allegheny post office. The rotunda was heavily draped in black; back of the platform on which the casket lay was a forest of palms, and about the platform were heaped American Beauty roses. At the foot of the casket stood the Naval Reserves as a guard of honor; all young fellows, standing motionless and silent as statues, but with tight lips and flashing eyes. The great windows were all open; outside the sunlight flashed with blinding brightness upon the gilded dome and the curves of the river; the morning wind whispered through the hall and rustled the green fronds of the palms. There were no flowers on the casket; across it lay only the flag, his flag, and despite the heavy fringes the long end caught again and again in the breeze and strained and fluttered to be free. From the thousands who filed by not a word, not a breath; the only sound that soft fluttering of the flag. It was as though the flag itself had spoken.

The body was then taken to the county courthouse in Pittsburgh, and at two o'clock the funeral cortege was almost two hours in passing; there were four thousand men in line, all in uniform. All the troops in the state were out carrying the old banners that had been through the Civil War, some of them were faded strips of silk, so burned and rent that it seemed

36. Cather reviewed *The Ensign* by William Haworth in the *Journal*, March 2, 1894, p. 3.

as if the wind would rend their tattered ends flying from the staff. Regiment after regiment passed in silence, band after band each with some dirge more solemn than the last until the last band came playing Chopin's "Marche Funèbre." Behind it came hearses full of flowers, and after them on a low gun carriage, fitting hearse for a soldier, was that black casket wrapped in the flag, and that new young flag seemed to flutter back the challenge of the old banners in front and to say, "I too have my heroes!"

Last fall, when the President of the republic was driven down that same street, the bands played very different music, and the crowd swayed and surged and men shouted and waved their hats in the air. That was the enthusiasm of a holiday but this was something deeper. An old Englishman told me the next day it was the most genuine demonstration he had ever witnessed in America. The impressive feature of the scene was not the soldiers nor the sailors, nor the glittering guns and regimentals, but the men and women packed by thousands and tens of thousands behind the ropes along Fifth Avenue, each of whom was a soldier or mother of soldiers to be. Young and old men, laborers and capitalists, stood bareheaded, shoulder to shoulder; women held their babies high and men lifted their little sons to their shoulders to let them see that low gun carriage as it passed. The procession passed on across the bridge, down the river to the old Uniondale Cemetery; through the ways where many a time he had scampered when a boy, they bore the hero home.

Is it any wonder that here in the streets, in the markets, in the foyers of the theatres, in the vestibules of the churches, in the glowing mills where stripped to the waist they hammer out the iron plates for battleships, men talk of war?

Courier, April 23, 1898, p. 3.

Mrs. Collier: "the most influential woman in this city"

Willa Cather had frequently commented on Lizzie Hudson Collier when she appeared with the Avenue Stock Company during the season of 1896–97 (see The Star System [III], above). On January 8, 1898, the Leader *reported that Mrs. Collier would be the leading lady of the New Grand Opera Stock Company, and on January 10 Willa Cather wrote to Mariel Gere of attending a supper party given by Mrs. Collier for William H. Crane and his wife.*[37] *In a later article (see "One of Our Conquerors," The* Library,

37. Cather had reviewed Crane in *Brother John* in Lincoln (see The Theatre [I], above), and she reviewed him in *A Virginia Courtship* for the *Leader*, January 11, 1898, p. 6.

below), Cather revealed that she learned of the following "pretty incident" because she "chanced to be standing in the lower hall of the Duquesne Hotel when Mrs. Collier came in at midnight."

Every now and then a pretty incident occurs that quite surpasses the storyteller's art. Such a one happened here a few weeks ago. Lizzie Hudson Collier is the leading woman of the Grand Opera House Stock Company here. A mighty handsome leading woman she is, by the way, and an actress of most unusual talent and versatility. You can count on the fingers of one hand the other leading women of this country who are a match for her in all-around work. She has been here now for three seasons and her life has been even more beautiful than her work. I think those of us who know her intimately sometimes fail to do complete justice to the actress, so much do we admire the woman. She is probably the most influential woman in this city of half-a-million souls. She has entered completely into our lives "and the deaths we died she has watched beside." I think nothing illustrates the power of her personality more forcibly than the attitude of young men toward her. Take the boys in our office, for instance. They are all good fellows and gentlemen but they all saw the black side of life too early and they have the reporter's cynical attitude toward actresses. Yet they always speak of this woman in the language of chivalry, as the knights of old spoke of women. They believe in her. And the good of such a belief cannot be estimated or measured. I could weary the most patient listener with instances of her goodness and tact and charm, and of course she is unconscious of it, she doesn't know that she is good. She simply has the high talent for living beautifully, and lives so. Such virtues, in so fair a setting, are a source of perpetual fragrance in the heart of this great, gloomy, jostling town, breathing perfume into the lives of thousands.

But now for the story: They were playing *Jane* at the Grand some weeks ago, and, as you remember, there is a baby in *Jane* that plays no inconspicuous part. Well, on this occasion it was a wonderful baby, positively the best I ever saw on any stage. It was just a poor little waif from the slums with a stupid, half-starved mother, who had a whole troupe of children and a husband out of work. Why such an attractive child should have been born into such misery and poverty is one of the ugly problems. It happens so every day. Well, she could act, this little thing of fourteen months. She didn't just lie blinking in Mrs. Collier's arms as the babies who have played in *Jane* aforetime. She sat up looking delightedly about her and kissed the leading man and shook hands with the comedian and flirted with the leader of the orchestra, and wanted to get over the footlights to examine his bald head. The louder the applause, the more interested she became. She demanded the center of the stage, and the brightest glare of the calcium, she was touchy about her cues and refused to have her "business" cut. The louder the applause, the more animated this infant became. She shook hands with the leading man, and kissed the leading juvenile, and made eyes at the conductor of the orchestra. Well, on one of those fearful cold nights when the weather man hung sinkers on the thermometer and the mercury dipped way below zero, Mrs. Collier discovered that this poor little waif lived somewhere down in the tenement district, and that its mother proposed to take her home, thinly clad as it was, through the biting cold. Mrs. Collier didn't do a thing but bundle the baby up and take it over to her room at the Hotel Duquesne and keep it all night. When she arrived at 11:30, all dressed in black and carrying this unaccustomed burden through the snowy winter night, she looked for all the world like the betrayed and deserted heroine of a Bijou melodrama who returns to receive the paternal curse. The elevator boy naturally had a spasm when she entered, and the chambermaids stood aghast. As for the baby, it had a milk toddy and a hot bath and was wrapped in soft, silky things and tucked into the leading lady's bed and was warmer and happier than it had ever been in its life before, and perhaps than it will ever be again. She has done many a pretty thing in her time, our leading lady, but she never did a prettier one than that.

Courier, March 18, 1899, p. 5.

Books and Authors (III)

(December 20, 1896—October 21, 1899)

During 1897 and early 1898, when Willa Cather was writing "Old Books and New" for the Home Monthly, *there were relatively few direct comments on literature in "The Passing Show," and those that appeared there were of a more serious nature than she directed to her "Helen Delay" audience (see p. 333). Most of the discussions demonstrated her continuing interest in books and authors whom she considered important before she left Nebraska. In this period the chief literary innovation in "The Passing Show" (after it passed from the* Journal *to the* Courier) *was interviews with guests of the Writers Club of Pittsburgh, to which Willa Cather belonged.*

In March 1898, after "Old Books and New" had been discontinued in the Home Monthly, *reviews signed "Sibert" began to appear in the "Books and Magazines" column of the* Leader. *In fact, however, Cather had been contributing unsigned pieces to the column since the preceding fall, sometimes reviewing the same books she discussed in the* Home Monthly. *For a time after the first signed "Books and Magazines" review on March 4, the column ran weekly, then fortnightly; and there was a hiatus when Willa Cather was in Nebraska on vacation. (For the dates of columns, see the Bibliography.) "Books and Magazines" included reviews running three or four paragraphs in length and also briefer comments, sometimes less than a paragraph, which frequently seemed to be derived from dust-jacket blurbs. Magazine stories and articles occasionally were reviewed; and sometimes following the "Sibert" signature there were additional brief notices of books, perhaps written by other staff members or taken over from publishers' handouts. Although the column carried notices on many currently popular titles, Cather reviewed only one of the 1898 best sellers—Kipling's* The Day's Work *(see below).*

Among the books which she considered significant enough to discuss in both the Leader *column and "The Passing Show" was Mrs. Harcourt Williamson's* The Barn-Stormers. *This novel, forgotten today, may have been singled out because it was concerned with actors, and, according to Edith Lewis, "at some time during the Pittsburgh period [Willa Cather] began a long story,* Fanny, *that had to do with stage folk."[1] In view of this fact, Cather's comments on* The Barn-Stormers *are of extra interest:*

> *Of all the novels in the world stage novels are usually the most trashy and flatly unnatural and impossible, at least American and English novels, Henry James' magnificent* Tragic Muse *of course excepted. In France, where the theatre holds a more assured and legitimate place among the arts than here, the local color of the footlights has been rather overworked in fiction but with us it has been left to the penny dreadfuls. . . .*
>
> *It is no easy thing to write a good stage novel and faithfully preserve the atmosphere which eventually forms the lives of the people who live in it. That profession has customs, technicalities, a parlance of its own of which the general public is as ignorant as of the technicalities of music or painting. Again, the "pirates," the camp-followers of the profession have mannerisms and expressions of their own, differing from those of legitimate players as a patois does from the legitimate speech.*
>
> *It would be well if all authors before writing of a particular class or profession would inform themselves as thoroughly as Mrs. Harcourt Williamson has done. . . . One whose knowledge of the theatre is confined to its aspects in large cities could scarcely realize how faithfully the experiences of these poor barnstormers are presented; the horrors of local trains and rural theatres, the small boys of the village hooting at the "show women," and the kindly condescension of the chambermaid at the hotel who says, "I always do feel sorry for you poor actresses; folks is so down on you, ain't they? Ma'd be as mad as fire if she knew uncle let me associate with actresses!" There is the provincial attitude for you![2]*

Willa Cather realized that the kind of life she was leading, with heavy journalistic commitments and many social activities, was not conducive to the production of the kind of fiction she wanted to write,[3] and from the time of her arrival in Pittsburgh until the end of 1898, there are only nine stories attributed to her, and only one, a dialogue, in 1899.[4] But she was writing regularly about

1. Lewis, *Willa Cather Living*, p. 46.
2. *Courier*, April 16, 1898, p. 3. The "Books and Magazines" review appeared in the *Leader*, March 18, 1898, p. 8. For other comment on stage novels see the second selection (*Journal*, March 29, 1896) in "The View from Red Cloud," Books and Authors (II), above.
3. Willa Cather to Will Owen Jones, August 31, 1897.
4. *CSF*, pp. 585–586.

literature, and as she became free of the demands of play reviewing, criticism of literature, and of fiction in particular, became an increasing preoccupation. Moreover, her attention shifted from the author to the technique of his art.

Henry James: "a really great artist"

In an early Journal *column from Pittsburgh, Willa Cather wrote at length for the first time on Henry James (1843–1916).*[5] *A description of the plot of* The Other House *(1896), omitted here, was quoted from the* Critic. *Briefly, the novel concerns Anthony Bream, who had promised his wife on her deathbed that he would not remarry so long as their daughter was alive. He is loved by two women, the self-sacrificing Jean Mantle and a* femme fatale, *Rose Armiger. Rose murders the child and arranges that Jean be suspected of the crime. To shield Jean, Anthony takes the blame, but the truth comes out. Two years after her discussion of* The Other House, *Cather reviewed* In the Cage *in her "Books and Magazines" column in the* Leader. *In the intervening year James had written* The Spoils of Poynton *and* What Maisie Knew. *Allusions to the latter occur in two selections in The Urban Scene, above.*

It is not every day that a book by a really great artist is capable of making a sensation. And of all men under heaven Henry James is the last man who would be expected to arouse any excited admiration in the mind of the public at large, yet he has done it. Yes, I repeat it, Henry James has made a sensation! Will wonders never cease? For many years Mr. James has contented himself with the devout admiration of the very, very few. He has gone on quietly producing perfect masterpieces of style, but eschewing the strange emotion[s] of humanity as if he were a little afraid of them or considered them somewhat vulgar. Everyone who thinks seriously about such matters at all has long acknowledged him as one of the most subtile analysts, perhaps the greatest living English master of the counterpoint of literary style. But aside from his delightful reflection there was little to hold the average reader. He thinks too much, which is fatal to a novelist's popularity.[6] His touch is true and perfect, delicate,

5. A brief appreciative comment appeared in the *Courier*, November 16, 1895, p. 6; *KA*, pp. 360–361.

6. Cf. "Mr. Hall Caine's income is twenty thousand pounds a year, and Mr. Henry James, the first living writer of pure English and the highest exponent of refined literary art, makes an income of three hundred pounds a year, a smaller sum than most expert accountants are content with. Now if the figures of the two men's incomes were reversed, it would indicate the millennial dawn of public taste." *Courier*, November 25, 1899, p. 2.

yet unerring, but scarcely broad enough to catch the eye of the crowd. People got to saying that he suffered from literary ennui; that it was impossible for him to handle active, passionate flesh and blood characters and strong climaxes. Now Mr. James writes *The Other House* and shows them that he can do their miserable little trick better than the best of them. As someone says: "He has had the card up his sleeve all the time." His new novel is the tragedy of a man who was liked too well. It is as concise as a drama, the whole thing occurring in two scenes.[7] . . .

Stated thus briefly, the plot may sound impossible and farfetched, but that's one of the most glorious powers of art, to make the impossible seem probable, and Mr. James does it. O, the interest, the terror, the tragedy, the passion of it! It is the sort of book that keeps one up until three o'clock in the morning. These great elemental, human emotions are stirring enough when they are unchained upon us by cheap men like Edgar Saltus, but when they are handled by a great master, they become terrific, overwhelming; they become Shakespearean.

[Anthony Bream] is a new subject in fiction, this big, blonde, easy-going, comely fellow, without a touch of romance in him for whom women go mad and commit murder. Novelists have neglected his type. The Greeks, indeed, who knew the secrets of art, used to use him. They had their Theseus who carelessly kept [left?] poor Ariadne upon the rocks, and their Jason, for whom the dark Medea betrayed her father's secrets, and their indifferent, commonplace Adonis who didn't care for anything more sentimental than hunting boars and whom even Venus went crazy about. Anthony Bream is a good deal like these gentlemen. He only wants to take life easily and here and there women make a tragedy for him because they are "smitten of the gods," as the Greeks used to say, and can't help themselves. The closing words of the book are deeply significant. After Jean Mantle has been proven innocent of the murder of Tony's child and poor Rose Armiger, the Medea, the Lady Macbeth of the book, is allowed to escape, Tony's friend assures him that he will never be accused of the crime, even indirectly, for, as he says: "'Tony, people like you too much.'

"Tony, with his hand upon the door, appeared struck with this; but it embittered again the taste of his tragedy. He remembered, with all his vividness, to what tune he had been 'liked' and wearily bowed his head. 'Oh, too much, my boy,' he said as he went out."

7. In fact, *The Other House* was "drafted first as a scenario and later, in 1909, converted from a novel into a play." Walter Wright, *The Madness of Art: A Study of Henry James* (Lincoln: University of Nebraska Press, 1962), p. 107.

Ah! it is good to welcome a novel like this into the language. It will live when *Prisoners of Zenda* lie forgotten in their dungeons and when *The Seats of the Mighty* are brought low.[8]

And what has come over Mr. James? Has he wearied of skill and craft and the fine, subtle distinctions of the intelligence merely as such? Or has he a passing fancy to catch the crowd? At any rate in this book he has thrown off his old mood of pale reflection, he has achieved that unity of great art with great emotions that made Balzac what he was. He has put aside his graceful studies in repose, his scholarly analysis of characteristics. He has taken love and fear and hate and pity and made a tragedy, throbbing with the aching pulse of life.

Journal, December 20, 1896, p. 13.

If I had the space to quote a few pages of this remarkable story [*In the Cage*], it would be quite unnecessary to name the author. No one but Henry James could have written it, and I think no one else would be likely to evolve the situation with which it deals. Given: a young lady telegraphist shut up for eight hours a day in a cage of a telegraph office fenced off in a grocery store, forever smelling of hams and cheese and dried fish, in a suburban district of London. Her business is largely to decipher and send the messages of people who do most of their correspondence by telegraph, ladies and gentlemen who spend in sending "sincere regrets" and "dear loves" and trite trivialities sums that would buy her a new gown or take her out of the sultriness of the London summer to the seaside. Granted that this girl reads greasy novels from a circulating library, that she has good looks and, after a manner, imagination. That she has, moreover, the instinctive desire, feels the instinctive right of youth for life and experience, though she is but a part of the great telegraph system of the world, as much a machine as the "sounder" or the "ticker" it is her business to mind. Now, the question is, what will all these communications of gentlefolk to each other, invitations, regrets, orders for flowers and gowns, mean to her, how will they affect her? Mr. James knows well enough where the romance of the world lives, and from what humble sources the illusions of the world are replenished, in what hearts the old ideals are kept warm. My Lady may laugh at love on her wedding day, but the seamstress who, with affectionate pride, sewed the lace and tulle of her bridal gown does not laugh; she believes. My Lord may leave to

8. These books are discussed in "Old Books and New," February and September 1897, The *Home Monthly*, above. For Edgar Saltus, mentioned above, see Books and Authors (II), above.

his valet the selection of the flowers his fiancée is to carry to the ball, but the florist's girl, who puts the violets tenderly into their box does not know that; she steals covert glances at the card which accompanies them and all her imagination follows that box out of the shop. The maid who admits madame's admirer every night believes in romance, though madame finds these seances tiresome enough. We may all become cynics and materialists, but our tailors and our coachmen will always be idealists. Out of all the patrons of the telegraph cage, the girl inside selects a man and a woman for the chief characters in an emotional drama, and there, in the conflicting odors of bacon and dried herrings, she constructs her romance, puts into it what some of us put into the pictures we like, and some into poetry, and some into music, her imagination and her "inner life," as the phrase goes, the part of her that she could not shut up into the cage. And this outlet became precious to her, as it does to all of us. The dream came to mean more to her than the realities of her life; became, indeed, its chief reality. She is offered an escape from her cage to another cage a few feet larger, but she stays on to see her romance through.

So much for the mere situation, the intellectual trick of the book. Its highest quality is in Mr. James' sympathetic handling of his subject. It would be very easy to make such a study cruel, even brutal. Somehow one would resent seeing an overworked girl who supported an alcoholic mother made sport of, and her sentimental illusions held up to ridicule, as one would resent seeing her credulity trifled with in actual life. But Mr. James is not even a little bit of a snob, or if he is, his is a universal, all-comprehensive snobbery that gently and suavely patronizes us all, undeserving creatures that we are. He treats the girl in the cage quite as respectfully as he would treat a princess of blood, and one feels the same courteous, unsparing hand that did such eminent justice to poor little Pinnie in *The Princess Casamassima*.

Leader, December 2, 1898, p. 13.

Kipling: "*a force to be reckoned with*"

Willa Cather met Rudyard Kipling soon after her arrival in Pittsburgh, but unfortunately there is no record of what they said to each other during the forty-six minutes their conversation lasted.[9] *His volume of verse* The Seven Seas (*1896*), *which stirred considerable interest, is considered in the first selection below. Cather quoted two stanzas of* "*Mandalay,*" *omitted here,*

9. Willa Cather to Mariel Gere, August 4, 1896.

and three stanzas of "When Earth's Last Picture Is Painted," only the first of which is given here. Two years later when she reviewed The Day's Work *(1898) Cather took the opportunity to appraise Kipling's work as a whole. The* Courier *column presented below reprinted verbatim her "Books and Magazines" review* (Leader, *February 18, 1899). For earlier comment, see "Stevenson and Kipling," Books and Authors (I) and "Old Books and New [December 1897]," The* Home Monthly, *above.*

"Our Friend from India," Mr. Kipling, is having an interesting time of it. He went to sleep condemned as a writer of ribald stories and awoke to find himself hailed as the great English poet. In spite of the fact that he had published two volumes of better verses before, it was not until Kipling wrote "Songs of the Seven Seas" that people began to talk about his "taking up the succession after Tennyson." I wish the critics would let Kipling alone and not spoil him with big words. I hate to think of him in the group of British bards. He doesn't go well with Byron's impossible collar or Tennyson's curls and Shelley's lace ruffles. I'd rather think of him loafing back of the barracks with Mulvaney and Learoyd and Ortheris and the dog that had the mange. He is really too much of a—well, too much of a man to be called a British bard. How much in the usual order of things it is that just because Kipling is the supreme master of the short story people insist upon considering him a poet! He does, indeed, write excellent verses and personally one may be much fonder of them than of much greater poetry, but for all that they are not great in the highest sense. It is the individual quality in them that most appeals to one. People who like Kipling like his verses because they are Kipling's. Take, for instance, an extract from "Mandalay," one of his best. . . .

Personally, I like that. It has all the freshness and vividness of a man who knows the world, a bigger, wilder part of the world than ours, and who has seen with a perception strangely keen and sympathetic into all the experiences of men. But compare it, if you will, with Keats' "St. Agnes Eve," or with anything of Shelley's. Then would you wish to place Kipling among the immortal bards? If his verses were lost, literature would be the poorer for it, but poetry, I think would not. Never, in any of his work in verse, has Kipling ever burst into those higher strains of perfect melody, those seductive phrases which seem to capture the very spirit of beauty herself and hold her up living to the gaze of men. Compare Kipling's best verses with the first book of *Hyperion*, or with the best parts of *Sordello*, and he becomes mere *opéra bouffe*, vaudeville. There is something tremendously virile and effective about those loose, vivid phrases of his, and one need not be ashamed to feel their spell, but for all that they are not the language of the hill of Helicon. Kipling's verse is deservedly popular because it is the most modern verse that has ever been written and is immeasurably closer than any other to the heart of the present. Poetry is retrospective; life precedes it always. Homer could only have written after the heroic age, not before it, and there were, perforce, crusades before Tasso could write *Jerusalem Delivered.* Our poets are always a generation or two behind us. Kipling is the first man who has at all adequately handled the life that we know and live. He has even made an admirable poem on machinery, "M'Andrew's Hymn." His verses are full of our own phrases, of our slang even. He is thoroughly an exponent of the human and the living present. But in all ages and in all tongues, whether they wrote epics or lyrics, Bibles or love songs, poets have struggled with something beyond the human, with the unreasonable and inexplicable unrest which gives us our highest and most unreasonable hope. For it is no light saying that the poet walks with God. Usually he is a man of sorrows and acquaintance with grief. A grief that, as de Musset says, tracks him step by step all the days of his life and finally sits forever on his grave.

It detracts nothing from Mr. Kipling's honor that he is not an immortal "bard." He himself wishes to stand or fall by his prose. That is his serious work as an artist; his verses are his recreations, he writes them offhand, just as a tune happens to get into his head. Shades of the ancients! This young man has glory enough, as someone has said he conquered an empire before he was out of his 'teens. When one considers what this fellow of thirty-two has done, the thought of what he may be expected to do in the future becomes almost alarming. He is already a master of things that usually men of his age are just beginning to grasp. Think of it! He wrote *The Story of the Gadsbys* when he was twenty, and before he was twenty-five he had written some fifty of the most perfect short stories in the language. I don't believe he cares whether he is a "bard" or not. I believe he cares for his works more than for the glory thereof; that he has lived by the creed he professes in the epilogue of *The Seven Seas:*

When Earth's last picture is painted and the tubes are twisted and dried,
When the oldest colors have faded and the youngest critic has died,
We shall rest, and, faith, we shall need it—lie down for an aeon or two,
Till the Master of All Good Workmen shall set [put] us to work anew! . . .

Journal, May 16, 1897, p. 13.

Mr. Rudyard Kipling is a force to be reckoned with. You can count upon the fingers of one hand the Englishmen from whom a new volume could excite as much interest throughout the entire English-speaking world, or could mean as much to English letters. He is read with pleasure by admirers of Miss Corelli, and he is read with unfailing astonishment and admiration by the clientele of Henry James, Limited. He has been published in the *Ladies' Home Journal*, side by side with Mr. Bok's advice to young men,[10] and he has been taken seriously in the pages of the *Edinburgh Review*. In short, he is a fact in English Literature, known and felt by the many, disputed, perhaps, but always admitted by the few. Aside from his prodigious dexterity of execution, his methods, always unusual and often unprecedented, which compel the admiration of all lovers of good craftsmanship, he has an impassioned, never wavering interest in things vital and present which appeals to all men of affairs. So he has accomplished the seemingly impossible, and is Greek to the Greeks and barbarian to the barbarians, honored by two factions that love not to mingle their incense.

The title of Mr. Kipling's last volume, *The Day's Work*, might be said to cover his entire literary output. No man has ever written more persistently or more vividly of the affairs which engage the daily life of men. If Mr. Kipling knows that there are men of leisure in the world, he has never said so. The dilettante, who has always so important a place in novels, and who is still not without honor in the fiction of Mr. Richard Harding Davis and Mrs. Constance Cary Harrison, Mr. Kipling holds as beneath his contempt. The world has been a great many centuries in evolving its present gigantic industries, but Mr. Kipling is the first man who has ever written of them seriously or sympathetically. Steam was discovered in 1769, yet mechanics and poetry first met in "M'Andrews Hymn," and de Musset half a century before had declared them forever incompatible and antagonistic. The English army has been fighting and sweating and dying in India, in Asia and the Sudan for a century or more, yet it was Kipling who first introduced the English soldier to the English people. The nucleus of Anglo-Indian society was formed when Clive's troopers marched into the interior, yet no one knew anything about it until the appearance of *Soldiers Three* and *Mine Own People*. Edmund Gosse said, years ago when Kipling was in his first vogue and his place

10. Although Edward Bok (1860–1930) was editor of the *Ladies' Home Journal*, he did not write "Side Talks with Boys," a column similar to Ruth Ashmore's for girls (see note 9, The Star System [III], above).

in literature not at all assured, that if the British empire in India should become a thing of the past, those stories would be more valuable to the historian of the future than all the tons of government reports ever mailed to England.[11] When Zola wrote *L'Assommoir* he declared that it was "the first story of the people that had the smell of the people." Certainly Mr. Kipling is the first English author who has abandoned the smug standpoint of the quarterdeck and gone down to find what life was like before the mast. "The Bridge Builders" is one of the most characteristic stories in the present volume. Findlayson was a civil engineer who was building a bridge over the Ganges. He had been building it for three years. He had changed the face of the country for miles around; burrowed out pits and thrown up embankments, and seen a village of workmen grow up and about him. "He had endured heat and cold, disappointment, discomfort, danger and disease." Meantime the bridge grew, "plate by plate, girder by girder, span by span," and Findlayson built his life into the bridge.[12] Even Peroo, the native overseer, says, "My honor is the honor of the bridge." That is Mr. Kipling's idea of work. I fancy, moreover, that it is the spirit in which he works. He finds energy the most wonderful and terrible and beautiful thing in the universe; the energy of great machines, of animals in their hunt for prey, of men in their hand-to-hand fight for a foothold in the world. He has found in this energy subject matter for art, whereas it has previously been considered the exclusive province of science. An inevitable accompaniment of this worship of force is his keen interest in the entire physical world, and his sympathy for workmen in every field, and his insatiable avidity for the details of every trade. Give him the routine of a man's business, and he will make the man for you. Where he has acquired all his minute technical knowledge of bridge building, cod fishing, railroading, jungle creatures, army and civil life, his accurate and sympathetic knowledge of topography, that is a part of his genius and nature's secret. Enumeration, which has somehow come to be reckoned as one of the innovations of realism, is as old as the Catalogue of the Ships in the *Iliad*, and Mr. Kipling's use of it is not unlike Homer's. He can take a list of facts as dull as an extract from a report of the treasury bureau of statistics, and with a few deft touches, behold! it is a-throb with life, clear and vivid, and complete as a sketch by Meissonier. Take the following extract from his remarkable railroad story, "007," descriptive of a freight yard in a great city.

11. Edmund Gosse (1849–1928), prolific English man of letters, wrote an essay on Rudyard Kipling in the *Century*, October 1898, pp. 901–910.

12. Willa Cather was also to write of a bridge builder, Bartley Alexander, in her first published novel, *Alexander's Bridge* (1912).

007 pushed out gingerly his heart in his head light, so nervous that the sound of his own bell almost made him jump the track. Lanterns waved, advanced up and down before and behind him; and on every side, six tracks deep, sliding backward and forward, with clashings of couplers and squeals of hand brakes, were cars—more cars than 007 had ever dreamed of. There were oil-cars, hay-cars and stock cars full of lowing beasts, and ore-cars and potato-cars with stove-pipe ends sticking out in the middle; cold-storage and refrigerator cars dripping ice water on the tracks; ventilated fruit and milk cars; flat cars and truck-wagons full of market stuff; flat cars loaded with reapers and binders, all red and green and gilt under the sizzling electric lights; flat cars piled high with strong-scented hides, pleasant hemlock plank, or bundles of shingles; flat cars creaking to the weight of thirty-ton castings, angle-irons and rivet-boxes for some new bridge; and hundreds and hundreds of box cars, loaded, locked and chalked.

There is just one other man alive who could have written that paragraph, and that is Zola himself. But he would not have stopped there; he would have gone at length into the sufferings of the hearts in the stock cars, and insisted that the potatoes were rotten, and that the hides dripped with blood; he would have described the reapers and binders individually and separately; it is not unlikely that he would have catalogued the different bridge castings, and he would remorselessly have extracted every evil smell that is to be got out of a freight yard. Yet these two men, different as they are, are the only living writers who have at their command the virility of the epic manner, unless one include the author of *With Fire and Sword*.[13] Each is, in his own way, a master of detail, and their management of it is different as the men themselves. The one at his herculean tasks throws up mountains of facts that it is impossible to remember; the other concentrates all his knowledge into a few sharp, stinging sentences that cut clean to the heart of the matter and that it is impossible to forget. It is the old story of the hammer and rapier.[14]

It is in this vast and minute knowledge and in an effective and amazingly original use of it that Mr. Kipling has grown. But in depth, in grace, in noble seriousness he has advanced not at all. For the last ten years his

13. *With Fire and Sword: A Historical Romance of Russia and Poland* (1884; English trans. 1890), by Henryk Sienkiewicz. See also "Old Books and New [February 1898]," The *Home Monthly*, above.

14. For a discussion of the source of this phrase, see *KA*, p. 136 n. For earlier and later uses, see *Journal*, November 4, 1894, p. 12, quoted in introductory note to Books and Authors (I), above, and "On Language: French and English," below.

development has been of the hand rather than spiritual. Had *Captains Courageous* and *The Day's Work* been his first productions they would have made, doubtless, a noise in the world, but they would not have done for their author what *Plain Tales from the Hills* and *Soldiers Three* did. In his new book one finds no such masterpieces as "The Man Who Would Be King" or "On the City Wall," no such poetic paragraphs as once kindled the dullest imagination, no such depth of tenderness as awed the most irreverent of us in "Without Benefit of Clergy." I find in *The Day's Work* no such passages as this, from "Dray Wara Yow Dee."

> Come back with me to the north and be among men once more. Come back, when this matter is accomplished and I call for thee! The bloom of the peach orchards is upon all the valley, and here is only dust and a great stink. There is a pleasant wind among the mulberry trees, and the streams are bright with snow-water, and the caravans go up and the caravans go down, and a hundred fires sparkle in the gut of the pass, and tent-peg answers hammer-nose, and the pack-horse squeals to pack-horse across the drift smoke of the evening. It is good in the north now. Come back with me. Let us return to our own people! Come!

That, by your leave, is worth all the descriptions of all the freight yards in the world. Time was when Mr. Kipling brought into our lives a beauty wild and strange, when he promised to create a literature as unique as the *Arabian Nights*, when he was very near indeed to the face of "The True Romance."

A part of the greatness of a man of genius is to know what subjects are worthy of him, what of all the things he can do well are best worth his doing. In this instinct Mr. Kipling seems to be woefully deficient. He is dangerously clever and he has a taste for farce, and these two propensities lead him into many a *tour de force* unworthy of his high talent. Admitting that the Mrs. Hauksbee stories were cheap in their knowingness; that *The Story of the Gadsbys* was an atrocious precocity in a youth of twenty, they were better worth doing than Tom Brown schoolboy stories, or the conversation of horses in a Vermont pasture. He has the most vertiginous imagination of his generation, and it is not to be wasted on *Youth's Companion* stories. It found its fittest material in lands near the sun; lands of mystery, where there are mountains that have not been scaled, rivers that have not been bridged, deserts that have not been crossed. Surely, the temple bells are calling him "on the road to Mandalay." There are a dozen men who could have written *Captains Courageous* very nearly as well as Mr. Kipling—no, not half as well—but there is only one hand in all the living world that could have written "Without Benefit of Clergy" or anything like it.

In *The Day's Work* Mr. Kipling's experimental playfulness of mood seems to have affected his workmanship. Several of the stories exhibit an alarming departure from the single purpose and swift, vivid execution which has been one of his most meritorious qualities. The opium dream and the conversation of the Hindu gods in "The Bridge Builders" is an entire departure from the original theme of the story, and has nothing whatever to do with the fate of Findlayson's bridge. Mr. Kipling has dropped the familiar "but that's another story"; he now tells two stories in one. In "William the Conqueror" the love story is certainly forced unduly into the foreground to make it a love story at all, and, moreover, it is somewhat conventionalized. The elaborate discussion of Georgie's military career in India is diametrically opposed to the mystic strain in "The Brushwood Boy," and cannot be excused as a means of contrast, as can the recital of his experience at school. Georgie, indeed, smacks a little of Bobby in "Only a Subaltern," and yet he has a very different part to play, and is supposed to have a poet shut up inside of him somewhere. I could understand the hero of *The Light that Failed* having possessions in a dream world and riding the Thirty-Mile Ride with Maisie, but I cannot understand it in Georgie Cottar and the girl who lisped. In Georgie's Indian experiences the writing has a jocular ring that detracts from the dignity of the main theme, and if Mr. Kipling had subordinated Georgie's obtrusive virtues to the poetic mysticism of the background, he would have made a better story. It might have been one of the greatest stories that bear his name, and it is not. When he wished to use women for a high end, he used not to make them lisp, though his attitude toward the gentle sex has never been overly chivalrous. In "The Brushwood Boy" I miss something of the intense earnestness and tenderness which were so terribly present in "Without Benefit of Clergy"; something of the imperious splendor of imagination which made "The Gate of a Hundred Sorrows" one glorious debauch of color. I miss them, and I am unconsoled for their loss.

Courier, March 4, 1899, pp. 2–3.

Stevenson: "that blithe and gallant spirit"

In Pittsburgh Willa Cather had the opportunity to talk with two people who had known Robert Louis Stevenson well—the artist Will H. Low and Mrs. Isobel Strong, Stevenson's stepdaughter, who later collaborated with her brother Lloyd Osbourne on Memories of Vailima (*1902*). *The chat with Low occurred at the dinner described in "Will H. Low and Bouguereau," The Urban Scene, above.*

... When a seasonable opportunity came, I quoted a phrase or two of some verses that Stevenson once wrote to Mr. Low. The genial dinner-table expression left his face in a moment, he gave me a penetrating look and then dropped his grave eyes to his plate. I saw my break in a moment. The personal pain and sense of loss were acute still—after three years. I apologized simply and directly. He said he hoped he had not been rude, but that the subject was too painful a one for a dinner party. I said no more, but he inconsistently would talk of nothing else that evening. The name once mentioned was not to be forgotten. "The sad part of it," he remarked, "is that the world really never got the heart of Louis. I have lived in many countries and known many men, but the personal charm of that woman-man was the sweetest experience I have had ... [*Scrambled line*] on personality and quite froze up at the mention of his family. I could see he did not love the hoard of stepsons and stepgrandsons that lived on that one poor stricken genius. Of Stevenson's work he said more than I could write in a week, though he agreed with me that his manner was greater than his matter and his art alone his inspiration. But the strange part of his conversation was the way in which he spoke. He is the third man I have met who knew Stevenson personally, and it is the same with them all. At the mention of his name strong men melt and become tender as bereaved women. Nothing in life seems to fill the sense of personal loss they will carry to their graves with them. What was there in this man to make men love him so, I wonder? ...

Courier, October 30, 1897, p. 3.

I believe that as one's experience enlarges one loses the more physical attributes of hero-worship, that is, the personality and individual life of brilliant men ceases to interest one keenly, and that one is quite content to take the work apart from the workman and to lose sight of the man in contemplating the artist. But certainly when Mrs. Isobel Strong, Stevenson's stepdaughter and amanuensis arrived in Pittsburgh, I felt a very sharp attack of that devotional curiosity which one usually knows very little about after one is eighteen. I wanted to see this woman who had lived under the same roof with that blithe and gallant spirit, who had shared his exile in the South Seas, who had witnessed that long, manful struggle against disease, who had written down the text of those incomparable romances as they first fell from his lips. This personal affection for Stevenson is common among all people who find a peculiarly delicate pleasure in his words, and who are, as Andrew Lang put it, sealed of the tribe of Louis. Without doubt Stevenson's was the most winning and lovable personality in modern letters, and those who have come fully under his subtile influence are more jealous of his reputation than was he himself. I fancy Charles Lamb must have had something of this potent personal charm, but certainly no writer of this generation has approached it.

As to the lecture which Mrs. Strong delivered here on "Stevenson in Samoa" I can say very little for it. It was all Samoa and no Stevenson. She told us how clothes are made in Samoa, and instructed us carefully as to the roasting of pigs and the sauces wherewith they should be eaten, but of R. L. S., she said no effectual word. Moreover, I dislike the principle of the thing; one resents the commercial uses which Mr. Stevenson's family persistently make of his memory. It was only after the lecture was over, in the seclusion of a quiet room looking out upon the hills of the park where the autumn sunshine burned upon the colored foliage and the amber leaves rustled down through the blue hazy air, that I persuaded Mrs. Strong to talk of Stevenson himself. There, with the pictures she had taken of him in Samoa, and pages of his dictation still fresh in her memory, one began to feel quite in his atmosphere, and the blue hills off against the sky line recalled a little that mountain far away in the Pacific, where he sleeps, who is so well remembered. . . .

"His method of composition," said Mrs. Strong, "O it was slow and laborious—laborious sometimes even to painfulness, as he believed all good work must be. He would pace the floor with a tiny slip of cardboard full of notes in his hand, dictating to me so slowly that I was easily able to write it out in long hand, and he was scrupulously careful to dictate the punctuation, as that was rather a hobby of his. Perhaps he would finish a chapter that day. Then, the next morning he would read it over, usually with many a shake of the head, and with a sigh would rise and gird himself for the battle, probably throwing the entire chapter into the fire and carefully dictating it over again, recasting and revising it until it was sometimes scarcely recognizable. Perhaps it would remain in that form, but the chances were that he would lay it by for a week and then take it up and work it over again and again. Only once did I know him to shorten this process and write without revision, and that was in his last and uncompleted novel, *Weir of Hermiston.* He abandoned *St. Ives* in a fit of boyish enthusiasm for the new tale, and it came from his brain white hot, full formed and word perfect. He was master of it from the first, his hand never faltered or knew uncertainty. On the very morning of his death he said to me, 'I see the whole thing as clearly as I see you, the book already exists, it is!' He, who was always so modest about his work, always ready to poke fun at it, said that *Weir of Hermiston* would be his masterpiece. On that last morning he dictated with astonishing ease and fluency, at the very high tide of his power."

Only a few hours later the stroke came which stilled the delicate machinery of that subtile brain forever, and from that low coral shore there went out a tidal wave of loss and sorrow that was felt around the world. . . .

Courier, October 21, 1899, p. 3.

Anthony Hope

The announcement in the Courier, *October 23, 1897, that "in this number . . . Miss Willa Cather, now the dramatic critic of the* Pittsburgh Leader *begins her dramatic and literary critique under the familiar title of 'The Passing Show'" mentioned that her weekly contribution would include interviews with distinguished men and women. "In particular there is Anthony Hope Hawkins who will soon lecture in Pittsburgh and as he will not come to see us, it will be a rare pleasure to hear how the author of* The Prisoner of Zenda *looks to a friend and what he says." Hope read from his works in Pittsburgh on October 29, 1897. Much of Willa Cather's report in the* Leader *the next day was incorporated in her account for the* Courier.

I first met Anthony Hope Hawkins at a reception given him by the Writers Club. Now the Writers Club is composed of poor wretches who have the misfortune to earn their bread by the sweat of the ink pot and is maintained for the express purpose of torturing celebrities. When one of the Great comes to town "we" of the Writers Club issue invitations and hie us to a florist and invest in palms and chrysanthemums, and find a pianist and a man who can growl out bass solos and proceed to give the great man a reception. That is, he is compelled to stand on his feet for an hour and shake hands with hundreds of people he cares nothing whatever about, and make brilliant replies to their inane questions. This sort of a program was all very well for Dr. [John] Watson—"Ian Maclaren"—as he is a public man and a clergyman, and knew exactly how to conduct himself under the circumstances and to give you that fatherly handgrip and suave, meaningless smile that a rector bestows upon as you pass out of his church on Sunday morning. But Mr. Hawkins is different. He is simply a novelist and an English gentleman: quiet, conservative almost to shrinkingness, with the traces in his face of having lived a good deal, and with the kind of eyes that go to dreaming in the midst of a crowd. Not at all the sort of man for public functions, but rather to live quietly with his pipe in his law chambers in the Temple, making imaginary excursions into Ruritania.

I never pitied a man more sincerely. Major Pond[15] was not with him, and he was absolutely alone and stranded among those idiotic people. Even sensible people become unaccountably silly under such circumstances, and the club and their guests outdid themselves. It was a motley assemblage; there were university professors who stood and looked over their glasses at the "distinguished guest" as though he were a type specimen of some new species of mammal; there were pert reporters with their trousers turned up, and giddy society maidens who had come with the reporters; there were female reporters of uncertain ages in sloppy rubbers—which they would not lay aside in the dressing room, having no faith in the honesty of their sex—wearing glasses and carrying notebooks in which they occasionally wrote, stealing furtive glances at the bewildered Mr. Hawkins as they did so. Then there were a few of the society people present, who patronized the poor man in the frankest manner, and were anxious to know his "impressions of America."

While it is quite beyond me to give any adequate notion of the colossal stupidity of that reception, or of the indignities to which the helpless victim was submitted, I will endeavor to repeat a little of the conversation from memory—not having been wise enough to take a notebook, as did some more knowing ladies of my craft.

Heavy Society Lady, with a motherly smile: "Well, Mr. Hope, I suppose you don't like New York quite as well as London yet?"

Mr. Hawkins: "Well, you see I'm very partial to London, though they have treated me very nicely in New York, I'm sure."

Heavy Lady: "I expect you find the weather in Pittsburgh more homelike than in New York—the fogs, I mean."

Mr. Hawkins: "Now the truth is, that in London we have just about four fogs in the year, real fogs you know. We should call this a clear day."

15. Major James B. Pond (1838–1903) conducted the Lyceum Lecture Bureau.

Heavy Lady: "But in your last novel you have fogs enough."

Mr. Hawkins, nervously: "O! One can have all the fogs one desires in a novel, especially when one wants to get someone out of the way unobserved."

Young Society Lady, in a Gainsborough hat and ermine cape, with a troop of her kind behind her: "So this is really the man who wrote *The Prisoner!* We are so crazy to meet you and yet we're so afraid you might put some of us in your novels and say mean things about us!"

Mr. Hawkins, with deep meaning: "I am quite incapable of such an act, I assure you."

Young Lady: "I know writers hate to tell about their books before they're out, but won't you please tell us about the sequel to *The Prisoner*, whether you're going to have the King die and bring Rudolf and Flavia together?"

Mr. Hawkins: "I'm afraid I had scarcely considered that contingency—so careless of me."

Young Man, with literary aspirations: "Mr. Hawkins, there are several of us who want to know just a little about your methods of work, if we may venture on such a subject."

Mr. Hawkins, civilly: "I am at your service, gentlemen."

Young Man: "We want to know if you begin a novel with any definite plan as to how you will accomplish your end, that is, if you first decide upon the incidents by which you can best develop your characters?"

Mr. Hawkins, with a puzzled air: "I fear I don't entirely comprehend you."

Young Man: "Do you first make sketches of your characters, as a painter does for a figure piece?"

Mr. Hawkins: "I don't think the analogy will hold at all."

Young Man: "Well, do you prefer the positive or the negative method of art or do you consciously pursue either?"

Mr. Hawkins, with embarrassment: "I, I really fear, gentlemen, that I do not."

Young Man: "Then you have just stumbled upon your results?"

Mr. Hawkins, with abject humility: "Stumbled, merely stumbled."

My opportunity to really know Mr. Hawkins a little came just after this reception, where they encircled him between two pots of chrysanthemums. A clerical friend of mine here attended the same college with Mr. Hawkins, and after the reception carried him off to a private smoking room with me in tow. I had requested that I should be ignored as nearly as the ordinary laws of civility would allow. What I wished was to hear the tortured victim converse with someone he had known and who cared for him and was not merely trying to pump him.

The room was small and furnished in red and was a trifle less bleak than the reception room. Although it was only three o'clock the gas was lighted, for the mist was heavy outside, and a fire was burning in the open grate.

Mr. Hawkins sank exhausted into a leather reclining chair, and for the first time I felt that I could look at him squarely without impertinence. He is very tall and thin with a slight stoop in his shoulders and there is an indifference in his bearing that seems to come rather from preoccupation than listlessness. His hair looks as though it were pushed down over his ears. About the back of his head it is thick and touched with gray, but on the top of his head it is conspicuously absent. His cheekbones are high and prominent, his face thin and the youthful glow of his skin is at variance with the stoop in his shoulders and the gray in his hair. His high, full forehead and his eyes are his distinguishing features. They are really very remarkable eyes; very large and of a changing shade of gray, with something almost feminine in their expression. When he is in repose they are always dreamy as a maiden's are supposed to be, but when he looked into the face of his friend they lit with an opalescent glow, beautiful to behold. I never saw a man more retiring, more sensitive, less fitted for the role of a lion. Even the scars on his hands, acquired with a jackknife when he was a boy, seemed to attest to his thoroughly wholesome commonplaceness. Somehow it was amusing to think of this modern, scholarly English gentleman sending his soul off masquerading into Ruritania, fighting duels and wooing a Princess. And yet, I am not sure but that it should be put the other way about, and that magnificent young Howard Gould,[16] with a figure like a captain of the guards, who was playing *The Prisoner of Zenda* down at the Alvin last week and looking the part even better than he played it, was not masquerading in the knightly chivalrousness of this man's soul.

Mr. Hawkins did not sit still long. He forgot his exhaustion, and putting his arm about his friend's shoulder began to pace the floor and talk of old Oxford days and people, while I sat by the fire effacing myself

16. See note 34, The Urban Scene, above.

as nearly as possible. I noticed the serious vein of his conversation, though perhaps that was only natural in meeting an old friend in a strange country. He talked of old dons and tutors, of death and failures, of good fellows who had gone to the bad and bad fellows who had got the prizes of life, until one began to feel rather afraid of living.

I knew that Mr. Hawkins had married the charming English actress who played Flavia in *The Prisoner of Zenda*, and I began to be rather impatient because the clergyman did not ask him about his wife. The subject came around indirectly after awhile. They were talking about the change his literary success had made in his life, when the clergyman remembered, "But it was *The Prisoner* that brought you the multitude wasn't it?"

"Ah, my dear boy," replied Mr. H. Hawkins, "it did so much more than that—it brought me the One!" And it was good to see his hand tighten on his friend's shoulder as he said it. And if I repeated the rest of his conversation upon that subject, I should be a very hardened journalist indeed.

Just as we were going, Mr. Hawkins remarked that he had seen and admired Howard Gould's Rudolf. I asked him whether he had suffered much from Fanchon Campbell's Flavia.[17]

He smiled and answered, "Well, you see there is just one Flavia to me."

"And I suppose," put in the clergyman, "that she is just the antithesis of the dream Flavia?"

"Well, I really can't say as to that," said Mr. Hawkins, "you see, since I have known her I have forgotten the dream."

Was ever a neater gallantry spoken? I hope Madame Flavia Hawkins appreciates her blessings.

In the evening Mr. Hawkins read from his novel at the Carnegie Hall. To hear an author read from his own books is more or less depressing. He seems out of place. Granting this much to start with, one must admit that Mr. Hawkins did all that could be expected of him under the circumstances. When he got his "cue" he rose and went to the speaker's stand, leaning rather helplessly against it. He made no reply to his flattering introduction; he made no complimentary remark about America or Americans; he "taffied" no one, he flattered no one. Like a courteous and well-bred gentleman whom popularity has not spoiled he proceeded directly to the work in hand without any gilded phrases.

17. Frances Campbell died in 1947.

The charm of his reading is that it is not dramatic. He makes no gestures, though his voice and eyes get in a good deal of telling work.

His first selection was "The Philosopher in the Apple Orchard," that delicate study in the eternal feminine, that one-sided love story in which the girl does all the love-making. Everyone in reading Mr. Hawkins' books feel that he has a peculiarly sure touch with his women. He writes of them with understanding, or perhaps it is only with that respectful and sympathetic misunderstanding which is quite as effective. But in his reading this comes out even more prominently than in the printed page. Yes, the thing is clear; he wrote those stories for the sake of the women in them; for Dolly and the Duchess and Osra and Flavia,—Flavia most of all.

The feminine, the even girlish quality which Mr. Hawkins sometimes introduces into his voice is quite baffling. It is not really in his voice at all, which is deep and rather heavy. It is rather the audible translation of a psychic quality.

His second reading was that notable last chapter "If Love Were All," from *The Prisoner of Zenda*. In that his reading was almost monotonous at times, but that was done with a purpose, as the romance is written in the first person and supposed to be related by the hero. Mr. Hawkins adopts the careless, unostentatious air of a gentleman telling of his own exploits. Only into Flavia's replies did he throw any dramatic intensity, and it seemed as if he put all his life into those. "I do not know why God has let me love you. But this I know: then you must go and I must stay." If a few of the actresses who play Flavia could hear him read those lines, they might receive some enlightenment.

Mr. Hawkins seems to cherish an author's usual fondness for his more unpopular works, for when he read from the Princess Osra stories, he selected the least liked and probably the least deserving, "The Miller of Hofbau."[18] I believe he cherishes a personal weakness for Osra. He seems to have the same sort of lenient, half-regretful fondness that the rest of us do for that wilful, winsome Princess.—By the way, in pronouncing the name Flavia, he uses the long and not the broad sound of *A*.

The readings from *The Dolly Dialogues* were of course, the best—as readings at any rate. They were written to be read aloud. As he read them,

18. Cather had written approvingly of the Princess Osra stories in her "Helen Delay" column ("Old Books and New [February 1897]," The *Home Monthly*, above) and specifically of "The Indifference of the Miller of Hofbau" in the *Courier*, November, 9, 1895, p. 6; *KA*, p. 321.

the man seemed now and again to quite forget that they were his own and to be quite unconsciously amused by the delicate, volatile humor which plays through them. He makes Mr. Carter rather "harder hit" than he is usually supposed to be, but Mr. Hawkins leans just a little towards sentiment. Who wouldn't after Marie Delahesse and Osra and Dolly and—Flavia? No wonder he does not care for the society of ordinary women!

After his "lecture" he was seized by the multitude and dragged off to supper parties and smokers and other grewsome festivities. Poor man!

Courier, November 13, 1897, pp. 2–3.

John Oliver Hobbes

The American-born English novelist and dramatist Pearl Mary Teresa Craigie (1867–1906), who wrote under the name of John Oliver Hobbes, had published a half-dozen novels, including The Sinner's Comedy *(1892) and* The Herb-Moon *(1896), prior to* School for Saints *(1897), reviewed here. As Willa Cather notes, one character in the novel was said to be based on the famous French courtesan Liane de Pougy, whose admirers ranged from monarchs and millionaires and poets and painters to the heavyweight boxing champion James J. (Gentleman Jim) Corbett (1866–1933). For additional comment on Mrs. Craigie, see "Tales of John Oliver Hobbes and Ambrose Bierce," below.*

Mrs. Craigie has at last written a full-fledged novel: what Rudyard Kipling would style a "three-decker." It is more than a long novel, it is one of those most precarious ventures, a political and historical novel. To attempt to give a clear outline of the plot would be to attempt what Mrs. Craigie herself has not done. It is a book full of clever things, which bear no particular relation to each other. The style is somewhat heterogeneous and quite different from that in which *The Herb-Moon* was written. It looks very much as though Mrs. Craigie had taken a dignified pose, girded herself up for politics and determined to be highly serious and profoundly intellectual. Her hero is a young Englishman reared in France and brought up on cloisteral dreams and *Amadis of Gaul*, who at eighteen follows a beautiful actress to Paris on foot for the purpose of telling her that she is unworthy of his juvenile passion. The actress, by the way, is said to have been partially suggested by the haughty, naughty Liane de Pougy, of Jimmy Corbett fame. The denouement of the story—if one may apply so humble a term to a political novel—is that the monastic hero marries the daughter of the haughty, naughty one. Mrs. Craigie herself admits that her hero is a politician who should have been a priest. The novel is clumsily constructed and is singularly lacking in directness and continuity. Incidents are loosely strung together with small regard for their relative importance. Mrs. Craigie seems never to have dreamed of subordinating any one part of her story to throw another into bolder relief, or of conserving her forces for a particular end. She goes into trivial details so lavishly that she has no reserve power left for a climax. She does not attempt to make all the threads of her rambling plot strengthen each other for her own purposes. Her characters do not keep within the picture, do not focus the interest of the picture, but sit about in individual isolation like the figures in Puvis de Chavannes' canvases.

As to the historical and political features of the novel, and they seem to be the principal ones, they scarcely do more than divert the interest from the story and perplex the reader. Politics is not Mrs. Craigie's strong point; she does not succeed in giving it living interest. She has tried to write a Disraeli novel in a Bulwer-Lytton manner and she has succeeded in embodying the faults of both. The consciousness of this effort was so manifestly upon her that she has even introduced Disraeli, a dim, gaunt figure, swathed in epigrams and theological discussions. She assumes all the prodigalness of Bulwer and all his ponderous affectation of erudition. Her distant characters constantly shout Greek and Latin and Italian quotations at each other across the shadowy void between them, all of which Mrs. Craigie considerately translates, just as Bulwer always did. Even her French phrases she religiously renders into English. That kindly habit of translating always seems a bit impertinent on the part of an author, but when Mrs. Craigie translates that ancient Latin hymn, "Dies irae, dies illa," which is as common as a nursery rhyme, she rather oversteps the bounds of courtesy. Has all knowledge of Latin died out of England?

Mrs. Craigie in the course of her book several times takes occasion to assail Flaubert; a dangerous business for a lady of England, whose literary standing is by no means fixed to attack one of the classical masters of France! She has one of her characters remark that Flaubert had "the morals of a sick devil and the philosophy of a retired dancing master." What she means by that she alone knows. But let Flaubert's morals and philosophy be what they will, if literary perfection be the wages of endeavor, what countless centuries of unremitting toil lie between Mrs. Craigie and the author of *Madame Bovary!*

Leader, January 7, 1898, p. 13.

The Death of Daudet

The death of Alphonse Daudet (b. 1840) on December 16, 1897, elicited three articles from Willa Cather. The first, "Phases of Alphonse Daudet," appeared in the Leader, *December 26, 1897, and was adapted for the* Courier *column reprinted below. Some sentences were omitted including the following: "Now it is Alphonse Daudet who has laid aside his pen; and out in Père-Lachaise, that burial ground of genius where, beyond the glittering lights of Paris, Death keeps his court, there is another of those graves marked by a single name which Balzac said made the passerby dream."*[19] *The third piece, which appeared in "Old Books and New," the* Home Monthly, *February 1898, drew material (much abridged) from both the* Leader *and the* Courier *and added: "Daudet has been called the 'French Dickens' and I suppose no other French novelist, Victor Hugo excepted, is so popular in English-speaking countries." When Willa Cather began to read French once or twice a week with the George Seibels, the first book they took up was Daudet's* Femmes d'Artistes *(1874) and on her first trip to Europe she visited the land of Daudet.*[20]

Alphonse Daudet's funeral was one of the dramatic events of the season in Paris. A demonstration which could have occurred only in the capital of the world of letters. With honors such as other nations pay only to kings, they bore him through the streets of Paris, that same Paris to which he came from the South some forty years ago, a boy of eighteen with a bundle of manuscript and forty sous in his pocket. Ah, what labors herculean! what battles and what triumphs lay between that entrance and that exit!

That he died in his prime, before his glorious powers had failed him, before the cold of age had chilled the hot boy's heart of him, is only another proof that Fortune loved him with a more enduring constancy than is her wont. Not for him was the pitiable weakening so often attendant upon the age of genius, the senile vagaries and follies, the ossification of imagination, the blind groping for a dead inspiration. When Alphonse Daudet said adieu to life and art, the warm kiss of youth was yet upon his lips. God send us all [such a?] good ending!

And he had lived: No man of his time more deeply and more richly. He was the North and the South, the Provençal and the Parisian, the

19. For other uses of this reference, see "Carvalho," The Musical World (I), above, and "Two Poets: Yone Noguchi and Bliss Carman," below.

20. Seibel, p. 169. See also "In the Land of Daudet," The European Scene, below.

Bohemian and the man of family. He went through the noisy bazaar, among the lying merchantmen and bought only what was precious.

The story of his first experiences in Paris, Daudet himself wrote ten years ago; how he went there in a third-class railway carriage, penned in with a crowd of drunken sailors, and how, on arriving with a capital of forty sous, he enters the profession of letters. He lived in an attic—the most commonplace thing he ever did—on the fifth floor of the Hôtel du Senat in the Rue de Tournon with a horde of hot-blooded young Southerners like himself, among whom was Gambetta.[21] All were desperately poor; all confidently expected to become famous, and all were citizens of that "Bohemia of the roaring Forties," not then extinct in Paris, which Murger described as "an intermediate stage which leads either to the morgue or the Academy." It was from this corner of the Latin Quarter that, when he had neither fire nor breakfast and all Paris was wrapped in fog, Daudet used to steal out to watch the great dome of the Odéon emerge slowly from the mist, that Odéon where the audience was one day to rise when he entered. It was from there, too, that, attired in his first dress coat, he went to his first reception at the home of Augustine Brohan, the actress. He told in his *Thirty Years in Paris* what agonies of bashfulness he suffered on that occasion and how, in spite of his gnawing hunger, he could not eat, and in trying to get a drink of water upset a decanter and tray of glasses and sent them crashing to the floor. After this embarrassing mishap he made his escape as soon as possible and trudged homeward through the snowy streets with no overcoat and with the icy wind whistling through the tails of that sacred dress coat, stopping on his way at the market to drink a bowl of cabbage soup among the fishmongers and venders of vegetables. Years afterward Sarcey tried to recall the incident to Mme. Brohan and she said it must be a mistake, she only knew Daudet through his books. The long-haired Provençal youth who broke her wine glasses she had forgotten. A Parisian wit of the last decade once remarked: "Whenever I meet a particularly stupid boy from the South I have a horror for [of?] him, for I am haunted by the fear that he will become great."

When Daudet's first play, *La Dernière Idole* [1874], was brought out in Paris he had been ordered out of France for his health. On the very night of its first production he was in the further end of Algeria living with a

21. Léon Gambetta (1838–1882), president of France, 1879–1881, premier, 1881–1882. For Murger, mentioned in the next sentence, see "Murger's Bohemia," Books and Authors (II), above.

couple of Arabs in a tent under a clump of dwarf palms, and lay looking through the flap at the burning orient stars, longing for Paris. The telegram announcing its magnificent success was brought to him across the desert by a red-coated horseman riding at full gallop. Immediately he was seized with the fever for Paris, that city which all the geniuses of France have equally loathed and loved, from which they are always fleeing but never escaping. Daudet was annually taken with a revulsion for the place; always wandering back to the South; living now in complete isolation in a lighthouse with only the sea birds for company, now in a windmill in Provence, now in the desert. But the end of every journey was Paris. Once, when he was working in an old farmhouse down in the Rhone country, a reporter from Paris came down to write up a country fair and dropped in to breakfast with Daudet. Daudet had never seen him before, but as they talked of the happenings on the boulevards that unnamable fever for the city came over him, and though he was just in the middle of *Le Petit Chose* [1868] and knew that he could never finish it away from the Rhone Valley, by nightfall he was on his way back to Paris.

This delightful vagabondage, half the restlessness of a boy, half the caprice of a poet, was never quieted until his marriage. What a superb piece of irony that the man who wrote *Les Femmes d'Artistes* and so bitterly condemned marriage for artists, should have married the woman he loved and should have loved her through a lifetime. As he wrote of it years afterward: "I married! How ever did that happen? To what magic art did such a wild gypsy as I fall a victim? What spell was cast over me? What charm was strong enough to bind fast my once ever-changing caprice?"

By the English-speaking world Daudet is known chiefly as a novelist; in France his rank as a dramatist is almost as high. The only one of his dramas which has been produced in America is *L'Arlésienne* [1872] which Minnie Maddern Fiske played under the rather inadequate title of *The Liar*. Beside his work as a playwright Daudet did a great deal for the French stage in criticisms. He was the first critic in Paris to demand a scientific *mise-en-scène*, and he wrote the first history of dramatic criticism in France. It was he who first designated Napoleon I as the benefactor of the French stage and the father of modern criticism.

To place Daudet in the front rank of French novelists, with Balzac and de Maupassant and Flaubert, is to do him an injustice; it is applying a measure too large for him. Between their works and his there is that same indefinable shade of difference that you find between the pictures of

Millet and those of Jules Breton.[22] He had neither their technical mastery nor their elemental power. They were the giants of letters, those three, and this was only a gay troubadour from the South, with a lute as sweet as a nightingale's note and a song always dipping from laughter to tears. He left no novel which, in days to come, will carry the conviction and power of *Notre Coeur* or *Madame Bovary* or *Cousin Pons*. He has place among the men who, from the recesses of a single brain, fashioned a world, and who created a humanity of their own. He was a temperamental artist. He was not profound either in his observations of life or his interpretation of it. He saw the beauty which glitters upon the surface and reproduced it with a delicacy, a pleasure, a vividness only possible to a temperament so alert, so capricious, so exquisitely sensitive. Sentiment continually tempted him, and he was often dramatic before he was true. He had a thirsty, never-satisfied eagerness for life and art. He could perfectly reproduce all experiences; he described things utterly inexpressible; he mastered the language of sensations. That very ever-present personal quality which disqualifies him for a place among the greatest creators of fiction, is his most potent and persistent charm. He conquered by the element which was his weakness; he made his deficiencies gloriously triumphant. "O, wind and fire of the South, ye are irresistible!"

Kings in Exile will always be Daudet's most popular work in the Anglo-Saxon world. Henry James says that it is "a book that could have been produced only in one of these later years of grace. Such a book is intensely modern, and the author is in every way an essentially modern genius."[23]

But once and only once did Daudet rise to the full measure of his power, only once did Tartarin become wholly serious and possessed of a great creative purpose, only once did Daudet entirely sacrifice the Provençal to the artist; that was when he wrote *Sapho* [1884]. Then he gave the world his best; reserving nothing, hesitating at nothing. It is through that book that he will live.

22. Jules Breton (1827–1906), French genre painter, whose painting "The Song of the Lark" is associated with Willa Cather's novel of the same name. See *The Song of the Lark*, p. 249 and also the preface, p. v.

23. Quoted from Henry James's review of *Mon Frère et Moi: Souvenirs d' enfance et de jeunesse* by Ernest Daudet in the *Atlantic Monthly*, June 1882. Reprinted in Henry James, *Literary Reviews and Essays*, ed. Albert Mordell (New York: Grove Press, Inc., 1957), p. 189. The essay was collected in James's *Partial Portraits*, but, as Mordell points out, the early version was much altered and the sentences Cather quoted were eliminated from the discussion of Daudet's "modernism" (see pp. 206–207). For Cather's comments on *Kings in Exile*, see "Old Books and New [February 1897]," The *Home Monthly*, above.

One of the saddest and most cruel episodes in Daudet's life occurred shortly after the death of his friend and fellow-novelist, Turgenev. The great Russian novelist had been ranked as one of Daudet's warmest admirers, had spent days at his house, been tended by him in his last illness. Yet when his *Mémoires* were published he expressed in them the heartiest contempt for Daudet, both as an artist and a man. Worse than all, he called him openly a liar. The most painful part of it was that Daudet could not flatly deny the latter assertion. Like his countrymen of the South, like Gambetta, he saw the world through an opera glass, unconsciously magnified trivial details. He exaggerated, not because his sense of truth was less than that of other men, but because his sense of mental vision was more fervid. Yet all his friends knew that his heart was true as gold. He knew his own weakness, had made the confession of himself and his countrymen in *Numa Roumestan* [1881]. But all this was wasted on the cold-blooded stolidity of the Slav. Daudet never sought to revenge himself upon the dead. The men of the South are truer of heart than of tongue. He wrote one of the most tender and appreciative critiques of Turgenev ever published. Of Turgenev's treachery he merely said: "I can see him in my house, at my table, gentle, affectionate, kissing my children, I have yet many exquisite warmhearted letters from him. And this was what lay concealed behind that kindly smile. Good Heavens! How strange life is!"

And now Daudet, too, is dead, carrying perhaps in his own heart secrets and reservations as strange. For is the soul of any man ever known to his brother?

Courier, January 22, 1898, pp. 2–3.

William Wetmore Story and the Kingdom of Art

Perhaps the most important of Willa Cather's unsigned contributions to "Books and Magazines" was her review of Reminiscences of William Wetmore Story *by Mary E. Phillips (1857–1939?). Story (1818–1895) was the son of Joseph Story, Chief Justice of the Supreme Court, and the friend of that other son of Salem, Nathaniel Hawthorne. After a brief, successful career as a lawyer, Story lived many years in Rome as an expatriate writer and sculptor. He wrote a number of books about Italy, including* Roba di Roma *(1862) and* Graffiti d'Italia *(1868), and a novel* Fiammetta *(1886); earlier he had published* Poems *(1845). Among his sculptures, his* Cleopatra *was described glowingly by Hawthorne in* The Marble

Faun (*1860*). *Henry James's commissioned biography,* William Wetmore Story and His Friends (*1903*), *characterized him as a failure in art, but as a success in the art of life. Margaret Fuller Ossoli* (*1810–1850*), *whom Cather alludes to twice in the following review, wrote on feminism, edited a transcendentalist quarterly, served as critic for the New York* Tribune, *and was an ardent supporter of Mazzini in his struggle for the unification of Italy; she was the prototype of Zenobia in Hawthorne's* Blithedale Romance (*1852*) *and of the title character in* Elsie Venner (*1862*) *by Oliver Wendell Holmes.*

Whether by intention or not, Miss Phillips has confined herself to Story the man rather than to Story the artist, and in dealing with him, as with many of the great New Englanders of his time, such a course is the only rational one. His life, the breadth, the fullness, the many-sidedness of it, was tremendous. Compared with the force of the living man his achievements in art must take a very inferior place. To estimate such a character by the output of his craft alone would be manifestly unfair. The personality of the man towered always above his work. That has been the history of art in New England. It was so with many of Story's great contemporaries; with Bronson Alcott, with Margaret Fuller, with Thoreau, even, to a certain extent, with Emerson; their dynamic power seemed incapable of in any adequate measure communicating itself to art. They seemed incapacitated by their very greatness. They entered the kingdom of art like a catapult, and what they touched they crushed. Wide awake and alert, they came into the land of dreams and found there but shadows. Perhaps that which they brought was greater than that which they sought. But be that as it may, certain it is that our Lady of Art was sorely affrighted by this stern Puritan wooing, and fled from it to suitors much more frivolous and unworthy, she being from of old a pagan lady with a decided taste for things material and never having been quite persuaded to change her creed.

William Wetmore Story was born in a period of revolt: in the dawn of transcendentalism; a time when ministers' sons were taking to poetry, judges' sons to sculpture, merchants' sons to music. A generation of young men sprang up who, without equipments of temperament, without inherited tastes or standards, without mental elasticity or abandon, determinedly laid siege to Parnassus, and that they did what they did will be the wonder of all time. They left their mark. Among the fair and frail creations of art they planted a block of granite, as strange, as unique, as exotic as was that altar to an unknown god among the Athenian temples to Apollo and Aphrodite.

Story was one of these men whose spiritual influence in art so vastly surpassed their achievements, and it is on this dominating, magnetic personality that his present biographer dwells. She has vividly set forth the circumstances of his boyhood, incorporating into her text letters from his old associates speaking of him as being "looked upon as a sort of 'Steerforth' at Harvard; very handsome, courteous, always ready and bright, already accomplished, dabbling in music and painting and a capital mimic and actor in private theatricals." He must indeed have cut as strange a figure among the Harvard youths of his generation as did Burns when he went with his plaid artistically draped and his hair done in a worldly fashion to worship among the Covenanters at Alloway kirk. . . .

While Story was still a student his father wrote him a most characteristic letter, in which he speaks of re-reading Horace. "Happening the other day to be at Mr. Webster's, I saw an old edition of Horace, which I borrowed, and have been re-reading more than half the odes. After all there is little material in Horace. His principal merit is in a certain gracefulness and elegant form of phrase. But he was a mere fawning sycophant, and as gross a debauchee as lived in his day."

Ah, Horace, sweetest of all singers, most lovable of poets, most charming scapegrace of the ancient world, all too fond of thy Lydia and thy well-seasoned Massic, not according to the deeds done in manuscript, but the deeds done in the body art thou judged before the awful tribunal of Plymouth Rock!

So Judge Story taught his son, and his son was accordingly a better man than Praxiteles, though he made no Venus who will "smile back triumphantly over the centuries her invincible beauty has conquered."

Miss Phillips has treated fully of Story's life in Rome, his friendship with Browning and the invigorating influence he exerted over art and artists there. She quotes a part of Browning's exquisite letter on the death of Story's little son, Joseph. . . .

In her summary of Story's works, Miss Phillips notes the fact that he made two statues of Cleopatra and wrote his best verses on the same subject, and she seems to see nothing amusing in the fact. They are indeed his best verses and very fine ones indeed, and they are rather his best statues; still they are not at all like the Cleopatra of Shakespeare, or that of Gautier, much less that of Sardou, whom Marcus Antonius would probably bill as "l'Étoile laiteuse d'Egypte," today. She was something of a Margaret

Fuller, Story's Cleopatra, a lady capable only of frenzies of the intellect, who would have held long conversations on the destiny of the soul in the famous library of Alexandria, and perhaps would have started a little Brook Farm movement somewhere down on the delta. Ah, the world would never have been lost for such a Cleopatra! And at Actium Antony would have stuck to his ship like the exemplary youth in Mrs. Hemans' celebrated poem.[24]

Leader, January 28, 1898, p. 5.

Two Poets: Yone Noguchi and Bliss Carman

Willa Cather was acquainted with two volumes of poetry by Yone Noguchi (1875–1947), Seen and Unseen: or Monologues of a Homeless Snail (1897) *and* The Voice of the Valley *(1898). Noguchi was born in Japan, but spent nine years in the United States, particularly the West, where he lived for a time with the American poet Joaquin Miller (1839–1913), and where the Yosemite Valley inspired some of his poems. Cather maintained a continuing interest in Bliss Carman—whose name she continued to misspell long after she had identified him as the vagabond companion of Richard Hovey (see Books and Authors [I] and [II], above). Her review of Carman's* By the Aurelian Wall *(1898) showed increased appreciation of his work, perhaps because of her predilection for eulogies of literary figures.*

A few months ago a second volume of verse by Yone Noguchi made its appearance. For some time this young Japanese has been living in a cabin on the mountainside out in Joaquin Miller's country, "where the flowers are like trees, and the trees touch with heaven," and this is the second volume of poetry he has sent into the world from his solitude. While Noguchi is by no means a great poet in the large, complicated modern sense of the word, he has more true inspiration, more melody from within than many a greater man. He is one of the fervid singers, who sang when poetry was a passion merely, not an art. There is a long stretch of time between such verses as are written in the Occident today and such simple, spontaneous, unstudied songs as Yone Noguchi's. These verses are so naive, so fragile, so entirely the children of an hour and a mood, like the songs of the unknown Hebrew poet who wrote the so-called books of Solomon. They are conspicuously Oriental. The hurrying of the clouds toward the western horizon, he describes as "A glorious troop / Of

24. The allusion is to "Casabianca" ("The boy stood on the burning deck," etc.) by Felicia Dorothea Hemans (1793–1835).

the unsuffering souls of gods / Marching on with battle-sound / Against the unknown Castle of Hell."

Could anything be more suggestive of a simple, joyous indulgence of the imagination, such as we find in Japanese carving or painting? We have over-elaborated everything in the West; we have made whist so difficult that few of us can play it, wine so good that few of us can afford to drink it, poetry so difficult that few of us can read it. We must make a science even of recreation and kill all the joy of it. But here is a poet who has not tried to be profound. He sings because the sun shines, because the roses bloom, because there is love and laughter in the world. He has the full measure of oriental melancholy, and that warm languor of the spirit found in lands of perpetual high noon.

"Come," says the young poet, "buy my tears, for I have sucked them from the breasts of Truth."

Courier, February 8, 1898, pp. 2–3.

Mr. Bliss Carman has been so pronouncedly the poet of the joyous, of the happier moods of nature, of the subtile temptations of the dusty highway and the climbing sap and the autumn woods, that it was scarcely expected of him to write a book of elegies upon the great dead. And yet these songs [*By the Aurelian Wall and Other Poems*] are not so much of the great dead as the dear dead, and therein lies much of their spontaneity and charm. They are not written in the lofty and forbidding manner of elegies; no muses are bidden to lament the untimely loss of their favored sons, no nymphs are implored to weep. They are the verses of a man to men he loved, to fellow-voyagers who have slipped their cables and crossed the bar, sailing now in seas that he knows not, but this at least he knows, that whatever waters smite their prow, whatever strange winds fill their sails, the old warm hearts, the old potent fancy, something even of the old love of earth are still theirs. It is this prevailing spirit of friendliness that relieves Mr. Carman's verses from any shadow of funereal gloom. In what other spirit than a brave and manly one could he write of Stevenson and Phillips Brooks and Andrew Straton,[25] men who feared death less than any other of the contingencies of living. Although he writes of death, Mr. Carman does not forget his old belief that the first duty of a poet is to be joyful.

25. Phillips Brooks (1835–1893), American Episcopal bishop; Andrew Straton, a young friend of the poet. Poems to Stevenson and Verlaine (discussed in the last paragraph) and an unidentified quatrain have been omitted, as indicated by the ellipses. More than half the column consisted of Carman's poems. See also "The Death of Verlaine," Books and Authors (II), above.

He writes of his brothers, "perfection's lovers," men who gladly lived and gladly died and laid them down with a will. To men so near the earth as Stevenson and Paul Verlaine the final union with the earth was not the saddest of things to contemplate, men who loved the sigh of the wind and the scent of the fresh turned earth and the wet of the rain upon their cheeks living, would have small cause to fear it dead. It is no dreadful thought that the grass is growing over earth's tried and constant lovers. So sweet a brotherhood was theirs with her always, that the tender and beautiful intimacy can scarcely have been broken by the long, ultimate contact with her, breast to breast. One fancies that in the springtime those great, exulting hearts still throb with the starting roots and feel the climbing sap and sleep a little less soundly when nature wakes. . . .

Mr. Carman writes of the beautiful graves which are to us beacon lights of hope, like those graves marked with a single name which Balzac said made the passerby to dream. Certainly if death "keeps his court" anywhere it is near such graves as those, where sleep the brothers of that "mystic fellow-craft of joy," joyous still, believing still, attesting still, though with silent lips, to the "ultimate rightness of things."

Mr. Carman's verses on Robert Louis Stevenson will find an echo in the hearts of all who loved him, and who can number them? . . .

Mr. Carman's verses upon Paul Verlaine are particularly fortunate. Verlaine upon whom so much has been written in all tongues, dissected by all psychologists and who remains as inexplicable now as when he used to sit about in the cafes of the Latin Quarter drinking absinthe from a dirty glass and writing on scraps of paper verses that transmitted [transmuted?] the French language into gold. Vagabond, criminal and poet: I suspect Mr. Carman is wisest in leaving him to "loving kindness of the grass." Nature knows and cherishes her own; her justice will not be harsh. . . .

Leader, July 22, 1898, p. 6.

On Language: French and English

Occasionally in "Books and Magazines" Willa Cather discussed stories or articles in the Atlantic Monthly, Harper's, Scribner's, *or* McClure's. *Here she comments on an article in the current (March 1898)* Atlantic, *pp. 289–298: "English as Against French Literature," by Henry D. Sedgwick (1861–1957), a lawyer and brother of Ellery Sedgwick (1870–1960), future editor of the* Atlantic.

The initial article of the March *Atlantic* is a comparison of English and French literature by Mr. Henry D. Sedgwick, Jr. The gist of Mr. Sedgwick's article is a word that needs to be spoken, a truth that cannot be too often told, viz., that no lasting good can come to English letters from the largely artificial taste for French literature that has sprung up throughout the English-speaking world; that a man of letters cannot be cosmopolitan, that he must speak the message of his own people and his own country or be forever dumb; that truth, for him, is that which he reverenced in his childhood; and that poetry, for him, is the language which his mother spoke. All of which is of grave import and self-evident. The artist is bound to his native soil more closely than the serf who plods in the furrow. The Saxon, like the Hebrew, must wed with the ideals of his own people, though the daughters of the Amorites and the Egyptians be fair. Miss [Mary E.] Wilkins will never write stories of Creole life, and Hawthorne carried his Puritanism even into Italy, carried it with such conviction and power that the Faun of the Capitol has scarcely smiled so joyously since that grave New Englander looked into his eyes, with mute misunderstanding, across the gulf of so many centuries.

But to prove the futility of a Saxon's imitating the French masters, it is not necessary to attack French literature, which Mr. Sedgwick does with a provincial perverseness unworthy of so scholarly a man. He asserts that "the heart of all literature is poetry," and that "English prose is better than French prose because of the poetry in it." Has Mr. Sedgwick forgotten the prose of Gautier, or the earlier prose of Flaubert? He continues: "If a man admits that for him poetry is the chief part of literature, he must confess that French prose can not awaken in him those feelings which he has on reading the English Bible, Milton, Ruskin, Carlyle or Emerson." At length we begin to perceive what species of poetry it is that Mr. Sedgwick designates by the generic term. It is the poetry of the seer, not of the bard, the poetry which gave birth to religions, the poetry of the over-soul.

The French literature is not a language capable of high religious expression, of exalted spiritual fervor. It was born of a tongue in which faith was dead. The Latin colonists carried no ark of the covenant with them on their journey into Gaul. They took only the names of gods whose altars were already cold and the rituals of faith outworn. The French people from its earliest beginning had no illusions, no childhood. It was the offspring of a loveless union, of a father grown old and gray in the enervating excesses of decadent Rome. The French people never had the highest privilege accorded a nation, that of groping after faith in darkness, of fashioning for itself and with its own hands its god, whether of marble, or wood, or mud. No gods ever sprang from the soil of France; no Druids ever chanted in its forests, no nymphs bathed in its rivers. Over that land the spell of childish enchantment was never cast. Its people was born old, worldly-wise, critical, cynical.

When the intelligence no longer derives inspiration from the unseen, it employs itself wholly with the visible, leaves the speculation of alchemy for experimental chemistry. It confines itself either to analysis of, or enjoyment of, the tangible. In short, it becomes critical.

The French language is primarily the language of sympathetic criticism; criticism of life, of manners and of art. No other language can so exactly describe, nay, almost reproduce, an artistic effect, a physical sensation, a natural phenomenon. But it does no more than that. The "over-soul" has not learned that facile tongue. It is a totally uninspired language, save for the perennial inspiration of beauty which is perhaps the truest and most lasting inspiration of all, the sole one, at least, which has survived the death [of] nations and their creeds and the dissolution of gods. So flexible and exact is his tongue, that the Frenchman may say exactly and completely what he means, and, usually, to his reader, he means no more than he says. The epigram has no spiritual suggestiveness; it satisfies rather than incites the imagination. The French language like Andrea del Sarto's pictures, has the fatal attribute of perfection.

The Anglo-Saxon, on the other hand, came without an inherited classical sense of fitness and proportion, into a language as dark and unexplored as his own forests, unwieldy as his own giant battle-ax matched with the French rapier. It has never been perfected. Every English author has known the continual torment and stimulus of writing an inexact tongue. The Anglo-Saxon could not make a literary language. He made a religious language. Unable to build a pyramid or a Parthenon, in his titanic struggle, he cast up a mountain. Unable to fit his thoughts exactly to words, he made the most spiritually suggestive language ever written. He made it the tongue of prophecy, he gave it reverence, that element of which French is as barren as a desert of dew. He learned to mean more than he said, and to make his reader feel it.[26] He learned to write a language apart from words. You feel it in Emerson, when his sentences seem sometimes to stand dumb before the awful majesty of the force he contemplates;

26. Cf. the famous passage in "The Novel Démeublé," which begins: "Whatever is felt upon the page without being specifically named there—that, one might say, is created" (*Not Under Forty*, p. 50). The essay first appeared in the *New Republic*, April 12, 1922.

it is in the pages of Carlyle, when those great, chaotic sentences reach out and out and never attain, and through them and above them rings something that they never say, like an inarticulate cry. That is the cry of the over-soul, present to a greater or lesser degree in all the English masters. Mr. Sedgwick calls it poetry. It is the highest of all poetry. It will never be spoken in the tripping dactyls of any Latin tongue. It is the Anglo-Saxon's heritage, and it has cost him dear.

But there is a poetry apart from spiritual frenzy, from religious fervor. There is a poetry wholly human, physical, if you will. The poetry that thunders in the resonant verse of Homer, that breathes still through the lips of Sappho as softly as a sigh; the poetry of Arms and Men, of love and maidens. And this has found in France its most perfect expression. It speaks through the virile romances of the elder Dumas, through the exquisite prose of Gautier, the palpitating verse of Alfred de Musset, the irresistible songs of Béranger.

Mr. Sedgwick states that Victor Hugo is becoming obsolete as compared with Walter Scott. Let the public libraries answer him. Scott is placed on the shelves of the boys' library, while Hugo still retains a present and vital interest. Even Dumas, who owed his inspiration to Scott, has outlived his master. Mr. Sedgwick finds fault with Hernani and Ruy Blas, because in their conduct they did not manifest the quality of common sense. In the matter of common sense they can certainly stand comparison with Hamlet or Romeo. The pre-eminent quality of Hamlet and Romeo is not of Denmark, or of Italy, it is of England, and it is that overtone of the soul which is the life and power of English art.[27]

Leader, March 4, 1898, p. 8.

Tales by John Oliver Hobbes and Ambrose Bierce

Willa Cather had suggested some of the qualities that she admired in short stories and tales in her review of The Borderland of Society *by Charles Belmont Davis. Davis's stories, she wrote, had "a certain grace in the telling, a certain practiced air, and a quiet faculty for getting at the heart of*

27. In the concluding paragraph of this column, Cather added a comment on a new French magazine: "I have said that French is the language of criticism. I know scarcely a better evidence of the critical adaptability of that tongue than the new dramatic monthly *Le Théâtre*. . . . France is the only country today in which the drama is an entirely legitimate and honest art, in which it appeals always to the highest intelligence and draws always from the highest talent. To compare our dramatic publications with such a periodical as *Le Théâtre* is humiliating. . . . Without hesitation one affirms that it is the best theatrical magazine published."

things that made them difficult to forget. They were all stories of incident, studies in those critical moments of life which reveal character more clearly and define it more sharply than a chronicle of years of ordinary humdrum existence. There is in every life a moment which might be called the artist's opportunity, a moment which contains all the essential elements of a story, a play or a picture. It is the ability to seize and develop this third act of life, to take advantage of the lights and shadows of that fleeting moment, to point a life in a gesture, a history in a situation, that makes the short-story writer" (Leader, *January 20, 1899*). *Cather preferred the stories of Ambrose Bierce (1842–1914?)—whose volume* In the Midst of Life: Tales of Soldiers and Civilians *(1891) was reissued in 1898—to those of Mrs. Craigie (see "John Oliver Hobbes," above), whose* Tales *(1892) are also reviewed here.*

Mrs. Craigie is, on the whole, much more satisfactory in short stories, like these, than in tedious political novels like *School for Saints*. There are in that book many strong and telling passages, but they were poorly placed, like pictures badly hung, and their effect is lost in the chaotic maze of the whole. Mrs. Craigie's gifts are of the sprightly order; let her regard Mrs. Humphry Ward and *Sir George Tressady* and eschew politics.[28] Edmund Gosse once said that had Mrs. Craigie lived in an age of pure literature, she would have been one of the most entrancing of essayists. Her mind is certainly engrossed in the things of which great novels are not usually made. Her critical sense makes itself felt too keenly in her fiction and her fondness for all the arts runs riot. Her selection of characters is too much limited by her personal taste. They are usually either artists or amateurs with aspirations. They are shadowy figures who have an excellent command of language and a facile wit—and "temperament." O, they are generously supplied with temperament, rolling in it, so to speak, it is their meat and drink. They gloat over their temperaments like the man in Stephen Crane's poem who ate his heart and said he liked it because it was so bitter.[29] It is in this, I think, that Mrs. Craigie's chief fault lies; she despises too much everything that smacks of the bourgeois, the common passions and the common sorrows of the common man. Yet it is from these that the meat and marrow of art must come, not from the temperamental perplexities of poets, painters or actors. Shakespeare was too wise to make actors the heroes of his dramas, and Thackeray only once wrote

28. See "Old Books and New [May 1897]," The *Home Monthly*, above.

29. Poem III in Stephen Crane's *Black Riders* (1895). For comments on his poetry, see "Crane and Norris," Books and Authors (IV), below.

a novel on a novelist. When you step into a world of productive art you step into a world distorted and your novel is misshapen from its inception. Of all romances that of an artist's life is usually the most cheap, the most tawdry, the most vulgar. He would not disgrace his craft by writing a shilling shocker on it. An artist's life, aside from his work, is much like a machinist's shop after the engine he built has gone out; there is nothing but broken tools, the tanks of black water where hot metal was cooled, and gray ashes in the furnace. We want heart rather than temperament in a novel, and the two seldom go together. I am not sure but that what we call temperament, the sort of temperament that is utilized professionally, only develops when the heart is dying, like some showy fungus that is born of decay. At best it is only a gaslight imitation of the sun, as cold as the calcium moonlight that falls on Juliet's "made-up" shoulders when, from the property balcony, she sighs to give Romeo his cue. That is not the atmosphere in which Mrs. Craigie will find the stuff for great novels. George Eliot knew that well enough. She handled only ordinary people; she abjured artists. She tarried not in the studio or the greenroom, but went down to where the Floss winds through green meadows to the sea; where life ran still and deep and emotions were as virginal and fresh as they were to the first man and the first woman when they felt them first. She cared for the smallest details of this life; she made Mrs. Tulliver's preserves immortal. She knew from where the red blood of art comes. Thomas Tulliver, Sr., is worth more than all the temperamental fops that Mrs. Craigie can collect; the tragedy of his losing that mill is more terrible than all the artistic fiascos that ever foundered, and the simple, homely love of Tom and Maggie is greater dramatically, artistically, anyway you choose to view it, than all the grand passions that were ever stolen from France and smuggled to London.[30]

Mrs. Craigie has literary powers of the highest order, and a gift of expression as beautiful as it is rare, but she must get closer to the earth.

Leader, March 11, 1898, p. 4.

This is a new edition of a volume of very remarkable stories [*In the Midst of Life*] that never won in America the popularity their high merit warrants. In Germany they have met with a more appreciative audience. They are strange stories; they speak like bullets and come with the swiftness of death in battle. Mr. Bierce adopted Poe's method of

30. For comments on *The Mill on the Floss*, see "Old Books and New [November 1897]," The *Home Monthly*, above.

working swiftly and surely for a single effect, but his hand is firmer, rougher, more compelling than his master's often was. In each story his final effect [hits?] you like a sudden blow, so swift and overwhelming is it. Like Poe, too, he seems to have a taste for the horrible, a penchant for depicting pain and the passion of terror. I know of nothing else written since Poe at all like the masterly story of the young man who was stopping in a naturalist's house and found a snake under his bed. . . .[31]

You cannot escape the persistent horror of the thing; it haunts your memory and confronts you in the dark like Kipling's "At the End of the Passage."

The soldier stories are equally powerful and gruesome, each a triumph of craft. Utterly devoid of the sentiment and poetry of war, they freeze the blood as Mr. Stephen Crane's stories never do. After reading one or two of these stories, you begin each with apprehension, knowing that, no matter how innocently they open, a knife thrust awaits you at the end. In each story there is a single, deadly effect, and not one word is wasted for any other purpose, not one sentence written that does not drive you toward that final shock. It is seldom one's good fortune to meet more perfect workmanship.

Leader, March 25, 1898, p. 9.

Richard Le Gallienne: "a bankrupt genius"

Possessor of a minor but varied talent, Richard Le Gallienne (1866–1947), poseur and Pre-Raphaelite literary critic, wrote R. L. Stevenson and Other Poems *(1895), a novel,* The Quest of the Golden Girl *(1896), and* Prose Fancies *(two series: 1894–1896). Willa Cather was referring to the last-named when, in her review of his novel* Young Lives, *she wrote that "the patronizing assurance of Mr. Le Gallienne's prose style at one time led many susceptible people to expect great things of him, but I fancy most of them have grown weary of his saccharine attempts at fiction"* (Leader, *June 17, 1899*).

The public has ceased to expect any considerable degree of literary perfection from Mr. Le Gallienne. It is tired of waiting for him to grow up. The flaws which were once hopefully considered the pardonable imperfections of youth are now recognized as fundamental faults, and his affectations of diction have become essential mannerisms. Mr. Le Gallienne has now reached years of some maturity and is still masquerading in the

31. A summary of the story "The Man and the Snake" is omitted.

erratic precocities of youth. Much was forgiven his earlier works, *Prose Fancies, The Book-Bills of Narcissus,* etc. because they promised better things. *The Romance of Zion Chapel* is like its predecessors; a promissory note written with violet ink on scented paper, signed by a bankrupt genius whose paper is at a discount in the market.

This book is Mr. Le Gallienne's first attempt at a novel, and it is really a series of essays interlarded with a story. He will never write a novel; he is too subjective. He cannot leave his own interesting personality long enough to give his characters a chance to assert themselves. He simply crowds them into the background, buries them in a careless flow of saccharine sentimentality. Mr. Le Gallienne troubles himself very little about local color. Zion Chapel was located in an English village where, presumably, people worked and ate and slept and led normal and healthy lives. But with these people Mr. Le Gallienne is not concerned. Kipling has found very effective material in the common man who earns his bread, but Mr. Le Gallienne has no taste for such. Out of this community he selects for his hero a weak-kneed minister who is addicted to Morris wallpaper and reads Rossetti and flirts with elocutionists. This young minister we are permitted to know only casually. There are many chapters about the artistic opportunities of a minister and about a literary man's religion, but of the minister himself we see very little. Apparently he serves in the capacity of understudy to Mr. Le Gallienne and appears only when that gentleman is indisposed. We know, however, that his name is Theophilus Londonderry, and that he prefers to call himself Théophile to resemble the author of *Mademoiselle de Maupin.*[32] I fancy we care to know very little more than that about Theophilus Londonderry; he is altogether too much like a young man whose name is Galloon, and who calls himself Le Gallienne. One would expect such a man to flirt with anything—even an elocutionist. Well, this Theophilus is engaged to a sweet young girl called Jenny, who writes essays on "Dress as a Form of Self Expression," and who loves him even to the extent of reading *Marius the Epicurean;* and allowing her chamber to be hung with Morris wallpaper. To explain this love affair Mr. Le Gallienne says: "God gives a man a little measure of porcelain and a handful of stars and leaves him to construct the woman he needs for himself." . . .

The book is not without its merits but they are scarcely the merits of a well-constructed novel. When Mr. Le Gallienne is in his favorite role of

32. *Mademoiselle de Maupin* (1835), by Théophile Gautier. See "Three Translations," Books and Authors (IV), below.

an essayist and is exploiting his own personality, he says some very good things, and in so many pages of effort it would be strange if he did not. . . .

Mr. Le Gallienne's views on ethics have been severely censured, but on that point it is scarcely necessary to speak. Another man might hold the same views on ethics and art and boldly announce them without being questioned. The art of literature, like the art of acting, is so largely a matter of personality. A tiger is a noble object in its rage and awakens awe in the most unimaginative spectator, while an infuriated kitten is always more or less ridiculous, no matter how good its provocation.

Mr. Le Gallienne has not infrequently been likened to Heine, and among his verses there are some with a Heine flavor. But Le Gallienne is fond of literary poses, which Heine scorned, and that effeminate sentimentality which is the keynote of Le Gallienne's work could never have been laid at Heine's door. Heine, pinioned on a "mattress grave," sightless, and dead from the hips down, had more virility than this man in his prime. Mr. Le Gallienne is as narrow in range as he is liberal in ethics. His entire literary equipment might be called a mood of Heine's, and Heine was a man of many moods, while Mr. Le Gallienne knows but one. In one Heine there were many Le Galliennes.

Leader, April 8, 1898, p. 11.

An Old-Fashioned Novel: The Two Standards

Father William F. Barry (1849–1930), Irish-born Roman Catholic priest in England, wrote widely on social, ethical, and theological questions, and incorporated his views into his romantic novels. The first, The New Antigone *(1887), which Cather had read, was an attack on nihilism and free love. In* The Two Standards *(1899), Marian Graystoke, a singer married to a fabulously rich London promoter, appears in an opera by Gerard Elven, a young composer obviously suggested by Wagner. She leaves her husband expecting to elope with Elven, but Elven is dissuaded from the step by his brother, a priest, and Marian goes alone to America to pursue her career. When her husband is exposed as a crook and loses his reason, she returns to England to nurse him. Cather concluded her long plot summary (omitted here) in this fashion: "She has learned that speculation in art is as ruinous as speculation in trade; that the speculator is always the victim. The result of her experience is summed up briefly as follows: 'The commercial idea allowed to reign is an insanity, is the destruction of art and reduces life to a monomania as vulgar as imbecile!'"*

. . . in this novel of five hundred pages there is much more than the story. There are many characters introduced, apparently, solely for their picturesqueness, many pages on music, on German literature, on sociology, on religion, all rich in reflection, in sound philosophy and scholarly comment, in varied and vivid imagery. But the question presents itself, have they or have they not place in a novel? The *Saturday Review* goes so far as to state that Father Barry's novel is a combination of Ouida and Mrs. Humphry Ward, and that it unites the faults of both. But the man who can compass the extremes of both these ladies has not been born. True it is that the rhetoric of *The Two Standards* is almost uniformly florid, . . . and true it is that the characters think rather than live. Yet, after all the tense, impressionistic fiction, written with conscious method and pride of craft, thrust upon us from the four quarters of the world, all the white heat, record-breaking, ocean-greyhound fiction that crowds the sensations of a lifetime into a short story, it is rather restful to stumble upon a man who has leisure for reflection; who seems not to be aware that life is shorter even than it used to be, and who is serene in the knowledge that art is infinitely long—five hundred pages long!

Though the novel deals with present problems and conditions, it is an old-fashioned novel, written in the old-fashioned manner. For the first hundred pages one flounders along, merely getting acclimated. Then one begins to realize that this is what good fiction was like in the days when it took two weeks to get news from across the Atlantic. Like the old-fashioned novelists, Father Barry sees to it that things come his way. All his patient and minute study of the society he depicts has not made him a realist, as the following incident will illustrate: During the rehearsals of Gerard Elven's opera, we are told that Marian studied the title role alone and without the composer's knowledge, and that she used to practice it down by the seashore. Now, so far as one can discover, Marian had no further musical training than ordinarily falls to the lot of a village curate's daughter, and her stage training had been acquired in amateur theatricals, yet on the night of the opera's production, when the world-famous prima donna, who sings the title role, falls ill, and is forced to leave the stage, Marian assumes the part "at a moment's notice," as they say at the Metropolitan, goes on and sings with a passion and fire that quite eclipse the humble efforts of the celebrated professional. What could be more characteristic of the old-fashioned novel, and what could be more absurd from the impresario's standpoint? Thank heaven! something more than passion and fire and a schooling in amateur theatricals are required to make an opera singer, or all our typewriter girls would be caroling Santuzza and

Carmen tomorrow. The musical interest of the novel suggests a comparison with Mr. George Moore's[33] *Evelyn Innes* [1898], a book much less profound and narrower in range, but withal a novel, and a novel admirably constructed, in which nothing superfluous is tolerated, and in which all the incidental philosophy and moralizing is made to support and strengthen the story proper; a book full of strength and enthusiasm, vivid, human characters; strong situations and brilliant episodes that cling to the memory. It is, moreover, a searching and sympathetic study of the artistic temperament, and the effects of the exhilaration of artistic endeavor and achievement on the conduct of life, which *The Two Standards* is not. Father Barry's treatment of Marian Graystoke is charitable and generous but never sympathetic. He fails to convey to the reader the emotional experiences of his characters. The chief value of the book lies in its ripe thought and spiritual power. It strikes a deep, rich tone, not unlike organ music. It has breadth and majesty of style and splendid serenity; an ecclesiastical calm pervades the book. The author stands among his creations like his own Father Rudolph, in the world but not of it. His message is noble, his faith strong, his wisdom sound, his sadness not without hope. He has chosen his characters impartially from the men and women about him, good and bad, representing all strata of society; he has studied them closely and judged them gently and generously, but he chloroformed them before he put them into his books, and they remain inanimate unto the end.

Leader, March 10, 1899, p. 12.

Zola: "Dante of Paris"

When Zola was rejected from the French Academy, Willa Cather was prompted to express her attitude toward him and naturalism (see Books and Authors [I], above). After his conviction for his "J'accuse" letter about the Dreyfus case, some of his books were reissued, including a translation of Le Ventre de Paris, *which Cather reviewed in the* Journal *under the title* The Fat and the Thin. *The following* Leader *review borrows a phrase or two from her first discussion and takes over almost entirely the later* Journal *review. Cather did, however, omit the magnificent last paragraph, which reads in part: "You may heap the details of beauty together forever, but they are not beauty until one human soul feels and knows. That is what Zola's books lack from first to last, the awakening of the spirit. An artist*

33. George Moore (1852–1933), Irish novelist.

may be clever when he answers you, he may be skilful when he pleases your senses, but when he speaks to the living soul within you, then and then only is he great. Only a diamond can cut a diamond, only a soul can touch a soul" (Journal, *February 16, 1896;* KA, *pp. 367–371). For her review of* Germinal, *see Books and Authors (IV), below.*

Zola's *Le Ventre de Paris* is now published in English under another title [*The French Market-Girl*], worse, if possible, than the one given the first English edition, which was, I believe, *The Fat and the Thin*. It is unfortunate that the book should be presented under titles which can appeal only to shop girls, as it represents Zola at his best, and contains comparatively little that is offensive to Anglo-Saxon taste. The story is soon told: Florent, a law student, was knocked down by the mob during the *coup d'état* of 1851, and a woman near him was shot. In endeavoring to lift her he got blood on his hands. He was found by the soldiers, and because of the suspicious appearance was tried and transported. Years afterward he returned penniless and hungry and rode into Paris on the vegetable cart of a kindly peasant woman. "When at length he reached Courbevoie the night was very dark. Paris, looking like a patch of star-sprent sky that had fallen upon the black earth, seemed to wear a forbidding aspect as though angry at his return. As he crossed the Neuilly bridge he sustained himself by clinging to the parapet, and bent over and looked at the Seine, rolling inky waves between its dense, massy banks. A red lamp on the water seemed to be watching him with a sanguineous eye." After wandering hungry among the markets, he found that his brother had become a well-to-do pork butcher. His brother received Florent kindly, if not gladly. He got work in the fish market and was favored by a handsome fishwife who smelt always of herrings. Then he got mixed-up in politics, became a mild sort of Socialist, was arrested, tried and again transported. So much for Florent, a rather colorless character in spite of his exaggerations. Zola is not strictly successful with characters of the Jean Valjean type. But the bulk of the book and the charm of it are the incidental descriptions of the markets of Paris. Those markets into which all the delicacies of the world are poured, that are "like some huge central organ beating with giant force and sending the blood of life through every vein of the city. The uproar of them is akin to that of mighty jaws." One can fairly see it, that great stronghold of plenty in the midst of want, that storehouse of food that is set up in the midst of aching poverty for an eternal temptation. You can feel in some of the descriptions the freshness of the morning. You can see the sunrise over the markets. "The luminous dial of Saint Eustache was palling as night light does when surprised by dawn. The gas jets in the wine shops in the neighboring streets went out one by one as stars extinguished by the brightness. And Florent gazed at the vast markets now gradually emerging from the gloom, from the dreamland in which he had beheld them, stretching out their ranges of open palaces." The author manages without too great a burden of detail to get it all before you, the piles of fragrant greenery, the heaps of flaming carrots with the black soil still clinging to their roots, the gray shimmer of the dripping fish-counters, the roses in their glass cases and the booths of fresh picked violets. And all about them the frugal bartering of hungry people, and the roar and clamor of Paris.

As for the rest of the *dramatis personae*, there is the fat butcher and his wife, whose complexion is like the fresh pork. Then there is "La Normande," the queenly fish wife, who befriended poor Florent, and there are Cadine and Marjorlin, two children brought up by an old market woman. The boy and girl lived in the markets, eating what they could steal, selling flowers when they were not too idle, loving each other by way of pastime, lunching in empty cellars, clambering over the roofs in the moonlight, happy as the sparrows that twittered about the towers of St. Eustache, and just as good for nothing. The most cheerful figure in the book is the young painter, Claude, who never had enough to eat and wore an old streaked overcoat to hide his lack of other clothing. He hung about the markets day and night, wild with enthusiasm over the profusion of colors, never vexed save when the seductive odors of the food made him hungry, and tightening his belt that his empty stomach might not interfere with the satisfaction of his eyes. He used to go down every morning to watch the effect of the sunrise upon the rows of bullock's lights. "And when a ray of sunshine fell upon the lights and girdled them with gold, an expression of languorous rapture came into his eyes, and he felt happier than if he had been privileged to contemplate the Greek goddesses in their sovereign nudity or the chatelaines of old romance in their brocaded robes." It was he, too, who said: "Do you know the battle of the Fat and the Lean? Cain was certainly one of the fat, Abel one of the lean. Ever since the first murder there have been rampant appetites which have drained the life blood of the smaller eaters. It's a continual preying of the stronger upon the weaker; each swallowing his neighbor and getting swallowed in turn. Beware of the Fat, my friend!"

In spite of its undeniable power, this is only a novel of the butcher shop with a fishwife for a heroine. Once again the foremost novelist of France has written a book full of repulsive odors, about another kind of unhappiness. Surely of all the men under the skies, the one most to be pitied is this Zola the miserable, the Emile the unhappy, this Dante of Paris who sees all the infamies of the pit but to whom the vision of Paradise will never open. He is a past master of the art of letters; he has the searching eye and the strong hand of his generation. No burden of detail is too heavy for him, no type of distorted, misshapen humanity baffles his keen penetration. In indefatigable, painstaking industry, he is second only to Balzac himself, and yet who of all the kindly race of men would change places with him? Better be a ditchdigger whistling in the sun than this man who has mastered all the technique of his craft only to find its soul unattainable to him forever. I suppose in his time this man has described, analyzed and catalogued every color, scent, sound, sensation; and yet out of them all he has never created one effect of absolute beauty. He is like a miser who has gathered together all the delights of the world, but who has lost the capacity to enjoy. That delicate fiber, lurking somewhere in the brain, which responds to beauty, has in him been paralyzed from birth. M. Zola claims that most of us are born under a curse. Certainly his is a heavy one; to be conscious only of evil; never to escape from it a moment; to have its blight always before his eyes, its filth under his feet, its reek in his nostrils. Artistically, he is an anomaly; a Frenchman, of the land of light phrases and elegant expression, his heavy, labored style smacks almost of the Teuton. He has the Gothic earnestness without the Gothic faith. He is no decadent, no scoffer, there is not an ounce of the charlatan in him. With a seriousness and devoutness worthy of a better end, he celebrates dark rites in the house of Baal and before the altar of Ashtoreth. Spiritually, he presents to us the man of the Stone Age. The dream gardens are closed to him; he sees only the potter's field and the marshes stagnant with decay. Like a Caliban, he trails always in the primal slime, from which he has no wings of faith, or hope, or love to rise.

Leader, May 27, 1898, p. 5.

Shaw's Plays, Pleasant and Unpleasant

Willa Cather had reported on Richard Mansfield in The Devil's Disciple *(see The Theatre [III], above) and, earlier, had commented on* Arms and the Man[34] *when he introduced Shaw to the American stage, but she had not reviewed any of the plays in the two volumes of* Plays, Pleasant and

34. *Courier*, August 24, 1895, p. 6; *KA*, pp. 254–255. See "Richard Mansfield," The Star System (II), above.

Unpleasant (*1898*). *She clearly was acquainted with* The Quintessence of Ibsenism (*1891*), *in which Shaw attempted to combat the influence of Scribe and Sardou, though she disagreed with his interpretation of Ibsen. In this "Books and Magazines" review, Cather virtually ignores the "pleasant plays"* (Arms and the Man, Candida, The Man of Destiny, *and* You Never Can Tell) *in favor of the "unpleasant" group* (Widowers' Houses, The Philanderer, *and* Mrs. Warren's Profession).

Browning was finally forced to go over *Sordello* and write for it a system of what a printer would style "subheads," that is, to place at the top of each page of the poem an explanatory line indicating what his intentions in that page might be. The insufficiency of the supply of cerebral tissue in the world has forced Mr. G. Bernard Shaw, much against his will, to vaguely indicate in the preface to his published plays what he is driving at, why he writes plays at all, and why he writes such plays. He informs us that his crusade is against Romance, pure and simple; Romance in morality, in ethics, in politics, and in religion. He adds: "I do not see moral chaos and anarchy as the alternative of romantic conventions. On the other hand I see plenty of good in the world, working itself out as fast as the idealists will allow it; and if only they would let it alone and learn to respect reality, which would include the beneficial exercise of respecting themselves, and, incidentally of respecting me, we should all get along much better and faster. To me the tragedy and comedy of life lie in the consequences, sometimes terrible, sometimes ludicrous, of our persistent attempts to found our institutions on the ideals suggested to our imaginations by our half satisfied passions, instead of on a genuinely scientific natural history."

So Mr. Shaw, who has spent a dozen splenetic years vilifying crusades and crusaders, is himself upon a crusade, a crusade of negation. For the gentleman offers no tangible substitute for the factor in life which he modestly desires to eliminate, and "natural history" is a vague term. In each of his plays he attacks a particular institution or tradition, and by a series of intellectual gymnastics and wit thrusts, demonstrates its fallacy; then he gives his trick away and takes you into his confidence, and gleefully admits that the weapons with which he slew your illusion are as false as the illusion itself, and cheerfully bids you go back to your lie again, as it is really much better than anything he has to offer. This dog-in-the-manger attitude toward the illusions of the humble Philistine is scarcely generous of Mr. Shaw. He should fight only with his equals. We are not scintillating geniuses; we cannot all write plays that bankrupt the managers who produce them; some of us have to pay for our seats at the theatre and otherwise respect the conventionalities of life. Mr. Shaw demonstrates in a jocular way that romance is the source of all the afflictions of life; certain[ly], for it is the source of all its pleasures. Why not leave us our illusions, since this is a short journey and cold, and mostly in the dark, and we believe, at least, that they comfort us. Did Mr. Shaw but know it, they are worth all they cost us, and all the tears we shed for them and all the wisdom we forgo. Let Mr. Shaw turn him to his master, Ibsen, and read *The Wild Duck* over again, and he will find that it is a dangerous business, this tearing our life-lies away from us. But we must eliminate Romance, and all, forsooth, because it incapacitates us to appreciate the plays of Mr. G. Bernard Shaw!

The seven plays which make up these two volumes are really remarkable instances of good dramatic writing. But so distorted and disfigured are they by egotism, flippancy, burlesque, whimsical exaggeration and indulgence in petty personal prejudices that only by sober analysis does one realize their skillful construction and clean-cut, definite, unconventional characterization. These plays are made by a man who knows the capacities and limitations of the stage, even though he has small consideration for the limitations of actors. They are not the work of a literary hack, nor of a long-winded novelist afflicted with a moral purpose. Their people are not "persons of the drama" merely, but people of the world, not flattering specimens of the race, certainly, most of them are unscrupulous and all of them are disagreeable, but they live, they have blood in their veins, not ink. It is really lamentable, when there is so little dramatic writing worth while, to see such fine talent and facile wit wasted and perverted and degraded by petty personal animosity and overweening self-conceit, to see a man breathe such dirty poison on his Venice glass. It has been urged that Mr. Shaw's egotism is largely assumed. I think, then, that I prefer the genuine and unconscious article; it is less aggressive.

Take, for example, the play, *Widowers' Houses*, which deals with the tenement-rent problem, in which the hero, in a burst of righteous indignation, breaks his engagement with a most unattractive heroine when he finds that her dowry is wrung from the starving wretches who inhabit her father's tenements. When he finds that the landlord must exact this rent in order to pay a usurious interest on the borrowed sum with which the tenements were built, and that he himself (the hero) holds the mortgages drawing this interest, he walks meekly back into the yoke. If Mr.

Shaw had kept within the uttermost bounds of the possible truth, and had, out of mere poetic license or literary courtesy, permitted even one of his characters either a conscience or a heart, he would have made a great play. As it is, he has only a whimsical travesty for his pains. There is only one honest man in the drama, a clergyman, and he does not appear on the stage.

On the other hand, examine *Mrs. Warren's Profession*, much the strongest and most orderly and least farcical of Mr. Shaw's published plays. Mrs. Warren's profession is one which, for the convenience of all parties concerned and unconcerned, the world has decided to leave nameless, though various euphemisms have been applied to it. Mrs. Warren's philosophy is that "The only way for a woman to provide for herself decently is to be good to some man who can afford to be good to her." Mrs. Warren's temperament is eminently romantic, and she treats her profession much as she treats her figure and her complexion; she laces it in here, and pads it out there, and powders it and rouges it until it makes quite a fair showing. Mrs. Warren has an intellectual daughter, who won a tripos in mathematics at Cambridge. When she discovers the extent of her mother's infamy she leaves her, not because her mother is bad, but because she is romantically bad. The gloss of sentiment nauseates her, and she throws over her sweetheart and goes to London to make mathematical calculations for civil engineers, and the curtain drops on her smoking a cigar and doing problems in calculus.

That is just what Mr. Shaw would leave us; to men, "natural history"; to women, a cigar; and to both, mathematics. And then there is death; I suppose Mr. Shaw will allow us that?

Well, some fine morning when the larks are in tune, and the sun comes back, who is the best romanticist of us all, up comes even so slight a fellow as the "Prisoner of Zenda" from Strelsau and the clank of his tin sword is heard around the world. Or over comes Cyrano from France, with his rapier in his hand and a song on his lips and a chivalrous passion in his heart, and we turn to him and cry like Roxane that we love him for his soul despite his face; that Romance disfigured is better than the Apollo of "natural history"; that the whole tired world is listening for that song, hungry for that passion. And then, Mr. Shaw, where are your Philanderer, and Mrs. Warren and her loathsome profession, and your "chocolate cream soldier," and your crusade of negation?

Leader, December 2, 1898, p. 13.

Richard Realf: "that erratic genius"

Willa Cather twice devoted part of "The Passing Show" to Richard Realf (1834–1878). On the first occasion she wrote of his Poems *(1898), which were published with a memoir by his friend Richard J. Hinton, and followed Hinton very closely both in factual matters and in interpreting Realf's career. The second piece was in response to an editorial (March 11, 1898) by Sarah B. Harris, editor of the* Courier, *disagreeing with Cather's estimate of Realf. A "Helen Delay" article, "Richard Realf, Poet and Soldier," appeared in the* Home Monthly, *May 1899; it was adapted from the first* Courier *column, revised to take into account that the local readers included "hundreds of men who remember Richard Realf." Cather replaced the last sentence of the* Courier *column with the last sentence of her early essay "Concerning Thomas Carlyle": "He dreamed always in life—great wild, maddening dreams. Perhaps he sleeps quietly now; perhaps he wakes."*

At last the poems of Richard Realf, poet, soldier and workman—some would add the harsher title, adventurer—who spent the six cleanest and happiest years of his disordered life in Pittsburgh—have been collected and edited. Twenty-one years ago Realf's tragic death in San Francisco attracted universal attention. He committed suicide there by drinking laudanum, driven to desperation by domestic troubles and pursued by the malignancy of an almost incredible hatred. His death was called a tragedy; it was, however, merely the end of one, the falling of the curtain on a tragedy which had lasted forty-four years. There are men who are simply cast for the tragic parts in life. Such a role was assigned the man who was once the Byronic genius of the Pittsburgh press, and he played it fiercely and well, up to the limit of his heart and brain and strength, played it to the death. Though the man has not yet been dead a quarter of a century, the story of his life is so wild, so horrible, so fantastically grotesque that it reads like a romance evolved by some disordered brain.

Richard Realf was born in Sussex County, England, in 1834. He was born one of the heirs of poverty and worked at gardening to pay for his schooling. When he was eighteen, he published a volume of verses, *Guesses at the Beautiful*, which attracted the attention of Eliza Cook, Gerald Massey, Lady Byron and her daughter, and a nephew of Thackeray's, and unfortunately secured him their patronage. The young man became the idol of Brighton, the most fashionable watering place in England, at the height of the season—and for a season only. This untimely adulation affected him as disastrously as it had done Burns years before, and completely disarmed him for the struggle before him. For, as George Eliot remarked, "To be an uncommon young man is to have an uncommon difficulty in getting along."

He was made steward on one of the Byron estates and there became entangled in a disastrous love affair with a Miss Noel, a relative of Byron's, the first of those baleful attachments which eventually wrecked his life. As if prophetic of the end, the first love affair was terrible in its consequences. He contracted large debts, wandered over England indulging in freakish excesses which called his sanity into question, and was at last found barefooted and in rags in the streets of Southampton, singing ballads for the pennies which passersby threw in his hat. So most of his dreams of love—and they exhausted arithmetic—began in the clouds and ended in the streets. The "eternal feminine" which was to thwart him at every turn, wait for him in every path, despoil him of every honor, hold his feet forever in the mire and at last track him to his death, was first born into his life with madness and destitution and shame in its wake. And whenever and wherever it crossed and recrossed his life, it left that same black stain. The influence which has lifted other poets to the stars, for him put out the sun and more than once threatened to extinguish the light of reason itself.

In 1855 Realf landed in New York. In 1856 Richard Realf and literature parted company and he went to Kansas to take part in the anti-slavery struggle there, having been one of that convention which pledged its members to death in the cause of liberty. He was a member of John Brown's band, but left for England before the raid on Harper's Ferry. On his return he entered a Jesuit college, remained there three months, then wandered over the country lecturing for some months, and then went out in one of those strange disappearances which clouded his life and perplex his biographers. He had periods of total disappearance, absolute lapses, as it were, from the world of the living. During these disappearances nothing whatever could be learned of him. At this time he was seemingly blotted out for almost two years. When he again rose to the surface and cast a shadow amongst living men, he enlisted in the Union army. His military career was brilliant. His name was recorded several times in eulogistic general orders for high personal heroism during the two years of mighty fighting in which the Army of the Cumberland bore so large a part. His bearing of the colors to the front at Missionary Ridge has been splendidly described by his biographer, Colonel R. J. Hinton. . . .

In 1845 [1865], while Realf was still serving as a soldier, he contracted his first legal marriage with Sophie E. Graves, whom he met in a small western town. When he was ordered south he left her in Indiana, apparently with every intention of returning to her. His letters to her were warm and frequent. But while he was serving in the south a fancy seized him for a society woman who lived in Washington, and when he received his discharge he hastened to that city against the promptings of his own reason, swayed by one of those violent and apparently irresistible caprices which governed and wrecked his life, and led his eager feet through such weary wanderings in despair and night. Of his latter marriage his biographer says: "The marriages of Richard Realf have been much discussed. I use the plural, though legally there was but one marriage. The second ceremony was bigamous in character .... The third relationship entered upon after he had obtained from one state court a divorce from the woman [Catherine Cassidy] he contracted marriage with at Rochester, N. Y., was, if any validity could attach, of the common law order. His partner in this third union was [Lizzie Whappham] the mother of children by him, and everywhere in his latter years he spoke of her as 'my wife.'" ...

The six years he spent in Pittsburgh as writer and editor on the *Commercial* were the least tempestuous and most useful of his life. There he became a convert to Francis Murphy's[35] temperance movement, for a time overcame the liquor habit and lectured as co-worker with the reformer. His wife appeared on the scene and he obtained a divorce. He went to England and on his return was completely unmanned to find that the decree of divorce had been annulled by a higher court. That moment was the one which prefigured the end, the "fatal third act" of the grim tragedy he played. Scandal engulfed him, he lost his position and became a vagrant again, took up the old course of dark ways and blind wanderings under a starless heaven. He drifted from place to place, from strait to strait, from disgrace to disgrace, always pursued by an implacable fury—a hate which never slept. His flight was only stopped by the Pacific Ocean. In San Francisco he hid himself deep. He was working industriously and hoping to bring his third wife to him when his Pittsburgh pursuer came. He returned to his lodgings one night to find her destroying his manuscripts and effects. He asked no questions then. The time had come, the supreme moment. It was time for the curtain. The finest steel has its

35. Francis Murphy (1936–1907), a nationally known Pittsburgh gospel-temperance evangelist.

yielding point. He spent his last money for laudanum and got a room in a hotel. He wrote letters to his friends explaining his act, saying: "... I have had heavy burdens to bear, such as have set stronger men than I reeling into hell. I have tried to bear them like a man, but can endure no more."

He wrote, moreover, one of the most remarkable poems in the language, the last lines blurred by the poison which had numbed his hand but not chilled his brain. He was buried with a circlet of yellow hair on his arm, a love-token from his first love, Miss Noel. The first madness and the last; there was very little difference between them save of time and circumstance. In the first folly was the essence of the last. But the verses, which were the bloody sweat of all this anguish, they will live as long as American letters.

Genius is the one thing indestructible.

The following is a part of his last poem [omitted here], the swan song which he wrote alone, penniless and dying on that last fateful night in San Francisco. A man's lips never uttered a braver death cry. A man's soul never went out in greater agony....

George Moore, in his critique on Paul Verlaine, says that a great poem is the most indestructible thing in the world; that if a great poem were cast in the sands of the Sahara Desert or dropped upon one of the remote islands of the sea it would be recovered and accorded its place among the world's priceless possessions. The theory accords well with the fact that these scattered poems, written for obscure journals published in out-of-the-way places, sired by a wandering vagrant, now a soldier, now a tramp, now a reformer, now a debauchee, who spent half his life fleeing from the consequences of his own mistakes, have been at last ferreted out, collected, published and accorded the place of distinction which is their due. Of all the storm and stress of this man's life, of all his innumerable follies and unspeakable anguish, of all his dreams which were born on the mountain tops only to die in the gutter, of all his tenderness and pity and courage, these three-score poems are what remains. In the language of Mr. Henry James, "How much of life it takes to make a little art!"

Every expression of the human soul through the medium of art is valuable either as art, or a documentary evidence upon life itself, as psychological data. It is impossible to judge the verses of Richard Realf merely as poetry. They were born in the stormy atmosphere of overwrought emotions and to the emotions rather than to critical discrimination do they appeal. Simple human anguish is outside the province of criticism. Of a death scene enacted on the stage, deliberately planned, no matter how intensely played or how complete the abandon of the actor, one may say that it is well done or ill done. But before death itself, criticism is dumb. There are two sonnets by Realf, among his best, which are wonderfully revelatory of the two sides of his character, the imperious frenzy of his personal needs and desires to which he sacrificed everything, and which drove him from folly to folly, and the beautiful tenderness, the true poet soul that lived and suffered amid all these tempests until the end, and made him beloved by all men, and by all women, save one. . . .[36]

That is certainly poetry of a high order, but its emotional vehemence is such that it is impossible to judge it purely as an art product. It is rather a man's heart's blood spilled out on paper; it is the cry of [a] man who probed the wound in his bosom with his pen. And apparently only in moments of such travail of soul, of such acute and almost physical agony could Realf strike so high a note. Under ordinary circumstances he wrote much that is ordinary. Yet in his most hasty and careless work, and he was often both, there is always the unmistakable stamp of power, always a line or two to serve as an autograph of the poet in him, often asleep, but never dead. For instance, in a poem which has little to say and which ends cheaply enough, one finds so exquisite a beginning as this:

> Sometimes when the wind goes roaring
>   Thro' the city's streets and lanes,
> And the homeless night is pouring
>   Blind tears on your window panes;
> When you shudder for the sailor,
>   Cast on the moaning sea,
> And the stranger in the forest—
>   Then, beloved, think of me.

In short, it is scarcely just to judge this man exclusively as a poet. If we consider him at all it must be as "poet, soldier or workman"; the soldier who bore the colors over the rifle pits at Missionary Ridge, the romantic adventurer who joined John Brown's band, the impassioned defender of liberty, "who smote for her when God himself seemed dumb." His profession was life, not letters, and the fever of living consumed the flower of his strength. A literary artist he never pretended to be, perhaps never seriously tried to be. Poetry was to him a means to life, not life a means to poetry. It is scarcely possible for a man to be both a poet and a reformer. Even Victor Hugo was not great enough to feed two

36. The poems "Passion" and "Silence Till" were given here.

flames so consuming. The evidence of the ages would seem to indicate that the best art is that done purely for art's sake, not for God or home or native land. To realize how little of Realf's heart was really in the profession of letters, one has only to compare his career with that of Edgar Allan Poe, a man similarly misunderstood and unhappy, like Realf, "a genius bound to the hackwork of the press," but a pauper prouder than princes, a beggar who never let a piece of slovenly work leave his empty hands.

One can only wonder what the results would have been had Realf never gone to Kansas and had given himself wholly to letters. But from the very nature of the man that could not be. He was athirst for storm and action, and the heat of battle went into his blood and burned there till he died. He drank life to the lees and found them bitter, a discovery which men are never tired of making. He loved unwisely and passing well and was still alone. The sonnet "Passion," already quoted, is perhaps one of the most poignant expressions ever written of that impenetrable loneliness which wraps about the souls of the great. He could speak when he suffered, then his hand was strong, and then fell upon him the "bright tongues of flame" of which he speaks in his last poem, but they burned his life out and burned it quickly. At forty-four he had known the sorrows of a lifetime and was glad to lay life down.

Years—years.
So long the dread companionship of pain,
So long the slow compression of the brain,
So long the bitter famine and the drouth,
So long the ache for kisses on the mouth;
So long the straining of hot tearless eyes
In backward looking upon Paradise,
So long tired feet dragged faltering and slow,
So long the solemn sanctity of woe.
Years—years.

Surely no one can deny him honor great as was his talent, commiseration great as was his agony.

Courier, February 25, 1899, pp. 3–4.

Gentle Northumberland,
If thy offenses were upon record,
Would it not shame thee in so fair a troop
To read a lecture on them?

Richard II

I am surprised and rather disconcerted to hear that my remarks on the subject of Richard Realf should have been construed as a defense of that erratic genius' life. Nothing could have been further from my intentions, and I think I said nothing to warrant such an interpretation. I did, indeed, write for my own paper an interview with Francis Murphy, the temperance reformer, which was a very ardent defense of Realf, but that presented Mr. Murphy's view and not my own. However, very much better people than I have taken up the argument for the defense. Col. R. J. Hinton, who wrote the sympathetic memoir of Realf which appears in the published volume of his works, is a temperance reformer and a writer on that radical temperance organ, the *Voice*. Francis Murphy, who certainly needs no certificate of character wherever his great work has been heard of, says of Realf that "his weaknesses, grave as they were, to those who knew him best seemed small beside his noble qualities." Now one of three things must be true: either these men are fools, or they are hypocrites, or Realf had his redeeming virtues. To call a man a sot and a bigamist is not characterization. It does not explain his paradoxical existence, nor reconcile his contradictions. A man may be both of these and yet be of our common species, in many things very like the best of us. If my article seemed to palliate his faults, it must have been merely because I tried to get at the man's motives, to understand the impulses which drove him to wreak such wretchedness upon himself and others. For I maintain that of all his victims, he himself suffered most, and then perhaps I sympathize with him a little because I know his wife, Catherine Cassidy, whom my friends in Nebraska do not. Knowing her, I can forgive him much. Shortly after my interview with Murphy was published, she turned up, that terrible woman whose name is known and dreaded in every newspaper office in Pittsburgh, and whose face, by her long cherishing of one fierce passion, has become a veritable mask of hate. It was the same woman who rented a child from an orphan asylum when she wanted to claim alimony from Realf, and who has kept the manuscripts of his poems all these years, refusing them to every publisher, as a sort of supreme vengeance against the dead. She appeared at the office speechless with fury, her features twitching and jerking with the bitter hate which twenty years have not cooled. When she was calm enough to listen to reason, I promised to write and publish her story, entirely from her standpoint, in her own words, which I did, though they were not pretty words by any means.[37] This woman has been for years the most notorious termagant in

37. Catherine Cassidy's answer to Murphy appeared in the *Leader*, February 15, 1899, p. 6, under the head "Mrs. Realf's Story."

Pittsburgh, and she has accumulated a vocabulary which freezes one's blood. As nearly as I can judge she and Realf answer to Daudet's famous description of the two cats sewed up in a leather bag and thrown in the hot sun to scratch each other to death. Her chief grievance was, of course, "them other women," and she had a crazy story which she was never tired of reiterating about Realf once taking forty dollars which she had hidden "in the family Bible, on the center table, a marble table it was, too, in the parlor," and buying champagne for an actress with it. That seemed to be her *casus belli*. When I asked her why in the name of goodness she ever married him at all, she rolled her gloves up into a wad muttering, "He was so handsome to look at—so handsome!" When I remarked that handsome articles usually came high, she flashed out, "Yes, and I'd do it agin, too, I reckon." When I asked her what kind of a woman Lizzie Whappham, the mother of Realf's children, was, her little beady eyes glittered at me a moment and she retorted, "O, she wasn't so much to look at!" It was almost pathetic, that little feminine burst from this old termagant, fairly shrivelled up by her sleepless hate. I believe she really loves the fellow yet and can't help herself, and hates him and herself and the world and especially "them other women" accordingly. Decidedly Catherine Cassidy is more than a scold and a vixen, just as Realf was more than a sot and a bigamist. Life is not to be measured in a phrase. It would take no less a person than M. Honoré de Balzac himself to do justice to those two strange people.

Courier, April 8, 1899, pp. 2–3.

Frank Norris's McTeague

Willa Cather reviewed McTeague: A Story of San Francisco, *by Frank Norris (1870–1902), for the* Leader *in "Books and Magazines," March 31, 1899. For her* Courier *column, presented below, she added only the first two sentences. Norris, who had attended the University of California (1890–1894), wrote most of* McTeague *at Harvard (1894–1895) under the direction of Professor Lewis Gates, to whom the novel is dedicated, and finished it in San Francisco, where he worked for the* Wave *(1896–1898).* McTeague *was published in 1899 on his return to New York after reporting the war in Cuba. Cather's interest in the "power and promise" of Norris (only three years her senior) was exhibited in her later comments (see Books and Authors [IV], below).*

A new and a great book has been written. The name of it is *McTeague: A Story of San Francisco*, and the man who wrote it is Mr. Frank Norris.

The great presses of the country go on year after year grinding out commonplace books, just as each generation goes on busily reproducing its own mediocrity. When in this enormous output of ink and paper, these thousands of volumes that are yearly rushed upon the shelves of the book stores, one appears which contains both power and promise, the reader may be pardoned some enthusiasm. Excellence always surprises: we are never quite prepared for it. In the case of *McTeague: A Story of San Francisco*, it is even more surprising than usual. In the first place the title is not alluring, and not until you have read the book, can you know that there is an admirable consistency in the stiff, uncompromising commonplaceness of that title. In the second place the name of the author is as yet comparatively unfamiliar, and finally the book is dedicated to a member of the Harvard faculty, suggesting that whether it be a story of San Francisco or Dawson City, it must necessarily be vaporous, introspective and chiefly concerned with "literary" impressions. Mr. Norris is, indeed, a "Harvard man," but that he is a good many other kinds of a man is self-evident. His book is, in the language of Mr. Norman Hapgood, the work of "a large human being, with a firm stomach, who knows and loves the people."

In a novel of such high merit as this, the subject matter is the least important consideration. Every newspaper contains the essential material for another *Comèdie Humaine*. In this case McTeague, the central figure, happens to be a dentist practicing in a little side street of San Francisco. The novel opens with this description of him. . . .

Then Mr. Norris launches into a description of the street in which McTeague lives. He presents that street as it is on Sunday, as it is on working days, as it is in the early dawn when the workmen are going out with pickaxes on their shoulders, as it is at ten o'clock when the women are out purchasing from the small shopkeepers, as it is at night when the shop girls are out with the soda-fountain tenders and the motor cars dash by full of theatregoers, and the Salvationists sing before the saloon on the corner. In four pages he reproduces the life in a by-street of a great city, the little tragedy of the small shopkeeper. There are many ways of handling environment—most of them bad. When a young author has very little to say and no story worth telling, he resorts to environment. It is frequently used to disguise a weakness of structure, as ladies who paint landscapes put their cows knee-deep in water to conceal the defective drawing of the legs. But such description as one meets throughout Mr. Norris' book is in itself convincing proof of power, imagination and literary skill. It is a positive and active force, stimulating the reader's imagination, giving him an actual command, a realizing sense of this world into which he is suddenly transplanted. It gives to the book perspective, atmosphere, effects of time and distance, creates the illusion of life. This power of mature, and accurate and comprehensive description is very unusual among the younger American writers. Most of them observe the world through a temperament, and are more occupied with their medium than the objects they see. And temperament is a glass which distorts most astonishingly. But this young man sees with a clear eye, and reproduces with a touch firm and decisive, strong almost to brutalness. Yet this hand that can depict so powerfully the brute strength and brute passions of a McTeague, can deal very finely and adroitly with the feminine element of his story. This is his portrait of the little Swiss girl, Trina, whom the dentist marries. . . .

The tragedy of the story dates from a chance, a seeming stroke of good fortune, one of those terrible gifts of the Danaë. A few weeks before her marriage Trina drew five thousand dollars from a lottery ticket. From that moment her passion for hoarding money becomes the dominant theme of the story, takes command of the book and its characters. After their marriage the dentist is disbarred from practice. They move into a garret where she starves her husband and herself to save that precious hoard. She sells even his office furniture, everything but his concertina and his canary bird, with which he stubbornly refuses to part and which are destined to become very important accessories in the property room of the theatre where this drama is played. This removal from their first home is to this story what Gervaise's removal from her shop is to *L'Assommoir;* it is the fatal episode of the third act, the sacrifice of self-respect, the beginning of the end. From that time the money stands between Trina and her husband. Outraged and humiliated, hating her for her meanness, demoralized by his idleness and despair, he begins to abuse her. The story becomes a careful and painful study of the disintegration of this union, a penetrating and searching analysis of the degeneration of these two souls, the woman's corroded by greed, the man's poisoned by disappointment and hate.

And all the while this same painful theme is placed in a lower key. [Here is summarized the episode dealing with the murder of Maria, McTeague's former housemaid, by Zerko, the junkman, who believes Maria knows where a gold dinner service is hidden.]

From this it is a short step to McTeague's crime. He kills his wife to get possession of her money, and escapes to the mountains. While he is on his way south, pushing toward Mexico, he is overtaken by his murdered wife's cousin and former suitor. Both men are half mad with thirst, and there in the desert wastes of Death Valley, they spring to their last conflict. The cousin falls, but before he dies he slips a handcuff over McTeague's arm, and so the author leaves his hero in the wastes of Death Valley, a hundred miles from water, with a dead man chained to his arm. As he stands there the canary bird, the survivor of his happier days, to which he had clung with stubborn affection, begins "chittering feebly in its little gilt prison." It reminds one a little of Stevenson's use of poor Goddedaal's canary in *The Wrecker*. It is just such sharp, sure strokes that bring out the highlights in a story and separate excellence from the commonplace. They are at once dramatic and revelatory. Lacking them, a novel which may otherwise be a good one, lacks its chief reason for being. The fault with many worthy attempts at fiction lies not in what they are, but in what they are not.

Mr. Norris' model, if he will admit that he has followed one, is clearly no less a person than M. Zola himself. Yet there is no discoverable trace of imitation in his book. He has simply taken a method which has been most successfully applied in the study of French life and applied it in studying American life as one uses certain algebraic formulae to solve certain problems. It is perhaps the only truthful literary method of dealing with that part of society which environment and heredity hedge about like the walls of a prison. It is true that Mr. Norris now and then allows his "method" to become too prominent, that his restraint savors of constraint, yet he has written a true story of the people, courageous, dramatic, full of matter and warm with life. He has addressed himself seriously to art, and he seems to have no ambition to be clever. His horizon is wide, his invention vigorous and bold, his touch heavy and warm and human. This man is not limited by literary prejudices: he sees the people as they are; he is close to them and not afraid of their unloveliness. He has looked at truth in the depths, among men begrimed by toil and besotted by ignorance, and still found her fair. *McTeague* is an achievement for a young man. It may not win at once the success which it deserves, but Mr. Norris is one of those who can afford to wait.

Courier, April 8, 1899, pp. 2–3.

The Musical World (III)

(October 25, 1898—May 12, 1900)[1]

As was to be expected in a city as musical as Pittsburgh, Willa Cather had many friends actively interested in music. Her desk at the Leader *was next to that of the music critic, Arthur Burgoyne, of whom it was written: "He is a musical composer and critic of much ability and can play on any sort of instrument, be it brass or string."*[2] *She was often at the George Seibels', "where music and pfeffernüsse were somehow mingled," and she was "constantly invited" to musical parties by Mrs. John Slack, whose house in suburban Sewickley—next door to that of the Nevins—had "a large and beautiful music-room."*

Most important of all her musical friendships at this time was that with Ethelbert Nevin (see The Urban Scene, above). He was the first famous artist whom Willa Cather knew intimately, and quite apart from the glamor of his celebrity, she valued his friendship deeply.[3] *The degree of their intimacy is suggested in a letter Nevin wrote to his wife—"Oh, my dear little girl, I am dependent on you. Miss Cather was right."*[4]*—which clearly indicates that they had talked over his personal situation. Moreover, when Nevin's biographer, Vance Thompson, wished to portray Nevin's home life, he reprinted excerpts from Willa Cather's article, "An Evening at Vineacre" (see below).*

Opera and opera singers continued to fascinate Cather, but—no doubt because of her involvement with Nevin—a significant proportion of her musical

1. For narrative interest and for the purpose of contrast and comparison, this chapter includes two articles which appeared later than the May 12, 1900 date. See "Ethelbert Nevin," below.

2. "The Men Who Make the Pittsburgh Papers," *Library*, August 4, 1900, pp. 13–14. For a discussion of the authorship of this article (signed "C.W.S."), see the introductory note to The *Library*, below. The first quoted phrase following is from Brown, p. 84; the rest of the information in this paragraph is from Lewis, *Willa Cather Living*, p. 47.

3. Willa Cather to Mariel Gere, January 10, 1898, and n.d. [November or December 1898].

4. Vance Thompson, *The Life of Ethelbert Nevin* (Boston: Boston Music Co., 1913), p. 203. See also note 19, below.

comments from the fall of 1898 to the spring of 1900 are devoted to piano virtuosi. During the two years that she knew him her musical world combined her old interest in opera with a new interest in pianists, a combination that was to reappear in her portrait of Thea Kronborg.[5]

John Philip Sousa

> *Sousa's rousing marches were well adapted to the chauvinistic spirit of the day, and he remained for years the unquestioned "March King." Willa Cather reviewed his first operetta,* El Capitan, *in 1897 (see "Three Operettas," The Musical World [II], above), and the following year she reported on* The Bride Elect, *for which he also wrote the libretto. After a run of sixty-four performances following its New York opening in April 1898,* The Bride Elect *went on the road, with Pittsburgh an early stop on the tour.*

The town is full of Sousa; you can hear him at the Alvin or on Fifth Avenue; where you choose and where you don't choose. When he comes, we capitulate. Sousa's music has played an important part in recent history. From the heights of San Juan, the coast of Puerto Rico and the trenches before Santiago those marches come back to us like war-stained veterans, bearing their blushing honors thick upon them.[6] They have accompanied the fluttering of victorious banners and the tramp of moving squadrons and the march of feet that were to return no more, have rung out above death groans and farewells; and now it seems almost incongruous to hear them playing to the tap-tap of high-heeled leather boots and the flutter of spangled skirts and the flash of gay tin swords of comic opera.

Seriously speaking, *The Bride Elect* marks a notable advance in Mr. Sousa's career as a composer of comic operas. It shows a marked growth in his handling of lyric themes, a kind of expression in which *El Capitan* was deficient. The fine adaptation of those familiar lines from Longfellow's "The Children's Hour," at the opening of the second act, is an example of this, and is one of the most melodious arias in the whole opera. The "Snow Song" is another instance of graceful composition, while La Partorella's card song is finely dramatic and makes a brilliantly effective climax. And, by the way, it could hardly have been sung better than Miss

5. In *The Song of the Lark* Thea studies piano until her teacher, Harsanyi, discovers her voice is her true gift.

6. The Battle of San Juan Hill had been fought on July 1, 1898, and at this time (October 1898) The United States and Spanish peace commissioners were meeting in Paris.

Hilda Clark sang it. The book is very flat indeed; the sort of book freshmen sometimes write for college dramatics, and most of the humor in the lines was introduced by the members of the cast along with slabs of local color. The orchestration throughout is remarkably good and the harp accompaniment is so alluringly tuneful that I wonder it is not used oftener in music of that sort. The entire composition has that vivacious quality so essential to light opera. It is full of movement, the score seems continually to be getting somewhere. Moreover, it has what all Sousa's music has—nationality. Say what you will, it is a bandmaster's opera, excellent within its limitations, but nevertheless very limited, marked by strongly personal mannerisms, yet withal thrilling and tingling with martial spirit and giddy with the exultant gayety of arms. "Unchain the Dogs of War" would not surprise anyone, even if it were heard for the first time, for although Sousa never reminds you of anyone else, he not infrequently reminds you of himself. It is a great march, all the same, like its predecessors, and when, after it had been encored until the singers were exhausted last night, the band took it up to the waving of Cuban and American flags, the house simply had a hot-box and got up and pawed the air. . . .

Leader, October 25, 1898, p. 2.

Three Pianists

Except for her report on Teresa Carreño (see The Musical World [II], above) Willa Cather had not written for her Lincoln readers of the solo instrumentalists whom she heard perform at the Carnegie Music Hall in 1896 and 1897. The following selections were written after her meeting with Ethelbert Nevin, who probably kindled her interest in piano virtuosi. The artists discussed are: Moritz Rosenthal (1862–1946), a Polish pianist, who made frequent tours of the United States and taught for a time at the Curtis Institute in Philadelphia; Rafael Joseffy (1852–1915), who was born in Hungary and lived in New York, teaching at the National Conservatory of Music after 1888; and Vladimir de Pachmann (1843–1933), Russian interpreter of Chopin, who toured the United States frequently after 1891.

Last Friday evening Moritz Rosenthal played at the Carnegie Music Hall with the Pittsburgh Symphony Orchestra, of which Victor Herbert, author of the *Wizard of the Nile*, is conductor.[7] Mr. Rosenthal played several of his own compositions, so preposterously difficult of execution

7. Victor Herbert had been chosen to replace Frederic Archer as conductor. For additional comment on Herbert, see Guest Editor of the *Courier*, below.

that probably no other living pianist would care to attack them. The *pièce de résistance* of his program, however, was Chopin's famous Concerto in E Minor with orchestral accompaniment, which has been so cleverly edited and adapted and exemplified that it affords just the opportunity for an absolute master of the keyboard like Rosenthal to bewilder his auditors. I believe it is esteemed one of the noblest compositions in all the literature of the piano. Ethelbert Nevin styles it an apotheosis of the instrument. I believe the largo movement has suffered less from editing and interpolation and has retained more of the original poetry of Chopin than the allegro and rondo, and it was in that, that Rosenthal exhibited his wonderful pianissimo effects. In those involved, intricate melodies, more delicate than the strands of a spider's web or the fantastic traceries of the frost upon the window pane, a mere lacework of sound, the pianist displayed all those subtleties of execution whereby he fairly illuminates a composition. He takes up a pianissimo passage and actually whittles it down until it is but a ghost of sound, a mere breath of the strings. Throughout the romance he used the soft pedal almost continually, checking the vibrations of the notes sharply, skimming the surface of the tones, making tone bubbles, as it were. Surely this man has in a wonderful degree that element of classic grace which so distinguishes Joseffy. That quality stood out above all others in his exquisitely simple phrasing of the passage in the latter part of the allegro, which is accompanied only by the melancholy French horns. Heavens! what variety there is in that composition! what brilliant runs, what ravishing melodies, what dazzling passages of bravura, what whispering of the strings weird and sweet as the music of a wind-harp. So delicately does Rosenthal intone those softer passages that we seemed indeed to hear "the horns of elf-land faintly blowing." The rondo was executed without the elision of a note, the runs fairly whistling after each other, and the marvellous finale was played with a brilliancy, a depth, a crashing, impetuous power which completely subordinated an orchestra of sixty pieces. After nine encores Mr. Rosenthal played the Chopin waltz that Paderewski always plays, but in a very different manner, making thirds and sixths out of those charming runs, as Joseffy always does.

In his personal appearance this Herr Rosenthal suggests a Polish workman rather than an artist. Be not deceived by his leonine photographs. He is a short, thickly built man with the shoulders of a porter and a shaggy unkempt head of hair. His clothes are rumpled and ill-fitting and he does not even take the trouble to brush the cigarette ashes from his coat when he enters the concert room. At the hotel where he stopped they tremble at his name. Well, if one were a Rosenthal one could afford to have all the carpets pulled up from one's rooms, and the curtain torn down and the furniture fired into the corridor, and even to empty a lobster Newburg down the waiter's neck if it pleased one to do so.

Courier, February 4, 1899, p. 3.

So Joseffy has come forth from his retirement at last, come forth no whit older, with the same wonder in his hands and the same severity of countenance. He takes to the ground periodically and buries himself, giving lessons and studying and abjuring concerts. This time he has come out of his shell with the marks of hard work on him, and he even plays the heavier sonatas of Brahms, and even that one stupendous sonata of Tchaikovsky's at his recitals now. One never used to find such ambitious and noisy people on his programs. I had not heard him for five years, and I somehow expected him to be very much older, but the man must be on good terms with life. When he stepped upon the platform, I could see no trace of *embonpoint* to detract from the dignity of his figure; his hair, though cut close, curled about his high forehead in the way it used to do, and his hands, those white, shapely, elegant hands that colorists have loved to paint, swept the air with the same curt, apologetic gesture, the hands of a gentleman and an artist. There was of old a sort of atmosphere of retirement and self-respect about this man that he still retains and that somehow makes one feel certain that he would never be implicated in dog-fights, or lost by his manager, or elope with a restaurateur's daughter to find a royal road to fame. There is, too, a certain distinction of manners, a certain aristocracy of the Race of Song, a classic grace and repose that goes well with that very poetic name, Rafael Joseffy.

His first number was the Brahms' Sonata in F Minor. I heard Rosenthal play it last winter and I have heard Ethelbert Nevin play the andante and scherzo and intermezzo often and often. Then I have heard Eugene Heffley, who is as big as Sieveking and as strong as Sandow,[8] bang splendid crescendos and build up great tonal cathedrals out of the allegro. Joseffy played it as I had expected, unevenly. He did not, I think, rise to the almost impossible possibilities of the allegro, and even his playing of the scherzo seemed to lack breadth of treatment. It is not that the allegro is

8. Martinus Sieveking (1867–1950), Dutch-born pianist, taught at the conservatory in Lincoln, Nebraska (1893–1895) and had a great success as a soloist in Chicago, Boston, and New York, 1896–1897. Eugene Sandow (1867–1925), a famous strong man, exhibited his physical-culture techniques at the Chicago World's Fair, 1893.

without melody, that it is all musical dynamics and shrapnel, that makes it so difficult of execution. There are no mannerisms which demand that the performer surrender his soul and better judgment, no inverted difficulties, no obscurities. The difficulty in the F Minor sonata, as in all Brahms', is simply a difficulty of dimension. He is hard of complete apprehension, simply because he is many-sided and big on all sides, because to master one of his sonatas, you must unravel it, like the cable of a war ship. When people of a merely external knowledge of music and literature speak of Brahms or Browning, they refer to their "obscurity" as though it were a quality of their work, whereas it is merely a matter of the quantity of the man's ideas, the teeming fertility of his brain, from which thought comes, not a clear and lucid stream, but it gushes torrent-wise, confused and confounded by its own turbulence and mass. If Browning had dug no deeper into the roots of things than Tennyson, I have no doubt that his meaning would always be as clear. If Brahms' piano compositions were not packed as they are with the very brain-stuff and soul-stuff, out of which music is made, I have no doubt that they could be played as easily as Felix Mendelssohn's. When people fail to play Brahms well, it is simply because their reach is not long enough; they may be artists and true followers of the Prophet, and yet not equal to this system of prodigious intellectual gymnastics—for intellectual gymnastics they are, not digital gymnastics. It seemed to me that Joseffy simply looked at the allegro through the wrong end of the opera glass. He did not make it big enough. His prime excellence lies in the grace, the quality, the timbre of his playing, and there is no reason why he should go forth with Brahms to slay. His allegro lacked brilliancy, breadth, variation, contrast, power. It was not big enough.

The andante he played much, much better than I have ever heard it, and if any one doubted that Rafael Joseffy is a poet, he knew better then. Ah, that andante! Heine knew moments as sweet, Tennyson and Paul Verlaine both knew that alluring, mystic shimmer of Romance, that fair uncertain light that comes song-laden from the past. The man at the piano sat weaving this poem, painting this landscape, making the brain quiver under the new, indefinite, tender sensations which he looked. He sat there calling out those clear, pure silver tones, silver as the waters of the lake whence Arthur drew Excalibur, silver as the armor that the knights of the Grail wore, silver as the moonlight that sleeps on the moss banks under the frosty pines of the North German forests. One felt as though it ought to be possible to catch those tones and hold them, to gather them up in some way and not let them waste away in empty air like that. As he sat there, his fingers making those limpid sounds, those crystal tones, I thought of Midas, that Cretan king, whose fingers turned all that he touched into shining gold.

Then came the Chopin music that Joseffy plays with such deference, such understanding, such discrimination; Ballade no. 4, a mazurka, that strange posthumous waltz that is so little heard, and a polonaise, one of those "cannons buried in flowers."

The second part of the program was wholly given up to Tchaikovsky's colossal sonata, the opus 37, which is fifty pages long, and which treats the piano in a fashion that should be answered by a charge of assault and battery. It is not piano music at all; it is a sonata for the orchestra, an attempt to batter orchestral work out of the black and white keys. And the piano was avenged, for the sonata has been practically dead for years and Joseffy is one of the few men who have revived it for concert purposes.

It was with one of his pupils that I went to hear Vladimir de Pachmann. "When you have heard him," he said, "you will have heard the best living player of Chopin, and you will have heard one of the men who make the history of art, an artist to his fingertips, vain as a woman, whimsical as a child, gifted as one of the sons of light." Although he no longer affects the long black hair and beard which once concealed his countenance and made him look like a Will H. Bradley illustration to a Stephen Crane poem, there is no mistaking the Russian pianist's vocation. He wears his hair brushed straight back now, very much à la Toby Rex, and his heavy body and broad, powerful shoulders look queer enough on the absurdly short legs which toddle them about. His feet are small and he is very vain of them. "But then," remarked the Pachmann pupil, "he is vain of everything; he is the vainest man I ever knew, and when I was with him I was almost as vain of him as he was of himself. One falls under the enchantment of the man and Pachmannism becomes a mystic cult, an intellectual religion, a new sort of theosophy. His pupils usually copy his walk, his gestures, I think I used even to wish I had his nose and his little slits of Tartar eyes. But listen!"

He first played Weber's Sonata in A Flat, wishing, I suppose, to give a certificate of his general musicianship and his complete dominion over his instrument before he began to "specialize." But in that, as in his Chopin numbers, one noticed first his unexpectedness. He does not deign to play a number as you have heard it before. He has a technique full of tricks and wonderful feats of skill, full of tantalizing pauses and willful subordinations and smothered notes cut short so suddenly that he seems to have drawn them back into his fingers again. In his thin and bearded days he looked like a wizard of the Svengali type, and even now is not unlike the portly, comfortable magicians of the Eastern fairy tales. The magician resemblance keeps occurring to one as he plays. He is very much of a trickster, in spite of that fiery quality, that temperamental intensity. But it is an intellectual variety of trickery, a sort of impassioned sleight of hand. There is indeed a kind of bravado about the astonishing liberty he permits himself in the matter of phrasing, and when he did something particularly startling he would look down at his pupil and screw up his brows and wrinkle his nose and wink slyly with one of his little Tartar eyes, very much as Jack Horner must have done when he pulled out the plum and said, "What a great boy am I."

It was not until he began playing the third prelude of Chopin that the Pachmann pupil utterly collapsed and murmured, "The tone—the singing tone! His own tone!" And singing tones they were; living things that lived a glorious instant of life and died under his fingers, "trembling, passed in music out of sight." The Pachmann pupil assured me that no one else had ever been able to produce a tone just like that, and he remarked that that peculiar bird-like tone would die with Vladimir de Pachmann, and then he told me a funny story of this quaint Russian egotist. When he was in Pittsburgh on his last American tour, he was playing the Chopin Valse Brilliante, opus 34, to a crowd of musicians in a wholesale music store here. He played even better than usual, and when he had finished, he looked up and said with a sigh and a gesture of ineffable regret, "Ah, who will play like that when Pachmann is no more!" There were actually tears in his eyes, for he was overcome with the sense of the great loss which the world must some day suffer.

Courier, December 30, 1899, p. 2.

The Perfect Wagnerite

In 1925 Willa Cather declared that she knew of "only two books in English on the Wagnerian operas that are at all worthy of their subject; Bernard Shaw's The Perfect Wagnerite [*subtitled* A Commentary on the Ring of the Nibelung] *and* The Wagnerian Romances *by Gertrude Hall."*[9] *Shaw, whose reputation as a music critic antedated his success as a dramatist,*

9. In Willa Cather's preface to Gertrude Hall, *The Wagnerian Romances* (New York: Alfred A. Knopf, Inc., 1925), collected in *On Writing*, p. 60.

published The Perfect Wagnerite *in 1898. The ellipsis in the following selection appeared in the original. For Cather's views on Shaw as a dramatist, see Theatre (III), above.*

From Mr. G. Bernard Shaw one always expects the unconventional. With his reputation as a whimsical iconoclast so firmly established, it possibly occurred to him that the most unconventional thing he could do was to write a thoroughly conventional book. At any rate, he has done so, and his essays on the Nibelung Ring may safely be introduced into musical libraries, or quoted in musical lectures, and parts of his book, at least, may even be read with impunity by young ladies cramming for their first opera season. One must admit, however, that these parts are not the most interesting and brilliant of the work. In short, Mr. Shaw does Wagner the honor to take him quite seriously and praiseworthily refrains from making merry at his expense. There are only four people, I believe, whom Mr. Shaw does take seriously—Ibsen, Wagner, Eleonora Duse and himself. It appears that he is entirely straightforward in his work on the *Ring*, and that he wrote it with genuine sympathy for the people who derive pleasure from the performance of the operas without being able to discuss counter-subjects, or codas, or strettos or pedal points. In his chapter "Preliminary Encouragements," he declares boldly: "My second encouragement is addressed to modest citizens who may suppose themselves to be disqualified from enjoying the *Ring* by their technical ignorance of music. They may dismiss all such misgivings speedily and confidently. If the sound of music has any power to move them they will find that Wagner exacts nothing further. There is not a single bar of 'classical' music in the *Ring*—not a note of it that has any other point than the single direct point of giving musical expression to the drama. . . . The unskilled, untaught musician may approach Wagner boldly; there is no possibility of a misunderstanding between them; the *Ring* music is perfectly single and simple. It is the adept musician of the old school who has everything to unlearn; and him I leave unpitied, to his fate." Mr. Shaw's discussion of the plots of the four music dramas of the *Ring* is perfectly orthodox in matter, though scarcely in manner, for it is neither pretentious nor stupid and the thoroughly orthodox discussion is usually both. Of course, in the last analysis all criticism is purely subjective, and any man's conception of the ultimate meaning of a work of art must be merely a personal impression. So in his chapter "Siegfried as Protestant," Mr. Shaw's summing up of the causes and effects of Wotan's complications is eminently characteristic and is not unlike his theory of Ibsen's art as expounded in his volume of essays entitled *The Quintessence of Ibsenism*. He says: "The philosophically fertile element in the original project of 'Siegfried's' death was the conception of 'Siegfried' himself as a type of the perfectly healthy man raised to perfect confidence in his own impulses by an intense and joyous vitality above fear, sickliness and conscience, malice and the make-shifts and moral crutches of law and order which accompany them. The world has always delighted in the man who is delivered from conscience. From Punch and Don Juan down to Robert Macaire and the pantomime clown, he has always drawn large audiences." The majority of society, Mr. Shaw says, can never attain this emancipation from conscience, and like Wagner's giants must be governed by laws. "Governments are, of course, established by the few who are capable of governing, though, its mechanism once complete, it is generally carried on unintelligently by people who are incapable of it, the capable people repairing it from time to time when it gets too far behind the advance or decay of civilization. These capable people are thus in the position of 'Wotan,' forced to maintain as sacred, and themselves submit to, laws which they privately know to be obsolescent makeshifts, and to affect the deepest veneration for ideals and creeds which they ridicule among themselves. No individual 'Siegfried' can rescue them from this bondage. Indeed the individual 'Siegfried' has come often enough, only to find himself confronted with the alternative of government or destruction at the hands of his fellows who are not 'Siegfrieds.'" This is very naturally Mr. Shaw's view of Wotan's predicament, but the evidence is certainly not wanting that it was also Wagner's, or at least a part of Wagner's view, which taken all in all, was rather too large to be restated by anyone. Mr. Shaw's volume is scarcely satisfactory on the strong love theme in the *Ring*, which after all concerned Wagner much more nearly than the perplexities of his gods, for as Mr. Shaw admits "Wagner always sought for some point of contact between his ideas and physical senses, and on all occasions he insists on the need for sensuous apprehension to give reality to abstract comprehension." It is encouraging to observe that throughout the book Mr. Shaw's splenetic personal prejudices are kept becomingly in the background, but like the naughty little boy who, having been good throughout the dinner, must perforce spill his dessert, in the very last page he breaks out with a reference to Campanini as "A bawling Italian trooper, without art or manners, accepted by fashion as principal tenor during the long interval between Mario and Jean de Reszke."

Leader, May 27, 1899, p. 5.

Lohengrin *and* Die Walküre

In the spring of 1897 Willa Cather reported to her Lincoln readers that the performance of Lohengrin *by the Damrosch Opera Company "was not strictly first class" (see "A Week of Wagner," The Musical World [II], above). Two years later, when the Metropolitan Opera Company for the first time added Pittsburgh to its spring tour, she had no such reservations about the production. In addition to Nordica, who sang Elsa, and Jean de Reszke as Lohengrin, the cast included Ernestine Schumann-Heink as Ortrud, Edouard de Reszke as King Henry, and David Bispham as Telramund.*[10] *The opera was conducted by Franz Schalk (1863–1931), who had succeeded the recently deceased Anton Seidl. Cather was even more delighted with the production of* Die Walküre, *with Lilli Lehmann as Sieglinde, Andreas Dipple (1866–1922) as Siegmund, Marie Brema (1856–1925) as Brünnhilde, Anton Von Rooy (1870–1932) as Wotan, and Schumann-Heink as Fricka. Both these operas figured importantly in* The Song of the Lark, *and it is interesting to compare the later fictional treatment with these "Passing Show" accounts.*[11]

The Pittsburgh Grand Opera season, the last engagement of the Metropolitan Opera Company before it disbanded and severally parted for Europe, was something long to be remembered. It was the closing of the most glorious opera season America has ever seen, and this dirty, gloomy city arrayed itself in dress coats and imported toilettes and just got up and did itself proud in honor of the event. Pittsburgh is noted for taking itself seriously, and it is frantically busy seven days out of the week the whole year round, but when it decides to take a holiday, it does it with a vengeance, as the great financial success of the opera season proved to Mr. Maurice Grau, to whose stony heart only dollars speak.[12]

Lohengrin, with the following cast [see headnote], was the opera selected for the opening night. . . .

Certainly all the living talent of the world could not furnish a better cast. It was Jean de Reszke's sole appearance and it took much tact and

10. The principals of the cast were those who had performed the opera at the Metropolitan on January 8, 1899, a performance which drew from Henry E. Krehbiel (1854–1923), distinguished music critic of the New York *Tribune*, the exclamation: "Fortunate public, destined to be the envy of future generations!"

11. For *Lohengrin*, see *The Song of the Lark*, pp. 498–502; for *Die Walküre*, see pp. 567–572. See also the description of Raymond d'Esquerré singing the first act of *Die Walküre* in "The Garden Lodge," first published in *The Troll Garden* (1905); *CSF*, pp. 193–195.

12. Maurice Grau continued as director of the Metropolitan after the death, in 1896, of his partner, Henry E. Abbey (see "Two Impresarios," The Theatre [III], above).

more gold to woo that haughty tenor so far from the coast. As for the performance, no company can uniformly give performances of such merit, it was one of those fortunate things that happens only occasionally. Madame Nordica told me in the afternoon when she was running over the score at her hotel that she had a premonition that the night would be a triumphant one. Perhaps she thought so because she found herself in unusually good voice, but she was not mistaken. It was not the first time I had had the pleasure of hearing her Elsa, but it was the first time I ever heard her sing it so well. She is less attractive physically this season than I have ever seen her, for she happens to be unpardonably stout. She has the most mercurial avoirdupois I know of, one winter she is almost slender, the next, she is like a matronly dowager. As G. Bernard Shaw says, "You never can tell." But after all she is a mere sylph beside Schumann-Heink. I never saw her give herself out to her audience as she did that night. She is becoming a proficient actress, that determined woman from Maine with the strong chin and big, firm hands, like a man's. It is difficult for her to act, but her whole life has been one long, laborious vanquishing of difficulties. Her very entrance in the first act gives you confidence in her. This is no timid, simpering Elsa. She comes in regally, confident, fearlessly, unstained by that serene hope in a mystic deliverance. When the herald calls for her defender, she awaits him with perfect assurance. Not until the call has been given the third time does she begin to doubt, and even then, when she rises from her knees at the close of her prayer, her face is shining with the fullness of her faith. And then he came, the great Jean, the deliverer, the greatest tenor and one of the greatest actors of his time. He was past fifty when I heard him in Chicago four years ago, yet he stood there in the swan-boat the radiant incarnation of youth and chivalry, the dream-knight of all dreams. And his entrance does what the entrance of a great artist always does, it imparted convincing reality to everything and completed the illusion of the theatre. The swan which drew this splendid figure in silver armour was a real swan, the painted river flowed along like any other river, there was a wind playing in the rushes, and there was a real Mount Monsalvat somewhere in the world, for this man could only have come from that place "which is bright forever." At the first note of the song to the swan, one felt that it was Jean indeed, and at the close of his long and arduous season his voice was fresh, unworn, exquisitely flexible, and his manner of using it is as wonderful as ever, when all is said, it is in his vocalization that De Reszke is unparalleled. Had he next to no voice at all, like the superb Maurel who can sing with a completely worn-out organ, he would still be a consummate artist. His voice is indeed a thing of beauty, but his method of using it is a joy forever. It is the method that makes the artist. The organ itself is purely accidental, and like most of the gifts of God is frequently ill-bestowed, but the use of [it]—ah, that is where the cerebral tissue comes in, and energy and taste and ambition and superhuman industry and all that makes a man. Here is a baritone who has made himself the prince of tenors, who arranges every phrase as a painter lays on his colors, who produces every tone in his brain as well as in his throat, who makes tone but the garment of the mind as flesh is the garment of the soul, who makes of his voice an instrument under perfect control and plays upon it what he wills. The mechanical perfection of the registration, the breathing and placing, they are the achievements of a lifetime of endeavor and are the joy of all young artists. But of the emotional resources of this voice, of its perfect adaption to every shade and degree of every passion, of its freshness and sweetness and bloom, its poetic quality blended with robust virility, what shall be said? The language has been beggared of adjectives to describe it, yet none of them reach it. Someone has called his singing of the Swan song "the milk and honey of music." Certainly he is the only tenor we have today whose tenderness is wholly without effeminacy, or whose voice can rise clear, melodious and true, to the full measure of tragedy, and then there is, undeniably, a deep sentimental quality, that baffling minor tinge that is in the acting of Modjeska and the music of Chopin. Perhaps it is only the cry of unhappy Poland, for which we have no name, a sort of echo that Polish mothers sang.

When the swan had gone and Lohengrin turned to Elsa there seemed nothing abrupt or hasty about his wooing. It was the day of the Arthurian legends come back again, when the knight came with his nobility stamped upon his face, and the maiden's helplessness was her strength. And this Elsa and this Lohengrin have sung that duet so often that their very voices seem to woo each other. When De Reszke sings "On the king of kings I call," he looks King Arthur indeed, and one can well believe that in the days of knighthood there was a Grail indeed.

It is that wonderful artist Mme. Schumann-Heink who dominates the second act. Bispham's Frederick is wonderfully dramatic, but this Ortrud was like none ever seen before. This Schumann-Heink, with her peasant face and her absurd dumpy little figure and short arms simply has unlimited power. She sings down everything before her. She makes you forget that she is not beautiful, and Heavens! what a triumph a woman achieves when she does that. Her scornful taunts at her lover's cowardice and weakness, her impassioned appeal to Elsa, her insatiable hatred, her crafty poisoning of that guileless maiden's mind, are all very triumphs of art. She so completely subordinates Nordica in that act that there can be no question that, within her limitations, she is the greater artist of the two. The second act was not, on this occasion, Nordica's best. In her solo "Ye wandering breeze" on the balcony, one noticed that old inflexibility, that hardness of tone that in her younger days used so often to detract from the effectiveness of her singing.

The third act, when De Reszke sings Lohengrin, is something never to be forgotten. The music of that nuptial duet is probably the most poetic Wagner ever wrote, and certainly the man who sang it has a poet's soul shut up in his throat. When he led Elsa to the window, I assure you he brought the stillness and beauty of the summer night into the hot air of the playhouse. I wish that every analytical student of literature, every misguided person who counts the false rhymes in Spenser and exultantly tears Browning's figures to pieces, or kills a flower to find its name, could have heard him sing that tender remonstrance:

> Dost thou breathe the incense of the flowers,
> Bearing a tide of deep, mysterious joy?
> And would'st know whence this rapture showers?
> Ask not, O love, lest thou the charm destroy!

It was like some divine, compassionate wisdom pleading with the narrow vision and petty pride of fretful pedantry. But poor, dull Elsa was a German lady of a philosophical bent of mind and she wanted a name for everything and could not believe in a joy which she could not analyse. So gently he entreated her, so fair the moonlight was, so sweet the night, so lovely all the world, yet poor practical Elsa could only cry "The name, give me the name!" Well, she got it, and so do the people who construct systems for measuring the value of poetry, but at what a cost! They get the name, and perhaps acquire vast erudition, but they lose the knight, and Mount Monsalvat, and the bright temple of the Grail and all the rest of it. I have heard a good many arguments against the methods of the people who count the poetic words in Tennyson, but I never heard one so powerful or so beautiful as that which Jean de Reszke sang that night.

I was talking with Mme. Nordica about Elsa's particular variety of stupidity after the performance, when she was getting from the airy draperies affected in Brabant into a Paris street dress. "Yes," she said, "that is in all Wagner, that too much analysis destroys; that, and the opportunity of the moment. For the gods there is Walhalla and forever and a day, but for mortals there is only the moment, and that is dying even while it is being born."

Courier, June 10, 1899, p. 3.

Of the four operas[13] given here by the Metropolitan company, I should say that *Die Walküre* was the most brilliant performance. Herr Van Wyck, who was to have sung Siegmund, was ill, but I scarcely see how anyone could have sung that difficult part better than did his substitute, Herr Dipple. From the first moment when, after that ominous prelude of the storm music, he rushes exhausted into Hunding's hut, to his last passionate rejection of immortality, he sang with matchless intensity and vigor, and he at all times sang perfectly in tune. Not every man can do that in the *Ring* operas. Sieglinde was sung by Frau Lilli Lehmann, who did not particularly distinguish herself. The truth may as well be told; whatever Frau Lehmann's past glories may have been, her voice is worn out, her methods are antiquated, and her self-conscious, declamatory German style seems very artificial and stilted beside the more natural methods of the younger singers. She was certainly unequal to that first stormy scene, and Herr Dipple and Mr. Bispham, who sang a most dramatic Hunding, bore the weight of it upon their shoulders. The mutual attraction between Siegmund and Sieglinde begins, you remember, the moment she discovers him at her husband's hearthstone, a refugee from his pursuers. She ministers to his needs, Hunding enters and the guest tells his story, sitting by the table, beneath the tree where the sword itself is waiting for him where his father thrust it on Sieglinde's wedding night. During his recital Sieglinde gazes at him enraptured, and Hunding sits in the shadow, his hands clenched at his side, his eyes blazing like live coals, while his guest sings of the beginning of the woes of the children of Wotan. After Hunding is drugged and safely disposed of by his resourceful wife, Siegmund is left alone by the fire. Then he begins the great sword song, praying for the weapon his father had promised him in his hour of need, the sword with which he can free this woman he loves. It begins with quiet melancholy, rising to that great cry, "Volsung, Volsung, Wo Ist dein Schwert?" Surely if the elements ever answered the cry of human need they would have answered Herr Dipple then. The flames on the

13. The company performed *Roméo et Juliette* and *Faust* in addition to the two reported here.

earth leap up and cast a glow upon the handle of the sword buried in the ash tree. Then in a burst of power which is the very apotheosis of the magnificent sword motif, Herr Dipple leaps upon the table and wrenches the weapon from its unwilling scabbard, and the sword song, glorified, flashes up from the orchestra like the steel itself.

Sieglinde enters, and seeing the sword in his hand knows that her deliverer has come. She tells him how the stern man with his hat drawn low over his eye, had put the sword there, and then he knows that this woman is his sister and bride. The scene which follows is probably the most exalted love scene ever set to music, and all Frau Lehmann's stilted posings could not mar it. When Siegmund throws open the door, letting the moonlight in, and sings his song of spring and love, then for the first time the human element enters the cycle of the *Ring*, and already, so far as dramatic purposes are concerned, Siegfried, the man waited for of the gods, is born.

During the intermission between the first and second acts I left the theatre and was crossing the bridge between the stage entrance of the grand opera house and the Avenue Theatre, when I was arrested by a most marvelous sound. The bridge extends above the dressing rooms of both theatres; in the dressing room just below me the skylight was open, and from it there streamed up a flood of light and a perfect geyser of the most wonderful notes that were quite unmistakable. It was Mme. Brema practicing the "Hi-yo" song of the Valkyries. The night was murky and starless; only the red lamps of the Hotel Henry and the line of river lights above Mount Washington were visible; on every side rose the tall black buildings that shut out the sounds of the streets. Those free, unfettered notes seemed to cut the blackness and the silence, seemed to pierce the clouds which lay over the city and reach the stars and the blue space of heaven behind, and to carry me up with them. . . .

[In the second act Brema, as Brünnhilde, is instructed to protect Siegmund and to slay Wotan], and the joyous Valkyrie leaps up the mountainside singing her "Hi-yo" song—and Lieber Himmel! how she sang it! The very pasteboard mountains seemed to echo it, as in the storm scene in *Childe Harold*, where

> Every mountain now hath found a tongue,
> And Jura answers through her misty shroud,
> Back to the joyous Alps, who call to her aloud.[14]

14. The last three lines of stanza XCII, Canto the Third. *Poetical Works of Lord Byron*, p. 222.

Then Fricka enters, the wonderful Schumann-Heink, whose Ortrud I had heard only the night before. She came not in her ram-drawn car in which she enters at Bayreuth the Holy, but on foot, like common mortals, and she came in a bad humor. I should like to see this incomparable Schumann-Heink in a good-humored part just once, for I know that she is capable of simulating every sort of bad humor and spitefulness known to woman or goddess. She comes, of course, to lecture Wotan for his countenancing the unholy love of Siegmund and Sieglinde, and to express herself upon the sanctity of the marriage vow. Then the deeper tragedy of the drama unfolds; the god bound by the laws of his own making, the strong man pilloried by the weakness of the race. . . .[15]

I suppose that if there was one man in that strong, well-balanced cast who stood out head and shoulders above the rest, it was Herr Van Rooy [Wotan], by reason of the vitality, the intimateness, the flesh and blood which he has given to that wooden part, full of long theological discussions and lectures on the civil government of Heaven. He does not always, I think, interpret Wagner perfectly, but it is an interpretation which commands attention, respect, admiration. He presents a figure not to be forgotten, with his iron jaw, his resolute mouth and a single gray lock drooping over the maimed eye, which was the price he had paid for wisdom, when, overcome by the authority of his wife's arguments, by the insatiable law that he had himself created, he sits down upon the rocks and his shield falls from his hand, he makes you feel how much more terrible it is to be a helpless god than to be a helpless man, and something in his attitude recalled the helpless god of the Greeks, Prometheus chained to Caucasus. He calls back Brünnhilde, the "wish maiden," she who executed his heart's desire, and reinstructs her, and so the wish is subordinated to the law, even with the god.

Herr Van Rooy's last scene is scarcely so satisfactory. His denunciation of Brünnhilde is too furious, too much washed by anger and resentment. Surely Wagner never meant that. Wotan's heart never changed an instant toward his daughter, he hated her no more than one hates his own desire that is impossible of fulfillment. He was too big a god to bear malice. He was driven against his will, by the inexorable law that tires out even the heats [hearts?] of the gods, that binds and fetters in Walhalla just as it does in Pittsburgh or in Lincoln. In his parting from Brünnhilde, Van Rooy is more impassioned than Emile Fischer, but not so tender. He is the irate god rather than the father.

15. Here Cather quoted the passage beginning: "Governments are, of course, established by the few . . ." from Shaw's *The Perfect Wagnerite* that appears in the preceding selection.

That night, when the singers boarded their special streetcar to take the long run out to the Hotel Schenley, where they were stopping, I got on the same car with several local musicians who were going out to a supper party. When the car was bowling off across the hill tops, I noticed a man in the further end, fast asleep. His coat collar was turned up, his linen crumpled, the make-up still discolored his eyes, his face was damp with perspiration, and he looked gray and drawn and tired. It was Herr Anton Van Rooy, late of Walhalla, tired as a laborer from the iron mills. It is hard work apparently, this being a god.

Courier, June 17, 1899, pp. 2–3.

Ethelbert Nevin

Willa Cather had introduced her Lincoln readers to Ethelbert Nevin in February 1898 (see The Urban Scene, above). She was frequently a guest of Nevin and his wife at their home, "Vineacre," and George Seibel recalled that "often she would bring home a bit of music for Mrs. Eyth [her landlady] to play—some new composition of a Sewickley friend named Ethelbert Nevin."[16] *Part of her account of a musical evening at the Nevins', "An Evening at Vineacre," which appeared in "The Passing Show," was later incorporated into "The Man Who Wrote 'Narcissus,'" published in the* Ladies' Home Journal, *November 1900. Nevin's sudden death in February 1901 was a great shock to Willa Cather. Her account of his death and funeral appeared in the "Music" column of the* Nebraska State Journal, *and her ode, "Sleep, Minstrel, Sleep," almost certainly was written in his memory.*[17] *Her portrait of Nevin's life is a sunny one, but when she came to fictionalize elements of this part of her Pittsburgh experience, Cather created in Valentine Ramsay a composer bitterly at odds with his wife, a representative of Philistine wealth.*[18]

AN EVENING AT VINEACRE

I

Gaily the troubadour
  Touched his guitar,

16. Seibel, p. 200.

17. First published in *April Twilights* (Boston: Richard G. Badger, 1903); *AT(1903)*, p. 14.

18. "Uncle Valentine (*Adagio non troppo*)," *Woman's Home Companion*, February and March, 1925. Another character clearly derived from Nevin is Adriance Hilgarde in "'A Death in the Desert,'" first published in *Scribner's*, January 1903, collected in *The Troll Garden; CSF*, pp. 199–217. See Bennett, "Willa Cather in Pittsburgh," p. 75.

As he was hastening
Home from the war.

Old Song

Half a dozen beautiful songs have come to the world lately daintily published by the Church Company under the fanciful title, *Songs from Vineacre*. They are the works of that young American composer who makes the most beautiful of songs, Ethelbert Nevin. They were published only this winter, but they are already known and sung all over the world, and [David] Bispham is singing them in London even now. It is not easy for a man who wrote "O, That We Two Were Maying," when he was in the middle of his teens to improve on himself, for it means that he must go very high, but this man has kept doing it from year to year, and the Vineacre series of songs are among the most exquisite he has written. With Nevin, this last winter has been one of ceaseless activity, of such splendid achievement along so many lines, that it would seem he has grown completely into his greatest self, and that, so young a monarch, he is coming into his kingdom, of which, since he was twelve years old he has been heir apparent. To the thousands of people who follow this man's work and progress with an interest almost personal, it may have occurred to wonder just where and what Vineacre is, and just where is the fortunate spot from whence these melodies come. Down the Ohio River some fifteen miles from Pittsburgh in Edgeworth.[19] There, on the green, wooded hills that rise abruptly from the river, is Vineacre, the old mansion where Ethelbert Nevin was born and where he spent his boyhood, a happy, happy boyhood it was, for there was music in the river and in the trees and music in the boy's heart, and the woods were full of his singing feathered brothers and the world was a good place to live in. It was there that he wrote his "Serenade," and "O, That We Two Were Maying," and "Doris" and it was there that he wrote "Narcissus," that melody as familiar now as the world's oldest classics, that everyone of us seemed to have heard some summer days in the fields and woods when we were children, and then

19. The remainder of this paragraph and the first three sentences of the next were included as the view of "a sympathetic visitor" in Vance Thompson's *Life of Ethelbert Nevin*, pp. 9–10. Sections II and V were also included (pp. 204–207), and from section IV the program notes for "A Day in Venice" (pp. 183–185). The son of a Pittsburgh pastor, Vance Thompson (1863–1925) had degrees from Princeton and the University of Jena. During 1895–1896 he and James Huneker published eleven issues of a daring magazine, *M'lle New York*. It is not known whether Willa Cather and Thompson were acquainted, but she made use of his program notes for "May in Tuscany" (see "Ethelbert Nevin: Return of Narcissus," The Urban Scene, above).

lost it again, until this boy on the banks of the Ohio brought it back to us from Arcady.

But back to Vineacre. It is a big rambling old house that has been frequently added to and rebuilt to conform to the tastes of its occupants. Mr. Nevin has four brothers, all men of decided tastes, and they each have apartments to suit their hobbies. In the center of the house is the library, the big room lined with books from floor to ceiling where Robert Nevin, Ethelbert's father, student and man of letters, still spends his tranquil days in study. It was in that room that the boy told all his childish troubles, and it was there he went, after a brief clerkship with the Pennsylvania Railroad Company, to ask his father to release him from his irksome duties, to let him be poor all his life and be a musician. God has been good to Ethelbert Nevin from the beginning, and he has given him other good things than genius. Next to getting the right wife, the best fortune which befell him was in having the right father. He was too fragile and too highly strung a lad to have brooked much opposition, and an unsympathetic father might have wrecked his boy's career at the beginning. Last Sunday, on the porch at Vineacre, I got the old gentleman to tell me again that story I have heard so often and never tire of hearing, of how he used to find the boy picking out tunes on the piano when he was in kilts, and how when his little sister went to take her music lesson, Ethelbert used to roll up a newspaper for a music roll and trot after her and play he was taking lessons, too. "One day," said Mr. Nevin, "when he was a little chap, I was coming down the hall and heard him *drumming* something I had never heard. I stopped and asked him what it was and he said he was 'making it up.' It was not just like the things other boys 'make up' and I stepped out on the porch here and for the first time thought about the child's taste seriously and decided to put him under a teacher." When Ethelbert was eleven years old his first composition was published, a polka of which some few copies are still extant, and on the cover was printed: "By Bertie Nevin, / Aged Eleven." The rhyme was sung to him at school until he was very sick of it.

He was rather a girlish little boy, always much concerned about his mother's dresses and fond of masquerading in dresses himself, so sensitive and tender of heart and so grieved for anything in pain that his family instinctively kept unpleasant things from him. He was always wanting to play boys' games, but lacked the strength and persistence to succeed. They tell a funny story of how he one day ran in flushed and panting to his mother and proudly announced that the big boys had taken him into their ball nine.

"Is that so, Bertie, and what do you play?"

"Why, mother, I'm umpire, think of that!"

And then he ran away to the piano and had it out with himself and forgot his honors.

II

Queen Ann's Lodge

To Arcady has't never been?
Hark, while I give the mystic key,
The password that shall let thee in
To Arcady!

Memories[20]

Now and then one finds one of Mr. Nevin's earlier songs "dedicated to Miss Ann Paul." Miss Paul is now Mrs. Nevin and that is why Mr. Nevin's music room at Edgeworth is called Queen Ann's Lodge. When Mr. Nevin returned from his long sojourn in Europe last year, he decided to work at home for a time. He was tired of wandering and tired of excitement; he had a brain full and a heart full of material, and he wanted to settle quietly down and use it. Then he fitted up Queen Ann's Lodge. A music room! It is a house of song, rather, a five-room cottage across the fields from Vineacre, and someone has called the vine-covered walk that leads to it "The Road to Arcady." There is a music room, a study, a bedroom with severe little iron bedstead, a bathroom and a kitchen. There are divans and easy chairs and Turkish rugs and an old Venetian lamp and desks and a concert piano and shelves of music and copies of old pictures, portraits of Wagner and Chopin and Mr. Nevin's own portrait done for Mrs. Nevin by Charles Dana Gibson, photographs of singers and artists and *littérateurs*, from all over the world, such lumber as an artist brings with him when he returns from going to and fro in the earth and from walking it up and down. There the songs of the Vineacre series were written, and there so many more are being written. There I heard his "A Day in Venice" while it was still in manuscript, and there are the scores and notes of songs and pianoforte compositions yet to be.

20. J. R. White wrote the words to this song of Nevin's. The epigraph for section III, below, is from *Sordello*, Bk. II, ll. 501–505, *Works of Robert Browning*, I, 223–224. The section IV epigraph, ll. 2–3 of "A Toccata of Galuppi's," will be found in the same source, III, 160; and the Byron quotation in that section occurs in *Childe Harold's Pilgrimage* Canto IV, stanza xviii, ll. 1–4. *Poetical Works of Byron*, p. 229.

III

Il Rosignuolo

He built on man's broad nature—gift of gifts
That power to build! The world contented shifts
With counterfeits enough, a dreary sort
Of warriors, statesmen, ere it can extort
Its poet-soul.

Sordello

It was twilight; some half dozen of us were seated around the music room when Nevin began to sing. He makes no pretention to being a vocalist. . . . He never sings in public now, but it is possible to sing very well indeed without much voice, and he can do it. . . . First came a love song in Italian, not yet published. Then a song to the words of Catulle Mendès, also yet in manuscript. Then he warmed to his work, and sang because he wanted to and they came one after another without preface or prelude; "The Rosary," "O That We Two Were Maying," "When the Land Was White With Moonlight," "Dites-Moi," "'Twas April," "A Fair Good Morn," "The Mill Song," "The Necklace," "There, Little Girl, Don't Cry." He seems to have written nearly all the songs one greatly cares for, this man, and when you stop to think of it, there is seldom a concert anywhere at which one does not hear a song that, at some time or another, has come "from Vineacre."

There was only the candlelight in the room, lamps are never used there. The composer's face was in the shadow but the light fell on that noble head and touched the hair already gray with the labor of giving five hundred compositions to the world in the last ten years. Gray hair above a face so young, so lyric, so mobile is a strange thing to see. It is as though the kiss of the muse had left its visible mark, and tells that if his wooing of her has been happy it has not been altogether painless. His wife sat leaning against the piano, in black and white, looking more than ever like one of the more tender and compassionate of Botticelli's Madonnas. Somehow Mrs. Nevin has always seemed to me a good deal like her husband's music, there is in her something of the same idealism and delicate sympathy and sweetness. Perhaps the music has grown to resemble the woman, perhaps the woman has grown to resemble the music, but in fancy I can never quite separate them.

The music went on and on for two hours, as mortals count time—I don't know by what system they compute it on Parnassus or in Arcady, but a Greek said that sometimes the hours of men are the years of the gods. The stars came out, and the frogs kept up an accompaniment outside, perhaps from some pool into which, years ago, Nevin looked and found Narcissus.

IV

Un Giorno in Venezia

> What, they lived once thus at Venice where the merchants were the kings,
> Where, St. Mark's is, where the Doges used to wed the sea with rings?
>
> *A Toccata of Galuppi's*

Last of all, Nevin played for us his "A Day in Venice" which is rivaling "Narcissus" in popularity. He lived in Venice for a year on the Grand Canal, and today a big black gondola glides in and out of the ancient waterways with a spray of yellow jonquils and the name "Narcissus" painted on the prow. The Venetians have been a music-loving people from time immemorial, and Nevin's old gondolier saw fit to commemorate his sojourn in Venice in that poetic fashion.

I. *Alba*—(Dawn)

The first movement begins with a few drowsy harmonies, as the sun touches the spires of St. Mark's with fire and the gondolier rouses and stretches himself in the sunlight on the steps of some old church where he has been sleeping. The lagoons are silver and a thousand scents are in the air, and the freshness of morning is upon the water. The gondolier laughs —at nothing—at everything, at life and youth, laughs because the sky is blue and the sun is warm, laughs for joy at the gladness and beauty of another day—a day in Venice.

II. *Gondolieri*—(The Gondoliers)

> She to me
> Was as a fairy city of the heart;
> Rising like water columns from the sea,
> Of joy the sojourn and of wealth the mart.
>
> Byron

The swing of the paddle is in the first measures, the rhythmic theme haunts one, carries one out upon dream highways fairer even than the waterways of Venice. It is a short cut to poetry and dreamland. The gondoliers are off for the day, out upon the historic waterways, gliding down the Grand Canal, under the arched stone bridges, through deep, still streets where the stone walls on either side are mossed with age, and the shadows make the water green and the air is cool,—and out again into the broad sunlit lagoons. It is in Venice, where people believe in happiness, even at work, and the gondolier has no other creed. He is not ambitious, he desires nothing but to be always a gondolier, as his fathers were before him. He will live a little, laugh a little, love a little while he is young, pray a little when he is old; what more would you have? Perhaps he has heard how one of his forefathers, long gone, carried guests down those same waterways to the fetes at the palace of the Doges; perhaps that he carried some doomed victim of the Forties out into the Adriatic and brought him back no more. But that and all the dark history of Venice is forgotten in the sunlight and the swing of the paddle and the rhythmic, haunting melody of the gondoliers' song. Life is good on the lagoons.

III. *Canzone Amoroso*—(Venetian Love Song)

The love song is written in the key of A flat, the key in which beautiful things happen. The work of the day is over, and the gondolier has his little sweetheart beside him, and in all the world there are but two people and the moon. It is a safe and happy love song, yet there is an intense fervor in the opening melody, for he has been away from her a whole day—and that is so long sometimes. The second subject, softer, more tender, than the first, rising to a climax in one voluptuous, languishing chord over which, in the score, the composer has written: "*Io T'Amo!*" (I love you). Few greater things are written nowadays than that love song.

IV. *Buona Notte*—(Good Night)

As the gondolier and his sweetheart glide out toward the Adriatic they pass an old church from which the Ave Maria is sounding. Perhaps the lovers sing a snatch of the hymn, perhaps the little girl crosses herself. Night sleeps deep and peaceful over Venice, the lights glimmer behind them, the moon draws a little fleecy veil over her face, like an abbess who demurely draws up her surplice, said de Musset. They are happy, and they hope that all the world is so.

V

L'Envoi

In the afternoon, as we all sat upon the porch at Vineacre, the talk ran hither and thither and some of us were drifting into a discussion of utilitarianism, when Mr. Nevin's father spoke up, as one having authority and said calmly: "We are all creatures of sentiment, we live and die by it, dispute it as we will, and it is the strongest force there is." The remark set me to thinking. I fancy it explains Ethelbert Nevin and his music. In his childhood he was never taught to be afraid of sentiment, and he has never learned to fear it. That is why his musical invention is so singularly free, why the influence of no school has ever touched him, why in all his music he is so entirely and gloriously himself. If MacDowell is king of France, this man is king of Navarre.[21] He has a province of his own in the music of the world—in the art of the world. No other man has ever set foot into his kingdom; it is wholly his own and he is the only man among all men living who can tell of it. His message is for his lips alone, no other could ever speak it. His work is unique among the world's beautiful creations. He carries so much of our pleasure and delight under that hair that is tinged with gray. His harmony and melody are his own, like no one's else. He has no affectations; he is not afraid of simplicity, of directness, as some one has said his melodies "gain a certain distinction from their very unconsciousness of the danger of vulgarity." To everything he writes, however slight, that rare grace and distinction clings, an aroma of poetry, a breath from some world brighter and better than ours, an exhalation of roses and nightingale notes and southern nights. Take, for instance, the little Negro melody he did for the Dartmouth College boys; if any one else had written that it would have been cheap. Is it? Try it and see! Even in his children's songs there is the same grace and tenderness. What he touches he dignifies. Of a simple lyric he can make a noble tragedy. And he has the courage of genius. I was asking his little daughter, Doris, who is just six, about some little French and Italian songs she sings when she startled

21. This comparison refers to a paragraph in "The Passing Show" earlier in the year: "Edward MacDowell [has been in Pittsburgh] in a concert of his own compositions, among them some of his wonderful 'Ocean Studies,' the result of his summer by the sea. He has been here several days, but he and Ethelbert Nevin were together so constantly that one had small opportunity to see anything of either of them. It is an experience to see them together, those two men so absurdly young, so world famous, who stand for about all there is of American music. Two young emperors they are, a Caracalla and a Geta who share an empire without strife. I made some such remark to Nevin the day after MacDowell left, but he threw out his hand with one of those quick, nervous gestures of his and answered: 'No, he is the king of France, while I, I am only the king of Navarre'" (*Courier*, March 18, 1899, p. 5). The Caracalla-Geta allusion was not a happy one; for once Willa Cather's classical learning seems to have let her down. Sons of Septimius Severus, Caracalla and Geta reigned jointly for a year only; then Caracalla murdered his younger brother and had himself proclaimed sole ruler (A.D. 212). For more on MacDowell, see Guest Editor of the *Courier*, below.

me by saying, "But best of all, I like 'Onward Christian Soldiers.'" I told her gravely that I didn't believe her father would consider that much of a song at all. "I don't care," replied the young lady. "I like that best." Not so much unlike her father, after all. For if Ethelbert Nevin liked "Onward, Christian Soldiers," he would say so, and he wouldn't give a snap of his gentlemanly fingers what the rest of the world said.

Courier, July 15, 1899, pp. 4–5.

The personality of Ethelbert Nevin, the man who wrote "Narcissus," is little known, and of the thousands of people who sing "O, That We Two Were Maying!" and "The Rosary," few have even the scantiest information as to their composer. The man is both retiring and uncertain, and it would take a globe-trotter to keep track of his whereabouts. When he is not in Paris, or Venice, or Berlin, or New York, he is usually to be found at "Vineacre," the family mansion, at Edgeworth, Pennsylvania, a little village on the banks of the Ohio.

There Ethelbert Nevin was born in 1862, and there he spent the first fifteen years of his boyhood. A happy boyhood it was, for there was music in the river and in the trees, and music in the boy's heart, and the woods were full of his singing, feathered brothers.

In the center of the old house is the library, a big, dark room lined with books from floor to ceiling, full of shadows and peopled with memories, where Robert P. Nevin, Ethelbert's father, student and man of letters, still spends his tranquil days in study. It was in that room that the boy told all his childish troubles, and it was there he went, after a brief clerkship, to ask his father to release him from his irksome duties, and let him be poor all his life if only he could be a musician. He was only eleven when his first composition, a polka, was published. His serenade, "Goodnight, Goodnight, Beloved," one of his most popular songs, was written when he was thirteen years old. When he was fifteen, he happened upon a volume of Charles Kingsley's verses, and, deeply stirred by their rare lyric quality, he wrote the air to "O, That We Two Were Maying!" in a little exercise book that he carried to school. The accompaniment, which is rather difficult, he did not write until he was twenty-two, but the air stands just as he jotted it down in his old notebook.

Everyone about the village knows Ethelbert Nevin, calling him familiarly by his first name, and no one is in the least in awe of him. Though he is but thirty-eight years of age now his hair is touched with gray at the temples. He is quite as much a boy as in the day when he used to gallop bareback over the hills, or, still in knickerbockers, used to stand on a table and sing "The Flowers of Sleep" at the village concerts. He is a slight, delicately constructed man, all nerves, with a sort of tenseness in every line of his figure, and the mobile, boyish face of the immortally young. His hands are unmistakably those of a musician, small of palm, with long, supple fingers, and a strong, well-developed thumb. They are never still when he is talking, and his gestures are quick and impulsive, like his manner of speech.

Temperamentally Mr. Nevin is much the same blending of the blithe and the *triste* that gives his music its peculiar quality, now exultantly gay, now sunk in melancholy, as whimsical and capricious as April weather. Although he is often ill he works almost incessantly, having a dozen or more compositions on hand at once, correcting the proofs of one the same day that he writes the first sketch of another. He is not in any sense a recluse, and though crowds annoy him and social functions exhaust him he is peculiarly dependent upon the society of his friends, and can work best in the company of his wife and children. He sleeps a very few hours out of the twenty-four, usually working late into the night, wandering restlessly about the house or reading the later French poets, among whose verses he finds his most congenial texts. Indeed, when one considers that in the last ten years he has given nearly six hundred compositions to the world, one wonders that he has found time to sleep at all.

At the beginning of his musical career Mr. Nevin intended to become a concert pianist, devoted his studies chiefly to that end and made several extensive concert tours. It was Karl Klindworth who persuaded him to give his attention solely to composition. Though he practices comparatively little now he is a pianist of rare ability, his execution being sympathetic rather than brilliant, colored by the same highly temperamental and romantic quality which gives his compositions their individual stamp.

Certainly he is the jolliest father in the world, and no one can play with a better heart. Neither of his two children (Paul and Doris) has any musical talent, yet he spends hours teaching them scales and exercises, and telling them stories in French, German and Italian, for they have lived over the world so much that they are in a fair way to become infant polyglots. Next to his piano he loves romping with children better than anything else.

Sunday is a great day at "Vineacre." All the relatives and all their friends troop into the big, rambling old house, and Mr. Nevin plays and sings for them all day long. He has a choir of little girls, selected from among the neighbors' children, who practice with him every Sunday evening before the lamps are lit. After they are hustled off to bed he sits with his old boyhood friends singing the old songs they used to sing together when he was just "Bert," and telling stories of those good old days in the valley.

These musical Sundays are never interrupted at "Vineacre," and in all of his wanderings in Europe Mr. Nevin always kept the day as they kept it at home. Music is a necessary feature of daily life there. Mr. Nevin's father is himself a composer and writer of verses, and the first grand piano that was ever shipped west of the Alleghenies was carted over the mountains for Ethelbert's mother, then Miss Elizabeth Oliphant, of Uniontown, Pennsylvania. When, a little over a year ago, his mother was dying, she would not allow this musical routine, this old habit of song, to be broken. On the night she died, sitting in the room next to hers, he played to her as he had done since he was a boy. . . .

It is almost impossible to write of Mr. Nevin without writing of his wife, so closely are they associated in everything. She is practically his business manager, is thoroughly posted in all her husband's work, and is his most constant if not his most impartial critic. Mrs. Nevin is an excellent linguist, and has lived so much among artists of all kinds that she is practically one of them in sympathy. She was originally a Pittsburgh girl, though now she is thoroughly cosmopolitan. Mr. Nevin was engaged to her before he went to Berlin to complete his studies under Karl Klindworth. At the end of two very lonesome years for both of them Mrs. Nevin, then Miss Paul, went to Germany with her father and sister, and Klindworth, in despair, gave his distracted pupil a vacation. There, under the vigilant chaperonage of a relentless German *hofdame*, the young couple pursued their courtship and were married upon Mr. Nevin's return to America. . . .

Of the composition of "Narcissus" Mr. Nevin gives the following account: "I had suggested to my publishers a suite of water scenes in five numbers, and had completed four of them: the 'Barcarolle'; 'Ophelia,' suggested by Shakespeare's heroine; the 'Water Nymph,' which is pure phantasy, and the 'Dragon Fly,' which was a reminiscence of the big fellows that used to dart their blue wings in my face and frighten me when I went swimming. The fifth number was still to be written, and I had neither a title nor theme for it. We were living in Boston then, in a little house facing on Pinckney Street. It was one bitter, bleak February afternoon in the winter of 1890; my wife had gone down to Florida with her father, and I was quite alone, and as gray and melancholy as the weather. I set to work to drive away the blues and finish the 'Water Scenes.' I remembered vaguely that there was once a Grecian lad who had something to do with the water, and who was called Narcissus. I rummaged about for my old mythology, and read the story over again. The theme, or rather both themes, came as I read. I went directly to my desk and wrote out the whole composition. After dinner I rewrote and revised it a little. The next morning I sent it to my publisher. Until the proofs came back to me I had never tried it on the piano. I left almost immediately for Europe, and my publisher wrote me there of the astonishing sale of the piece."

Although Mr. Nevin considers "Narcissus" one of the most trivial of his compositions it has certainly done much to establish his wide popularity, and its sale has gone beyond one hundred and twenty-five thousand copies. It is played in Cairo as well as in Paris and New York, and a returned Klondiker told me that he heard it played on a mouth-harp in Dawson City by a miner with his frozen feet in bandages.

If Mr. Nevin has any favorite among his compositions I would say it is his first "Love Song," written long ago and published in his "Sketch Book," though he recognizes "May in Tuscany" as his most ambitious work. I think Mrs. Nevin might almost be said to prefer all of them, but if one holds a warmer place in her heart than the rest it is "A Day in Venice."

Ladies' Home Journal, November 1900, p. 11.

Lie down, lie down, young yeoman,
The sun moves always west;
The road one treads to labor
Will bring one home to rest,
And that will be the best.
A. E. Housman[22]

On the seventeenth day of February, Ethelbert Nevin, the foremost of American songwriters entered into the sleep that has made him one of the immortally young, in the thirty-eighth year of his life and in the full vigor of his splendid talent. It was to meet such inexplicable decrees of destiny as this that the Greek proverb was framed: "Whom the gods love die in youth." Many of the composer's friends had, I think, a premonition

22. The last stanza of poem VII, *A Shropshire Lad*, p. 17.

that he would not escape the heavy penalty exacted from men whose extravagant precocity in youth seems to bankrupt maturity. Indeed it was almost impossible to conceive of his outliving youth, or that there should ever come a winter in his Arcady. His art was so completely and exclusively the expression of youth, so wholly youthful alike in its limitations and its scope. His personality had preserved all the waywardness, freshness, enthusiasm and painful susceptibility of youth, and he had never become accustomed to the routine processes of living, but found life always as new, as perplexing, as untried, as violent and as full of penetrating and wounding experiences as he had found it at eighteen. He had never developed the fortifying calm which usually comes to a man of genius in his thirties, the interior life which goes on undisturbed by external mischances. Within he had no vacuum in which the soul is held free from atmospheric disturbances and the contraction and expansion of a changing temperature. He had been unable to place any sort of non-conducting medium between the world and himself, no sort of protection to break the jar of things. His creative power was often retarded and congested by his very receptiveness, by the multiplicity and acuteness of mental sensations which not only moved but convulsed him. Every day that he lived he got up to meet life as barehanded and raw to the weather, disturbed by the roughness of the machinery of life, oppressed by the slightest neglect from anyone near him, sensitive to the criticism of strangers, enervated by the gloom of an overcast sky, like a weathervane at the mercy of the uncomprehending and unheeding universe.

The Nevins have been in New Haven since November. Several years had passed since their return from Italy, and most of that time Mr. Nevin had spent at his father's home in Sewickley, fifteen miles down the river from Pittsburgh. Last summer he grew exceedingly restless. Frequent change in his environment was almost necessary to him, and all his life he was torn by the conflict between his love for the old and intimate surroundings of his childhood and the feverish restlessness that periodically took possession of him. After settling down for the winter in New Haven, he passed three of the busiest and quietest months of his working life. He went out almost not at all and wrote constantly. Mrs. Nevin will soon send a sheaf of unpublished work to his publishers. . . .

During the first week of February he went to New York on business, expecting to return immediately but from New York he telegraphed his wife that he was going on to Sewickley. He seldom did what he planned or planned the things he actually did, and he particularly insisted upon keeping his own comings and goings and the motives for them to himself. So no one was particularly surprised when he suddenly appeared in Pittsburgh. He seemed thoroughly well and was as gay as only he could be. On the morning of his arrival he explained that he had come rather under his own protest and could remain only two days, but that in New York he had had a persistent feeling that unless he saw his father now he never would again. Old Mr. Nevin had been in bad health all winter and Ethelbert's sister was somewhat alarmed at his premonition on her father's account. He returned to New Haven and died little more than a week later. His death occurred on Sunday afternoon and on Saturday he was at his piano most of the day. Sunday morning he told Mrs. Nevin that he was ill and did not go down to breakfast. At one o'clock his wife went to his room and found him unconscious. The doctor who was called stated as soon as he had seen his patient that a blood vessel had burst in his brain and that life was only a matter of a few hours. The composer recovered consciousness an hour before the end and was immediately aware of his condition. He called his wife to him and gave her some instructions about his work and talked to her of the children and the year that had gone so quickly and prepared to die with greater calmness than he had ever prepared for anything in life. Like so many men who have found the matter of living inordinately hard and perplexing he seemed to find death exceedingly simple and natural and sweet, the potion that put out a fever, the decent cloak that covered the scar of a wound. So ill did he fit the world, so little was he of it, or bound to it, or hardened by it, that there seemed almost no ties to break. He was very much nearer to the sun and wind than most of us, and to the everlasting wash of air, so that the natural laws of change spoke plainly to him and dissolution was immediate resolution. With a willingness that was more than resignation, a gentleness naive and boyish, a truthfulness childlike and sweet, and with scarce more gravity than he had bestowed upon the other serious considerations of life, he set his face toward sleep and he seemed to meet the earth with an embrace, rejoicing in her fairness to the last. So the Grecian singers knew no fear of annihilation, no death-tragedy of which the Hebrew psalmist wrote, but were changed into flowers, or became singing fountains, or sighing trees, still in nature's kingdom and still in [the] care of the warm red hands that had first fashioned them.

There were those of his friends who wished for him a resting place on some sunny slope of the Italian hills that he loved so well, or in the Protestant graveyard at Rome, but he lies now on one of the hillsides where he played when he was a boy and gathered the May flowers through many a spring, perhaps the very hill he thought of when he wrote the music for the last verse of "O, That We Two Were Maying."

Funeral services were held both in New Haven and at the family church in Sewickley. The body arrived on Wednesday morning and was taken immediately to the house where a service was held for the family. In the afternoon the casket was borne into the crowded church, where the people of Pittsburgh gave the musician his last welcome home. Only last April hundreds of the same people gathered at the Schenley to show their appreciation of his year's work and to hear a recital of his new compositions. On that occasion Mrs. Katherine Fisk,[23] well known in Lincoln, sang a number of his new songs, among them "La Lune Blanche," which bears my initials in the dedication, then sung for the first time in Pittsburgh. Some of the same songs were sung at the church that bleak Wednesday when the snow was driving outside and "the land was white with winter."

The air inside the church was heavy with the odor of the flowers. The altar rail was transformed into a screen of narcissus blooms. The casket was opened full length, and the body of the man so well beloved was covered with his own flowers, so that his head and shoulders rose out of a bank of bloom. He looked much as he had always looked, except that the youthful face under the gray hair seemed more a boy's and a poet's than ever before, and was full of the peace that was never to be broken and the youth that was now to be immortal. There seemed even something of his old gayety about him still, for there were narcissus in his buttonhole. His wife, whose complete understanding of him was one of the most wonderful things I have ever known, who knew so well all that was most fitting for him, had put them there in New Haven, before he began his long, lonely journey through the night. So [t]hen in the dignity of death our troubadour came back to us debonair and triumphantly young. The services were appropriately simple, consisting chiefly of his own music. The soloist sang "O, That We Two Were Maying," the song first written in his early youth, completed soon after his marriage and dedicated to his

23. In the *Journal*, July 7, 1895, p. 9, Cather noted that the Chicago contralto Mrs. Katherine Fisk—"She is great enough as a woman to become a great artist"—was singing in concerts with Melba in England. Cather first wrote of Mrs. Fisk in a newly discovered group of nine signed articles for the Lincoln *Evening News*. See Bernice Slote, "Willa Cather Reports Chautauqua, 1894," *Prairie Schooner*, 43 (Spring 1969), 117–128, esp. 125–128.

wife. Then "The Rosary," the song so full of poignant meaning to those who now indeed must learn "to kiss the cross," and last the song written in his boyhood, "Goodnight, Goodnight, Beloved," which seemed to voice the long goodnight that all had come to say to him. There are those who believe that death will befriend him better than did life; that this rare and precious personality will not be lost, but will live in his works, and that his shall be one of those "tapers that burn throughout the night of time wherein suns are extinguished."

The chief characteristics of his music are spontaneous melodies, an unerring lyric discrimination, a suggestive lightness of touch, remarkable simplicity combined with the most nervous and highly articulated chromatic treatment, unqualified and undisguised sentiment and an utter lack of pedantic affectation. His style was that of a composer neither prophetic nor profound, but a poet and singer of changing seasons and of the fleeting surfaces of things. He was the poet of fancies sad and slight and tender, of the grief of little children and the unrestrained sentiment of youth. He frequently chose themes that in the hands of any other man might have been trivial, but which were saved from cheapness by the refined and exquisite treatment which he gave to everything he touched. Above all, one recognizes in his melodies, whether for voice or instrument, the spontaneity of a man who sang for the joy of singing, who was frankly subjective and wholly temperamental, and who made every bar he wrote the signature of his musical personality. His work is as fragile as it is exquisite, and the charge of lightness which has been made against it was not altogether unjust, but time has sometimes been very tender with those exquisite and fragile things. The songs of the minstrels of Provence have outlasted empires and the sweetness of *Aucassin and Nicolete* has survived many a stillborn epic, and today we think it truer poetry than the lofty flights of Pope or Dryden. The most unpretentious art is sometimes the most perfect and revelation comes to men not only by the comet's rush [but] by the rose's birth. It took as true a genius to fashion the Tanagra figurines as to chisel the Elgin marbles.

By ties of birth and blood this sprite-like apparition, with "a deal of Ariel, just a streak of Puck," who insisted that life should be a sort of perpetual May dance, was bound to this city of mechanical industries and hard-handed practicality. He was as incongruous here as though he had strayed out of a Greek pastoral with a flower-wreathed crook, so that he seemed to the eyes of the vulgar to be always in masquerade. Out of the soot-drift of the factories and amid the roar of the mills where the battleships are forged, he sang his songs of youth and Arcady and summertime. The songs, I think, will live when the battleships have rusted in far-off seas and when the roar of the mills is silent.

Journal, March 24, 1901, p. 13.

An Open Letter to Nordica

This was one of the pieces that Willa Cather hoped to collect and publish under the title "The Player Letters" (see "An Open Letter to Nat Goodwin," The Star System [III], above). Although the tone is different, much of the material appeared in an earlier discussion of Nordica (see The Musical World [II], above).

My Valiant Countrywoman:

I will acknowledge at the outset that your career has always interested me more than your art. Had you limited your ambition to a church choir, appearing occasionally in a limited oratorio repertoire, as many other women quite as talented as yourself have done, there would be little in you to marvel at. Had you, on the other hand, chosen an easy and remunerative career abroad, like your compatriot, Mlle. Sanderson,[24] you would have insured a wiser form of notoriety, would have appealed more strongly to the vulgar imagination, and would have encountered, I think, but few reproaches. It is your taste for difficulties that has always interested me. I think some strain of the zeal of the camp-meeting exhorter, John Allen, your grandfather, must prompt in you that Puritanic tendency to consciously master whatsoever is difficult in the world. The most remarkable thing about you is that you should have chosen the career you have. Having once seriously set out to be a singer, I fancy it was but natural that the granddaughter of John Allen should be a good one, and that whatsoever her hand found to do, she should do with her might.

You were born at Farmington, Maine; a name culpably easy of pronunciation for the birthplace of a singer. In early life you had the still greater misfortune to remove to Iowa; Patagonia would have been more

24. Sybil Sanderson (1865–1903), operatic soprano. Her Manon was scheduled for the week in March 1895 that Cather attended opera in Chicago, but Sanderson cancelled the performance. Cather later wrote: "Last winter Sybil Sanderson, the fair Californian whose voice and acting and general ensemble drove Paris wild, . . . came back to astonish her native land. She did astonish us—by her complete and unqualified failure. She did not sing more than half a dozen times in America, and then she was always in bad voice. . . . The rest of the time she was busy making excuses to her managers as to why she could not sing" (*Journal*, July 7, 1895, p. 9).

auspicious. Your youth was passed among people bitterly prejudiced to the theatre and indifferent to music of the better sort. It was a handicap that you ran with fortune from the outset. During the earlier part of your career you were persistently dogged by misfortunes, your connection with Mr. Gilmore's European fiasco being not the least among them. But you were abundantly endowed with that peculiarly practical and aggressive form of courage in America termed "grit." I believe there is no synonym for the word in any other language, and certainly the women of no other nation possess that quality so largely. It is not always an attractive quality in woman, but it is invaluable to ambition.

When you made your debut in opera, you had studied indefatigably and your musical education was unusually broad and comprehensive. Your memory has always been excellent, and you were able to sing a large repertoire at an hour's notice. But your inborn inaptitude for dramatic expression, your Puritanic aversion for emotional display, clung to you, fettering you like heavy armor. It was not until you sang at Bayreuth, when you were carried beyond yourself by the new possibilities opening before you, by the whole associations of the place, the flattering companionship of great artists, intoxicated by your own success, stimulated by the music itself as by a draught of Rhine wine, that you began to learn that hardest of lessons for American women; to let yourself go, in the argot of the greenroom, abandon, and that, my valiant countrywoman, is the only lesson you have never learned thoroughly; the easy thing, which is not a matter of labor, or sleepless nights, or incessant practice, but of a look, a touch, a sigh. But here that difficulty-defying brain was put at a loss; that iron will, trained so long to stubborn opposition in an unequal contest, refused to soften. Far from relaxing, you girded yourself up for a new assault, only to find that one thing, at least, is not to be got by conscientious endeavors, though it be the property of many a vagabond who sleeps in the sun.

I remember hearing you sing *Cavalleria Rusticana* in the West, shortly after it was first produced in this country. Not only was it impossible to conceive you as Santuzza, but as having any sympathy for or understanding of her. The music you sang remarkably well, but your indifference to the character was obvious, and to consider you seriously in the part seemed like offering an insult to a well-bred American woman. Passional crimes are not rife among the pine forests of Maine, nor are they encouraged even in Iowa. You have lived in many countries and have studied the language and manners of many peoples; intellectually you are free from prejudice. But sentiment is a thing inborn; it forms before the parietal bones have closed, is made up of the first lights and shadows and echoes of the great world that comes to us across the great threshold upon which we play, and education cannot change it. To your credit, you have remained an American woman, and it were easier to melt the stony hills of Maine than the proud marble of your body, easier to teach the pines a sensuous melody than the splendid Amazon warrior, full armed and girded for the fray.

Even since you returned to us with the hallmark of Bayreuth, we, your own people, have done you scant justice. Were you a *Deutsche frau* of mountainous physique, or a rawboned Russian giantess, or a frowsy-haired Hungarian Jewess, no doubt you would be very much the fashion. But since you are a gifted gentlewoman of our own blood, with the fresh color and frank eyes that bespeak such fine things of your country, we are prone to neglect you and take your merits for granted. We find the gypsies who consume black liqueurs and spoil their complexions with tobacco more interesting.

The manner in which you have held your own in the Metropolitan Opera Company should be a source of pride to your countrymen. With the exception of Mme. Eames you are the only American woman who has made herself indispensable to that heterogeneous organization. In that motley assemblage of bohemians, ex-cab drivers, ex-innkeepers, swarthy beings drummed up from every corner of Europe, speaking every gibberish and dialect, you have maintained your dignity and ours in a way that makes one long to cry, "A health to the native born!" Great artists, all of them, these foreign folk, of the aristocracy of genius, whatever their pedigree, of a blood more royal than that of princes, but people of strange manners and foreign sympathies and, withal, exceedingly bigoted. The overwhelming importance of these personages has never abashed you. What you know, you know, though you came from Maine, and you have made even the Poles—"Alas," said Cherbuliez,[25] "this sad world, full of accidents and Poles!"—feel the righteous indignation of the Puritan. As artists, you have given these personages their due, but in your personal and professional relations with them you have exacted courtesy, respect and fair dealing, and have carried your colors right gallantly, unawed by titles and splendors and the favors of kings. In much the same spirit did our great Franklin, in his coonskin cap, walk unperturbed through the halls of the Tuileries, conversing confidently with savants and princes, the

25. Victor Cherbuliez (1829–1899), novelist, critic, and composer.

equal of any of them; watching with keen interest the follies of the bewigged and bejeweled gentlemen about him, preserving himself, the simple, homely manners and severe, strenuous life of a newer world, washed clean by the blue sea water.

Whatever of international reputation you have acquired, you have won without servility, by courageous endeavor and unceasing effort. You have made the masterful New England character, come down to us no whit weakened from the days of Winthrop and Roger Williams, felt and respected abroad. Of this fine force of character in you, there can be no doubt. It is a softer and more elusive quality that we sometimes miss in you, the thing which, in the makeshift of our linguistic poverty, we vaguely designate as temperament. And I fear, my valiant countrywoman, that the two seldom thrive together. Even in your voice itself, that powerful and splendid organ, I miss a certain life-giving quality; yes, even in those round, full, unclouded tones, tones of silver, shaken from your throat as lightly as the water drops from a sea bird's wing, when it flies upward in the golden dawn. In them, to me, there is always a certain unyielding quality; scarcely metallic, but white and cold rather, like the glitter of the diamonds in your tiara. Ah! if you would sometimes let your heart go out with that all-conquering voice! if you would but sometimes be a woman!

Yours has been an admirable career, fair kinswoman; you have matched the better traits of your own people against the world, and we have no right to complain, since you have shown us all our worthiest virtues in so fair a setting. Yet genius does not always consort with industry and uprightness; some times with idleness and folly rather. It is because you climb so well that you have never tried to fly. You plan, you execute, you dare, but I think you never dream. You have mastered much, but I think nothing has ever mastered you. Music has become an exact science, and you have made that science your own.

Yet, forget it not, music first came to us many a century ago, before we had concerned ourselves with science, when we were but creatures of desire and before we had quite parted with our hairy coats, indeed; and that it comes to us as a religious chant and a love song. I believe that through all its evolutions it should always express those two cardinal needs of humanity, carrying the echo of those yearnings which first broke the silence of the world.

I am not yet convinced that, were the taste of the public more advanced, you would not do well to limit yourself to the concert stage. There is the dominion of pure tone; there less is demanded of phrasing than in opera, and the intrinsic beauties of the voice are judged in the light of their own splendor.

In opera, I prefer you in Wagnerian solos: warrior maidens, clothed in chastity and iron; women of the white robe and the bright sword, helpers of men and councilors of gods. Elsa, Brünnhilde, Elizabeth—Isolde? Ah, no! Never was the sting of the potion on your lips, never have the waves that lash so madly on the Irish coast told you the reason of their fury, nor of how many centuries they have quickened to the mystic wooing of the moon, able to escape it never.

American prima donnas of the future will look back upon your memory with pride and gratitude. You seem to me to embody all that is best in American womanhood. I think if anywhere on the continent, among the thousands of strange faces that pass one, I chanced to see yours, I should joyfully know under what sky to place it. About you there seems always something suggestive of a new hope in the world, not to be encountered in tired Europe; something altogether wholesome and invigorating like the clean smell of the pine woods, mingled with the fresh sea breezes. Something in your face, with its resolute chin, so powerfully modeled, bespeaking such potency for resistance and constancy—"resistance unto death," your grandfather would have said—recalls to me always the granite hills of the New England coast and the silent, enduring strength of its pioneers.

Courier, December 16, 1899, p. 3.

Clara Butt: "a voice without a soul"

The English contralto Clara Butt (1873–1936) gained her reputation on the concert stage. In 1920 she was made a Dame of the British Empire. The epigraph in all likelihood was Willa Cather's own translation.

In that voice what darker magic
  Lurks to wake forgotten pain?
Why do all the wounds recovered
  Break within my breast again?

Keep your tragedies, dark woman,
  Veil from me that languid eye,
When you sing the loves departed
  Wake again, again to die.

After Heine

The real Trilby has come across the seas in the person of Miss Clara Butt, the Trilby whose voice differed from other voices as the flavor of the peach differs from apples, the Trilby with the voice without a soul. Certainly she is unique among contraltos and unique among women. Conceive, if you will, a woman six feet two by actual measurement, slender, willowy, serpentine; long, long arms, narrow shoulders, a trifle stooped, outlines almost epicene, a small head set on a long, curved throat, heavy-lidded, languid eyes, a face common and middle class, and a nose which belongs to the genus of Cheapside and you have Clara Butt. Then give this long, swaying creature a contralto voice as big as a choir of ordinary contralto voices, with a range uncertain but unlimited, tones as deep as a pipe organ or as light as flutes. There is something uncanny about the mere dimensions of her voice, as there is about the long, straight lines of her figure, something that makes you shiver a little and still holds you. She is not an artist, not a bit of it, she is simply a wonder. Not that she is a freak, like Miss Yaw,[26] but rather a phenomenon, with something quite magical and a little bit gruesome shut up in that long, slender throat. Her methods are good, for she has been well taught, but her execution is slovenly, and she sings as she pleases, not as she was taught. She has been told that her voice is a full orchestra, and she believes it. Her lower tones are good by nature; there, if she but knew it, lies her strength. Her upper tones are artificial and her continual abrupt and showy transitions from her full, sonorous lower tones, to her weaker upper register is sometimes unpleasant. Her middle tones are uncertain and she has not perfected them by ceaseless toil. Indeed, Miss Butt is averse to toil. Her natural vocal equipment is so remarkable she found that she could succeed with a minimum of labor. She was too gifted to aspire to perfection. Her early triumphs unfitted her for industry. Having begun her career as a wonder, a wonder she has continued to be, and it is as a wonder, not as an artist, that one must consider her. Her physical proportions forever bar her from attempting anything in opera, and just so her peculiar vocal limitations and unusual vocal powers keep her always a little outside the pale of the rigidly "legitimate" and make her more or less a musical curiosity.

At one of Miss Butt's recitals, however, all these things are forgotten, or rather they do not occur to one. It is only afterward that one figures them out in cold blood. When I heard her, her first song was [John] Hatton's "The Enchantress." This tall creature, dressed in a dark green gown embroidered with silver serpents, accentuating her slenderness,

26. Ellen B. Yaw (1868–1947), American soprano noted for her C above high C.

swayed to the front of the stage with a sweeping bow, like a tall tree bending to the wind, and with her head thrown back, her chin raised, her heavy, lusterless eyes half closed, she sang:

Warriors I have brought to shame,
  Turning glory to disgrace;
Kings have trembled when I came,
  Reading doom upon my face.

But for thee, but for thee,
  My wild hair shall braided be
With the rose of richest breath,
  With the jasmine, white as death.

And my voice in music flow,
  And mine eyes all gently glow,
O believe me, love like ours
  Is the power of magic powers.

"But for thee, but for thee," after the crashing crescendo of the first verse, how the subtile, insinuating tenderness of that refrain steals through one, how heavy and dark and Circe-like are those tones, such as the witch of the Aegean isle might have used when she turned Odysseus' comrades into swine, and that tall creature with the silver serpents and the terrible eyes was the woman to sing it. She is wonderfully like Burne-Jones' women, like those tall, angular, bloodless women with the sensuousness of the soul in their pale, worn cheeks, chained by a fever that is never fed. There is something of their unwholesomeness about this Clara Butt of the trumpet tones, for she is not at all like the rose, but like "the jasmine, white as death."

I cannot say just why this young woman gives one a creepy feeling as she does. She made me think of all the verses of all the Degenerates, and sometimes I thought she was more terrible and pessimistic than Yvette Guilbert herself. She recalls a little the paintings of the Pre-Raphaelites, and somewhat the sorrows and deadly verse of Baudelaire. She sings, indeed, much church music, but her singing of it affected me much as Paul Verlaine's religious poetry, as feverish, overstrained, unnatural. It is the faith of pessimism. Miss Butt's second number was Beethoven's "In Questa Tomba," which she followed by Schubert's "Death and the Maiden." That, of course, came directly within her scope, that haunting, horror-begetting quality of her low tones finds its most proper expression in songs of death and enchantment and languor and dark magic. Next she sang Chaminade's "Silver Ring" and quite spoiled the effect of it by over-dramatic phrasing, dragging the last verse horribly in conformation to a cheap conception of pathos. Then came "He Giveth His Beloved Sleep" and there again Miss Butt seemed in her element. It was an ocean of voice that we listened to, deep, sonorous, self-sufficient, like the moan of the sea or the sighing of the forest in the night wind. The grand climax of the recital was that noble hymn of Riddle's, "Abide With Me," sung with pipe organ obbligato. It filled my ears like the sound of many waters, it crashed through sleep for nights afterward!

> When helpers fail, and captains flee,
> Help of the helpless, abide with me!

It seemed as though it must be heard up aloft there, above all the singing of the celestial choirs. The concert hall could not contain it, it rang out into the night and the starlight. It was the most effective piece of emotional, religious, singing I ever heard. If Miss Butt had joined her gifts for a season with those of Mr. Moody, Sankey would have been forgotten.[27] People would surge in hundreds up to the altar rail. This hectic emotionalism of Miss Butt's would stir up a conscience if the rudiments of conscience were left.

Now there is a mystery about Miss Butt, as there was about Trilby. I happen to know one of Miss Butt's teachers very well and it is from him that I have the disclosure. The girl has absolutely no musical intelligence; no musical memory, no musical taste. The brain cells are not fashioned the right way, the nerve tissue is not of the right fibre, and Miss Butt will never while time endures be an artist. When she was "discovered" ten or twelve years ago she had, as she has still, one of the most remarkable voices in the world, a physiological wonder. It was, he said, the most wonderful voice he had ever taught; it was capable of everything but certainty, precision, that unfailing exactness which distinguishes the artist from the amateur. To teach her was like building ropes of sand. One day those wonderful tones would do what you willed, they obeyed like the keys under your fingers. The next there were little inaccuracies and lapses and she would never seem conscious of them. She was not particularly ambitious and not fond of work. When she did work, it was without fervor.

27. Ira D. Sankey (1840–1908), evangelical singer who appeared with Dwight Moody (1837–1899), revivalist preacher. They were in Pittsburgh in December 1897.

She was good-natured, and took reproof, and smiled her middle-class smile and had some trouble with her h's. She boned away at *Alceste*, Schubert and Schumann, but she preferred "Kathleen Mavourneen" and "Abide With Me," and she freely acknowledged her preference. There simply is not one fibre of the artist in all her six feet two. So, in spite of her success in America and her popularity in England, the voice is practically lost, a sort of runaway engine that may pull up anywhere. It is perhaps the most wonderful contralto voice in the world, but there is no mind to direct it. It is very much as if an organ builder, having completed his masterpiece, should lock it and throw the key into the sea; and only chance winds, blowing into the reeds, make an echo there. Therefore, there is something ghastly about that great, triumphant voice when it sings what it has been taught. One feels as though the voice itself were under an evil spell, as though it had been put to sleep, or frozen, or in some way subjected to dark enchantment. There is something mortuary about it, like "the jasmine, white as death."

Courier, January 6, 1900, pp. 2–3.

Mark Hambourg

Mark Hambourg (1879–1960), Russian-born British piano virtuoso (lately a child prodigy), stopped in Pittsburgh during his first tour of the United States in 1899–1900. His brother Jan Hambourg (1882–1947), a violinist, later married Willa Cather's close friend Isabelle McClung (see The Gazette, *below). Though Cather casts herself as "Auditor" of the conversation she reports between Hambourg and Ethelbert Nevin, the opposition of poetry and inspiration to philosophy and analysis were familiar to readers of "The Passing Show." The title of this column was "The Pianist of Pure Reason."*

I believe Mark Hambourg went no farther west than Milwaukee, so you have not heard him. He has been the musical sensation of the hour in the east, and in Pittsburgh he scored an overwhelming triumph. He came from Europe unknown and little advertised, and he has made revelations to us about the technique of the piano, about the possibilities that lie in ten human fingers. When he first stepped upon the platform of the Carnegie Music Hall here, a general sigh of disappointment went up from the audience. Here was a little fellow, below middle height, pink and white like a girl, slender, with a look of callow and beardless boyishness absurd in a man who was to wrestle with that old war horse of the concert stage, Rubinstein's Concerto in D Minor. When he left the stage, after the deed was done, he seemed a splendid young giant, a youth with gifts miraculous, a boy with the technique of a master.

But the purpose of this article is not to discuss Hambourg's playing, but to tell how a Materialist and an Idealist and an Auditor breakfasted together. It was eleven o'clock when I arrived at the Hotel Schenley that stands in big windy Bellefield Square out by the Carnegie Music Hall. Outside, the weather was doing everything disagreeable that it could, snowing and blowing and spitting fine frozen rain. The mud and slush were ankle deep and the gray fog ate into your bones. The instantaneous transition from this gray and wet and cold into the red Turkish breakfast room, where the palms grew in a soft, even heat like that of a Polynesian summer, was not disagreeable. The clang of the cars was not heard there, all those pale, anxious faces in the street were forgotten, and the long, serpentine parade of black umbrellas. The carpets were soft and red, the linen was white, Nevin and Hambourg were waiting for me, ready to order breakfast. In the breakfast room there was an air of ease and leisure, and a feeling of the deliberateness of art. It was the morning after the concert, but Hambourg looked as fresh as a schoolboy. His twenty-one years and his boyishness were so manifest that it was almost impossible to recognize in this the hero of last night's triumphant assault upon the piano. It seemed out of the question that the arms and hands of this young fellow were capable of such things. Meeting him casually, out in the world, one would glance at his head and figure and say that he was a student, possibly with a speculative bent. His shoulders are very broad for so slight a man, and are the seat of much of his astonishing power. They are slightly stooped, which is the mark of the student, and his head is of the kind that nature models carefully and for a purpose—large and well-developed all over, broad of brow, with a heavy mane of chestnut-brown hair that falls back over his coat collar. His eyes are brown as sloes, shaded by long, light lashes which give them a peculiarly kindly and gentle look. The rest of his face is by no means gentle; he has a big, strong masterful nose, a square jaw, and a hard, young mouth. In spite of the energy and ambition and intellectual alertness stamped upon it, one wonders where a man with a face so boyish and undisciplined by life ever got so mature and well-developed a technique. It seems almost as though he must have cheated time and got more out of twenty-one years than other people.

We sat down at the table, and the grapefruit turned Hambourg's conversation upon India, and the strange sights one sees there and the good things one gets to eat there, and upon Australia, where he has made two concert tours.

"I always travel when I rest," he remarked. "It was India last time, next time it shall be China and Japan. O, I must get clear out of civilization to work, out of Western civilization at least. I think Tennyson said something about fifty years of Europe using a man up more than a cycle of Cathay. One doesn't rush so among those older people. Time seems less fleet, what one can do less important."

One began to see that he had not found a shorter road to fame than others, he has only run faster and slept less. I fancy that energy and ambition and intellect, good brain-stuff, explain Mark Hambourg. He has a greed of labor, a passion for difficulties. His eyes glow when he talks of work, his cheeks flush as though he spoke of his sweetheart. He has been overworked most of his life. I notice it is only people who have worked very little who are always afraid of overtaxing themselves. He was ill a great deal when he was a boy, he kept up his studies in mathematics and philosophy and mastered all the more generally spoken European languages, he has played in all the principal cities of Europe, studied two years under Leschetizky, made two concert tours to Australia—remember the gentleman is twenty-one—and all the while he has been mastering his instrument, getting it in hand, battering away at the technical difficulties of the keyboard, working out that tempestuous technique of his, like young Siegfried hammering at the sword Nothung.

"Did it ever occur to you, Hambourg," said Nevin, "how little people in general really know of work? I mean the people who hurry along outside there and sit in offices eight hours a day and do what they are bid, and think they toil prodigiously. They simply know nothing about work, the real work that one must drive one's self to, where one is one's own master and one's own fate, the work that goes on in the nerve centers and that takes it out of one." He began to break the eggs into a chafing dish for a complicated omelette such as are dear to certain tribes of the North Germans, which it took forever to make, for Mr. Nevin is as dainty about his cooking as he is about his music, and his dishes are as complicated as his accompaniments.

Hambourg thrust his feet under the table and leaned back in his chair, running his fingers through his hair.

"Work?" he ejaculated, "O, that is everything, and that is everlasting, the only enduring thing on the program. One is sick or well, one is sad or happy, one is in love or one isn't in love, one is old or young, but one always works. An instrument is a rebellious spirit, a wicked genii that one must be forever subduing or be vanquished. It means eternal warfare.

I have seen the time when it was a pleasure to be very ill, so ill that I could not stand or sit and must rest."

"Let me see," said Nevin, "you have been a concert soloist for nine years, and you are twenty-one. You can do things in the D Minor concerto that Rubinstein himself didn't attempt when I studied it under him. Now I want to know where you have found months enough in the year and days enough in the months to have annihilated the technical difficulties of the piano in this fashion?"

Hambourg laughed and shrugged his broad shoulders, "Ah, that's my secret. That is the gist of life, the heart of success, what one can get into the twenty-four hours of a day—everything hinges on that. When I was a student I worked fourteen hours out of every day and never more than six of them went to music. The rest were put on mathematics, philosophy and history. I'm very fond of mathematics, but fonder still of philosophy. You'll laugh at me, Nevin, but I'm going to try for my degree in philosophy next year; I think I can make it."

Nevin sat down and pushed back the chafing dish. "A degree in philosophy?" he gasped. "What for? It would be about as useful to you as an engineer's certificate would be to me."

"Well, I want to have it," replied Hambourg.

"Nonsense, boy; that's sheer vanity of the silliest kind, sillier than a girl who likes a string of sweethearts to show that she can have them. And how much poetry do you read, young man?"

"None; I don't like it, and I do like philosophy; Schopenhauer, Swedenborg, Kant, all of them." The youth rattled the glasses in his enthusiasm. Nevin looked grave, for he loves not the names of the great philosophers and agnostics and the men who kill faith. He confined his attention to the chafing dish and brought out a big narcissus-colored omelette.

I was moderately sure of Hambourg's attitude toward poetry before Mr. Nevin questioned him, but I was not sure that his answer would be so frank. He is not a temperamental player, this young Russian, and he does not pose as one. He believes in the omnipotence of the human intellect. "I like the exact physical sciences," he remarked, "where one can prove everything. I have read much philosophy, to the detriment of my religion, and I am unable to accept things on faith."

"'Hang up philosophy! Unless philosophy can make a Juliet transport a town, reverse a prince's doom,'" quoted Mr. Nevin vaguely.[28]

28. From *Romeo and Juliet*, III, iii, 55–57.

A pianist of the twentieth century, this Mr. Hambourg, a pianist of the atomic theory and the Darwinian laws. Whenever there is adverse criticism upon Mr. Hambourg's work, it is to this effect; that he lacks the romantic element, that for poetry and color he has substituted speed, a whirlwind of intellectual and digital gymnastics, that he takes the piano by storm and wins at the cost of everything but success, that he merely astonishes and does not truly and deeply delight. These remarks are all very well from people with a modest little technique, and with only one pair of hands—for I am convinced that this young fellow has an extra pair concealed about him somewhere.

All these criticisms, and even harsher ones, were once made on Rosenthal,[29] and yet no one who has heard him play the "Linden Baum" can accuse him of coldness or colorlessness. Like Mr. Hambourg, I have great faith in the human intellect, when it is united with such industry and ambition as his. Life usually softens people, as it has done Rosenthal, and is absurd to expect mature feeling in a boy of twenty-one who has been busy making for himself hands of iron strength and lightning speed. Granted that he is not a man of "temperament"—and he certainly does not pose as one—if I am not mistaken he has been intellectually apprehensive of things, and the mere experiences attendant upon living in the world will put into his playing what Mr. Philip Hale[30] finds lacking. Certainly in his mastery of technical difficulties this young man stands absolutely alone, and it was anciently remarked "to him that hath shall be given."

The conversation ran from one thing to another, for Mr. Hambourg is interested in many things, and his mind never sleeps. He is, as I have said, an unassuming young man with an immense faculty for application and a taste for difficulties. It will be interesting to see what life does for Mark Hambourg. I wonder whether he will remain the Pianist of Pure Reason, or whether some day those hard, white fingers of his will grow warm upon the keys they have mastered so perfectly, and the consciousness of poetry will come to him.

Some fancy like this must have been in Nevin's mind, for when the cigarettes were brought on he leaned back in his chair and looked at the boy fondly and sadly, with the glance that men who have worked and loved and suffered and sounded the whole range of life cast upon younger men who have it all before them.

29. See "Three Pianists," above.

30. Philip Hale (1854–1934), music critic for the Boston *Journal*. Cather alluded to him in her essay "148 Charles Street," *Not Under Forty*, p. 61.

"My boy," he said, "you have done so much, so much that is difficult. I know what work is, and I know how to value it. You have left most of the easy things of life until the last. I hope you will miss none of them. You are wonderful, sir, but I think you place too much value upon mere facility. I remember once in Paris Mme. Marchesi sent me a note asking me to come and hear her most gifted pupil, who has one of the most wonderful voices in the world, but little art and no message, nothing to tell with all those splendid tones. She sang and sang. When she was through Marchesi asked her daughter, Blanche, to sing. That unattractive little woman with next to no voice at all, but with her splendid art, her lyric soul, began to sing, and I felt as a traveler in arid deserts when he comes again to springs of living water and the green hills of home. Then I knew that it is art, not gift, which is divine, and that the only beauty which ever has been or ever can be is the beauty of the soul."

Hambourg sat staring at his plate, his attitude a little like Mephisto's when he heard the mass chanted in the church. As Stevenson wrote to Rudyard Kipling: "Surely all the fairy godmothers were present at this young man's christening; what will he do with their gifts?"[31]

Courier, January 27, 1900, p. 3.

Three Operas

After an uneven season because of the absence of Melba and Jean de Reszke, the Metropolitan brought five operas to Pittsburgh—Tannhäuser *and* Carmen *in addition to those commented upon here.*[32] *Willa Cather compared the performance of Marcella Sembrich (1858–1935) in* The Barber of Seville *with that of Melba, whom she had heard sing Rosina two years before; Emma Calvé she had previously heard in concert (see The Musical World [II], above, for both selections). Cather had frequently commented on* Cavalleria Rusticana *before, but the discussion of Mozart's* Don Giovanni *was new.*

The Pittsburgh opera season opened brilliantly this year. A splendid and enthusiastic audience contributed much to the general spectacular effect, and Mme. Sembrich, Mlle. Calvé, Campanari, and Edouard de

31. Stevenson wrote to Henry James, December 29, 1890: "Certainly Kipling has the gifts; the fairy godmothers were all tipsy at his christening: What will he do with them?" Sidney Colvin, ed., *Letters of Robert Louis Stevenson* (2 vols.; New York: Charles Scribner's Sons, 1899), II, 256.

32. The company gave *The Barber of Seville* and *Cavalleria Rusticana* on April 16; *Tannhäuser* on April 17; *Carmen* at a matinee on April 18; and *Don Giovanni* that evening.

Reszke were greeted with ovations. The first performance was *The Barber of Seville* and *Cavalleria Rusticana*, and was notable not only for such singers as Calvé and Sembrich in their strongest roles, but in the opportunity of comparison between two of the leading Italian operas of divergent schools.

The Barber of Seville has held its own longer than any of Rossini's operas and, indeed, has outlived all the compositions of its day and style. Its vivacity and gaiety, its naive artifice of melody, and its three excellent comedy roles have prolonged its popularity among singers and with the public. Spirited and gay *The Barber* certainly is, ornate and decorative after the manner of the Italian school of half a century ago, but showy as it is, it is never truly brilliant, and its floridity is without richness. Entertaining as the opera is to the general public, and interesting as it is to students of musical history, it is a composition that can never be taken very seriously. Had operatic composition never advanced beyond the frank artifice and blithe triviality of Rossini, operagoing would scarcely have become a serious avocation.

Comparisons are usually unfair but anyone who has heard both Mme. Melba and Mme. Sembrich as Rosina must reflect somewhat upon the many things which distinguish an artist from a singer. After the finesse and bewitching comedy of Mme. Sembrich, the endeavors of Mme. Melba seem not a little clumsy, and her comedy savors of the kittenish maidservant. Only an artist so resourceful in pantomime as Marcella Sembrich and so gifted in delicacy of comic suggestion can make the vapid Rosina at all attractive to operagoers of this generation.

When Wagner called his goddess women down out of Walhalla, they relegated the fragile heroines of the old Italian operas to oblivion of antiquated dolls on the shelves of a toy shop, and only a true artist can endow them with any vitality whatsoever. Mme. Sembrich is perhaps the prima donna with a natural aptitude for comedy, and certainly she is one of the most intellectual of singers, and her wide culture and thorough musicianship is manifest in every part she sings. She sings with superb beauty of style and perhaps her exquisite vocalization is responsible for her freshness of voice at the end of a long and trying season. In speaking of her voice in itself, of its richness and mellowness and that haunting beauty of pure tone, I believe it was Charles Henry Meltzer[33] who said, "It is a Slavonic voice, with all the sentiment of the Slav in it." . . .

33. Charles Henry Meltzer (1853–1936), dramatic and music critic for the New York *Herald*, and at this time assistant and secretary to Maurice Grau.

Certainly Sig. Campanari shared the honors very evenly with Mme. Sembrich. Only his inimitable vivacity and grace kept the opera from dragging at times. The *esprit* and picturesqueness of that admirable baritone gave all his works a potent dramatic force, but his Figaro is absolutely unique. It is seldom that one sees such absolute identification with a part, and as an actor he greatly surpassed most actors who do not sing. I remember in the Melba production he absolutely carried the whole opera through on his sturdy shoulders. Edouard de Reszke was greeted with wild applause, and as Basilio gave an admirable comic impersonation, his generous proportions adding much comedy to the timid priest.

After a short but torrid intermission, the curtain rose again on *Cavalleria Rusticana*. From old to new Italy, what a leap! From the rondos and cadenzas and quaint elaboration and foolish ornamentations of Rossini, to the intensity and passionate abruptness of Mascagni. Here is music that means something more than pleasing sound, here is music that becomes a notable emotional language, the speech of the soul. Surely Emma Calvé is the singer of singers to speak this lofty language, the greatest singing actress of her time, whose inimitable art so far subordinates its medium that the mere beauty of her voice is well-nigh forgotten. Yet what a splendid organ it is, what richness and color and throbbing vitality in her every tone! But after all, it is Calvé the actress, it is Santuzza that transfixes one. Someone has said that Calvé is the greatest of Wagnerian singers though she has never sung a Wagnerian role. She is the exponent of Wagner's message indeed, and no singer has been so permeated by the modern doctrine of music for art's sake. Having studied peasant life in Italy among the very people out of whose lives this opera grew, and having studied, too, under Duse until she assimilated much of her method, it was as Santuzza that Calvé first took her place among the world's greatest singers.

When you have seen her, you have seen but a flatfooted peasant woman in a shawl, with a great passion and a great despair. Mlle. Calvé handles the score freely, subordinating it completely to the tempestuous emotion it conveys. Her impersonation is as great for what she omits to do as for what she does. She has followed Duse in the study of "what ought not to be done," and she omits as superfluous more than most singers ever master. That Easter morning in a peasant woman's life she has made tense with all the oldest and most perpetual tragedies of living, and seeing how much is concentrated into that half hour, one recalls again the frequent words of Henry James, "How much of life it takes to make a little art!"[34] . . .

From the enthusiasm of the audience and the frequent recalls I am led to believe that Mozart's *Don Giovanni* was more pleasing to the people than any other opera given here. Now this is a trifle perplexing as Mozart is supposed to be the musician's composer, just as Keats is the poet's poet. It would be interesting to know whether it was the limpid melody or the touch of *opera buffa* that delighted the general public. Wagnerian enthusiasts of course find that uninterrupted flow of pure melody monotonous and almost exasperating. Having become acclimated to the wild gorges of *The Valkyrie* and the storm-swept sea of *The Flying Dutchman*, they soon weary of this Mozart who is forever leading them among the same green fields and by identical still waters. Not that there is anything similar in the melodies themselves, certainly, but the pitch, the intensity, is always the same, and all these entrancing arias, duos, trios, quartets, quintets, sextets, in which everybody sings different words to the same air, totally destroying the possibility of any dramatic significance, what of it all, *Pourquoi?* say the Wagnerists. What are all these airs about, where is the dramatic coherency, who cares about the woes of weeping ladies who trail about the country roads in party dresses and about the soprano who sings trills over her murdered father's body? Why is all this melody wasted upon a plot insincere, grotesque and trivial, why is it not given direction and purpose and made to tell something of human experience and human passion? This is all because that malicious man Wagner has stung the palate so that all other styles seem insipid, and it recalls the story of the South Sea islanders who, having tasted the champagne in the hold of a wreck, threw their wholesome native drinks into the sea and proceeded to abuse their gods because the rivers did not run champagne. It is simply a question of whether the incomparable melody of Mozart does or does not compensate you for the naive artifice of his plots. . . .

Courier, May 12, 1900, p. 11.

34. Seibel noted that Cather read James's *French Poets and Novelists* (1893) in Pittsburgh (p. 203), and a variant of this quotation appears in the essay on Musset: "It takes certainly a great deal of life to make a little art!" (p. 30).

The Star System (IV)

(January 14, 1899—April 21, 1900)

So far as I can determine, Willa Cather wrote only a dozen pieces of dramatic criticism during her last eighteen months on the Pittsburg Leader. *Of the eleven selections in this chapter, ten are reprinted from "The Passing Show," and only four among them were based on* Leader *reviews.*

With the exception of Sir Henry Irving and Ellen Terry, the stars that Willa Cather wrote about were those already familiar to readers of her column. It is testimony to her instinct and taste that the men and women who commanded her continued attention were the most important figures on the American stage at the turn of the century. Although her engagement with the theatre was declining, its great personalities still excited her interest, for they were the flesh-and-blood embodiment of talent, genius, art.

Minnie Maddern Fiske in Person and as Becky Sharp

Willa Cather interviewed Mrs. Fiske in Pittsburgh during a week that she was appearing in A Bit of Old Chelsea, *a one-act play by Mrs. Oscar Beringer, and* Love Finds a Way *by Marguerite Merington. Both had been in Mrs. Fiske's repertory in 1896, but were not seen in New York until April 1898. Commenting on the plays in "The Passing Show," Cather celebrated Mrs. Fiske's ability to play comedy as well as tragedy: "You see that penetrating intellect of hers is like a searchlight, she has only to turn it upon a character to master it. She materializes mental and emotional conditions before your eyes, and when all is said, her modernness is the compelling power in her acting. She throws aside all traditions, traditions of elocution and of stage business and the lofty manners of the tragedy queens. She comes down by your side, into the pulsing, complex life of the present. She has that ardent sympathy which is the very root of all realistic art—and, in another form, of all romantic art, for that matter."*[1] *In the second selection Cather discusses Mrs. Fiske in* Becky Sharp *by Langdon Mitchell, adapted from Thackeray's* Vanity Fair. *The play ran for one hundred and sixteen performances after its opening in New York on September 12, 1899.*

An hour with Minnie Maddern Fiske—that is an hour to be singled from among the rest, an hour touched with highlights and standing out boldly in the long calendar of hours so gray and so like each other. It is an hour spent in a powerhouse where great forces are generated, an hour that leaves one humbled and exhausted, rather glad to descend into the street and mingle again with the common, lazy-going world, to chat with the newsboy on the corner and to discuss the weather with the streetcar conductor. For the most of us cannot live at white heat all the time, and a very little of that atmosphere, so surcharged with electric forces, in which genius lives, makes our breath come hard and reminds us that we are of the earth.

I found her very pale and weary looking, but that did not last for long. A little conversation on the one thing on earth or in heaven that matters to her, and the color glowed in her cheeks as in live coals when you blow upon them. She was attired in some sort of a loose pink arrangement that caught and accentuated the colors in that wonderful titian hair of hers. She was seated at her breakfast table, where a place was waiting for me, and she had a volume of Browning in her hand, reading while she waited. I really think I made a feeble Browning joke, but I am not sure. The furniture swayed around the room in a rather suspicious manner and on the whole it was a rather trying moment. Apropos of Browning, she remarked: "He seems to me the most modern and full-grown of poets. So many of the others are boys, carried away by their own emotions and enamoured of boyish fancies. But he has attained his majority, the manhood of poetry. Play Browning? O no, that would be midsummer madness. The Queen in *Two in a Balcony* is my favorite part, but I shall never play it in public. We are not so very unlike, that queen and I."

The whole secret of talking to artists, whether it be a professional interview or otherwise, is to enter completely into their mood, not to ask them to come to yours; for the moment to make their gods your gods, and to make their life the most important thing on earth to you. If you ask

1. *Courier*, December 24, 1898, p. 3. See also "Minnie Maddern Fiske as Tess," The Star System (III), above.

questions you are doomed, moreover, that is impertinent. But if you can stir a little of that enthusiasm by which they live, fan a little that fire which makes them great, then you no longer feel like an intruder, the hour becomes worth many hours of our comatose existence, and the day is made memorable.

I saw that, as she spoke, she glanced again at the volume in her hand and half opened it. I knew that moment was mine. By the grace of heaven I remembered the first few lines of one of the Queen's speeches to Constance:

> O to live with a thousand beating hearts
> Around you, serviceable hands
> Professing they've no care but for your cause,
> And you the marble statue all the time.[2]

There she caught up the lines and finished them. When she concluded, her eyes were as bright as the Queen's, her cheeks as hot, that fragile, drooping little figure which lounged back in the arm chair a moment before, was erect and tense, her fingers trembled as she swept the hair back from her forehead, and I was to have an hour, not with the tired woman, but with the artist. The brilliancy, the richness of the experience I cannot even suggest. I can repeat some of her words, but the personal element is lost. The breakfast was a name, nothing more. She sat beside the table rolling the bread crumbs up into little balls and stacking them up like reserve ammunition, and talked on and on in that hard, dry staccato which can outmatch in its wonderful effects the most sonorous elocution. "Of course no one can act who hasn't lived tremendously; and yet people who act well can't afford to spend much time living.[3] But the little of life we get we take very hard, we have hungry palates and our taste is keen. The mere suggestion of an experience is enough to make us realize it fully. This faculty makes sad havoc of our lives sometimes—but that doesn't matter. In fact, the work is all that does matter. I think that we often live again moments of our own lives on the stage, experiences wholly different

2. The one-act play *In a Balcony* first reached the stage in New York in October 1900, with Mrs. Sarah LeMoyne and Otis Skinner. After the first line, the speech quoted should read: "Around you, swift eyes, serviceable hands, / Professing they've no care but for your cause, / Thought but to help you, love but for yourself,— / And you the marble statue all the time. . . ." *Works of Robert Browning*, IV, 195, ll. 405–409.

3. Cf. Thea Kronborg in *The Song of the Lark:* "'Your work becomes your personal life. You are not much good until it does. It's like being woven into a big web. . . . It takes you up and uses you, and spins you out; and that is your life. Not much else can happen to you'" (p. 546).

from that which we portray, but alike in kind. One has perhaps at sometime accidentally hurt an animal, and then one knows how it would feel to kill a man, the nausea, the physical revulsion which would follow. Yes, I think we feed our art with everything in our lives. Other things come in for a moment and we pursue them and clutch at them, but in the end we come back, always back, and in one way and another our experience colors and enriches our work. You see the work is all, or it is nothing. One gives body and brain and soul, or one is a dilettante. And then there is another thing; it sounds rather absurd, but I believe that to play well one must have suffered. Sometimes I think that it was sorrow which first called any art into being. Such a statement savors of sentimentality when it is made boldly, but I believe that the trouble with the work of half our young players is that life has been too easy for them."

The talk drifted to the new play which Mrs. Fiske is to bring out next year, the dramatization of Thackeray's *Vanity Fair*. The adaptation is by Langdon Mitchell, son of Dr. S. Weir Mitchell, of Philadelphia, the *Hugh Wynne* man.[4] Mrs. Fiske is already studying her part—need I say that it is Becky Sharp?—and will be hard at it all summer. In October she will put the piece on in New York, afterward taking it to Chicago and Boston only. . . .

"The second act," said Mrs. Fiske, "is one of the strongest. The scene in which Becky, who is quite without irresistible personal charms, makes herself irresistible to George by sheer force of will, seduces him by intellect, as it were, is a very great opportunity. Throughout the whole novel, Thackeray never allows you to lose your respect for Becky's intelligence for a moment. In a sneaking sort of way, you even like her, at least I do. This regard is just what I shall try to keep for her. In the old English comedies you are made to sympathize with women who are neither virtuous nor sentimentally naughty, who never deceived themselves or called their vices by petty names. The same thing can be done today. She was a woman possessed of power, and force is force, it tells, it moves, it commands irrespective of morality, just as electricity does."

The hour had passed, and several of them, and I rose to go looking long at that strange little wisp of a woman with the titian hair, the compressed lips, the searching eyes, and the bright spot burning on either cheek, upon whose frail shoulders the hope of our stage so largely rests.

4. For S. Weir Mitchell, see "Old Books and New [January 1898]," The *Home Monthly*, above.

And the old question came back to me, how long can so slight a body endure the friction of a mind so great and so incessantly active. When one thinks of the red blood that is wasted all over the world every day, of the health and strength that are squandered, one protests at the injustice of it. Ah, well, "Other heights in other lives, God willing."[5] When I have been for a little while with minds like that, then I know that somewhere, sometime there is a resurrection and a life, that nothing can destroy or entirely disintegrate a personality so unique, so dominating, so pregnant with power.

What a strange figure she is among our gay mummers and masquers, that pale, fragile little one with the thin nervous lips, and eyes fixed always upon the distance. And life has never been easy for her. No player ever served a harder novitiate. She began life on the stage; she has never known anything else. Her cradle was one of the theatre trunks in her mother's dressing room, and the trunk lid was propped up to keep the light out of her eyes. But that was not for long, she loved that fierce light even as a baby, and could stare at it without blinking. She was not an easy child to take care of, and as she was more contented at the theatre than at the hotel, her mother always took her along. The playground she loved best was that dusty green carpet behind the footlights. The hard pitiless light of the calcium was the sunlight of her childhood, and in it she shot up as pale and slender as a cellar-grown plant, and this world grew to be very real to her; the painted skies and seas and the canvas trees were to her what the real skies and woods are to other children, and she learned to think and dream and live with them. So from the first the unreal was reality to her, and the life of the imagination her only life. All her most acute needs and desires and experiences were those of the imagination.

When she was but seven years old she was already going with her father's company, a poor, bedraggled little company of strolling players, wandering from town to town across the prairies of the blizzard-swept West, performing on tables lashed together in tavern dining rooms, often stranded and without money for days together. The child danced the highland fling, brought up in the rear of the Amazon march, played the Duke of York in *Richard III*, played in *Ten Nights in a Bar Room*, in short went through the whole repertoire of irksome duties attendant on the lower walks of the profession she leads today.

5. Line 115 in "One Word More," *Works of Robert Browning*, IV, 175. For an earlier use of this quotation, see "Walker Whiteside's Hamlet," The Theatre (II), above.

When she was ten she was doing the child prodigy with Barry Sullivan[6] in New Orleans, and a sad time of it the poor fellow had with her. It took the most persistent coaxing to make her learn her lines, as she always insisted that she could improvise something quite as good, and held the text of the playwright in utter contempt. Even in Shakespearean plays she frequently improvised in blank verse to the astonishment of the audience and the utter confounding of her fellow players. One night she was cast for the apparition which bids Macbeth be "lion-mettled," and the appearance of this funny little ghost in a white nightgown sent the audience into a convulsion of laughter.

Then came the long, hard, hopeless year of wandering about the frontier, starving in cheap melodramas, living at cheap hotels, in the companionship of cheap people. She played only soubrette parts and she did not play them remarkably well. She was poor, unknown, unnoticed, unattractive. *Tess of the D'Urbervilles* had not been written then, Ibsen had not been translated into English. What noble faith, what miracle of hope supported her in a struggle which seemed so hopeless? When she was fifteen she was married to Legrand White, an xylophone soloist she met somewhere in the west. It seems that the Fates have a sense of humor after all.

Her New York debut was no more successful than her western starving ventures. She appeared in a soubrette part in a wretched play *Fogg's Ferry*, and played it indifferently. Then she married Harrison Grey Fiske, editor of the *Dramatic Mirror*, and weary, disheartened, disgusted, she left the stage, saying that she was leaving it forever. Then came nearly six years of retirement, recuperation, ceaseless and tireless study. It was during those years that she found herself, found within her own breast the power she had thirsted and starved for. When she came back upon us, it was like the coming of a storm. So great a reputation was never built so quickly. Since then her career, covering less than five years, has been one of constant triumph, her talent the most conspicuous and the most hopeful on the American stage. Who has a better right to say that to be great, one must have suffered?

Courier, January 14, 1899, p. 3.

Minnie Maddern Fiske has been here in her new play, *Becky Sharp*, an adaptation of Thackeray's *Vanity Fair*. The play has been somewhat of a disappointment to the public and to Mrs. Fiske herself. Not that it is not

6. Barry Sullivan (1822–1891), actor and manager.

clever enough, and interesting to boot, but it lacks—well, nobility. I believe it was Mr. Zangwill[7] who said, "There is a force within the heart of things that makes for beauty," and when that force is not strong we feel the lack of it, even in a work of art. Of course, Mrs. Fiske is always artistic, but, ah! she can be so much more than that.

The play *Becky Sharp* is by Mr. Langdon Mitchell, and the young man has shown remarkable skill in selecting the essentials of his play out of the great mass of material before him. He has taken only as much of the novel as concerns the fortunes of Becky, introducing, of course, the fragile Amelia, by way of a contrast. . . .

If for nothing else, this play would be notable in that it is the occasion of one of those fitful revivals of energy which have occasionally graced Maurice Barrymore's indolent career.[8] His Rawdon Crawley is another illustration of how true an artist can be when he takes the trouble to try. It is only fair to say that his Rawdon is nearer to Thackeray than is Mrs. Fiske's Becky. He plays the character, not a caricature of it. He is the only noble figure in that sad assemblage of sordid and selfish people, stupid, slow, powerful in any last resort, the kind of fellow who lives badly and dies well, as hard as iron in an extremity, otherwise as soft as a woman. His good-bye to Becky before he leaves for the field of Waterloo, was, I think, the finest bit of acting in the play. This duffer of a Rawdon, who never pretended to pay his debts and couldn't keep out of the bailiff's hands, came out strongly just where other men were weak, and he was staunch where other men were disloyal. He goes out with tears in his eyes and Becky stands at the window and watches the troops go by, laughing good-naturedly to herself as she says, "There they go to die for their country—and I am dying for my breakfast!" . . .

. . . Rawdon had a code of ethics, somewhat original and rather inconsistent, but what he believed he stuck to, and he wanted to do the square as nearly as one may do it on nothing a year. As for Becky, the one admirable quality about her, now and always, is her grit. Mrs. Fiske believes that Becky's pluck, coupled with her cleverness, was enough to make her more dear to Thackeray than were any other of his women, and it is upon these qualities that the actress bases Becky's claim to public interest. Even in that splendid dramatic moment when she is discovered

7. For Israel Zangwill, see "'The Drama as a Fine Art,'" The Theatre (III), above.

8. "According to Modjeska, '[Barrymore] was much admired by women, but too intellectual to be a mere matinee idol.'" Quoted in Hughes, *A History of the American Theatre, 1700–1950*, p. 265. See also note 12, The Theatre (II), above.

at supper with the Marquis of Steyne, her nerve does not fail her and she lies to the last, lies even when the marquis' banknotes are in her husband's hands. Great as Mrs. Fiske was in that scene, I think Barrymore was greater. Her magnificent acting recalled that phrase of Stevenson's, that if that blow from Rawdon Crawley's fist had not descended upon the marquis' head *Vanity Fair* would cease to be a work of art. For dramatic purposes Mr. Mitchell has added a few flourishes to Becky which I think a little inconsistent. Take, for instance, that soliloquy by the fire, in which Becky says: "I am so tired of it all—my God, the very muscles of my face are tired with smiling to the people I hate." That is not Thackeray's Becky. She liked the game for its own sake, regardless of the stake. Next to winning, she liked losing.

The last act is in Becky's lodgings in Pumpernickle, where she lives with the old hope of getting back into respectability, wearing soiled evening gowns and drinking beer with noisy German students. The atmosphere is meant to be cheap and sordid, but I found it no less attractive than the rest of the play. *Vanitas vanitatum* is all very well in a book, and one can stand the meanness and petty vices of humanity in type, but in actual flesh and blood, clothed in selfishness as with a garment, flaunting their miserable ambitions as they flaunt their jewels, these people are hateful beyond the limits of one's patience. Some way these envious, scheming, snobbish, stupid English folk seemed very much more detestable than the suave, worldly people in the French dramas. After all, they are only conventional Don Juans and their wickedness is only stage wickedness. But these Thackeray folk are too much like the sad caricatures of humanity that we know every day, not the rare victims of grand passions, but the countless slaves of petty and sordid ones, the people who love money better than blood, who wait for dead men's shoes, blackmail their neighbors or leer at their neighbors' wives. *Becky Sharp* will not be a popular piece. Not even the genius of Mrs. Fiske, nor the admirable efforts of her company can secure for the play a long run. Ten righteous men would have saved Sodom, one would save Becky Sharp, but there is only poor, stupid Rawdon, much more sinned against than sinning. There is not enough beauty in the play to save it. If our fellows are like these people, we at least will not admit it. We will wear dominos and masks and play that there are gentlemen and gentlewomen behind them. The soul refuses to be stripped bare of its disguises in this fashion. The mirror which William Thackeray held up to nature was too true a one, we shudder and drop the glass.

Courier, April 21, 1900, p. 3.

Nat Goodwin in Nathan Hale

Willa Cather had followed the career of Nat Goodwin attentively and wrote of him often; indeed, he was the recipient of an "open letter" (see The Star System [III], above). When at last he attempted the serious role so long urged on him, playing with his wife Maxine Elliott in Clyde Fitch's Nathan Hale, *he tried out the play on the road. Willa Cather reviewed it in the* Leader, *November 27, 1898, and incorporated much of the review in the following "Passing Show" column, which appeared after* Nathan Hale *opened in New York, January 2, 1899.*

I see that Mr. Goodwin's first elaborate venture in serious drama is being treated in New York with the consideration which it deserves. Everyone is familiar with the schoolboy's hero, Nathan Hale, and everyone is familiar with Clyde Fitch, the dramatist who wrote *Beau Brummell* when he was twenty. *Nathan Hale*, as presented by Mr. Goodwin, is a splendidly staged production; it deserves to, and doubtless will, succeed. As to the play itself, *Nathan Hale*, like all Clyde Fitch's later works, *De Grammont* and *The Moth and the Flame*, it has brilliant moments, flashes of dramatic intensity almost, but not quite, great enough to redeem the whole play. It is full of good material, clumsily utilized. The first two acts are poorly constructed and wasteful in time and opportunity, contributing little to the serious motif of the piece. The first act is laid in the schoolroom at New London where Nathan Hale—Mr. Goodwin—is making love to his oldest pupil, impersonated by Maxine Elliott and she is "the biggest girl" in very truth, as heavenly fair as ever but grown amazingly matronly and rather elephantine in the kittenish pranks of a schoolgirl. But what a lover he is, that impudent comedian, Mr. Nat C. Goodwin, how fine and tender, and how incongruously delicate—for Goodwin. We used to catch glimpses of it in *The Gilded Fool* and *An American Citizen*, but as this New England schoolmaster he is a Romeo indeed. . . . There is something as spontaneous about Goodwin's lovemaking as about his humor. Tenderness, not of the overdone stagey sort, but quiet and manly, seems to be a part of him, and this rakish comedian has kept it strangely sweet and fresh and ingenuous through all these riotous years. . . .

In such a character as [Nathan Hale], Mr. Goodwin labors under obvious physical disadvantages. Nathan Hale was but one-and-twenty when he died, was a famous athlete and the handsomest youth in all the colonies. Now Mr. Goodwin has said a long and sad farewell to forty, and his "cheek is but a map of days outworn" at that. But for all that, he deserves hearty commendation for the sincerity and good taste which he displays in the part throughout. While Nathan Hale is by no means Mr. Goodwin's best impersonation, it demonstrates beyond question his power of self-restraint and a marked ability for serious drama. Ability, but scarcely aptitude, I think. When I saw him in this drama it did not occur to me, as it so often has when I have seen him play *The Gilded Fool* or *An American Citizen*, that no other actor could play the part quite so well. He played the dramatist's character as it was written, and played it vigorously and well, but I missed the strong personal note which has given him the high place he holds in his profession. After all, the best thing about Goodwin is Goodwin, and he will have to go a long way to find anything better. He may make of himself a serious actor if he will, I do not deny it, but I say that God made him a comedian.

Miss Maxine Elliott steadily improves as an actress, and yet I almost wish she would be content just to be beautiful. I remember that there was a time when I took a very haughty attitude toward the beauty of professional women and considered it an index of insipidity. But I am beginning to find out how little of it there is in the world, and I take humbly and gratefully all that comes my way and I no longer scorn Julia Marlowe because she is so passing fair. But I am dodging the question. It is necessary to forget Miss Elliott's eyes for a moment and to say that *Nathan Hale* was written for her rather than for her husband, that she plays the leading part and that she is unequal to it. I have seen her do some highly creditable acting, but she does not do it in *Nathan Hale*. In her lighter moments she is heavy and almost graceless, and in her emotional climaxes she is as hard as iron, displaying again and again a crudeness and self-consciousness almost amateurish. I can only account for this latter fact by judging that she realizes that that part is too girlish for her and feels ill at ease in it. Her love scenes are thoroughly cold even when they are most emotional; there is no warmth in her caresses and no grief in her tears. It is a portrayal of frozen passions from end to end. Miss Elliott is a most tasteful and picturesque leading woman; she is not and never will be a convincing romantic actress.

It is unfortunate that for his first extensive effort in serious drama, Mr. Goodwin should have so uneven a play, and it is more than unfortunate that Clyde Fitch, who wrote a great play at twenty, should never have been able to repeat to himself: "And too soon marred are those too early made."

Courier, January 21, 1899, p. 4.

Julia Marlowe as Rosalind and Countess Valeska

Willa Cather's view of Julia Marlowe altered over the years (see The Star System [I], [II], and [III], above). Sharp criticism yielded to grudging admiration, and at last Cather emerged as a positive supporter of Marlowe, particularly in her Shakespearean roles. The Countess Valeska, *adapted from a German work,* The Tall Prussian, *by Rudolph Stratz, was added to her repertory, opening in New York on January 10, 1898. Exactly a year later Cather reviewed the play for the* Leader, *using much of the review in her subsequent* Courier *column.*

Oui, c'est une rêve, une rêve d' amour, that Rosalind of Julia Marlowe's. Shakespeare dreamed her, and as a dream presented her. The very title suggests that, *As You Like It,* as you would have it, if dreams came true. Leigh Hunt, in a volume of the best dramatic essays ever written in English,[9] says that Rosalind was Shakespeare's ideal mistress and that he put into her mouth the words he would have had his ideal mistress speak, made up for himself the sweetheart that nature was not deft enough to make for him and gave to her all the attributes that Anne Hathaway and Mary Fitton lacked. And as a dream Miss Marlowe plays her, scarcely tangible and earthly enough to be a thing of flesh. For the simple satisfying effect of beauty, of lyric loveliness, I know of nothing now on the stage like her Rosalind. If she has not ensnared the very dream of Shakespeare, then I think, had he seen her play it, he would have forgot the dream.

I have seen her now three times in the past, and I begin to think that she could not play it badly if she tried. I also begin to distrust that legend always whispered behind the scenes when her name is mentioned, that Ada Dow[10] drilled her in all her Shakespearean parts so thoroughly that she is absolutely bound to the letter of Ada Dow's teaching, that her every intonation is but the echo of another woman's intelligence and that this beautiful Miss Marlowe is but a fair mouthpiece for another woman's soul. I do not believe it. I have watched her reading too closely to be further deluded by any such spiteful myth. Anyway, the story is usually told by jealous ladies whose husbands have managed Miss Marlowe or played with

9. Leigh Hunt, *Dramatic Essays*, ed. William Archer and Robert Lowe (London: Walter Scott, Ltd., 1894), p. 189: ". . . she is the beau ideal of one of Shakespeare's mistresses in Shakespeare's time, and talks (we have no doubt) precisely as the poet would have had her talk to himself."

10. Ada Dow (1847–1926), actress and teacher of acting.

Miss Marlowe. Take Rosalind's first scene with Celia and Orlando at the Duke's court. I have yet to see her play that twice alike. When Celia, after Orlando goes out, crosses to her at the sundial and asks her if all her melancholy is for her banished father and Rosalind replies, "No, some of it is for my father's child." Last year she read that line with a droll affectation of melancholy, this year she read it with a frank gaiety. The line spoken when she gives Orlando the token, "Sir, you have wrestled well, and overthrown more than your enemies." Last year she spoke it timidly, with the deeper meaning in her eyes. This year she spoke it archly, merrily, with a challenging dash of coquetry, and either way it was equally charming. On my life, I could not choose between two moods so bewitching and both so admirably in the spirit of the character. You see, *being* Rosalind, Miss Marlowe can afford to be rather free in her reading, that is just the point; she speaks, she does not read. It is the language of lyric youth, the lovely tongue of Arcady, not elocution. Why, she speaks all that blank verse as though she meant it, loved it, lived it. She is not afraid of it because it is Shakespeare. There is not a line of the play into which she does not infuse life and wit and youthful charm, and she does not infuse too much, she does not overdraw the color of Rosalind's passion, she does not make her too much a thing of flesh and blood, she leaves her half in dreamland, where she should be. After witnessing Ada Rehan's reckless, hot-headed tomboy of a Rosalind,[11] what a joy to see again this poetic creation, as fresh, as mild, as fragrant as an English springtime.

Yet, in spite of its prevailing delicacy, Miss Marlowe's Rosalind is by no means lacking in variety, differentiation and color. Take her reply to her uncle, the Duke, when he exiles her in the first act. How often have I heard that speech whimpered forth with grovelling humility and maudlin pathos. Miss Marlowe replies to her uncle with dignity and spirit. In Elizabeth's time the women of England had begun to demand justice, and Rosalind was a new woman, the first that appeared in literature. Contrast with this gaiety of her banter with Orlando in the forest, her little touch of seriousness and wayward tenderness in the mock-marriage scene, which Miss Rehan makes absolutely farcical, and then there is that beautiful faint when she receives the bloody handkerchief. It is the best stage faint I know, and yet it isn't a stage faint at all, just a weakening of the knees and

11. This is the first mention that Cather has made of seeing Ada Rehan as Rosalind; so far as I can discover, she never reviewed her in that role. Rehan had played Rosalind ten times in 1897–98, but not in Pittsburgh; her last New York performance was on April 17, 1898. She then went on tour, playing Boston, Philadelphia (but not *As You Like It*), and Chicago.

a slipping to the ground, indescribably girlish and graceful and beautiful. She fainted that same faint the next night in *The Countess Valeska*, and I, for one, was mighty grateful to her.

Of Miss Marlowe's qualifications for the character, I shall not attempt to speak, for that would involve a discussion of her beauty, her melodious vocalization, her personal grace and charm, in short, of her whole unique personality, which is nature's secret and no business of mine. But I think her success in her treatment of the character is largely due to the fact that she presents it intellectually rather than emotionally, and fancifully rather than in the broadly humorous vein which Miss Rehan adopts—and without which Miss Rehan can do nothing. Miss Marlowe realizes so completely the nimble wit, the quick imagination, the volatile humor of the Duke's daughter. She is amused at the very extravagance of the passion she feels for Orlando and mocks herself by drolly exaggerating it still further. Those lines about Hero and Leander and the short enduring woes of lovers, actresses have usually spoken lifelessly, merely because the lines were set down for them. But Miss Marlowe speaks them with spirit, as though she had read those old tales many a time in her uncle's castle and had drawn her own conclusions about them.

The scene in which Rosalind discovers the verses which Orlando has hung upon the trees has usually been played ill enough. You remember how Miss Marlowe strolls in, attired in the page's toggery which becomes her so wondrous well, kicking the dried leaves carelessly from her path, singing an old air which is heard before she comes in sight. She reads the verses quite without the usual cheap affectations of surprise, yet with such freshness and spontaneity that I could but believe their contents new to her, and her laughter was fresher than the grass beneath her or the morn above.

The secret of Miss Marlowe's charm is largely, very largely, in her satisfying beauty and in the delicate and almost epicene outlines of her singularly girlish physique. How has she preserved that beautiful immaturity of figure which lends an almost sacred attribute to the parts of virtuous maidenhood she plays? Why, she is now thirty-five at the least calculation, and I cannot see that her virginal loveliness has grown one whit heavier, more earthly, less elusive. It is the old, bitter irony of her profession that when a woman has acquired the art and experience which enable her to play Juliet understandingly, lines have come into her face which make the scene with the nurse a cruel travesty. But Miss Marlowe's face seems married to the lines she speaks, and she seems to breathe and be the very poetry she utters. Youth and art! the two fairest things the sun shines upon—and the two most unmateable! For the moment she holds them both within the compass of her arms. Never shall I forget her in the last act of *As You Like It*. She does not speak the epilogue as Modjeska always did, but contents herself with mingling in the dance. May I always remember her so, under the mottled shadows of the forest, dancing as though she were in truth seventeen, spurning the earth with a light foot—*pede libero*—as Horace bade the nymphs to do. To some women it is given to dance like that when they are seventeen, only a few of them even at that age, and yet Julia is now five-and-thirty. Ah! may the winds of winter never blow on Arden Wood,[12] and she who dances there, may her springtime last long to gladden the eyes of us all! It is a strange wood, that forest of Arden, lying forever at our doors, a place where we may forever renew our first youth. Even to those of us who are walled up in the hearts of great cities, that fair wood lies ever green just across the threshold of our library, a goodly *plaisance* in which the soul may lose itself and forget. And never do I enter it now, that I do not see there this fairest of Rosalinds, whose ethereal youth has given such pleasure to us all.

The very next night I saw Miss Marlowe as the Countess Valeska, saw her drooping about the stage in Empire gowns and become incoherently emotional, marring her fine elocution with spasmodic gurgles and sighs. For ten weary years Miss Marlowe clung to the legitimate drama with a persistence highly praiseworthy in so young a woman. Then she decided that since the public hungered and thirsted after uniforms and Empire gowns and mamelukes and melodrama, she would produce them. And who can blame her? The "legitimate," like virtue, is so lonesome. And she produced them in very good form, too, through the medium of a romantic drama from the German of Rudolph Stratz. Yet I think that the slender audience which greeted Miss Marlowe here that night proves that *The Countess Valeska* is not so popular in all cities as in New York. The play is well made. The plot is well developed, the action is swift, the situations are picturesque and dramatic. But the trouble with all these exciting situations is that they do not excite. And for why? Because all this agitation and anguish is about a thoroughly impossible and most unlikeable hero, Achim Von Lohde. The ladies of Poland must be even more susceptible than their reputation would lead us to think them, if

12. Cf. the poem "Arcadian Winter," which begins: "Woe is me to tell it thee, / Winter winds in Arcady!" First published in *Harper's Weekly*, January 4, 1902; *AT*(*1903*), p. 11.

such a hulking bear of a fellow could so distract the countess. The man's love is so thoroughly selfish and unchivalrous that one doubts that it is even sincere of its kind—and it does not pretend to be a very choice variety. His use of his physical influence over the countess to save his life is an atrocious piece of cowardice. By the way, I cannot but think that Miss Marlowe rather strains the hypnotic suggestion in the lines in this scene by her cataleptic symptoms. Surely the only "hypnotism" meant is one so old and so familiar that it need scarcely be named. No, even the public, which likes queer things sometimes, will never like Achim Von Lohde. There are some things which are neither fair in love nor war, and a base and calculating use of what Miss Marlowe and her gentle company would call "hypnotism" is one of them. . . .

As to Miss Marlowe, I hate to see her slopping about the stage in petticoatless Empire gowns and going daft over a big sawdust man of a Prussian. She is fit for so much better things. There is no doubt that in this play she demonstrates her ability to portray intense emotions with admirable sincerity, if not with power. But, after all, she is not for them, nor they for her. It is like trying to force the tones of a 'cello from a violin. She is a poetic actress, not an emotional one. In those graceful old English comedies, for which she seems expressly fashioned by heaven, I believe her equal does not live today. Where is there another Rosalind or Viola who so satisfies us up to the very level of our dreams? But when the gentle Julia appears in sloppy Empire gowns and asserts that her Polish veins run fire, then I long to go off and drink ice-cream sodas or do something wicked.

Courier, January 28, 1899, pp. 2–3.

Maude Adams and The Little Minister

The sensation of the 1897–98 season was Maude Adams' debut as a star in James M. Barrie's The Little Minister. *Barrie adapted the play from his 1896 best seller expressly for Miss Adams, after seeing her and John Drew in* Rosemary[13] *(see The Star System [III], above). For Willa Cather's views on Maude Adams in* L'Aiglon, *see "Bernhardt and Maude Adams," Washington Correspondent, below.*

Maude Adams and her production of *The Little Minister* are the talk of the town. Certainly Mr. Barrie's little play is a delightful one, full of quiet, poetic situations, quaint, natural comedy, and with a delightfully

13. Lloyd R. Morris, *Curtain Time: History of the American Theatre* (New York: Random House, 1935), pp. 280–282.

literary flavor about it. It is not at all a great play, but it is a mighty pretty one, well constructed, though it is so light, logically developed and perfectly sustained and abounding in deft, clean-cut characterization. As for Miss Maude Adams, I wish I could admire her, people do seem to get so much pleasure out of it. There is no middle ground in the case of Miss Adams. Either she carries you all the way or she moves you not at all, and I have the misfortune to be without the charmed circle. To me, she is merely a clever ingénue, very unattractive to look at. Her perpetual "girlishness" bores me to extinction, and the nasal twang in her voice is unpardonable. In her self-conscious primness, her artful artlessness, there is a fake note. There is something very cheap about her startled-fawn glances and her affectations of shyness when she is called before the curtain. She has been coming before the curtain for some ten years now, and it is quite absurd to assume this shrinking timidity. She knows well enough that the audience will not eat her. She is the only player in her excellent company who fails to contribute anything to the atmosphere of the piece. She does or says nothing to indicate that Babbie is Scotch at all, yet in the play she is not a gypsy, but Lord Rintoul's daughter masquerading. In the comedy scenes Miss Adams was unctuous and kittenish, but quite without humor. In the more serious scenes she was jerky and hysterical and insincere. Her winning ways do not compensate for her lack of imagination. In short, her work seems to me quite without finish, repose, distinction, flavor, charm. And as for temperament, Miss Adams has no more than a sucking dove, but offers in place of it a presumptuous artlessness. Girlishness and greatness are alliterative, but that is the only thing they have in common. The graces which charm in the drawing room are seldom effective either in the study or the portrayal of human problems and passions; yet I know women of genius, splendidly gifted, the props and mainstays of our stage, who consider Miss Adams irresistible. Ah well, it is so in every girl's boarding school; you will always find some unattractive, putty-faced, backachy, headachy little minx, who can never get her lessons unaided, and about her you inevitably find a dozen fine, sound, clever girls who ask no greater bliss than to be her handmaidens and get her lessons for her and "do" her hair and clean her gloves and offer her violets and sighs. For if there is one thing strong people love better than another, it is being gulled by weak ones. In May, Miss Adams is to appear as Juliet in New York with a magnificent company, and I intend to go over and see her. A Juliet right out of the Elsie books, a Juliet well brought up and after Ruth Ashmore's own heart is not to be missed. It will be the greatest libel on William Shakespeare that has ever been perpetrated in all the centuries. Yet this young woman is so popular and so idolized, that I am always half afraid it is an indication of some horrible moral depravity in me that I cannot admire her. In defense of my position I can only say that I think an actress ought to be able to act—a little.

Courier, March 18, 1899, p.5.

Mansfield as Cyrano

After seeing Richard Mansfield in Cyrano de Bergerac, *Willa Cather wrote at length about the dramatist and the play in "The Passing Show" (see "Rostand and* Cyrano de Bergerac," *The Theatre* [*III*], *above*). *The following week she discussed Mansfield's performance.*

Mr. Richard Mansfield's interpretation of the chief and, indeed, the only character of the play, *Cyrano de Bergerac*, is entirely worthy of the foremost American actor of his time. It is by no means one of his most brilliant efforts, for Mr. Mansfield is a character actor, not a romantic actor. It is such a complete departure from anything he has ever done, or that any other living American actor ever attempted, that he is entitled not only to our admiration, but to our gratitude for having addressed himself to so serious an intellectual effort and enriched us by so unique and exotic an experiment. It has cost him much money and study and has been a continual provocation to his unfortunately irascible temper.

The character is one which gives Mr. Mansfield little opportunity to display his most prominent merits; his subtle underplay, his inimitable finesse, his penetrating analysis of personal motives and mental attributes. On the other hand, it attacks him from the side on which all Americans are weakest, that of the academic requisites; physical repose, grace of carriage and rhythm of motion, sonorous and rich and varied elocution. The French think more of those technical beauties than we do, it is a part of their partiality for elegant form. The demands which the role makes upon the actor's physical strength and technical skill of execution are enormous. The part is one of the longest ever written, and memorizing is exceedingly difficult for Mansfield. He often stumbles in his lines after he has played a part for years. There are a dozen or more long, involved speeches, crowded with fantastic imagery and bristling with abrupt transitions and violent contrast, perfect rifle volleys of words, that require a richer and broader and more versatile elocution than any other modern play demands. . . .

The moon extravaganza in the third act, Mr. Mansfield intones, chants as a sort of recitatif, but even sung, it is not more melodious than his fervid reading of the balcony scene, in which all the romance of night since night began seems breathed between his lips. Anyone who knows Mr. Mansfield's temperament will appreciate what a magnificent effort he makes in that act. He is not a man who wears his heart on his sleeve and he loves not to be sentimental. I think only in the stage darkness and the stage moonlight would he play the lover so ardently, and even then he was by no means the most ardent lover that I have heard. For under all this great man's disguises, under all his wigs and rouge and powder, at the bottom of every passion he assumes, one always feels his own personality; a personality intense to fierceness and tinged with bitterness. At the bottom of his crucible there is a hard substance which all the flame of his great genius has never fused, a kind of final negation, a drought of the soul. . . .

And again this Richard Mansfield, this restless and prolific genius, has made stageland the richer by one great character the more. As "Biff" Hall said, "After all, there are just three kinds of actors; there are good actors, and bad actors, and there is Richard Mansfield." What a great example do you offer to the frivolous young actors of our generation, Mr. Mansfield.[14] You have realized that the traditions of stage points have nothing whatever to do with life or the interpretation of it, that they are the accidents rather than the essentials of your art, and that a dramatic effect is worth nothing save in so far that it illuminates the soul behind it. You build your characters up from the very beginning of life. Incidentally, you lay bare the primal causes, the inherent traits, the conditions of nature which lie at the roots of the man's life and account for his conduct in the play. You get down to the subconscious personality of the man, to the framework of his being, analyze those delicate combinations which are nature's art problems wherewith she beguiles the long tedium of the centuries. You know something of the chemistry of the blood, of those wasting fevers not named in the literature of medicine, of those warring elements which, under a seeming unity of character, from the man's first sobbing breath continually rend him. You have stood, I think, like Omar in the Potter's house at eventide, surrounded by the Things of Clay, and you have learned something of the secrets of his craft; how for his diversion he combines his rarest clay with the mud of the streets; how a

14. The shift to direct address suggests that Cather may have contemplated including an "open letter" to Mansfield in her unpublished book, "The Player Letters" (see "An Open Letter to Nat Goodwin," The Star System [III], above.)

turn of the wheel may subvert the fine vessel to base uses and how a little care in finish may destine the basest earth for honor and high offices.

It is in this deeper knowledge of the products and by-products of nature's combinations that you outstrip your playwrights, make your characters actual personalities, each with his own personal traits, mannerisms of speech, methods of thought and peculiar habits of body, each as complete as a creation from the pages of Balzac. It is difficult to believe that the same blood flows in your Beau Brummell, and Rodion, that the same heart can feed two beings so different. Surely the same flesh cannot clothe the shrunken jowl of Chevrial and the youthful cheek of Don Juan. You seem to give to these beings different nerve fibre, different cellular structure. Each night you seem to wear the livery of a new master and to make your body the receptacle of a different soul. Each night your limbs seem moulded, your cheek seared, your eyes burned by the despotic usage of the particular passion you assume, as a house, long occupied, seems at last to conform to and even share the caprices of its tenant.

Courier, April 22, 1899, pp. 2–3.

Two Pinero Heroines

Olga Nethersole (see The Star System [III], above) added The Second Mrs. Tanqueray *to her American repertory in January 1899. Performed by the Kendals in 1893 (see The Star System [I], above), the play had established Arthur Wing Pinero's reputation in the United States. His* Trelawney of the Wells, *a story of backstage life, was the hit of the 1898–99 season. It afforded the English actress Mary Mannering (1876–1953) her first important starring role as a member of Daniel Frohman's Lyceum Company, which also included John Mason (1858–1919) and William Courtenay (1875–1933). Among the other players was Olive May, whom Willa Cather had interviewed before (see The Star System [II], above). For comment on another Pinero play,* The Gay Lord Quex, *see Washington Correspondent, below.*

One of the most interesting and artistic performances I saw at the theatre last winter was Olga Nethersole's production of *The Second Mrs. Tanqueray*. In the first place, it is a great play, the greatest play written in the English tongue for many a long day. I suppose there is no question that Arthur W. Pinero is the first living English playwright. For many years an actor himself, he knows all the limitations, requisites and possibilities of the stage, and he never writes a play that is not an acting play.

He realizes what a distinct form of literature the drama is, and he makes no endeavor to distort it from its original purpose. He is a consummate artist, and he knows a great deal about life. He is not deep, he makes no revelations, but he is subtile and he knows the tricks of his trade. He has an unusually light touch for an Englishman, just a spice of Congreve, and he has written some of the most delightful of farces, of which *The Amazons* [1895] is probably best known in this country. But in the presentation of Paula Tanqueray he has turned to more serious things. Of course the play is a "problem play" which every play is, at the bottom. It is the old question [of] Camille and her past treated more candidly and honestly, if less brilliantly, than Dumas treated it. Now here is a woman who had much bad and much good in her. She had lived a bad life and honestly wanted to quit it. She tries with all her strength, and she has a good man to help her. How far will she be able to do it ? . . .

Had Paula Tanqueray been a thoroughly bad woman, there would have been no tragedy. She had plenty of money, liberty, beauty, admiration, and a husband both foolish and fond. But she had married Aubrey for none of these things; she married him to become respectable, respectable inside. It was in herself that she wanted the change, to be born again. This was what she had honestly hoped for, and she fought and fought and broke her life against the bars, she could not "get back," as the phrase goes, over that line she had crossed so lightly once. That is the grimmest tragedy in life, the finding that, in this world at least, there is no resurrection of the soul. That part of hers which could enjoy the simple pleasures and experiences of life, she had seared away with a red-hot iron, and there can be no future for what no longer exists. What is it that Paula says crouching down by Aubrey's side, with her cheek on his shoulder and her heavy eyes staring off into vacancy.

"I believe that the future is only the past again, entered through another gate."

And Aubrey says truly "That's an awful belief."

Courier, July 22, 1899, pp. 5, 9.

When Frohman's New York Lyceum Company came to town presenting Pinero's delightful comedy *Trelawney of the Wells*, about the most attractive person in the company was Miss Olive May, formerly of Beatrice, Nebraska, and sometime Mrs. Henry Guy Carleton. That is saying a good deal, for it was an excellent company and in it some very exceptional people, such as the dashing young William Courtenay, that beautiful Mary Mannering, and John Mason, now fully recovered from the baleful influence of light-opera morphine and Marion Manola,[15] and doing the splendid work that he is so capable of doing. The play of course offers rare opportunities for good acting, and there is not a part in it that is not full of individuality and flavor. Of all the living English playwrights, I pin my faith on Mr. Arthur W. Pinero. He never writes a play unless he has something to say in it, and he never says it other than effectually and artistically. He has written, in *The Second Mrs. Tanqueray*, one of the strongest and most merciless dramas of our time, and he has written some of the most poetic and idyllic comedies. Since I saw his *Trelawney of the Wells*, I have believed in him more completely than ever. The play is the least garish, the most dignified and untheatric that I have seen in many a long day, and it has a literary flavor rare enough in these degenerate times. Miss Trelawney, the heroine of the piece, is the leading lady at the Wells Theatre, London, and the plot of the play hinges on her engagement to a London society youth, her attempt and failure to adapt herself to the humdrum life of his family and her return to the theatre to discover that she had lost the trick of the florid declamation then in vogue, and that having tried two worlds she now belongs to neither, and is neither a gentlewoman nor an actress. Her lover himself goes upon the stage and finally wins her in her own world and among her own people. The play is quiet, full of subtile elegance, and it reads almost as well as it acts. The declamatory actors who have outlived their period and who are reduced to want by the new school of naturalistic actors, form a pathetic background for the story. And just here, let me say that it is time to denounce the old fallacy that "plays about actors don't go in America," since *Trelawney of the Wells* and *Zaza* were the two most popular plays in New York last year, and Charles Coghlan's *Royal Box* held its own for two seasons.[16]

But to return to Olive May: she had, after Miss Mannering, rather the best part in the play, and I am inclined to think that she made it quite the best part. For Miss Mannering, although her exquisite beauty is worth any price of admission and her personality is one of the most elusive and charming behind the footlights today, has always seemed to me rather a conventional actress. Miss May, on the other hand, is clever to her fingertips, and has animation enough for half-a-dozen women and a pair of eyes

15. For John Mason and Marion Manola, see the second selection in "The Perils of Journalism," The Urban Scene, above.

16. David Belasco's *Zaza*, starring Mrs. Leslie Carter, ran for one hundred and eighty-four performances after January 9, 1899. For *The Royal Box*, see "The Lesson of Dumas *père*," The Theatre [III], above.

that tell very much more than her lines. Indeed, she seems to have invented a system of optic elocution of her own. She is fairly bubbling over with that vivacity which won her her first notable success in *The Butterflies.* I suppose one might call it *esprit,* but it is something more than that, for by her reading of some most unostentatious lines in the third act she achieved the truest note of pathos struck in the play. . . . After the matinee I had a long talk with her at her hotel and found her quite as young and as good to look at and as full of vivacity as when I first met her four years ago. Her enthusiasm for bicycling has been transferred to golf, that is about the only change. It interested me to see how staunch is her loyalty to the West and how warmly she remembers her friends there, and I got more Nebraska news while the Lyceum Company was in town than I had heard since I last crossed the Missouri. After dinner, when we left the Lincoln Hotel for the theatre, the city was shrouded in a veil of smoke and fog, through which the lights in front of the theatre burned murkily, and she made the usual protests against Pittsburgh weather. I remarked that we both knew a country where the air was clear enough and where the wind was galloping forty miles an hour over interminable stretches of red-brown prairie. . . .[17]

Courier, December 23, 1899, p. 2.

An Open Letter to Joseph Jefferson

This "Passing Show" column was one of three which Willa Cather collected for her rejected book, "The Player Letters" (see note 14, above). She had reviewed Jefferson in Rip Van Winkle *(see The Star System [III], above), and doubtless had seen him as Bob Acres in* The Rivals, *which he brought to Pittsburgh the week of October 30, 1899. In the following comments, Cather drew freely on Jefferson's* Autobiography. *For her view of him as a painter, see Washington Correspondent, below.*

Venerable Sir:

When recently a man of letters, M. Octave Mirbeau,[18] made an attack upon the profession and person of actors, M. Coquelin, answering him in a courteous manner common among actors, but alas none too common among men of letters, merely recalled the names and profession

17. Cf. the description of the "great prairie the color of wine-stains" in *My Ántonia:* ". . . more than anything else I felt motion in the landscape; in the fresh, easy-blowing morning wind, and in the earth itself, as if the shaggy grass were a sort of loose hide, and underneath it herds of wild buffalo were galloping, galloping . . ." (pp. 15, 16).

18. Octave Mirbeau (1848–1917), dramatic critic for *L'Ordre.*

of Molière and Shakespeare, adding "It is sweet, monsieur, to be insulted in such company." In every country there are certain names, which men whose feeling for the drama is deep and vital evoke in vindication of the art they love. Yours, sir, is one of those names, the very utterance of which renews our loyalty to the theatre. Your name can never be spoken or written, can never greet the eye from the printed page without contributing a peculiar lustre to the art which you have so long adorned. There have been other careers in the history of the American stage quite as valuable as yours, but about your life and work there is a singular fitness and evenness and completeness which give you the authority of a classic master in your own lifetime. Your career has been one of the beautiful incidents of dramatic history. Future chroniclers will delight to write of it, and many an actor yet unborn will consecrate to you the purest aspirations and find in your name a weapon to refute (combat) the mockery of the world.

I have noticed, sir, that in writing of you, even critics doff their air of licensed superiority, and fall into the language and feeling of the man who pays for his seat and reserves the right to enjoy and admire unconditionally. And, indeed, you seem not to belong to the quibbling world of analytical criticisms and conflicting estimates and hairbreadth distinctions, but to the common world of all of us, where the real sun shines and real brooks flow. You have reached out of art into life. You have touched the large world of men who feel more closely than the small world of men who formulate. Your art has given a tangible delight that is quite independent of the intellectual or critical faculties; a beauty which the simplest divine and which the most astute cannot define, which retains the vitality outside the radius of the calcium, and which the backwoodsman can carry back to the hills and find it as real in the sunlight as it seemed to him in the theatre. This, sir, is the art which endures, because it concerns itself with men's sympathies, which are changeless, rather than with the intellect, which is constantly modified by external conditions, and developing new tastes at the expense of old passions. Yours, sir, is the *vox humana* of art, the element which survives transition of form, revolution of method, and the decadence of schools, contributing actually and measurably to the sum of human happiness. And perhaps after all, sir, that is the only thing which gives art the right to be.

Your growth and development has been, up to a certain point, almost one with that of the American stage. You yourself have esteemed it fortunate to have been born, as it were, into the theatre. Whatever may be the merits and talents of actors recruited to the stage from other walks of life, the man who is born an actor may well claim the advantage. For the stage is a world in itself, a world apart, and one to which it is difficult to become acclimated; a world which awakens only when the humdrum world of the everyday is asleep, which is created and supported by the fancies of men, which is every night born anew out of dreamland, like the cloud palaces of the Fata Morgana. And this world has an atmosphere, a perspective, laws of vocalization and motion distinctively its own, with which one can best familiarize himself in childhood. You have told, better than anyone else could tell it, how the stage was your first playground, how its settings and properties, Juliet's balcony, the throne of the stage kings, the tomb of the Capulets, were your first playthings. How the star's dressing room was a sort of throne chamber to you, and how many a time you slipped from your nurse's arms and stole down in your white nightgown to behold the elder Booth, or Macready, or Fanny Kemble posing in their robes of state before the mirror. Yet I think, sir, that much of that rich humanity which makes your character seem less a stage creation than people of our own world and guests at our fireside is due to the influences that came from the world without, and to certain peculiar and trying conditions with which churlish fortune saw fit to hedge about your youth. The life of the strolling player, as you knew it, is now almost a thing of the past. Its hardships, its privations, its reproach, its vagabond wanderings, its jovial acceptance of the chances of sun and rain, its glorious liberty and its touch of veritable, first-hand romance, are now become legends. I have often wondered whether those fortunate spectators who tremble before the demoniac fury of Kean's Overreach[19] or the bursts of vindictive hatred of his Richard, bethought them from what strange sources, from what wracking experiences, the actor had distilled such passion and such bitterness: from what weary miles tramped over the frozen slush of winter roads; from what miserable shelters in hayricks and stables whither he and his wife had crept for warmth; from what rope dancing at country fairs, hooted and jeered by rustic bumpkins, from what frenzied debauches in low taprooms, amongst the most depraved of human kind, Edmund Kean had learned so well to suffer and to hate. And you, sir, found honey, even where he found gall. Like him, you felt the world's rough hand and learned life and art amongst the people, far enough from the pinnacle you were destined one day to grace. When

19. The part of Sir Giles Overreach in Massinger's *A New Way to Pay Old Debts* was in the repertory of Edmund Kean (1787–1833).

in your autobiography, one of the most engaging and least pretentious works in the literature of the drama, I read of those early Thespian wanderings of yours; of that memorable trip to Chicago by boat, when the shores of the Great Lakes were dotted with Indian villages, of your playing in flatboats, drifting down the turbid Mississippi, of those barn-storming nights on the prairies of Illinois, of your following the army into Mexico, of all the various extremes of life you tasted and the manful manner in which you mingled among men while yet a boy, then I think with compassion of our young actors whose world lies between Broadway and Fifty-first Street; who spend half their lives in theatres and hotels and the other half in the dawdling monotony of a Pullman car. You were never beset by the temptations of premature or cheaply bought success. Poverty made you a man before you became an artist. To your long and hard apprenticeship, to your slow and natural growth, to the stubborn difficulties which confronted you, you owe much of that perfect finish, that ability to completely develop the possibilities of a past and throw it into a strong relief which imparts a singular and final authority to all your impersonations and makes the task of your successor a fearsome one indeed. It was a relentless school, sir, in which you acquired your training, with hunger for a taskmaster, and the harshness would have been well-nigh fatal to a man less resolutely cheerful. Yet it was there you learned your scale of values, formed your estimate of things, that cold, practical, unerring estimate which has been so potent a factor in your success. It was there, moreover, that you gathered at first hand a knowledge of men as they are, a knowledge not to be acquired in polite society, much less among actors and artists.

We hear much in these days of the "artistic temperament," and, like charity, [it] is made the cloak for many unsightly things. I wonder if one of our temperamental players, who offer temperamental excuses alike to their wives and their tailors and are forever demanding temperamental consideration, had one of these been set down in a barn in Mississippi to amuse the country folks for his dinner and a night's lodging, whether his temperament would have kept his heart light or his heels nimble? Yet I think you learned something in the barn that our dramatic schools have not been able to teach. To have cultivated a timely tolerance for the failures and failings of men; to have valued all men for the potential good in them; not to have been blind and stopped with personal ambition, but alert and awake to every humor, every passion, every beauty, however fleeting, in God's great playhouse; to have been serious without pretentious gravity, to have cheerfully welcomed fair days and foul; to have lived joyfully and kept the inner delight in things alive until one is six-and-seventy, this, it seems to me, bespeaks the true temper of the artist more than do all the exaggerated eccentricities of distorted egotism, so often mistaken for genius.

It is this happy temper which has prolonged your youth for three-quarters of a century and given to your work that exquisite polish, that even serenity, that refinement of grace which our younger comedians would do so well to emulate, which has infused into your creations a mellowness of humor, a gentleness of pathos akin to the modest beauty of the English classics of a hundred years ago.

It is greatly to be wondered at that an actor so perfectly equipped should have been so seemingly dormant in artistic ambition, so satisfied by a few creations, well-nigh perfect though they are. Yet strangely mingled with the poetry and humor of your nature there is a vein of hard Yankee practicability. There is no gainsaying that your managerial success limited your artistic growth, that you made the actor subservient to the manager, which, from the professional point of view, is quite as it should be. The enormous financial success of *Rip Van Winkle* checked your career gloriously, but finally. Your ambition went to sleep with Rip upon the mountain top, and though thirty years and more have passed, it has never wakened. You have chosen the placid waters and sheltered harbors. No craving for versatility has ever tempted you into broader highways of dramatic experience. Unlike Mr. Mansfield, that restless spirit "forever roaming with a hungry heart,"[20] you have risked nothing and lost nothing. You have been content to concentrate yourself upon a few dramas, all of which were, or have become, classics, and to attain in these almost absolute perfection, you have been singularly lacking in that insatiable, that holy curiosity, usually so impotent [potent?] a factor in the artistic constitution. You have evinced a kind of classic conservatism and content, as opposed to that feverish thirst of soul which drives men to seek various and multiform expression, which limits your register to a single mellow octave in the vast scale of dramatic passions and experiences. Within this limit we have accepted you with all gratitude and admiration, as one of the noblest geniuses of our time, regretting occasionally, perhaps, that Fortune turned her smiling face upon you quite so early, that one so equipped should have lacked the acute passion for creation,

20. Line 12 of Tennyson's "Ulysses" reads: "For always roaming with a hungry heart. . . ." *Poetical Works*, p. 89.

and that having the clue and the sword you did not care to explore the labyrinth.

George Moore somewhere says that to have a personality worth expressing and to express that personality perfectly is the essence of dramatic art. We all know in what character you have formed your most adequate expression; a character perhaps the greatest which the American stage has yet produced, and which will scarcely outlive you. For almost forty years the public, so fickle and so fond of new toys, has never wavered in its loyalty to *Rip Van Winkle*. How few historical creations, sir, have ever really installed themselves in our affections! How few of those reverend cardinal virtues behind the footlights are really dear to us in our heart of hearts. Some amuse us, some we admire; but toward how few do we feel the warmth of a personal affection; yet for nigh upon half a century this improvident, dream-drinking Dutchman has been beloved by the whole English-speaking world. Only an actor ripe in judgment, rich in sympathy, gentle by nature and very lovable himself could so have endeared such a character to us. Judged by purely intellectual canons, your impersonation of Bob Acres is doubtless a more remarkable performance. But it is as Rip that future generations of playgoers will know you. Alas! not know you. For what written accounts of your performance can convey to them its dignity and tenderness, the dramatic power of that utterance to Gretchen when, pointing to your child, you say, "You say that I have no part in anything in your house?," the poignant pathos of your farewell to Meenie, or the greatness of that moment in which you go out into the storm and the night? In this tippling vagabond whom even the dogs loved, who squandered his life and fortune and yet possessed more of this world than most of us, in this wayward lover of Old Earth who was so close to her that the trees talked to him, who got so much of the sweetness out of life while other people were doing their duty, you have found expression for all that is best in you, and you assume the character only to ennoble it. Only half awake in this tippling Dutchman are those fresh, childlike perceptions that have made poets of so many of the world's vagabonds. It is on this ground that you meet the character. It is this dominant note of poetry that makes your Rip unique among the creations of comedy, this light, fanciful touch that makes the supernatural experiences through which he passes seem not extravagant or impossible. No scene has ever been made more weirdly poetic than that on the moonlit Catskills, with its long, trying monologue so gracefully and naturally delivered. What a feeling of the hills and the forest do you bring into the hot, dusty atmosphere of the playhouse, what a spirit of running water and dew-drenched woods. We forget that we are in a theatre at all. We seem to sniff the clean air of the mountains and feel again that elation which sometimes seizes us upon the top of the Catskills or the Alleghenies when the pines are white with frost, and yet there are but the painted trees and waterfall, the pasteboard rocks which we see in the theatre every night and which move us not at all. All that is marvelous, eery, poetic, you yourself bring to us, and you clothe those poor mimics with all the freshness and wonder of life; you carry the verdure of the woods in your heart. At some time during those wanderings on the lower Mississippi, through the forests along the lakes or on the western prairies, you must have lain very near to nature, watched lovingly her face and listened for her secret whisperings, and all your life you have carried them with you, as the shell carries the whispers of the sea.

I maintain, sir, that, in all your impersonations, the pre-eminent charm is not your art, but your humanity—a rare quality which life sometimes gives to art. You and Mr. Richard Mansfield represent two extremes of dramatic art. There can be no question that Mr. Mansfield's is the more fertile and creative genius, that his reach is wider, his art more brilliant, more complex, richer in startling surprises. But he lacks the human touch. His characters come to us white hot from the brain, rather than blood warm from the heart. It is not your art alone, sir, not your easy and melodious elocution, your grace and elegance of gesture, nor your wonderful bits of stage business, nor the suggestiveness and wit of your byplay which have made us all your friends and lovers. In your dramatic impersonations, in the pages of your autobiography, in some of the pictures from your brush, we feel that genial glow of personality, the reflection of a noble and generous soul. Only the soul, sir, can wholly satisfy the soul, and we Saxons love to prove the heart of a man and know that it is beating sound and true under all the creations of his genius. We continually demand this personal understanding, even with authors. So it is that the personal asides which completely spoil Thackeray for a Frenchman, are what most endear him to his countrymen. Yet though you have furnished us with this certificate of your integrity upon which we lay such stress, you have been very little of a preacher and have kept apart from all the ephemeral vexations of the drama. You have never conceived it to be your duty to make the stage a pulpit or to set about denouncing the sins of the world. You have been content to produce the beautiful, knowing well that man must desire virtue, because it is fair and goodly to possess, or not at all.

Would that we could adequately thank you, sir, for the pleasure which you and your fellows have given us in our overwrought, over-practical world, where we have overelaborated everything. We have made whist so difficult that few of us can play it, wine so good that few of us can afford to drink it, poetry so fine that few of us have wit enough to read it. We make a science even of recreation and kill all the joy if it. But the drama is still the art of the people, not dominated by purely intellectual passions, concerning itself rather with the experiences of the many than the tastes of the few. So genial and generous an art that it is still beloved of the children and the aged, a thing of laughter and tears, still simple and human, touched with our infirmities and acquainted with grief. Yours, sir, has been an art, helpful and wholesome, and you have aroused the kinder nature of men. It is the fashion nowadays for actors to give a serpent when we ask for meat and to furnish us with clever studies of the brutality of men, revealing hitherto unsuspected depths of depravity in our old stage friends. But you have read into the part of a vagabond the feelings of a gentleman. You have given us of the living waters which brings contentment and peace. You have not found virtue dull or insipid, nor folly altogether vicious. You have given us a message of hope and cheer and bidden us all a hearty Godspeed on this journey through the dark which must shortly end for you. And may it all return to you; as the flowers fall to enrich again the generous lap of earth, so in the remaining years may all the pleasure which your life and genius have bestowed come back to you an hundredfold, and your downward way break out ablossom with the kindly smiles and generous moisture which you have brought to the faces and the eyes of men. If your years should be too few to contain so much felicity, then perchance something of our love may follow you across the uncertain void where man may bear neither riches nor honors, and even death may not be able to quite unclasp our hands, so warmly clasped upon your own. When you lay aside the crown your talents won and your life honors, worn blamelessly through so many years, fear no successor. In our hearts, sir, you reign always, the Prince of Players, best loved, most honored of them all.

Courier, December 2, 1899, pp. 3–4.

Olga Nethersole as Sapho

The Pittsburgh performance of Nethersole as Fanny Legrand in Daudet's Sapho *preceded the New York opening by almost a month. Adapted by Clyde Fitch from the play by Mme. Daudet and M. Belot,* Sapho *opened in*

New York on February 5, 1900, and after twenty-nine performances was closed by the police on the ground that it was immoral. Nethersole was acquitted in the subsequent trial and resumed the play for fifty-five performances, beginning April 7.[21]

The largest and certainly the most enthusiastic audience of the season greeted Olga Nethersole at the Alvin last night, in her new role as the heroine of Alphonse Daudet's greatest novel.[22] Mr. Clyde Fitch no longer writes plays; he manufactures, combines, revamps them by the half dozen. It is only fair to him, however, to say that it has been a long time since he has made so creditable an arrangement as this of Daudet's novel. To be sure, there is very little original work about it, for he had Daudet's own drama, and the opera libretto by Henri Cain, to guide him, but this is no time to quarrel with sources; if we get a passably good play, for goodness sake let us rejoice and be glad, [whether it?] bring with it airs from heaven or blasts from France. At least Mr. Fitch's arrangement of *Sapho* presents many of the strong situations of the novel, preserves something of its finesse and artistic color scheme, and is, with the possible exception of the last act, a well-made play.[23]

The entire interest of the play, of course, centers about one character, about one theme, what M. Daudet called "the glorious, the horrible beauty of Sapho." Miss Nethersole has given a performance greater in the mere matter of degree in her Carmen, and a character delineation more subtle in Paula Tanqueray, but never one which was so absolutely unique, more original in conception, more finished or brilliant or various in execution than her Fanny Legrand. There is no other character just like this in English drama, and certainly no one will ever play her like this strange Englishwoman with a Russian name and eyes of the Orient. Not an idealized consumptive like Marguerite Gauthier, nor a frankly and joyously wanton nature like Carmen, this character involves shades and semitones and complex motives, the struggling birth of things and burnt-out ghosts of things that it baffles psychology to name. And Miss Nether-

21. Burns Mantle and Garrison P. Sherwood, eds., *The Best Plays of 1899–1909* (New York: Dodd, Mead & Co., 1944), pp. 361–362.

22. Willa Cather had read the book as early as 1891 and owned a copy that she prized. Willa Cather to Mariel Gere, July 16, 1891; Willa Cather to Mariel Gere, January 2, 1896.

23. Norman Hapgood, at this time dramatic critic of the *Commercial Advertiser*, stated: "Mr. Fitch's adaptation improved the French play theatrically, on the whole, though in a literary sense it is inferior; while to compare it with the novel would be to contrast an ordinary, insincere, made-to-order piece of work, adequate for its purpose, with a masterpiece of finesse, experience, taste, and sincerity." *The Stage in America: 1897–1900*, p. 357.

sole has gone at this character with that strange intensity, that sort of ferocity of attack by which she makes her character her own, takes them in through her pores and absorbs them into her blood as she did Carmen. She has idealized the character no more than was necessary, and with admirable verity she drops now and then back into her part, the part which is never left behind, but always with us, and ever and again returns a look, a gesture, a word which comes from the pavement. Aside from the vividness of her general conception of the part, of her vigorous presentation of the great "points" of the play, Miss Nethersole has brought the finesse of her work up wonderfully. She resorts less frequently to those more individual and personal modes of expression called mannerisms, her use of those stirring contralto tones is more artistic and discriminating, and she makes her every attitude on the stage a picture, her every movement beautiful to see. Only Mme. Bernhardt herself can make picture follow picture in that dazzling succession. . . .

Leader, January 9, 1900, p. 4.

Sir Henry Irving and Ellen Terry

Though Willa Cather had commented on Sir Henry Irving (see "The Training of Actors," The Star System *[II]), she did not see the Irving-Terry Repertory Company until the week of January 15, 1900, when it played in Pittsburgh. Irving had selected Ellen Terry (1847–1928) to be his leading lady in 1878, and the two made a great and immediate impression on the English public. They visited the United States frequently after their first success in 1882–83, and were acclaimed for their repertory, particularly Irving's scenic productions of Shakespeare. For a later view of Ellen Terry, see* "Merry Wives of Windsor," *The European Scene, below.*

Last week I saw Sir Henry Irving and Ellen Terry in *The Merchant of Venice*. It was not only a play, it was the reconstruction of an historic period, the restoration of a bygone civilization, it was the glorious history of Venice animated and made flesh. I not only believe that I never saw Shakespeare adequately played before, but that I never saw him played at all. I have indeed seen Shakespearean characters well played, but never an entire play so presented as to bring out the playwright's complete conception, his full purpose, every light and shade that go to make the piece as a whole a perfect work of art. Now I know why it is that Irving's "stagecraft" is so much talked of, it is because he plays in every character on the stage, because he governs this puppet world like a sort of inexorable Providence, making all the players work together for one end and to produce one great harmony, as the conductor of an orchestra does. You felt that great central intelligence in Gobbo as well as in Shylock, in the grouping of the characters, in the very painted canvas.

Speaking of canvas, any one of Irving's Shakespearean productions is enough to convince one that scenery may have a noble meaning, like all else that is fitting and beautiful, and that any actor has a right to enhance or elaborate the playwright's scheme by scenic accessories, just as a conductor has a right to transcribe a Liszt rhapsody for a full orchestra. Certainly it can only add to the effectiveness of the first act of *The Merchant of Venice* to have the first act beautifully staged upon the square of St. Mark's and to suggest in the promenade of the gallants all the gay, luxurious life of the Venetian nobles. Certainly the trial scene gains in dignity when the pomp of the Venetian court is put tangibly before your eyes.

When I first saw Richard Mansfield's Shylock,[24] I maintained that masterly and convincing as it was, it was the Shylock of Richard Mansfield, and not that of Shakespeare. Mr. Irving handles the text more respectfully, and his interpretation is more orthodox and, strange as that may seem, at the same time more free and immensely more varied. Mansfield voices the tragedy of the ghetto; he presents the patriarch burning under the accumulated wrongs of centuries, the picture of age in exile and subjected to insults. His Shylock knows the passion of bitterness but not that of personal hate, and he values money only as a means to power. But Shylock himself said, "And if you wrong us, shall we not have revenge?" and this quality of personal hatred against Antonio as the exponent of Christian doctrines and practices, which is touched very lightly by Mr. Mansfield, is the point of strongest emphasis with Irving. It is a hate that the Jew himself cannot control, that breaks out when he would not let it be seen and endangers the plan of revenge he broods upon. It is the hysterical hate of an old man, that breaks the voice and glitters in the eye and shakes the body as with palsy. The ferocity and malice under that cackle of tremulous laughter with which the Jew first proposes the terms of the bond to Antonio makes the listener shudder. With Irving's Shylock the passion for his ducats is a material passion, simply that of a miser and no more. When he says of Jessica, "Would she were hearsed at my foot, and the ducats in her coffin!" he means just that. Yet the patriarchal side of the Jew is not forgotten, only Irving scores in a single scene the point

24. See "Mansfield as Shylock," The Star System (III), above.

that Mr. Mansfield devotes the entire play to. It is in the scene at his own house, before he goes out to sup with the young Venetians, that Irving's Shylock is the patriarch. And what a wonder Irving makes of that scene! The curtain rises on that dark house on the canal, the light burning before it. The maskers of the Venetian carnival, clad in rainbows of color, troop through the street; a gondola hung with colored lanterns, full of youths and maidens singing to the accompaniment of a guitar glides down the canal. As the laughter of the maidens dies in the distance and the music goes to sleep on the waters, you hear the rap of Shylock's staff, and the Jew enters, muttering and cursing the gaiety he hates and the opulence and splendor of his oppressors. The scene with Jessica is solemn and dignified almost to pathos, for in his own house the Jew is still high priest and representative of Jehovah on earth. After he goes out, again the maskers, the gay gondolas, the arrival of Lorenzo and his friends, the amorous passages with Jessica, and the flight. Then the Jew returns to his desolated house, the song and laughter heard across the canal mocking his despair. In the trial scene he is less theatric than Mansfield and much more dramatic. Mansfield gave Shylock in his momentary triumph a sort of cynical satisfaction, while Irving's Shylock is no more of a cynic than the child who kicks the door that pinched his fingers. As he plays it, the scene is full of fine "points" like this: When Bassanio offers him six thousand ducats for his three, Shylock approaches him and taps the bag of gold with his sharpened knife, listening to the clink of the coins, and then answers him. "If every ducat in six thousand ducats" etc. The final blow of Portia's decision he receives with a sort of tottering apathy, like a man stunned by a physical blow. Creditable and ingenious as Mr. Mansfield's performance is, it will scarcely stand comparison with an interpretation so rich, so varied, so complex, so full of subtile analysis and so quickened with dramatic power. This is the work of a larger intellect, a larger experience, a more conscientious study.

I wonder how she ever happened, I wonder what she really is, that strange combination of sentiment and comedy, of witchery and mirth, of carelessness and happy intuitions, that incarnate grace that they call Ellen Terry? That Portia with a voice of dreamland and the dignity and exquisiteness of all the queens of old Romance, who after playing the fair lady of Belmont for lo, these fifteen, nay twenty years, still catches in her lines and dares to improvise in the "quality of mercy" speech. I don't believe Sir Henry himself knows her much better than the rest of us do. I had a long chat with the stage manager about her, and I'm convinced he doesn't know her. "Naw," he said, "she doesn't know the lines of any of her parts, and in blank verse of course that's awkward. Why doesn't Sir Henry call her down do you say? Dear me! then there would be stormy times for all of us! Why the Governor would never dare suggest that Miss Terry ought to know her lines. Why the Governor hasn't hung up in a star's dressing room since we've been in the states. She takes the best one every stop and the Governor he takes what's left. Then she puts up her hammock in her dressing roon and sleeps between acts, and we have to hold scenes for her. She's not in a good humor this trip anyhow. She hates her part in *Robespierre*[25] and is never done finding fault about it. O, he's a good man, is the Governor, a good man and patient."

I have an old picture of Miss Terry as Mamillius to Charles Kean's Leontes,[26] taken when she was five years old, and even there the grace of that little body is as the grace of an elf child, and the face has the same exquisite mobility and sensitiveness that she has kept into her fifties.

But to Belmont: Ah! that was a Portia to dream on! I never want to see another. There is comedy and comedy and then some; but hers is the comedy of grand dames and princesses of the blood, done regally and blithely and to the tune of silver bells. The scene with Nerissa in which she describes the suitors is simply inimitable and indescribable. In the casket scene the great lady was careless and seemed in a bad humor with Bassanio. Indeed I quite forgot her in the magnificent acting of the Prince of Morocco. He was an impressive figure as he swept in with his twelve dusky slaves, big and black and ablaze with jewels, and he delivered those long, flowery speeches set down for him with a fire and fervor that made his suit a noble one. I shall never forget the great dignity with which he drew his mantle about him and bowed himself from her presence with his "Thus losers part."

The trial scene of course is one of the most perfect expressions of Miss Terry's more serious art. But it was in the last act that I liked her best, that wonderful last act where the play becomes a comedy again, where picturesqueness and happiness is allotted to every one and every flower in the moonlit garden exhales poetry. The laugh that is half a sigh, coquetry that is half pure enchantment, comedy in the summer moonlight, that is Miss Terry's own art.

Courier, February 17, 1900, pp. 2–3.

25. *Robespierre* by Victorien Sardou had been adapted by Laurence Irving, Sir Henry's son. It opened in New York on October 30, 1899.

26. In Kean's production of *A Winter's Tale*.

Books and Authors (IV)

(April 22, 1899—April 7, 1900)

During her last year as a regular contributor to the Leader *and to the* Courier, *it is safe to say that Willa Cather discussed nearly a hundred books. The bulk of her comments appeared in the "Books and Magazines" column of the* Leader, *with some of the reviews reappearing in her* Courier *column, and she continued to write about books in "The Passing Show" after she ceased contributing to "Books and Magazines" in December 1899. In that month, too, she made her last contribution to the* Home Monthly. *In March 1900 Cather stopped writing drama criticism for the* Leader *and at an undetermined time during the spring, perhaps in May, resigned her job at the telegraph desk. By this time she was turning out work for the* Library, *a short-lived literary magazine (see The* Library, *below), and in May "The Passing Show" made its last appearance in the* Courier. *The preceding month her story "Eric Hermannson's Soul" came out in* Cosmopolitan.[1] *It was the first signed story by Willa Cather in a national magazine since "On the Divide" was published in the* Overland Monthly *in January 1896.*

George Seibel has written about the "new planets [that] swam into Willa's ken during these years," among them A. E. Housman and Sarah Orne Jewett, and of her "habit of bringing along books by new men—there was Differences, *a first novel by Hervey White, for whom we predicted great things which never came to pass."*[2] *Indeed, though many of the books Cather discussed reflected her earlier interest in such writers as Eugene Field and Zola, she was deeply involved in the literature of her age. She did not, it is true, review* David Harum *and* When Knighthood Was in Flower, *the leading best sellers of 1899, because—as a passing reference to the latter made plain—she could not take these kinds of*

1. As early as August 1896 a manuscript reader for *Cosmopolitan* said the magazine would pay Willa Cather one hundred dollars for her story "The Count of Crow's Nest," but it already was committed to the *Home Monthly*. Willa Cather to Mariel Gere, August 4, 1896. For "Eric Hermannson's Soul," see *CSF*, pp. 359–379.

2. Seibel, p. 202. *Differences* (1899) was a novel of settlement work in Chicago. Hervey White (1866–1944) wrote several other books and founded the Maverick Press in New York.

books seriously. (Her interest in Mary Johnston's To Have and To Hold, *the leading best seller of 1900, was aroused by its Old Dominion setting.) But in general her choices for significant commentary comprise a cross section of the work being published by representative American, English, and French writers at the turn of the century.*

Four Women Writers: Atherton, Ouida, Chopin, Morris

Willa Cather had expressed herself firmly more than once on the subject of women writers.[3] *Among novelists she honored the "great Georges" and Charlotte Brontë and Jane Austen, but for the most part she had "not much faith" in women fiction writers. Of the four discussed below, Gertrude Atherton (1857–1948) was chiefly known at this stage of her career for her historical romances about her native state of California. Willa Cather earlier had recorded her opinion of Ouida;*[4] *the comments presented here occurred in a review of Max Beerbohm's* More *(1899). Kate Chopin's novel* The Awakening *(1899) evoked one of Cather's most interesting critical statements. Mrs. Chopin (1851–1904) had written three earlier books on Creole life, beginning with* At Fault *(1890). After the vicious critical attacks on* The Awakening, *which was widely denounced for immorality,*[5] *she stopped writing fiction. The last author considered, Clara Morris (see The Star System [I] and [II], above), had made a great name for herself as an emotional actress before she turned to writing. When Willa Cather reviewed her collection of stories for children,* Little Jim Crow, *she declared that both as an actress and a writer Clara Morris knew how to "touch . . . the secret springs of tears and laughter"* (Leader, *December 16, 1899*).

And here, too, is dear Mrs. Atherton taking to the psychological and pretentiously analyzing things which she was once content to admire. The trophies of Henry James and Mrs. Craigie will not let her sleep, and she will produce "literature" at any cost. Dear! Dear! How the ladies do fall in. I should not be surprised to hear at any day that Mrs. Ella Wheeler

3. See, for example, "Three Women Poets," Books and Authors (I), "The Literary Situation in 1895," Books and Authors (II), and "Old Books and New [May 1897]," The *Home Monthly*, all above. Cather admired Sarah Orne Jewett's *Country of the Pointed Firs* (1896); she gave a copy to George Seibel, who wrote that he was fonder of Mary E. Wilkins, "but Willa preferred [Jewett's] austere and unsentimental *Country Doctor*" (Seibel, p. 202).

4. *Courier*, November 23, 1895, p. 7, in "The Literary Situation of 1895," Books and Authors (II), above.

5. Arthur Hobson Quinn, *American Fiction: An Historical and Critical Survey* (New York: D. Appleton-Century Co., 1936), pp. 356 ff.

Wilcox[6] had entered the field of "conscientious" literature, or that Marie Corelli had abandoned the *Sorrows of Satan* [1895] for those of realistic fiction. Ah, we thought we had been punished enough for ever having countenanced the psychological novel, but our real punishment is now, when the ladies have taken up the war cry. I suppose that Mrs. Atherton, whose fervid pen once labored solely in the interests of love and longing, now loses sleep over character development and comparative values and unity of structure and all the rest of it. I predict that Patty Thum, of the *Ladies' Home Journal*, will be the next convert to Art. Well for Ruth Ashmore that she did not live to see this day! Now that the ladies have left us, whither shall we turn for the old-fashioned love story in which they always married and flouted art? Who will now supply the pages of *Munsey's* and *Lippincott's?* It all reminds me of the experience of a certain emancipated lady, who wished Gautier's much-abused watchword, "L'Art Pour l'Art" engraved on her book plates. But the engraver was a good man and he had not read *Mademoiselle de Maupin*, and he turned out the book plates with the inscription, "L'Art Poor l'Art," which, by the way, would apply to many more books than Gautier's phrase. *The Daughter of the Vine* [1899], the "leading lady" of Mrs. Atherton's latest psychological novel, is a charming and gifted young woman addicted to an excessive use of intoxicants, and the hero is a young Englishman in quest of experiences. The scene, of course, is laid in San Francisco. . . .

Since she has openly avowed that her desire is to emulate Henry James, why does Mrs. Atherton select such hectic subjects? She should remember that Mr. James' men are never tempted to indecorously blow aside a wandering curl that hangs over a lady's forehead, no matter how disorderly the lady's hair or emotions may be, and that never, never, do Mr. James' men take down a lady's hair and put her hairpins in their pockets. Any James man would blush at the thought of such a deed. No more do Mr. James' ladies ever say, "We'll take this week off and do what we please, and then afterward this week won't count." That would be a convenient arrangement in life, but eventually it did count most fatally with the Daughter of the Vine. In the end she dies of alcoholism and requests to be buried by her child.

I remember a good while ago, before Mrs. Atherton went to England, before she ever dreamed of art or James, she wrote a story called *The*

6. Ella Wheeler Wilcox (1850–1919), author of *Poems of Passion* (1883) and of syndicated daily poems. Patty P. Thum (186?–1926), mentioned below, was a magazine illustrator.

Doomswoman [1892], which was fairly good of its kind. True, it was a pretty bad kind, the kind that summer hotel ladies term "light literature" and that schoolgirls keep hidden in their desks and weep over. Nevertheless it had some kind of coherent structure because it was spontaneous, and some sort of spirit because it was done without an ulterior purpose and was not an imitation. It was frankly "light" and did not try to be anything else; yet I remember it gave one a vivid impression of the wealth and vastness and variety of old California, and a striking, if not a true, picture of Spanish society. It was a story that, in spite of its faults and unsubstantialness, held your attention. Its exaggerations were a part of its author, and one can put up with them. I shall be greatly surprised if Mrs. Atherton ever does so well again. To be entertaining is something. But Mrs. Atherton can never make psychology even entertaining. "Not every man who saith unto me Art, Art! shall enter, etc." Art has done for Mrs. Atherton.

Leader, April 22, 1899, p. 5.

. . . To one who can take Ouida seriously, there is scarcely anything to say. It is like using perfumery or wearing Nethersole bracelets: There is no reform for it, no way to convince the perpetrator that it is in bad taste. Yet there are two sides to the Ouida question. Since George Sand, no woman has had such a vivid and brilliant fancy, such an active imagination, such running fluency of pen, or such untiring industry. And yet she scarcely deserves great credit for a passionate pursuit of what, to her, is not labor, but indulgence; not gestation, travail, but relief, a pleasurable exercise, a freedom from irksome restraint. . . .

But the core of the whole matter is this: That no one was ever less of an artist, that she is absolutely deaf and blind to niceties of form and color, and insensible to good craftsmanship in letters; that she never sacrificed or toned down one of her constantly-reiterated phrases to further the beauty of a passage, strengthen a situation, or advance the effectiveness of a story. She gives you absolutely everything that comes into her mind, good and bad; sometimes she gives it to you in excellent English, sometimes in the doubtful periods of the penny dreadful. She has wide information of a kind, but like many of these things that cover a great deal of ground, it is apt to be rather thin. She affects a knowledge of mythology as wide as that of Miss Lulu Glaser,[7] who I believe has written

7. Cather reviewed Lulu Glaser (1876–1958) in the comic opera *The Little Corporal* in the *Leader*, May 2, 1899, p. 2. Glaser also is mentioned in "Stage Celebrities Who Call Pittsburgh Home," Pittsburgh *Gazette*, March 2, 1902, p. 8.

a mythological dictionary, and she uses it with offensive liberality. Her *Ariadne* [1877] is full of display of this sort and of information and misinformation on Greek sculpture, dispensed with haughty assurance. To realize fully the garish superficiality of such work one has only to compare it with a masterpiece like George Moore's *Evelyn Innes* [1898], which deals understandingly with the art which is its central theme. Even the finer chapters of *Wanda* [1883] and *A Village Commune* [1881], which Mr. Ruskin so much admires, are spoiled by a lack of taste, true elegance, verbal precision and restraint, and marred by those debauches of the imagination in which she continually permits herself to indulge.

Even her best productions have only the vulgar display, the florid attractions of an over-dressed woman whose magnificence never quite conceals the fact that she is dowdy.

Yet nature was generous with her; she possessed many of the good mental qualities of George Sand, and all of the bad. She is seldom dull, never stupid, and she never makes a demand upon her untiring imagination that is not granted. She had a fine talent, but she spoiled it, and spoiled it utterly. It is impossible for any but schoolgirls and ribbon-counter ladies to take her seriously, and in the world of letters proper her name is spoken only in jest. . . .

Leader, June 17, 1899, p. 5.

A Creole *Bovary* is this little novel of Miss Chopin's. Not that the heroine is a Creole exactly, or that Miss Chopin is a Flaubert—save the mark!—but the theme is similar to that which occupied Flaubert. There was, indeed, no need that a second *Madame Bovary* should be written, but an author's choice of themes is frequently as inexplicable as his choice of a wife. It is governed by some innate temperamental bias that cannot be diagrammed. This is particularly so in women who write, and I shall not attempt to say why Miss Chopin has devoted so exquisite and sensitive, well-governed a style to so trite and sordid a theme. She writes much better than it is ever given to most people to write, and hers is a genuinely literary style; of no great elegance or solidity; but light, flexible, subtle, and capable of producing telling effects directly and simply. The story she has to tell in the present instance is new neither in matter nor treatment. Edna Pontellier, a Kentucky girl, who, like Emma Bovary, had been in love with innumerable dream heroes before she was out of short skirts, married Leonce Pontellier as a sort of reaction from a vague and visionary passion for a tragedian whose unresponsive picture she used to kiss. She acquired the habit of liking her husband in time, and even of liking her children. . . . At a Creole watering place, which is admirably and deftly sketched by Miss Chopin, Edna met Robert Lebrun, son of the landlady, who dreamed of a fortune awaiting him in Mexico while he occupied a petty clerical position in New Orleans. Robert made it his business to be agreeable to his mother's boarders, and Edna, not being a Creole, much against his wish and will, took him seriously. . . . The lover of course disappointed her, was a coward and ran away from his responsibilities before they began. He was afraid to begin a chapter with so serious and limited a woman. She remembered the sea where she had first met Robert. Perhaps from the same motive which threw Anna Karenina under the engine wheels, she threw herself into the sea, swam until she was tired and then let go. . . .

Edna Pontellier and Emma Bovary are studies in the same feminine type; one a finished and complete portrayal, the other a hasty sketch, but the theme is essentially the same. Both women belong to a class, not large, but forever clamoring in our ears, that demands more romance out of life than God put into it. Mr. G. Bernard Shaw would say that they are the victims of the over-idealization of love. They are the spoil of the poets, the Iphigenias of sentiment. The unfortunate feature of their disease is that it attacks only women of brains, at least of rudimentary brains, but whose development is one-sided; women of strong and fine intuitions, but without the faculty of observation, comparison, reasoning about things. Probably, for emotional people, the most convenient thing about being able to think is that it occasionally gives them a rest from feeling. Now with women of the Bovary type, this relaxation and recreation is impossible. They are not critics of life, but, in the most personal sense, partakers of life. They receive impressions through the fancy. With them everything begins with fancy, and passions rise in the brain rather than in the blood, the poor, neglected, limited one-sided brain that might do so much better things than badgering itself into frantic endeavors to love. For these are the people who pay with their blood for the fine ideals of the poets, as Marie Delclasse paid for Dumas' great creation, Marguerite Gauthier. These people really expect the passion of love to fill and gratify every need of life, whereas nature only intended that it should meet one of many demands. They insist upon making it stand for all the emotional pleasures of life and art; expecting an individual and self-limited passion to yield infinite variety, pleasure, and distraction, to contribute to their lives what the arts and the pleasurable exercise of the intellect gives to less limited and less intense idealists. So this passion, when set up against Shakespeare, Balzac, Wagner, Raphael, fails them. They have staked everything on one hand, and they lose. They have driven the blood until it will drive no further, they have played their nerves up to the point where any relaxation short of absolute annihilation is impossible. Every idealist abuses his nerves, and every sentimentalist brutally abuses them. And in the end, the nerves get even. Nobody ever cheats them, really. Then "the awakening" comes. Sometimes it comes in the form of arsenic, as it came to Emma Bovary, sometimes it is carbolic acid taken covertly in the police station, a goal to which unbalanced idealism not infrequently leads. Edna Pontellier, fanciful and romantic to the last, chose the sea on a summer night and went down with the sound of her first lover's spurs in her ears, and the scent of pinks about her. And next time I hope that Miss Chopin will devote that flexible, iridescent style of hers to a better cause.

Leader, July 8, 1899, p. 6.

It is now several years since this well-known actress [Clara Morris] began to contribute short stories to periodicals. Before that, she wrote only essays on dramatic art, and unusually clever ones they were. In so far as I can see, Miss Morris plays her new role much as she did all her old ones, with a sort of ferocious violence which at once repels and fascinates. She is as crude in her literary methods as in her dramatic ones, and as effective. These stories of hers [*A Silent Singer*] have little beauty of form, but they have force; no symmetry, but considerable power. Mentally, the woman was always strong. She had a message, and a message which could only be spoken in her own way. When she went to New York, a frail slip of a girl, with big burning eyes and a great talent over which she had no power of control, Augustin Daly, who always trained where he could, let this woman alone. He realized that the raw, fierce genius of her would win its own way, and that she must speak her message through the violent, erratic, unartistic medium that was natural to her. In her stories one recognizes the same power, the same lack of restraint, the same strange combination of shrewd humor and violence, above all one recognizes that old tendency of hers for probing the depths of physical and mental anguish. She is never content to suggest, she must say it all. In the poignant pathos of *A Silent Singer* one finds the same power to depict the most heart-breaking suffering that evinced itself in Miss Morris' *Camille* and *Leah* and *Article 47*. It is a sort of ungloved method of attack, a tendency to lay bare the horrible and painful which amounts almost to a mania. The effectiveness with which Miss Morris does all this is evidence of her sincerity, but it is an unfortunate and a misdirected power. To use a pretty phrase of Stevenson's, it "sins against the modesty of life." There are certain extremes of all emotions over which it is well to draw a veil, certain paroxysms of pain, of which it is not best to speak. But Miss Morris never was known to let any detail of agony escape her. Hers was a realism which knew not suggestion. She could never understand that it is only the thing of beauty which is a joy forever. The artist proper cultivates method to save himself, he makes his brain work, and learns to cherish and guard his emotional force. Miss Morris either could not, or would not, learn this; she burned the wick; and she burned it out quickly. She was a physical wreck when she should have been in her prime. Her violence wore her out, like the mill that grinds itself to pieces. Now, in an exhausted body, the old fierce soul of other days is still rampant, and she is seeking to let it out by a new channel. And behold! in her stories are the same faults and the same power that she displayed on the stage. . . .

Leader, July 15, 1899, p. 9.

Stephen Crane and Frank Norris

Willa Cather had an encounter with Stephen Crane (1871–1900) in Lincoln in February 1895,[8] *but she did not make a significant mention of him in her columns until she reviewed his volume of poems* War Is Kind *(1899). Herself kind only to the title poem, which she quoted in full, Cather wrote acidly of "Intrigue," an admittedly inferior group of poems,*[9] *from which she drew most of the examples for her criticism. The ironic and satirical* Active Service *by Crane and the lyrical* Blix *by Frank Norris (both published in 1899) were based on the writers' experiences as newspapermen: Crane as a war correspondent and Norris as a reporter in San Francisco. In* Blix *Cather found proof that Norris was fulfilling his early promise (see Books and Authors [III], above).*

This truly remarkable book [*War Is Kind*] is printed on dirty gray blotting paper, on each page of which is a mere dot of print over a large I of vacancy. There are seldom more than ten lines on a page, and it would be better if most of those lines were not there at all. Either Mr. Crane is

8. See "When I Met Stephen Crane," The *Library*, below. See also *KA*, pp. 19–20 for the circumstances of Crane's visit to Nebraska.

9. Joseph Katz, Introduction to *The Poems of Stephen Crane* (New York: Cooper Square Publishers, Inc., 1966), p. xlix.

insulting the public or insulting himself, or he has developed a case of atavism and is chattering the primeval nonsense of the apes. His *Black Riders*, uneven as it was, was a casket of polished masterpieces when compared with *War Is Kind*. And it is not kind at all, Mr. Crane, when it provokes such verses as these—it is all that Sherman said it was.

The only production in the volume that is at all coherent is the following, from which the book gets its title:

Do not weep, maiden, for war is kind, . . .

Of course, one may have objections to hearts hanging like humble buttons, or to buttons being humble at all, but one should not stop to quarrel about such trifles with a poet who can perpetrate the following:

Thou art my love,
And thou art the beard
On another man's face—
Woe is me.[10]

Now, if you please, is the object of these verses animal, mineral or vegetable? Is the expression, "Thou art the beard on another man's face," intended as a figure, or was it written by a barber? Certainly, after reading this, "Simple Simon" is a ballade of perfect form, and "Jack and Jill" or "Hickity, Pickity, My Black Hen," are exquisite lyrics. But of the following what shall be said:

Now let me crunch you
With full weight of affrighted love. . . .

This is somewhat more lucid as evincing the bard's exquisite sensitiveness:

Ah, God, the way your little finger moved
As you thrust a bare arm backward. . . .

Mr. Crane's verselets are illustrated by some Bradley pictures, which are badly drawn, in bad taste, and come with bad grace. On page 33 of the book there are just two lines which seem to completely sum up the efforts of both poet and artist:

"My good friend," said a learned bystander,
"Your operations are mad."

10. Quoted here were stanzas 6, 7, and 8 of "Intrigue," *Poems of Stephen Crane*, p. 111. Quoted below were, in this order, stanzas 18 and 19 of "Intrigue" (p. 114), stanza 21 of "Intrigue" (p. 115), and lines 7 and 8 of "Forth Went the Candid Man" (p. 90).

Yet this fellow Crane has written short stories equal to some of Maupassant's.

Leader, June 3, 1899, p. 6.

If you want to read a story that is all wheat and no chaff, read *Blix*. Last winter that brilliant young Californian, Mr. Norris, published a remarkable and gloomy novel, *McTeague*, a book deep in insight, rich in promise and splendid in execution, but entirely without charm and as disagreeable as only a great piece of work can be. And now this gentleman, who is not yet thirty, turns around and gives us an idyll that sings through one's brain like a summer wind and makes one feel young enough to commit all manner of indiscretions. It may be that Mr. Norris is desirous of showing us his versatility and that he can follow any suit, or it may have been a process of reaction. I believe it was after M. Zola had completed one of his greatest and darkest novels of Parisian life that he went down to the seaside and wrote *Le Rêve*, a book that every girl should read when she is eighteen, and then again when she is eighty. Powerful and solidly built as *McTeague* is, one felt that their method was carried almost too far, that Mr. Norris was too consciously influenced by his French masters. But *Blix* belongs to no school whatever, and there is not a shadow of pedantry or pride of craft in it from cover to cover. Blix herself is the method, the motive and the aim of the book. The story is an exhalation of youth and spring; it is the work of a man who breaks loose and forgets himself. Mr. Norris was married only last summer, and the march from *Lohengrin* is simply sticking out all over *Blix*. It is the story of a San Francisco newspaperman and a girl. The newspaperman "came out" in fiction, so to speak, in the drawing room of Mr. Richard Harding Davis, and has languished under that gentleman's chaperonage until he has come to be regarded as a fellow careful of nothing but his toilet and his dinner. Mr. Davis' reporters all bathed regularly and all ate nice things, but beyond that their tastes were rather colorless. I am glad to see one red-blooded newspaperman, in the person of Condy Rivers, of San Francisco, break into fiction; a real live reporter with no sentimental loyalty for his "paper," and no Byronic poses about his vices, and no astonishing taste about his clothes, and no money whatever, which is the natural and normal condition of all reporters. Blix herself was just a society girl, and Condy took her to theatres and parties and tried to make himself believe he was in love with her. But it wouldn't work, for Condy couldn't love a society girl, not though she were as beautiful as the morning and terrible as an army with banners, and had "round full arms," and "the skin of her face was white and clean, except where it flushed into a most charming pink upon her smooth, cool cheeks." For while Condy Rivers was at college he had been seized with the penchant for writing short stories, and he worshiped at the shrines of Maupassant and Kipling, and when a man is craft-mad enough to worship Maupassant truly and know him well, when he has that tingling for technique in his fingers, not Aphrodite herself, new risen from the waves, could tempt him into any world where craft was not lord and king. So it happened that their real love affair never began until one morning when Condy had to go down to the wharf to write up a whaleback, and Blix went along, and an old sailor told them a story and Blix recognized the literary possibilities of it, and they had lunch in a Chinese restaurant, and Condy because he was a newspaperman and it was the end of the week, didn't have any change about his clothes, and Blix had to pay the bill. And it was in that green old teahouse that Condy read Blix one of his favorite yarns by Kipling, and she in a calm, offhanded way, recognized one of the fine, technical points in it, and Condy almost went to pieces for joy of her doing it. That scene in the Chinese restaurant is one of the prettiest bits of color you'll find to rest your eyes upon, and mighty good writing it is. I wonder, though if when Mr. Norris adroitly mentioned the "clack and snarl" of the banjo Condy played, he remembered the "silver snarling trumpets" of Keats? After that, things went on as such things will, and Blix quit the society racket and went to queer places with Condy, and got interested in his work, and she broke him of wearing red neckties and playing poker, and she made him work, she did, for she grew to realize how much that meant to him, and she jacked him up when he didn't work, and she suggested an ending for one of his stories that was better than his own; just this big, splendid girl, who had never gone to college to learn how to write novels. And so how, in the name of goodness, could he help loving her? So one morning down by the Pacific, with Blix and *The Seven Seas*, it all came over Condy, that "living was better than reading and life was better than literature." And so it is; once, and only once, for each of us; and that is the tune that sings and sings through one's head when one puts the book away.

Courier, January 13, 1900, pp. 2–3.

After reading such a delightful newspaper story as Mr. Frank Norris' *Blix*, it is with assorted sensations of pain and discomfort that one closes the covers of another newspaper novel, *Active Service*, by Stephen Crane. If one happens to have some trifling regard for pure English, he does not come forth from the reading of this novel unscathed. The hero of this lurid tale is a newspaperman, and he edits the Sunday edition of the New York *Eclipse*, and delights in publishing "stories" about deformed and sightless infants. "The office of the 'Eclipse' was at the top of an immense building on Broadway. It was a sheer mountain to the heights of which the interminable thunder of the streets rose faintly. The Hudson was a broad path of silver in the distance." This leaves little doubt as to the fortunate journal[11] which had secured Rufus Coleman as its Sunday editor. Mr. Coleman's days were spent in collecting yellow sensations for his paper, and we are told that he "planned for each edition as for a campaign." . . .

[Coleman, who has just been jilted by his sweetheart, takes his mind off his troubles by playing poker and going on a bender. Willa Cather quotes passages describing these activities.]

The atmosphere of the entire novel is just that close and enervating. Every page is like the next morning taste of a champagne supper, and is heavy with the smell of stale cigarettes. There is no fresh air in the book and no sunlight, only the "blinding light shed by the electric globes." If the life of New York newspapermen is as unwholesome and sordid as this, Mr. Crane, who has experienced it, ought to be sadly ashamed to tell it. . . .

After this Coleman went to Greece to write up the war for the *Eclipse*, and incidentally to rescue his sweetheart from the hands of the Turks and make "copy" of it.[12] Very valid arguments might be advanced that the lady would have fared better with the Turks. On the voyage Coleman spent all his days and nights in the card room and avoided the deck, since

11. The New York *World*, for which Crane worked.

12. The reference here is to the war between Turkey and Greece in 1897, which Cather—in a review of *Going to War in Greece* by Frederick Palmer (1873–1958)—described as "this *opera buffa* war in which the soldiers gave more attention to the polish on their boots than to the condition of their fortifications." The review continued: "It is interesting to compare this narrative of the last Greek war against the Orientals with Herodotus' account of the revolt of Hellas against eastern despotism twenty-four centuries ago. Yet the scene was the same: this miserable travesty was brought out on the stage where men had played the roles of demigods and history herself became inspired. As Victor Hugo said of the *coup d'état* under Napoleon III: 'It was a farce—after a tragedy.' One can but hope that the graves of the three hundred at Thermopylae are deep, and that the Turkish artillery awoke no echoes in the underworld. In that pass the glory of Greece was born, and there, after twenty-four centuries, she touched the bottom of national dishonor" (*Leader*, March 4, 1898, p. 8).

fresh air was naturally disagreeable to him. For all that he saw of Greece or that Mr. Crane's readers see of Greece Coleman might as well have stayed in the card room of the steamer, or in the card room of his New York hotel for that matter. Wherever he goes he carries the atmosphere of the card room with him and the "blinding glare of the electrics." In Greece he makes love when he has leisure, but he makes "copy" much more ardently, and on the whole is quite as lurid and sordid and showy as his worst Sunday editions. Some good bits of battle descriptions there are, of *The Red Badge of Courage* order, but one cannot make a novel of clever descriptions of earthworks and poker games. The book concerns itself not with large, universal interests or principles, but with a yellow journalist grinding out yellow copy in such a wooden fashion that the Sunday *Eclipse* must have been even worse than most. In spite of the fact that Mr. Crane has written some of the most artistic short stories in the English language, I begin to wonder whether, blinded by his youth and audacity, two qualities that the American people love, we have not taken him too seriously. It is a grave matter for a man in good health and with a bank account to have written a book so coarse and dull and charmless as *Active Service*. Compared with this "War was kind," indeed.

Leader, November 11, 1899, p. 9.

Yeats and Housman

Willa Cather's first published book was to be a volume of poetry, but she brought out few poems between 1896, when four appeared in the Home Monthly, *and 1900, when more than a dozen came out, most of them in the* Library.[13] *Nor did she often review poetry in "Books and Magazines." The following review of* Wind Among the Reeds *(1899) by William Butler Yeats (1865–1939) ran in the same column with the review of Crane's* War Is Kind *(see above). The appearance of the second American edition of* A Shropshire Lad *gave Cather an opportunity to write at length on A. E. Housman, whose poems she had discovered (see "Old Books and New [October 1897]," The* Home Monthly, *above). Her interest in the poet led her to visit Shropshire on her first trip to England (see "Out of the Beaten Track," The European Scene, below).*

Mr. Yeats' verse purports to have some very close and involved connection with Celtic mythology, such an important and mystic connection

13. See *AT* (*1903*), pp. 78–80.

indeed that while there are only sixty-five pages of poetry, there are forty-three pages of notes. Now unless actuated by promptings of duty or business necessity, I would never read, or even begin to read, a volume of poetry with forty-three pages of notes, nor do I care to study Celtic myths in verse. Poetry that has to be explained, by its author's own confession usually would be as well unwritten. If a young man wishes to devote himself to folklore or etymology, he had better forswear the flowery paths of poetry. "All poetry," said William Watson,[14] "is merely a love-confession." It is certainly not an exposition of the researches of folklore students or of ethnological hypotheses. Even with Browning, erudition was but a means, an incidental, a store of richness gathered unconsciously, lavished unsparingly.

But in spite of his notes and the fact that Mr. Yeats is probably an ethnologist, he can write real poetry. The following[15] is, I think, the best in the book, because it relates an experience of the heart, illumines a little the comedy of life, and can be read without notes by the simplest, for this particular fool was not the first who, having given his heart and soul, "honor and faith and a sure intent," bethought him to spend the pitiful tricks of his craft, which he had deemed unworthy, and through them has won. . . .

Leader, June 3, 1899, p. 6.

There is nothing so unmistakable as a true poem; there is nothing over which the conventions of men and the laws of the schools have so little control as poetry. There is no art in which ambition and effort and culture count for so little. This is peculiarly exemplified in a recent volume of verse by that eminent scholar and critic, Mr. George E. Woodberry.[16] This volume contains many ideas set forth in verse, many musical lines, but not one poem. It is not within the power of any man to attain unto poetry by much labor or wide learning or faultless taste. A man can no more write a poem by mastering poetics than a botanist can make a rose, or an astronomer fashion a star. Even true poets do not always write true poetry. The true poem is and must remain largely a happy accident, and the gift of the man who writes it is accidental, unquestionable. And about

14. William Watson (1858–1935), English poet, best known for his "Lacrymae Musarum" on the death of Tennyson, in his *Collected Poems* (1899) and for *Excursions in Criticism* (1893).

15. "The Cap and Bells," quoted in full.

16. *Wild Eden* (1899) by George E. Woodberry, at this time professor of literature at Columbia University. Woodberry taught at the University of Nebraska in 1877–1878 and 1880–1882.

this gift there is a mystery so impenetrable and so beyond the range of our analysis that it has among all peoples, even the most skeptical, been accounted as a certain touch of divinity in man. In all other arts perfect execution and complete mastery of form insure a large measure of success, but a man either is a poet or he is not. Burns, who was a plowman, might make poetry, Mr. Woodberry, who is a scholar, may not. This is as far as we are enlightened on the matter.

Some three years ago an Englishman calling himself simply A. E. Housman published a volume of lyrics which carried the hallmark of true poetry. Their quality is as unmistakable as it is rare. I do not know who Mr. Housman is, but I know that he is a poet. I have sought far and wide for some information concerning this man, and have been unable to obtain even the most meager. Miss Louise Imogen Guiney[17] has tried to locate him and has met with no better success. I have decided to let him remain a literary mystery and the theme of many imaginings. He called his single little volume of verse *A Shropshire Lad*. The lyrics composing it bear no titles, but there seems to be a vague sort of plot running through them all, binding them together. They might be grouped under two general headings; songs of Shropshire, and songs of exile. It seems that Mr. Housman was once a Shropshire lad himself, and that there were many lads there who fished and danced at the fair and worked in the fields and were staunch comrades and true. Then the lassies began to figure in their lives and there was trouble a-brewing. Ah! such sad endings they came to, those merry Shropshire lads, and to what dark havens and down what black streams were they borne, those gay crafts that put out into the Severn tide in the gladsome morning. One lad, an athlete, died young, before the laurel of his triumphs had withered, and his sweetheart married his best friend. One killed his brother by the haystack and was hanged in Shrewsbury jail. . . .

Another of the Shropshire boys went into the army, and fell into some black disgrace and shot himself, and still another, the singer of these Shropshire songs, wandered to London town and dwelt there in a comfortless exile. . . . [Miss Cather here included poem LII, "Far in the western brookland"—"that is true poetry, and there is a touch as genuine as Heine's, an expression simple, complete, perfect; a mood, a personality, a

17. Louise Imogen Guiney (1861–1920) gave the first important American review to *A Shropshire Lad* in the *Chap-Book*, February 1, 1897, pp. 245–246. In an omitted portion of this review, Cather remarked parenthetically of Miss Guiney: "And ah! what songs she has sung herself, that sad, little New England woman." See also "Poets of Our Younger Generation," The *Gazette*, below.

lifetime in sixteen short lines." It was followed by poem XVI, "Look not in my eyes," which "Mrs. Ethelbert Nevin had me copy in her own edition of Mr. Nevin's 'Narcissus.'"]

For exquisite grace of form and delicacy of fancy I scarcely know its equal. This is Mr. Housman's first volume of poetry, but he seems to have learned the important thing at the beginning. There is not one lyric in the collection which has not this absolute genuineness. This Shropshire lad has an existence in literature as actual and indisputable as Childe Harold's. This homesick boy is one of the dwellers on Helicon. But hear him further, and at his best:[18]

> On your midnight pallet lying,
>   Listen, and undo the door!
> Lads that waste the light in sighing
>   In the dark should sigh no more. . . .

That is what it means to write poetry; to be able to say the oldest thing in the world as though it had never been said before, to make the old wounds of us all bleed fresh, to give a new voice to the *Weltschmerz*, that, perhaps, is the most exalted lyric of the entire collection. Yet he can be as light as he is sad:

> When I was one and twenty
>   I heard a wise man say:
> "Give crowns and pounds and guineas,
>   But not your heart away. . . ."

But after all, it is the homesick songs that I love the best:

> 'Tis time, I think, by Wenlock town
>   The golden broom should blow;
> The hawthorne, sprinkled up and down,
>   Should charge the land with snow. . . .

Here is another, exquisite as it is brief:

> The winds out of the west land blow,
>   My friends have breathed them there;
> Warm with the blood of the lads I know
>   Comes east the sighing air. . . .

18. The column was virtually a Housman sampler, including here and below verses from, respectively, poems XI, XIII, XXXIV, and XXXVIII of *A Shropshire Lad*.

Sometimes I wonder whether this man is old or young, whether these verses are the first output of youth and loneliness, or whether they are the slow secretions of long, lonely, dreamful years, the cry of an unhappiness that has well nigh exhausted the singer's life; whether he will have more to say, or whether, having told of his solitude, he will be silent, and in this volume has given his whole heart. Well, if he should never be heard from again, there is more poetry in this little book than in any half-dozen volumes of contemporary verse I know of. Again I wonder who and what this man Housman may be. But at least I know that he has eaten the bitter bread of exile, and trod the hostile streets of great cities and hungered for the little village where he was a boy and suffered in the lives of the lads he knew in the years agone and died in their dead. I know that he has dwelt among thousands more solitary than the last man will be, that he has tramped the desert of brick and stone and seen such monstrous distortions of life that he has wept for the west wind and the brown fields and the quiet country stars. And in so far, many of us are his brothers in exile. I only hope that he too, at last, has found how delightful companionship is after loneliness, and how kind Destiny can be in the way least looked for, and how much better life can be than song; that that has come to him which can make exile sweet and rob distance of its weary pain and set the maddening tramp in the streets to music; that an infinite kindness has made him forget the long, black loneliness of those first London years, and that in eyes that look summer into his he sees his Shropshire skies again, and once again believes in life a little.

Courier, March 10, 1900, pp. 2–3.

Harold Frederic

After eight years on the Albany Evening Journal, *Harold Frederic (1856–1898) was the London correspondent for the New York* Times *from 1884 until his death. Frederic, a Christian Scientist, suffered a paralytic stroke that proved fatal, partly because he refused medical help. His novels and stories were set in New York and London.* The Damnation of Theron Ware, *among the best sellers of 1896, had a New York background;* March Hares *(1896)*, Gloria Mundi *(1898), and* The Market Place, *a best seller of 1899, were set in London. The latter is reviewed below.*

Unusual interest is attached to the posthumous work of that great man whose career ended so prematurely and so tragically. The story is a study in the ethics and purposes of money-getting, in the romantic element in modern business. In it finance is presented not as being merely the province of shrewdness, or greediness, or petty personal gratification, but of great projects, of great brain-battles, a field for the exercising of talent, daring, imagination, appealing to the strength of a strong man, filling the same place in men's lives that was once filled by the incentives of war, kindling in man the desire for the leadership of men. The hero of the story, Joel Thorpe, is one of those men, huge of body, keen of brain, with cast-iron nerves, as sound of heart as most men, and a magnificent capacity for bluff. He has lived and risked and lost in a dozen countries, been almost within reach of fortune a dozen times, and always missed her until, finally, in London, by promoting a great rubber syndicate he becomes a multi-millionaire. He marries the most beautiful and one of the most impecunious peeresses in England and retires to his country estate. There, as a gentleman of leisure, he loses his motive in life, loses power for lack of opportunity, and grows less commanding even in the eyes of his wife, who misses the uncompromising, barbaric strength which took her by storm and won her. Finally he evolves a gigantic philanthropic scheme of spending his money as laboriously as he made it. . . .

It is very fitting that Mr. Frederic's last book should be in praise of action, the thing that makes the world go round; of force, however mis-spent, which is the sum of life as distinguished from the inertia of death. In the forty-odd years of his life he wrote almost as many pages as Balzac, most of it mere newspaper copy, it is true, read and forgotten, but all of it vigorous and with the stamp of a strong man upon it. And he played just as hard as he worked—alas, it was the play that killed him! The young artist who illustrated the story gave to the pictures of Joel Thorpe very much the look of Harold Frederic himself, and they might almost stand for his portraits. I fancy the young man did not select his model carelessly. In this big, burly adventurer who took fortune and women by storm, who bluffed the world by his prowess and fought his way to the front with battle-axe blows, there is a great deal of Harold Frederic, the soldier of fortune, the Utica milk boy who fought his way from the petty slavery of a provincial newspaper to the foremost ranks of the journalists of the world and on into literature, into literature worth the writing. The man won his place in England much as his hero won his, by defiance, by strong shoulder blows, by his self-sufficiency and inexhaustible strength, and when he finished his book he did not know that his end would be so much less glorious than his hero's, that it would be his portion not to fall manfully in the thick of the combat and the press of battle, but to die poisoned in the tent of Chryseis. For who would foresee a tragedy so needless, so blind, so brutal in its lack of dignity, or know that such strength could perish through such insidious weakness, that so great a man could be stung to death by a mania born in little minds?

In point of execution and literary excellence, both *The Market Place* and *Gloria Mundi* are vastly inferior to *The Damnation of Theron Ware*, or that exquisite London idyl, *March Hares*. The first two hundred pages of *Theron Ware* are as good as anything in American fiction, much better than most of it. They are not so much the work of a literary artist as of a vigorous thinker, a man of strong opinions and an intimate and comprehensive knowledge of men. The whole work, despite its irregularities and indifference to form, is full of brain-stuff, the kind of active, healthful, masterful intellect that some men put into politics, some into science and a few, a very few, into literature. Both *Gloria Mundi* and *The Market Place* bear unmistakable evidences of the slack rein and the hasty hand. Both of them contain considerable padding, the stamp of the space writer. They are imperfectly developed, and are not packed with ideas like his earlier novels. Their excellence is in flashes; it is not the searching, evenly distributed light which permeates his more careful work. There were, as we know too well, good reasons why Mr. Frederic should work hastily. He needed a large income and he worked heroically, writing many thousands of words a day to obtain it. From the experience of the ages we have learned to expect to find, coupled with great strength, a proportionate weakness, and usually it devours the greater part, as the seven lean kine devoured the seven fat in Pharaoh's vision. Achilles was a god in all his nobler parts, but his feet were of the earth and to the earth they held him down, and he died stung by an arrow in the heel.

Leader, June 10, 1899, p. 5.

Richard Whiteing's No. 5 John Street

Richard Whiteing (1840–1928), English journalist and editor, resigned from the London Daily News *when his second novel became a best seller of 1899. The success of* No. 5 John Street *led to the reissue of his first novel,* The Island *(1888), which Willa Cather reviewed in the* Leader, *December 2, 1899: "The writing is quite as remarkable as that in* No. 5 John Street, *and indeed it rather gives one a turn to come upon pregnant, solidly built sentences like these nowadays when slipshod English seems to satisfy everyone. It is a luxury to recognize the hand of a scholar and a thinker in type,*

> *and to note that ideas still have a place in literature, as they did in the days of Amiel and Carlyle. Mr. Whiteing, by his gift of penetration beneath the shell of things, his weird second sight into the awesome mystery of things which have lost their poignant meaning to the rest of us through their commonplaceness, not infrequently recalls the Carlyle of* Sartor Resartus; *a Carlyle somewhat tamed, as it were, got up in respectable evening dress, with his rampant locks smoothed, and redeemed from his habit of breaking the furniture, of swearing in German.*"

This book, I fancy, is one of the few permanent contributions to literature that the year has produced. It is seldom enough that one encounters a book that carries one along from page to page by the pure excellence of its literary form, by its grace and novelty of fancy, its richness of illustration, its aptness and nicety of expression, the coherence and force with which its theme is developed. Socialistic studies in the guise of fiction are usually unattractive, not infrequently dishonest, and almost never have they anything new to say. Usually they falter with painful indecision between the theme and the plot, and introduce a fragile and superfluous love story at the expense of sociology. Mr. Whiteing's story is the personal narrative of a man of fortune who voluntarily accepts the life of the extremely poor in a swarming metropolitan region, lives their life without knowledge of any of his friends, and in complete disguise, as a wage-earner. After he takes up his residence at Number 5, John Street, he lives with the people. He cultivates them in a kindlier and more human sense than as mere sociological studies, draws them so close to him that they become to him and to the reader not studies, but real folk of the real world, of the most real of worlds, indeed, with a convincing actualness of speech and manner and the blessed warmth of blood in them. Mr. Whiteing handles these people in the only satisfactory way possible, which is to say that he does not "handle" them at all. He thinks of them, feels for them, knows them, lives with them, until one feels that here is an explorer who has gone into that dark interior of the lost half of civilization, who did not leave his heart behind. He tabulates not at all; gives no statistics, makes no cold-blooded observations, offers no theories, draws no conclusions. Mr. Walter Wycoff,[19] indeed, made a conscientious tour into this Darkest Africa, and slept in unpleasant places and ate ill-tasting things and inhaled

19. Walter Wycoff (1865–1908) taught political economy at Princeton. *The Workers—East* (1897) and *The Workers—West* (1898) were the result of socioeconomic study while he was an itinerant worker for eighteen months.

bad odors for a worthy object. His observations will be valuable to sociologists, but when all is said they are but stiff-necked, colorless reports, thorough and conscientious, but with no more life in them than a college thesis on "Our Vagrant Classes." Like Mr. Richard Harding Davis' account of the Cuban war, they have a certain supercilious air of the man who stood off afar and watched the battle and suffered because his linen was not clean. This may be because Mr. Wycoff is merely a student and a sociologist and not a poet, and because he received his impressions wholly through his cerebral apparatus. Nobody yet ever knew anything thoroughly through study, much less are they able to adequately impart that knowledge by a purely intellectual process. To know anything about any class of people, one must ascertain how and what they feel, and to do that one must not only observe but feel himself, and that is what it never occurred to Mr. Walter Wycoff to do. The sculptures on the old Egyptian monuments of the slaves who drew water and fed the oxen and ploughed the rice fields and quarried sandstone six thousand years ago are quite as instructive and quite as much alive as his "Workers." But in *No. 5 John Street*, we enter a different world, an actual world which comes close to us, because a man who has that touch of nature that makes all worlds akin reveals it to us, and because he speaks in the common tongue of pain and pleasure and joy and sorrow, which is the same in John Street and in Piccadilly. Through the doorway of a rare and exalted idealism we enter here upon a kind of realism that is real indeed. After all, in art imagination is the only verity, and the poet is more reliable than the statistician. Only a literary artist can tell the truth by means of literature, just as only a painter can tell the truth with colors. That is why most socialistic novels, written by sociologists, are barren and unconvincing. The student may arrange his facts ever so carefully, and yet the ensemble of his work may mislead, just as the painter may take all his measurements and yet paint a lie. But, as Browning wrote long ago:

> This is the glory and the good of art,
> That art remain the one way possible of speaking truth. . . .[20]

This Mr. Whiteing recalls *Sartor Resartus* more than once, and the reflections of his hero are not unlike the musings of Teufelsdrochk when he saw humanity weltering beneath him like a pot of Egyptian vipers, each trying to get its head above the others, while he [was?] above it all, "alone with the stars." Yet Mr. Whiteing is not content with idealizing

20. *The Ring and the Book*, Part XII, ll. 841–843. *Works of Robert Browning*, VI, 321.

and fancifying; he goes down and sweats and welters with his kind, and he is not afraid of the sordid details of the life he pictures. He knows the tragedy of environment. . . .

Perhaps it is only in John Street that real friendship is possible. About two years ago a workman at Homestead fell into a live cinder pit, disabling his back in the fall. A friend of his, who was a workman like himself, jumped in after him and stood up to his knees in the burning cinders holding his friend's body in his arms until a ladder reached them. He has not walked since. Somehow one would like to live in a society where things like that happen, even if the people ate onions and bathed infrequently. There are some of us tired enough of the world we live in to go to this man who has lived in John Street and to ask him to take us there.

Leader, June 17, 1899, p. 5.

George Borrow and William Knapp

In 1895 William Knapp (1835–1908), professor of Romance Languages at the University of Chicago, resigned to go to Europe to complete his two-volume work, George Borrow: Life and Correspondence. *Borrow (1803–1881) had traveled for the Bible Society in Russia, Spain, Portugal, and Morocco studying languages, especially Romany. One result was a travel book,* The Bible in Spain *(1843). It was followed by his famous romance,* Lavengro: The Scholar, the Gipsy, the Priest *(1851) and its sequel,* The Romany Rye *(1857).*

. . . With the notable exception of Edgar Allan Poe, no character in literature is more difficult to treat biographically than Borrow. Only a man sharing Borrow's enthusiasms, understanding his taste for wild life, and able to fully appreciate the marvels of his versatile and voracious, if somewhat slovenly scholarship, could at all comprehend a life governed by such fierce intellectual passions, or mete out to him that justice which is the prime essential of effectual biography. George Borrow has been to Prof. Knapp all that Turner was to Ruskin, all that the prophet is to the disciple or the hero to the hero-worshiper. This monograph of two volumes is actually and literally the work of a lifetime. Knapp was, at the outset, that rare combination, a gypsy and a scholar. Like Borrow, he had the faculty for easily acquiring multifarious tongues and dialects, and a feeling of brotherhood with all wild, wandering peoples. And he had a third mania as strong as either of these; an overwhelming desire to sift the thousand and one lies that enshrouded the memory of the author of *The*

Bible in Spain, to brush aside the mists of years and to see and know the real George Borrow. He spent fifty patient years collecting from the four quarters of the earth Borrow's manuscripts, letters, notebooks, and the scattered remains of his library. For fifty years he has gathered and weighed the evidence pro and con in the case of George Borrow. He has followed the trail of Borrow's wanderings, learned the tongues and gypsy gibberish that Borrow loved. With sleuth-like persistency and the constancy of a shadow he has followed, every inch of the way, the path of that involved and mysterious career, jumping from one quarter of the globe to another, ferreting out the trails that Borrow himself carefully covered, until he has actually wrested its secrets from a heart that is dust. Such monomanias fortunately do not occur often, and fortunately do occur sometimes. Prof. Knapp has held various professorships, among them one at Yale and one at the University of Chicago, which latter he gave up to [go to] Norfolk, and write Borrow's biography in Borrow's own atmosphere. I fancy that most of the professor went into his hobby, however, and that after fifty years he gives us, in these two volumes, his own life along with that of George Borrow. After all, there is nothing in the world much more awe-inspiring than the consecration of the scholar—nor much more pathetic. It reaches heights that the cloth never dreams of. Occasional instances of devotion of this sort give us comforting reassurance that the enthusiasms of youth sometimes outlast the morning, and that not every man forgets the star that called him and settles down to tend pigs with Audrey.[21] In his youth Mr. Knapp's imagination—sometimes even professors do have it—was ensnared by that most romantic figure in letters, that gypsy, polyglot, adventurer, scholar, trickster, that passionless Byron of scholars who posed by instinct and wore the masque and buskin from choice. He was a brilliant figure, that Borrow, and well calculated to reign in a young scholar's fancy. But here at the end of fifty years, behold Mr. Knapp as enamoured of his hero as ever and only drawn the closer to him by the vigils and journeys and appalling labor which he has incurred for his sake. And I doubt not that as when Jacob served for Rachel, the fifty years "seemed to him but a few days, for the love he had for him." The madness of the scholar, the madness of the poet, the madness of the lover—for these there is no cure but death, say the Japanese.

The outcome of Mr. Knapp's lifelong enthusiasm, is one of the most valuable biographies that has been written in recent years, and a work that

21. For another use of the Endymion-Audrey allusion, see "*The Devil's Disciple*," The Theatre (III), above.

will take its place beside Sidney Lee's *Shakespeare*,[22] though its merits are of a very different order. It is not a critique, it is a reconstruction; "George Borrow, restored by William Knapp." There is scarcely a paragraph of literary criticism, analytical or appreciative, in the work. Mr. Knapp simply fits together all the disjointed, contradictory data about this man, carefully testing every stone. He builds up his life again year by year, and leaves the summarizing to the Borrovians. Next to its exhaustiveness, the most remarkable feature about his work is its accuracy and merciless veracity. In spite of his avowed devotion to Borrow, his methods are the impartial, unsparing methods of a scientist. He evades nothing, he palliates nothing. He exposes and throws aside the romances which Borrow told about himself, as well as those that other people told about him. . . .

Even more interesting than the adventurous career of George Borrow, and the luxuriant stage settings of the Alhambras and fountains and Spanish nights which he insisted upon having about him, I find this strange Frankenstein of a biographer, who is both hero-worshiper and vivisectionist, cynic and enthusiast, and who, having devoted almost an entire lifetime to an impassioned study of one man, proceeds to laugh at him through a good share of seven hundred pages, and seems to derive a droll amusement from all his eccentricities and infirmities. Certainly the professor has himself well in hand, and he does not thrust his own sentiments down your throat. He practically admits that Borrow used the Bible Society as a means to his own end, and rather suggests that the Bible Society should have felt honored at being used for an end so creditable. It is, indeed, quite probable that the Bible Society did more for the world in providing an income for George Borrow than it has ever done before or since. In so doing it enabled him to write ten books invaluable to English prose, and great stylists are scarce enough anywhere in the world, and particularly scarce in Bible societies. . . .

Although Mr. Knapp's personal enthusiasm for Borrow is so great, it would be erroneous to convey the idea that his biography of him is in any sense a sentimental one. Indeed, it is singularly barren of sentiment and rhetoric, and is written in the terse, cold language of a scientist rather than in the florid phrases of an appreciation. Biographies of the newer school, indeed, are not so much inclined to idealism and to indulging in personal impressions as those of fifty years ago. They read more like a botanist's series of notes on the growth of a plant than like the vivid portraitures of Carlyle and Macaulay. Carlyle usually thought it necessary to

22. Sidney Lee (1859–1926), editor of the *Dictionary of National Biography* and author of *A Life of William Shakespeare* (1898).

realize a character completely, and went about it much as an actor does when he creates a character for the stage. And like most actors, he only succeeded in projecting himself into the part in hand. In his Cromwell, in Mohammed, in Burns, in Dante, we find only phases of Thomas Carlyle. Mr. Knapp, on the other hand, gives only the scenario of the drama, and leaves each of us to create the character for ourselves. But what a brilliant scenario it is! That mysterious gypsy-scholar who never seemed quite of this world, now starving like Chatterton in London, trying to earn his bread by verse writing; now among the frozen steppes of Russia, now in the oleander gardens of Spain, now on the wild hills of Wales. . . .

Then began his period of active literary production, the least interesting and most fruitful period of his life. Mr. [Edmund] Gosse somewhere remarks that men who have lived and felt up to the limit of human capacity are usually men who are wholly unable to reproduce their experiences in ink. François Coppée, hinting at the same thought, says that a poet's life consists of ink and reams of paper;[23] that he has no leisure or opportunity for adventure. Henry James regards the fact that Alfred de Musset did not visit Spain when he had the opportunity as one of the saddest proofs of his intellectual limitation, and finds de Musset's "contented smallness of horizon" the most regrettable thing in his life.[24] Now Borrow was a man who could both experience and relate, and therein lies his value to literature. The reason is not far to seek; his experiences were purely intellectual, he was thoroughly emotionless. His mind operated in a vacuum, as it were; there was no emotional friction to limit or disorganize it. Thus protected, thus inoculated against the weaknesses and virtues of men, he passed among the outermost and uttermost camps of the earth and brought back his spoils. He added a new province to English letters, a province peopled by nomad tribes and the sons of eternal unrest. Yet he lived as much alone as he died. He was always with men, of them never. He wrote the best narrative style of his time; he spoke thirty languages, yet he never spoke the human tongue. He was a highwayman on the paths of knowledge, a brilliant adventurer of the intellect, a scholar, having little in common with men. As Stevenson said of Thoreau, he was not a man to love, for he was "not touched with the feeling of our infirmities."[25]

Leader, July 15, 1899, p. 5.

23. See "François Coppée," Books and Authors (I), above.

24. Henry James, *French Poets and Novelists*, p. 4.

25. Robert Louis Stevenson, *Familiar Studies of Men and Books* (New York: Charles Scribner's Sons, 1882), p. 138.

John Buchan and Maurice Hewlett

After World War I, John Buchan (1875–1940) went on to a distinguished career as a diplomat, ending as Governor General of Canada (1935–1940). Willa Cather's review of his A Lost Lady of Old Years *(1899) appeared in the* Leader, *July 22, 1899, and a week later in the* Courier. *She had reviewed his earlier novel* John Burnet of Barnes *(1898) in the* Leader, *December 2, 1898. Another writer of romances, Maurice Hewlett (1861–1923), achieved his first popular success with* The Forest Lovers *(1899). Cather was acquainted with his* Earth Works out of Tuscany *(1895) and* Pan and the Young Shepherd *(1898), a poetic drama. In her review of the latter, she called it "a prose poem of high merit. It has an atmosphere of its own, one that we seldom scent in books, and you catch a whiff of it in the first pages. The first scene admits you into a world remote and little heard of, often sought but seldom visited. Puvis de Chavannes found that country, probably he got further into it than anyone that has done so since Virgil, and in that lost land of content and pastoral calm, this little two-act piece is placed"* (Leader, *May 27, 1899).*

It seems that it is still possible to write a novel of Scotland which is not kailyard fiction.[26] I believe Hamlin Garland is credited with once saying that the time had come when a man could take a sod house and a sunflower and make literature. Recently much literature has been made of a stout Scotch dialect, a bit of heather, a funeral and a parson or two. The parson and the heather were sometimes, though seldom, omitted, but the dialect and the funeral, never! The sameness and the dreariness of their inventions has begun to pall on the world. Is there nothing but funerals in Scotland, pray? Are people never born, or do they never get married there? Is the entire population composed of ministers—"little" or big—and have the Scotch got a corner on death and are they running the mortality of the world to suit themselves? Yet there was a time when a certain cheerful gentleman, one Robert Louis Stevenson, wrote tales of the highland and the heather, when a tale from Scotland brought other tidings than those of woe and another message than one from the grave, when stories came to us from Scotland full of high doings by land and sea, and of gallant gentlemen who were not above being merry sometimes and who could talk of something beside their "kirk" and their prayers, stories

26. See *Courier*, November 30, 1895, in "The Literary Situation in 1895," Books and Authors (II), above.

with the ring of swords in them and stout hearts and high hopes and the faith of "Charley over the water." Ah! those were indeed the days "when the wind was blowin' bonny in the North Countree!"

Well, since I have read Mr. John Buchan's *A Lost Lady of Old Years*, I have almost fancied that those good old days, or some like unto them, might come again. At any rate this is the first book I have read that I have felt like comparing with the incomparable romances of Mr. Stevenson, and indeed I feel myself almost a traitor while I do it. Mr. John Buchan is not unknown to fame. Certain people about the world have had their eye on him ever since the publication of a highly meritorious novel *John Burnet of Barnes*, reviewed in these columns last winter. But *A Lost Lady of Old Years* shows a long stride to the forward. It is more dramatic, more direct, the author has struck a better balance between atmosphere and action, and above all he has gained immensely in the massing of his material and the mastery of form. This is one story to which one does a gross injustice to attempt to give even an analysis, for the plot and the style here are inseparable, and the style is a living thing, not to be dissected in cold blood. . . . This Mr. Buchan seems, indeed, to be a man to whom we may look with hope. He is impregnated with the spirit of the true romance, not the pseudo romance which animates Mr. Max Pemberton and Robert Chambers[27] and, too frequently, Mr. Anthony Hope. He is no mere constructor of situations, he deals not in catchwords nor cheap sentiment. There is a sort of elegant reserve about him. Moreover, his story, without sermonizing or setting down in black and white a moral purpose, has moral fiber, an element of strength which many young English writers are trying to get along without, and a sorry stagger they make of it. The book is written in a style intrinsically beautiful, a style fertile, rich, humorous, often quaint and at all times delicate, reserved and touched by a certain reflective gentleness and melancholy not easy of description. A man must feel considerable of a fellow after he has written half a dozen pages of prose such as that. When Louis Stevenson died, he died without an heir and he left his kingdom desolate. Mr. John Buchan has more of that

27. Max Pemberton (1863–1950), English novelist and editor, who wrote the romance *The Iron Pirate* (1893). Robert W. Chambers (1865–1933), popular and prolific American novelist. In a review of his *Ashes of Empire*, Willa Cather wrote: "Myself, I have always read Mr. Chambers for the pictures I find in his books, not for the people I meet there" (*Leader*, December 10, 1898, p. 10). And of *Outsiders* she said: "Mr. Chambers' episodes are conventional, his characters wooden, his plots machine-made. . . . [He] has the storytelling faculty, and has it strongly. He overcomes your scruples and simply interests you without trying to do more. He puts up a good bluff" (*Leader*, July 8, 1899, p. 6).

kingly blood in his veins than any of the romance writers, unless it be Quiller-Couch.[28]

Courier, July 29, 1899, p. 3.

If ever the tints and odors and sounds of summer were caught between the pages of a book, they are in Maurice Hewlett's *The Forest Lovers*. The novel is a mediaeval romance, the old story of a knight and a maid and another woman. It is one of the strongest examples of direct treatment that I know, and as different from the conventional historical novel as possible. Consider, for instance, the masterly and yet laborious method by which Scott constructs his stage, assembles his *dramatis personae* and produces his atmosphere. In *Ivanhoe*, if I remember rightly, there are some pages devoted to the historical situation, the condition of the country and the relations of the Normans and Anglo-Saxons. Then there are pages of geographical explanations, and detailed descriptions of the costumes of each character. All this is certainly very fine and very effective and done as no living man today could do it. Yet it is interesting to see how this young Mr. Hewlett dares to be different. He constructs no stage, he finds one and steps in. He produces no atmosphere, he is already submerged in it before he begins his books. He does not tell you what people wore in the Middle Ages, but suddenly you find that you begin to have a pretty distinct notion of how they felt. He does not design [deign?] to tell you in what century his romance transpired, nor what was the political situation, nor, indeed, in what country it transpired. Either this gentleman has not "read up" on mediaeval affairs, or, if he has, he has the grace not to show it. Because the names are French, one supposes that his forest is somewhere in France, but on sober second thought I should say that it is located in the Domain of Pure Phantasy somewhere between Arcady and Shakespeare's Forest of Arden. Mr. Hewlett makes no more effort to produce an historical setting than Shakespeare did in *As You Like It*. Yet from the first pages of his delightful romance you drop into his world, the antique world reconstructed in dreamland. Before you have turned many pages you are incalculably far away from the world of steam and telegraph and W. D. Howells. The strangest feature of this forest romance is its convincing flavor of reality. Like the wood of Arden, the forest is more real than a real forest; the people smack of the soil, the shepherds smell of their flocks, the maids are brown as hazelnuts, and red as wild strawberries. I remember Ethelbert Nevin said that the book ought to be made into a woodland

28. Arthur Quiller-Couch (1863–1944) completed Stevenson's *St. Ives* (1898).

symphony, but that Brahms was the only man who could get close enough to the soil to do it, and he, unfortunately, is dead. I am inclined to think that Brahms would have got altogether too close to the soil, and Germanized the thing and crushed the fresh, sturdy spirit of romance under his ponderous tonal architecture. Whether it is ever supplemented by music or not, *The Forest Lovers* remains a masterpiece of imaginative literature, exhaling into our arid atmosphere a fragrance bucolic and pastoral, a humor rich and robust, a sentiment delicate and poetic. The whole performance announces the advent into the world of letters of a vigorous, virile mentality, a hand skillful and exquisite, a craft unique and somewhat exotic and which is a law unto itself. Surely the wood nymphs were abroad and the pipes of Pan were playing in the hour when Maurice Hewlett was born. His other two books, *Earth Works out of Tuscany* and *Pan and the Young Shepherd*, are quite as remarkable as this, and wholly different in atmosphere and feeling.

Courier, August 26, 1899, pp. 3–4.

Arnold Bennett and Eden Phillpotts

Arnold Bennett (1867–1931) was an assistant editor on the fashionable magazine Woman *when he published his autobiographical first novel,* A Man from the North *(1898).*[29] *Another new English novelist was Eden Phillpotts (1862–1960), whose second novel,* Children of the Mist *(1898), is reviewed below. For additional comment on Phillpotts, see Guest Editor of the* Courier, *below.*

A curious instance of a bad thing well done is Mr. E[noch] A[rnold] Bennett's new novel, *A Man from the North*. It tells the single [simple?] story of a young man who comes down to London with little in his pockets and high hopes in his heart, and ambitions of the literary order. Like nine hundred and ninety-nine men out of every thousand, he fails, and fails in the bitterest way that a man can fail; he fails himself. Circumstances do not crush him, he voluntarily renounces all that he had hoped for, chiefly because it is too much trouble to get it. His dreams are not high enough or strong enough to lead his life upward. He renounces his literary ambitions, obtains a comfortable clerkship and marries the red-haired cashier in a restaurant he patronizes, whom for the moment

29. Fifteen years later Cather wrote about Arnold Bennett as a playwright in "Plays of Real Life," *McClure's*, March 1913, pp. 70–72, and in "New Types of Acting," *McClure's*, March 1914, p. 51.

he desires. Well, we, most of us, start out to write epics and end by writing advertisements. When once the human side of us begins to grow, we, most of us, honestly prefer cabbage soup to ambrosia. For all that, it is a tragic moment when a young man says good-bye to his dreams, and the commonness of the tragedy does not lighten it. Yet I fancy the transaction is never quite so sordid as Mr. Bennett would have us believe. His young man must have seen something more in the red-haired cashier than Mr. Bennett ever tells us of, or he would not have married her. So with a hundred homely romances that go on under our eyes every day; we see only the outside which may be vulgar and ludicrous, but to the actors the play may be full of poetry. In this Vanity Fair we only see and marvel at the extortionate prices that men pay for their toys, we never know what treasure they may find in those bonbon boxes they snatch so eagerly. We see but the baseness of the sin; we never know the fairness of the temptation. That novelist who does not tell me what men dreamed and by what sweet delusions they cheated themselves is to me no artist at all, for assuredly I myself can go forth any day and see men munching their food in cheap restaurants or brawling in the street.

Courier, July 29, 1899, pp. 3–4.

A new writer of promise has come up in England in the person of Mr. Eden Phillpotts. His new book, *Children of the Mist*, has been pronounced by some critics the novel of the year, though I think it should scarcely be rated above *No. 5 John Street* [see above]. One of the most daring innovations of M. Rostand's novel *Cyrano de Bergerac* was its astonishingly long list of *dramatis personae*. Playwrights have found that a drama can be worked out very well with a dozen characters, or even fewer, and that this economy of time gives the opportunity to develop the really important people of the play more fully. The same change has taken place in the novel in France, in Russia and in England. Mr. Howells and Henry James enjoy fewer characters in a single novel than did George Eliot. As the drama has grown more like the novel, so the novel has taken upon itself more and more the limitations and direct methods of the drama, and contents itself with situations which involve all the characters concerned. But Mr. Phillpotts has returned to the older manner, and his book takes up the lives and fortunes of an entire Dartmoor community. His novel deals not with a few persons and a problem, but with many people and the universal, ever present problem of getting through the world somehow. He considers the life of a town, the influence of the environment upon the people, of the people on each other. His canvas is wide enough for comedy and tragedy. He takes up the village hero, the village belle, the village scholar and the village clown and follows them through the checkered drama that they play. I am not sure that this is worth doing quite as well as Mr. Phillpotts does it. I am not sure that his rich and exhaustive writing would not be more effective if it were governed and tempered by a little artistic discretion. The novel is not closely knit together, it seems not to have been carefully planned. Scenes of noble pathos lose their force because they are followed by chapters more or less irrelevant. The comedy is not always tactfully placed and is persistently placed, sometimes to the extent of being *de trop*, like the later comedy of Dickens. The current of the story is split up into so many channels that one somehow loses the force of it and scarcely realizes how splendidly the whole thing is written. A man with a much narrower range, without half Mr. Phillpotts' wide grasp of divergent types of life, without half his vividness and richness of style, by a more skillful arrangement might have made his joints better. In *The Mill on the Floss* George Eliot had much the same problem to confront.[30] She too wrote the drama of an entire community, she too wished to make a complete picture of country life and took a large canvas and brought a company of stolid, earthly people about her more feverish characters. But she knew when to lay all of them aside and saved herself for that one supreme dramatic moment in which she brought about her tragedy. The crescendo begins with Maggie's ride down the river with Stephen and from there on the dominant theme is brought steadily to the front. At the proper time she subordinates every interest to one, throws all the lesser characters of her book into the shadow, destroys the scaffolding by which she built this tragedy and leaves Maggie Tulliver's cross and expiation above and supreme. The tragedy rises like the black flood that came down the Floss, engulfing field and hamlet and town and mill, leaving those two figures to stand out alone above all the world for a moment before they sink into the flood. "The boat reappeared, but brother and sister had gone down in an embrace never to be parted; living through again in one supreme moment the days when they had clasped their little hands in love, and roamed the daisy fields together." And so the reader, in one great moment of illumination, sees the whole of these two lives, as a man sees a whole city by a flash of lightning. Ah Heavens! when will the man or woman be born

30. For earlier discussions of *The Mill on the Floss*, see "Old Books and New" columns for May and November 1897, The *Home Monthly*, above; also "Tales by John Oliver Hobbes," Books and Authors (III), above.

who can write like that again? Perhaps sometime Mr. Phillpotts, whose career began not long ago, may give us something as full of nature and truth as his *Children of the Mist*. Yet fashioned with a more rigorous and compelling hand. He has the temper from which all health in literature springs. He sees the world freshly, as though it had been made but yesterday, and he ceases not to wonder at it. His book is full-blooded, free from literary affectations, lusty and wholesome and full of joy in out-of-door life, with roots that reach deep into the soil and a florescence pale and beautiful as the Dartmoor mists.

Courier, September 16, 1899, p. 4.

Zola's Germinal

On September 9, 1899, the retrial of Alfred Dreyfus (1859–1935) ended with his being sentenced to ten years on Devil's Island (eventually, of course, he was freed). Emile Zola, whose famous "J'accuse" letter (January 1898) precipitated the retrial, had fled to England when he was convicted of libel, returning in triumph in June 1899. Reversing the usual order of publication, Willa Cather's review of Germinal *appeared first in the* Courier,[31] *then in the* Leader *(November 18, 1899). See also "Zola: 'Dante of Paris,'" Books and Authors (III), above.*

Now that the Dreyfus matter is ended or at least one stage of it, the one man who will stand out pre-eminent above all the great and little men who have figured in the matter is Emile Zola, perhaps the greatest mind in France today. It is the man's first appeal to the popular sentiment, the first time that the eye of the world has taken stock in him seriously. Yet the courage of the hand that penned the "J'accuse" letter had been demonstrated long before when an author, poor, young and comparatively unknown, he took upon himself the great task of writing the twenty volumes of Rougon-Macquart, a series of novels which should completely depict one epoch of French society, which is, as he himself has said, "a world, a society, a civilization." Certainly it took much less courage to attack the French army in behalf of justice than to challenge the whole world in behalf of a theory of art. M. Zola's greatness as a man has not always been to his advantage as an artist. He is a theorist and the artist has never quite mastered the theorist. In his novel *Germinal* [1885], however, the man and the artist are in perfect unity and perfect balance, all that is best

31. As an epigraph for this column, Cather quoted eighteen lines of Edwin Markham's "The Man with the Hoe."

in his magnificent genius and titanic power goes to make this greatest of labor novels. In *Germinal* we reach the third generation of the Rougons; we have Gervaise [*L'Assommoir*, 1877] drink herself into the gutter and die of starvation in an attic in Paris; we have seen her daughter Nana [*Nana*, 1880] rise from the streets to the theatre, from the theatre to noblemen's houses, we have seen how she wrecked the oldest families and squandered the largest fortunes in France, how the forests of Brittany were cut down to fill her wardrobe, how, leagues from Paris, miners toiled in the black bowels of the earth to buy her jewels, how she drove a whole city mad and corrupted an entire civilization. Now it is to Etienne that the master turns, Nana's elder brother, who went to work in the Voreux mines. *Germinal* is more than a novel, it is the epic labor. Nowhere are the forces of master and workmen arrayed in so tremendous a drama. Etienne is a socialist without the power of reasoning, an uneducated man who reads Ruskin and Darwin and reads them just as the son of Gervaise who drank herself to death. His blood was heated and his reason distorted before he was born, he was crippled before the fight began. His brain is fired by a Russian exile who had been implicated in a plot to kill the Czar and who had seen his wife hanged in the streets of Moscow. Etienne incites the miners to revolt, and the strike which follows is the *raison d'être* of the book. What can a revolt of labor under the present conditions of society mean, and how must it end? That is the problem which M. Zola takes up. The strike is best followed through the fortunes of the Mahue family. Father Mahue is the best workman in the mine, sober, orderly, law-abiding, industrious. His ancestors have been miners for centuries, they have lain on their bellies pecking at the coal until they have hewn out gallery after gallery, undermined the country mile upon mile. All of them, men and women have lived in the darkness, in the foul air below the surface of the earth, where nature buries her dead of the ages and hides the secrets of her past. They have been covered with the grime of the mines and marked with soft soap until the hair of the race has become bleached and the skin discolored. Mahue's old father, who worked for fifty years in the mines, still lives with him, and Mahue himself has seven children, most of them too young to work. The comeliness and intelligence of the family are in the daughter, Catharine, who fills a car in the mine. The family has run a little into debt and owes a hundred sous and cannot pay it. Every payday their immediate necessities swallow up their earnings, leaving nothing for the debt. Wages are cut, despair seizes Father Mahue, and he joins the strikers. Then comes the step from half a loaf to no bread. Every want and necessity is reduced to one, bread. The Mahues, who were once so self-reliant and proud, send their children out to beg upon the highway. Mother Mahue pawns her betrothal gifts, the little ones' clothes, the cooking utensils. Nothing is left in the home but the colored picture of the Emperor on the wall. The children steal from each other and one boy becomes a precocious criminal. One of the girls dies, but the Mahues never weaken. When the strikers charge on the soldiers Mother Mahue, with her child at her breast taunts her husband with cowardice when he lags behind. He is shot down at her feet. Then only the young, helpless children and the mother are left, and the old, old man, who has witnessed so many tragedies and seen the mine swallow up generation after generation of his race. In every other family in the village the ravages of the strike are equally terrible. Etienne stands appalled at the desolation of the hurricane of revolt he had raised, heartsick at the ruin of the Mahues, whom he loved. Still Mother Mahue sits by her dead, famished, and curses Catharine who begs to be allowed to return to the mine to earn bread for the little children. Then, in the midst of all this misery, it dawns upon Etienne that when capital and labor war, capital can wait, while labor starves. That is what capital means; something ahead. He recalled the words of his Russian friend, Jouvarine:

"Increase the salaries. Why, they are fixed by an inexorable law at the smallest possible sum, just enough to allow the workmen to eat dry bread. If they fall too low, the workmen die and the demand for new men makes them rise again. If they go up too high, the losses are so much greater that they drop again. It is the equilibrium of empty stomachs, the perpetual condemnation to a fate like that of the galley slave."

Then Catharine Mahue, whom Etienne had long loved but who had married big Cheval, another miner, returned abused and deserted by her husband and turned to him for help. That swings the scale. The problem of life took on another form, and a new duty pressed closer than the old. He could starve himself, but he could not see the woman he loved go hungry. He bowed to the inexorable necessity which has defeated every revolution, the necessity of men for love. Together he and Catharine set out for the mine. On their way they met the Russian who started to warn Etienne that the strikers intended to wreck the mine and kill their comrades who returned to work. Then he looked at Catharine and understood why Etienne had recanted. "When there was a woman in the heart of a man, the man was finished, he could die. Perhaps he saw in a quick vision his mistress who was hung at Moscow,—the last link broken, which left him free as to the life of others or his own. He said simply, 'Go'!"

After Etienne's moral defeat and his return to the mine, the perspective in the great novel narrows, like the galleries of the mine itself. Everything is then concentrated upon the struggle of the man and woman for life and for each other, which of course is the immediate cause of all labor problems and the origin of labor itself. Etienne and Catharine are cut off in the mine, buried in the same gallery with Cheval, the woman's brutal husband. There, in the darkness, these men, already in the grave, fight a duel to the death for the possession of this woman who is already the bride of Death. There is something awesome about that combat, something of the savagery of the stone age. So, when the world is cold, the two last survivors of their race may fight for the last woman in the world. Etienne is the victor, and Cheval's body falls back into the water that rose from the broken pumps. For nine days Catharine and her lover lie there in hunger and madness, listening to the picks of the rescuers from above. The water rises and brings them company. The body of big Cheval floats back to Catharine's feet. They push it away frantically, but always it floats back and rocks there in the water, jostling against them. He even floated between them in his obstinate jealousy. When the rescuers arrived, Catharine was dead.

It might seem that this is climax enough for any book, but Zola follows it by a greater and a nobler, a climax that would be almost unendurable, like some of Hugo's, were it not tempered by a simple and almost gentle approach. When Etienne recovers from his long illness in the hospital, he goes to the mine to bid farewell to his old comrades and asks for Mother Mahue, Mother Mahue who had been the strongest of them all, who had seen her children beg and die and cheered her husband to his death, who had cried defiance still when he lay dead before her. . . .

[Etienne finds that La Mahue, who had threatened to strangle the first of her family who went down in the mines again, is preparing to work in the mines herself, as well as her children.]

So Etienne went forth upon his journey, giving up forever the problem of the equilibrium of empty stomachs, knowing himself to be the prisoner of poverty, and realizing that if he should wander to the world's end he would only change his prison house.

Courier, September 16, 1899, pp. 3–4.

Elia W. Peattie

When Mrs. Elia W. Peattie (1862–1935) was a columnist on the World-Herald *in the 1890's she had become a friend of Willa Cather's, and was one of the first to predict a great future for her.*[32] *Cather had announced Mrs. Peattie's book* A Mountain Woman *in the* Journal, *March 29, 1896, and during her tenure on the* Home Monthly *had published one of Mrs. Peattie's stories (see note 9, The* Home Monthly, *above). In late 1897 Mrs. Peattie moved to Chicago, where she was a member of The Little Room, which helped to spark the Chicago Renaissance, and in 1901 she became the literary editor of the* Chicago Tribune.[33] *The following review of an* Atlantic *story appeared in the* Courier; *earlier Cather had reviewed Mrs. Peattie's children's book,* 'Ickery Ann and Other Boys and Girls *in the* Leader, *April 22, 1899. She said that after so many "violet musings" about children, accompanied by decadent Beardsley drawings, she was delighted with these stories for "kids."*

The September *Atlantic* contains a story of more than passing interest, "The Man at the Edge of Things," by Mrs. Elia W. Peattie. It is certainly the best western story that I have chanced to read. By that I do not mean that it has more of the West in it than a good many other western stories, but I have not happened to see elsewhere so exquisite a literary effort concerning itself with the problems of life in the Middle West, and I am not forgetting some remarkably brilliant [ones] by young Wolcott Balestier.[34] It is not by any means the first good western story that Mrs. Peattie has written, but it stands out so prominently above all her previous work that one might say it begins a new era with her. In the first place, it is good reading merely as a story, it has incident enough to attract the most indifferent eye, and that, of course, is the prime essential in a short story. In constructing a story as in building an airship the first problem is to get something that will lift its own weight. But the abiding delight in "The Man at the Edge of Things" is the masterly manner in which the incidents are used, the light and shade, the perspective and bold foreshortening which give the story its unusual vividness and directness. Ordinarily the most unattractive feature about western stories is their monotonous cheerlessness, a feature so indigenous to the atmosphere of a prairie country that perhaps only people that have lived there can understand its inevitableness. This, Mrs. Peattie has deftly avoided by placing the first part of her story in the east. The story begins amid the college festivities of Dilling Brown's

32. See *KA*, p. 27.

33. Duffey, *The Chicago Renaissance*, p. 57.

34. Charles Wolcott Balestier (1861–1891), Kipling's brother-in-law and his collaborator (on *The Naulaka*, 1892), and author of *Benefits Forgot* (1892), a novel of the Rocky Mountain mining camps.

Commencement day, and jumps then to Dilling's old home in a quiet village in New York State, where there are comfortable maiden relatives who look after him, and nice girls who play tennis and dispense lemonade; and all the quiet, easy friendships that spring from long acquaintance and normal conditions of living. The closeness and intimacy of their quiet village life, the friendly, sheltering atmosphere created by the old home, the old boxwood walks, the old china and old memories, the devoted old women who serve him, is insisted upon just enough to bring about the vigorous contrast the author wanted, and in the latter part of the story the arid airs, the scorching winds and hot horizons are haunted by vague suggestions of that sweet, cool, green spot on the Atlantic coast and the odor of boxwood and mignonette. For Dilling Brown was not content with the narrow horizons of happiness, and he went to seek his fortune in the free-grass country of California. The whole of the ranch life is treated with virility and vigor and color. Brown took up his abode at the edge of things with many hundred sheep and a few herdsmen and a Chinese cook, living in an adobe house formerly inhabited by a luckless sheepman and his sister who had been overtaken by disaster and fled the country, leaving their shack furnished and standing empty in the painted desert. All about the room in which Dilling Brown slept there were reminders of that courageous woman who had lived there, and over the fireplace she had written on the wall: "He, watching over Israel, slumbereth not, nor sleeps," and it occurred to him that no nice, white muslin, tennis-playing girl he had ever known would have thought of writing that "in an adobe house, in a sun-cursed desert." So Dilling fell into the habit of thinking of that woman when he was exhausted or lonely. "As the weeks went on, trailing along as slowly as wounded snakes, as the wool lengthened on the sheep, and the hair hung lower on the shoulders of the herdsmen"—and that is phrasing worth the doing, by the way,—and everything grew longer but money, he turned more and more to his visionary feminine presence which haunted the place. That exaltation of femininity in the desert, that subtile, tantalizing suggestion of a woman's presence conjured up by an old glove and a few yards of white muslin, is one of the most skillful things in that skillful story, and recalls the manner in which Maupassant used to achieve effects of that kind, absolutely impalpable, yet so close and physical that they penetrate one at every pore. The tale reaches its climax when Brown learns that this woman's brother, his immediate predecessor at the "Edge of Things," went crazy after the manner of sheep herders, and used to drop on his knees and crop the grass with his sheep. Brown himself is saved from a similar fate by an old college chum and a Shakespeare-reading Frenchman who was overseer at a neighboring ranch. The story is evenly worked up from every side, the texture is close and firm, not a point has been slighted and every play scores. The Frenchman contributes nicely to the color of the thing. The grotesque comparison between the idyllic shepherds of Arcadia, garland decked and piping under soft skies and by peaceful streams, and these scorched, shaggy, vacant-eyed sheep keepers of the free-grass country is a piece of ironic byplay that amounts to artistic cruelty, but art is generally cruel, and Mrs. Peattie's almost always so.

Courier, November 4, 1899, p. 3.

Three Translations: Maupassant, Gautier, Omar Kháyyám

Maupassant and Gautier were among the writers whom Willa Cather read in French with Mr. and Mrs. George Seibel. In these excursions, as George Seibel has written, "Henry James was the guide whose hand held ours, and his critical standard was our polestar on those voyages." [35] *A slightly different version of the first of the following selections, a review of Maupassant's* Fort comme la mort *(1899), appeared in the* Leader, *October 28, 1899. Gautier's* Une Nuit de Cléopâtre *was translated in 1882 by Lafcadio Hearn (1850–1904), and a reissue of that volume is reviewed in the second selection.*[36] *Commenting on Willa Cather's poems, George Seibel recalled that some "had a drop of absinthe from Verlaine, whom we had been reading, or wine-wet rose petals from FitzGerald's* Omar, *whom she had first imported into our home one Christmas in a green corrugated cardboard edition published by Dodge at San Francisco in 1896, at the prodigal price of 25 cents."* [37] *The translation of the* Rubáiyát *reviewed here is that of Mrs. Jessie Cadell (1844–1884), reissued by Richard Garnett (1835–1909), keeper of books at the British Museum.*

A new translation of Maupassant's *Fort comme la mort* is made by a gentleman with the exotic name of Teofilo Comba, and is an unusually

35. Seibel, p. 203. The books of Henry James which they consulted were *Partial Portraits* and *French Poets and Novelists.*

36. Seibel, p. 197. Gautier's *Mademoiselle de Maupin* (see "Four Women Writers," above), "secretly sold in paper covers throughout Illinois," was read by Eden Bower in "Coming, Aphrodite!" *Youth and the Bright Medusa*, p. 30.

37. Seibel wrote a play based on the *Rubáiyát* for Richard Mansfield, and Willa Cather planned to do an article on it, but unfortunately Mansfield never produced the play. Willa Cather to George Seibel, n.d.[1900?], in the possession of Mrs. George Seibel, Capitola, California.

satisfactory piece of work as translations go, with not a few of the commendable features of Mr. Lafcadio Hearn's efforts in translating French fiction. French fiction masquerading in English phraseology always reminds one of an English actress—say, that gifted but matronly artist, Mrs. Kendal[38]—disporting herself as Frou-Frou or Denise or Manon Lescaut. There is apt to be something a trifle heavy about it, a trifle brusque, a trifle too direct, and the whole is apt to resemble an attempt to filigree in bronze. Of all the French masters, with the possible exception of Gautier, none is more difficult to render into English than Maupassant. The two mediums of expression are so essentially different that it is almost like translating the odor of violets into speech. The translator's choice is a happy one. It is a question as to just how much of Maupassant is possible or desirable in English, but no one who is inclined to take literature seriously can have any valid objections to *Fort comme la mort*. In short, while there is no necessity to introduce it into the boarding-school curriculum, it is not one of those novels which, as Mrs. Phelps-Ward[39] once primly put it, "give more pain by their indelicacy than their art gives pleasure."

Technically, the book is one of Maupassant's best. However uncertain his later work may have been, in *Notre Coeur* [1890] and *Fort comme la mort* he was in possession of the full measure of his power, and these two novels, at least, are constructively as flawless as the short stories which are usually considered his masterpieces. The story is that of a Parisian painter, very much in vogue, who has all his life been the lover of one woman who, fortunately for his happiness and his art, has entertained for him not a caprice but an affection, genuine and constant, which grew with habit and association until when he reaches fifty and his creative power begins to fail him somewhat, he is more necessary to her than he was in his youth and the flower of his genius. . . . At this juncture the Countess' daughter, who has spent her childhood with her grandmother, returns to Paris, and her marvellous physical resemblance to her mother is a matter of universal comment. The artist has preserved the tastes and sensibilities of a young man, or he would not be an artist. In Annette he finds the youth of the mother reincarnated, she seems indeed but another phase of the mother, having the same flesh and the same soul. She charms and soothes the man for whom the tragedy of age is beginning, she compensates for the

38. See "The Kendals," The Star System (I), above.

39. Mrs. Elizabeth Stuart Phelps-Ward (1844–1911), writer of religious novels including the best-selling *Gates Ajar* (1868), whose autobiography, *Chapters from a Life*, ran in *McClure's* in 1896.

domestic ties which he has missed in his own life, in her youth he lives again the romance of his own. He loves her without conscious infidelity to the mother whom she so marvelously resembles, and it is the helpless, despairing love of an old man, laying hold for the last time upon youth, and he clung to it as the old cling to youth, as the dying cling to life. . . . The situation is a supremely difficult one, but Maupassant seldom did anything which was not difficult, and like all master craftsmen, he had a penchant for experiments in pure skill, and like all writers of modern feeling he had a passion for psychological studies the most intricate and complex. The struggle of the old painter against their Indian summer of love, the fluctuations of the two loves in his heart, his constancy and pity for the mother and himself, are handled with that delicacy and subtileness and poignant vividness always at Maupassant's command, and chastened by that sense of fitness and beauty which always restrained him. But the chief pleasure derivable from the book is an esoteric one, and lies in the simple beauty of the writing, the rare felicity of the phrasing, and the style has that integral value, that individual and exalted grace which alone gives art a right to be. . . .

One notices continually Maupassant's usual freshness of observation, his old trick of forever comparing the real to the artificial to give it verity to a public with whom good artifice has become the only reality. An eyeglass is a "small circle of glass at the end of a black silk hair," the butterflies flutter above the turf "as if they had been suspended on the end of an elastic thread." When the great ladies of Paris are out driving in the Bois one spring morning, "a breath of cold air swept by, come from afar, from the country that was hardly awake yet, and the whole Bois shivered, that coquettish, chilly, and worldly park. All the women with an almost simultaneous motion brought up on their arms and bosoms the wraps fallen behind them, and the horses, from one end of the avenue to the other, began to trot as though the sharp breeze had lashed them like a whip."

That is the sort of thing language was made for. . . .

Courier, November 4, 1899, pp. 3–4.

[Here is] a beautiful new edition of Mr. Hearn's celebrated translations of Gautier's masterpieces of French prose. Probably no stories have ever been written which represent a higher quality of art and artifice than these. They are the *Thousand and One Nights* of an advanced civilization, the elegant fairy tales of illusionless people and incredulous age. *One of Cleopatra's Nights* [*Une Nuit de Cléopâtre*] and *La Morte amoureuse* translated under the title of "Clarimonde," have never been surpassed in any language.[40] They are among the priceless things of art, and had Gautier never written anything else, he would have died one of the world's master craftsmen. Unique enough they are in literature, these stories in the original meaning of the word, these graceful inventions, with all their frank and joyous hedonism, their naive and yet over-subtle delight in all physical beauty, in all rococo things, in all white flesh and rare fabrics and clear gems and lustrous fruits and graceful furniture, in all the elegant trappings wherewith Théophile Gautier loved to clothe his dreams. And all these details, these wonders of wood and fabric and gold and stone, belong to the inspiration, are a part of and inseparable from it, as the queen is inseparable from her state, the singer from her art, the thyrsus from the god. Such were the blue opium dreams he dreamed, that Gautier, whose mind was in Alexandria while his body was in Paris, whose mind was of the East, simple and strangely sensitive, though his style, as Henry James has said, is one of the latest products of time. Mr. Hearn's translation is the best that exists, and one could scarcely conceive of a better one.

Leader, November 18, 1899, p. 9.

Although Mr. Richard Garnett in his preface pays a high tribute to Mrs. Cadell's Persian scholarship, as well as her facility in rhyme making, it is scarcely likely that this translation will ever rival the FitzGerald. With reference to the literalness of FitzGerald's translation and the liberties he took with Omar's text, much has been said. But if it was by adhering but loosely to the original and supplementing the thought of the Persian poet that FitzGerald gave us that masterpiece of Oriental philosophy and elegant expression known as the English *Rubáiyát*, then the greater man FitzGerald. . . .

[Mrs. Cadell's] translation throughout is without melody, and seems to have been made with regard for the letter rather than the spirit, and reads like a set of maxims and proverbs unillumined by poetic feeling or imagination. It may be a more literal translation than FitzGerald's *Rubáiyát*, but it is very inferior to it as literature. It may be a more scholarly piece of work than FitzGerald's, but FitzGerald was more than a scholar, he was a poet, and he left but one masterpiece, into which he condensed thirty years of loneliness and inactivity and dreamful misery. According to the

40. The title character in "The Count of Crow's Nest" (*Home Monthly*, September and October 1896) claimed *La Morte amoureuse* as an old favorite, though he thought that "'Poe surpassed even Gautier in using some effects of that character.'" *CSF*, pp. 453, 454.

exorbitant rates at which such masterpieces are paid for, he got it rather cheaply at the price of a lifetime, for it is unique in literature. Since FitzGerald's time various poetasters have tried their hand at it, notably Mr. Richard Le Gallienne [in 1897], who produced a young ladies' version in pink and white, redolent of musk. As for Mrs. Jessie Cadell, Mr. Garnett remarks in his preface that she studied Persian because the education of her children was not in itself enough to engross the energies of her active mind. There is, indeed, no moral law to prevent the study of Persian as a recreation from pedagogical labors, but neither is there any good and sufficient reason why Omar should be combined with kindergartening.

Leader, November 25, 1899, p. 6.

A Shaw Novel: Cashel Byron's Profession

Between 1879 and 1883 Bernard Shaw wrote five novels, the best of which was Cashel Byron's Profession *(1882, published 1885–86). Reviewing the 1899 American edition in the* Leader, *Willa Cather called it "a novelized drama." Shaw did, in fact, dramatize it as* The Admirable Bashville *(1901). For comments on Shaw's plays as literature, see Books and Authors (III), above.*

If Mr. G. Bernard Shaw gets as much fun out of the gentle gibes he pokes at existing society as existing society does out of reading them, his life must be a sweet and joyous one. Mr. Shaw has been notably indulgent of his caprices, and the managers who have attempted to produce his plays in England have paid for his whimsicalness to the tune of many thousands pounds per night, in which Mr. Shaw feels a pardonable pride. But never has Mr. Shaw thrown down the bars and allowed his eccentric fancy such free rein as in this novel. The world has somewhat painfully acquired a knowledge of the dramatized novel, but I should call Mr. Shaw's latest a novelized drama. The leading man thereof, Mr. Cashel Byron, is first introduced to us as an overgrown, blubbering schoolboy, with hard fists and scanty Eton jackets. He is the son of a favorite London actress who found him inconvenient, and who kept him secluded in a school for small boys when he was a small boy no longer, and the longer his legs grew the more of a problem he became, an awkward, unattractive problem that cost so many pounds a quarter. At last Cashel settled the matter by knocking down one of the instructors and running away to sea. He eventually pulled up in Australia, where he adopted his profession, i.e., that of a prize fighter. Now, while Cashel was busy learning to punch people under the belt, the fates were busy in another part of the world getting ready a bride for him, and as Mr. Shaw attributes a high and refined sense of humor to the fates, this is the way they went about it. There was a certain English critic and philosopher, Carew by name, who was a man of active mind and bad digestion and a taste for art. This gentleman, who declared that his wife had the distinction of being the most disagreeable person he had ever known in a wide acquaintance with mankind, had one daughter for whom he had no affection but a great respect. Miss Lydia Carew translated many works of the German philosopher[s], spoke all the languages of the civilized world, and assisted her father in writing his books of travel and criticism. . . . For many pages Mr. Shaw dilates on this erudition, which it is his glee and pride to bring to naught. The lady is rich, pursued by men, though no longer in the first pink of youth, and as Mr. Shaw dryly remarks is much "incommoded by her involuntary power of inspiring affection in her own sex," and much of her vitality was consumed in keeping impulsive young girls at a distance.

After her father's death, Cashel Byron returns to England, the king of the prize ring, and sporting lords risk their fortunes on his fists. While he is training for a great combat, his trainers rent a cottage on the Carew manor for him. One day Miss Lydia lays aside the second part of *Faust* and goes for a stroll in the hot noon sun, and in a sylvan haunt descries Cashel at his exercise, innocent of clothing, and decides that she has stumbled upon an antique god in his woodland glade. . . . But though Cashel could not speak English grammatically, and was innocent of the German philosophers, and fervently declared that art was rot, he was very large and pink and white, and Miss Lydia Carew closed the second part of *Faust* and said: "If it be possible for a child of mine to escape this curse of autovivisection, it must inherit its humanity from its father, not from me—from the man of emotion who never thinks, not from the woman of introspection who can not help thinking."

So Miss Carew marries the prize fighter out of consideration for the nerves of the next generation, a stage of lofty self-command which few of her sex ever reach.

Cashel Byron's Profession is interesting from a constructive point of view. I fancy the brilliant and flippant Mr. Congreve, had he written novels, would have written them much after this manner. The dialogue is sparkling, the characters clear, the humor bitter and all but coarse, the style full of irrational and innumerable excesses, the tone of the whole rather splenetic, and the ideas are thick as persimmons before the frost. The book is strangely without perspective and the effects of distance and the restful out-of-door atmosphere. The plot is carried out by cleverly drawn types on a cramped stage amid canvas trees and painted lakes and in the glare of the calcium sunlight. It is a brilliant farce in the form of a novel. Mr. Shaw is too humorous to write a novel, as novels go. He is too knowing, too self-conscious, too critical; he is deficient in blindness and faith and the trick of taking things seriously and of making other people take them so.

Leader, November 25, 1899, p. 9.

Eugene Field: The Love Affairs of a Bibliomaniac

Much of this review originally appeared in the Journal, *February 23, 1896* (KA, *pp. 332–333*), *when Eugene Field's* Love Affairs of a Bibliomaniac *was published shortly after his death. When the book was reissued in 1899, Willa Cather exhumed the piece and ran it again in the* Leader. *See also "Stevenson and Eugene Field," Books and Authors (II), above.*

Eugene Field was all his life a cheerful sort of a fellow, and everything he wrote bore the marks of his genial personality. But the best and cheeriest of his work appeared after his death in his *Love Affairs of a Bibliomaniac.*

It is only fair to this book to say at the outset that it is nothing whatever like the *Literary Passions* of William Dean Howells,[41] in which that gentleman informs the astonished world that Dumas was a romanticist and discusses in an authoritative manner the charms of Tolstoi. It has nothing whatever of the pedantic, autocratic, exclusive flavor of Mr. Howells' work. If ever a volume was filled with a genuine, humble, reverent love of the very leaves and covers and odor of books it is this little chronicle of Field's love affairs. It is not strictly biographical, it is not critical, and from cover to cover the word "art" does not once occur! It is not an analysis of the power of books, but rather a humble expression of their charms. He does not write of them constructively from the inside, but objectively from the outside. He does not write of books as "art," but as personalities. He does not see them as studies in environment or character, but as trusty companions, and he speaks of them as "a plain, blunt man who loves his friends" might speak. In this century books and women have been subjected to a most painful system of analysis. Every youngster before he is out of kilts, announces that he likes in a woman this trait, and in such a

41. See "Howells: *My Literary Passions,*" Books and Authors (II), above.

book that feature. It's a downright comfort to come across a man who loves a book *in toto*, with a personal affection and who feels its charm without insisting upon dissecting it. This little book is so brimming with downright affection for all printed things that when you open it you lose your bearings for a moment and fancy that you are reading some old fellow of Goldsmith's or De Quincey's time before the fashion of analysis came over from France.

Eugene Field was a queer fellow; he was a man of letters of the old school, yet he lived in Chicago; he was a man who loved the classics and read them daily, yet he was a journalist, a strange and, unfortunately, rare anomaly. His *Love Affairs* is a sort of autobiography of his tastes. . . .

Leader, December 16, 1899, p. 3.

Booth Tarkington: The Gentleman from Indiana

When Willa Cather reviewed this best-selling novel by Booth Tarkington (1869–1946), a Courier *editorial—"Sophomorical Stories," by Sarah B. Harris—supported her point of view. The editorial complained about the hero worship of the "few distinguished men in their college who can kick or run or throw a curved ball. . . . He [the football hero] is carried on shoulders and ranks everybody in the college world and undergraduates know no other. For and to these worshippers the college yarns of the deeds, poses, favorite drinks, sacred oaths and costumes of a football Saladin are written. It is a large and tempting clientele, which if the publisher can secure, means large profits. The rest of the world which has got beyond skittles and beer, but reads the new books is still obliged to listen to the college boy in literature and make one of his audience"* (Courier, *January 20, 1900*).

You may cut him clean of his football hair,
An' lock his toys away,
But you can't make a man of a college star
If you try till his dyin' day.

The Gentleman from Indiana is a lucky book; it has been much talked about and it has had a large sale. I believe that Mr. Booth Tarkington, the author, was graduated from Princeton in '93, and that he has since been employed with this novel in which he wished to transcribe that part of the *Comédie Humaine* which transpires in a little town in the Middle West. He takes John Harkless, who had been a great man at college, and sets him down in Plattville, Indiana, to work out his destiny as the editor of a small country newspaper. Harkless apparently had been one of those perennial college stars of whom "great things" are expected—Lincoln has known a few of them, and concerning most of them it is still "expecting." He had been surrounded by that luster which occasionally incapacitates a man for usefulness in active life; so he went off into the wilderness where he could hide his halo and be comfortable. But even then he was not comfortable, his college popularity having spoiled him for any sort of grown-up living. Indeed, he was a most uncomfortable young man, and had he not impoverished himself by buying a perfectly worthless newspaper from a Chicago agent at a fancy price, he would never have stuck it out in Plattville, but would have returned to the country where he was considered a great man, and would have attended fraternity banquets and gone to football games with his college colors tied to his cane, and tooted a fish horn and talked about college spirit even after the gray hairs had begun to come, and he might even have sunk to the device of "posting" in the hope that callow freshmen would still point him out as the man who used to be "the great Harkless." Have we not of old time seen them thus in Lincoln, these remarkable students who somehow fail to make any deep impression in wider fields, and who drift back to post and cultivate a standing with lower classmen and passionately insist upon being "great." Probably Mr. Tarkington would not agree with my opinion of his hero, but he must admit that his hero hungered after all these things as a boarding-school girl does after the chum who used to eat caramels with her and curl her front hair and sew bows on her slippers.

Well, Harkless worried through some seven years of this kind of life, and then a girl came to Plattville whom he had known when she was a child. . . . Naturally this young lady brought back many pleasant memories of better days, . . . and she sang Schubert's "Serenade" and looked like a marquise, and Harkless made enterprising love to her just the first chance he got. When the Marquise, whose everyday name was Helen, slightly discouraged him, he rushed wildly, madly out into the storm—at least I think that is the way he did it—and let the Whitecaps [Ku Klux Klan] get him. Now the Whitecaps had been after him for a long time because of the lofty moral tone of the Carlow County *Herald*, and when they got him they left as little of him as possible. . . .

Finally Harkless was found shot to pieces in a hospital in a neighboring town, and in his delirium he sang songs and "heard the seniors singing on the stairs," and was always trying to steal the clapper from the college bell, which childish trend of thought shows how little seven years of the world had done for him. While he was ill the Marquise from the Philadelphia finishing school ran his paper for him and wrote political editorials and leaders on the petroleum possibilities of Indiana, which craft it is the especial aim of all finishing schools to impart, and when he recovered she recompensed him for his sufferings with her affections. . . .

The first few chapters of Mr. Tarkington's novel are exceedingly well written. The wide-streeted prairie town with its low framed buildings, its sidewalk loafers and store-box whittlers who, when the sun got hot, slouched over to the courthouse yard and whittled at the fence under the trees where the farmers tied their horses, are well done. But as Mr. Kipling once remarked, local color is a dangerous thing in the hands of a novice, and you can't make a novel out of good bits of description. The young editor's former glorious career is much overdone, and the frequent references to it are often in bad taste. . . .

As we well know, the great and good are never known as such in their own town. I had only to go to Lawrence, Kansas, to hear that Frederick Funston[42] was a coward and averse to telling the truth. Yet Mr. Tarkington tells us that the good people of Plattville were as dust beneath the feet of their dear young editor, and that the young men so loved him for his virtues that they mounted guard every night to keep the Whitecaps from him. A home trader or a pugilist might stir the youths of Indiana to such a degree of enthusiasm, but I know well enough that the inhabitants of a western village would not have left enough of this sentimental "tender strong" college youth for the Whitecaps to carry off. *À bas* the "tender strong" college man in fiction anyhow! The day will surely come when he will be called to render an account of all these things.

The chapters which deal with the raid on the Whitecaps' village and the hospital episodes are considerably above the rest of the book. Mr. Tarkington's descriptions of nature are almost invariably fake and far-fetched, and come dangerously near "fine writing." I think some of them must be made up of the "daily themes" the young author did at Princeton, when his professor told him to go out and observe nature and duly chronicle what he saw. Nature is very nasty and unreasonable about being "observed," and they who seek her critically shall not find her. Mr. Tarkington's English is not always faultless. I find this astonishing sentence, which

42. Frederick Funston (1865–1917), Colonel of the 20th Kansas Volunteers, was made a brigadier general in May 1899 for bravery in the Philippines, and was awarded the Congressional Medal of Honor shortly after this review appeared. See *Courier*, August 17, 1901, in "Literary Notes," Guest Editor of the *Courier*, below.

surely his professor neglected to underscore—"a crescendo of portliness was playing a diminuendo with his youth." Now a Harvard student might so express his feelings, if he had been to a Boston symphony concert the night before, but why should a Princeton man be thus tempted? . . .

The execution of Mr. Tarkington's novel is so amateurish that it will scarcely be seriously considered among literary people—outside of Indiana—and his view of life is so shallow and puerile and sophomorically sugary that grown-ups will have very little patience with it. Appearing as a serial in a college weekly it would be all very well, and might strike one as a promising piece of work. The Princeton brand of novels opens up new vistas before us. The fiction of the Harvard school and the Barrett Wendell Method[43] has entertained the Philistine aforetime, but, God wot it has never offered us anything so refreshingly youthful as this.

Courier, January 20, 1900, pp. 2–3.

To Have and To Hold

The second novel by Mary Johnston (1870–1936), To Have and To Hold, *headed the best-seller list in 1900, but no doubt its primary interest for Willa Cather resided in its period and setting: it was a tale of colonial Virginia. In the* Nebraska Literary Magazine, *June 1896, she herself had published "A Night at Greenway Court," a story of Virginia in the days of Lord Fairfax.*[44] *And her fondness for the olden times in her native state comes through in her review of Eugene E. Presbrey's* A Virginia Courtship: *"[The play] deals with a period when men had time to notice and regard the picturesque element in existence and when life moved slowly enough to preserve the elements of courtliness and grace. The world went very well then, before electrical appliances were born, when chivalry was the code of men and the duty of women was to be fair, when the hiss of steam and the glare of arc lights had not yet frightened away romance, and life was less from the brain and more from the heart. They were golden days, those days of the Old Dominion, and it is just possible that in the transition from that century to this we have lost something quite as precious as electricity"* (Leader, *January 11, 1898*).

At last an historical novel worth having and holding. Since the days of Hawthorne, attempts to utilize American history in fiction have, for

43. Barrett Wendell (1855–1921), professor of English at Harvard, author of *English Composition* (1891).

44. *CSF*, pp. 483–492.

the most part, miscarried. Historical novels we have had in generous measure, but they have been histories without accuracy and romances without romance. Recently Mr. Paul Leicester Ford [in *Janice Meredith*, 1899] has so vulgarized history and so caricatured human nature that it takes some courage to set out upon the reading of a novel that has anything to do with the history of the colonies. One has not traveled very far with Miss Johnston, however, before he discovers that he has quite another sort of authorship to consider, and a work which must be taken seriously. Miss Johnston displays again the qualities that stood out so prominently in her former novel, *The Prisoners of Hope* [1898]; an illuminative imagination and a deep vein of sensitive romanticism. The historical novel is the field for which she is peculiarly and eminently fitted. In no other department of letters is a heated imagination more necessary, and nowhere is it more rare. In these deplorable days when Knighthood is in Flower to the tune of half a million copies, and when novels of the same literary fibre as *Molly Bawn* and *Red as a Rose Is She*[45] are tricked out in crinoline and powdered hair and odds-bodikins—whatever those may be —and sent forth heralds of the revival of Romance, it is a pleasant experience to encounter such a novel as Miss Johnston's bearing the stamp of a superior mentality and of an individuality strong enough to do freshly and well what has been done often and badly.

Because Miss Johnston does not sink history into the slough of sentimentality I do not mean to say that she has written an historical commentary. If she has "read up" she has the grace not to show it, and she has spared us her cross references.

The history of Colonial Virginia is peculiarly rich in romantic suggestion. The state was settled by gentlemen, men of birth and education with a thirst for adventure and, many of them, with the wanderlust in their blood. Unlike their New England neighbors they were not reformers and had no mind to take the color out of life by an ascetic morality or to reduce existence into a grey uniformity of exacting social codes. They lived for this world and were not averse to pleasure. They were of the element which had made the picturesqueness of English history under Elizabeth. Some of them had left romantic pasts behind them, and a romantic disposition is like a bad reputation; a man may leave a good deal of it wherever he goes, but he always takes more of it with him. To such a likely source Miss Johnston has gone for her material. For the persons of

45. *Molly Bawn* (1878) by Margaret Hungerford ("The Duchess"); *Red as a Rose Is She* (1878) by Rhoda Broughton (1840–1920).

her drama she has selected a Captain of the Low Country wars, a ward of James I who had fled the court to escape a distasteful marriage and come in disguise into the Virginia Wilderness, the king's favorite, Lord Carnal, as handsome and dissolute a villain as heart could wish, John Rolfe, and a giant of a play actor who had turned preacher but who still sang Master Shakespeare's songs on sunny days in summer. To how much historical accuracy Miss Johnston may lay claim I cannot say. But certainly she has a kind of spiritual verity, a faculty of making other times and other conditions stand forth in their beautiful perspective, of calling back forgotten tragedies across the years like the strains of distant music. She has the instinct of contrast, the feeling for color, the sense of values that goes to make up the true romantic novelist. What a stroke of art it is to bring Lord Carnal, with his Venetian goblets and cloth of gold, his Italian physician and courtier's ways and the king's favor like a visible nimbus about his handsome head, into this stern, dark Virginia wilderness. There is something about Miss Johnston's way of dealing with these "old, unhappy, far off things" that minds me not a little of Charles Kingsley and bids me turn to *Westward Ho!* again.[46] Her use of the physical features of Virginia is a source of perpetual charm throughout the book. There is a high quality of imagination about it that at times is almost lyric. Miss Johnston's Indians are less like those of the tobacconists than any that I have previously encountered in fiction. Indeed I can think of no other novel since Cooper in which the Glorious Red Man has been lifted much above the Old Sleuth series. The heroine of the tale is worthy of her setting, picturesque enough to grace any romance or turn the head of any captain, though she seldom condescends to step out of her canvas and one feels her presence most when she is silent and seen only through Captain Percy's eyes. As for Miss Johnston's hero, I suppose he is the sort of man that women would have peopled the world with, though I have a sad conviction that such a one never fought and lived and loved in the old Virginia colony, and I think he acquits himself best and is more of a man when he is away from his lady and in the forest with Diccon. Miss Johnston has succeeded better with the men whom she cherished less, Diccon and the inimitable Master Sparrow, preacher and play actor, and even with that attractive villain, Lord Carnal. In denying them some of the virtues she has given them a more than compensating humanity and blood

46. Charles Kingsley (1819–1875) wrote *Westward-Ho!* (1855) and *The Roman and the Teuton* (1864); the latter was the source for one of the epigraphs in *The Troll Garden*. See *KA*, pp. 442 ff.

that we know the color of. Certainly Miss Johnston has struck a new note in American fiction, remote and plaintive and sweet, and from her voyagings into the past she has brought a richer cargo than all the plate and cloth of gold and Venice glass of my Lord Carnal's ship.

Courier, March 24, 1900, p. 3.

Jane Addams on Tolstoi

European intellectual history was made when Count Leo Tolstoi (1828–1910) renounced his art and his worldly goods to devote his life to a mystical religion, the social equality of work, and didactic art. His social and economic ideas and practices drew adherents and observers from all over the world, including the famed social worker Jane Addams (1860–1935), who founded Hull House in 1889. Tolstoi's ideas on art were expressed in his 1898 essay, What Is Art?[47] *In an unpublished fragment, "Light on Adobe Walls," collected posthumously, Willa Cather wrote: "Art is too terribly human to be very 'great,' perhaps. Some very great artists have outgrown art, the men were bigger than the game. Tolstoi did, and Leonardo did. When I hear the last opuses, I think Beethoven did. Shakespeare died at fifty-three, but there is an awful veiled threat in* The Tempest *that he too felt he had outgrown his toys. . . ."*[48]

Of course everyone has heard of Jane Addams, the founder of Hull House, in Chicago, who has done such remarkable work among the poor of that city. Ordinarily I am not interested in philanthropy, and I have an absolute aversion for women who lecture. But Miss Addams lectured here on Tolstoi, and I went to hear her. I think I have met no one since I met Nansen[49] who impressed me as being so full of power, so keen and so unafraid. She rides no hobby. She is not a lady who talks about the rum curse, she does not believe that cigarettes will destroy civilization. She is a student and a member of that reckless fraternity that hunts for truth. She is not fortunate enough to believe that any one thing, such as the abolishing of saloons, or the prohibition of cigarettes will right the wrongs of the people among whom she works. She would be much happier if she could only be a fanatic. She does not believe that society will ever be very much

47. Kitty Ayrshire, prima donna heroine of "A Gold Slipper," discourses at length on the essay to a Pittsburgh businessman. *Youth and the Bright Medusa*, p. 142.

48. *On Writing*, p. 125.

49. See "Nansen: 'that unmistakable Norse accent,'" The Urban Scene, above.

better off. I think she sometimes doubts even the effectualness of her own work, and so much the greater must her courage be in doing it so loyally.

She is a grave, quiet woman, perhaps forty-five years old. She is slightly stooped and somewhat indifferent to her appearance. Her iron-gray hair is knotted carelessly and plainly at the back of her head. But her face, as you look at it, seems the face of a conqueror, of one who lives far above the tides of feeling. You are conscious of a purpose and an intelligence that burns like the lamps of a lighthouse, above the toiling of the waves and the stress of the sea.

Miss Addams began her lecture by a discussion of the relations of the Russian peasant to his lord, and a brief analysis of that strange being, the Russian peasant himself, his heavy Slavonic nature and his fondness for the soil.

Miss Addams is not a Tolstoian to the full extent, indeed Miss Addams is not an extremist in anything, but a candid, large-minded student of men and measures, a fearless critic of life. She spoke calmly, dispassionately, with unfailing fluency and conciseness. Miss Addams is strangely unlike the well-known woman with a hobby, or woman with a theory, or woman with a wrong. She seems rather to be a woman with a mind, and a large, large humanity. . . .

Miss Addams believes that the great quality of Tolstoi's art and the distinguishing feature of his novels is his broad and compassionate humanity. No mind, she thinks since Shakespeare's has been so keen in discerning the springs of action in other people, has had such a complete intuitional realization of just what those people would do under all circumstances. This same quality, she says, is evinced in his conduct of life. . . .

While Miss Addams was talking I could not help thinking of the letter that Turgenev wrote Tolstoi from his deathbed, urging him, begging him to abandon his philanthropic madness and give himself again to the great art which he had once enriched. When Count Tolstoi lived in the world and was, as he assures me [us?], a very bad man, he wrote some of the greatest novels in the world's literature. Now that he lives like a serf and spends his strength for his convictions, he writes fables for heavy-browed peasants. The comparison is a poor argument for godly living. But the gist of the whole matter is this, in these times a man cannot live away from the stress of the battle. A weak man or a vicious man who in the long run makes for good is more useful than a saint who hides in the cloister.

Count Tolstoi argues that art has grown too far away from the people. No, it is the people who have grown, and art with them. He argues that no greater poetry has been written than the *Iliad* which came almost directly from the people. But verses from the people of today would be very different stuff. The life of the peasant today is less independently personal, more complex than that of the Argive kings. The life and fortunes of the humblest laborer today are influenced by telegraph reports, stock markets, questions of transportation. So the art that expresses life today must be more complex than the art of the Homeric Greeks.

As to Tolstoi's theory of labor, of one man's doing several kinds of labor and of throwing the disagreeable work wholly upon no one class, its absurdity is plain enough. If Tennyson had gone every day into his tulip bed and sent his tulip gardener in to work at *Maud*, I fancy neither *Maud* nor the tulips would have prospered. It seems unfair enough that some should be doomed as the hod carriers of the world, but even Count Tolstoi cannot unmake and refashion God's universe. Nature did not mean all things to be equally beautiful or equally happy. She made the skylark and she made the toad, and not all the passion of our prayers could give the reptile wings. There is no means among all the resources of science whereby we may communicate to an oyster the beauty of a symphony.

Courier, March 17, 1900, pp. 3–4.

Frank Norris: "An Heir Apparent"

A year before the following selection appeared, Willa Cather had reviewed Norris's McTeague *(Books and Authors [III], above) and nine months later wrote of* Blix *("Stephen Crane and Frank Norris," above) with unabated enthusiasm. She revealed part of the basis for her response to Norris in a review of* The Helpers *by Francis Lynde (1859–1930), in which she referred to Blix as a model western woman: "Since Mr. Lynde wished to write a novel on the helpfulness of men and women to each other, it was very proper that he should stage it in the west, where the newness of the civilization and excess of transient life brings about an almost colonial condition of society. Everyone is practically away from home; everyone has left his friends behind him, and the common exile draws men and women very close to each other and makes quick friendships. Naturally the chief factor in Jafferd's rehabilitation was a woman. . . . She was as strong and loyal and frank as a man, and as tender and compassionate as a woman. Perhaps it was because her mental horizons were so wide that her heart was so large, and perhaps her love was enduring not because it was blind, but because it saw all, and knew the ways of life. After Mr. Norris' tribute to western women in* Blix, *and Mr. Lynde's apotheosis of them in* The Helpers, *some chivalrous fellow should feel it incumbent upon him to take up his quill in defense of young ladies born within the pale of the more rigid conventionalities*" (Leader, *December 2, 1899*). *The title of the following column was* "*An Heir Apparent.*"

Last winter a young Californian, Mr. Frank Norris, published a novel with the unpretentious title, *McTeague: A Story of San Francisco*. It was a book that could not be ignored nor dismissed with a word. There was something very unusual about it, about its solidity and mass, the thoroughness and firmness of texture, and it came down like a blow from a sledge hammer among the slighter and more sprightly performances of the hour.

The most remarkable thing about the book was its maturity and compactness. It has none of the earmarks of those entertaining "young writers" whom every season produces as inevitably as its debutantes, young men who surprise for an hour and then settle down to producing industriously for the class with which their peculiar trick of phrase has found favor. It was a book addressed to the American people and to the critics of the world, the work of a young man who had set himself to the art of authorship with an almighty seriousness, and who had no ambition to be clever. *McTeague* was not an experiment in style nor a pretty piece of romantic folly, it was a true story of the people—having about it, as M. Zola would say, "the smell of the people"—courageous, dramatic, full of matter and warm with life. It was realism of the most uncompromising kind. The theme was such that the author could not have expected sudden popularity for his book, such as sometimes overtakes monstrosities of style in these discouraging days when Knighthood is in Flower to the extent of a quarter of a million copies,[50] nor could he have hoped for pressing commissions from the fireside periodicals. The life story of a quack dentist who sometimes extracted molars with his fingers, who mistreated and finally murdered his wife, is not, in itself, attractive. But, after all, the theme counts for very little. Every newspaper contains the essential subject matter for another *Comédie Humaine*. The important point is that a man considerably under thirty could take up a subject so grim and un-

50. *When Knighthood Was in Flower* by Charles Major (1856–1913), the leading best seller of 1899. In the review of *To Have and To Hold*, above, "Knighthood is in Flower to the tune of half a million copies."

attractive, and that, for the mere love of doing things well, he was able to hold himself down to the task of developing it completely, that he was able to justify this quack's existence in literature, to thrust this hairy, blonde dentist with the "salient jaw of the carnivora," in amongst the immortals.

It was after M. Zola had completed one of the greatest and gloomiest of his novels of Parisian life, that he went down by the sea and wrote *La Rêve*, that tender, adolescent story of love and purity and youth. So, almost simultaneously with *McTeague*, Mr. Norris published *Blix*, another San Francisco story, as short as *McTeague* was lengthy, as light as *McTeague* was heavy, as poetic and graceful as *McTeague* was somber and charmless. Here is a man worth waiting on; a man who is both realist and poet, a man who can teach "Not only by a comet's rush, / But by a rose's birth."

Yet unlike as they are, in both books the source of power is the same, and, for that matter, it was even the same in his first book, *Moran of the Lady Letty* [1898]. Mr. Norris has dispensed with the conventional symbols that have crept into art, with the trite, half-truths and circumlocutions, and got back to the physical basis of things. He has abjured tea-table psychology and the analysis of figures in the carpet and subtile dissections of intellectual impotencies, and the diverting game of words and the whole literature of the nerves. He is big and warm and sometimes brutal, and the strength of the soil comes up to him with very little loss in the transmission. His art strikes deep down into the roots of life and the foundation of Things as They Are—not as we tell each other they are at the tea-table. But he is realistic art, not artistic realism. He is courageous, but he is without bravado.

He sees things freshly, as though they had not been seen before, and describes them with singular directness and vividness, not with morbid acuteness, with a large, wholesome joy of life. Nowhere is this more evident than in his insistent use of environment. I recall the passage in which he describes the street in which McTeague lives. He represents that street as it is on Sunday, as it is on working days, as it is in the early dawn when the workmen are going out with pickaxes on their shoulders, as it is at ten o'clock when the women are out marketing among the small shopkeepers, as it is at night when the shop girls are out with the soda fountain tenders and the motor cars dash by full of theatregoers, and the Salvationists sing before the saloon on the corner. In four pages he reproduces in detail the life in a bystreet of a great city, the little tragedy of the small shopkeeper. There are many ways of handling environment—most of them bad. When a young author has very little to say and no story worth telling, he resorts to environment. It is frequently used to disguise a weakness of structure, as ladies who paint landscapes put their cows knee-deep in water to conceal the defective drawing of the legs. But such description as one meets throughout Mr. Norris' book is in itself convincing proof of power, imagination and literary skill. It is a positive and active force, stimulating the reader's imagination, giving him an actual command, a realizing sense of this world into which he is suddenly transported. It gives to the book perspective, atmosphere, effects of time and distance, creates the illusion of life. This power of mature and comprehensive description is very unusual among the younger American writers. Most of them observe the world through a temperament, and are more occupied with their medium than the objects they watch. And temperament is a glass which distorts most astonishingly. But this young man sees with a clear eye and reproduces with a touch, firm and decisive, strong almost to brutalness.

Mr. Norris approaches things on their physical side; his characters are personalities of flesh before they are anything else, types before they are individuals. Especially is this true of his women. His Trina is "very small and prettily made. Her face was round and rather pale; her eyes long and narrow and blue, like the half-opened eyes of a baby; her lips and the lobes of her tiny ears were pale, a little suggestive of anaemia. But it was to her hair that one's attention was most attracted. Heaps and heaps of blue-black coils and braids, a royal crown of swarthy bands, a veritable sable tiara, heavy, abundant and odorous. All the vitality that should have given color to her face seems to have been absorbed by that marvelous hair. It was the coiffure of a queen that shadowed the temples of this little bourgeoise." Blix had "round, full arms," and "the skin of her face was white and clean, except where it flushed into a most charming pink upon her smooth, cool cheeks." In this grasp of the element of things, this keen, clean, frank pleasure at color and odor and warmth, this candid admission of the negative of beauty, which is co-existent with and inseparable from it, lie much of his power and promise. Here is a man catholic enough to include the extremes of physical and moral life, strong enough to handle the crudest colors and darkest shadows. Here is a man who has an appetite for the physical universe, who loves the rank smells of crowded alleyways, or the odors of boudoirs, or the delicate perfume exhaled from a woman's skin; who is not afraid of Pan, be he ever so shaggy and redolent of the herd.

Structurally, where most young novelists are weak, Mr. Norris is very strong. He has studied the best French masters, and he has adopted their methods quite simply, as one selects an algebraic formula to solve his particular problem. As to his style, that is, as expression always is, just as vigorous as his thought compels it to be, just as vivid as his conception warrants. If God Almighty has given a man ideas, he will get himself a style from one source or another. Mr. Norris, fortunately, is not a conscious stylist. He has too much to say to be exquisitely vain about his medium. He has the kind of brain stuff that would vanquish difficulties in any profession, that might be put to building battleships, or solving problems of finance, or to devising colonial policies. Let us be thankful that he has put it to literature. Let us be thankful, moreover, that he is not introspective and that his intellect does not devour itself, but feeds upon the great race of man, and, above all, let us rejoice that he is not a "temperamental" artist, but something larger, for a great brain and an assertive temperament seldom dwell together.

There are clever men enough in the field of American letters, and the fault of most of them is merely one of magnitude; they are not large enough; they travel in small orbits, they play on muted strings. They sing neither of the combats of Atridae nor the labors of Cadmus, but of the tea-table and the Odyssey of the Rialto. Flaubert said that a drop of water contained all the elements of the sea, save one—immensity. Mr. Norris is concerned only with serious things, he has only large ambitions. His brush is bold, his color is taken fresh from the kindly earth, his canvas is large enough to hold American life, the real life of the people. He has come into the court of the troubadours singing the song of Elys, the song of warm, full nature. He has struck the true note of the common life. He is what Mr. Norman Hapgood said the great American dramatist must be: "A large human being, with a firm stomach, who knows and loves the people."

Courier, April 7, 1900, p. 3.

Part III

THE WORLD

❈ ❈ ❈

Chronology for Part III

1900	
May (?)	Willa Cather resigns from the staff of the *Leader*.
August 11	Last signed contribution to the *Library*.
Fall	Moves to Washington, D.C.; works as translator in a government office.
November	"The Man Who Wrote 'Narcissus'" in *Ladies' Home Journal*.
December	First letter from Washington in *Nebraska State Journal* on December 9; "Winter Sketches from the Capital" begins in *Index of Pittsburg Life* on December 22. During 1900 Cather published nine poems.
1901	
February 17	Death of Ethelbert Nevin. Cather attends funeral in Pittsburgh.
March	Final contribution to *Index* on March 16; final Washington letter in *Journal* on March 17. Nevin obituary in *Journal* on March 24. By this date Cather probably back in Pittsburgh. On March 30 a story, "Jack-a-boy," in *Saturday Evening Post*.
Spring	Teaches spring term at Central High School. Now living with the McClung family at 1180 Murray Avenue.
July—August	In Red Cloud and Lincoln. Guest editor of the *Courier* for issues of August 10, 17, and 24.
September	Resumes teaching at Central High School.
November 17	First signed article ("Henry Nicklemann") in *Pittsburgh Gazette*.
1902	
January—June	Teaching at Central High School. Continues to contribute to *Gazette*. Poems in *Harper's Weekly*, *Lippincott's*, *Youth's Companion*.
June—September	Abroad with Isabelle McClung. Sends travel letters to the *Journal;* articles also appearing in *Gazette*.
Fall	Resumes teaching at Central High School.
October 19	Last contribution to *Nebraska State Journal*.
November 30	Two articles in *Gazette*.
1903	
January	Story, "'A Death in the Desert,'" in *Scribner's*.
April	A volume of verse, *April Twilights*, published by Richard G. Badger.
Summer	Vacationing in Nebraska.
September	Begins teaching at Allegheny High School.
November 29	Article in the *Gazette*.

The *Library*

(March 24, 1900—August 4, 1900)

Willa Cather had been in Pittsburgh nearly five years when she ended her connection with the Leader *and embarked upon her career as a free-lance journalist. While the reasons that prompted her resignation—and even exactly when it occurred—are not definitely known,*[1] *the acceptance of her story "Eric Hermannson's Soul" by* Cosmopolitan *surely would have been encouraging, and at this time she still had hopes of finding a publisher for "The Player Letters."*[2] *But the immediate impetus may well have come from the launching of a new magazine by Charles S. Clarke, a young man who had inherited twenty thousand dollars and who "decided that Pittsburgh needed a literary journal like the London* Spectator, *only more so."*[3] *A five-cent weekly described as "handsome and interesting,"*[4] *it was called the* Library *and the first of its twenty-six issues appeared on March 10, 1900. I have found no evidence that Willa Cather was ever a member of the staff, but among contributors apparently she had the inside track, for during a period of less than six months (while the proprietor's money was melting away) she contributed twenty-six proved items—poems, stories, and articles—under her own name and under pseudonyms. In addition, six articles and columns signed "C.W.S." and two poems and one article signed "Clara Wood Shipman" have been attributed to her.*[5]

1. According to Brown, *Willa Cather*, p. 91, she was still listed as a reporter for the *Leader* in the Pittsburgh directory of 1900, but I have discovered no identifiable *Leader* pieces later than March 13, 1900. Willa Cather's "Passing Show" column came to an end on May 12, 1900, and this too suggests a change in her circumstances.

2. In January 1900 Willa Cather wrote a friend that the letters "are now with R. H. Russell & Co. of New York. . . . Rupert Hughes, of the Criterion, says they will surely go somewhere." Quoted in Adams, "Willa Cather," p. 92. Since "Eric Hermannson's Soul" appeared in the April *Cosmopolitan*, it must have been accepted no later than the first of the year.

3. Seibel, p. 205.

4. Mott, *History of American Magazines*, IV, 88–89.

5. John P. Hinz, "Willa Cather in Pittsburgh," *New Colophon* 3 (1950), p. 201, made these attributions, in part on the basis that Willa Cather transposed the initials W.S.C. to

Of the seven proved poems, five appeared under Cather's own name, one was signed with her initials, and one was signed "John Charles Asten." Of the seven proved stories, including revisions of two which had been published before she left Nebraska, six were signed and the seventh appeared under the pseudonym "Henry Nicklemann." Two of the twelve proved articles were signed by her own name; there was one each by "Helen Delay," "George Overing," and "Goliath"; and seven were signed "Henry Nicklemann." The name Nicklemann, according to George Seibel, was "borrowed from a folklore figure in Gerhart Hauptmann's Sunken Bell, *which we read once as an interlude of our French program."*[6] *The "Helen Delay" pseudonym has been discussed earlier (see the introduction to The* Home Monthly, *above); "George Overing" was the name of a Red Cloud acquaintance; and "Goliath" carries out the idea of the article to which it is signed, "A Philistine in the Gallery."*

The "Helen Delay" article, omitted here, was titled "Out of Their Pulpits" and concerned the Pittsburgh clergy. The unproved pieces, also omitted, were of purely local interest. That by "Clara Wood Shipman," which appeared on June 30, 1900, was called "Pittsburgh Summer Amusements." The others, by "C.W.S.," were: "Pittsburgh People and Doings" (July 7 and July 14); "The Pittsburgh Firemen" (July 21); "Pittsburgh People and Points" (July 21); "The Men Who Make the Pittsburgh Papers" (August 4); and "Pittsburgh on the Ocean" (August 25). Arthur G. Burgoyne, Sr., the Leader *music critic, whose desk was next to Willa Cather's, is one of the newspapermen discussed in "The Men Who Make the Pittsburgh Papers," and whether or not Cather wrote the piece, there are some interesting points of resemblance between him and Scott McGregor in* The Professor's House, *who wrote a daily poem for his newspaper and "'uplift' editorials."*[7] *Of Burgoyne it was said: "His 'All Sorts' column is best known, perhaps, of all his work, though he writes more seriously when he is fighting trusts or straightening out municipal politics, editorially. Like all men who write funny things, he is of a very solemn cast, almost to the point of gloom. But it is no contradiction that he should find life a little strenuous. To write a*

---

indicate her identity. But, as Bernice Slote has pointed out, "Clara Wood Shipman" was publishing in the *New England Magazine* in June 1896, and Willa Cather did not use Sibert as a middle name until 1900 (*KA*, p. 28 n). Slote states elsewhere that "up to now I have been unable to find unassailable proof that all writing with that signature [Clara Wood Shipman] is Willa Cather's" (*AT(1903)*, p. 76).

6. Seibel, p. 206. Interestingly enough, the first issue of the *Library*, March 10, 1900 (to which Willa Cather did not contribute), announced that E. H. Sothern and Virginia Harned would give a charity performance of *The Sunken Bell* during their run in Pittsburgh, March 19–24.

7. *The Professor's House*, pp. 44, 73.

poem every day, a poem with a point to it, and to have it a funny poem with no lack of rhymes, is as serious a task as one cares to imagine, and to have an opinion or an observation at hand about everything, every day, from Boxers to Cuban Post Offices, is also a task requiring the versatility and quick-wittedness of a man like Mr. Burgoyne. . . . The fact that Mr. Burgoyne lives about eleven miles out of town and has his own piece of land, which he hoes and digs to his own satisfaction after he leaves his work, is probably the reason why his newspaper work is always full of a crispness and terseness, for he never takes his newspaper cares home with him."

Willa Cather's first proved contribution to the Library *was a poem ("In the Night") appearing in the second issue, March 17, 1900, and she had two other contributions in March, both in the March 24 issue. The distribution of other proved pieces is as follows: April—six contributions in four issues; May—one (May 12); June—six (including a two-part serial) in four issues; July—seven in four issues; August—three in two issues (ending with a story, "The Conversion of Sum Loo," on August 11).*

"*Some Personages of the Opera*"

Willa Cather's first signed article for the Library *is interesting to contrast with her numerous earlier newspaper pieces on prima donnas (see The Musical World [I], [II], and [III], above). While she makes some familiar points, the article is by no means a rehash; her approach is more detached and sophisticated, and the whole production is a good deal more polished.*[8] *The article is given complete except for the three concluding paragraphs, which dealt in summary fashion with three male singers—Edouard de Reszke, Pol Plançon (1854–1914), and Ernest Van Dyck (1861–1923).*

A Chicago critic in comparing the four great sopranos of the Metropolitan Company once said, "Eames is ice water; Nordica, Rhine wine; Melba, champagne; but Calvé is a whole drunk."[9] His rhetoric was not elegant, but his imagery was expressive. Undoubtedly Calvé is the most conspicuous figure among the singers who are to appear in Pittsburgh during Easter week, and throughout the season she has done more than any other member of Mr. Grau's Company to fill the void created by Jean de Reszke's absence. When all is said, it is personality that counts in

8. See also Willa Cather, "Three American Singers," *McClure's*, December 1913, pp. 33–48.

9. For an earlier use of this quotation, see *Journal*, October 21, 1894, p. 13, in "The Critic's Province," The Theatre (I), above.

art as in everything else, a personality that reaches out of art into life, commanding alike the wise and the foolish, and Mr. Grau has found that when Jean de Reszke stays abroad, he must have Emma Calvé.

The greatest compliment paid to Calvé as an artist is, that one hears so little about her voice. She herself has eclipsed it, she is so much greater than the mere gift she possesses. It is impossible to consider her in a coldly critical spirit; if you accept her at all, you must consider her *in toto*, her magnificent dramatic impulses, her abounding vigor, her warmth, her power, her caprices, her whole dynamic personality.

Though she has proved so invaluable to Mr. Grau, none of his sopranos have caused him more annoyance. She is capricious as a child, superstitious as a peasant, and vain as an artist. She is at once the most indolent and energetic of women. She never hurries; it is a physical impossibility with her. She is always late, and is the despair of rehearsals. She insists upon having two hours to dress before every performance, and then is never ready for the call boy. When she has a matinee performance, she goes to the theatre as soon as she gets out of bed. She will never dress without two maids to assist her and her companions,who read aloud to her from the latest novel by Paul Bourget or Gabriele D'Annunzio. Calvé has a profound conviction that heat dries up her lungs and injures her voice, and she abominates American methods of heating. She is utterly impervious to cold, and in the rawest nights of a New York winter has the heat turned off in her dressing-room and the doors and windows wide open. Her maids, poor things, who have neither the Calvé "temperament" nor the fire of her genius, are always wretchedly cold. She is genuinely sorry for them, and pats them upon the cheek quite affectionately, but they have tonsillitis none the less. By her fellow artists Mlle. Calvé is sincerely admired and feared, but few of them lead a placid existence near her. Her quarrel with Emma Eames is now ancient history, but it was during the last of her former seasons in New York that she sang at a charity concert with M. Plançon, and when he innocently ordered some of her flowers removed from the stage before the performance began, as their odor annoyed him, she rushed hatless and furless from the theatre and was found in the street hailing a cab.

Calvé's great operatic success is a matter of recent date, for she is yet a young woman. After an impoverished and laborious girlhood, she made her debut in Brussels in 1881. She then received a salary of one hundred and forty dollars a month. In the very beginning of her career she spent much time in Italy, where she came under the influence of Eleonora Duse, whose consummate art has permeated all Calvé's impersonations. In 1892 she created the role of Santuzza in Mascagni's new opera, *Cavalleria Rusticana*, and then for the first time really took her place among the world's great artists. Her next triumph was her Carmen, in which she first appeared in Paris in 1894. It was one of the greatest events in all the history of opera. Other women had played Carmen, but this, by grace of God, was Carmen herself.

Among the young American art students in Paris, Emma Eames holds much the same place that Julia Arthur[10] used to hold among college boys in this country, something between a patron saint and a subject for sonnets. Her house there is open to all her ambitious young countrymen, and both she and her husband are most generous to young artists. Mme. Eames has good reason to feel kindly towards art students; when she was studying in Paris years ago, she posed for one who afterwards became her husband. Young Story[11] called his picture "Song," but Miss Eames left Paris before it was completed, and he sold it to Mrs. Henry Kirke Porter, of Pittsburgh, and during the engagement of the Grand Opera Company here last season, Mr. and Mrs. Story went to call at Oak Manor, and the prima donna saw the finished picture for the first time. It was exhibited at the Carnegie Gallery here this winter. Mme. Eames' marriage to Mr. Story was the cause of much newspaper romancing. The simple facts are these: her mother opposed Mr. Story's suit most vigorously, and the young singer, who is as determined as she is calm, quietly eloped and was married to Mr. Story in the old church at Bray.

Mme. Eames is not a great actress, and it is very probable that she has never tried to be one. Her very bearing when she steps upon the stage seems to say, "I am a gentlewoman, and I sing for you; I am not an actress." Her voice appeals more particularly to musicians, her power is largely an intellectual one, her personal charm [lies?] in a certain dignity and severe, patrician beauty. Her greatest successes have been in Wagnerian parts. In 1891 she first sang Elsa in *Lohengrin* after only one rehearsal. In 1895 she first sang her Elizabeth in *Tannhäuser*, which is considered the noblest and most original rendition of the part ever given. Cold she is, but it is the coldness of reserve, not of apathy, and in her very inactivity upon the stage there is a significance and the classic grace of Grecian marbles.

10. For Julia Arthur, see "The Training of Actors," The Star System (III), above.

11. Julian Russell Story (1857–1919), American portrait painter, son of the sculptor William Wetmore Story (see Books and Authors [III], above).

Frau Ernestine Schumann-Heink is certainly the foremost contralto of the Metropolitan Company, if not of the world. Her dramatic Ortrud and superb Fricka are still remembered here. The lot of a contralto is, for the most part, an ungrateful one, since all the operatic virtues are supposed to express themselves only in the soprano register. It would be an interesting experience to hear Frau Schumann-Heink sing a good, natural part, for well we know that she can simulate every manner of spitefulness and treachery known to the day of Scalchi's prime. No contralto has sung with such dramatic fervor. In the matter of industry and capability Frau Schumann-Heink is simply amazing. In addition to the rigorous labor of her profession, her domestic duties are most onerous. When she arrived in St. Louis this season, a would-be wit said, "Here is Schumann-Heink, but where are the nine?" He referred, of course, to Frau Schumann-Heink's nine children, the youngest of which was born in New York last winter. It has been the custom of the itinerant Schumann-Heinks to name their children after the hotel in which they happened to be born, and last winter Frau Ernestine astonished Mr. Grau by suddenly packing her chattels and decamping from the Astoria, declaring that she would inflict on no child such a name as Waldorf-Astoria Schumann-Heink.

Frau Schumann-Heink is rabidly domestic, and during her stay here last winter was chiefly interested in baby foods, and had very little to say to anyone not informed upon that absorbing topic.

Theodore Thomas once said, "If a man had Lillian Nordica's chin, he could take an empire." Anyone who knows what it means for an American girl with New England training and traditions to fight her way up to the thrones of the great operatic sopranos, will say that Mme. Nordica has done almost more than that. He who has conquered Bayreuth is mightier than he that taketh a city. There are many theories as to how much environment and heredity have to do with the making of an artist, but certainly anyone will admit that an operatic singer born at Farmington, Maine, of a non-musical family, and the granddaughter of a Methodist revival exhorter, had some disadvantages to begin with. But Lillian Norton's life has been one long conquest of difficulties. She has lived up to that determined chin of hers. She had much of the Valkyr in her before she ever sang Brünnhilde. She has never lost the hallmark of New England—did any New Englander every lose it?—and in that strange assemblage of polyglots which constitute the Metropolitan Opera Company, she has always stood out as distinctly and unmistakably American.

Mme. Nordica's musical education was begun at the New England Conservatory of Music in Boston, and she once stood in high favor there, though I believe she has since estranged the affections of that city by once, in a moment of irritation, declaring that the Boston Symphony Orchestra played like a Kalamazoo band. She has studied incessantly, and her musical scholarship is unusually broad and comprehensive. The beginning of her career was clouded by difficulties which would have appalled a woman of less indomitable ambition. "Put your heart under your foot, Kate!" she once said impatiently to a pupil who was trying to decide between a domestic and an artistic career. She made her debut in opera at Brescia in 1879. Ten years ago she attacked Wagner with characteristic vigor, and in 1894 her Elsa was pronounced the greatest ever heard at Bayreuth.

Mme. Nordica's first marriage was to her cousin, Roland Gower. Many and strange as have been the fates of prima donnas' husbands, Mr. Gower's certainly was the most unique of all. Shortly after their marriage he made a balloon excursion in France, and neither he nor the balloon were ever heard of again. Ten years later Mme. Nordica became engaged to a Hungarian tenor, Zoltan Doehme, and their courtship was a somewhat stormy one. Nordica finally broke the engagement, and announced that she was "happier than she had been for years." Six months later, however, when she was singing in Indianapolis, Herr Doehme's card was sent up to her at her hotel, and she found him in the parlor, whither he had come all the way from Hungary. His explanation must have been satisfactory, for they were married that same night.

Of Patti's great rivals, only Marcella Sembrich now remains, and the curious public probably knows less of her life and personality than of any other singer of her rank and fame. In the most public of all professions, she has managed to live behind closed doors, and to keep herself within herself. Perhaps her Polish blood may somewhat account for her exclusiveness. The Poles are a clannish people, and not given to conviviality. Mme. Sembrich is a musician of remarkable versatility; a better pianist than many a so-called virtuoso, an accomplished violinist, and one of the greatest singers of our time, who for almost twenty years has helped to make the history of opera. She was born in Galicia in 1858, and first appeared in concert when she was twelve years old, playing both piano and violin. She intended to devote herself entirely to the piano, but when she went to Vienna to study under Liszt, Lamperti the younger discovered her vocal possibilities, and persuaded her to study for the opera. In 1880 she was Patti's most formidable rival. She married her former teacher, Stengel, and when she is not touring, lives in her sumptuous home in Dresden.

Mme. Sembrich is exceedingly fond of riding, and the Emperor of Germany says that she is the best horsewoman in his empire. . . . [March 24, 1900, pp. 18–20]

"*A Philistine in the Gallery*"

This article originally appeared with the subtitle "Some Remarks on the Pictures at the Carnegie," and was signed with the name of the Philistine giant, "Goliath."[12] *Willa Cather previously had written in "The Passing Show" about the Carnegie Institute Art Galleries and some of the artists mentioned here, including Bouguereau and William Merritt Chase (see "Will H. Low and Bouguereau," The Urban Scene, above). In the light of later developments, perhaps the most interesting comment attaches to the work of the French painter Pierre Puvis de Chavannes (1824–1898), best known for his murals in the Sorbonne and the Boston Public Library, who had two paintings in the original Carnegie collection. In an open letter to the* Commonweal *on* Death Comes for the Archbishop *(1927), Cather wrote: "Since I first saw the Puvis de Chavannes frescoes of the life of Saint Geneviève in my student days, I have wished that I could try something like that in prose."*[13]

I have noticed that there is a general reluctance among artistic folks, and particularly among amateurs and very young art students, to admit that the Philistine has any right to an opinion. The whole duty of the Philistine is to pay the bills and to gratefully accept such diluted information as the Young Art Student believes him capable of grasping. Now I am merely a Philistine myself. I once saw a picture of a little peasant girl by Bouguereau that I thought very pretty. I admire a certain novel of Ouida's, and I sometimes go to comic operas, and these things are indisputable proofs of my humble station. Yet, with many others of my kind, I go to look at pictures, and, in our own unenlightened fashion, we enjoy

12. Identified by Bernice Slote, who found passages which had appeared in Willa Cather's column in the *Journal*, March 1, 1896, p. 9; *KA*, pp. 415–417; and who noted that "some of the same article was used in a signed piece in the *Courier*, August 10, 1901" (*KA*, pp. 77–78 n). See "The Chicago Art Institute," Guest Editor of the *Courier*, below. A later Nicklemann piece was called "The Philistine in the Art Gallery"; see The *Gazette*, below.

13. Letter to the Editor, *Commonweal*, 7 (November 27, 1927), 713, collected in *On Writing*, p. 9. The frescoes of the life of St. Geneviève are in the Pantheon in Paris, so Cather probably first saw them on her first trip to Europe in the summer of 1902.

them, and we have as good a right to our fun as the Young Art Student has to his.

The pictures now on exhibition at the Pittsburgh Carnegie Gallery are, with the exception of three loans, the pictures owned by the gallery, some of them new acquisitions, some of them old friends with which the general public have become thoroughly familiar.

It is suggestive to observe how often the greatest work combines the qualities which appeal to the artist and those which appeal to the people. Take, for instance, the most remarkable of the new pictures, a loan by the way, Josef Israels'[14] "Mother and Child." Its popularity must be a source of chagrin to the Young Art Student. The simplicity of its directness and treatment, the somber tenderness of the coloring are in no wise lost upon the Philistine, though he may [not?] stop to reason about it, and may attribute the whole of the pleasure he experiences to the beauty of the subject—maternity. Yet he will go away with some sort of a notion that Israels was the tenderest painter of Dutch women; and that is the most important thing to know about Israels, though his technique was the best of one of the best schools in all the history of painting. Alfred Sisley's "Village on the Shore of the Marne" will scarcely be so popular. A marshy, slow-moving river, a stretch of wind-blown rushes, a pool mottled with water lily leaves, a dozen Breton peasant houses on the shore, a sky that is a monotone of cold, bluish gray. I think only people who have played by the marshes when they were children and heard the rushes sigh in the November winds, and found how satisfying that monotony of color can be, will get the full poetry of it. People who have a little of that chilly gray in their blood, and people who have tried to paint skies like that and come to grief will seek it out, but for most of the people who saunter through the galleries it will remain dumb. It is an intensely temperamental picture, and its message is for the few. Some peculiarly poignant recollection of the place, or some impression painfully sharp, got mixed into the paint as the artist worked, and his mood, somber and beautiful, was caught and transfixed there.

The other loan picture, "The Mark," by Charles Sprague Pearce, deserves small favor and gets little. The painting is certainly good, the

14. Josef Israels (1842–1911), Dutch genre painter. Others mentioned in this paragraph and the next are: Alfred Sisley (1838–1899), French landscape painter, leader of the Impressionist school; Charles Sprague Pearce (1851–1931), whose allegorical murals are in the Library of Congress; Giovanni Boldini (1845–1931), Italian genre painter and fashionable portrait painter; and Jules Bastien-Lepage (1848–1884), French painter, whose well-known picture of Joan of Arc is in the Metropolitan Museum.

painting of the fabric excellent indeed, but the subject is unpardonable. The woman is of a worse sort than Boldini's "Woman in Black," she is more than plebeian, she is common, from the curl of the finger of her left hand to the turquoise on her right. Commonness in itself is not objectionable, but commonness in white satin is odious, no matter how well the satin is painted. One is glad to turn away from this smug, vain, much bepowdered Miss to Bastien-Lepage's splendid peasant girl, who hangs beside her in fatal contrast. Here is a noble style for you, and here is a man who painted with the strength of the soil on his palette. She is the noblest thing in the whole gallery as she stands there with her hand on her hip, this little low-browed peasant girl who speaks all the tragedy of her people.

One of the pictures recently purchased by the gallery is "Judas," the work of that brilliant young Negro painter, H. O. Tanner,[15] who has shown such a marvelous aptitude for the treatment of Oriental subjects, and who seems to have found his metier in painting Biblical subjects in an entirely modern spirit. The theme of the picture is the suicide of Judas. The body hangs near the wayside, swaying in the wind, while a Jew hurries by on the other side of the road, his hands upraised in protesting horror. There is something about Tanner's insistent use of the silvery green of the olives, of the yellow of the parched clay hills of Palestine, that reminds me of Pierre Loti's faculty of infusing absolute personality into environment, if one may compare two such dissimilar mediums as prose and paint. He produces the most Oriental effects with low color tones, and his is not the Orient of the Midway and bazaar, dressed up and tricked out for a show, it is the work-a-day Palestine, the place where men plowed and sowed and prayed. There is a tradition that Biblical subjects should be painted in a highly decorative manner, and Orientalism means crimson and ultramarine. Mr. Tanner long ago struck out on a new path, and he paints pictures like "Judas" with a realism so unaffected, a sympathy with the life of the people so deep, that he has painted them with an almost national touch.

Among these graver performances, one comes upon a bit of Venice done by gay Master Rico, San Trovaso, on a sunny morning. A very blue sky, a silvery canal, white and red houses, bridges and gay gondolas, and in the foreground the dear Lombard poplar, the gayest and saddest of trees,

15. Henry O. Tanner (1859–1927) was a native of Pittsburgh. In the next two paragraphs: Martin Rico y Ortega (1850–1908) and Gari Melchers (1860–1932), who won second prize at the Inaugural Exhibition of the Institute.

rustling green and silver in the sunlight. Now Master Rico the Young Art Student always passes by in commiserating silence, for Master Rico chooses to be pretty, and mere prettiness is, in the eyes of the Young Art Student, a sin. The Young Art Student can find no place in life for the trivial and the dainty and the gay, but would have us live in Gothic cathedrals, and marry the noble but angular ladies in the mural paintings of Puvis de Chavannes. Rico is only a humming bird, if you will, or a yellow rose in June, but the Philistine will stand by him because he adds somewhat to the gaiety of life.

I have heard Gari Melchers called a hard painter, but it must have been an Art Student who said that. He has got more of the poetry out of common life than any man since Millet. The Carnegie Gallery now owns his "Sailor and His Sweetheart," and this is a picture before which the Philistines throng. They are quick enough to appreciate the striking character touch in the big white buttons on the sailor's red shirt. One who has seen the woman can never forget her, the robust uncorseted figure, the heavy, thick hands with blunt fingers, on her head just a spoolful of that peculiar sandy shade of red hair that Melchers loves, yet, after Lepage's peasant girl, I think she is the prettiest girl of the lot, and it is a mighty subtile little touch of sentiment that makes her so.

"The Bridge at Grez," by John Lavery,[16] is a wonderful piece of still water painting. There is a peculiar atmosphere about a stone bridge, and any Philistine who has ever boated about the arches of masonry and noted the peculiar greenness and coldness of the water there, will realize that Mr. Lavery had got it.

Tryon's "May" is another picture "popular with the people." I believe it is Tryon's custom to go off somewhere in the woods in the spring, and build himself a pine shack, and work up and finish his pictures on the spot. Long after they leave his hands they keep the atmosphere in which they were done. This is a windy May, of blues and violets and light greens and yellows, with the cleanest of color and treated with great elasticity and delightful enthusiasm and freshness.

There is a grave misconception about the popular attitude towards Whistler. I do not mean to say that everybody is ready to accept some of his more extreme pictures, which Ruskin described as a pot of paint slung

16. John Lavery (1856–1941), British portrait and figure painter, who won a gold medal at the Inaugural Exhibition of the Institute. In the next two paragraphs: Dwight W. Tryon (1849–1925), American landscape painter and James A. McNeill Whistler (1834–1924), who had one painting in the original collection.

at the canvas. Certainly the lack of detail in some of his night scenes is calculated to puzzle the unimaginative. But his portrait of Sarasate is one of the most popular pictures in the gallery. Everyone has appreciated the skill which brought that black figure out of the black background and has felt the almost malignant mystery about that dark, lithe man, the character in the nervous hands and bold black eyes and the full red lip.

Some very clever, and I doubt not, very young Art Student saw fit to paint a caricature of Raffaelli's works while that eminent artist was in Pittsburgh,[17] and the young impressionists here decided that he was very little of an artist. Nevertheless his "Boulevard des Italiens" has been admired by men who have much larger pasts than the young impressionists have futures. The flavor and atmosphere of the picture, its freedom and strength are characteristic of Raffaelli at his best. The woman in the foreground is painted with exquisite refinement, the battered-looking gentleman rolling a cigarette has his whole history painted in the set of his clothes.

Chase's "What Did You Say?," a study of his little daughter prettily posed in his studio, is one of the recent acquisitions of the gallery. Chase, as everyone knows, is the pet abomination of the Young Art Student. They score him because he has the trick of color, and because his pictures are pleasing to the eye and convey no lofty message. Mr. Chase is not, indeed, a poet, much less a seer. He is an admirable colorist, and he believes that there is a sort of divinity in color itself. He has at least marvelous facility and craft, and it ill becomes folk with large ideals and scant technique to belittle him. Technique is the base of every art, and the noblest sentiment may be shipwrecked in the perilous voyage from the brain to the hand. A pretty little girl, daintily posed in a studio, painted with a beautiful refinement of color, has as good a right to exist in the catholic kingdom of art as the pale, primeval shades of Puvis de Chavannes. [April 21, 1900, pp. 8–9]

"*One of Our Conquerors*"

For this article on her friend Lizzie Hudson Collier (see The Star System [III] and The Urban Scene, above), Willa Cather borrowed the title of George Meredith's 1891 novel, an engaging portrait of the New Woman. She signed it "Henry Nicklemann," her second use of this pseudonym in the

17. Jean François Raffaelli (1850–1924), French impressionist, won a prize at the Third Annual Exhibition in 1898 and was a judge at the exhibition the next year, at which time he made some condescending remarks about America in a *Leader* interview, November 5, 1899, p. 20.

Library.[18] *Charles Henry Meltzer (1853–1936), who translated Hauptmann's play* The Sunken Bell *in which "The Nicklemann, an elemental spirit," appears, described the character as a symbol of "Doubt and materialism,"* [19] *but that is hardly the tone of this tribute. The day after the article appeared, Mrs. Collier gave the final performance of her spring season with the Grand Opera House Stock Company. A* Leader *piece of June 4, 1899—"How Lizzie Hudson Collier Has Been Feted in Pittsburgh"—reported that she had become a pet of society and that "her warmest admirers, it is said, are found among the members of her own sex."*

One rainy night last winter a stranger at the Baltimore & Ohio station, observing a crowd of people who had assembled to greet a woman alighting from an in-bound train, asked,

"Is she a missionary back from the Cannibal Islands, or a society girl who has been nursing in the Philippines?"

When a native informed him that the lady in question was a popular actress getting back to town for a few days, the gentleman began to reflect upon the ways of inland cities. In a city full of transient life, like New York, it would be impossible for any public woman to attain the degree of personal popularity which Lizzie Hudson Collier has attained in Pittsburgh. A journalist once laughingly remarked, "That woman has entered into the lives of more people than anyone I ever knew, except Henry Ward Beecher."

Mrs. Collier next week completes her fourth season in Pittsburgh. During the years of '97, '98 and '99, she played the entire winter and spring seasons here as leading woman of the Grand Opera House Stock Company, and this year, having played the winter season in Cincinnati, she was engaged here for the supplementary spring season of four weeks. Her return engagement here has been a sort of continual reception, and her dressing room has supplied the hospitals with flowers. Indeed, the money spent on this fair lady's flowers since her first season here would found a hospital or buy a cottage at Long Branch. The test of time is a crucial one with an actress, and the public is notoriously fickle. In its admiration, the public is indeed fickle, but not in its affections; for the public, after all, is made up of individuals, and of individuals with hearts as well as caprices. The secret of Mrs. Collier's prolonged success here is, that, in some

18. "Henry Nicklemann" appeared in the issue of April 28, 1900, signed to a story, "The Dance at Chevalier's"; *CSF*, pp. 547–555.

19. *The Sunken Bell* by Gerhart Hauptmann, "freely rendered into English verse" by Charles Henry Meltzer (New York: Doubleday, Page & Co., 1911), p. viii.

mysterious manner, she has laid hold upon the personal affections not of a few, but of hundreds. She is the friend of people absorbed in domestic life, who seldom go inside of a theatre, and the street urchins grin all over their grimy faces when she gets back to town. I remember seeing among the costly presents that crowded her room last year at Christmas time, several quaint little offerings bought with children's pennies, for with all her arduous professional and social duties, she is never too busy or too tired to see a child. Socially, her life here has been most brilliant, though this feature of her career has already been dwelt upon more than she wishes. It is enough to say that the most conservative families of the two cities have been proud to call her their guest, and that she has been taken into the hearts and homes of the people, not because she is an actress and beautiful, but because she is a gentlewoman and altogether charming. Of course, for this sort of substantial, personal popularity, one must always pay, and pay dearly, and the many and impetuous demands made upon Mrs. Collier have often proved a severe tax upon even so warm a heart and spontaneous a sympathy as hers. She has lived much in the lives of others and suffered not a little in their misfortunes. But earth usually gets its price for what earth gives us.

Mrs. Collier is known to be generous to a fault and stranded professionals know the way to her door only too well. Her Christmas shopping last year was something fearful to contemplate and was accomplished only by the aid of her faithful maid, Alice, and many market baskets, as every one, from the manager to the stage hands and scrubwomen, was remembered. But after all, generosity of this sort is very little when compared with that rich gift of personal sympathy, so precious scarce in our Christian civilization. I recall a little incident that occurred last season when the stock company were playing *Jane*. A real baby is a necessary property in the play, and the manager secured a frail, wan little waif from the slums, eighteen months old, whose mother brought it night after night to the theatre. The cold weather came on, and one night the thermometer sank to twenty degrees below zero, and the child's mother prepared to take it home through the biting cold after the play. The actress interfered, but what was to be done? I chanced to be standing in the lower hall of the Hotel Duquesne when Mrs. Collier came in at midnight, attended by her maid, gowned in black and hugging that baby in her arms for all the world like the betrayed and deserted heroine in the fifth act of a Bijou melodrama, while the elevator boy had a paroxysm. In the morning I saw Miss Sarah from Soho comfortably taking a milk toddy in a bower of roses while the actress was preparing to give her a hot bath.

Like most actresses, Mrs. Collier has had a "past," but not such a very dreadful one. She has had, however, what most actresses have not had, a thorough education, which laid the foundation of her discriminating work in her remarkable memory, and versatile conversation. She was born Elizabeth Hudson, and as her father died in her infancy, her mother's brother, James W. Collier, who was for years manager of the Union Square Theatre in New York, largely took his place. She was educated at the New York State Normal, from which she graduated when she was seventeen.

"One reason," says Mrs. Collier, "why I am particularly fond of *Captain Letterblair* is that it was written by Marguerite Merington, who was my old Virgil teacher at school. She was the cleverest woman I ever knew, and sublimely absent-minded as to whether her skirt and waist missed connection in the back, or how many inches of skirt binding were trailing from her gown. How I have pinned that dear woman together after class!"

The year after her graduation, Miss Hudson overcame her mother's objections, and was permitted to join one of her uncle's companies in Kansas City, to take a child's part. She started off on her first long journey in the company of a child who was also to join Mr. Collier's company. Dining cars were less frequent then than now, and the two youthful travelers ate at the hotels on the road. Miss Hudson's mother had thought best to give her just about enough money to defray her expenses, and the young lady's experience in eating at hotels had been confined to little treats her uncles had given her at fashionable New York restaurants, where everything you ordered cost a fancy price. Table d'hôte service was unknown to her, she decided to be very economical, and for her first dinner on the road ordered only toast and tea. The child, who had traveled before, ordered pretty much the whole bill of fare, and when Miss Hudson saw that the bill was two dollars, she decided that if she ate very much she would never get to Kansas City. For the rest of the journey she confined herself to toast and tea in order not to stint the child, who fared sumptuously, and when she arrived at the Coates House in Kansas City, her uncle and John T. Raymond were convulsed over the story of her needless privations. She made her debut in Kansas City as the maid in *The Banker's Daughter*. When the leading woman, Mrs. Charles Walcott, fell ill, Miss Hudson took her place. Next season she played leading business in *The Lights O'London* under her uncle's management.

When she was nineteen, Miss Hudson married her uncle's only son Walter Collier, and the union has been such a satisfactory one that she has never had any inclination for further matrimonial ventures. She was married in New York on a Sunday, and on the Monday night played with her husband in Pittsburgh. Last year, at the close of the season, Mr. Collier, who is engaged in managerial business, joined his wife in Pittsburgh at the close of her engagement, and he remarked that "it was an awful strain on a man to have a popular wife, for the town fairly stared him out of countenance."

After her uncle retired from managerial life, Mrs. Collier joined Joseph Jefferson's company, playing Bertha in *The Cricket on the Hearth*, Mrs. Phobbs in *Lend Me Five Shillings* and Gretchen in *Rip Van Winkle*. Jefferson grows very fond of his people when they are the right sort, and used to read his young leading woman long extracts from his *Autobiography*, then in preparation. His youngest son, then a lad in short trousers, was so much attached to Mrs. Collier that the old actor used to say he "would have her for a daughter yet, if Walter didn't look out."

Mrs. Collier's next engagement was as William H. Crane's leading woman, playing Mabel Denman in *The Senator*, and taking the leading part in Brander Matthews' play *On Probation*. Professor Matthews, like most professional gentlemen, was exceedingly anxious that his own ideas should be brought out in his play, and wrote Crane that the leading woman must be "an actress—but, oh! so much more than an actress,—a gentlewoman, turned on a fine lathe." When he saw the dress rehearsal he remarked contentedly, "I guess you got her, Crane."

Mrs. Collier next played with Nat C. Goodwin, with whom she created the part of Margaret Ruthven in the original production of *The Gilded Fool* at the Fifth Avenue Theatre, New York. She then returned to Crane, playing Hetty in *Brother John* and Mrs. Page in *The Merry Wives of Windsor*. After that, she came to Pittsburgh, and her history since that time is inscribed in the hearts of the people.

She has played many parts in this city, played them all admirably, with grace and sympathy and dignity, but in no role has she been so popular as in that of Lizzie Hudson Collier. That rare and elusive personal charm, which is what style is to an author, or timbre to a voice, or perfume to a flower, has never failed, has always delighted and charmed. "An actress—and oh! so much more than an actress." Her kindliness and sympathy will be remembered here even longer than her art, the sweetness of her womanhood will outlive her beauty. How many generous actions are told of her, how many blue moments she has made bright! What a cordial hand clasp she has given us all on this weary way that we travel in the dark. Easy must lie the head that wears such a crown. [June 2, 1900, pp. 3–4]

"*Letters to a Playwright*"

In this signed article, the letters were addressed "To Wm. Shakespeare." Charles Frohman had produced Romeo and Juliet *with Maude Adams, William Faversham (1868–1940), and James K. Hackett (1869–1926) on May 8, 1899, and the production closed after only sixteen performances. William Winter's comment was typical of the withering criticism it received: "Mediocrity has seldom made a more judicious endeavor or encountered a more decisive defeat."*[20]

Empire Theatre, New York, June 1

Dear Sir:

Before trying a second experiment with your play *Romeo and Juliet*, I must insist upon certain alterations. Mercutio is sacrificed too early in the play, and Mr. Hackett thinks it due his professional reputation to have the part extended through the fifth act. I have always thought highly of the play as a sweet, pure love story, but the role of Juliet is not a sufficient exponent for Miss Adams' many-sided genius. While it offers ample scope for her exquisite sentiment, it offers no opportunity for that bewitching and sprite-like comedy in which she is peerless. I have thought, however, that following her production of Rostand's *L'Aiglon*, it might be expedient for her to play Romeo for a season, as in the line of feminine portrayals there is little left for her to achieve. She might profitably give a short special season of *Romeo* at ten dollars per seat.

Sincerely,
Charles Frohman

Thousand Islands, June 1, 1900

Dear Sir:

Your play *Romeo and Juliet* has greatly interested me, and I think, with a few changes, I could use it as a successor to *Kate Kip, Buyer*. In the first place, I must insist on playing it all on the ground-floor. For personal reasons I consider balconies unsafe, and I carry no accident policy. In the potion scene, I prefer to use champagne. The public is always suspicious if you drink anything muddy or mysterious on the stage. They're sure

20. Winter, *The Wallet of Time*, II, 214.

to think it's dope and decide you're a morphine fiend. Any American champagne house will furnish it by the case for the ad. You of course would have no objection to introducing a cakewalk at the Capulets' party, it would be a good way to bring the young people together. Introduce a song. Something of a ragtime nature, or "I'd Leave My Happy Home for You" would be suggestive and appropriate. I would like to play your heroine; it is a heavy part and suited to me. But no balcony, please, for

Yours truly,
May Irwin[21]

✥

Waldorf-Astoria, June 1, 1900

Dear Sir:

Miss Nethersole has read with much pleasure your play *Romeo and Juliet*, and we think, with a little strengthening of the love interest, it will be admirably suited to her purpose. I would suggest that the scene with Mercutio be cut out, and good, live love episodes be inserted in their stead. If Juliet could be given a previous entanglement, it would add greatly to the interest of the piece. Nothing takes like Redemption by Love. Allusions to a dark past would give Miss Nethersole many opportunities for strong emotional work. The chamber scene, we think, should be prolonged and more vividly written. There are great opportunities for realistic acting in the scene, if somewhat expanded. In the ballroom scene Miss Nethersole would wish to appear in fleshings and recite one of Mrs. [Ella Wheeler] Wilcox's *Poems of Passion*. Could you not arrange to have Juliet come down from the balcony in the second act, and then allow Romeo to carry her up again? Miss Nethersole has found this bit of business most effective. We think the Capulet ball scene should be written more along comic opera lines, and that the supper should take place on the stage, and perhaps it would be well to introduce a few models and chorus girls. With these changes, we think we could use your play.

Respectfully,
Louis Nethersole

21. The American comic actress May Irwin (1862–1938) starred in *Kate Kip, Buyer* by Glen Macdonough, which opened in October 1898 and ran for one hundred twenty-eight performances. Miss Irwin was celebrated for her "coon song" singing and for her ragtime renditions of "Ta-ra-ra-boom-der-é" and Harry Tilzer's "I'd Leave My Happy Home for You" (1899).

Rye, N. Y., June 1, 1900

My Dear Sir:

Your play seems to have been written by a man of some intelligence, therefore it is damned from birth and totally unfit for an American audience. I would not object to playing Romeo if you introduced a little Italian phraseology into his lines, but the part has, I understand, been played before, and I create all my parts. Besides, there is no actress alive who could play Juliet. In fact, if there are any actresses alive, I have never seen one.—*L'art, c'est moi.*

Richard Mansfield

Atlantic City, June 1, 1900

Dear Sir:

When I formerly put on *Romeo and Juliet*, I regret to say the profits did not pay for Mr. Taber's dog biscuit. That is the bitter truth. Still, I have a large wardrobe of Shakespearean costumes, many old editions of your plays and other Shakespeareana, and with such accoutrement would regret to shelve your charming play altogether. I would suggest that you give it modern interest. Mr. Clyde Fitch believes that the American play is the opportunity of the hour. You might lay the scene in Chicago, exiling Romeo to Milwaukee. The Spanish war might be touched upon to give the flag a chance. I would like to produce the play without changes, but I am an unprotected woman, and I must live.

Faithfully,

Julia Marlowe [June 9, 1900, p. 7]

"*When I Knew Stephen Crane*"

The death of Stephen Crane in England on June 5, 1900, inspired this major statement on the man and his art. Unlike Willa Cather's customary eulogy on the death of an artist she admired, the essay took the form of a reminiscence of a "chance meeting." It appeared first in the Library *under the "Henry Nicklemann" pseudonym and then three weeks later, on July 14, 1900, under her own name in the* Courier.[22] *As Bernice Slote has pointed out, the essay "is fictional in a number of details. Most striking is the time of*

22. This important article was identified by Mildred R. Bennett when she was working on her book *The World of Willa Cather*. Mrs. Bennett called it to the attention of the late Lowry C. Wimberly, who published it in *Prairie Schooner* 23 (Fall 1949), 231–236.

Crane's visit as it is represented in the article—not the actual bitter-cold February [1895], but late spring, 'oppressively warm' with a dry wind blowing up from Kansas."[23] *In 1926 Willa Cather wrote an introduction to Crane's* Wounds in the Rain, *in which she praised him as a "post-impressionist" who "simply knew from the beginning how to handle detail."*[24]

It was, I think, in the spring of '94 that a slender, narrow-chested fellow in a shabby grey suit, with a soft felt hat pulled low over his eyes, sauntered into the office of the managing editor of the *Nebraska State Journal* and introduced himself as Stephen Crane. He stated that he was going to Mexico to do some work for the Bacheller Syndicate and get rid of his cough, and that he would be stopping in Lincoln for a few days. Later he explained that he was out of money and would be compelled to wait until he got a check from the East before he went further. I was a Junior at the Nebraska State University at the time, and was doing some work for the *State Journal* in my leisure time, and I happened to be in the managing editor's room when Mr. Crane introduced himself. I was just off the range; I knew a little Greek and something about cattle and a good horse when I saw one, and beyond horses and cattle I considered nothing of vital importance except good stories and the people who wrote them. This was the first man of letters I had ever met in the flesh, and when the young man announced who he was, I dropped into a chair behind the editor's desk where I could stare at him without being too much in evidence.

Only a very youthful enthusiasm and a large propensity for hero worship could have found anything impressive in the young man who stood before the managing editor's desk. He was thin to emaciation, his face was gaunt and unshaven, a thin dark moustache straggled on his upper lip, his black hair grew low on his forehead and was shaggy and unkempt. His grey clothes were much the worse for wear and fitted him so badly it seemed unlikely he had ever been measured for them. He wore a flannel shirt and a slovenly apology for a necktie, and his shoes were dusty and worn gray about the toes and were badly run over at the heel. I had

23. *KA*, pp. 19–20. Miss Slote observes that "'Henry Nicklemann' as the narrative voice . . . is not bound to factual autobiography, and may be a precursor of a later persona like Jim Burden in *My Ántonia*." See also her article, "Stephen Crane and Willa Cather," *The Serif*, December 1969, pp. 3–15.

24. Introduction to *Wounds in the Rain and Other Impressions of War*, Volume IX of *The Work of Stephen Crane* (New York: Alfred A. Knopf, Inc., 1926), p. x. Collected in *On Writing*, p. 69.

seen many a tramp printer come up the *Journal* stairs to hunt a job, but never one who presented such a disreputable appearance as this story-maker man. He wore gloves, which seemed rather a contradiction to the general slovenliness of his attire, but when he took them off to search his pockets for his credentials, I noticed that his hands were singularly fine; long, white, and delicately shaped, with thin, nervous fingers. I have seen pictures of Aubrey Beardsley's hands that recalled Crane's very vividly.

At that time Crane was but twenty-four, and almost an unknown man. Hamlin Garland had seen some of his work and believed in him, and had introduced him to Mr. Howells, who recommended him to the Bacheller Syndicate. *The Red Badge of Courage* had been published in the *State Journal* that winter along with a lot of other syndicate matter, and the grammatical construction of the story was so faulty that the managing editor had several times called on me to edit the copy. In this way I had read it very carefully, and through the careless sentence-structure I saw the wonder of that remarkable performance. But the grammar certainly was bad. I remember one of the reporters who had corrected the phrase "it don't" for the tenth time remarked savagely, "If I couldn't write better English than this, I'd quit."

Crane spent several days in the town, living from hand to mouth and waiting for his money. I think he borrowed a small amount from the managing editor. He lounged about the office most of the time, and I frequently encountered him going in and out of the cheap restaurants on Tenth Street. When he was at the office he talked a good deal in a wandering, absent-minded fashion, and his conversation was uniformly frivolous. If he could not evade a serious question by a joke, he bolted. I cut my classes to lie in wait for him, confident that in some unwary moment I could trap him into serious conversation, that if one burned incense long enough and ardently enough, the oracle would not be dumb. I was Maupassant mad at the time, a malady particularly unattractive in a Junior, and I made a frantic effort to get an expression of opinion from him on "Le Bonheur." "Oh, you're Moping, are you?" he remarked with a sarcastic grin, and went on reading a little volume of Poe that he carried in his pocket. At another time I cornered him in the Funny Man's room and succeeded in getting a little out of him. We were taught literature by an exceedingly analytical method at the University, and we probably distorted the method, and I was busy trying to find the least common multiple of *Hamlet* and the greatest common divisor of *Macbeth*, and I began asking him whether stories were constructed by cabalistic formulae.[25] At length he sighed wearily and shook his drooping shoulders, remarking: "Where did you get all that rot? Yarns aren't done by mathematics. You can't do it by rule any more than you can dance by rule. You have to have the itch of the thing in your fingers, and if you haven't,—well, you're damned lucky, and you'll live long and prosper, that's all."—And with that he yawned and went down the hall.

Crane was moody most of the time, his health was bad and he seemed profoundly discouraged. Even his jokes were exceedingly drastic. He went about with the tense, preoccupied, self-centered air of a man who is brooding over some impending disaster, and I conjectured vainly as to what it might be. Though he was seemingly entirely idle during the few days I knew him, his manner indicated that he was in the throes of work that told terribly on his nerves. His eyes I remember as the finest I have ever seen, large and dark and full of lustre and changing lights, but with a profound melancholy always lurking deep in them. They were eyes that seemed to be burning themselves out.

As he sat at the desk with his shoulders drooping forward, his head low, and his long, white fingers drumming on the sheets of copy paper, he was as nervous as a race horse fretting to be on the track. Always, as he came and went about the halls, he seemed like a man preparing for a sudden departure. Now that he is dead it occurs to me that all his life was a preparation for sudden departure. I remember once when he was writing a letter he stopped and asked me about the spelling of a word, saying carelessly, "I haven't time to learn to spell."

Then, glancing down at his attire, he added with an absent-minded smile, "I haven't time to dress either; it takes an awful slice out of a fellow's life."

He said he was poor, and he certainly looked it, but four years later when he was in Cuba, drawing the largest salary ever paid a newspaper correspondent, he clung to this same untidy manner of dress, and his ragged overalls and buttonless shirt were eyesores to the immaculate Mr. Davis, in his spotless linen and neat khaki uniform, with his Gibson chin always freshly shaven. When I first heard of his serious illness, his old throat trouble aggravated into consumption by his reckless exposure in Cuba, I recalled a passage from Maeterlinck's essay, "The Pre-Destined," on those doomed to early death: "As children, life seems nearer to them than to other children. They appear to know nothing, and yet there is in

25. An allusion to Professor Lucius Sherman's critical method. See "Practical Education," The Local Scene (II), above.

their eyes so profound a certainty that we feel they must know all.—In all haste, but wisely and with minute care do they prepare themselves to live, and this very haste is a sign upon which mothers can scarce bring themselves to look."[26] I remembered, too, the young man's melancholy and his tenseness, his burning eyes, and his way of slurring over the less important things, as one whose time is short.

I have heard other people say how difficult it was to induce Crane to talk seriously about his work, and I suspect that he was particularly averse to discussions with literary men of wider education and better equipment than himself, yet he seemed to feel that this fuller culture was not for him. Perhaps the unreasoning instinct which lies deep in the roots of our lives, and which guides us all, told him that he had not time enough to acquire it.

Men will sometimes reveal themselves to children, or to people whom they think never to see again, more completely than they ever do to their confreres. From the wise we hold back alike our folly and our wisdom, and for the recipients of our deeper confidences we seldom select our equals. The soul has no message for the friends with whom we dine every week. It is silenced by custom and convention, and we play only in the shallows. It selects its listeners willfully, and seemingly delights to waste its best upon the chance wayfarer who meets us in the highway at a fated hour. There are moments too, when the tides run high or very low, when self-revelation is necessary to every man, if it be only to his valet or his gardener. At such a moment, I was with Mr. Crane.

The hoped for revelation came unexpectedly enough. It was on the last night he spent in Lincoln. I had come back from the theatre and was in the *Journal* office writing a notice of the play. It was eleven o'clock when Crane came in. He had expected his money to arrive on the night mail and it had not done so, and he was out of sorts and deeply despondent. He sat down on the ledge of the open window that faced on the street, and when I had finished my notice I went over and took a chair beside him. Quite without invitation on my part, Crane began to talk, began to curse his trade from the first throb of creative desire in a boy to the finished work of the master. The night was oppressively warm; one of those dry winds that are the curse of that country was blowing up from Kansas. The white, western moonlight threw sharp, blue shadows below us. The streets were silent at that hour, and we could hear the gurgle of the fountain in

26. Maurice Maeterlinck (1862–1949), in *The Treasure of the Humble* (New York: Dodd, Mead & Co., 1899), pp. 45–46.

the Post Office square across the street, and the twang of banjos from the lower verandah of the Hotel Lincoln, where the colored waiters were serenading the guests. The drop lights in the office were dull under their green shades, and the telegraph sounder clicked faintly in the next room. In all his long tirade, Crane never raised his voice; he spoke slowly and monotonously and even calmly, but I have never known so bitter a heart in any man as he revealed to me that night. It was an arraignment of the wages of life, an invocation to the ministers of hate.

Incidentally he told me the sum he had received for *The Red Badge of Courage*, which I think was something like ninety dollars, and he repeated some lines from *The Black Riders*, which was then in preparation. He gave me to understand that he led a double literary life; writing in the first place the matter that pleased himself, and doing it very slowly; in the second place, any sort of stuff that would sell. And he remarked that his poor was just as bad as it could possibly be. He realized, he said, that his limitations were absolutely impassable. "What I can't do, I can't do at all, and I can't acquire it. I only hold one trump."

He had no settled plans at all. He was going to Mexico wholly uncertain of being able to do any successful work there, and he seemed to feel very insecure about the financial end of his venture. The thing that most interested me was what he said about his slow method of composition. He declared that there was little money in story-writing at best, and practically none in it for him, because of the time it took him to work up his detail. Other men, he said, could sit down and write up an experience while the physical effect of it, so to speak, was still upon them, and yesterday's impressions made today's "copy." But when he came in from the streets to write up what he had seen there, his faculties were benumbed, and he sat twirling his pencil and hunting for words like a schoolboy.

I mentioned *The Red Badge of Courage*, which was written in nine days, and he replied that, though the writing took very little time, he had been unconsciously working the detail of the story out through most of his boyhood. His ancestors had been soldiers, and he had been imagining war stories ever since he was out of knickerbockers, and in writing his first war story he had simply gone over his imaginary campaigns and selected his favorite imaginary experiences. He declared that his imagination was hidebound; it was there, but it pulled hard. After he got a notion for a story, months passed before he could get any sort of personal contract with it, or feel any potency to handle it. "The detail of a thing has to filter through my blood, and then it comes out like a native product, but it takes forever," he remarked. I distinctly remember the illustration, for it rather took hold of me.

I have often been astonished since to hear Crane spoken of as "the reporter in fiction," for the reportorial faculty of superficial reception and quick transference was what he conspicuously lacked. His first newspaper account of his shipwreck on the filibuster *Commodore* off the Florida coast was as lifeless as the "copy" of a police court reporter. It was many months afterwards that the literary product of his terrible experience appeared in that marvellous sea story "The Open Boat," unsurpassed in its vividness and constructive perfection.

At the close of our long conversation that night, when the copy boy came in to take me home,[27] I suggested to Crane that in ten years he would probably laugh at all his temporary discomfort. Again his body took on that strenuous tension and he clenched his hands, saying, "I can't wait ten years, I haven't time."

The ten years are not up yet, and he has done his work and gathered his reward and gone. Was ever so much experience and achievement crowded into so short a space of time? A great man dead at twenty-nine! That would have puzzled the ancients. Edward Garnett wrote of him in the *Academy* of December 17, 1899: "I cannot remember a parallel in the literary history of fiction. Maupassant, Meredith, Henry James, Mr. Howells and Tolstoy, were all learning their expression at an age where Crane had achieved his and achieved it triumphantly."[28] He had the precocity of those doomed to die in youth. I am convinced that when I met him he had a vague premonition of the shortness of his working day, and in the heart of the man there was that which said, "That thou doest, do quickly."

At twenty-one this son of an obscure New Jersey rector, with but a scant reading knowledge of French and no training, had rivaled in technique the foremost craftsmen of the Latin races. In the six years since I met him, a stranded reporter, he stood in the firing line during two wars, knew hairbreadth 'scapes on land and sea, and established himself as the first writer of his time in the picturing of episodic, fragmentary life. His friends have charged him with fickleness, but he was a man who was in the preoccupation of haste. He went from country to country, from man

27. A slip. The copy boy would escort home Miss Willa Cather, but not "Henry Nicklemann," a chap "just off the range." See Slote, "Stephen Crane and Willa Cather."

28. Edward Garnett, "Mr. Stephen Crane: An Appreciation," *Academy*, December 17, 1898, pp. 483–484.

to man, absorbing all that was in them for him. He had no time to look backward. He had no leisure for *camaraderie*. He drank life to the lees, but at the banquet table where other men took their ease and jested over their wine, he stood a dark and silent figure, sombre as Poe himself, not wishing to be understood; and he took his portion in haste, with his loins girded, and his shoes on his feet, and his staff in his hand, like one who must depart quickly. [June 23, 1900, pp. 17–18]

"The Hottest Day I Ever Spent"

This piece, signed "George Overing," was identified by John P. Hinz,[29] *who recognized that it incorporated portions of a newspaper story on Brownville by Willa Cather in the* Journal, *August 12, 1894 (see "Brownville," The Local Scene [II], above). The disaster conditions that brought Stephen Crane to Nebraska as a reporter in February 1895 were the result of three years of terrible drought, climaxed in late July 1894 by a day of record-breaking heat.*[30] *As in the Stephen Crane essay above, elements are fictionalized in this account, which purports to tell of a visit to Brownville by "a young Swede, who had been in the West but a few months, a Japanese, my brother, . . . and myself ['George Overing']." In actuality, the party consisted of Mariel Gere, Willa Cather, and her brother Roscoe.*

Hot weather grumblers in the Mountain States know nothing about it. Ask the man from St. Louis, and he will tell you what hot weather is. The territory along the Missouri River is the only really hot place on earth, and the river itself is the hottest thing out of Inferno. I spent one day in a town on [the] Missouri River when the government thermometer registered 115 degrees in the shade and 135 degrees in the sun. That was a day to remember; it cost more in money and suffering than the Charleston earthquakes or the Johnstown Flood, and wrought greater destruction than the Chicago fire. That one day ruined the wheat and corn crops of two of the greatest agricultural states in the Union, Kansas and Nebraska. It was about the middle of July, 1894, when I went to Brownville, Nebraska, one of the most historic towns in the Middle West, with a party of

29. Hinz, "Willa Cather in Pittsburgh," p. 201.

30. The state had almost total crop failures in 1893 and 1894; see Olson, *History of Nebraska*, p. 239. Just about the time Willa Cather made her trip to Brownville, newspaper dispatches of July 26 and 29 from Hastings, Nebraska, forty miles north of Red Cloud, report a five-day effort by rainmakers to break the drought, at the end of which time "the rainmakers gave up in disgust and left." Louise Pound, "Nebraska Rain Lore and Rain Making," in *Nebraska Folklore* (Lincoln: University of Nebraska Press, 1959), p. 51.

newspapermen to write up its historical features. There were four of us in the party, a young Swede, who had been in the West but a few months, a Japanese, who boasted that he had no conscience, my brother and myself. The town, besides being the hottest place on earth, is one of the deadest, it is a Town That Was.

Brownville is built in a little horseshoe-shaped Gulch. Behind it on either side rise the steep, wooded bluffs, from which one can look out over four states: Nebraska, Kansas, Iowa and Missouri. In front of it rolls the turbid yellow river. The first settlement in the state was made there about forty-eight years ago, when Richard Brown, the Missourian, crossed the river with his cow and hens on a raft and pitched his lodge in the Wilderness. The first telegraph wire that ever crossed the Missouri was run into Senator Tipton's big house on the hill, and the first message that came over the wire to the waiting frontiersmen who thronged the hall and porch was, "Westward The Course of Empire Takes Its Way." We saw the old yellow telegraph slip there under glass. Brownville happened because of the steamboat trade, and when the steamboat trade went under it carried Brownville with it. The big river steamers that used to come up from St. Louis and New Orleans brought all the supplies for the wagon trains which ran from Brownville to Pike's Peak and Cherry Creek, which is now Denver. The *Montana* and *Silver Heels* brought up parties of Europeans to hunt buffalo, and the old *Hannibal* brought to Brownville the rails for the building of the Union Pacific railroad, the first road that crossed the plains. When the river channel became so capricious that the river trade was impossible, the high tide of prosperity went out in Brownville, and all the merchants and traders who had made fortunes there left their big stone houses and went away. When we arrived by the six o'clock train, we thought we had unearthed a little Pompeii. All over the hills were handsome residences windracked and gone to ruin, terraces plowed up for potato patches and sloping lawns grown up in wheat and sunflowers. The main street was lined with empty, windowless brick buildings and gaping cellar holes, where the buildings had been pulled down or had fallen. Even the Lone Tree saloon is falling to pieces, and in a western town that is an unfailing indication that all is lost. Yet the town did not strike us as an unsightly place, as we stood in the empty street, watching the accommodation freight pull out, leaving us to our fate. The cows were coming back over the hill tops, old men were cutting wood in their back yards, the smoke was beginning to curl from the chimneys, there was a smell of supper in the air, and the little town lay passive in this picturesque dilapidation, as though it had lain down with Rip Van Winkle among the hills and was busy putting in its thirty years.

That night, as we sat on the hotel verandah after supper, watching the heat lightning play over the river, we remarked that the night was warmer than the day had been and discussed the probabilities of getting any sleep in such weather. There was a stiff, steady breeze from the south, but, as the Swede remarked reflectively, "Him wind not vera cold."

My brother and I looked at each other and said nothing, we knew what a warm night wind in that country means, but we left the Swede and the Jap to come into a fuller knowledge by experience.

I awoke at five in the morning, dripping wet as though I had been in a Turkish bath. The pillows and the sheets under me were wet; I was faint and deathly sick. My brother called,

"Come and help me with the Swede, he's in a bad way."

The Swede lay on the edge of his bed, panting like a dog, his tongue hanging out, and his eyes rolling when he spoke, the nature of his conversation was exceedingly foolish. We were all sick. We stood around Hanns, mopping our faces and wondering what we had eaten and whether we had been poisoned. We rubbed him with some brandy we had with us and threw water over him to get some sort of reaction. We noticed that the water was hot, and my brother cried: "By Jove! we're hot, that's what's the matter with us!" It was the first time this had occurred to any of us. We made a break for our own rooms, having got Hanns on his feet.

For breakfast we wanted nothing but ice, but the landlord said he never "took ice" until August. We went out on the porch, and the government thermometer registered 104 degrees in the shade, though it was then but seven o'clock. By nine o'clock, the mercury was at 110, still going up. The yellow Missouri rolled before us like a torrent of molten brass, the wind blew furiously from the south, hot as the breath of a furnace. The leaves of the cottonwoods were curling under it, and the corn on the hills was wilting.

"Where the Devil he come from, this wind?" groaned the poor Swede, tearing off his collar.

But we were unable to explain the genesis of the wind; we only knew what the result would be to the state at that critical period when the young corn was just in tassel, and we knew that mortgages would be foreclosed, homesteads lost; that banks would break and long lines of white-topped wagons drawn by jaded horses would creep across the state like ambulances, carrying the defeated and discouraged farmers back to their old homes somewhere farther east. Those hot winds are not matters of mere discomfort, but of life and death; whole communities go down before them, and whole villages are left desolated by them, and they are more dreaded than cyclones. This one, coming as it did after a long season of dry weather, we knew would plunge the whole state into poverty for another year. By noon the thermometer had risen to 115 in the shade and 130 in the sun. The Japanese had lived in New Mexico and had crossed the Arizona deserts, and he assured us he had never known anything like it. We started out on an expedition after ice, and we were quite as desperate as the starving Polar crews who hunt for food on the frozen islands of the North. We would have shot a man who refused to sell us ice. We got it by paying twenty-five cents a pound for it, and I think we got all there was in the town, though it was little enough. We all crowded into the Swede's room, which was the largest, and hung wet sheets over the windows to cool the wind a little. In fifteen minutes a wet sheet would be as dry as a board. We tied ice on our heads and played jokes and used much profanity until sundown. Then we went out to see whether anyone was left alive. The inhabitants were sitting on the sidewalks, whittling.

They are a placid people who never work. The river is the only feature in their lives. They live on the catfish they catch and burn the driftwood that is washed up on the shore. The boys never know anything but the river; they run away from school to fish or swim, and their one wild dream is to go "down the river" to St. Louis some day. The sidewalk tenants said we'd be all right if we'd keep calm. This was a pretty hot day; two babies had died in the town, and one old woman had drowned herself in her well, but calmness would see us through.

That night we sat on the verandah looking down on the desolated streets, conjuring up memories of the time when those dark broken glass fronts were ablaze with light, when the streets were full of ox teams and loaded wagons bound for Pike's Peak, and the teamsters were singing and twanging their banjos in front of the Lone Tree saloon, and on that same verandah the cabin passengers and wealthy traders sat and smoked and, looking out over the river, watched their steamers lying at the wharf and listened to the hoarse whistle of the boats as they came around the bend in the bluffs, with their dancing lights and train of sparks and cinders blown back into the darkness. We sat there until morning.

The next day we left and went westward through the state that had been green as the Garden of Eden two days before, and it was burned as brown as though it had been swept by a prairie fire. From one end to the other Nebraska and Kansas had been visited by a plague worse than the death of the first-born or the turning of the sea to blood, and the tragedies that followed in its wake, only those who dwell in that country can know. [July 7, 1900, pp. 3–4]

"The Personal Side of William Jennings Bryan"

When the Democratic National Convention renominated William Jennings Bryan for President on July 5, 1900, Willa Cather wrote an article about her fellow Nebraskan, just as she had written about his wife in 1896 (see "Two Women the World Is Watching," The Home Monthly, *above), incorporating some of the paragraphs from the earlier article with minor cuts and changes. This was another "Henry Nicklemann" piece, and was identified by Mildred R. Bennett.*[31] *Mr. Dillon, in "Two Friends," had heard Bryan make his "cross of gold" speech in 1896,*[32] *but it is highly unlikely that Willa Cather did—as "Henry Nicklemann" claimed. A letter to Mariel Gere at that time makes no mention of the speech, although she tells of going to an art exhibition while she was in Chicago en route to Pittsburgh.*[33] *In any case, the "Boy Orator of the Platte" stimulated her imagination, even if he could not change her solidly Republican principles (see introductory note to The Local Scene [II], above).*

When I first knew William Jennings Bryan he was the Democratic nominee for the First Congressional District of Nebraska, a district in which the Republican majority had never fallen below three thousand. I was a student at the State University when Mr. Bryan was stumping the state, which he had stumped two years before for J. Sterling Morton, now his bitterest political enemy.[34] My first meeting with him was on a streetcar. He was returning from some hall in the suburbs of Lincoln where he had been making an address, and carried a most unsightly floral offering of large dimensions, the tribute of some of his devoted constituents, half concealed by a clumsy wrapping of tissue paper. The car was crowded,

31. See note 22, above. The Bryan article also was reprinted in *Prairie Schooner* 23 (Winter 1949), 331–337.

32. *Obscure Destinies*, p. 222.

33. Willa Cather to Mariel Gere. See note 4, The *Home Monthly*, above.

34. J. Sterling Morton (1832–1902), an early-day Nebraska "boomer," was territorial secretary and acting governor in 1858, founded Arbor Day in 1872, and served as U.S. Secretary of Agriculture (1893–1897). Cather is referring to the gubernatorial election of 1892 in which Morton ran a poor third.

and the candidate had some difficulty in keeping his "set piece" out of the way of the passengers. A sympathetic and talkative old lady who sat next him looked up and enquired sympathetically: "Is it for a funeral?"

Mr. Bryan looked quizzically at his encumbrance and replied politely: "Well, I hope not, Madam."

It certainly was not, for that fall he carried the Republican district by a majority of seven thousand. Before that time Mr. Bryan had been a rather inconspicuous lawyer in Lincoln, by no means ranking among the ablest members of the bar. He had come there in 1887, I think, bringing with him little more than his family and law books, for his practice in Illinois had not been particularly remunerative. He came at the solicitation of his old college chum, A. R. Talbot, with whom he went into partnership. He was never a man who frequented ward caucuses, for he was an idealist pure and simple then as now, and he had practically nothing to do with Nebraska politics until he stumped the state for Morton. Then he began to make a stir. His oratory "took hold," just as it did at the Chicago convention, and his own nomination came to him entirely unsought. In those days Mr. Bryan used to have leisure to offer occasional good advice to university students, and I believe he drilled several for oratorical contests. He wrote occasionally for the college paper of which I was editor, and was always at home to students in his library in the evening. The man's whole inner life was typified in that library. The walls were hung with very bad old-fashioned engravings of early statesmen, and those pictures were there because Mr. Bryan liked them. Of books there were many, but of the kind of books that are written for art's sake there were very few. There were many of the old classics, and many Latin and French books, much worn, for he read them constantly. There were many lives of American statesmen which were marked and annotated, schoolboy fashion. The works on political economy were mostly by quacks—men who were mentally one-sided, and who never rose to any true scientific eminence. There was much poetry of a didactic or declamatory nature, which is the only kind that Mr. Bryan has any taste for. In the line of fiction there was little more recent than Thackeray. Mr. Bryan used always to be urging us to read *Les Misérables* if we hadn't, and to re-read it if we had. He declared that it was the greatest novel written, yet I think he had never considered its merits or demerits as a novel at all. It was Hugo's vague hyperbolic generalizations on sociological questions that he marked and quoted. In short, he read Hugo, the orator and impractical politician, not Hugo, the novelist.

The last ten years have changed Mr. Bryan very little personally. He is now, as he was then, a big, well-planted man, standing firmly on the soil as though he belonged there and were rooted to it, with powerful shoulders, exhilarating freedom of motion, and a smile that won him more votes than his logic ever did. His prominent nose and set mouth might have belonged to any of the early statesmen he emulates. His hair is rather too thin on top and rather too long behind. His eyes are as sharp and clear as cut steel, and his glance as penetrating as a searchlight. He dressed then very much like a Kentucky judge, and I believe he still clings to the low collar and black string tie. He was never anything but a hero to his valet—too much of a hero for comfort. I have seen him without his coat, but never without a high moral purpose. It was a physical impossibility for him to loaf or dawdle, or talk nonsense. His dining room was a forum. I do not mean that he talked incessantly, but that when he did talk it was in a manner forensic. He chipped his eggs to the accompaniment of maxims, sometimes strikingly original, sometimes trite enough. He buttered his toast with an epigram, and when he made jokes they were of the manifest kind that the crowd catch quickly and applaud wildly. When he was at his best, his conversation was absolutely overwhelming in its richness and novelty and power, in the force and aptness of his illustrations. Yet one always felt that it was meant for the many, not the few, that it was addressed to humanity, and that there should be a stenographer present to take it down.

There is nothing of familiarity or adroitness in the man; you never come any closer to him than just within the range of his voice. The breakfast room was always too small for him, he exhausted the air, he gave other people no chance to breathe. His dynamic magnetism either exhausted you or overstimulated you. He needs a platform, and a large perspective and resounding domes; and he needs the enthusiasm of applauding thousands to balance his own. Living near him is like living near Niagara. The almighty, ever-renewed force of the man drives one to distraction, his everlasting high seriousness makes one want to play marbles. He was never fond of athletics. He takes no care of himself. After his own fashion he studies incessantly, yet his vitality comes up with the sun and out-burns the street arc lights. He has the physique of the dominant few.

In his business relations, in his civic relations, in his domestic relations, Mr. Bryan is always a statesman, large minded, clean and a trifle unwieldy. If all this were not so absolutely natural to the man, so inseparable from him, it might be called theatric.

Mrs. Bryan's life is simply a record of hard work. She first met Mr. Bryan in Illinois when he was a college student, and she was attending the "annex" of the institution. He graduated a valedictorian and she achieved a like honor in her class. Two such brilliant and earnest young people were naturally drawn to each other. Then from the very outset there was between them a mutual enthusiasm and a great common purpose. It was a serious wooing. The days of their courtship were spent among books and often passed in conversations upon dry subjects that would terrify most women. They were both voracious readers, readers of everything; history, fiction, philosophy, poetry. From the outset their minds and tastes kept pace with each other, as they have done to this day. Bryan never reads a new book, never was seized by a new idea that she did not share. Their minds seemed made for each other. Away out West, where there are no traditions, no precedents, where men meet nature singlehanded and think life out for themselves, those two young people looked about them for the meaning of things. Together they read Victor Hugo, and Dante, and Shakespeare, and had all those sacred aspirations that we can know but once. And the strange thing about these two people is, that neither of them have lost that faith, and fervor, and sincerity which so often dies with youth. It is not wholly practical, perhaps, but it is a beautiful thing to see.

Mr. and Mrs. Bryan were engaged when she was nineteen and he twenty, but they were not married until four years afterwards. They lived in Illinois a little time then moved to Lincoln, Nebraska. There Mr. Bryan, a young man and a poor one, began to practice law in a country none too rich. In order to be better able to help him, Mrs. Bryan studied law and was admitted to the bar. She has never practiced law, but when her husband began to mingle in politics many of the duties of the law office fell upon her. To society she paid little or no attention. For there is such a thing as society, even in Nebraska. There are good dancing clubs and whist clubs, but she never found time for them. Except at political meetings and University lectures, and occasionally at the theatre, she was seldom seen in public. Into one social feature, however, Mrs. Bryan has always entered with all her characteristic enthusiasm. She is a most devout clubwoman. She organized the Lincoln Sorosis and has been an active worker in the State Federation of Women's Clubs. She and Mrs. [Elia W.] Peattie,[35] of Omaha, the gifted authoress of *A Mountain Woman*, were probably the most influential clubwomen in Nebraska. There is in Lincoln

35. See "Elia W. Peattie," Books and Authors (IV), above.

as in all university towns, a distinct college clique, and in this Mrs. Bryan has always figured prominently. Mrs. Bryan is a wheelwoman, but she has never gone wild over it or made any "century" runs. She is an expert swimmer, and Wednesday mornings she and her friends used to go down to the plunge in the sanitarium and spend the morning in the water. But she carried none of these things to excess. Mrs. William Jennings Bryan has but two "fads"; the Honorable William Jennings Bryan, and the political doctrines which she believes will be the salvation of the people of the West.

Decidedly the strongest and most characteristic side of this woman is the mental one. Before all else she is a woman of intellect, not so by affectation or even by choice, but by necessity, by nature. Eastern newspapers have devoted a great deal of space criticizing Mrs. Bryan's dress. It is doubtful if she ever spent ten minutes planning the construction of a gown. But many and many an hour have she and her husband spent by their library fire talking over the future of the West and those political beliefs which may call in question their judgment, but never their sincerity. In Washington they worked out that celebrated tariff speech together, line by line. When the speech was delivered she sat unobserved in the gallery and by signals regulated the pitch of her husband's voice, until it reached just the proper volume to fill the house. She knew every word of that speech by heart, and at the finest passages her lips moved as she repeated them under her breath. Much of the reading, searching for historical references and verification fell upon her. She spent days in the National Library. Several days before the speech which made Bryan famous was delivered, he was called upon to make eulogy upon a dead comrade. Mrs. Bryan sat in the gallery and carefully noted what tones and gestures were most effective in that hall. They prepared that speech and its delivery as quietly and considerately as an actor makes out his interpretation of a role. At the reception given the Bryans, Mrs. Bryan did not appear in evening dress, and the couple stood about ill at ease until the affair was over. The people who work most earnestly do not always play the most skilfully, and the peculiar inability of the Bryans to carry off social honors gracefully reminds people of that great gentleman of history who rode down to the White House and tied his horse to the palings. Mrs. Bryan held aloof from Washington society, and neither accepted nor gave invitations. She dressed plainly and stopped at a quiet hotel. She most sensibly lived within her husband's salary and helped him do his work, and this is just what she is doing now.

The distinctive feature of Mr. Bryan's career is that he began at the top. At an age when most lawyers have barely succeeded in building up a good practice, he was the leader of one of the two great political parties of America. He attained that leadership quite without financial backing or an astute political impresario, attained it singlehanded. He would not know how to manage a machine if he had one, and certainly no machine could manage him. The man himself would scorn a machine; he is by nature unfit for such campaigning methods. His constituents are controlled not by a commercial syndicate or by a political trust, but by one man's personality.

Behind this personality there is neither an invincible principle nor an unassailable logic, only melodious phrases, a convincing voice and a hypnotic sincerity. Though he is in politics, Mr. Bryan is not a politician; he has [no] resources to fall back upon if his main position were routed, he has not built up a power, no great captains have developed under his generalship. During these last four years, instead of planting a fort here and a base of supplies there, and sealing influential allies to himself, he has been engaging in various crusades of sentiment. If he were struck dumb, he would be as helpless as a tenor without his voice. In his brilliant study of Bryan, in *McClure's Magazine*, Will Allen White quotes the following passage on Bryan's early oratorical flights from Mrs. Bryan's biographical sketch of her husband:

"A prize always fired William's ambition. During his first year in the academy (the preparatory department of Illinois College), he declaimed Patrick Henry's masterpiece, and ranked well down the list. Nothing daunted, the next year found him with the 'Palmetto and the Pine' as his subject. The next year, a freshman in college, he tried for a prize in Latin prose, and won half the second prize. Later in the year he declaimed 'Bernardo del Carpio,' and gained second prize. In his sophomore year he entered another contest, with an essay on 'Labor.' This time the first prize rewarded his work. An oration on 'Individual Powers' gave him a place in the intercollegiate contest held at Galesburg, where he ranked second."[36]

It is the elocutionary phases of political economy which have always appealed to Mr. Bryan most strongly. Had he attended a more sophisticated Eastern college, where a young man who talked of righting the wrongs of the world would be held under a pump, and where dramatic

36. William Allen White, "Bryan," *McClure's*, July 1900, p. 232. For White, see "Old Books and New [December 1897]," The *Home Monthly*, above.

societies are more in vogue than debating societies, he might have felt that his call was for the stage and declaimed Shakespeare with a noble purpose and bad grace. He is an orator, pure and simple, certainly the greatest in America today. After all, it is not a crime to be an orator, and not necessarily ridiculous. It is a gift like any other gift, and not always a practical one. The Hon. William McKeighan[37] was one of the first free silver agitators in Nebraska and had gone from a dugout to the halls of Congress. When McKeighan died, Bryan came down to the sun-scorched, dried-up, blown-away little village of Red Cloud to speak at his funeral. There, with an audience of some few hundreds of bronzed farmers who believed in him as their deliverer, the man who could lead them out of the bondage of debt, who could stay the drouth and strike water from the rock, I heard him make the greatest speech of his life. Surely that was eloquence of the old stamp that was accounted divine, eloquence that reached through the callus of ignorance and toil and found and awoke the stunted souls of men. I saw those rugged, ragged men of the soil weep like children. Six months later, at Chicago, when Bryan stampeded a convention, appropriated a party, electrified a nation, flashed his name around the planet, took the assembled thousands of that convention hall and moulded them in his hands like so much putty, one of those ragged farmers sat beside me in the gallery, and at the close of that never-to-be-forgotten speech, he leaned over the rail, the tears on his furrowed cheeks, and shouted, "The sweet singer of Israel!"

Of Mr. Bryan's great sincerity there can be no doubt. It is, indeed, the unsophisticated sort of sincerity which is the stamp of the crusader, but in a man of his native force it is a power to be reckoned with. His mental fiber is scarcely delicate enough to be susceptible to doubts. There is nothing of the Hamlet about William Jennings Bryan. Then his life has not been of a very disciplinary kind. It is failure and hope deferred that lead a man to modify, retrench, weigh evidence against himself, and Mr. Bryan's success has been uninterrupted.

It is scarcely necessary to say that he has no finesse. His book, *The First Battle*, is an almost unparalleled instance of bad taste. But his honesty is unquestionable. He had the courage to stick to his party when he went, a poor man, into a state where the only way to success lay through Republican influence. He favored the ratification of the treaty with Spain when his party opposed it. In the Kansas City convention he drove his

37. William A. McKeighan (1842–1895), a Democrat who was elected to Congress (1891–1895) with Populist support, was described as "the fiery Red Cloud orator." Olson, *History of Nebraska*, p. 235.

party to the suicidal measure of retaining the 16-to-1 platform. He is the white elephant of his party, and yet they cannot escape the dominant influence of his personality. It is an interesting study in reactions that the most practical, and prosaic, and purely commercial people on the planet should be dazzled and half convinced by a purely picturesque figure—a knight on horseback.

Alphonse Daudet all his life made notes for a book he never wrote, a book which should be *Tartarin* and *Numa Roumestan* in one, and which should embody in the person of Napoleon the entire race of the south of France. So I think William Jennings Bryan synthesizes the entire Middle West; all its newness and vigor, its magnitude and monotony, its richness and lack of variety, its inflammability and volubility, its strength and its crudeness, its high seriousness and self-confidence, its egotism and its nobility. [July 14, 1900, pp. 13–15]

"*A Houseboat on the Land*"

This was the last "Henry Nicklemann" piece to appear in the Library; *a signed poem, "Are You Sleeping, Little Brother?," ran in the same issue. It is also the last proved article to appear in the* Library, *although a signed story, "The Conversion of Sum Loo," came out the following week (August 11).*

Sewickley can probably show up one of the most unique residences in all the environs of Pittsburgh, and I doubt whether there is another like it anywhere in the world. It is a cross between a houseboat on the land and a palace car off the rails. Mr. Lemuel Miller, the owner and architect, says that he never got enough "camping out" when he was a boy, and he is determined to get even with fortune and have a go at it now that he is gray headed. He pitched his tents in the following manner. He placed two streetcars parallel with each other on brick foundations about thirty-five feet apart. Between these cars he has built a conservatory. Around the entrance end of each car there is a circular entrance, which looks like the stern of a fishing tug. In these two streetcars Mr. Miller has fitted up luxurious bachelor apartments. The interior of the front car is not unlike that of Richard Mansfield's private car. It is richly carpeted with Indian rugs, and the double glass windows which run along the side, as in an ordinary streetcar, are covered by tapestry which is hung on rings. The seats on the side have been torn out, and it is astonishing how effectively this widens the car. There is plenty of room for easy chairs, potted palms, a dainty table and a mammoth music box. One of the most curious features of the room is the owner's bed, a marvel of substantial comfort, which is fastened to the wall, like a sleeping car berth. At one side is a gas fireplace, which blazes cheerfully in winter. The motorman's box is handsomely decorated and is curtained off from the car, containing a marble lavatory. The whole car is lit by electricity, and is so tight and snug that when I called on Mr. Miller one bitter day in January, not a breath of cold air penetrated it.

Now another strange feature of this strangest house is, that under each car there is a comfortable basement, just the size of the car above. These underground rooms are lined with cement and fire brick, then plastered and frescoed until they are entirely dry and free from moisture, though they retain the advantage of being delightfully cool in summer. Mr. Miller, who used frequently to suffer from rheumatism, declares that he has never felt a touch of it since he has lived in his houseboat. The basement under the first car is used as a sort of library and sitting room. There is a small combination desk and bookcase, a library table, and a large, soft couch, which, when you remove the padded top, proves to be a bathtub underneath. The walls are painted a light yellow, the ceiling and floors done in dark red. Another little lavatory is partitioned off from this room. Electric fans are kept buzzing to cool the air, and another giant music box trills and warbles away phlegmatically.

The second streetcar is Mr. Miller's dining room, for he is a consistent bachelor and keeps a man of all work. There he gives oyster suppers, bachelor dinners, and late lunches. The basement below the second car is the kitchen, and is very much like the kitchen on a well-appointed steam launch. There are closets stocked with canned fruits and canned meats, pickles, crackers and viands ready for quick lunches. The range is one of the best and most modern makes, with an ample hot-water attachment. The refrigerator is built back in the wall, a little cave bricked and lined with zinc, and in the morning the ice man comes along, opens a trap and drops a chunk down, and the refrigerator is loaded for the day.

The conservatory is the room in which Mr. Miller spends most of his time, and it is certainly the most beautiful thing in his unique housekeeping system. Only the glass roof is above ground, and all efforts to successfully photograph the interior have failed because of the relentless blaze of light. I only wish I were able to offer a picture of it, as it looks more like a place where things were grown for pleasure and less like a place where they were grown for business than any conservatory I have ever seen. There are none of the cheap and gaudy flowers which people grow because they are easily taken care of. The room is in harmony throughout, and when I saw it, it was a little bit of tropical forest shut in out of a bitter, northern night and clouds of whirling snow flakes. The roof is hung with tropical vines. A passion flower that has gone mad and run over everything, hangs in twisted ropes and cables and mats over the rafters. There are bread fruit and banana plant and orange trees. There are palms of every description and rich, florid blossoms of the nightshade family. The only non-tropical flowers I saw were some cold, pale English violets that grew with maidenhair ferns behind a thicket of palms, and their faint, cool fragrance somehow seemed all the more exquisite and desirable amid all this exotic splendor. Then there is the fish pond, a big clear pond full of water lilies, and aquatic plants, and frogs, and big turtles, and goldfish. This pond lies directly under the palms and the riotous passion vines. An electric light of great power which is submerged in the water gives a startling effect at night. It is like a sub-marine sun; every moss and lily root, every green frog and yellow turtle is visible. It is a favorite trick of Mr. Miller's on winter nights to turn out all the lights in the conservatory except this submerged one, get his music box to going, light his pipe and sit quietly and observe the life of the fish people. For an hour or more I watched them glide back and forth about the incandescent globe, big Japanese goldfish with tails like lacework, and some with tails like pale, lilac fleur de lys in water. They were continually busy; whether they swam for business or pleasure I can't say, but they took it very seriously. With stately grace they advanced and retreated, crossed over and "went up the middle." I could only think of the Mock Turtle's song:—

> See how gracefully the lobsters and the turtles all advance.
> They are waiting on the shingle.
> Won't you come and join the dance?

While the grounds of Mr. Miller's stationary palace cars are not extensive, they are beautifully kept. He has one of the finest lotus beds I have ever seen, and I doubt whether there is another such in the city. Both his land-grown cars are surrounded by latticework which is covered with vines.

Taking it altogether, its odd origin, its luxurious internal fittings, its flowery surroundings, its lotus bed and its goldfish, this strikes me as about the most delightful home a man of unconventional taste could make for himself. [August 4, 1900, pp. 17–18]

Washington Correspondent

(December 16, 1900—March 17, 1901)

Willa Cather's first extended visit to Washington came in 1898, when she spent the first two weeks of May with her cousin James Howard Gore and his wife, the former Lillian Thekla Brandthall. Together the Gores introduced their young kinswoman to the cosmopolitan world of diplomatic Washington. The beautiful Mrs. Gore, whose father had been Norwegian ambassador to the United States and who was a cousin of King Oscar of Sweden, enraptured Willa Cather with her stories of court life, her Ibsen readings, and her singing of Grieg's songs.[1] *Dr. Howard Gore (1856–1939) was a professor of geography at Columbian University (now George Washington University), a frequent consultant to government agencies, and a founding member of the National Geographic Society. He also was the author of* Holland as Seen by an American, *which Cather reviewed in the* Leader, *May 27, 1899. The book, she wrote,*

> *does exactly what M. Paul Bourget signally failed to do in his* Outre-Mer,[2] *it gives a sharp and vivid impression of a country and an indirect, yet convincing analysis of the life and national fiber of a people. It is an appreciation of rather than a study of Holland, and it certainly meets the final requirement of appreciative description—it makes one want to take the first boat to Holland. The informality and brevity of the sketch add greatly to its attractiveness, and on reading it, it occurs to one that if D'Amici's* Holland *were boiled down to about one half of its bulk, it would be a more readable book and lose none of its beauty. In descriptive works the merit is usually in inverse ratio to the length. Felicitous description is almost always accidental or incidental. It is not at all a question of presenting information, but of suggesting the character of a place, or reproducing an atmosphere.*

1. Willa Cather to Frances Gere, June 23, 1898.

2. For Paul Bourget and *Outre-Mer*, see "Mark Twain: 'impossible as a man of letters,'" Books and Authors (I), above.

Maupassant's incidental description of Corsica in his little story, "Le Bonheur," suggests more of the country than all the volumes that have been written about it.

In 1900 Willa Cather returned to Washington for a stay of several months, but it is difficult to say exactly when she arrived there. As previously discussed, it seems likely that she resigned from the Leader *in late spring, and the volume of her contributions to the* Library *suggests that she must have been based mainly in Pittsburgh through July and perhaps part of August. Contrary to her normal custom, she did not visit Red Cloud that summer; and, according to Elsie Cather, she secured a job in a Washington government office as a translator sometime during the fall or winter.*[3] *At any rate, in December Cather began sending a weekly Washington letter to the* Nebraska State Journal, *the first one appearing on December 9. In the same month, on December 22, she began a column consisting almost entirely of material reprinted from the* Journal, *in a magazine called the* Index of Pittsburg Life.

The Index, *which had absorbed the* Library, *had made its debut on September 1, 1895, "as a quarto of sixteen pages and a cover at a dollar a year. It chronicled society, literature, and current events, and was well edited by Robert Galloway Paull. Its price was increased to a dollar and a half in 1900, and its scope was enlarged in various directions."*[4] *By the time Willa Cather began to contribute to the magazine its length had been increased to twenty-six pages and its contents included features on topics of interest to Pittsburgh society—women's clubs, golf, automobiles, collegiate sports (particularly at Princeton and Yale), music, theatre, art, and literature—an occasional story or poem, and letters on New York and Atlantic City society. In all, twelve pieces signed "Willa Sibert Cather" appeared in the* Index. *The first nine, covering the period from December 22, 1900, to February 16, 1901, were called "Winter Sketches in the Capital." The tenth, in the issue of February 23, was an account of the Gridiron Club dinner. After a two-week hiatus came a review of Pinero's* Gay Lord Quex *and a week later (March 16) an article, "Literature in the Capital," the final contribution.*

Thirteen signed pieces with Washington datelines appeared in the Journal, *the first, as noted, on December 9, 1900, and the last on March 17, 1901. Frequently material in the* Journal *letters was omitted from the* Index, *and two pieces which appeared in the* Journal*—a review of Bernhardt in* La Tosca *and* Camille *(February 4) and "Hunting the North Pole" (March 17)—were not*

3. Elsie M. Cather in an interview with the editor, August 16, 1963.
4. Mott, *History of American Magazines*, IV, 88.

reprinted in the Index. *On the other hand, an* Index *piece of January 5, 1901, on the Chinese minister Wu T'ing-fang, did not appear in the* Journal. *On March 24, the* Journal *published Willa Cather's eulogy of Ethelbert Nevin (see The Musical World [III], above), but it did not carry a Washington dateline. In all probability by this date Cather had returned to Pittsburgh, for during the spring term she taught Latin and English at Pittsburgh's Central High School.*[5]

Willa Cather's months in Washington must have been strenuous in the extreme. It was "a winter of continuous theatre and concert-going,"[6] *and she was doing other writing—her article on Nevin appeared in the November* Ladies' Home Journal *and a poem in the* Critic *in December—in addition to the weekly letters and the translator's job. At some time during the winter, possibly as early as Christmas, the idea of securing a teaching position occurred to her,*[7] *and when the opportunity presented itself Willa Cather disembarked with alacrity from the Washington merry-go-round. Although she was not ready to give up free-lancing, in the future she would operate from a more stable center.*

A Carreño Concert

This letter to the Journal, *largely devoted to a concert by Teresa Carreño (see The Musical World [III], above), was datelined "Washington, Dec. 12," but when it was reprinted in the* Index *in the first of the "Winter Sketches in the Capital," the dateline read, "Washington, D.C., December 20." In the* Index *the account of the concert was much abridged; and the column included a tribute to the recently deceased Senator Cushman K. Davis of Minnesota, which had appeared in the* Journal *on December 9.*

The opening session of the Senate was not unlike a high school commencement in the matter of flowers and admiring friends. The Chamber looked like a conservatory, or seen from the gallery, like a big German flower garden where the flowers were portioned off in little beddies. There was not one desk without a bouquet when the Senate was called to order, except that of the late Senator Davis, and before the first hour was over one of the members sent some of his flowers over to

5. Brown, *Willa Cather*, p. 92. However, according to Mildred R. Bennett, Willa Cather taught Latin only during her first term at Central; subsequently, "to her relief" she was transferred to the English department. *CSF*, p. xxii.

6. *Index*, February 16, 1901, p. 8.

7. *CSF*, p. xxii.

the empty desk by a page. Senator [Mark] Hanna's desk was piled with flowers until it looked like a high altar, and on the floor beside him stood an American Beauty rose tree that his desk was not large enough to hold.... Senator [Thomas H.] Carter, of Montana, had a bunch of fierce yellow chrysanthemums that lit up his corner, and tiny Senator [George G.] Vest was completely hidden by roses and carnations. All the members of the Senate were in afternoon dress, and with one or two notable exceptions presented an unusually tidy appearance. "Lonnie" Stuart, the chief of the pages, wore a Prince Albert coat, a white vest, light trousers, and a frowsy white chrysanthemum in his buttonhole.

The gallery was crowded long before the house was called to order and women were greatly in evidence. As a rule the best known women of the capital do not turn out on the opening day, unless as a personal tribute to some statesman who will be watching for them; that day being given over to the country relatives of the member, who come to Washington to see him make his debut. But on this occasion the anticipated floral display brought nearly all the women who are prominent socially, and many of the women of the foreign legations.... The unusual crush was caused by the presence of many women from out of town who had come to the city to attend the W.C.T.U. convention here. These ladies all took the proceedings very seriously, and many of them asked to be shown the seat and desk which Roberts tried to hold. Whether they wanted to exorcise it or to tie white ribbons on it I do not know. A brilliant figure in the gallery assembly was Mme. Teresa Carreño, who was billed for a concert in the city that night. She sat near the rail in an enormous black hat and black Russian sables, looking like Catherine the Great come to life again. I never should have suspected the lady of having any interest in politics, but if she had taken to them, in a republic or an empire, or any other form of government where men were men and where sleepless ambition counted for anything, what a howling success she would have made of them.

I had not intended going to Carreño's concert that evening, but after getting a glimpse of her at the Senate chamber, I changed my mind and decided that even if one were too tired for music it was a good deal of a privilege to look at her, in these days when royalty is growing more tolerant and losing its old prerogatives and when an imperatrix is not to be met with every day. When madame appeared that night it was in a gown of blue satin, with a sort of armor plate overdress of black net with huge round disks of jet set here and there over it, that made her look like the Black Knight. She is a trifle grayer than when she played in your city a few years ago, but I could see no trace of the humility of age in either her face or manner. Washington, which is strangely deficient in some of the things that a full-grown city is supposed to have, has no auditorium, and Carreño played in a church. She didn't seem to like it, and I'm sure I felt the inappropriateness of it all evening. The Ten Commandments were frescoed in red and yellow above the platform on which she played, and between whiles she read them attentively. Indeed, at one time she became so intent on them that she very nearly forgot to begin the Chopin Barcarolle at all. The church was as cold as a country meeting house. Someway it never seems necessary to have churches warm, and when madame came out from the Sunday-school room which had served her as a dressing room, she wore, over all her magnificence a little blue shawl, such as people sometimes wrap about babies. Her timid little maid reasoned with her and did her best to persuade madame to take off her funny little wrap, but not so, madame played Mozart's Fantasy in C Minor quite through in her little blue shawl. The conductor of the musical society under whose auspices she appeared, a little Dane with a serpentine figure and no shoulders whose conducting was a series of spasms, tried vainly to give madame assistance in going up and down at the stairs of the platform, but she was much larger than he and she brushed him impatiently aside.

The concert came in like a lamb and went out like a lion, since it began with Mozart and ended with Liszt. During the course of the recital Carreño played fifteen numbers, the program including Mozart, Beethoven, Chopin, Schumann, and Liszt's arrangement of several Schubert airs.

In spite of the blue shawl, I am inclined to think that the most remarkable work of the evening was done in the first number, comprising the Mozart Fantasy and the Beethoven Sonata No. 3, of opus 31. I have heard Carreño exploit her peculiar power more vividly, but it is not always in the compositions peculiarly her own by taste and sympathy that her highest work is done. In compositions of a more classical mould and moderate tone, the real wonder of the woman is revealed, the locked, unshaken force that lies behind the tempest, the scholastic mastery of tonal relations, quite apart from their dramatic or emotional effect. It is in this respect that Carreño so far surpasses even that gifted artist, Fanny Bloomfield Zeisler,[8] in that deeper and more exhaustless virility, the scientist under the artist.

8. Fanny Bloomfield Zeisler (1863–1927), European-born American pianist.

I wonder how Mr. James Huneker reconciles all his theories about the emasculating of Chopin by women,[9] the continual enslavement of that mighty spirit which women have accomplished from the days of Mme. Dudevant down, with Carreño's playing of him? Surely there is little of the saccharine in the way this Latin American attacks him. What would Mr. Huneker say to her when she goes a-castle storming in the Scherzo, opus 31? The sentimentalizing of Frédéric Chopin can never be laid at Carreño's door. Here, as always, I was minded of the remark of a young Russian pianist, who described Carreño's manner of attack as equivalent to "There, damn you, take that!" If Mr. Huneker were to make any criticism at all, he might make an argument of the statement that on the other hand Carreño divests Chopin of some of that suggested lassitude which properly belongs to him.

It was the Schumann Fantasy in C Major that Carreño found the medium for her overwhelming individual power, and most effectually displayed that marvelous technique which, however brilliant it may be, is always warm. Then followed several Schubert-Liszt numbers, closing with the "Erlkönig" which is one of her old war horses. The coloring in these last numbers was of course incomparable. The terrific power of the woman is as amazing as ever, the commanding, militant attack and the panoramic impressions of purple and crimson that somehow are left on the brain by the barbaric splendor of sound, this opulent richness of tone, were as vivid as ever. Her message is eminently the one spoken in the thunder and flame and with the call of the trumpet. In person, as I say, she has changed but little, and she still acknowledges the applause of her audience very much as Cleopatra might have acknowledged the cheers of the populace. "*Non humilis mulier*," said Horace.[10]

Journal, December 16, 1900, p. 19.

Hedda Gabler

Henrik Ibsen's plays had been unenthusiastically received in the United States, beginning with Modjeska's 1883 production of A Doll's House. *Cather's favorite from Lincoln days, Maida Craigen (see "Shakespeare," The Theatre [I], above) played Mrs. Elvsted in the first American*

9. Huneker's *Chopin: The Man and His Music* was published in 1900. Later in this sentence George Sand is referred to by her married name, Mme. Dudevant.

10. From the *Odes* of Horace, Book I, Ode XXXVII (to Cleopatra), line 32. Willa Cather's translation of Ode XXXVIII in the same book appeared in the *Hesperian*, November 24, 1892, p. 12; Shively, *Willa Cather's Campus Years*, p. 112.

production of Hedda Gabler, *March 30, 1898. In the performance described below, the title role was played by Blanche Bates (1873–1941), who had won stardom in* The Senator *with Sol Smith Russell and had played in* A Doll's House *on the road. In "The Passing Show" Willa Cather had reported that Fridtjof Nansen had talked with her of "the great dramatist of the century," Ibsen: "[Nansen] thinks the American idea that Ibsen's dramas lack dramatic interest and are coldly intellectual for stage purposes a mere misapprehension, and says that they are the most effective acting plays that have been written this generation"* (Courier, *December 25, 1897). The following selection, which comprised the second "Winter Sketches" column, carried a Washington dateline of December 27, 1900. It had appeared in the* Journal *on December 9.*

Ibsen is played so seldom in America that to every performance of his dramas some particular importance may be attached. The production of *Hedda Gabler* by Blanche Bates at the Lafayette Theatre here was a notable one in many respects. In the first place, the character of the audience was exceptionally interesting. It was made up of the most violently contrasting elements. Many of the most noted scientists and scholars of the city were there, people from the libraries and the Coast Survey and officials from the various government departments, and people of quite another character were much in evidence, people who usually go to the variety theatres. Whether the latter contingent merely came because the play had been much advertised, or whether there is a particular interest in Ibsen among that class of people, I was not able to decide. An interesting feature of the audience was the presence of Sol Smith Russell and his party. They occupied one of the boxes near the stage, and the actor looked so worn and changed after his long illness that I would scarcely have known him. His physical strength has largely come back to him, but his memory shows no sign of return. He haunts the theatre, heavy-eyed and seldom smiling, waiting for the change of some sort that must come soon.

As to the playableness or non-playableness of Ibsen people will doubtless always differ, as they differ about the readableness of George Meredith, but I have never seen an audience more intent upon what went on before them. Of course, the audience was rather exceptional, and there were many serious people present who prefer psychology to acrobatic art, and who are not averse to thinking in the theatre. The only doubt entertained about the performance by people who had read the play was occasioned by the youth of the actress. Could a young woman, with limited dramatic experience at all cope with a character so unusual and so complex? From the moment Miss Bates entered, I knew that she held the reins in her hands, the only question was, would she drive too hard? The chill of her greeting of her husband's kind, silly old aunt, I thought a little overdone, but it may have been nervousness, for until the curtain fell on the tragedy in the last act, that was the only point on which a student of the play could seriously differ from the actress. Miss Bates has so absorbed the character that it is difficult to think of her in any other, her intellectual grasp of the part is enviable, for anybody is to be envied who can so entirely enter into and possess an abstraction. Her effort seemed to be not so much to present the moods and caprices of General Gabler's daughter, but the mental constitution of the woman, the battery where all these fierce and terrible demonstrations of force were generated. Miss Bates' identification with the character was such that she had felt it unnecessary to make up in the least. When Hedda stepped upon the stage I at once decided that she was one of the most intelligent faces among the actresses of the younger generation, and, in an odd way, one of the handsomest. She certainly looks very unlike a professional, and she seemed to have made absolutely no attempt to make herself pretty. A sharp, bold chin, a rather hard mouth, a broad, full forehead, eyes sometimes green and sometimes blue and sometimes gray, and always inscrutably deep, a commanding figure and a pair of wonderfully expressive hands, and there you have a bloodless outline of her.

Her analysis of the character was thorough, her conception of it clear, and her execution wholly spontaneous and unfaltering.

I confess that the insufferable vixen that I had got from a reading of the play, was a very much more improbable creature than the highly strung woman, maddened by the inactivity and narrowness of her life, that Miss Bates presented. From the first she made Hedda's desperation clear enough, and the causes of it. She had been tired of dancing, she had reached the age where women in Christiania marry; she was rather afraid people would begin to wonder, maybe. She had a chance to carry off one of the university lights, a man who never looked at women, and out of bravado and a taste for experiments, she did it; she was General Gabler's daughter, whose playthings were her father's pistols, and a taste for adventure ran in the blood.

Then came the long wedding journey, and she did not find the great historian interesting company. Wherever they went he did nothing but regret that he had forgotten to bring his carpet slippers and grub in libraries. As Hedda tells Brack, "Always the same person, forever and a day. Always the libraries, and the History of Civilization, forever and a day." At this juncture Eilert Lövberg turns up, the fellow whom, in her keen thirst for knowledge of the life of the world, she used to question about his escapades; who had misconstrued this purely intellectual curiosity and who had taken advantage of her confidence and against whom she had raised her father's pistol. But Lövberg has found himself again, and is getting along much better out of Hedda's company than he ever did in it. Moreover, he has found a woman who cares more for his work than he does himself, and who is helping him do it at a heavy sacrifice to herself. So Hedda finds that she is not really a moving power in anything, and with the consciousness of ability—which people of executive power are pretty sure to have—hot in her, she swears that she will have an influence in some destiny. Hedda's power, had she known it, lay in other lines than in playing the enchantress. She might have done a hundred things at first hand, but her talents were not at all to admire, encourage and console. She may have made herself believe that by bringing Lövberg out of the fear of himself into a broader moral freedom, she could make of him a greater man than ever Mrs. Elvsted could, but I think her desire was chiefly to pull down Mrs. Elvsted's work, at whatever cost. Miss Bates emphasized the only condition which makes the destruction of Lövberg's manuscript at all endurable, even from a woman half-deranged by physical conditions, and that is the slight value that she put on all intellectual things, and her total ignorance of the way in which a man's work may take hold even of his emotional nature. It is a terrific scene, that in which, maddened by the thought of an unwelcome maternity, she destroys this brain child of Lövberg's and Mrs. Elvsted's, and it is only from that point that the play becomes a tragedy.

I had often wondered whether in the actual presentation of the play it would be possible to make Hedda's repeated allusions to Lövberg with vine leaves in his hair other than ridiculous. But when the character stands in life before you, you somehow understand that whatever Lövberg was in the old days, he was always picturesque, always gratified her fancy and stimulated her imagination. Now, in all the ugliness and narrowness of this genteel poverty in which she finds herself, in the uncontrollable spasm of physical repulsion for her dry, bookish husband which has seized her, she turns longingly back to that old childish fancy of Eilert Lövberg, splendid and serene, living his free, passionate life, unafraid of any penalty, with vine leaves in his hair, like the youths who shook the thyrsus in the train of Bacchus. Every element of beauty has died out of her own life, her every relation with the world has become nauseating, and she looks at this old ideal of pagan freedom as a sort of reminder that the whole world has not turned to ashes, as one who had become a curse unto himself might look at one of the Attic marbles and forget his own debasement. It is when the details of Lövberg's filthy death reach her, when her Greek statue is spattered with mud, that her overwrought nerves give way completely.

As I came out of the theatre I was talking about the play with one of the Congressional librarians, and remarked that after all nothing in the play seemed to me to entirely account for Hedda, or to explain her. He reminded me that Hamlet is not explained, and that the inexplicable mystery of the character has been the secret of its power. Nevertheless, I am not at all convinced that a tragedy can properly be built on a temporary physical condition, and one which varies with the individual.

Index, December 29, 1900, p. 14.

Christmas in Washington

The following selection is excerpted from a Journal *letter, datelined December 28. Other portions of the column—about life in Washington in the early 1800's and paragraphs about Olga Nethersole and the English playwright Haddon Chambers—were reprinted in the* Index *on January 19, 1901, but not this holiday vignette.*

Christmas in Washington is a strange experience to anyone bred in a less kindly climate and in less leisurely cities. Then the drifting population of the city, people who spend half the year wandering about the four quarters of the globe, return home. The congressional retinue departs, and the hotel corridors are empty. This year people did their Christmas shopping in their summer clothes. The week preceeding Christmas was like a western September, presenting a succession of cloudless skies and sunny days. The avenue was thronged with carriages and automobiles. The men wore no overcoats, the women drove in afternoon toilets without wraps. The street corners were gay with flower stands, and the forest of Christmas trees and holly bushes about the old market place looked more like the decorations for a flower carnival than for a midwinter festival. Every Negro one met wore a broad smile on his face, and whenever a street piano came along a dozen newsboys were doing a ragtime dance in the street before the first air was over. Even the beggars in this easy-going, good-natured city are never the unfortunate degenerated creatures that they are elsewhere. The old blind "auntie" who sits on the steps of the G Street Congregational church is singing hymns every morning as I pass her and rattling the pennies in her box. I have known men in Pittsburgh who did business in six figures who never seemed on such good terms with life as the colored boy who sells roses in the street before the office. He always takes his hat off as the President drives out of the White House grounds, and the President never forgets to nod to him. The President himself does not get off easily at Christmas time. His secretary has a week's work before him, acknowledging gifts of every description, except wines and liquors, which are not accepted. Early in the week express wagons began to make hourly calls at the White House, with packages from all over the United States and even from Cuba, Puerto Rico and the Philippines. This year the list included almost all known manufactures from hand-pieced bed quilts to hammered silver. Turkeys and cigars were especially in evidence. When all these native offerings are collected, and those from the personal friends of the McKinleys are sorted out, the remaining are divided among the servants or taken up to the White House attic, which is a junk shop devoted to such tributes. During the W.C.T.U. convention here I heard one lady complain that an oil painting, executed by herself, which she had sent the President last Christmas was nowhere to be found in the White House reception rooms. People are fond of sending the President his picture, snapshots that they have taken of him in different cities where he has made speeches; oil portraits and life-sized crayons "enlarged" from cabinets. He has received numerous transparencies of himself, and portraits in painted "cut glass." One enterprising dentist sent him, the President, his portrait made of hundreds of colored teeth which he had extracted, a sort of dental mosaic. Many little girls send him drawn-work handkerchiefs and pen wipers, and the bracelets he has received from the scroll saws of small boys would supply a poor family with kindling wood for a month. And for all these curios poor Mr. Cortelyou[11] has to express the President's "profound thanks."

Journal, December 30, 1900, p. 13.

11. George B. Cortelyou (1862–1940), secretary to President McKinley, later Secretary of the Treasury. From 1909 to 1935 he was president of what became the Consolidated Edison Company.

The Chinese Minister

In "A Chinese View of the Chinese Situation," which appeared in the Library, *July 28, 1900, Willa Cather reported an interview with Lee Chin, a Pittsburgh importer, in which she was unable to secure a comment on the Boxer revolt against foreign influence and presence in China. For political discussion, Lee Chin referred her to Wu T'ing-fang (1842–1922), Chinese minister to the United States: "'Wu can do all that, down in Washington, . . . he's paid for it, and I guess he earns his salary.'" Two weeks later the* Library *published Willa Cather's story "The Conversion of Sum Loo," which, like the interview, stressed the sense of exile and isolation of the Chinese in the United States.*[12] *The following column on Wu T'ing-fang, the third of the "Winter Sketches," did not appear in the* Journal.

I think a speaker has seldom made a deeper impression than that made by Mr. Wu T'ing-fang, the Chinese minister, when he delivered the Founder's Day address at the Carnegie Institute in Pittsburgh last month, so soon after the embarrassing and trying position in which he had been placed by the political convulsions in his country.

The Chinese minister has the reputation of being one of the greatest wags in Washington, as well as one of the best informed men politically. His humor is always ready and usually kindly. Before I left Pittsburgh so many rumors of his attainments had been the rounds of the press there that one might have fancied Mr. Wu a man of letters as we understand that designation, as well as a critic of painting and music; in short, that impossible thing, a completely Europeanized Chinaman. The Chinaman has held his identity through too many centuries of adverse conditions to lose it in a few years of European culture; his nerve cells, brain stuff, and even his emotional instincts are totally different from those of the nations of the West. Mr. Wu is a Chinaman down to the end of his attenuated queue; European art of any sort is incomprehensible to him. He talks fluently about the elevating influence of music, but by music he means the monotonous beating of a brass gong, or a few high, shrill notes on a flute, or at best the twanging of a mandolin. Of orchestration, of polyphonic composition, of the symphony, Mr. Wu knows about as much as an oyster. He can see nothing in English or French poetry at all, except that

12. "The Conversion of Sum Loo," *Library*, August 11, 1900, pp. 4–6; *CSF*, pp. 323–331. For Cather's review of a similar story, *The Bride of Japan* by Carlton Dawe, see *Leader*, May 6, 1898, p. 9. Cather wrote a later article about Lee Chin, "Pittsburgh's Richest Chinaman," Pittsburgh *Gazette*, June 12, 1902, p. 5.

of Tupper,[13] which expresses worthy sentiments. The poetry of Proverbs and Ecclesiastes he thoroughly enjoys, and anything in the shape of maxims seems to him the highest form of literary art. That you should tell a truth indirectly, or indicate it by a negative process, which Browning says is the glory and the good of literary art, seems to him an absurd waste of time and strength.

On the other hand, when you come to matters of general scientific knowledge, to a comprehension of comparative law and the science of government, I doubt whether there is a man in the city with a wider outlook than Mr. Wu.

The Wus do not entertain very often, but several times each winter and once in the fall the legation house is thrown open, and these occasions are red-letter days in Washington society. If it is a dinner, the cuisine is sure to be of the best; if a reception, the greenhouses of the city are left bare after festooning the high walls of Mr. Wu's residence.

Mrs. Wu is always present at the entertainments given by her husband, and even if the guests are exclusively men they are expected to ask permission to pay their respects to the lady of the house, whose smile is as broad as her English vocabulary is narrow. Every now and then some enterprising lady in short skirts and an Alpine hat and nose glasses, who calls herself a "journalist" and avails herself of all the privileges that are believed to go with that title, walks up to the legation house and demands an interview with Madame Wu. But she never goes again. "It isn't that she is hard to get at," such a lady recently explained to me, "but she asks so many embarrassing questions." Reporters never like being interviewed. Madame Wu is always ready to see an interviewer, but she questions them so incessantly they seldom get a word in edgeways. When Mr. Wu was in Pittsburgh, some of the questions he asked were considered rather impertinent, but personal questions are the highest form of Chinese etiquette. The minister practices this method of making his guests comfortable much less vigorously than Li Hung-chang,[14] however, whose interrogations used to create the most awkward situations. The Oriental is naturally boastful, but he loves not to boast openly, and the most considerate thing you can do for him is to question him and give him an opportunity to say how much he is worth, whether his wife is handsome, or his sons are scholars, etc.

13. Martin Tupper (1810–1839), author of *Proverbial Philosophy* (1838).

14. Li Hung-chang (1823–1901), called the "Bismarck of Asia," was prime minister of China (1895–1898), visited Europe and the United States in 1896, and was commissioner to restore peace after the Boxer uprising (1900).

Madame Wu always wears the native costume, of course. She particularly abominates the dress affected by the mannish woman, and she objects even to shirtwaists. "It is not that they are improper," she explained, "but they are so ugly." She attends personally to all the details of her household. Her servants are all Negroes who have been trained in American households, with the exception of one expert Chinese cook, who is kept to prepare certain Chinese dishes, incomprehensible to the American mind, but very dear to the palate of Mr. Wu. Madame usually rises at six o'clock in the morning, and about nine she goes shopping or marketing if the weather is at all good. As her feet are too small to permit of her walking about the shops, she is waited on in her carriage. There is no subject to which Madame Wu brings more enthusiasm than Washington weather. During the years they spent in London, she was miserable most of the time. She hated the fogs and she dreaded the cold. The warm winter sunlight of Washington suits her exactly, and in the big east window of her sleeping room she has a divan built as a sort of window seat, and there she takes sun baths all through the chilly months. "I be much contented to live in Washington always," she remarks placidly.

The house of the Chinese legation here is one of the handsomest of the legation houses, and the interior sets one to reading the *Arabian Nights* over again. I have never seen so much elegance or so little comfort. The ceilings are high as those of a chapel, vaulted and frescoed and gilded and arched with heavy dark woods until it makes your head whirl to try to puzzle out the different designs on them. Everywhere there are oriental tapestries and rugs and paintings of the most gorgeous color, but the general effect of the rooms is dark and high and cold for all that. In the Oriental Room the ebony cabinets stand eight feet high, laden with such treasures in ivory and jade and silver and alloys of the precious metals as are beyond price because they are not made in the world at all any more, not even by the patient craftsmen of China. Vases in bronze and porcelain stand as high as your head, and everywhere there [are] inlaid chairs and tables made from scented woods and woods of many colors, priceless bronzes of the most exquisite workmanship, sulky demons and sulkier gods, tiny fir trees that are hundreds of years old, yet so small that they can be kept in jardinieres, things curious and rich and wonderful, but never a place where a man could sit down and smoke with any comfort or where an American child would want to stay, unless it stayed to play it was Sinbad or one of the unfortunate Calenders.

The Wu automobile is used more constantly than any vehicle in the city except the streetcars. When the minister and his wife are not riding together, they are riding alone, and when they are not using it, the minister's little son and one or two of his little friends are sent to ride in care of a servant. This little boy goes to the public school, but he is not at all at the head of his class, as the story went in Pittsburgh. He finds western learning difficult to put into a yellow head, and though he is by no means the lowest in his class, he is scarcely up to the average. He certainly is, however, one of the most patient, earnest, industrious little boys that ever bent over a book. I met the little chap through the twelve-year-old son of a German diplomat here, a handsome boy, with blue-black curls all over his head and flashing eyes, and that red and white North German skin, who is at the head of a class of boys a great deal older than himself, and who learns things by intuition, as it were. This dashing little fellow, to whom everything comes so easily, is the little Asiatic's dearest friend, and I never saw anything more pathetic and quaint than the look of pride and amazement with which the little yellow boy watches the red-and-white boy rattle off a string of names and dates in a history recitation.

The Chinese boy wears the Chinese dress and queue, and he is a queer little figure on the playground with his skirts and wadded shoes, trotting along with his arm over the German lad's shoulder and his mild eyes full of admiration for his gifted comrade. When the boys play active games, the little chap gathers up his skirts in one hand and goes in with a will. Among his amusing Chinese toys he showed me a translation of a Chinese book of children's rhymes that are as old as the name of Confucius himself. The translation was made by Prof. Headland, of the University of Peking.[15]

Index, January 5, 1901, p. 22.

"*Joe Jefferson, the Painter*"

Willa Cather had a great deal of admiration for the dean of American actors (see "An Open Letter to Joseph Jefferson," The Star System [IV], above). The exhibition of his paintings, reported here, was not a sentimental tribute to a popular favorite, for Jefferson was recognized as a serious artist. One of his paintings had been in the original collection of Pittsburgh's Carnegie Institute Gallery, and when he was elected to the American Academy of Arts and Letters in 1905, it was as much in recognition of his painting as of his work in the theatre. The following selection appeared in the Index *with a*

15. Isaac T. Headland (1859–1942), American Methodist missionary to China and professor of science at Peking University (1890–1907), author of *Chinese Mother Goose Rhymes* (1900).

Washington dateline of January 10, 1901. It had appeared in the Journal *on January 6, datelined January 3. The* Index *omitted the concluding paragraph, which described an oil in the Raleigh Hotel "that has amused a good many people in its time. It was done a good many years ago and is a portrait of N. P. Willis and Nathaniel Hawthorne fishing. They are nicely posed on a flat rock in the middle of a pearly brook; N. P. is attired in a kilted frock coat, . . . and is daintily baiting his hook, with his little finger carefully curved. Hawthorne, in the background, stands in blousing trousers and a stiff hat shaped like an umbrella jar, and is casting his line."*

An exhibit of fifty-four of Joseph Jefferson's oil paintings at the principal art store of the city kept the veteran actor in the city nearly two weeks. I met him dining at the Raleigh with some friends one evening and got him to talk of his pictures. If enthusiasm and good humor alone could keep a man young, this gentleman would be younger than either of his sons. Talking to him is a good deal like talking to a boy with a Santa Claus mask on, you have to keep reminding yourself of the discrepancy between the man and the mask. "You see I come honestly by having two strings to my bow," he said. "My ancestors were painters and players, sometimes one, sometimes the other, about evenly divided. I can't remember the time when I didn't want to be both. But painting required leisure and comparative financial security; so I didn't get at that so early. I had to hustle when I was a youngster, and I was fairly successful as an actor before I even got started at my brushes, otherwise, who knows? I might have been the founder of a religion, like Whistler, instead of a poor play-actor at whom people clap their hands. I suppose it would never do at all for me to say that I would rather be a painter than an actor, for the public insists that a man shall be entirely loyal to his *premier amour*. Indeed, I have always concealed my work with colors, rather than vaunted it, and one of the articles of the Philistine's creed is that a man cannot excel in two things. So outwardly I have been devoted to one art and have carried on a lifelong liaison with another. It is only behind the shelter of my grey hairs that I dare to brazenly exhibit my pictures."

I could not forbear asking the gentleman how the limitations of the stage seemed to a man fortunate enough to be master of the mediums of two arts.

"Of course, the painter does his work under more fortunate conditions, but I am always the man to say a good word for the buskin. I've worn it on sunny roads and stormy, and I've never been tempted to quit it. It is the most difficult of all the arts, because it is not necessary to do your best to succeed. Its conditions are the hardest and most irksome for a sensitive soul to endure, and yet they have a sorcery all their own, and one becomes wedded to them and can't get on without them. We're a good deal like the tramp who loves the misery of sleeping out of doors. I shall be very content to die an actor."

While the pictures were on exhibition here, Francis Wilson bought one of the largest, "The King of the Forest," an immense oak on the White Mountains. Sol Smith Russell purchased a Florida scene, and several more were sold to nonprofessional people. Individual pictures by Jefferson may be seen almost anywhere, but a collection of them speaks more strongly than any single picture could do. It was the excellence of the painting that most surprised one, the way in which the painter's medium responds to him, the sureness of his execution. There are none of those affectations of the bizarre so often seen in the painters who are forever talking about "strengthening their style." This is downright good painting, a sound technical skill, modestly used, and responding to the fancy of a poet. The collection was made up exclusively of landscapes, and, with the exception of a few Australian scenes, of American landscapes. One of the most striking canvases was a study of the Everglades, in sepia and Chinese white, with no other color discernible, with broken trees and grey mosses, and snakey creepers over everything. It is very different from the tender green woods which Mr. Jefferson usually paints, and for an effect of density of shadow, of still, dead light and decaying wilderness, it is certainly a piece of work which any painter might be proud of. "After Trout" and "Forest and Streams" are two brook studies, and the latter picture is especially poetic, being entirely submerged in that peculiar yellow shade of green, the green of high noon and early spring in which Jefferson delights as Inness did in the colder and bluer tint. In both these pictures, and in many others in this exhibit, the willow trees were treated with peculiar feeling and tenderness, the color so completely in character, the lines of the trunk through the yellow green of the slender leaves so truly those of the willow and of no other tree.

It is an interesting thing to watch, that feeling of certain painters for certain trees. With Corot it was always the wide-topped elm, the most exquisite tree of all for shape and line; with Sisley it was the silver poplar, the whole tree permeated and riddled with light like a lattice. Certainly these men must have played when they were little under their peculiar trees, and got on a personal footing with them, so to speak, got the individuality of the tree established in their inner consciousness. Somehow or other Jefferson has got all the glad message of the willows in the spring, all their freshness and wetness and gay yellow, and their appeal to every man to be a boy again and to cut his pole and bait his hook and hunt for a warm spot along the bank where the current is not too swift.

But "Moonrise" and "The Tug Boat" are good examples of the strongest technical merit of Mr. Jefferson's work, his handling of skies. In "The Tug Boat" the tug has just made fast to the vessel, and is saving her steam. There is no action of any kind in the picture, and a light, fog-like cloud hangs over the water, but where the mist is thin the cold, clear blue night sky of the winter time shows bright behind it, with its stars glittering and bright. It is as blue and as cold as some of Fritz Thaulow's[16] wonderful night skies, and looks at you through an atmosphere of still, piercing cold.

In "Moonrise" the painting of the sky is more conventional, but the sentiment of the piece is exquisite. The storm clouds coming over the Adirondacks, yellow-brown and full of motion, is perhaps the most remarkable work in the collection.

"A Smoky City" is a long, somber picture of the Chicago lake front, full of dull greys and reds. It is chiefly artistic through what it omits, and its avoidance of vulgar realism, so easy to turn to in handling such a subject, and so effective with the crowd. The grey of the slimy lake water, the soft colors of the smoke, the effect of height and murkiness are present, but beyond that I don't believe a Chicago merchant would know his town any more than a London cockney would recognize Whistler's picture of St. James, and that is the best I can say for it.

"A Street Scene in St. Augustine" is one of the most attractive of the pictures; a languid sunset sky, with the fiercest of its color burned out, a pale evening star, an old house of the architecture of another time and another country, a Negro and his cart. Why should this be a true work of art? "Because," said W. E. Curtis, "Rip Van Winkle is a poem."[17]

Of what a beautiful life are these pictures the record, these studies in nature made here and there for nature's sake, made in his resting time, deep in the woods or far in the country, where "Nobody works for money and nobody works for fame." As Jules Dupré[18] said of Jefferson,

16. Fritz Thaulow (1847–1906), Norwegian painter, who had one painting in the original Carnegie Gallery collection.

17. W. E. Curtis (1850–1911), journalist on the Chicago *Record* (1887–1901) and author of *Relics of Columbus* (1883).

18. Jules Dupré (1811–1889), French landscape painter, who had three paintings in the original Carnegie Gallery collection.

"He soaks up the poetry in nature like a sponge, only to go home and squeeze it out upon his palette." What invaluable memories this collection of paintings must recall, what a veritable Arcadian youth, that has never grown grey, what a lifelong love affair with the grass and trees and flowers, what comradeship with free winds and running water, what a deathless passion for beauty. Yet Mr. Jefferson belongs to a profession whose votaries spend their whole lives in the midst of crowded cities, who regard those precincts beyond the reach of bellboys and elevators and fizzing soda bottles, with a vague horror, much as the Romans regarded Britain, as a country of wilderness and savagery. So many of these people have become mere machines operated by steam and electricity and stimulated by complex drinks. Yet out of this world of false perspectives and all manner of tricks and shams, where the trees and flowers are mimicked, where the brooks are wretched things of glass and the very sun is basely counterfeited, comes this old wanderer with the breath of the fields in him. And yet people ask why he is a better actor than the men of the younger generation!

Index, January 12, 1901, p. 10.

Hubert Vos's Racial Studies

In 1892 Hubert Vos (1855–1935), Dutch-born court painter was sent to the United States as art commissioner for Holland at the Chicago World's Fair of 1893. He subsequently settled in Washington where he gained considerable fame for his portraits and still-lifes of oriental subjects. The following selection appeared in the Journal *datelined January 8, 1901; it also included an interview with Daniel Frohman, manager of the Empire and Lyceum theatres in New York, whose brother Gustave had been interviewed by Willa Cather in Lincoln in 1895 (see* The Theatre *[II], above). She said in part: "The most remarkable feature of Mr. [Daniel] Frohman's conversation upon the profession which he has cornered is that he insists upon mixing up rosy metaphors and remarks about 'human kindness' and 'divine poesy' and 'our Shakespeare' with his cold-blooded business statements. I have heard pickle manufacturers discuss their business with more impassioned enthusiasm and commendable earnestness and honest well wishing toward their employees. In a sense Mr. Frohman's great business is a public trust and lease from the people, but I assure you he has no sentimental notions about it, and if he feels there is any element of duty in it all, he carefully conceals it." The interview was omitted from the issue of the* Index, *January 19, 1901, which carried the discussion of Vos's work. As it appeared in the* Index, *the description of Vos's exhibit was marred by two dropped lines, which made one paragraph nonsensical.*

The Corcoran Art Gallery just now exhibits a peculiarly interesting collection of paintings called "racial studies," by Hubert Vos, formerly court painter of Holland. Mr. Vos came to Washington about four years ago, and opened a studio here. While his reputation was not greatly extended beyond the borders of the city in this country, many of the Europeans of Washington knew of him and patronized him loyally, and he has found a very select and remunerative field of usefulness here. He has been employed by most of the members of the Cabinet and officers of state to paint portraits of their wives and daughters, and has successfully treated several officers of high rank, though his specialty is painting women. About two years ago, he decided to go abroad and visit the more obscure countries of the world in order to put to the test a certain theory of his. His theory was this, that if any of the darker races were studied by a painter analytically, as the Caucasian types are studied, if individual faces of these races were painted with skill and penetration, that such paintings would be invaluable to anthropologists and would present these races in an entirely different light to home-staying Caucasians. In pursuance of this idea, Mr. Vos spent two years in Hawaii, China, Korea, and Java, and now he has returned with his spoils. He declares that these oriental faces, so much alike to the superficial eye of the white man, present all the delicate points of difference, all the baffling half-revelations of character that a European subject does. He says that they have usually been painted conventionally, showing only the conventional race features, just as we use a certain wooden sort of Indian in children's storybooks. Very few good photographs, even, have been made of the dark races. He claims that his portraits are, in so far as he was able to make them, character studies of the great men of Asia.

On the night of the opening of Mr. Vos' collection at the gallery nearly all the members of the diplomatic corps were there, and especially conspicuous were the Turkish minister and the Chinese minister, Mr. Wu, who had come to see the portrait of his mother's second cousin, Prince Ching.

Among the interesting pictures, there is one full-length portrait of the King of Korea, in a yellow robe and padded shoes, a foxy-looking gentleman of middle age with a well-contented smile. Mr. Vos had many things to say as to the complex character indexed on that face, but as for me, I confess I could see evidence of nothing but that he lived in a warm climate and ate a great deal of fat and did not often wash his hands and had an exceedingly high opinion of himself.

There was also a portrait of a Korean prince which was much more engaging. This gentleman was evidently a beau, and he wears a robe of the palest blue, with a black net cap on his head. His features are delicate and languid, and the coloring in his face exceedingly soft and beautiful, like the elusive brown of a hazelnut that has just begun to turn. His lips are full and red and yet quite delicately moulded, as though if he went in for pleasure there would be a point at which he would shrink back and become as immovable as an anchorite. It is a dreamer's face, and a mighty sensitive and critical one for a heathen.

The studies in Hawaiian men and women offer very little that is either interesting or attractive. The bodies are of powerful build and the faces expressing little but good health and good nature. They are more attractive than Negro faces, but have little more spirituality.

The studies in Chinese women are revelatory to people who have seen only the coolie women, such as we find in American cities. There are dainty little creatures, with faces as round and bright as children's, shining jet-black eyes, square white teeth, and soft brown skins with pink cheeks and ears. The pictures of Japanese women present an entirely different type; long faces, pale, with full lips that droop at the corners, heavy-lidded, dreamy eyes, and a general air of sentimental languor.

The most remarkable face in the entire collection is that of the wily Prince Ching of China. It is unlike any of the other oriental faces. The eye is quite round, instead of being elongated, and there is none of the fullness of eyelid and cheek which characterizes so many Chinese faces and gives them such a well fed and placid look. This man has the eyes of a European, eyes that seldom sleep. The lips and brows are wrinkled, covered with deep, broken lines, like the veining of a leaf, a most unusual thing in a Chinaman. A scraggy grey mustache hangs over his firm red mouth. His cheeks are a bit shrunken. He leans forward in an attitude of intense attentiveness.

Prince Tuan is painted in black furs; a big man with a genial face, though somewhat coarse, full blooded and full of Tartar arrogance and assurance, in the prime of life, his brown hair and mustache untouched by grey.

Journal, January 13, 1901, p. 9.

Bernhardt and Maude Adams

During the week of January 7, 1901, Maude Adams appeared in Washington in Rostand's L'Aiglon, *which she had introduced in New York in October 1900. The following week Sarah Bernhardt came to the capital with a repertory of five plays in French: Rostand's* L'Aiglon *and* Cyrano de Bergerac, La Tosca, Camille, *and* Hamlet *(in which she played the title role). According to George Seibel, Willa Cather went to see Bernhardt four nights in succession.*[19] *The first of the following selections appeared in the* Journal *datelined January 24; it was reprinted in the* Index *on February 2, but the final paragraph was omitted. The second selection, which was datelined February 1, appeared only in the* Journal.

William Winter, erstwhile Mme. Bernhardt's most severe critic, states, with a suggestion of fine writing which could only be permitted to so venerable a critic, that on her opening night in New York the applause that greeted her "was like the fall of a cataract, and it followed her like the waves of the sea."[20] Such a greeting was given her in Washington, where the audience included so many of her countrymen, whose pride in her is unfailing. This enthusiasm was no mere demonstration of rapacious curiosity, but a sincere recognition of one of the greatest artistic careers of the last fifty years, one of the most strenuous and ambitious and most rich in achievement. Since Mme. Bernhardt's professional career began a score of brilliant actresses have come and conquered and had their little day of fame and been forgotten, but this woman, who for many years was so frail that she used often to faint at rehearsals, has for nearly forty years stood the ravages of a most exhaustive life and the most exhaustive of all arts. Our own actresses are forever ailing and resting and seeking healing waters, but when has this woman ever rested? Every year new ambitions, every year new creations; tragic, comic, sentimental, romantic. She has kept herself always a vital factor in the art of the present, whatever trend it may take, and has interpreted the masterpieces of the poets of all nations. When she began her career in 1862 the classical school held even a more important place in the French theatre than it does today, and her *Phaedra* was declared equal to

19. Seibel, p. 203. The date given is "January, 1911," but in context this is an obvious misprint for 1901. For earlier comments on Bernhardt, see The Star System (I); for Maude Adams, see The Star System (III) and (IV), above.

20. Wrote William Winter: "Sarah Bernhardt, in contrast with Maude Adams, suggested the leopard alongside of the kitten." *The Wallet of Time*, I, 527.

Rachel's. While France was still glowing with the romantic vogue inaugurated by Victor Hugo, she made her name inseparable from that of Doña Sol. She was the highest exponent of the sociological plays of Dumas *fils*, which were by nature distasteful to her, and when the penchant for theatric effects spread over the world, she made the career of Victorien Sardou. When the study of oriental life and religions was a fad in Paris, she produced several dramas translated from the Sanskrit, and in these latter revolutionary days she has made another marked departure from the conventional lines usually adhered to by an actress of her standing in producing remarkable studies in the life of the women of the people in several socialistic plays. When the study of Shakespeare, insisted upon by Brunetière[21] and Paul Bourget, became recently more general among the literary cults of Paris, she produced *Hamlet* more worthily than it has ever been produced on a French stage. Her last, and certainly not her least, service to her country and her art, is the discovery, encouragement and introduction of M. Edmond Rostand, for it was at her instigation that he began writing *Cyrano de Bergerac*, it was she who presented him to M. Coquelin and sued for a consideration of his work, and it was she who, when the young poet was utterly unknown, was willing to produce and lose many thousands of francs on his first play, *La Princesse lointaine*.

So it is not because of her eccentricities that the French people feel so keen a pride in Mme. Bernhardt, but because for the last forty years she has been the most active and ambitious element in the glorious history of their theatre. The best answers to those extravagant charges of eccentricity formerly made against her in America is the magnitude, the scope and the perfection of her work.

The most interesting feature of Mme. Bernhardt's present tour is, of course, her production of Rostand's third play, *L'Aiglon*. I saw Miss Adams in the title role of that piece on Saturday night and Mme. Bernhardt on the following Monday. A complete analysis of the two renderings would be futile and would be little less than brutal to the young actress, whose schooling has been of the most superficial nature and whose head was early turned by the indiscriminating adulation of a fatuous and fickle public. Moreover, the *esprit français* is so large and vital a part of this play that it is peculiarly difficult for an English or American company.

Mme. Bernhardt's physical equipment for this role could scarcely be better. Her figure, at the present time, is excellent, and while by no

21. Professor Vincent Brunètiere (1849–1906), editor of *Revue des Deux Mondes*. The controversy over Sarah Bernhardt's *Hamlet* is alluded to in *My Mortal Enemy*, p. 58.

means meager, is easily adaptable to any style of costume, an ideal condition for a body that is made to hold and express so many souls. Her voice, that *voix blonde*, of which the French poets thirty years ago used to write and which has aroused wonder and admiration in two, yes, three generations of playgoers, remains practically unimpaired. In some of the higher head tones the bell-like clearness may be dulled a little, but the wonderful strength and evenness of her middle register, her resonant low tones are unchanged. One must feel and admit again the liquid sweetness which she imparts to the reading of verse, as spontaneous and free, withal, as the sound of running water. The piquant staccato which she employs so effectively in lighter passages, and the ineffable tenderness which, in her more feeling moments, trembles in that caressing voice, creating an effect of melodious pathos not to be found elsewhere outside of music itself. A voice? It is rather a consonance of beautiful instruments, an organ with many stops upon which this woman can thunder or entreat at will.

Miss Adams' Duke is such an exceedingly nervous and timid young gentleman that he is never still a moment, but prances about the stage looking for trouble in the most persistent manner, and the actress apparently quite forgets that lassitude and absent-mindedness are essential ingredients in the mental make-up of a dreamer, and that downright irritability is insisted upon by the playwright as a prominent feature of the Duke of Reichstadt's character. Her Duke is certainly a good deal of a crybaby and addicted to declamation. Mme. Bernhardt, on the contrary, was careful to give her Duke much of the grand manner, and it was clear enough that he had been reared in a palace, though an exile, and one might well believe that as a child he had indeed played in the Tuileries. I have heard many people assert that Miss Adams' is the more pathetic interpretation; and so there are people who find Dickens' Paul Dombey more pathetic than Daudet's Jack.[22] Certainly Mme. Bernhardt's pathos is more subtle, more restrained, less evident, more modestly colored, for it is curbed in its demonstration by a certain dignity, sustained even through physical weakness. She imparts to the character a little of the silent suffering of Hamlet, and even in his half-hysterical moments the Duke remembers that majesty which doth hedge about a king. In the first act, which is less given to declamation and more to a varied

22. The pathetic tale of the death of the invalid Paul Dombey is told in Dickens' *Dombey and Son* (1848); in Daudet's *Jack* (1876) death ends the misery of an illegitimate child.

characterization of the Duke than the following acts, she achieves her most delicate and subtle, though by no means her most forceful effects. Her entrance is marked by reason of its quietness and the seemingly unconscious trick of wearing a male costume in a male manner, yet without the slightest vulgar affectation of mannishness. Her place on the stage is inconspicuous and subordinate until she is left alone with the young conspirator, who is disguised as a tailor and thus wins an entry into the palace. Miss Adams was intensely interested in the samples the tailor showed, but Madame sat in an attitude of profound dejection and ennui, and the tailor talked to empty air. These lapses into entire absent-mindedness, recurring often through the play, lend a peculiar color and individuality to the character. The long monologue in which the Duke recites his father's conquest of Prussia to his tutors who had omitted it from their lectures, is of course done as only such an actress could do it, with a force and vigor, an elocution so melodious and various, a diction so faultness and pure, that if the actors of our country cared about such things one way or the other, they might well find only discouragement in listening. Immediately after this fiery passage comes the beautifully tender scene between the Duke and his mother, in which she attempts to reconcile him to his position as an Austrian archduke, and urges him to plunge into the gay life of the Austrian court. For the young Duke's reply to his mother—" Without ceasing I remember what I saw one day when I was a child; his little throne, with a round back like a drum, and which Saint Helena has made almost divine; in the middle of the back, plain and simple, the N, the letter which says 'No' to time!"—M. Rostand had given the stage direction *Une voix profonde*, and it is indeed a profoundly deep voice with which Mme. Bernhardt reads the lines, a tone that is almost that of a prayer, with a whole religion of sentiment in it. The splendid lines which follow are given with an exaltation that is almost ecstasy: "But when I tell myself that I am the only one in whose veins flows the blood of that Corsican lieutenant, I weep when I gaze at the blue of my wrists."

It is in passages of this ecstatic nature that the Oriental fiber in the woman comes to light, that strange undercurrent of warm, sleepy eastern blood that flows in this whimsical, capricious Parisienne. It is then that one catches that subtle and seductive quality of voice with which a snake charmer might have soothed his serpents to sleep, or a Persian fire worshipper sung his chant to the sun. The Duke's goodnight to poor, silly Marie-Louise is a marvel of playful tenderness, and when she leaves for the ball his heartbreaking "*Ma pauvre mère!*" once heard cannot soon be forgotten, is in a tone so sick with pity and full of his nausea of life.

The part of Flambeau, the faithful grenadier of Napoleon and the devotee of the son, is an easy one for such an actor as M. Coquelin, and the author has entrusted some of the finest lines of the play to him. His death on the field of Wagram is the most effective and simple I remember having seen on the stage. In the Duke's death scene Mme. Bernhardt rose to absolute sublimity, and it was in this scene that Miss Adams failed most utterly, getting from it nothing but a species of cheap pathos. But this French Duke of Mme. Bernhardt's tries very hard to die like a king and Napoleon's son. It is this dignity, supported so long by the boy, under intense physical pain and with every evidence of his immediate dissolution on his ghastly face, that arouses such poignant pity when at the very end his courage breaks, and he throws his arms about the miserable, foolish woman who bore that name and cries "Mama!" like a little child in pain or terror.

Of Mme. Bernhardt one can only say in Rostand's graceful phrase that she has in her name "the 'N,' that letter which says 'No' to time."

As to the play, while it is from no point of view the equal of *Cyrano de Bergerac*, it is a romantic poem of high merit, and most noble in sentiment. There can now be little doubt that a poet of the theatre speaks again in France, for the first time since Victor Hugo. It is not Victor Hugo, any more than the Duke of Reichstadt was Napoleon, but it is a great heart, a great talent, and a most indomitable ambition—shut, alas, in a body as frail as Reichstadt's.

Journal, January 27, 1901, p. 9.

During the latter part of Mme. Bernhardt's Washington season she recurred to two of her very old successes, *Camille* and *La Tosca*.[23] I saw her in the flimsy Sardou piece on a night when she was not at all well, and laboring under the dread of leaving for Chicago at three o'clock in the morning after two most exhausting performances crowded into one day, and her playing was as uneven as the circumstances would warrant. The part was handled with supreme cleverness and superb indifference at the same time. Only in the scenes with Scarpia did she at all rouse herself to that intensity which she was wont to impart to the role. Her scenes with Mario, while they were at all times exquisitely graceful, were neither

23. For another view of Bernhardt in *La Tosca*, see "Fanny Davenport Plays Sardou," The Star System (III), above.

very tender nor very sincere, and she plainly showed that she was glad enough to be done with them. Tony Benadika, her transportation agent, told me that she immensely overworked. "There is only just one woman in all the world who could work like that and still live," he remarked. "But the Jew was the greatest worker of antiquity, and the French were the busiest people of the Middle Ages, and the Dutch are the most incessant workers of modern times, and madame, she is of Jewish blood, of Dutch extraction, and of French birth, and she works like all three put together, and yet she can find time for her little fun and her little interests."

Of all the performances she gave here, *La Tosca* was the only one which betrayed this overworked condition, and it did so only by its unevenness. If a new actress were to rise up anywhere in the world and play so well as that, it would be the talk of the world for a long time to come, but when Mme. Bernhardt permits herself to play only as well as that, we feel that we have a right to be aggrieved. Her scenes with Scarpia, both the torture scene and the murder scene, seemed quite up to the exorbitant standard that she herself has set for herself. The burst of weeping in the torture scene is still the most perfect expression of desperate perplexity and sudden and unavailing grief to be met with anywhere, and her repulsion for Scarpia in the last act, the visible creeping of the flesh, are marked by all their old perfection of visible expression. But the delicate archness of the character which was there at its best, the inimitable coquetry, these were slurred and hurried over in a careless fashion most exasperating to witness. Indeed, by far the most powerful personality on the stage, as it seemed to me, was that of M. Coquelin, and the manner in which he contrived out of this cheap, conventional, trumpery villain, this "heavy" who roars for the groundlings, to make a character of indisputable force, is one of the magic secrets of his art. Repulsive as the character is, he gives it a certain dignity and power which makes it quite distinct from the blustering, vulgar thing it has always been supposed to be, if indeed it ever seemed a character at all and not a mere theatrical device. This baron of Coquelin's has a degree of muscular force, a measure of brute strength which one is bound to respect in proportion as one feels the loathsomeness of the character.

I saw Mme. Bernhardt in two performances of *Camille*, which I think on the whole must be accounted the greatest performances she gave here. It has been something like twenty years, I believe, since she first created the [title] role of Dumas' great play, and if her interpretation has lost anything of its original adroitness and finesse, what must it have been then? But it seems improbable that it can have suffered anything more than the cruel and inevitable loss of youthful charm in the actress herself, which is perhaps more than compensated for by the greater fixedness of purpose and more complete renunciation to her art which has characterized her later years. For if youth consists of an exalted enthusiasm and poignant sensibilities, surely this woman is younger than most of us. As Mr. Norman Hapgood, the ablest of all American critics, has said, surely we realize that after all it is worth while to be wholly great, when we see this great artist, after forty years of triumph, playing with all the buoyancy of spring and all the mellowness of autumn.

I suppose a perfect sense of proportion is the last and highest grace than an artist attains. The Greeks held it to be the most essential quality to greatness, and surely it is the quality which seems to be most lamentably lacking in the art of this generation. The presence of this aesthetic discretion, this admirable care for the perfection of the whole, seemed to me the most conspicuous merit of Bernhardt's Marguerite Gauthier.

Surely no play is more fertile in opportunities for crude effects, and in no play is it more easy for an actress to cheat us through our emotions and to make us forget our standards in the excitement of the moment. This drama, which was written as an experiment in realism and its possibilities in the theatre, is seldom enough played as such. It is made into a sermon, an appeal to humanity, the voice of an element of society, and what not. All these moralizations and conclusions seem more properly the privilege of the spectator of the play than the business of the players. The part, as Mme. Bernhardt played it, was specifically a study of an individual and not of a type, and on the whole no other treatment of the character seems either fitting or in strictly good taste.

Mme. Bernhardt's Marguerite is by far the most elevated and spiritual I have ever seen, and very different from that serpentine creature which Miss Nethersole presents.[24] This Camille was at all times a woman exquisitely refined, very pleasure-loving and beauty-loving, with a manner most charming, a diction most pure, and with more than a little culture, and an atmosphere of elegance preserved through all vicissitudes. This lifted the character so far beyond those vulgar and gross impersonations, Sapho and Zaza, that one wondered how people can endure their ugliness for the little of merit that they have. Mme. Bernhardt is too wise

24. For Cather on Nethersole as Camille, see The Star System (III), above.

a woman and too great an artist to for a moment outrage that almost religious feeling for beauty, that revolts against the crude and brutal, which first begot the passion for art in the race. So this Camille is neither a sermon nor an awful example nor a grewsome illustration, but a beautiful creation, replete in sentiment, in grace and in a pathos so dignified and delicate that one need not be ashamed to weep at it. The refined playing of the first act should put most of our actresses to shame, for they could not play a queen so elegantly. Her graceful refusal of all Armand's proffered caresses seems inevitable with this charming conception of the part, and one would be both surprised and shocked if she accepted them. It is the beauty of the feeling which his chivalrous devotion awakes in her no less than that devotion itself which calls from her that last ecstatic utterance as he leaves her, "Love, at last—perhaps!"

To the scene with Armand's father she gave an added beauty by her gentleness and admirable respect for his years. Even when, after his bitter reproaches, she reminds him that she is a woman and is in her own house, it is done with a sweetness and humility so much finer than the usual absurd affectations of dignity. After leaving Armand in the third act, it is customary for actresses to return and do a sort of improbable shadow-dance behind his chair. But Mme. Bernhardt makes her adieux to the house that has held her happiness before Armand enters, and the glances she bestows upon all the little familiar articles in the room are suggestive enough to anyone who has never [ever?] broken home ties. When she finally leaves her lover, she goes out of the door with the swiftness and direction of a shot bolt, and one trembles at the strength of that going. It was in this act that I saw her do one of the most admirable bits of acting that I ever hope to see. At the first performance in which I saw her, she wrote the letter to Varville, called Prudence and gave it to her, asking her to deliver it, in the regular manner. But on the second night she let the letter fall to the floor in handling it, and Prudence had to stoop and pick it up. Then, in the same voice, shaken with grief and heavy with tears, she murmured, "Pardon, Prudence," a line not in the text at all. It seems to me that is what our American friends call "living in the character."

The death scene is usually made such an orgy of grief that it sometimes seems that Marguerite might, like Alice in Wonderland, literally float in her tears. But here it was played with that same unerring sense of fitness, that care for the truth and poise of the whole. Marguerite sick and dying still an exquisite, and still keeping a trace of her old gayety. As Miss Nethersole plays the role the woman of the last act and the woman of the first are two different beings. I believe there is some theory about "purification by suffering" or something of that sort. But this Marguerite never went through any transforming process. She keeps to the last the same charm and the same follies that made her so attractive and so pathetic in the first act. Even touches of her old gayety are preserved with admirable verity. When she goes to the window and laughs at the child outside, it is done with a sincere gayety, and a gayety merely, there is no hidden sermon and there are no suppressed tears. The tears are saved for that bitter rebellion against physical weakness at the end, when she says to Nanine, "Go tell the doctor that Armand has returned and that I wish to live, that I must live, that I must live!" After the vehement expression of this desire, and the heroic struggle to elude death, it is peculiarly fitting that she should die on her feet, as she does. And this Marguerite, who is no horrible example, but a woman who lives by bread as we do and cares for music and pictures and has her ethical code the same as other people, does not die smitten with thunderbolts, nor a sacrifice to divine wrath; she dies, in short, of being herself, as Stevenson said of Robert Burns. As the play was rendered, nothing could be further from the problem play, from sociological lecture; nothing could be more human, more individual, more graceful and tender, more truly a beautiful and poetic creation.

The weather happened to be exceptionally fine while the French company was here, and Mme. Bernhardt spent a great deal of her time driving and reading in Lafayette Park, which is about half a square from her hotel. Every morning at ten o'clock the money for her last night's performance was brought her, and she insists on being paid in gold. Referring to her business affairs she said blithely: "Well, it is always the same. When I first went into the Française to play I made a hundred francs a month and spent a hundred and fifty. Now I make a million a year and spend a million and a half. That is why I keep my son and his family. The money would go anyway. No other Jew ever had such a hand as mine, the money runs through it like water. I prefer not to think about the future. I have always been rather lucky, and I still hope that I may one day, before I become too ugly, be lucky enough to drop over on the boards and make a decent ending. But if I should have to stop playing from old age, Paris will not let me starve, I hope. But all this is an impossible contingency. When I cease to act I shall cease to live. When they lead me from the stage for the last time, I shall go out as a candle thrown out of doors into the dark. I cannot breathe that other air out there."

Journal, February 4, 1901, p. 8.

Ernest Seton-Thompson

In August 1898 Willa Cather had made a trip to the Black Hills, and she enjoyed discussing the region with a tea-party companion, Ernest Seton-Thompson (later known as Thompson Seton, 1860–1946). He was the author of books on natural history, which he illustrated himself, including Wild Animals I Have Known *(1898),* The Biography of a Grizzly *(1900), and a children's book,* Lobo, Rag and Vixen *(1900). The following selection appeared in the* Journal *datelined February 6; it was carried in the* Index *on February 16 (with Seton misspelled "Seaton" throughout). Comments on a performance in Washington of the Pittsburgh Symphony Orchestra and on the death of Queen Victoria appeared in the* Journal*; only the former was included in the* Index. *Earlier, on December 1, 1900, the* Index *had run an article, "The Personality of Mrs. Ernest Seton-Thompson," and a story by her, "A Woman Tenderfoot and a Grizzly."*

Ernest Seton-Thompson (his name is Seton in private life) spent a few days in town last week, and was seen at several dinners that were given to Mrs. Marion Crawford, who has just returned from Europe. I could only think, on meeting Mr. Seton, what a surprise the personality of this gentleman would be to a naturalist of the old school, some old gentleman from the more inaccessible parts of New England, who could still recall Thoreau and Audubon, and who took nature as seriously as Burroughs.[25] For Mr. Thompson is not a particularly serious man, at least the tea-party side of him is not, and I am quite sure that Audubon would have been grave and absent-minded even at a tea, with perhaps a few bird's eggs, or a snail, or a tiny snake or two forgetfully left in his pocket. But Mr. Thompson is a most unorthodox naturalist, in his methods of work and manner of life, and he is not the man to cause his hostess anxiety, like the Washington geographer who always draws maps on the tablecloth with his fork for the enlightenment and entertainment of the lady who is unfortunate enough to go out to dinner with him. Mr. Thompson is a man of about thirty-five, I should say at a guess, very tall and straight and dark, with thick black hair, worn parted in the middle and long enough to exhibit a most pronounced tendency to curl. His face is thin and rather oval in contour, and he wears a fierce, Spanish-looking mustache. He is something of an exquisite in regard to his clothes, and struck me as looking more like an actor than a literary man, and not at

25. John Burroughs (1837–1911), American naturalist, whose first book, *Notes on Walt Whitman as Poet and Person*, appeared in 1867.

all like the conventional type of kindly, ill-kept, buttonless naturalist. I was introduced to Mr. Seton by a portrait painter, so the talk naturally ran more to the pictorial than to the literary side of his work. He assured us that he had none of the freedom of execution which is often attributed to him. He puts his drawings, even the most unique bits, such as the tracks of animals scattered about his pages, together bit by bit, with painful accuracy. He has collected data steadily for twenty years for these drawings, and he goes about making them as though he were making the plans for a building, or preparing to cut a canal. He must have a record of the exact texture of the hair of the animal he draws, and the exact curl of it. He must know the animal from the skin out, besides knowing all that the animal painter must always know about positions, attitudes, and habits of body. He draws very slowly, sometimes working for several days on an animal's legs and paws.

The Black Hills are Mr. Seton's particular hobby. He speaks of them as Mr. Kipling might speak of India, with the paternal pride of a man who has introduced them into letters. He states frankly that he considers that region the most beautiful in North America, and I believe he further thinks that he is alone in his opinion and gets a good deal of satisfaction out of thinking so. Certainly, if there is anything in Emerson's definition of a landlord as the man who can carry the characteristic beauty of a place in his mind, rather than a man who has the right to rub his hands in the soil, Mr. Seton may claim the whole Black Hills region as his park and demesne. I never met anyone who could conjure up a part of the physical globe and transport it over a thousand miles in that black-art fashion. Perhaps Thoreau might have talked of the Maine woods as convincingly and picturesquely, but certainly no one could hear Mr. Thompson talk of the Black Hills without admitting that his picturing power does not stop at black and white or wash drawings. In a moment the Turkish rug became a yellow sand stretch, and the palms shrunk to sagebrush, and even the smell of the sage seemed actually there, so keenly he made one remember it.

Mr. Seton insists strongly on the personality of animals, declaring that it is quite impossible to generalize. The naturalist who only invents Latin names, and whose business is with dead animals may generalize, but not the man whose work is with the living. He says that there are good wolves and bad wolves, kind wolves and cruel wolves, stingy bears and generous bears, honest cats and dishonest cats. He says that there are the rich and poor among all animals, and that the poor are usually the stupid and unskillful, and not infrequently the indolent. He is convinced that all wild animals have been affected by civilization, and that their mental attainments are greater than they were a hundred years ago. To live to grow up, a wolf must be a cleverer wolf now than then. A century ago it was an easy thing to trap a wolf, now it is almost impossible. It is quite useless to suggest to Mr. Seton that the increasing scarcity of wolves may have something to do with this, for although he is the mildest of men when he talks about the weather, if you insist upon talking to him about his own business, you do it at your risk, and he becomes absolutely autocratic and even irritable, and I for one do not see how he could very well be anything else. It is a queer world, anyway. A man gives his nights and days to the study of one particular subject until his opinions or feelings on that subject are considered valuable enough to induce the world to pay for them, notwithstanding that the same thing has been discussed for centuries, which is proof positive that the man has actually added something to the subject from his own personality, has really, in short, given a new thing to the world. Then some good lady, who has never given one hour's honest study to his subject, asks him to dinner; perhaps she has read his "articles," perhaps she has taken her husband's word for them, perhaps, worst of all, she has misread them. Now the man who goes to her dinner is not a savage; he does not expect her to be versed in his specialty, he does not think any less of her because she is not, perhaps he even thinks more of her for that very reason. He is perfectly willing to talk about the weather, or anything else, to make himself agreeable; he may enjoy a good story, or he may be really fond of gossip; he may honestly like or admire his hostess. But she will have none of all this; if he is a painter, he must discuss art; if a musician, music; if a naturalist, the habits of birds or the tracks of quadrupeds. The man's position is pitiable; she is not a pupil whom he can instruct, an opinionated schoolgirl whom he can give a wholesome snubbing, or a person idly curious, whom he can ignore. He is expected to sit patiently and be practiced on through the dinner. If he is a charlatan, he may enjoy it, but if he is a gentleman and a man of genuine attainment, he is made exceedingly uncomfortable; he can neither correct her blunders nor assent to them. As Professor Benjamin Ide Wheeler[25] remarked of the wife of a prominent statesman when a dinner was given him here shortly after the publication of his *Alexander the Great:* "Why will a woman who can converse on American politics so well, insist on discussing Greek politics so badly?"

Journal, February 10, 1901, p. 9.

26. Benjamin Ide Wheeler (1854–1927), president of the University of California (1899–1919), author of *Alexander the Great* (1900).

The Gay Lord Quex

Arthur Wing Pinero (1855–1934) had interested Willa Cather from the beginning of her career as a dramatic critic (see especially "Two Pinero Heroines," The Star System [IV], above).[27] *His comedy* The Gay Lord Quex *opened in New York on November 12, 1900, and played for sixty-seven performances, with the actor-manager of London's Globe Theatre Company, John Hare (1844–1921), in the leading role. Hare was later knighted. The following review appeared in the* Index *datelined March 7 and in the* Journal, *with the same dateline, on March 10. A portion of the act-by-act synopsis of the play has been omitted.*

John C. Hare was with us recently, presenting the best English play of the year, *The Gay Lord Quex*. It is high time that someone said a word for the sinner that repenteth as well as for the sinneress. We have had enough Marguerite Gauthiers attired in the black cashmere gown and heavy veil which invariably betoken repentence, but we have hitherto heard very little of the Don Juan who does not wait for the rap of the Commander's statue, but gets a bitter taste in his mouth and tires of Sodom apples on his own account. The world is full of instances of the kindness of men of this sort; most young men have gone to them for money, and they have given most young women very sound advice, but for some reason they have stood without the pale of the indiscriminate pardons of sentiment. Certainly no one has recently tried to assert, dramatically, that such a man may prefer for his own sake to be a good man; that, not as a smirking hypocrite, but sincerely and with open eyes, and for his own more enduring pleasure he may decide to live the life of the family. Although Mr. Pinero has expressed himself on this point merely as a dramatist and for dramatic purposes exclusively, he does not specially object to our deducing a moral from it, since we are so given to that sort of reasoning.

The first act of the piece is laid at a manicurist's shop. The proprietor, Sophy Fullgarney, is the foster sister of Muriel Eden, niece of the Duchess of Strood, the young fiancée of the gay Lord Quex. Now the wild doings of Quex had been much noised among the tradespeople, who have always taken a peculiar delight in any scandals relating to the classes which they serve. This keen interest has never been exactly defined, I

27. Pinero was one of the dramatists Willa Cather discussed in a later article, "Plays of Real Life," *McClure's*, March 1913, p. 72.

think, but it seems to be only partially vulgar, being partly a species of misguided hero-worship and a hectic romanticism.

Sophy, in the light of my lord's past, has conceived it to be her mission to save the English lily, Miss Muriel, from falling a prey to the limitless rapacity of such a time-worn and weather beaten wreck of iniquity. To defeat Quex she has encouraged a former flirtation which Muriel had, half out of bravado, carried on with a young army man, and arranges meetings between the two at her shop. This Sophy Fullgarney is one of the most searching and unique bits of character study that Mr. Pinero has yet given us. She is quite simply a typical specimen of her class, individual enough, but quite submerged in the ideals and tastes and ambitions of manicure and hair-dressing people the world over. I should like to be able to get at the personality and standards of taste of one of the experts employed in the Roman baths as successfully as Mr. Pinero puts one *en rapport* with the inner life of Miss Fullgarney. If we had one such study left us from the reign of Tiberius, we should know a good deal more than we do about the flavor of the actual social life of Rome. It was quite time, too, that someone called our attention to the vast part that the middle [working?] classes play in our lives; to the singular power with which valets and ladies' maids are invested to influence the dispensations of Providence in the cases of their masters and mistresses.

In affairs of the heart, at least, a clever and devoted valet has often stood a man in better stead than a fortune, and the reputation of many a woman has been at the mercy of her maid. Furthermore, there is the devout interest that dressmakers and hat makers take in the careers of the people who wear their creations; their fond picturings of the adventures which these gowns are destined to grace, imaginings inspired by ecstatic readings of Ouida. These people are the most confirmed of sentimentalists, and they are forever demanding that their patrons should enact the highly colored scenes of which they have read, as children demand the most extravagant elegance of their dolls. So Miss Fullgarney undertakes to act the part of destiny for her darling and save her from the martyrdom of marriage of convenience, as she considers it, and to give her over to a dream of perpetual romance. And poor Fullgarney succeeds just as well as people usually do when they interfere in love affairs, and she is repaid just as you and I were when we interfered in a love affair, that is to say, she gets a cuff from everyone concerned; from the lover and the designing family and from the pining fair one herself. And that is just what Miss Fullgarney deserved, and what we deserved under like circumstances.

The first act merely gets the characters well introduced, according to Mr. Pinero's orthodox manner, for although Mr. Pinero is the most original of English playwrights he is also the most conventional and never introduces anything bizarre to gain an effect. . . .

I suppose it goes without saying that Mr. Arthur W. Pinero is the only living English dramatist who can be taken at all seriously, that is, he is the only one to whom the drama is a natural and inevitable mode of expression. There are plenty of men who revamp novels rather cleverly, and surely that is no reproach, for most of the Shakespearean plays are but revamped fiction, but for the most part these men do not make dramas when they throw the story they treat into dialogue, but only succeed in converting the printed novels into spoken novels. They seem to have no marked aptitude for dramatic expression, and are unable to make their point through the medium of dramatic form alone and by dramatic resources. Somebody must stand in the center of the stage and explain what the whole play is about and just what sort of people are in it, so that one might as well go to a lecture and have no play at all. As a result of this, a heaviness of touch coupled with a perfectly irrepressible sentimentality, has become the hallmark and chief characteristic of the English drama. Mr. Pinero has less sentimentality and more finesse than any of his contemporaries, but that is by no means his distinguishing trait. The remarkable thing about Mr. Pinero is that he sees the world through a pair of opera glasses. His is essentially a dramatist's vision. He sees people as the figures of a drama; life naturally falls into acts and scenes and dramatic incidents before him, as it does into paragraphs and chapters to Thomas Hardy. The drama is not only the means through which he has chosen to present life, but the only means at his command. Over and above the fact of his adroit uses of dramatic resources, stands the fact of his pre-eminently objective mind, the hallmark of the dramatist proper. Within the last hundred years this order of mind has had little to do with the British theatre. In British comedies and melodramas of the period it is the fashion to make every character a mouthpiece for a vice or virtue. No one is left in doubt for a moment as to what the playwright thinks of each and every one of his characters, or as to what he means you to think. He presents you with a complete card catalogue of his people. These prosy play people accept each other as texts and not as people. In Pinero we get back to the logical and colorless mind which reflects life. Who knows whether Pinero pities or condemns Paula Tanqueray? Who knows whether the humor of *The Amazons* is kindly or spiteful? Every play the man has written seems to be an advance. *The Gay Lord Quex* is certainly not the intense and commanding piece of work that *The Second Mrs. Tanqueray* is, but it is built upon broader lines, has a wider sweep of interest, and is in a true sense a drama of society and a mirror of contemporary life. It is such plays, usually, that make the classics of the future.

Index, March 9, 1901, pp. 8–9.

"*Literature in the Capital*"

This column, the last that Willa Cather contributed to the Index, *was datelined March 14, 1901; it had appeared in the* Journal *on March 3, with a February 28 dateline. The future Mrs. Payne Whitney, Helen Hay (1876–1944), one of the two writers discussed, was the daughter of Secretary of State John Milton Hay (1838–1905), himself an important literary figure. Reviewing Miss Hay's first poetry collection,* Some Verses *(1898), in the* Leader, *May 27, 1899, Willa Cather had written that "Miss Hay's verse, at least her sonnets, are by no means ordinary. The pure sonnet form is not an easy one, and, I believe with the notable exception of Mrs. Browning, it is not one in which women have been particularly successful. Miss Hay's sonnets have genuine quality, and the lack of spontaneity which is the gravest fault of her verses, naturally is little felt in the sonnets." A more professional literary lady was the late Emma Southworth (1819–1899), two of whose novels,* Ishmael *and* Self-Raised, *each sold more than two million copies.*[28]

Miss Helen Hay, the daughter of the Secretary of State, whose first published verse appeared some two years ago in a little gray volume modestly entitled *Some Verses*, has just completed a lengthy romance of the South Seas in blank verse. It is said that Miss Hay has no personal acquaintance with the South Seas, but that in preparation for her romance she dug industriously among the encyclopedias at the Congressional Library. This might strike some people as an unorthodox method of procedure, but her friends remind us that Keats had never been to Greece when he wrote *Endymion*. I confess I am anxious to see the outcome of this method of poetizing. Of one thing I am sure, however, and that is that Miss Hay's romance will not be dull, nor will it contain lines in which

28. "The most popular authoress in the annals of American publishing was Mrs. E. D. E. N. Southworth. . . . In all, Mrs. Southworth wrote over fifty novels, and nearly all of them sold in six figures." Mott, *Golden Multitudes*, p. 136.

one will be compelled to skip or suppress several feet to preserve the metre, as in the general run of feminine verse. Even in her earliest attempts at verse Miss Hay evinced a peculiar gift of rhythm, and considerable excellence of form. As she says she wouldn't know a trochee from an anapest and has had no formal training in the rules of prosody, her ear must be acute and her natural feeling for harmony very strong. However, Shakespeare's sonnets are Miss Hay's favorite literature, and they are not bad schoolmasters and are rather more likely to teach a young lady how to write sonnets than are most professors of literature. And Miss Hay can write sonnets of no mean pretentions. I recall one in her first volume which I have heard both Mr. Stoddard and Mr. Spofford pronounce an excellent performance, a true sonnet, admirably done.[29] It is somewhat unusual in both matter and manner to be the work of a very popular and much flattered young woman, and a very young one at that. Much the most admirable features of the sonnet are its melody and its restraint, its distinct lack of any sort of violence or exaggeration. . . .

Mr. Kipling, I believe, was the first person who ever encouraged Miss Hay to work seriously, and he is not a gentleman who encourages people merely to make himself agreeable, nor has he much use for a girl with inky aspirations. The Hays had a summer place near Kiplings' in Vermont, and Miss Hays and the irascible Anglo-Indian struck up an acquaintance across the fields. No one ever took life and the things that make life worth living with more gusto than the Secretary's daughter. She goes out as much as any young woman in Washington, and she makes no lofty pretenses to despise dinners and teas and theatre parties, but gets a normal enjoyment out of them all, and knows and likes more people than most women meet in a lifetime. She takes life as a schoolboy takes his holiday, and if you happen to meet her for five minutes, you stop to consider what an exceedingly decent world it is to live in, and how well it is arranged when one young woman, just turned twenty-one, can be so pretty, and so happy, and so gracious, and can write such exceedingly decent verses into the bargain.

Miss Hay's enthusiasm for Washington is altogether refreshing. She had always lived in Cleveland and other cities more or less smoky until she came here and made the acquaintance of the sky. I think no one in this

29. The sonnet, "Pity Me Not!," which was quoted in full, begins: "Cruel and fair, within thy hollowed hand / My heart is lying as a little rose. . . ." The men expressing admiration for it were Richard H. Stoddard (1825–1903), poet and literary editor of the New York *Daily and Express*, and Ainsworth R. Spofford (1825–1908), Librarian of the Library of Congress.

clean, white city enjoys it more than she does; the yellow sunlight, nor the blue skies, nor the white shafts and columns, nor the parks, so full of box and magnolia all the winter that they counterfeit the spring. Sooner or later Miss Hay ought to write some verse that will be of more than passing moment; she is young enough to wait, happy enough to work—and she can afford to indulge in the most unremunerative of occupations.

One of the quaint "literary landmarks" of Washington is the little red cottage in Georgetown where for nearly fifty years Mrs. Southworth planned adventures for self-sacrificing chambermaids and noble, though affectionate factory girls. It is a very humble dwelling, standing on a high bluff overlooking the Potomac, with the gray pile of the Academy of the Visitation a little way down the river, behind you the "domed city, white and wide still," and across the river Arlington and the wooded hills that every night the sunset fires. I am afraid I went to the place in a spirit of jest, with the cries of queenly servant girls, who were spirited away in cabs and married to disinherited lords, ringing in my ears. But somehow or other, when one stood on the little porch, where the withered vines swung in the wind, still holding a deserted birds' nest or two, one came into a more respectful frame of mind. It is rather appalling to think of the mere physical labor the poor woman accomplished, sitting in the little library facing on the river, writing thousands upon thousands of pages with a fine pointed pen, in her tiny, laborious chirography. One feels an ebb of energy at thinking of it. It is easy to see, or at least it is possible to see, why people bitten with the passion for creative experiments and for happy and complete expression as by the craving for a drug, should be able to support the herculean labors and brutal reverses of this ungrateful craft, but what could have made it worth while to her? worth an unremitting toil of sixty years, ending just where it had begun? For it must be understood that this woman was no mere mercenary; I doubt whether Mr. Henry James himself is more sincere, or whether his literary conscience is more exacting than was hers, according to her light. She took herself and her work with entire seriousness, and strange as it may seem, some of her novels were rewritten many times, were hoped and dreamed and prayed over. I went to her cottage with a man of such profound literary knowledge that he could afford to be charitable, and his telling of the story of the woman as he knew her made her life seem less grotesquely comic. To this little house for many years each mail brought appreciative letters from thousands of admirers, from young women who aspired to this wonderful craft, or from those who merely worshipped from afar, and who declared that her novels were their spiritual and intellectual food. And if this is not fame, what is it, please? How many of us ever think of writing to Henry James when we approve of him, or beg him to be merciful and recall his heroines to life when they perish, or care very much whether they perish or not? There is an element of unabashed romance in the untutored mind, and of hearty sympathy that we certainly lose in the course of social and mental evolution. Then we must remember that Mrs. Southworth was not always the butt of jests as now, particularly the jests of the very newly emancipated in the matter of literary taste, who are eager to attest their emancipation. Whenever I hear anyone go out of his way to show his cleverness by jesting at these tales that are quite too pitifully wanting to be subjects for mirth, I am pretty sure that once the gentleman thought them all very fine. There was a time when the old novelist was young, when she was very much sought after socially, and when it was very much the fashion for all young ladies of the "'first families" of the South to read her latest story as they reclined in hammocks on their wide verandas, recuperating after the strain of rural gaieties, which they considered quite the most important social functions in the world. In those days the "gifted authoress" was feted and banqueted in the capitals of the southern states, and young ladies sat at her feet and took counsel, and gray-haired men with war records and a family tree took her out to dinner and were proud to do it. If the position of Mrs. Southworth was ridiculous, I should like to know what is left to say of the criterions of American taste. We may talk very knowingly about the structural finesse of contemporary French novelists and air our cosmopolitan culture as we will, but most of us had mothers who in their youth considered this woman the inspired priestess of the softer emotions, and her style the most poetic and intoxicating in the world. In matters of literary taste we are so emphatically of the *nouveau riche* that we should be duly humble, and never forget that our grandparents were entirely convinced that the fiction of Mrs. Southworth was more engaging, more elevating, and of far higher literary merit than the stories of Master Edgar Allan Poe. Most of us, in these United States, cannot even claim as much as the Jewish lad whose father, ennobled by the queen for his financial services to the state, undertook to remonstrate with him on his indiscretions and who replied: "You have nothing to say to me, sir, for I am the gentleman here. At least I have one ancestor, and your father was a tradesman." I am not sure that we have even improved much upon our ancestors, for there are those among us who read Marie Corelli, some in secret and some openly and brazenly. It is true that Miss Corelli has greater facility at her command, a larger variety of adjectives, the advantages of a better education and a more restraining environment, but her real literary idea is much the same as Emma Southworth's. Her muse is also of the chambermaid variety; a chambermaid who has learned a little French now and who dresses better, who flashes jewels and wears ermine and affects absorbing intellectual interests, but you have only to watch her for a little while to recognize under all this finery the beautiful factory girl of Mrs. Southworth, or the virtuous lodgekeeper's daughter, more gaudy and less circumspect than she used to be.

Index, March 16, 1901, pp. 8–9.

"*Hunting the North Pole*"

Willa Cather had written of the current race to reach the North Pole when she reported on Fridtjof Nansen in December 1897 (see The Urban Scene, *above). The following May, according to a letter of June 7, 1898, she "spent two weeks in Washington, D.C., writing up the Wellman polar expedition for the Associated Press."*[30] *When Walter Wellman (1858–1934), journalist and explorer, was in Washington to seek the approval and cooperation of the National Geographic Society for his proposed dash to the Pole from Franz Josef Land, Howard Gore, Willa Cather's cousin, agreed to represent the society on the adventure and later wrote two articles about it.*[31] *The leader of the proposed expedition reported below, Evelyn Briggs Baldwin (1862–1933), had been a member of Wellman's 1898–1899 expedition. The dateline on this selection was March 16, and it included a description of the collection of weapons, vases, and saltcellars belonging to the Russian ambassador, Count Cassini.*

The North Pole mania is a constant one in Washington. There is always some geographer, or some member of the Geodetic Survey, or

30. Letter to the Secretary of the Class of 1895; see note 40, The Musical World (II), above. In another letter of this period Willa Cather refers to the imminent departure of her cousin on the North Pole expedition (Willa Cather to Frances Gere, June 23, 1898). There is no reason to doubt that Cather did undertake the assignment for the Associated Press, but her work has not been identified.

31. "Wellman Polar Expedition," *National Geographic Magazine*, July 1899, pp. 267–268; "Return of Wellman," *National Geographic Magazine*, September 1899, pp. 348–351. See also Gilbert Grosvenor, *The National Geographic Society and Its Magazine* (Washington: National Geographic Society, 1948), p. 53.

some man in the Weather Bureau who is preparing for an Arctic expedition or who is advancing a theory as to how such an expedition should be conducted. When I was in Washington three years ago Walter Wellman was outfitting his party, and this winter Evelyn Baldwin was here arranging for the Baldwin-Ziegler expedition. I was at several dinners given to Mr. Baldwin and met him frequently at the Geodetic Survey building and learned a good deal about his plans. The gentleman scarcely does himself justice at dinner parties, having much the manner of a sailor ashore, and the presence of many women visibly disconcerts him. He is a short, swarthy man, ill at ease in drawing rooms, whose heavily lined face bears the marks of exposure and of his hard schooling in the Arctic. Although his appearance does not convey the impression of great physical strength it is well known that he once made a journey of eighty miles over the ice hummocks north of Greenland in the teeth of the Arctic winter alone with his dogs and sledge. He has been a member of several expeditions, and was one of the first applicants to urge for a place on Andrée's fatal balloon.[32]

He went north twice with Peary and was one of Wellman's party. He has been planning for years to conduct an expedition of his own, but only recently found his backer in William Ziegler,[33] who formerly prospered in the manufacture of a well-known brand of baking powder, and who has offered a million of his hard-earned dollars to get Baldwin to the Pole. The explorer has purchased two vessels, the *America* and the *Frithiof*, and expects to leave Tromsö, Norway, about the middle of June. He has bought four hundred Esquimau dogs and fifteen Siberian ponies for draught purposes, and has his own devices for solving the polar mystery as all his predecessors have had before him. He has a plan to outwit the ice and a plan to make the drift serve his purpose. I have wondered whether these Pole seekers really feel the confidence they express, but I suppose it takes a rather genuine kind of enthusiasm to face the prospect of rations of raw dog meat and to induce men to forsake their beds for frozen sleeping bags. There seems to be something in the spell of the ice from which men never quite recover if they have felt it once, and a man who once sets out on that polar quest usually spends most of his life drifting northward.

32. Salomon A. Andrée (1854–1897), Swedish aeronaut, lost while attempting a balloon flight in the polar regions.

33. William Ziegler (1843–1905), an organizer of the Royal Chemical Company, manufacturer of Royal Baking Powder, patron of North Pole expeditions.

Even the crew employed in Arctic expeditions seldom settle down to the career of ordinary seamen again. Usually they become the companions of the north fisher folk or ship on board whalers until they get another chance to try their luck in the ice. At a reception given several weeks ago by the German ambassador, Baron von Holleben, I heard a group of men discussing Baldwin's outfit and prospects. In their midst was a tall, bloodless figure, with white hair and a grizzled beard and deep sunken eyes, the mere ghost of a man, all that the Arctic had left of General Greely, who commanded the memorable *Jeanette* expedition twenty-odd years ago.[34] Some of the men were expressing a doubt as to whether Baldwin would be able to improve on the Duke of Abruzzi's record.[35] "All the same," said the general, with a sigh, "if I had any health at all there is nothing I'd like so well as to take a little run up there with him." It would seem that if any experience could cure a man of the polar fever it would have been Greely's. It must be a fine song that the ice sirens sing.

I heard Mr. Baldwin tell one evening the story of the strange ordeal of the Norwegian Bjorvig, of the Wellman expedition, with a wealth of detail that affected everyone present very keenly. Surely never before has any man believed it to be his duty to spend eight weeks in a half-lighted hut with a dead man in the berth beside him. Bjorvig and his companion, also a Norwegian, had been sent on ahead into the northern part of Franz Josef Land with limited supplies to spend the winter in a stone hut and be ready to strike northward in the spring. Long before the winter was over Bjorvig's companion fell ill from poor food and lack of heat. They had a train oil lamp, but the man's circulation was unable to withstand the cold, and for days before his end he knew that he was freezing to death. The fellow was a fisherman and had been on the ice for a good share of his life and had seen the ugly side of the business. In short he had a horror of being eaten by the bears. He knew that to dig a grave in the frozen earth was out of the question, and every night he could hear the bears prowling about the hut, and this horror became a sort of morbid

34. General Adolphus W. Greely (1844–1935), founding member of the National Geographic Society, commanded United States Army expedition for the study of Arctic weather and climate, 1881–1884, author of *Three Years of Arctic Service* (1885). Thea Kronborg, in her cold loft room, "comforted herself by remembering all she could of 'Polar Explorations,' . . . and by thinking about the members of Greely's party: how they lay in their frozen sleeping-bags, each man hoarding the warmth of his own body and trying to make it last as long as possible against the oncoming cold that would be everlasting" (*The Song of the Lark*, p. 72).

35. Luigi, Duke of the Abruzzi, Prince of Savoy-Aosta (1873–1933), naval officer and explorer, was the first man to climb Mount St. Elias in Alaska (1897).

insanity with him. Bjorvig, who had shipped on the same vessel with the sick man since they were boys, promised to keep his body inside the hut, and when the man died the fisherman kept his word. His doing so was a piece of incomprehensible folly, if you will, but to Baldwin, who knows both the simplicity and the extravagant intensity of the Scandinavian and the loyal comradeship of the fisher folks, it seemed quite a matter of course. The sentiment that has become outlawed in all the complex machinery and intense activity of the temperate zones is a very real thing in slow, deep Scandinavia. When the relief party came on in the spring they found Bjorvig the wreck of a man and scarcely more alive than his silent bedfellow. He had lived with the dead man for eight weeks and lain down by his side to sleep, and eaten his food in his grim company. Afterward he told the members of the relief party that he had only saved himself from madness by committing to memory a volume of Ibsen's plays he had with him by the light of his train oil lamp. There is a tale to be told about Norwegian firesides, and it would make no mean saga. It was Tennyson who said: "Ah, dark and true and tender is the north!"[36]

Journal, March 17, 1901, p. 13.

36. Line 98 of "The Princess: A Medley," IV. Correctly the first word is "And" instead of "Ah." Alfred Tennyson, *Poetical Works*, p. 174.

Guest Editor of the *Courier*

(July 20, 1901—August 24, 1901)

As a teacher, Willa Cather had the summer months free—a compelling reason for seeking a teaching position. When she went to Red Cloud in the summer of 1901—her first trip home in two years—she said in a July 17 letter to the Seibels that she had lost twenty pounds during the spring term and was exhausted from the strain of teaching Latin and of final examinations.[1] *But she was not too exhausted to write, and on July 20 a column called "Comments and Commentary" appeared in the* Courier. *The next month, at the invitation of her friend Sarah B. Harris, Cather served as the* Courier's *guest editor for the issues of August 10, 17, and 24, writing the editorial column, "Observations." In addition, she contributed a book review to the issue of August 10. The review and the July 20 column are presented in full; excerpts from the three editorial columns are arranged topically. This was the last work that Willa Cather did for the* Courier, *although two of her poems were reprinted there the next year. She was not to have regular editorial duties again until she joined the staff of* McClure's *in 1906.*

Western Railroads

Willa Cather summed up her feelings about her frequent rail journeys back to Nebraska in her 1923 poem, "Going Home"—"How smoothly the trains run beyond the Missouri; / Even in my sleep I know when I have crossed the river"[2]*—and her admiration for the men like Captain Forrester who "'dreamed the railroads across the mountains'" is memorably expressed in* A Lost Lady.[3] *She enjoyed talking about railroads with men like Ernest Seton-Thompson (see Washington Correspondent, above) and Prince Michael Hilkoff, the Russian Minister of Transportation during*

1. Willa Cather to George and Helen Seibel, July 17, 1901. Letter in the possession of Mrs. George Seibel, Capitola, California.

2. *April Twilights and Other Poems* (New York: Alfred A. Knopf, Inc., 1923), p. 66.

3. *A Lost Lady*, p. 55.

the building of the Trans-Siberian railroad, whom she had met in Pittsburgh. During her tenure on the Home Monthly, *an editorial in February 1897 declared: "The Prince has very little in common with the dawdling noblemen of his country who ape French manners and French vices. He is more American than Russian in his manner. He is thoroughly a modern man; modern in his independence, his practicality and his unrivalled business sagacity."*

There is no experience of travel quite like the feeling of relaxation and comfort with which a western bred man or woman steps into his home bound Pullman or any one of the great western railroads running out of Chicago. When he settles himself in a Burlington or Rock Island train he is half way home already. There are several words on American travel that have never been written, you can only pick them up from tourists or prove them in your own experience. American travel has so far surpassed in comfort anything to be found in Europe that word of it has gone back to the Old World and, in Russia at least, has been productive of many reforms. Only a few years ago Prince Hilkoff, the Russian minister of transportation, spent a week in Pittsburgh when he was investigating American railroad improvements in behalf of the Trans-Siberian railway —then incomplete. His investigation covered almost every department of the railroad business, but the Prince himself was chiefly interested in the superior passenger service afforded by American roads. He admitted that while in Europe railway travel was a necessity, in America it is a recreation. Much of the disparity in the class of passenger accommodations furnished in the two continents, however, was, he said, directly due to the difference in governmental policy. In America, he said, everything proceeds from the average man and is made for his comfort; even luxury is provided at prices which the average man can occasionally meet. In Europe, that portion of the population which demands luxury is so small that, as the minister expressed it, "It would be impossible to get a rate on these superior comforts, and even unnecessary, according to our notions of the needs of the people."

The Trans-Siberian railway, however, opened a new problem. The length of the journey and the costliness of operating the road at all made comforts to the passengers and the additional revenue therefrom equally necessary. The Russian government wanted models for drawing-room cars, dining cars, observation and sleeping cars, and Prince Hilkoff knew where to find them.

Unfortunately for the Trans-Siberian road, however, the Minister confined his tour of inspection to the great railroad systems of the eastern part of the United States, and, as every American knows, the real comforts of travel are to be found between Chicago and the Pacific coast. I remember hearing this matter discussed at a dinner given to one of the officials of the Pennsylvania road. One of the guests present, a member of the governing board of an eastern railway, told most picturesquely the story of his first trip west of Chicago. The gentleman is an Englishman who was a man of affairs before he came to the United States and whose active and successful business life had kept him closely tied down to the territory between Pittsburgh and New York. He admitted very candidly that it was quite impossible for any eastern road to offer its patrons the same class of accommodations provided by the great systems of the west. One of the guests told a story of her first experience in the sagebrush country of northern Colorado. After five weeks in the monotonous gray of the sheep country, barren and bloomless enough in August, she boarded a through Burlington train at Holdrege and stepped into the dining car to find the white tables, clean table linen, and competent service of a New York hotel. After weeks of roughing it and wagon travel the sudden transition seemed to have something of the black art about it and seemed altogether unnatural. There were fresh white fish hundreds of miles from water and on the tables great bunches of La France roses, gathered from no man knew where in this brown windy sweep of blossomless land.[4]

I heard many of these same opinions voiced most heartily by Mr. Ernest Seton-Thompson during his stay in Washington last winter. Mr. Thompson, however, is so confirmed a lover of the Bad Lands and the Black Hills for their own sakes that he would be loyal to any road that brought him into that region. His enthusiasm for that country is at once that of an artist and a boy. I shall never forget the picture of the Bad Lands he conjured up before us at a dinner party one night in that deliberate white-and-gold southern city. At a single gesture of his long nervous hand over the table linen you could see the heat waves dancing above the sand. The candlesticks became granite boulders and the flowers gray sagebrush bushes and the soft lamplight the glaring splendor of a Dakota noon. He

4. Cf. the description of Thea Kronborg in the dining car on her way from Chicago to Moonstone: "The linen was white and fresh, the darkies were trim and smiling, and the sunlight gleamed pleasantly upon the silver and the glass water-bottles. On each table there was a slender vase with a single pink rose in it." *The Song of the Lark*, p. 275.

declared that there is no spot left in the world where nature is so willing to be seen and pursued and loved. Surely no class of thinkers or writers differ from each other so widely as naturalists. Nature seems to present absolutely different sides to different men; to some she is the pale nun and to some the red and brown gypsy. All that the green hills and willow-grown brooklands of New England are to John Burroughs, the Bad Lands are to Mr. Thompson. "There," he says, "is every imaginable effect of color and contrast, there is the last stand of the Old West, there nature has paused to breathe a moment before she takes flight and leaves us to our own devices, like the Moorish king when he paused to look back over lost Granada; there, as Balzac said of the desert, one has everything and nothing, God without mankind."[5] [July 20, 1901, p. 3]

Edward MacDowell and Victor Herbert

Willa Cather had attended a concert by Edward MacDowell (1861–1908) in Pittsburgh and had reported on it enthusiastically to her Lincoln readers in the Courier, *March 18, 1899.*[6] *MacDowell's career as a composer was crowned in 1896 with his election to the chair of music at Columbia University—the first professorship of its kind in the United States. After his untimely death, his widow founded the MacDowell Colony at Peterborough, New Hampshire, carrying out her husband's plan to establish a congenial retreat for artists. Willa Cather herself wrote part of* Death Comes for the Archbishop *there in 1926.*[7] *During her winter in Washington, Cather had attended a concert of the Pittsburgh Symphony Orchestra at which "Mr. [Victor] Herbert's symphonic poem, 'Hero and Leander,' was received with marked enthusiasm"* (Journal, *February 10, 1901). For her review of Herbert's* Wizard of the Nile, *see "Three Operettas," The Musical World (II), above.*

"What is the best thing that can be done for American art?" said Ignace Paderewski to Mr. Krehbiel,[8] the foremost of New York musical critics. "Why, buy pictures and get the people to look at them." "What

5. For another use of this quotation, see Willa Cather's review of Pierre Loti's *Romance of a Spahi*, *Courier*, November 9, 1895, pp. 6–7; *KA*, pp. 365–367, quoted in part in the headnote to "The Death of Verlaine," Books and Authors (II), above.

6. See note 21, The Musical World (III), above.

7. Elizabeth Shepley Sergeant, *Willa Cather: A Memoir* (Lincoln: University of Nebraska Press, 1963), p. 224.

8. See note 10, The Musical World (III), above.

is the best thing that can be done for American music?" "Why, give Edward MacDowell twenty thousand a year and make him quit teaching and write."

Yet every day one comes across pedantic music teachers who ask: "Who is Edward MacDowell?"

With the exception of Dvořák, Grieg, Massenet and Saint Saëns, there is probably no living composer who is writing music of such an intensely individual nature as MacDowell, or whose work seems to have more of that quality which gives unlimited youth and tenure to works of art. Ten or fifteen years ago his compositions began to appear in the repertoires of foreign concert pianists, and for the last eight years they have figured from time to time in American concert programs; but MacDowell seldom gives recitals himself, and, except by his pupils, very little is known about his personality.

He is a man of leonine head, with a physique not unlike Rosenthal's.[9] For some years he has been professor of the theory of music at Columbia University.

Although he has an assistant who relieves him of most of his pedagogical duties except occasional lectures, he writes very little except in his summer vacations. He has a cottage in the pine woods somewhere along the New England coast, and there every summer he gives himself up to his work.

The verses written under the titles of most of the collection of *Sea Pieces*[10] are his own. He has written a good deal of verse from time to time, though he has published very little, and is an omniverous reader of verse, French, German and English; his catholic taste including pretty much of everything that is good from Heine, whose form is flawless, to Walt Whitman, who has no form at all.

I never heard of any recognized verse that he did not like except Swinburne and Stephen Phillips;[11] and he objects to these as "effeminate and unsound."

9. For Moritz Rosenthal, see "Three Pianists," The Musical World (III), above.

10. MacDowell's works mentioned in this selection: *Sea Pieces* (1898), *Sonata Tragica* (1893), Sonata no. 2, *Eroica* (1895), and "To a Wild Rose" and "From an Indian Lodge" (not "Wigwam," as here) from *Woodland Sketches* (1896).

11. Of the poetic drama *Paolo and Francesca* by Stephen Phillips (1865–1919), Cather had written: "The piece might be played anywhere, in a garden, on the rude stage of the old Globe Theatre, so untheatric it is. Indeed the play is built on the lines of the Greek tragedies rather than of modern plays, and it is a drama of fate, in which the characters are driven to their doom by a force seemingly outside of themselves. . ." (*Courier*, March 3, 1900, pp. 2–3).

He has written the words for some of his own songs, though singers claim that his songs are most of them wanting in melody and practically unsingable.

On the whole, he is an instrumental writer rather than a song writer; and is most successful when he makes the instrument do his singing but no one who has heard his exquisite "To a Wild Rose" or "From an Indian Wigwam" can doubt his gift of melody.

The *Heroic* and *Tragic* sonatas and several of the *Sea Pieces* are certainly the highest and strongest work that any American has done in instrumental composition; and there is very little that is better in all contemporary music.

He has not a trace of the florid or exotic, governing all he writes by a sort of Puritanic self-control and a relentless melancholy that is but half expressed. The New England conscience, maybe, transmuted into art at last and put behind the throne where the Greeks set fate. [August 10, 1901, pp. 1–2]

Four years ago Victor Herbert went to Pittsburgh to conduct the symphony orchestra there. The managers of the orchestra had received several personal letters from Anton Seidl[12] stating that he considered Herbert the most promising orchestra material among the young men of this country, and that no concert-meister under him had ever shown such marked ability to manage the personnel of an orchestra and keep each man up to his best work. At that time Herbert was still one of the best concert cellists in America, had written several admirable suites for that instrument, and had written two very creditable light operas, *Wizard of the Nile* [1896] and *The Serenade* [1897].

The first of these two in melodic quality was certainly superior to any comic opera that had been originated in this country for many years. The instrumentation was broad and skillful and the opera was rich in naif and catchy arias. The first thing Mr. Herbert did after he took charge of the orchestra was to enlarge it from sixty to eighty pieces, putting in a large portion of brasses, which he declared indispensable to the production of Wagnerian music. "The trick of the ex-bandmaster," as Frederic Archer, the organist, contemptuously declared.

From a business point of view, Mr. Herbert's directorship has been a most successful one. He is a good business man and a born manager of men. His musicians swear that he's the best fellow in the world and the

12. For Anton Seidl, see The Musical World (II), above.

most generous. He has helped the orchestra to get clear of debt and to make money. He has discharged his duties faithfully and yet found time to swell his private income by writing such execrable musical nonsense as *The Ameer* [1898], *The Fortune-Teller* and *The Singing Girl* [both 1900], besides several orchestral suites and one symphonic poem, "Hero and Leander" [1901], which abound in cleverness, yet totally lack any reason for existence.

The truth of the matter is simply that Herbert is wholly mercenary and is in no sense a conscientious musician. With the constitution and animal energy of the Irish giants who may have been his direct ancestors, he is able to eat and drink and work enormously without showing any evidences of wear and tear.

An organizer, a clever workman and a good citizen the man surely is, but to ask for inspired composition or for irreproachable interpretation from him is, to reverse Charles Lamb's simile, like asking for champagne at a mutton shop. [August 10, 1901, pp. 2–3]

The Chicago Art Institute

In manner and content this piece leans very heavily on "A Philistine in the Gallery" (see The Library, *above), and the painters Willa Cather singled out for special notice were all represented in the collection of Pittsburgh's Carnegie Institute Art Gallery. See also "Will H. Low and Bouguereau," The Urban Scene, above.*

William Chase is another painter whom the people love and whom the Young Art Student affects to hold in scorn because he has the tricks of pleasing color, and because his pictures convey no lofty message. Mr. Chase is not, indeed, a poet; much less is he a seer. He is an admirable colorist, and he believes that there is a sort of divinity in color itself. He has at least marvellous facility and craft, and it ill becomes young folk with large ideals and scant technique to belittle him. Technique is the base of every art, and the noblest sentiment may be shipwrecked in that perilous voyage from the brain to the hand. Pretty little girls daintily posed and painted with exquisite refinement of color have as good a right to exist in the catholic kingdom of art as the pale, primeval shades of Puvis de Chavannes.

It is not unlikely that the Chicago Art Institute, with its splendid collection of casts and pictures, has done more for the people of the Middle West than any of the city's great industries. Every farmer boy who goes into the city on a freight train with his father's cattle and every young merchant who goes into the city to order his stock, takes a look at the pictures. There are thousands of people all over the prairies who have seen their first and only good pictures there. They select their favorites and go back to see them year after year. The men grow old and careworn themselves, but they find that these things of beauty are immortally joy-giving and immortally young. You will find hundreds of merchants and farmer boys all over Nebraska and Kansas and Iowa who remember Jules Breton's beautiful "Song of the Lark,"[13] and perhaps the ugly little peasant girl standing barefooted among the wheat fields in the early morning has taught some of these people to hear the lark sing for themselves.

Some of the most appreciative art criticisms I ever heard were made by two sun-browned Kansas boys as they looked at George Inness' "Prairie Fire,"[14] there in the Cyrus H. McCormick loan exhibition. Of all the lighthouses along the Great Harbor, there is none that throws its light so far.

Paderewski's theory of buying pictures and getting people to look at them has been exemplified in at least three cities in the United States: New York, Chicago and Pittsburgh. As a result those three cities contain nearly all the important private collections in the United States.

There is no reason why Pittsburgh, for instance, should display any greater interest in art than Kansas City or Denver or Omaha or San Francisco. It is not a city of culture; the city is entirely given over to manufacturing industries, and the only standard of success recognized is the pecuniary standard. But one thing Carnegie did; he bought pictures and got people to look at them.

Whether art itself can be propagated by infusion or no, has not been proven; but in some measure taste can be.

There is no reason why the common people of Chicago, the people who read Marie Corelli and go to see *The Pride of Jennico*,[15] should know any more about pictures than the people of any other big city, but they do. Any stranger in the city who spends much time about the Art Institute must notice the comparatively enlightened conversation of the people who frequent the building on free days.

13. See note 22, Books and Authors (III), above.

14. George Inness (1825–1894), famous landscape painter of the Hudson River school.

15. *The Pride of Jennico* by Abby S. Richardson and G. Furniss, starring James K. Hackett, had played one hundred eleven performances after its opening March 6, 1900.

For some reason the institution is much nearer to the people of Chicago than the Metropolitan art gallery is to the people of New York. Perhaps it is because the spirit of caste is less perceptible in western cities, and the relations between employers and employees are more cordial. When any one of the Deerings or McCormicks buys an Inness or a Corot, he exhibits the picture in the Art Institute and their workmen drop in to have a look at it some Sunday and decide that they could have done something better with the money, if it had been theirs. The convenient and attractive location of the building may also have something to do with its popularity.

The collection of pictures is such that it would be impossible to cultivate a false or florid taste there. With the exception of several Bouguereaus, there is not a poor picture in the gallery. Yet there are hundreds of pictures there that the veriest Philistine can admire and, to a great extent, appreciate; people who read *Under Two Flags* and enjoy comic opera and ice-cream soda.

The real fault of popular taste, when we get down to the heart of the matter, is that the people prefer the pretty to the true. That is a fault, certainly; but not so grave a one as the Young Art Student makes it. Indeed, there are times when I would take the Philistine's word for a picture, long before I would the Young Art Student's; for the Philistine is always governed by moderation, and he is always honest with himself.

There are certain painters whom the Philistine seems to get quite as much pleasure from in his way as the Art Student does in his. Take, for instance, Josef Israels' Dutch interiors, and especially his pictures of mothers and children. The simplicity and directness of his treatment and the sombre tenderness of his coloring are by no means lost on the Philistine, though he may not stop to reason about it and may attribute all the pleasure he experiences to the mere beauty of the subject.

H. O. Tanner, the colored painter, who handles Biblical subjects with the power and conviction of the Old Masters, is another favorite with the people. I have seen country preachers and solemn old ladies in ill-fitting black gloves stand before his "Suicide of Judas" with visible emotion.

There is something about Tanner's work that makes the people and places and life of Palestine real to us as nothing else has ever done. The Old Masters painted Italian Christs and Dutch Marys and Spanish Josephs; but this man paints the Orient, not the Orient of the midway and bazaar, dressed up and tricked out for a show, but the work-a-day Palestine, where men plowed and sowed and prayed.

There is a tradition that Biblical subjects should be painted in a highly decorative manner, and that Orientalism means crimson and ultramarine; but Mr. Tanner produces his most Oriental effect with low colors. He paints with a realism so unaffected, a sympathy with the life of the people, that there seems to be an almost national touch in his pictures. There is something about his insistent use of the silvery gray of the olives and the parched yellow clay hills of Palestine that recalls Pierre Loti's faculty of infusing absolute personality into environment, if one may compare two such different mediums as prose and paint.

Another great favorite with the Philistine is gay master Rico, whose name to the Young Art Student is as the red rag to the bull. Now, Master Rico chooses to be pretty, and that, in the eye of the Art Student, is an unpardonable sin. You will find a copy of one of his Venetian scenes in every picture-loving home of the middle class; very blue skies, a silvery canal, white and red houses, bridges and gay gondolas, and in the foreground the dear Lombard poplars, the gayest and saddest of trees, rustling green and silver in the sunlight. The people like to think of Venice as a pretty place, where people forget their troubles, and therefore they like Master Rico's pictures better than those of greater painters than he who have darkened the canals of the city with the shadows of her past.

The Young Art Student can find no place in life for the dainty, the trivial or the gay; but would have us live in Gothic cathedrals and marry the noble but angular ladies of Puvis de Chavannes. Rico is only a hummingbird, if you will, or a yellow rose in June, but the Philistine will stand by him because he adds somewhat to the gayety of life.

Painters sometimes call Gari Melchers a hard painter, but the people know his worth, and they feel the poetry in his subjects, even if they do not know the tricks of craft by which he presents it.

Every woman who has ever carried a baby will stop and smile at his young Dutch mothers, with their plump, uncorseted figures and their pudgy little children with wooden shoes on their feet.

The densest person cannot miss the beautiful and homely sentiment in "The Sailor and His Sweetheart." The Philistine is partial to fireside scenes and domestic and sentimental subjects generally. He knows that sentiment is the most vital motive in society, in his own life and in the lives of his friends. That it wrecks banks and controls the markets, directly or indirectly, and he demands that the comings and goings and courtings and festivals and farewells that make up the gladness and sadness of his life be somehow put into art. He will accept it even when it is badly done for the sake of the sentiment; but I believe that in time he will prefer it well done. Do we not all admit that the man who can make these homely subjects into art is the greatest of all artists, and that the peasant folk of Millet are worthier a man of genius than the ballet dancers of Degas? [August 10, 1901, p. 2]

A New Novel by Eden Phillpotts

Willa Cather's review of Children of the Mist *by Eden Phillpotts had appeared in the* Courier *on September 16, 1899 (see "Arnold Bennett and Eden Phillpotts," Books and Authors [IV], above).*

Sons of the Morning is the title of a remarkable new book by Mr. Eden Phillpotts. Mr. Phillpotts' first novel, *Lying Prophets*, attracted considerable attention because of its marked individuality and its picturesque and vigorous prose. His second work, *Children of the Mist*, which was reviewed in THE COURIER two years ago, convinced all critical readers that a new man had entered the ranks of the great English novelists. In his last work, *Sons of the Morning*, he has entirely avoided the fault of diffuseness which detracted somewhat from his second novel.

In *Children of the Mist* Mr. Phillpotts attempted to depict the life of an entire Dartmoor village, and to chronicle fully and sympathetically the lives of some twenty persons. In view of the difficulties of the task he set himself, his success was remarkable; but the diversity of interest in some measure detracted from the congruity and compactness of the novel as a whole.

The scenario of *Sons of the Morning* is much the same as in his former novels; but the plot is concerned chiefly with four characters, picturesquely attended by a train of country folk and retainers which Mr. Phillpotts handles with notable success. Indeed the most hopeful of this young man's many brilliant qualities is his clear and sympathetic understanding of the British yeoman and the laboring man of that part of England of which it is his pleasure and perhaps his necessity to write.

Thomas Hardy, George Meredith and George Moore are all of them old men, to whom very many more years of literary activity cannot be left; and among the newer writers there seemed none of sufficient vigor and body to succeed them worthily.

Sir Walter Besant[16] has chosen easy and flowery ways; Hall Caine, who even in his best days wrote always at the top of his voice, is now

16. Sir Walter Besant (1836–1901), English novelist, whose works included *The Seamy Side* (1881), with James Rice, and *All Sorts and Conditions of Men* (1882).

quite beyond the province of serious consideration. Mr. Anthony Hope Hawkins, who might have done what he pleased with us eight years ago and made us all for a space prisoners of Zenda, has since done nothing much above the clever dilettante, and Mrs. Craigie has never cherished any ambition other than to surprise.

For the sake of so much that was beautiful in *The Forest Lovers*, we willfully stopped our ears to that note of hysterical effeminateness which crept now and then into Mr. Maurice Hewlett's work; but the lamentable collapse of the latter third of *Richard Yea-and-Nay* demonstrated that he has not sufficiently matured to be absolutely trustworthy and that his taste is capable of very gross lapses.

Then there is a whole host of the disagreeable people of the Voynich[17] and Cholmondeley order and a host of the light and subtle people, passionate imitators of all genre work, ancient and modern.

The notable thing about Phillpotts is that he has withstood the temptations of the historical romance and the illusive and recompenseful short story and has gone back to the life of the real English people depicted by George Eliot, Henry Fielding and Thomas Hardy, and by Dickens at his best.

The world is weary unto death of stories about artists and scholars and aesthetic freaks, and of studies in the "artistic temperament." Mr. Phillpotts was wiser than his generation when he went back to racy, rugged chronicle of common life again.

In his *Sons of the Morning* there is a whole troop of working people, reapers and hay-makers and foresters and plow-boys and milkmaids, all presented with a brevity and vividness and impartiality almost Shakespearean.

Indeed as one Shakespearean reads of the black rages of Cramphorn, the wisdom of Churdles Ash and the courtship of Libby, one thinks continually of Audrey and William and Phebe and the old shepherd [in *As You Like It*]. The combat between the two sisters, Margery and Sally Cramphorn, in its rich humor and lusty spirit recalls the famous battle in *Tom Jones* in which Mollie, the forester's daughter, lost her new gown and most of her reputation. Both the sisters were known to be in love with Greg Libby, a weak-blooded, cautious country swain who could not make up his mind which of them would make the best housekeeper, and mightily feared the wrath of the rejected. After mature consideration he proposed to both and invited each separately to appear at a certain

17. Ethel Voynich (1864–1960), English novelist, best remembered for *The Gadfly* (1897); Mary Cholmondeley (d. 1925), another English novelist, whose works included *Red Pottage* (1899).

secluded spot on the same hour of the same day. He himself hid behind a rock and the maids met, began to twit each other and finally fell into a furious battle, fighting with stones and fingernails for weapons while Greg sat by and watched them, determined to wed the victor.

I am sure there is no other living man besides Thomas Hardy who could have written that scene. If Mr. Phillpotts were not absolutely without sentimentality, it would have been impossible for him.

Fiction writers are becoming more and more "sicklied o'er with the pale cast of thought"; given over to psychological studies so that they have lost all kinship and knowledge of that part of society which lives in its ears and eyes and stomach and uses its fists oftener than its handkerchiefs.

Old Dumas said that to make a play he needed but four walls, two people and one passion.[18] Now-a-days to make a story we need but a studio, a woman who is more than half man and a man who is more than half woman and an intellectual affinity. If there were one man who could write of the American common people, the people on whom the burden of labor rests, who plant the corn and cut the wheat and drive the drays and mine the coal and forge the iron and move the world, then there might be some hope for a literature of and from the American people. But so far our men who write of the people at all write of trusts and strikes and corporations and man-devouring railroads, of the mere condition of labor and not of men at all.

The wealth of descriptive writing which from the first marked Mr. Phillpotts' style is, if anything, enhanced in his last work. It seemed that nothing more could be said about Moorland rivers and trees and sky and birds and flowers, than was said in *Children of the Mist;* but the man's passion for the visible forms of nature seems inexhaustible.

I suspect it was to tell of these things that he first wrote at all. He paints a dozen different sunrises seen from practically the same place; all complete, presentive, and wholly distinct. He tells of nights and noons and morns over and over without ever wearying the reader's patience. Such a knowledge of botany, forestry, horticulture, geology, ornithology and zoology as underlies this fervid and pictorial descriptive writing.

Whether he will sustain his objective study and delineation of character as wonderfully as Thomas Hardy has done, it is too soon to say; but like him he has heard the heart-beats of the people, and he is more of a poet than Hardy ever was. [August 10, 1901, p. 7]

18. See "The Lesson of Dumas *père*," The Theatre (III), above.

Small-Town Life

From the point of view of a woman with considerable experience of the world, Willa Cather gives her opinion on two Midwestern phenomena, small-town funerals and Carry Nation (1846–1911), the renowned temperance agitator who took out after John Barleycorn with a hatchet.

It may be said the funerals make up the social life of many small towns. Social endeavors become discouraged in little western towns, like the crops in the south wind.

It has been argued before now that if the people in the villages all over the western states took more interest in each other, and could manufacture a smile when their neighbors had a stroke of good luck, or could find a sympathetic word to say when they were in trouble, that the corn itself would take heart o' grace and see some use in growing.

The privations that people suffer in our little western towns are of their own making, and are not brought upon them by God or the railroads or the weather.

Within the memory of all of us there was plenty of life and enthusiasm in every Nebraska town, as there is in Cheyenne or Deadwood today. The smallest village had its euchre clubs and whist clubs and dancing clubs, and nearly everybody spent money beyond their means. Then hard times and small crops came along for awhile, and everybody got remorseful and discouraged and more or less bitter.

People who met with financial reverses turned about and said spiteful things about their friends who had been more fortunate, and these friends, being human, withdrew within a wall of haughtiness and answered back with scorn.

As the phrase goes, people "got out of the habit of going" to see their friends, and soon enough they got out of the habit of caring about them at all. Now some of them are pessimistic and lay it on the weather or the corn. It would be no great wonder if the corn did get tired of growing to feed selfish and grouchy people.

In little eastern towns factions and indifference are to be expected. There are old blood feuds that have been handed down for generations and there are caste lines that everybody regards. But in a western town everybody has a second chance and begins again with no past behind him and a clean slate. He doesn't have to be mean because of tradition; because his father sanded sugar or watered his hay before he sold it.

Everybody has an opportunity to help in making a social side to life that will benefit him and his children, but he won't do it because he doesn't like this fellow or that fellow doesn't like him.

There is one thing the small-town man and woman will not do, and that is show courtesy to people whom they do not like; they hold such conduct to be bare deception. The fallacy of their theory is that nine times out of ten if they sat down beside these same distasteful people for an hour and did their part to sustain a conversation, their hatred would vanish and their action would cease to be a deception.

William James, the psychologist, has so admirably explained that so often the act precedes the feeling in matters of courtesy and kindness.[19] If it were necessary to feel a strong affection for people in order to conscientiously dine at their house or invite them to your own, there would be few dinner parties in the world.

Most of us don't try to love our friends after we are eighteen, unless we are fools or geniuses. We take them for what they are worth and let it go at that, knowing perfectly well that we ourselves are in need of reciprocal charity.

The small town lets its social arrears go and go until people are buried beneath an ashamed sense of their own remissness, and then they try to make it all up at funerals. When anyone dies whom they haven't broken bread with or called on for years, his fellow townsmen put on their black clothes and go to see him, and the women ravage their gardens to send him flowers. If a college student comes back to his native town and wants to see all his old friends together, he has to go to a funeral to do it. It's a futile and inexpensive sort of remorse and it's a dishonest way of paying social obligations.

Surely it is better to ask a man to dinner once during his lifetime than to go to his funeral, and surely it is pleasanter. It's a better plan to tell him that he's a good fellow and that he has deserved all the luck he's ever had, and more too, than to tell his widow about it someday. How many people have ever told the best lawyer in their town that they appreciate the fact that he is clever, or the best student in their schools that they take an interest in him?

Why is it that the common courtesies of life that make it easy sailing and compensate somewhat for the larger disappointments of life, come harder than blood in the small towns? [August 17, 1901, p. 2]

19. A reference to the famous James-Lange theory of emotion. "In the days before psychology became the happy hunting-ground of the erotic extrovert," wrote George Seibel, Willa Cather was "a devoted disciple" of William James (p. 202).

When David Nation made application for a decree of divorce at Medicine Lodge, Kansas, last week, the hearts of the people were with him. If he found the ridiculous position in which he has been placed at all endurable it would be an unfaltering indication of the manner of man he is.

Mr. Nation has for some time been living with a daughter in Iberia, under whose roof he has taken refuge. Mrs. Nation, in her comments upon the suit, scornfully stated that her husband had been an encumbrance upon her for years and that she had never had the slightest respect for him.

The mind refuses to picture the position of a man whom Mrs. Nation regarded as an "encumbrance": an old soldier and peaceful citizen deserved a better fate.

There can scarcely be any doubt that his wife's astonishing conduct is the result of her limitations and a soured and uncharitable nature. Given a woman with a passion for violence and bitter speech and place her in a small town where petty animosities thrive, and your result is a Carry Nation in word if not in deed.

There is no figure in society who can work more discomfort than the village Semiramis, whose prejudices are as violent as her information is limited, and who has an accepted outlet for her ferocious energy. [August 24, 1901, p. 1]

Literary Notes

Two men whose names were very much in the news in 1901 were William Allen White (see "Old Books and New [December 1897]," The Home Monthly, *above) and General Frederick Funston. White had written studies on three politicians for* McClure's: *William Jennings Bryan (July 1900); McKinley's political strategist, Senator Mark Hanna of Ohio (November 1900); and Tammany boss Richard Croker (February 1901); he also published a political novel,* Stratagems and Spoils, *in 1901. General Frederick Funston, a Medal of Honor winner, had captured the Philippine insurrectionist leader Emilio Aguinaldo in March 1901.*[20]

It is an old and accepted difficulty in the world of storytelling that the man who can knock about the earth "for to admire and for to see," never gets settled down to the chronicling of his experiences, and the man who is industrious enough to work up some skill in the telling of things, can't afford to take the holidays that would give him the best of material.

20. For Funston, see note 42, Books and Authors (IV), above.

While young men were scurrying about the world in search of material and adventure, the best of adventure stories came from the sick bed with blood-stained linen where Stevenson wrote *Treasure Island* and *The Master of Ballantrae*. One is often tempted to wonder which of those two likely Kansas boys gets the most out of life, Will White, or Funston. They grew up on the Deer Creek and fished and hunted together and made their own adventures, and they went to the University of Kansas together and were sorry scholars, both of them. Then they went out to find the goddess of their boyhood, seeking her by different trails.

I believe White has had more of her than Funston. There have probably been not a few of those priceless moments that only military achievement seems to give in the little general's life; but it is not improbable that White has gotten as much pleasure out of his friend's brilliant career as ever Funston has, minus the heat and dust and thirst and mosquitoes.

Pickett never saw the beauty of his charge at Gettysburg; that was left to the strategists who watched the movement.

After all Funston is only Funston, and he is limited to one game; but White is Funston and Piggy Pennington together.

The story-maker's recompense for being nobody in reality is that he can be everybody in theory. Mr. White has even shown himself able to be Mr. Bryan, Mark Hanna and Richard Croker in such rapid succession that one trembled for him, recalling the story of the versatile ogre who turned himself into an elephant, a bear and a mouse, in which last form Puss-in-Boots devoured him.

Secretary [of State] Hay has said to his friends that no writing in the history of American politics has equalled those three character studies of White's for astuteness and brilliancy. [August 17, 1901, p. 2]

Willa Cather wrote a number of columns about children's reading and she believed in storytelling as a means of interesting children in books. Discussing the programs for children at Pittsburgh's Carnegie Library in a 1900 article, she had written: "The librarians found that by this primitive method of storytelling, which has always been the beginning of literature, ever since the Iliad *and* Odyssey *were sung, they could unobtrusively direct the children's reading almost entirely. Surely we all know that the books we read when we were children shaped our lives; at least they shaped our imaginings, and it is with our imaginings that we live. . . ."*[21]

21. "The Children's Part in a Great Library," *Library*, July 7, 1900, pp. 16–17. For comments on children's books, see especially the "Old Books and New" columns, The *Home Monthly*, above.

The children's reading room and children's book list have gradually brought about a new division of labor in the larger public libraries, and now the children's librarian prepares for his or her work by a special course of study and kindergarten work. . . .

A new ruffle has been added to the children's librarian's duties in the shape of what is called the "story hour." Children whose mothers have little time to give them are assembled once a week and the librarian devotes an hour to storytelling. To this plan there could be no objection; but the enthusiastic librarians have conceived a gigantic plan of reducing all literature to the kindergarten dimension. They tell the story of the Trojan war, omitting the story of Helen's elopement; the story of Faust expurgated for the youthful mind; the story of Napoleon's energy, maintaining a careful silence as to his ambition.

In short, these enthusiastic librarians simply abolish the elements of evil from literature for the benefit of the "pure young mind." This would be well enough if they could also banish it from the world in which these children must live, but it is doubtful whether this milk-and-water training will make much impression on wise little Jewish girls whose backs are bent with carrying babies ever since they were old enough to stand alone, or on Negro boys who have just helped to clean their father's razor for a cakewalk.

I am not sure that the kindergartners have any particular right to rewrite Homer and Virgil and Faust and the Bible, even if they do it with a lofty purpose. The thing only goes back to that mistaken endeavor of kindergartners to make study easy, to make work play, to make duty inclination—paradoxes which it fairly staggers the mind to contemplate.[22]

To keep from a child the knowledge that the world is a hard place to live in, and that he will have to do many difficult and distasteful things before he gets through with it, is as disastrous as to keep him out of the reach of those childish diseases which are ten times as dangerous if contracted when he is older. [August 17, 1901, pp. 2–3]

It is rather strange, when one comes to think of it, now that the eyes of all the world are turned upon Asia and the nations of the Orient,[23] that

22. Kindergartens had been introduced into the United States in 1873, but had not yet gained a place in the educational system because of opposition to the theories of the originator, Friedrich Froebel (1782–1852), who stressed controlled play as a means of learning for pre-school children.

23. The Boxer Rebellion and the Philippine Insurrection were the major concerns of American foreign policy in 1901.

the man who most nearly speaks the voice of the people and the spirit of the times first called our attention to the old East ten or twelve years ago. Rudyard Kipling set the song of the East humming in a million brains, and long before he knew that bungalows and punkahs would ever figure in government expense bills, we began to use the names of them. Before Kipling's day we knew as little about the mixed religions and mixed nations of the Orient as we knew about the etiquette of Tibet, and cared as little.

There once lived a very subtle critic in England who declared that life imitates art to a much greater extent than art imitates life. At any rate, I should like to know how many of the men who boarded the transport for the Philippines were repeating "On the Road to Mandalay" under their breath.

Whatever indifferent work Mr. Kipling may have done in the last five years, and whether he is a literary artist or no, he is certainly the genius of the times, the man who speaks and prophetically foretold the spirit of the hour; the passing of old orders, the expansion of the white races, the passion for machinery and perfected system, the stroke for conquest and the renaissance of the spirit of war. He preceded by about ten years everything we are doing and thinking today. That is what the tribe singer, the original poet, did in the days before literary art or any wearisome theories about it had come into being, when the poet sang to his people of the things he knew that they would do, and told them where the fishing was good and where the bucks were fat, and of treasures that might be easily wrested from men on the other side of the mountain. [August 24, 1901, p. 2]

"*The Real Homestead*"

Homestead was the company town where the workers of the Carnegie Steel Corporation lived, the scene of the notorious Homestead Strike of 1892 by the Amalgamated Association of Iron and Steel Workers, when state troops were called out to protect Carnegie properties. In July 1901 the iron and steel workers began a strike against the newly formed United States Steel Corporation, which came into being when J. P. Morgan bought out Andrew Carnegie. Willa Cather had visited Homestead in March 1898.[24]

24. Willa Cather to Mariel Gere, March 7, 1898. Willa Cather made the trip to see her friend Mary Esther Robbins, who was cataloguing books at the Homestead Library, described in this article.

Whatever may be the real cause of the disturbances that come up from time to time in Pittsburgh steel circles, one fact is peculiarly significant, that strikes never occur when the demand for worked steel and steel products exceeds the supply. The press dispatchers, in figuring up the total losses to the steel corporations through the inactivity of the mills, have neglected to figure what the steel magnates would lose by meeting the weekly payroll when their warehouses are already overstocked, and an inevitable depression in the steel industry stares them in the face.

If all strikes are the fault of the workmen altogether, it would seem but a common sense measure to strike when their labor is indispensable, as, for instance, when the government orders that followed the declaration of war against Spain had to be filled, or when Russia's orders were heaviest.

The repeated occurrence of strikes when orders are light and work is slack would seem to indicate that the steel corporations of Pennsylvania and Ohio can avoid them when they find it expedient to do so, and that if they lose money through the idleness of their mills they would lose more in the long run through their operation. [August 10, 1901, p. 1]

There is probably no city in the United States which is more in the public eye just at the present time than the town of Homestead, and probably no steel town where there is less outward excitement about the strike.

The town lies about five miles up the river from Pittsburgh, built in the narrow valley between the Monongahela and the low line of hills beyond.

On the opposite side of the river the Baltimore & Ohio tracks wind under wooded bluffs where the trees are gradually dying from the chemical action of the smoke-laden atmosphere. The river is seemingly without current, still and yellow as a mud lake, and dotted with coal barges and puffing little tugs.

The great steel plant that will always be known as the Carnegie works is not in the town of Homestead at all, but just outside the town line in the village of Munhall. The majority of the mill workers, however, live in Homestead.

The town is neglected and unlovely in appearance, like most manufacturing towns, and the residences are built to eat and sleep in rather than to live in. There is very little green grass, few trees and fewer flowers. The meat shops and grocery stores carry goods of the best quality, as mill workers are prodigious eaters and insist upon the most nourishing sort of food. At the Carnegie Hotel, which stands just outside of the main entrance to the steel works, a dollar-a-day house of indifferent service where many of the chemists and testers and draughtsmen board, the meats are as good as can be got at any of the best hotels in the city of Pittsburgh.

The mill worker's notion of comfort is good eating. He buys strawberries in April and cantaloups from Colorado. The interior of his home usually is more indicative of prosperity than of taste. He always has an organ and a Brussels carpet and a "set" of cheap oak furniture and a crayon portrait of himself in a huge gilt frame. Ordinarily he is careless of his dress, but he invariably has a diamond to screw in his shirt front on Sunday. This, of course, is true only of the workmen who are more or less skilled. Nearly every man rides a bicycle to his work.

The Carnegie Library of Homestead stands on the hills overlooking the works, but just within the Homestead line. It is a French Renaissance building 228 by 133 feet in its exterior dimensions. Back of the library stands the residence of Robert Corey, former superintendent of the works. The library building includes under its roof a well-equipped music hall, gymnasium, billiard room, swimming pool, running tracks, smoking rooms and ladies' parlors and reception rooms.

The library, like the rest of the world, is full of good things that no one has leisure to enjoy. It was built and fitted up for the use of the mill men, but the mill men, when they are working, work twelve-hour shifts, that means from six in the morning until six in the evening. If a man lives any distance at all from the works he has to get up before five in the morning, and by the time he has cooled off and had a bath and his dinner in the evening it is eight o'clock. He has been working all day in a most exhausting temperature and probably drinking heavily to combat the heat, and he wants no music or books or athletics, but all the sleep he can get before four-thirty the next morning.

There are hundreds of the men who stand the strain of these twelve-hour shifts year in and year out without losing a day, but the margin left them of their lives for social relaxation is so small that clubs and libraries established in their interests seem almost absurdities.

Occasionally, when it is a question of a marriage or a funeral or a christening, a man can get his "buddy," the man who takes his work in the next shift, to relieve him; this arrangement gives the "buddy" a shift of twenty-four hours over the hot metal with no break except the half-hour allowed for lunch. There are plenty of cases on record where a substitute has stood his ground for sixty-four hours without sleep and with few breathing spells. It would seem that Mr. Carnegie's sense of humor must be deficient when he supplies Herbert Spencer and Wagner for these men.

The facilities of the library are made use of by the bosses and draughtsmen and office forces, but the mill workers proper very seldom go there and even their wives and children patronize [it] little.

Twelve-hour shifts are doubtless good economy, but they do not tend to make a literary or music-loving community.

The most objectionable element of Homestead, the foreign labor element which was met with such bitter antagonism when it was first introduced there, is carefully hid from the eye of the casual observer. Occasionally someone asks what is to be found in the ramshackle red buildings inside the company fence, and he is told, "That is only Pottersville." Pottersville is a collection of some sixty or seventy hovels made of thin planks and painted red, which are huddled in the soot and ashes and cinder heaps back of one of the rolling mills and inside the fifteen-foot stockade which surrounds the town-front of the steel plant.

In this collection of wretched habitations dwell nearly two thousand mill workers: Huns, Slavs, Poles, Italians, Russians and Negroes. The last census revealed a startling condition of things in Pottersville, but it is a condition that will last as long as the town lasts. One six-room boarding house reported seventy inmates, some of the rooms accommodating twenty lodgers. This, of course, is only made possible by the twelve-hour shift system. Every bed does double duty, and every floor is a bed. As soon as one set of men get up and go to work, another set, tired and dirty, creep into the same sheets and go to sleep.

Naturally a corporation can employ to advantage men who can live in this fashion. They seldom eat meat and need only rye bread and diluted wood alcohol and an occasional turn in a sort of tribal bed. When a Hun or a Pole gets crippled in the works, he usually opens a boarding house in Pottersville. No one house is ever occupied by a single family, even when the children run above a dozen in number, as they often do.

This world of barbarism that is shut in behind the stock-pen-like fence is not the work of any "soulless corporation," at least, not directly. During the great strike of 1892, when the company took on a great many foreign hands, the superintendent, John Potter, built the ramshackle houses inside the stockade to protect the "scab" laborers from the fury of the strikers. The "scabs" have never had ambition enough to get outside of the stock-pen, and it is well enough for the town of Homestead and the village of Munhall that they have not. All the riffraff of the town, the brute force that turns the wheels of the great steel mills, are hidden away from the citizen and visitor alike, and the heart of the boldest missionary fails him when he looks through the knotholes in the fence.

Like most unsightly things, Homestead has its picturesque side, or rather its picturesque phase. On Saturday night, when the mills are running, there is not a noisier spot on earth, nor a more interesting study for the sociologist.

Although the mill fires usually begin to go down about dusk on Saturday night, they are still bright enough to terrify the mountaineer, and a cloud of red flame hangs over the hundreds of giant smokestacks. The river is a red lake with green lanterns here and there on the coal barges. The rolling mills give out their periodic crashes of deafening sound, and the streets are full of men of every race and tongue who are getting rid of their money.

The whiskey drunk in Homestead every Saturday night would float an ocean steamer. Every nationality exhales its own peculiar odor of drunkenness, and men stand in long box-office lines before the bar-room doors. Dances and acrobatic feats are executed on the sidewalks to the music of a street piano. The click of the pokerchips sound from the windows of the card rooms, and there are drunken women in the streets reeling toward the hovels of Pottersville. Brutalizing toil is followed by brutalizing pleasures. [August 24, 1901, pp. 1–2]

An ideal democracy, that is, a complete and consistent democracy, would completely disprove all of Herbert Spencer's system of philosophy. The warfare of the world can never be eliminated and these pretty theories of friendly strivings are parodoxical on their very face. No man can strive at all and be willing to see the other fellow win under any consideration.

The struggle for power is essentially the same whether it is fought with railroad shares or the flint hatchets of the stone man.

Mr. J. Pierpont Morgan seems to have acquired control of more men and money than any other man the United States has produced. His army of workmen far outnumber the United States military, and he controls capital enough to buy any of the smaller kingdoms of Europe at auction.

Speculations upon his actual wealth are quite superfluous, for after money reaches a certain figure it ceases to be money at all and becomes power. It is not reckoned by its purchasing power any longer, but by its initiative and resistive power.

Mr. Morgan's real wealth is in his brain and not in his coffers. Surrounded as he is by the most complicated business machinery, a week of false estimates and bad judgment would wreck as many lives as a general sacrifices by a bad strategic movement. His life is given not to the enjoyment of wealth, but to the solving of problems and the amassing of power. He can eat but one dinner a day and wear but one coat at a time, like the rest of us.

Whatever civilization has done, it has not been able to expand by one inch the individual's capacity for enjoyment. Mr. Morgan could gratify the tastes of a thousand men, but it is only an infinitesimal part of his fortune that he can use upon himself. The only men who have the least excuse for envying him are men of ambitions; and, though every man imagines he is ambitious, the number of ambitious men is scarcely larger than the number of great men. [August 24, 1901, p. 2]

Rodin's Victor Hugo

The great French sculptor Auguste Rodin (1840–1917) had been commissioned by the state to create a monument to Victor Hugo for the Pantheon, but his conception was so shocking to public taste that he discontinued work on the statue to make a more conventional one. Photographs of the unfinished statue, which was exhibited at the Paris Salon of 1901, were frequently published in American periodicals and newspapers.

Auguste Rodin's contribution to the salon this year is an unfinished statue of Victor Hugo. The statue is of heroic proportions and full length, representing the poet lying nude on the rocks, his leonine head supported on his hand.

The enemies of the sculptor, and they are many and scurrilous, declare that the effect produced by taking a modern man of letters and a politician out of his frock coat and trousers and stretching him, Greek fashion, on the rocks is ludicrously shocking and absurd. Photographs of the work, however, lead one to believe that it is quite the most remarkable of all the many noble things Rodin has done. Seemingly he has achieved the impossible by treating a modern subject in the antique heroic manner with perfect success.

The figure is one of superb dignity, and might be mistaken for a resting Hercules. The idea in itself seems ridiculous enough; for who could imagine Wagner or Daudet treated in this unclothed manner by anyone save a malicious cartoonist? That Rodin has been able to do it with sublime seriousness in Hugo's case is a pure triumph of his genius. No other treatment could have been so noble, yet it is to be hoped that Rodin's imitators will not repeat this new note in portrait statuary and give us George Sand as a wood nymph or Alfred de Musset as a weeping Orpheus. [August 24, 1901, p. 2]

D'Annunzio's Il Fuoco

Il Fuoco *(1900) by Gabriele D'Annunzio (1863–1938) was available in America in Kossendra Viraria's English translation, titled* The Flame, *the year it was published, but Willa Cather seems to have read it in the French translation by G. Henelle,* Le Feu *(1901), passages from which she rendered in English for the* Courier *readers. For earlier comments on Eleonora Duse, the heroine of D'Annunzio's* roman à clef, *see "Duse and Suppressed Emotion," The Star System (II), above.*

Duse's delayed tour of the United States is now announced for the early winter of 1902–1903, and her managers state that among the number of plays by D'Annunzio she will produce a dramatization of his novel *Il Fuoco*, of which she herself was a heroine.

Whether this is a managerial fiction, or whether the persecuted actress actually intends to resort to this extreme measure of self-defense, remains to be seen. If she actually produces the play, her action will surpass anything in the history of feminine psychology or the most morbid perversion of D'Annunzio's pen.

How she can do it is a question which need perplex no astonished American; for how he could have written the novel at all, or how she could have permitted herself to live after he had done so, are questions quite as unanswerable to people on this side of the Atlantic.

The book is a study of two people; the author's rosy and highly flattering view of himself, his own power and gifts, and his brutal and shameless analysis of the emotions of the woman whom he claims gave up her entire life to him until he was weary of accepting her devotion.

For any man to sit down and set about computing on paper how greatly and in what manner a woman had cared for him, giving even the number of her house in Venice, lest the public should make any mistake, is a bad enough proposition; but *Il Fuoco* goes a great deal further than that. It is a shameless sale of confidence of the most sacred kind for money, a savage and shameless attack upon a woman who is still living and who is ill and unhappy.

Her age and physical infirmities are mentioned by the gentleman in comparison with his own splendid youth and resplendent beauty. The reptilian nature of the man as disclosed by his book has set up a bitter revolt against him in Italy where Signora Duse is deeply beloved, and many of his countrymen have sent him threatening letters. If he should ever be rash enough to visit England it is doubtful whether he would ever get out without a horsewhipping, for as likely as not some country squire who had never heard Duse at all would take pleasure in paying up humanity's score against D'Annunzio with his fists. There have been men without any sense of honor before in the world, but surely no man has ever been able to make such a masterly presentation of his destitution.

Il Fuoco, considered merely as literature, takes a high rank among modern novels. Even from a French translation of it one is able to gather that the man, always gifted with a superb power of language, has never fitted phrases together more melodiously, and in the Italian tongue the novel must approach as near to poetry as prose safely can.

The plot is concerned with a love affair between an actress and a novelist, in which the woman is considerably more than half the wooer. The scene is laid in Venice, and the city with its dark and stirring past, the present decrepitude and decay, are used to cleverly emphasize the picture of the aged and ailing actress.

The first part of the novel, which is almost purely descriptive of the city, if published alone would make one of the finest pieces of work of its kind in literature. The mental associations aroused by the city itself are presented so vividly that they become almost a part of one's personal existence, and you cannot deny that the man achieves the miracle of transferring his fancy to his reader with exactly the color and intensity that he wishes.

The associations of places with persons and events speak very strongly to D'Annunzio; that was the real source of the grewsome charm of *The Triumph of Death* [1894; English translation 1896]. The first fifty pages are full of presentive passages like the following, which describes the clamor of the city as heard by two people in a gondola: "A confused roar, like the imaginary rushing that animates the rushing of some sea shells, rose from between the two watchful columns of granite, as the barge came to shore by the crowded Piazzetta. Then suddenly the shout rose higher in the limpid air, breaking up against the slim forest of marbles, vaulting over the brow of the taller statues, shooting beyond the pinnacles and across, disappearing in the far distances of twilight. The manifold harmonies of the sacred and pagan architectures all over which the Ionic modulations of the Biblioteca ran like an agile melody, continued unbroken in the pause which followed, and the summit of the naked town rose like a mystic cry."

One knows well enough what he means when he says of the actress, "this lonely, wandering woman who seemed to carry in the folds of her dress the silenced frenzy of those far-off multitudes from whom her cry of sorrow or enthralled pause had wrenched the sublime pulsation of art." There lingers a little of that nimbus about every woman who has stood before the people and moulded them to her will.

If D'Annunzio's power could only have been given to a man, modern Italy might have given us something to keep in the treasure houses. [August 24, 1901, pp. 2–3]

The *Gazette*

(November 17, 1901—November 30, 1902)

When Willa Cather returned to Pittsburgh in the fall of 1901 to resume teaching at Central High School, her personal circumstances were more settled and serene than they had been in years. The previous spring she had been invited by her friend Isabelle McClung, daughter of Judge and Mrs. Samuel McClung, to make her home in the family mansion on Murray Hill Avenue. Willa Cather's several biographers have commented on the many benefits that accrued to her from this arrangement. As Edith Lewis has written, "she enjoyed a tranquility and physical comfort in the McClung house she had probably never before experienced. Isabelle McClung fitted up a sewing-room at the top of the house as a study for her, and she wrote here on week-ends and holidays, and during school vacations."[1]

There has been a tendency to assume that when Willa Cather began teaching and went to live with the McClungs, she dedicated herself wholly to serious writing and turned her back forever on ephemeral journalistic writing. But this is contradicted by the record. While undoubtedly 1901 was a watershed in her life, she was by no means finished with free-lancing.[2] *Apart from her work for the* Courier *in the summer of 1901—which might be dismissed as undertaken for auld lang syne—in the fall of 1901 she began to contribute to the Pittsburgh* Gazette. *This morning newspaper, founded in 1786, was the oldest and largest in Pittsburgh. In 1901 it began to put out a Sunday edition, and George Seibel, who had been associated with the paper since 1896, was made editor.*[3] *During a*

1. Edith Lewis, *Willa Cather Living*, p. 54. For accounts of the circumstances of the invitation and Willa Cather's friendship with Isabelle McClung, see Brown, *Willa Cather*, pp. 93–98; Moorhead, *These Two Were Here*, pp. 48–51; and Sergeant, *Willa Cather*, pp. 25–26.

2. While it is beyond the scope of this book, recent and continuing research indicates that Willa Cather was contributing feature articles (in addition, of course, to stories and poems) to periodicals even after she had published several novels. See Bernice Slote, "Willa Cather," in *Fifteen Modern American Authors: A Survey of Research and Criticism*, ed. Jackson A. Bryher (Durham, N.C.: Duke University Press, 1969), pp. 23–62.

3. Seibel, p. 202.

period of slightly more than a year, Willa Cather wrote at least twelve pieces for him, three under her own name and nine signed "Henry Nicklemann." [4] *Nearly all were concerned with Pittsburgh places and people—celebrities and characters. One article, "A School for Servants" (April 13, 1902), may have derived from her new life with the McClungs, for they "had a great rich house, with plenty of servants, conducted in the lavish style of half a century ago."* [5] *More characteristic was "On the Christmas Side," reflecting her enjoyment of Christmas at the Seibel home, rich with old German traditions: "The South Side could teach the rest of the city how to keep Christmas. The native American population is comparatively small there, and representatives of the nations of Northern Europe have things pretty much to themselves. The northern people have been the only ones that have ever really known much about Christmas-keeping, and nearly all of its beautiful accessories, the fir tree and the child-loving saint and the bountiful sledge and reindeer, are of northern origin" (December 22, 1902).*

Seven of the twelve pieces appeared before Willa Cather went abroad in the summer of 1902 (see The European Scene, below). Three appeared in August and two in the issue of November 30. Almost exactly a year later, on November 29, 1903, came still another signed contribution: "The Hundred Worst Books and They That Read Them" (see Appendix III).

"The Philistine in the Art Gallery"

Willa Cather reported the seventh annual Founder's Day Exhibition at the Carnegie Institute Art Gallery in two articles, both signed "Henry Nicklemann." The first has obvious connections with "A Philistine in the Gallery" (see The Library, *above) and with "The Chicago Art Institute" (see Guest Editor of the* Courier, *above). The second, called "Popular Pictures," uses a different point of view to press many of the same issues.*

When the young art student visits the Carnegie gallery he is inclined to wonder what pretext the thousands of visitors who are not art students have for going there at all. They either admire the wrong pictures, he says, or the wrong things in the right pictures, or they see the entire collection of paintings with a distorted vision, so he argues that they had far better go to see *A Guilty Mother*, or confine themselves to some form of recreation better suited to their state of enlightenment. But the truth

4. John P. Hinz also attributes to Willa Cather "The Real Poe," signed "Gilberta S. Whittle" (which can be rearranged to yield "Willa Sibert"). See Hinz, "Willa Cather in Pittsburgh," p. 202.

5. Dorothy Canfield Fisher, quoted in Brown, *Willa Cather*, p. 96.

is that there are thousands of people who go to the gallery in family parties, who do not stand squinting before a picture, through half closed eyes, or making measurements with a lead pencil and who do not talk about "atmosphere" or "color scheme," who sincerely and genuinely enjoy the exhibit, and it is for their enjoyment rather than the young art student's that these pictures are gathered together. There is this year in the collection an unusually large proportion of those pictures which the most unpretentious Philistine can enjoy, pictures that are not only well painted, but which treat subjects which the Philistine thinks worth treating.

For the first time since the annual exhibits at the institute were inaugurated, there is, among the prize pictures, one which is universally popular. Hitherto Sergeant Kendall's "Mother and Child" was the most popular picture which had ever received a prize at the institute, but, in the regard of the people who come and go, it has been quite overshadowed by Ellen Ahren's portrait of an old lady sewing, which was awarded the medal of the class.[6] The Philistine may not notice how simple, and yet how wonderfully effective is the composition, one of those things which we see every day, and which only a master can force us to regard seriously, but he will see something that to him is more important than this. He will see a wonderfully thrifty, executive old woman, one who is the prop of a household and community; who has brought her own family up well and, if need be, could bring up her son's children; who could take up a business that was run down, or a family of children that had run wild, and institute order and discipline and thrift; a woman of strong prejudices and narrow of sympathy, tireless in energy and unsparing in the administration of justice; who, with more of common sense than imagination, has made a decent, practical, substantial success of living, though she probably sees very little worth while in Browning or Chopin. The Philistine will note, too, the successful coloring of the hair and the lines in the forehead, and the decision with which the old lady speeds the needle with her middle finger. Only yesterday afternoon I heard a typewriter girl, viewing the pictures in her half holiday, remark that the "old lady made her think of one of Mary Wilkins' short stories, somehow," and that is a comparison that the young art student himself would not have been ashamed of.

The picture, which was awarded the medal of the first class, is less fortunate. Will there ever be a first-prize picture of which our mothers and great aunts will approve? This "Arrangement" of Maurer's[7] they

6. Sergeant Kendall (1869–1938), American painter; Ellen Ahren (1859–19??), won the thousand-dollar Founder's Day Prize in 1900.

7. Louis Maurer (1832–1932), best known for his watercolors.

declare aimless and meaningless. "It's nothing in the world, Myrtle, but a girl sewing the binding on her skirt," declared the typewriter girl, in a tone of amazement and disappointment. The peculiar difficulties in the drawing, the remarkable painting of the white silk shirtwaist appealed not at all to Edna, the stenographer, because a shirtwaist is a thing of common use and how can it possibly have anything to do with art? She sees nothing in the picture simply because it tells no story, because her imagination finds no delight, no pleasurable suggestion in "skirt binding." If the girl were leaning over to pick up a child, or to solemnly burn love letters, or to weep beside a bier, both Edna and Myrtle would have found the picture resplendent with beauty, they would really have experienced pleasure in looking at it.

Tarbell's "Venetian Blind" did not fare much better at their hands; the painting of it puzzled and altogether confounded them. They wanted to know where the light on the model's shoulder came from, and twisted themselves into the most grotesque positions trying to illustrate that it could not possibly have fallen on her in that way, and that the painter "didn't know what he was talking about." It seemed, too, that from the name of the picture they had expected to find a Venetian scene of some sort, and felt unjustly defrauded of blue canals, etc.

Certainly the most popular picture in the gallery is Louis Deschamps' "Abandoned."[8] I shall be surprised if the artist does not sell the picture here. It is no exaggeration to say that there has never been a painting in the gallery which has given such universal pleasure. People of all classes and conditions of servitude, young and old, have stood before it with smiles and exclamations of pleasure. Not the young art student himself can derive more pleasure from the picture than the yearning grandmothers in old-fashioned bonnets and skirts that dip behind, who declare that they "want to take it up."

As a rule, the Philistine likes Gari Melchers, he catches the spirit of the painter's Dutch mothers and fisher folk as he did of James Herne's *Shore Acres*. I saw Edna's face light up as she came upon his "Wedded." Myrtle, indeed declared that the girl was insufferably ugly, and that the whole thing was horrid. "Nobody could say that girl is pretty as a picture," she remarked contemptuously, and thereby revealed much as to her attitude. The gory Segantini[9] Myrtle declared resembled a fresco at

8. Louis Deschamps (1846–1902), French painter.

9. Giovanni Segantini (1858–1899), Italian impressionist. In the next sentence: Edwin A. Abbey (1852–1911), had three pictures in the original collection, best known for his *Harper's Weekly* illustrations and his murals in the Boston Public Library.

the Alvin, and the Alma-Tadema she not undiscriminatingly remarked looked like Sarah Bernhardt. Edna was much impressed by the Abbey, and the splendor of the nobles and prelates made her more indignant than ever with the "skirt-binding picture," as she called Maurer's picture, and she suggested that it might do for [a] streetcar advertisement by some binding manufacturer. She enthusiastically admired Cecelia Beaux's disagreeable portrait, not for its exquisite painting, but for certain *Ladies' Home Journal*ish mannerisms that have become more and more marked in Miss Beaux's work of late years. Both girls heartily admired Chase's "Japanese Print." Surely Chase has the trick of pleasing if ever a man had it; "the fatal trick of pleasing," the young art student terms it, with a curl of his lip, but he has an old grudge against Chase because he pleases so unfailingly and paints so well. Chase never painted a bad thing, and the young art student knows it, yet nobody calls him crazy, and American millionaires buy his pictures, therefore, he is a thorn in the flesh of unappreciated genius. [November 17, 1901, p. 5]

One widely popular picture in the corner of the art gallery is Marianne Stokes' "Little Brother and Sister."[10] The picture is an illustration of the old Grimm fairy tale about the little brother and sister who were driven out into the forest by their cruel stepmother, and when they came to a brook and stopped to drink the brook cried out:

"Who drinks of me
A bear will be."

For the wicked stepmother had laid a spell on all the brooks in the forest. When they came to another, it cried out:

"Who drinks of me
A bear will be."

But the little brother was so thirsty that he must drink at any cost, and the picture illustrates the moment of his transformation. The little sister is at that age when nothing seems more natural than such a transformation, and she accepts it quite unquestionably, as Alice did the transformation of the Duchess's baby into a pig, her only expression being one of commiseration and a grave "I told you so."

It is well enough that Fritz Thaulow's picture of Pittsburgh is protected by glass, or before the exhibit closes the paint would be literally

10. Marianne Stokes (1855–1927), whose "Aucassin and Nicolete" hung in the gallery.

worn away by the pudgy fingers of the countless small boys, who surround it every afternoon, pointing out exact localities. The people who stand peering at this picture with puzzled expression feel something there which is not in the actual scene; a certain power of co-ordination, a certain revelatory treatment. We all knew that the mills on the South Side opposite Second Avenue were impressive, but why had we never noted the picturesqueness of the old cobble-paved streets and bald, green-shuttered red and brown houses on this side of the river, and why had we never perceived their striking and peculiar relation to the river and the flaming mills along and point that out to us?

Scarcely a man has gone through the gallery who has not paused for a long look at Tuke's "Diver,"[11] and the older the spectator, the longer he pauses. This is only another instance of how good a popular picture may be. I stood near a family party who were showing an old uncle from Greensburg through the gallery; at first the old gentleman seemed somewhat uncomfortable because of the presence of his young great-nieces, but when they wandered off to conjecture about the "Assault of St. Quentin," he smiled long and wistfully at the picture, now with his spectacles on his nose, and now with them on his forehead. I daresay he thought little enough of the original treatment of the water, or the splendid sunlight, or the painting of the fine, firm young flesh, or the hitch of preparation in the diver's shoulder blades, but he knew why the face of the boy in the rear end of the boat is as radiant with happiness as with sunlight, and he knew that the state of kings is small pickings to that of the diver. I accosted him, and we became friends on the strength of old memories of a common and a lost kingship.

Becher's "Italian Landscape,"[12] the somber Italy of Guelph and Ghibelline, blood-drenched and legend-haunted, meets with but little favor, and is usually supposed to be a scene on the Rhine, the Rhine being the one river in Europe of which the popular mind has become convinced. Aman-Jean's delicate and subtle "Comedy" is passed with equal carelessness. Mary Macomber's sentimental picture, "The Hour Glass," on the other hand, causes the populace to think better of the judges than it otherwise would do. Everyone stops to look at the old lady who is watching the hour glass. "The sands are almost run for her," remarked Edna in a subdued tone.

11. Henry S. Tuke (1858–1929), English painter of youthful nudes.

12. Arthur E. Becher (1877–19??), American painter and illustrator. In the same paragraph, Edmond Aman-Jean (1869?–1936), French painter; Mary Macomber has slipped into obscurity.

Both De Forest Brush's pictures, "The Silence Broken" and "The King and the Sculptor,"[13] are, of course, popular, as they are so largely story. People like them because they know something of the subject matter, just as people who are not at all musical often like Tschaikowsky's "1812" symphony [Festival Overture] because they recognize the strains of the "Marseillaise" and the Russian national hymn, and because it makes them think about the burning of Moscow and Napoleon's retreat from Russia.

Among the landscapes that are best liked are André's "Autumn Scene on the Seine," hanging over the staircases, and Birge Harrison's "Christmas Eve,"[14] representing a quiet village, shrouded in snow and a sort of holy stillness, under a blue winter night.

The most pleasurable feature about the exhibit is that so many of the pictures are by artists who have exhibited frequently before and with whose work and style the city has grown fairly familiar. "Did any manufacturing city ever evince any taste for art?" they say in the New York studios; "Can you make a city in the likeness of Mammon and then introduce art by inoculation?" The question can only be answered by time and patience, but in the meantime the thousands of people who troop through the gallery yearly are becoming familiar with the work and style of hundreds of the best painters of their generation. There are just three kinds of people who visit the gallery; those who enjoy simply and know nothing about the technique of picture painting; those whose enjoyment is marred by the consideration of what they ought or ought not to enjoy, and those who are so apprehensive that they might enjoy the wrong thing that they cannot enjoy at all. [November 24, 1901, p. 6]

"*Pittsburgh's Mulberry Street*"

The title of this article was intended to remind the reader of the work of Jacob A. Riis (1849–1914), whose first book, How the Other Half Lives *(1890), had portrayed the downtrodden of New York. Willa Cather had reviewed his next book,* Out of Mulberry Street *(1898), in the* Leader *"Books and Magazines" column. Of the author she wrote: "No journalist has worked at this mill with a steadier hand, or more observant and sympathetic eye." As for the stories, "They run the whole gamut of human impulse and emotion, from pity and love to jealousy, greed and murderous*

13. George de Forest Brush (1855–1941), whose portrait of President McKinley hung in the gallery.

14. Birge Harrison (1854–1929), American landscape painter.

hate, giving authentic glimpses into the homes and hearts of the people of every race that swarm on the East Side of the great city, speaking all tongues, but actuated by motives essentially the same on Mott or Mulberry Street as on Murray Hill. His latest book will widen Dr. Riis' audience and strengthen his reputation as storyteller and student of sociology" (Leader, *December 10, 1899*).

It was some time in the latter part of November several years ago that I went to hunt temporary quarters in the region of Pittsburgh's Mulberry Street for the purpose of collecting certain sociological data.[15] I remember that there was much dressed poultry in the windows of the butcher shops, and grocer's windows were full of oranges and white grapes, as it was near Thanksgiving. I finally got a room in Pride Street next door to the house where Biddle, the burglar, afterward took up his residence. The choice of a landlady in Pride Street is a delicate matter, and a feud with one is no trivial matter of shrewish words and annihilating glances. On the day that I took possession of my quarters, a colored preacher's wife had a dispute with a female lodger as to whether the rent was or was not due, and bit off the lobe of the woman's ear. Several members of her husband's church assured me that she was esteemed a lovable and Christian character. I took good care to be deferential to my Italian landlady.

I was awakened every morning by the heavy groans of the master of the house. He was an Italian stone mason, and it took half an hour of sleepy profanity to get him awake. After beseeching all the saints in heaven to relieve him of the cruel necessity of getting up, he cursed them roundly for their disobliging nature, and that put some snap into him. While he dressed he kept calling his wife a lazy hen and a stupid pigeon, reminding her that he had to get up and go out into the cold, while she stayed at home. As soon as he was dressed and before he put his coat or shoes on, he took a heavy drink of whisky, nearly twice as much as an ordinary whisky glass holds. By this time the odor of his breakfast and of his neighbors' breakfasts would fairly drive me out of bed. Such breakfasts as those people eat! Fried meats of every sort, onions and potatoes and chunks of rye bread.

While I was dressing I would see an occasional darkey hurrying down the hill with an old pea jacket or no overcoat at all over his swallow tail and an absurdly incongruous hat on his head. They were not gay revellers

15. It must be remembered that Willa Cather is speaking here as "Henry Nicklemann." See note 23, The *Library*, above.

escaping late from rosy chains, I found, but waiters hurrying to various hotels and restaurants where they were employed, and usually they beat the stone mason down the hill by half an hour.

At about eight o'clock Aunt "Minty" would come to put my room in order. She lived in the cellar under the house—it was only by a sort of charitable euphemism that it was called a basement. She was a very old, spare creature, with a wizened, apish face under her red turban, her limbs bent and distorted by rheumatism, but for all that exceedingly active. She had seen better days, as she expressed it, and she did me the courtesy to say that she knew good breeding when she saw it. She had been a slave and was reared by a family in Georgia of whom I knew something. After she had made my bed she liked to sit down on the floor before the grate and smoke her pipe, and talk about our neighbors, of whom she entertained no flattering opinion. She was glad to have a clean room to smoke in and glad to talk about the old estate on which she had been brought up and where I had once spent a week in hunting season.

The retail shops on the hill are open early. At half-past five and six half-dressed children are sent scurrying all directions for bread or meat or onions. The shopping hour for that region, however, is from nine to ten, when the matrons market for their families. Even in very cold weather they seldom wear bonnets, and though those November mornings were chilly, only an occasional woman wore a shawl. They never carry market baskets, but stroll from shop to shop, piling their purchases in their aprons; carrots, cabbages, cauliflower, potatoes or live chickens, it is all the same. The women one meets marketing are most likely to be Hebrews or Negroes; if neither, then they are sure to be either Italian or German. They do a good deal of gossiping and visiting while they are waiting for the clerk and turning over the vegetables. Sometimes they talk about their children, but usually they are discussing the shameful conduct of some other woman's husband and expressing their appreciation of her virtues. If she overhears them she is seldom grateful for their sympathy, and is apt to tell them that they are liars, and to apply various direct and expressive adjectives to them.

I saw two Amazonian combats during the few weeks I spent on the hill, but they were beautiful things, spirited and fought to a finish. One of the combatants, an Italian woman, the cousin of my landlady, lost enough hair during the fray to make a wig. This she gathered up and preserved, and when she had her hearing took it into court to prove the extent of her injuries.

The Thanksgiving marketing was fraught with unusual excitement. The shops had made some slight attempt at decoration or display. The chaffering with the clerks was for the most part good natured, and the only conspicuous ill humor was displayed by the surly wife of a Hebrew butcher. The lady must have weighed three hundred pounds and her husband boasted that she could eat five pounds of raw beefsteak for breakfast any morning. Her diet had somewhat ensanguined her disposition, and she went about threatening and offending and pushing everyone, a bushel of apples and a pumpkin and bunches of celery in her apron, her loose-hung jaws open. While Thanksgiving is by no means an established holiday among them, many of the Jewish churches and families observe it, if for no other reason than because they are always glad of any excuse to eat poultry.

There are probably more fowls eaten on Pride and Bedford and Wylie in a week than are consumed in all the East End in months. This marked preference for poultry results in a secret industry which I discovered for myself.

I had often noticed how many live fowls were inconsiderately carried about by their legs and stuck into aprons, and I had never been able to conjecture where they all came from, as the crates that always stand in front of the butcher shops seemed insufficient explanation.

In passing a Jewish grocery in that district, I had often noticed a particularly rank and noisome odor which seemed to rise from the grated cellar window in the sidewalk. As the window was boarded underneath the sidewalk, it seemed improbable that the odor, singularly vile even for Pride Street, could not come from the cellar. One morning while I was buying grapes from the little girl who tended the shop I heard a sound that startled me in that dark, ill-smelling, smoky room, the self-congratulatory, indolent "all's well" salute made by a hen who has just left her egg somewhere in the clean, fragrant straw of the stack, or the hay in the mow, a sound which she never makes except upon the accomplishment of her duty.

In a sudden inspiration, I told the girl I wanted a chicken, a live one, and that I wanted to pick it out myself. After considerable hesitation and a weak protest or two, she told me to wait until she came back. She lit the lantern and went into the living room back of the shop, where she disappeared through a trap door. I held my handkerchief to my nostrils and followed her. There, back under the pavement and out under the street was a subterranean chicken house, a sort of Plutonian farmyard. Excited by the light from the lantern, the fowls fluttered and shrieked, and the air was heavy with dust and down and stench.

There must have been three hundred chickens in all. There were roosts for them in the middle of the cellar and piles of corn and cans of water. Along the sides of the wall were a series of nests, little caves cut back into the earth. The darkness, when not relieved by the lantern, was absolute; the poor fowls were as far from light as though they had been muffled in black velvet.

Yet I afterward learned that dozens of little chickens were hatched out in that cellar every spring and grew to maturity and laid eggs of their own in that Stygian blackness, surrounded by that damp, sour-smelling earth. The poultry business has always seemed so inevitably associated with wind and sun and open air, farmyards and cattle and work horses and barn fellowship, that there was a sort of unnameable horror clinging about this chicken pit, over and above the odor, which was horror enough. The creatures all seemed contented and stupid enough, but they must have had their moments of dull hennish frenzy, for there were holes scratched in the earth, full deep enough to bury a hen.

The two specimens the girl caught for me were fat, flabby-looking birds, with whitish feet, and were covered with vermin. There are more than several of these chicken cellars within the radius of a mile, though they are carefully guarded from the health authorities.

Social life on the hill is at its height in the afternoon, and on Sundays and holidays, such as Thanksgiving and Christmas, everyone who is not calling is being called upon. In warm weather the guests are usually entertained on the three or four steps that lead from the sidewalk to the front door. The women, and especially the colored women, are exceedingly informal about their dress, and often go calling or promenade the sidewalk in lace trimmed dressing sacques and colored silk underskirts.

Almost every day a street piano would find its way up the hill and there was a sudden raising of windows and opening of doors, for there is a keen appreciation of ragtime in Pride Street. Even the pale-eyed people who, like Aunt "Minty," live in the basements and cellars, will come forth like Lazarus at the first note of the "Holy City" or "Coal-Black Lady."

Occasionally in May, when the sun manages to be seen on this side of the smoke, and the trees, that are surrounded by green painted boxes and manage in some way to get moisture from under those flinty cobblestones, are in their leafing time, and a street piano is playing a lively air in front of a saloon, Pride Street manages to put on quite a recognizably springlike aspect.

On winter evenings, about four or five o'clock, there are always a number of fires lighted in the middle of the street. Any shopkeeper who has an empty barrel or box contributes to it. Around these fires the newsboys usually loaf, and the boys who have been sent out on errands, and an occasional broom seller, or paper-flower vender, and usually an umbrella mender and a scissors sharpener. Not infrequently a darkey who has received too warm a reception at home joins the circle and cracks jokes to assure his neighbor that he is not henpecked. Often when one fire dies out the crowd moves on to another, and it would be hard to say where some of them go when all the fires are dead.

The very little boys, who are young enough to wear some of their sister's cast-off clothes, like nothing better than to get a few matches and sticks and a wisp of hay and make a fire of their own. I have seen many a Rubens study of that sort up there. Two ragged little manikins who have never said "hello" to a bathtub, will bend for a quarter of an hour over a handful of sticks, and when at last a murky flame breaks out they will rise and clinch their hands and throw out their chests with a manful cry of triumph. There seems to be in every boy a sort of echo of glee of our hairy ancestors when they lit their first fires in a new cave and founded a new house. If it is not to be accounted for by transmitted tendency, it is not easy to explain a child's peculiar sense of victory and satisfaction at merely making wood kindle. [December 8, 1901, p. 5]

"*The Hotel Child*"

During the month of August 1902, while Willa Cather was in Europe, three articles by her appeared in the Gazette. *Two were derived from other pieces. "Lives in a Streetcar All Year Round" (August 24), about an eccentric gentleman in Sewickley and signed "Henry Nicklemann," re-used material from "A Houseboat on the Land" (see The* Library, *above). "The Strangest Tribe of Darkest England" (August 31) drew on "The Canal Folk of London" (see The European Scene, below), which had appeared in the* Journal *on August 3. "The Hotel Child," which appeared under her own name, with "Special Correspondence Sunday Gazette" in parentheses beneath it, might have been stimulated by her travel abroad, although the first paragraph points to Pittsburgh hotels.*

The hotel-bred child occupies a unique place in the wide democracy of childhood. He has experiences, afflictions and consolations all his own.

He exists everywhere, in all countries, wherever there are cities of considerable size. In New York, Washington and San Francisco he exists by the thousand; in Pittsburgh, which is for many reasons one of the most home-staying and domestic of cities, he is much less in evidence. One finds him here chiefly at the Schenley, the Monongahela House and the Seventh Avenue Hotel. Yet it is erroneous to say that one finds the hotel-child at all, for one of the most remarkable peculiarities of his existence is that he is neither seen nor heard, that he is as invisible as the elf people that live under the hills.

The hotel-child has, of course, a notoriously bad reputation; his mere existence is denounced, resented, concealed and even denied. Dean Swift himself was not more bitter against the young of the human species than the most mild and amiable people sometimes become on the subject of the hotel-child. In summer hotels, where he is necessarily present, he is subjected to the most humiliating slights and discriminations, and he will kill the reputation of a city hotel more certainly and effectively than people who are obviously disreputable.

I once heard the president of a children's flower mission say that she would rather live in a hotel infested by rats than one infested by children. It is a noticeable fact that the child's natural friends become his enemies when he lives in a hotel. They consider him out of his proper environment.

Many of the peculiar afflictions which beset the life of the hotel-child come about through this inexorable necessity of "keeping dark." He is a thing of odium in the corridors, he is not permitted in the parlors or reception room, nor in the dining room, except on his birthday or occasionally at lunch time. If circumstances are favorable and he happens to be in a venturesome mood, he may annex one or two of his small friends and slip down to the parlors when the guests of the hotel are at dinner. There he furtively tries all the sofas and easy chairs, skips from figure to figure over the carpet patterns, slips on tiptoe into the writing room and experiments with the pens and note paper.

He never remains very long, however. Either an anxious nurse who has been gossiping appears, or else a boy in the livery of the house, who whispers a magic word in the children's ear and they vanish like frightened little ghosts at cock-crow.

Children who live in a hotel are necessarily confined a great deal to their own rooms, and there they are permitted to indulge only in quiet games. As a result they depend very largely on their imagination for diversions and their fanciful powers thrive under their imprisonment. Like old John Bunyan, they dream dreams which would never have come to them in a state of freedom. I once knew a lad of twelve living at a Washington hotel who perpetually played that he was the Scottish pretender living in disguise in London and so accounted to himself for his state of hiding and soothed his vanity for the many and obvious slights put upon him.

In his hotel, children were allowed to ride upstairs only in the freight elevator, so it behooved them, if they expected any favor, to keep on very good terms with the colored man who ran the passenger elevator. Once when this boy was trying to wedge himself between two trunks in the freight elevator the passenger elevator boy called out: "Come over here, youngster, I'll take you up." When we got off at the boy's floor, he remarked to me in the most dignified manner: "That darkey is a gentleman."

His nurse is the hotel-child's worst bane. He is compelled to have one long after his years and dignity resent it, long after boys who live in the open have dispensed with theirs. He has, too, a nice sense of discrimination in the matter of nurses. If she is a French girl he endures her petty tyrannies with some sense of consolation; he believes that there is, after all, something rather distinguished in having a French nurse. He can at least say that she is a governess and tell the little girls that he only has her in order to learn the language. But if she is an American girl his sense of injustice is keen, and if she is colored he is full of dull resentment. But he tastes the dregs of the cup only when she is Irish—when she calls him "darlin'" and the other boys imitate her brogue.

In any case his life is a sort of perpetual death watch. If she is faithful he never breathes or smiles except under her surveillance. She is always there, always ready to brush, wash or comb; always ready to report to his mother, to say "hush!" and to remove from him "the means of all annoyance." To dodge her, to lose her, to trick her is the fascinating problem of his life. He warms toward her only when he can work upon her to bring him contraband sweets or permit him to have ice cream for his dinner.

The children's dining room is another perpetual source of humiliation to him. Unless he is exceptionally hungry he never enters it without a sense of indignity. He is always confident that everything worth eating is consumed in the big dining room downstairs and that the children's menu is nothing but various preparations of baby food. He groans when the nurse asks him whether he will have tapioca pudding or sliced orange for dessert.

The most envious moment of his life is when one of the older little girls is considered big enough to eat with her father and mother downstairs. She is put into her first stays and has her hair done up on her head and goes down in the passenger elevator attired in a dress longer than those in which her companions knew her. All the children on her floor peer out to see her go down the hall in solemn state, her head very high, her arms very stiff.

Of course the hotel-child has his daily outing. Usually he takes a walk with his mother in the morning and accompanies the nurse when she goes out to do errands in the afternoon. But there is one unnatural restriction laid upon him which weighs heavily. Whatever other children may be, a hotel-child must not be dirty or in any respect ill kept. His shoes, his clothes, his hair, his face and hands are subjected to constant attention. This oppressive neatness takes the brightness from the sunlight when he walks in the park, and the greenness from the grass. The snow, however white, the puddles, however deep, the mud, however thick and smooth, are not for him. The *plaisance* of boyhood is denied him and the ground is accursed for his sake. Even out of doors he feels that he is some way still surrounded by an impalpable case of some sort, tight and clean, that shuts him from the air. He spends his life in a sort of glass prison; very gay, very full of people and excitement, of flowers and music, but still a prison, and the out-of-doors is merely an adjunct conservatory.

There are, of course, compensations in the life of the hotel-child. To begin with, his life is deliciously exciting. He is placed in the midst of changing winds and crossing currents, a sort of great telephone exchange where hundreds of live wires cross and he manages to get a gentle shock from each of them. He is in a village packed under one roof, and he knows something about everyone in the hotel. He is keenly alive to changes and sensations. He knows what women do not like each other. He manages in some way to find out what boy's father is dissipated. He knows when a girl becomes engaged and whether her fiancé sends her candy. He never thinks much of one who sends only flowers. He hears from somebody's nurse when any of the young men have lost heavily in the bucket shops. He is prodigiously interested in singers or actors who happen to stop at his hotel and forms a corridor acquaintance with them if they are affable. He is intensely excited when there is a dance at his hotel, and sometimes he is permitted to go down to the ballroom to look on and hear the music for a time. And afterward there is no tiresome carriage ride and getting home when one is sleepy, no dull evaporation of his pleasure from getting his wrap on and off; he has only to take the elevator to reach his room and his bed.

The child's friendships are largely diplomatic ones. He pays court to such of the old ladies as would be likely to invite him to their rooms for afternoon tea, and he behaves charmingly to the nurses of pretty little girls whose mothers are very particular. He is ready to fetch and carry like a bellboy for such of the young men as keep horses, and sometimes will take a boy out in their cart. He makes flattering confidences to the head-waiter downstairs, so that if he slips into the dining room with an elaborately concocted message for his father he will not be snatched up at the door and sent off with a bellboy. He exerts all his powers of fascination upon the day clerks in the office, hoping to be graciously received when he goes down in the morning to ask whether there is any mail for his mother.

There is always some man about the hotel among the transient or permanent guests who is the hero of the little boys. Sometimes an army man who happens to be there for a few days, sometimes a retired naval officer who is living there, sometimes a young man of leisure who is reputed as a sportsman and in whose room there is the skin of a tiger that he shot himself. If this young man chances to smoke a bubble-bubble and wear a red fez and dressing gown in his own room, then his picturesqueness, according to the boy's notion is quite complete. If he can extract a gracious "good morning" from this hero, his heart thumps with pride.

If the hotel-child happens to fall ill he becomes suddenly quite an important personage. All the nice old ladies and the pleasant young men come to ask after his condition, with flowers and books and toys. But if he should be so unfortunate as to develop a contagious disease he early finds out the shallowness of friendship and the shyness of pity. If his presence in the hotel was resented when he was well, it is now the topic of general reproach. People are sorry for him, doubtless, but they are much more afraid of him. His floor is deserted, the nice old ladies could not be dragged past his door; the young man who shot tigers is the only one who is brave enough to come to inquire about the boy. Even the waiters who bring his mother her meals put the tray by the door and make haste to be well down the hall before she opens it.

People are frightened if the boy dies and resentfully impatient if he has the pluck to become convalescent. His mother always brings him out too soon to suit the kind old ladies. If he is so careless of the public weal as to have diphtheria or scarlet fever there is usually a panic of timorousness and selfishness in the hotel.

I was once stopping at a Denver hotel when a child died there of diphtheria. The proprietor and health officer were inclined to mercy, but the women stopping at the house almost mobbed the office. They consulted together and laid their demands before the proprietor. As a result the little girl was buried four hours after her death and the casket was lowered by ropes from the windows of the sixth story, as the stairways of the house were literally guarded by desperate and panic-stricken women. If the child's mother had been the mother of a criminal she could not have been more systematically shunned and left alone. [August 10, 1902, p. 4]

"*Poets of Our Younger Generation*"

This signed article for the Literary Section of the Gazette *was stimulated by Josephine Dodge Daskam's essay, "The Distinction of Our Poetry," which appeared in the* Atlantic Monthly (*May 1901*). *Willa Cather accepts Miss Daskam's central point but adds to it the notion that the preoccupation of American writers with form parallels developments in French poetry. The title of the article was taken from the book by William Archer, currently being reviewed: an anthology of poems by thirty-three young British and American poets, chiefly British, for Archer deferred to Edmund C. Stedman's* An American Anthology, 1787–1900 *in respect to a more complete collection of the Americans. All the poets mentioned in Cather's article, except the Canadians Carman and Roberts and the newspaper poet Post Wheeler, had a place in Stedman's anthology. A few months after the appearance of this article, in late April 1903, Willa Cather published a collection of poems,* April Twilights. *Reviewing the volume in the* Gazette *on April 26, 1903, George Seibel called it "a book of genuine poetry in unpretentious guise," found a perfection of form reminiscent of Gautier, and noted that she "disdains luxuriant words, and with homely Anglo-Saxon syllables paints pictures that will not fade."*[16] *Seibel placed Willa Cather in the tradition of poetry that she respected, the tradition that she defined in this article.*

The tendency, the distinction and the hope of contemporary American verse were admirably defined by Josephine Dodge Daskam in an article published in the *Atlantic Monthly*, May, 1901. It is not exactly to Miss Daskam that one would have looked for so able a piece of literary analysis;

16. Quoted in *AT(1903)*, p. xxi. In a letter dated April 28, [1903], Willa Cather thanked Seibel for the review. Letter in the possession of Mrs. George Seibel, Capitola, California.

her facility has seemed to lie rather in other lines and her early and uninterrupted success has, perhaps, somewhat prejudiced people of conservative opinion in literary matters. There is, however, in this article on "The Distinction of Our Poetry" nothing of the flippancy we are wont to expect from a young author whose productivity taxes the resources of publishers' presses, but every evidence of deep insight and mature judgment.

Miss Daskam names Emerson and Thomas Bailey Aldrich as the two men who first distinctly exhibited the tendencies which characterize the newer school of American poetry.

The schoolboy is taught that Bryant was the first American poet who was able to rid himself of English traditions and write of the flowers and hills and rivers of his own country, rather than of those familiar to him only through his study of English classics. But there is a deeper and less easily demonstrable truth which the schoolboy cannot be expected to comprehend—that a poet may write of American rivers and mountains and Indian tribes without infusing into his work any perceptibly national essence, that he may even write intensely patriotic poetry which is not even measurably national.

Beyond question the majority of our earlier poets showed very few of those qualities which seem to be, and which ought to be, the tendency of American verse of today. Longfellow, Bryant, Holmes, Lowell and even Whittier for the most part endeavored to apply the methods and sentiment of English poetry to their New World environment. During the last thirty or forty years America has nationalized intensely, and during this formative and intensive process has been written the verse which would seem to indicate something of the nature of the future poetry of America.

The dominant characteristics of this newer school of verse, which is wholly the outgrowth of our national life, are perfection of form, intensity of spiritual experience and extreme temperateness and delicacy of expression. Our present tendency, probably our ultimate and final tendency, is toward the shorter forms of verse, chiefly the lyric.

From the very beginnings of our verse this lyric inclination, coupled with a certain delicately temperate and almost reserved expression, has been evident. It is doubtful that American verse will ever be stormy, florid, abandonedly emotional or prodigal in color. It is equally doubtful that it will ever exhibit that tone of scholastic reflection or the traditionally pastoral strain which characterize so much of English verse. The classics of earlier ages occupy no such place in our life as they hold in that of the

English man of letters. We are more deeply concerned about even the small things of the present than the large things of the past.

One respect in which our poetry seems developing along the lines of the French masters of the lyric form is perfection of execution. Let who will cavil of carving cherry stones, it is the perfect thing, however small, that outlasts the ages wherein faulty epics are entombed without memorial. Mr. Aldrich's "Memory," a little masterpiece of ten lines, Emerson's "April," Poe's "To Helen," and Sidney Lanier's "Into the Wood[s] My Master Went"[17] will outlast many of the more ambitious efforts of our earlier poets. It was in these four poets, indeed, that the fundamental tendencies of our newer school of verse first found expression.

The two most typical representatives of this seemingly national tendency in verse, among the poets of the younger generation are probably Bliss Carman and Miss Louise Imogen Guiney. In England and Germany George E. Woodberry is believed to exemplify it strongly, and, in England, Mr. Lloyd Mifflin and Miss Lizette Woodworth Reese are believed to have rendered the movement stout service.[18]

Of Bliss Carman it is difficult to speak without prejudice, for he is altogether made up of contradictions. He is, I believe, a Canadian by birth, but like Charles G. D. Roberts[19] he has come to be regarded among the poets of our own nation, as he is of our own soil. He still suffers in the regard of serious people from having posed in his youth as the "poet of joy" and from having affected a good deal of superfluous bohemianism. Both he and Richard Hovey, along with their study of French literature, acquired a certain trick of attitudinizing which is manifestly as absurd in an Anglo-Saxon as it is natural to and pardonable in a Latin. But the days when Mr. Carman gave us *Songs from Vagabondia* are past, and his later work, though sometimes baffling, is usually sincere and often noble. Of his several volumes the one entitled *By the Aurelian Wall* is the most uniformly excellent and is entirely free from the touch of bravado and willful frivolity which detracted from much of his earlier work.

His poem on the death of Robert Louis Stevenson, included in this volume, is one of his most successful, and has appealed deeply to the

17. The title of the Lanier poem, of which this is the first line, is "A Ballad of Trees and the Master."

18. Lloyd Mifflin (1846–1921), editor and diplomat, wrote *Fields of Dawn and Later Sonnets* (1900). Lizette Woodworth Reese (1865–1935), whose most recent book of poems was *A Quiet Roadside* (1896). For Bliss Carman, see Books and Authors (I), "The View from Red Cloud," Books and Authors (II), and "Two Poets," Books and Authors (III), above. For Louise Imogen Guiney, see note 17, Books and Authors (IV), above.

19. The Canadian-born Roberts (1860–1943) published *New York Nocturnes* in 1898.

multitudinous lovers of that exquisite craftsman whose literary personality has laid hold upon this generation in a manner so singularly intimate. The poem is a long one and it is possible to quote but a few stanzas:

O all you hearts about the world
  In whom the truant gypsy blood,
Under the frost of thin, pale time,
  Sleeps like the daring sap and flood,

That dream of April and reprieve!
  You whom the haunted vision drives
Incredulous of home and ease,
  Perfection's lovers all your lives!

You brethren of the light heart guild,
  The mystic fellow-craft of joy,
Who tarry for the news of truth,
  And listen for some vast ahoy,

Our restless, loved adventurer,
  On secret orders come to him,
Has slipped his cable, cleared the reef
  And melted on the white sea-rim. . . .

The verses written on the death of Paul Verlaine, which appear in the same volume, have a wider significance than that of a mere personal appreciation. They express, I think, very subtly the attitude of the younger American artists toward the art of the old world, their guiltlessness of any inclination to patronize, their catholic sympathies and willingness to take whatever is good, judging clemently what is evil, their conviction that a rose is still a rose, whether it be grown on a muck heap or in the river-watered meadows.

Not much we gave you when alive,
  Whom now we lavishly deplore—
A little bread, a little wine,
  A little Caporal—no more.

Here in our lodging of a day,
  You roistered till we were appalled;
Departing, in your room we found
  A string of golden verses scrawled. . . .

Excellent as are these verses, it is in Mr. Carman's out-of-door verse that he is most truly a poet. I would give all of his mystifying philosophy and even his literary appreciations for one of his lyrics of the Canadian woods, the blue-misted hills and the valleys where the autumn maples mark the trail of his Scarlet Hunter.

The striving for perfection in form which is so evident in much of our verse of the last half century, is not only a hopeful thing, it is a reassuring evidence that our later verse is really of us, a thing indigenous to our soil and growing out of the larger trend of our national life. Certainly, taking all things into consideration, we insist more strongly upon good workmanship than any other nation in the world, and we are more fruitful in ingenious contrivances. Even our humblest manufactured products are better made than those of England. The French, our only rivals in this nicety of construction, send out better finished goods for the American market than they supply to their own.

This deftness in mechanism is evinced not only in our mechanical contrivances and in the heating and lighting of our houses, it has been from the first, and is becoming more and more one of the dominant characteristics of our art. Our painters are perhaps chiefly remarkable for their absolute mastery of their medium, the sureness and freedom of their technique. To realize how indisputably this is true one has only to examine the American pictures purchased by the French government for the Luxembourg Gallery. In the room devoted to foreign art the pictures by Whistler, Alexander, Sargent, Ben Foster and Winslow Homer[20] are conspicuous for their technical excellence and in this respect are comparable only to the work of the masters of modern France.

This passion for perfect form is also, if not equally, true of the best of our verse writers. In the achievement of excellence in expression and the mastery of meter none of our younger poets have equaled Miss Louise Imogen Guiney. In the mere matter of meters there seem to exist no difficulties for her. She has performed metrical miracles so deftly and so apparently without effort that only close study reveals their astounding complexity. But this is the least of her excellencies—if it can ever be the least of a singer's. She, I believe, more than any of her fellows, has evinced that nobility of conception, that fervor of sentiment admirably controlled and exquisitely delicate, which chiefly gives individuality to the best of

20. Not previously mentioned: John White Alexander (1856–1915), painter from nearby Allegheny, best known for his portraits of literary men and theatrical personalities; John Singer Sargent (1856–1925); Benjamin Foster (1852–1926), American landscape painter.

our verse. Take the following poem, which she calls "The Vigil at Arms":

Keep holy watch with silence, prayer and fasting
Till morning break, and all the bugles play;
Unto the One aware from everlasting
Dear are the winners; thou art more than they.

Forth from this peace on manhood's way thou goest,
Flushed with resolve, and radiant in mail;
Blessing supreme for men unborn thou sowest,
O knight elect! O soul ordained to fail!

There is no black flaunting of modern pessimism here, no bitterness affected, no rhapsodic exaltation of failure. The sentiment, calm and submissive to decree as it is, might be Emerson's own. It is one of those things which, he said, the centuries have taught us.

"The Kings," which is even more exalted in sentiment, is too long for quotation. Miss Guiney has a singular power of adapting her meters to her subject, so that the mere melody of her verse often takes the color of the sentiment and interprets it as the accompaniment does the air of a Schubert song. Take this, which she calls "Hylas":

Jar in arm, they bade him rove
Thro' the alder's long alcove,
Where the spring hid musically
Gushes to the ample valley.
(There's a bird on the under bough
Fluting evermore and now:
"Keep young!" but who knows how?)

Down the woodland corridor,
Odors deepened more and more;
Blossomed dogwood, in the briers,
Struck her faint delicious fires;
Miles of April passed between
Crevices of closing green,
And the moth, the violet-lover,
By the wellside saw him hover.

Ah, the slippery sylvan dark!
Never after shall he mark
Noisy ploughman drinking, drinking,

On his drowned cheek down-sinking:
Quit of serving is that wild,
Absent, and bewitched child,
Unto fiction, age and danger,
Thrice a thousand years a stranger.

Fathoms low, the naiads sing
In a birthday welcoming;
Water-white their breasts, and o'er him
Water-gray, their eyes adore him.
(There's a bird on the under bough
Fluting evermore and now:
"Keep—young!" but who knows how?)

It would be difficult to find anything more pertinently and beautifully suggestive than the refrain in parenthesis at the end of the first and fourth stanzas. We have not many such lines to our credit as the first four in the last stanza. On a first reading one might say they recalled something of Keats' vividness, but of what a graver color, and how infinitely more restrained!

There is a little poem of Miss Guiney's, called "Temperance," which I quote, not only because the sentiment is characteristic of herself, but because it is strikingly the temper of nearly all our best contemporary verse:

Take Temperance to thy breast
While yet is the hour of choosing
As arbitress exquisite
On all that shall thee betide
For better than fortune's best
Is mastery in the using
And sweeter than anything sweet
The art to lay it aside!

There is in all Miss Guiney's verse a marked lack of sensuous beauty, a marked absence of anything approaching to floridity, a sort of gentle, tolerant asceticism, tempered by her close sympathy with everything fresh and fragrant in nature. As she says, the rose appeals to the veriest clod, but only a fine perception lingers about the "noble peace" of scentless flowers. This poetry, spiritual rather than sensual, restrained rather than abandoned, intense rather than diffuse, seems to be that which we are destined to contribute to Anglo-Saxon literature. From the first our verse writers have had little to do with roses and raptures, or with lilies and languors; they have found a delight more exquisite, a passion more colorless but exhaustless, a beauty less apparent but more noble than those which have aforetime so often stirred the senses and fired the pens of poets.

Lloyd Mifflin has confined himself almost exclusively to the sonnet form, and has certainly written more good sonnets than any one of his contemporaries. There seems to be, however, no place in literature for the mediocre sonnet, and many of Mr. Mifflin's are scarcely more than that. There are few of his sonnets which are sustained throughout or which do not contain lines that were evidently written simply because the form demanded a certain number of lines. . . .

The sonnet, because of its inviting puzzlingness, and because of the popular notion that it is not bound to mean anything in particular, is a form which often tempts the dilettante, but nowhere is an amateurish hand more lamentably made manifest. Because its rhythmic form entails a certain vagueness, only a strong feeling, a hot conviction, a keen purpose can arrive unjaded at the end of the fourteen lines. One of these, Lizette Woodworth Reese must certainly have had when she wrote her sonnet on Keats:

> An English lad, who, reading in a book,
> A ponderous, leathern thing set on his knee,
> Saw the broad violet of the Aegean Sea
> Lap at his feet as it were village brook. . . .

Charles G. D. Roberts is one of the few men who have learned by slow degrees to write good poetry. Nothing could be further from promise than his first two volumes [*Orion and Other Poems*, 1880; *In Divers Tones*, 1887], which were both pedantic and imitative. Some of his later verse, however, is wonderfully beautiful; rich in expression and redolent of wood life and field life, of Canadian forests and meadows.

In the poetry of nature I should be inclined to give Joseph Russell Taylor a high place.[21] I think we have no one now who quite equals him in the power of woodland picture-making, of definite landscape coloring in words. There is a freshness and unconventionality in his treatment of nature that makes his verse distinctive. He has got so far away from all the platitudes of singing brooks and sighing pines that one feels a sort of nakedness and unprotectedness among these actual forests, these hot, fern-clad glens, these rainy mountain heads of his.

21. Joseph R. Taylor (1858–1955), a classicist at Boston University.

Mr. Taylor's passion for bird life is evident in most of his verse. From his poems one gets the ancient feeling that there is some unexplained relation between us and our feathered brethren, and that in consulting them the Attic soothsayers did more than perpetuate a laughable superstition. Writing of the flight of birds in the early morning, Mr. Taylor says:

> Over our drowsy heads,
> Death-beds and bridal-beds,
> Over the human hush,
> Swallow and sparrow and thrush.
> Over our life, if life be sleep,
> Hear my voyagers laugh and weep,
> Pipes of passage!

In the matter of taste American verse seldom errs. Our saving grace of humor, which is perhaps the most fruitful and hopeful of our literary attributes, generally shields us from the humiliation of becoming passionately or mawkishly ridiculous. This saving grace, however, was denied one of our most gifted contemporary verse writers quite as completely as it was denied Edgar Allan Poe. Madison J. Cawein[22] certainly possesses more fervor than most of our younger poets; he has a strong romantic bent, a luxuriant fancy, and, when he bestows the least care upon his work, a rare melodic faculty. Surely there came to his christening some unbidden and evily disposed fairy who so foully endowed him that the splendid gifts of her sisters should be well-nigh useless to him. William Archer, the English critic, affirms that Cawein has no sense of style whatever. It is scarcely too much to say that in taste he is almost entirely deficient. Much of his work is marred by excesses which indicate a lack of the most ordinary sense of propriety. Even the least scrupulous reader will not countenance such sentimental distortions of language as this:

> A mist on the deep that was ghostly,
> A moon in the deep of the skies;
> And the mist and the moon they were mostly
> In thee and in thine eyes.

George Edward Woodberry[23] has published comparatively little. To those to whom he appeals at all he appeals most intensely. There are not

22. Madison J. Cawein (1865–1914), whose most recent book was *Shapes and Shadows* (1898).
23. For Woodberry, see "Yeats and Housman," Books and Authors (IV), above.

a few students of poetry who find him cold and visionary, rather wanting in humanness, but every honest critic must admit his conscientious and graceful execution. However much he may lack in vividness, however studied some of his verse may seem, he certainly shares the spirit which animates the work of the newer school of American verse writers. His latest volume, *Wild Eden*, contains not a few lyrics which are genuine contributions to our literature. . . .

In any extensive article on our younger verse writers it would be necessary to comment at length upon the work of Richard Burton, Miss Alice Brown, John Vance Cheney, Clinton Scollard, William Vaughn Moody and Miss Josephine Preston Peabody,[24] though none of these writers are so typical as those from whom I have quoted.

Then there is the innumerable throng of newspaper poets, nearly all of them fettered to timely topics, except, perhaps, Post Wheeler.[25]

One fact seems clear: the trend of our poetry today was foreshadowed in the work of our best lyric poets of yesterday, and it exhibits to a very perceptible degree the salient characteristics of Emerson's verse. Certainly he, more often than many readers of verse ever realize, wrote with the pen "Which on the first day drew, / Upon tablets blue, / The dancing Pleiads and eternal men." [November 30, 1902, p. 24]

24. Richard Burton (1861–1940), whose *Songs of the Unsuccessful* appeared in 1900; his *Songs of Brotherhood* was reviewed by Willa Cather in the *Leader*, November 11, 1899, p. 9. Alice Brown (1858–1948) subsequently wrote the biography of Louise Imogen Guiney. John V. Cheney (1854–1921), author of *Poems* (1901). Clinton Scollard (1860–1932) in 1900 published *Lawton* and *Ballads of American Bravery*. William Vaughn Moody (1869–1910) published *Gloucester Moor and Other Poems* in 1901; and Josephine P. Peabody (1874–1922) published *Fortune and Men's Eyes* in 1900 and *Marlowe* in 1901.

25. Post Wheeler (1869–1956) published *Love-in-a-Mist* in 1901.

The European Scene

(*July 13, 1902—October 19, 1902*)

In mid-June of 1902 Willa Cather and her friend Isabelle McClung left Pittsburgh to spend the summer abroad. This first European tour was, as Edith Lewis has written, "a great imaginative experience."[1] *For someone like Willa Cather, "there is nothing quite like that first encounter with European culture on its own soil, in its age-old stronghold—it is a home-coming more deeply moving and transfiguring than any home-coming to friends and family, to physical surroundings, can ever be." The record of this journey has been preserved in a series of travel letters written for the* Nebraska State Journal.

In 1956 the letters were collected and edited by George N. Kates, and published under the title Willa Cather in Europe: Her Own Story of the First Journey.[2] *Although Mr. Kates stated that the text was published unaltered except for standardization of spelling and punctuation and "a few occasional small changes necessary for sense," some solecisms were emended and there were a number of omissions and other alterations in wording.*[3] *Consequently, in order to make available a more accurate text, the letters are reprinted here exactly as they first appeared in the* Journal, *except for the inserted words shown in brackets and the emendations listed on pp. 969–970. Extra space between paragraphs indicates where a bar appeared in the* Journal. *Each letter was signed either "Willa S. Cather" or "Willa Sibert Cather." The signatures are omitted here.*

"*First Glimpse of England*"

The twenty-sixth of June, the day that Willa Cather and Isabelle McClung landed in Liverpool, was to have been the coronation day of King Edward VII and Queen Alexandra. However, the coronation was postponed until

1. Lewis, *Willa Cather Living*, p. 55.
2. New York: Alfred A. Knopf, Inc., 1956.
3. For a list of the more significant alterations and omissions, see A Note on the Editing, pp. 967–969.

August because of the illness of the elderly monarch, who had been stricken with appendicitis. As in other selections in this chapter, the Journal *headline is used as a title.*

LIVERPOOL, Eng., July 1.—(Special Correspondence.)—On the 26th of June Liverpool presented such an array of color, flowers and banners as very nearly disguised the grimness of the city itself. We arrived at about 8 o'clock of the most radiant of June mornings, and our drive to the Northwestern hotel was under canopies, arches and flags. From pillar to pillar along the sidewalks ran chains of paper roses for miles. Everywhere hung pictures of the king and queen. The shops were all closed, and workingmen were standing about the streets, yet there was a palpable shadow in the air that did not belong to a festival. Even had the news of the king's illness not reached us at Queenstown, we would certainly have recognized symptoms of discomfiture in the streets of Liverpool. Moreover, in hundreds of places the silk draperies which bore the inscription "God Save the King" had been torn down and others substituted with the legend "God Raise Our King."

The Northwestern hotel at which my friend and I stopped is directly opposite the public square and St. George's hall, which is by far the finest building in Liverpool. The square was a sheet of blazing sunshine that morning and the Union Jack everywhere fluttered and tugged in the wind. A blind man with a concertina played national airs at the foot of a colossal statue of the Duke of Wellington that stands on a column 115 feet high. The "bobbies" were lined up on the steps of St. George's hall and a few red coats with their caps perched at their favorite jaunty angle and short canes under their arms came and went among the groups of people who thronged the square. A group of girls with their hair hanging loose over their shoulders and the most strident voices imaginable, sold flowers at the foot of an equestrian statue of Queen Victoria, done in bronze by Thornycroft when the empress was a young woman.

Although the whole effect was remarkably gay, there was nothing of the smartness and neatness and trimness of an American crowd. The square as a whole presented a beautiful variation of line and color, but the majority of the individuals who made up these dark splotches on the yellow plane were far from lovely. The dress of English women, and of English men of the working class is frankly a shock at first, no matter how catholic one may be in such matters. I have been in England a week now, and I have not seen one English girl or woman of the middle class who is not stoop-shouldered to a painful degree, or who does not stand with her chest sunk in and the lower part of the torso thrust forward. Even in the little, little girls one sees the beginning of it. The topping of the shoulders and contraction of the chest. This unfortunate carriage is so universal that it amounts to a national disfigurement among the women. Girls with [the] skin of a rose and well featured enough have the figures of riddled old dames. Their dress is almost as remarkable. The American idea of neatness, of being genuine as far as you go, of having little and having it good, which at home even the shop girls imbibe more or less of, prevails not at all here. The streets are always full of badly made, home concocted silks and satins and lawns and dimities. No shirt waist is complete without a daub of penny lace on it, no skirt is correct unless it trails in the back, is too short in front and is a cascade of draggled ruffles and flounces. The railway trains are full of young women traveling in white muslin, white stockings and white shoes. Their hats are something beyond belief. Hats have never at all been one of the vexing problems of my life, but indifferent as I am, these render me speechless. I should think a well taught and tasteful American milliner would go mad in England and eventually hang herself with bolts of green and scarlet ribbon—the favorite color combination in Liverpool. The flower girls have nothing in their trays half so brilliant as the blossoms on their bonnets. The English working girl and especially the country girl has a passion for cheap jewelry. She wears the most unblushing frauds of this sort even to the extent of half a dozen breastpins at once. However, I am not at all sure that I would be willing to exchange the pretty voice; after hearing only English voices for a few days, the first American voice you hear in a boarding house is very apt to suggest something of the nature of burrs or sandpaper.

On the afternoon of the 26th we went to see the poor of Liverpool fed at St. George's hall, just across the street. The lord mayor and lord mayoress had arranged to dine all the worthy aged poor there in honor of the new king's ascent to the throne, and in accordance to the king's wish that all the coronation festivities in which the poor were to receive gratuities should be carried out, the great dinner was given on the day set for it. There were over five hundred guests entertained in all, each of the guests being over sixty years old and some upwards of ninety. The dinner consisted of roast beef, vegetables, plum pudding, beer. As the guests left the hall they were each presented with packages of tea and sugar and the men with plugs of tobacco. While the old folks were eating, Mr. Roberts, organist of St. Paul's, played the coronation march written by Mackenzie for the coronation of Edward VII, and afterward "Zadoch, the Priest," one of the suite of four numbers written by Handel for the coronation of George II and Queen Caroline.

Constant comparisons are the stamp of the foreigners; one continually translates manners and customs of a new country into the terms of his own before he can fully comprehend them. There are so many thoroughly engaging and attractive things about English life and people, that it is not a little satisfaction to be able to say to one's self that in no American city could be nurtured such an array of poverty and decrepitude as filed into St. George's hall on that holiday. They seemed worn to the bone, some of them and all of them had had a sixty years' tussle with poverty in a land where the competition is exceedingly close. There was very little sullenness, however; they seemed as eager and pleased as children and as the caterer's men, all in white duck, carried huge cauldrons up the street and into the side door, the long line of the poor inhaled the savory odor from the kettles with smiling satisfaction.

Every old dame who had a red rag of a flower in her black bonnet was happy. The tickets which admitted guests to the hall had been distributed by the vestrymen and the guardians of the poor. Of course a great number of people arrived who had no tickets, hulks of drunken old sailors whom you see everywhere in Liverpool, poor old women who had every one an excuse, but never a ticket. When the cooks and their cauldrons arrived and the odor of the food whetted their appetites, some of them became quite desperate and tried by every means to smuggle themselves into the happy ticket line, fairly clawing at the bobbies who gently put them back. Some sat down on the steps and cried bitterly into their aprons; some railed upon the falseness and futility of human institutions in general. When we came out from the hall half an hour later they were still there, held by that tantalizing odor; scolding, crying, sulking, so old and tired and poor that one's heart went out to them who had not on the wedding garment. The cause of their misfortune was not apparent; perhaps they were professional beggars; perhaps they had bad records behind them, but their age was evident enough and their hunger, and when at last the bobbies drove them even from the steps, one could not help regretting their defeat.

The feeling of sympathy for the king seems to be a very genuine one. Most English people think he has not been altogether justly used. They believe Queen Victoria should have abdicated twenty years ago when she retired to nurse her private sorrow. These twenty years, they say, Edward has been doing the sovereign's work with none of the sovereign's perquisites. The evidence seems to be very much against the American notion that the king's life has been one rosy path of wine and song. A detailed account of the daily routine the king has gone through for the last twenty years rather staggers one. He embodies many of those qualities which the English people esteem most highly. He is a good sportsman, he can do a great deal of work without making any display, his personal courage is as unquestioned as his generosity. Even his extravagant taste for boxing and the turf endear him, not only to the smart world, but to the common people as well. His son, the present Prince of Wales, is the antithesis of his father and is exceedingly unpopular. He is said to be foppish and effeminate to the last degree. [July 13, 1902, p. 4]

"*A Visit to Old Chester*"

For a discussion of Maurice Hewlett, who is referred to in this letter, see "John Buchan and Maurice Hewlett," Books and Authors (IV), above.

CHESTER, July 1.—(Special Correspondence.)—Chester, which is considered the quaintest and most picturesque of all English towns, is about fifteen miles from Liverpool on the river Dee, in the region of where the sand bars are wide and the tide treacherous and where the fishermen still hear Mary calling her cattle home. The town is planted at the foot of the wildest of the Welsh hills, and is one of the oldest in England. In the business part of the town the streets are nearly all called "rows," that is, the second story of each building is built over the side walls and forms a sort of roof, being supported by heavy posts. Many of these buildings have endured from Elizabeth's time, some are even older, and when new ones are built they are put up in exactly the same manner. The dwellings are many of them very handsome, especially Eaton hall, the summer place of the duke of Westminster, which lies about six miles out. The chief charm of the town, however, lies in the dwellings of the common people. They are quaint red brick houses, the majority of them very old, with diamond window panes and high walled gardens behind. These high walls, the red brick beautifully toned and colored by age and overgrown with ivy, tea vines and Virginia creepers, form one of the chief beauties of these gardens. A hedge of holly or alder trees often rises even above the wall, which is seldom less than twenty-five feet high. Then there is always the matchless English green of the sod, the gravel walks, the fern bed, poppies and pale iris growing next the wall, and the apple and pear tree, under which the family take their afternoon tea.

The walls of Chester mark the boundaries of the old city, though now they simply form an oblong in the middle of the town. The exact date of their erection is not known, but they were probably built in the reigns of Elizabeth and James on the site of the walls of the mediaeval town. They are of red sandstone and are about thirty feet high. A rail has been put along one side and the top of the wall is now used as a promenade and forms a delightful walk from which you can look down into the walled gardens. The whole circuit of the old walls is about two miles. At the northeast corner is the Phoenix tower from which Charles I witnessed the defeat of his troops on Rowton moor, just outside the town walls. Before the arrival of the king, the city, which was one of the most loyal in the west, had stood a long siege by the parliamentarians. The citizens were reduced to eating all their cats and dogs, and every silver coin was cut into four pieces and stamped with the city arms, each fraction representing the value of a whole coin, to remedy the contraction of currency. When the king relieved the town it was only to see his forces routed outside the walls and Cromwell's enter the gates.

Hawarden castle, Mr. Gladstone's old residence, lies about six miles from Chester and lies back in a magnificent park about a mile from the village of Hawarden. The village is one of the prettiest and quaintest we have seen, though nearly all of it lies on one street. Nearly all of the cottages are thatched and overgrown with dog and climbing roses, while the yards are full of the most delicately tinted tea roses, roses that grow, not on bushes, but on rose trees from five to eight feet high. The new castle, as the Gladstone residence is called, is a nineteenth century building which came into Mr. Gladstone's possession on his marriage with Catharine Glynne, the heiress of the estate. This Miss Glynne was a direct descendant of Hugh Lupus, a cousin of William the Conqueror, who came over with the Normans and was given by William a large tract of land covering what is now known as Cheshire and Shropshire. It was this same Hugh Lupus who built the so-called "old castle," which forms the chief beauty of Hawarden. Of this only a splendid Norman tower, half its original height, roofless and ivy grown and a section of the wall that led from the keep to the living apartments, remain. The tower was built about 1075, but was repaired and restored and used as a fortress as late as 1664. This never has been out of the possession of Lupus' descendants, and was one of the strongest garrisons in the long struggle with the Welsh just across the border. The Welsh often saw fit to raid the rich plains of Cheshire, and a goodly number of troops were always kept at this garrison. My friend and I spent half of a June day in almost utter solitude at the foot of the tower. There is a sort of wall about it now that follows the line of the old moat. Generations of oaks have grown up over the site of the living rooms of the Norman baron. The hill on which the tower stands is wooded from top to base, and the solitude is so complete that the birds are nesting in the old loop holes of the keep. The rains and winds of a thousand years have given the masonry of the tower a white, clean-washed look, like the cobble stones of the street after a shower. One can understand, lying a morning through at the foot of the Norman tower, why there are Maurice Hewletts in England. The temptation to attempt to reconstruct the period when these things were a part of the living fabric of the world, is one that must necessarily assail an ardent imagination. The brighter the day, the greener the park, the more deep the significance of their ghost of Saxon oppression, the more mystically it speaks of "far off, old unhappy things, and battles long ago."

The Baron Hugh Lupus, who built this tower overlooking the swampy forests about the Dee, built the oldest part of the beautiful Chester cathedral. A man well on in years at the time of the conquest, and having blood enough on his conscience, he determined to found a religious house at Chester. He decided to introduce the Benedictine order from France, and sent to the great churchman St. Anselm, asking him to come over from Rouen and organize his church and cloister. Now there was at Chester an old Saxon church and a very holy one, where the remains of St. Werburgh reposed. St. Werburgh was the daughter of a heathen king of the Mercians who was buried in what is now Herefordshire. During the second Danish invasion, when the Danes were ravaging all the churches in their path, the daughter of Alfred the Great, who had devoted herself to a religious life and had founded a church at Chester, hearing that the Danes were approaching Hereford, dug up St. Werburgh's remains and mounting her palfrey rode over with her train to Chester. Here she reinterred St. Werburgh's remains in her own church. When St. Anselm arrived in England, he and Hugh Lupus decided upon St. Werburgh's shrine as the site for their Norman church. It was on St. Anselm's return from this mission in the west that William Rufus called him to be archbishop of Canterbury. The original Norman church was quite as large as the present cathedral except in height. Through the twelfth, thirteenth, fourteenth and fifteenth centuries, builders have built over and under and around the Norman church and destroyed most of it. Two sections of the original wall with their round arches, and the bases of many of the pillars are still to be seen. These enormous pillars are not made of single stones, but of large stones fitted together with perfect symmetry into a sort of thick stone tube, the hollow center of which was filled with smaller stones and mortar. This largely explains why so little of the Norman ecclesiastical architecture is left, as the super-imposed weight in time forced these composite arches apart. The building is of the soft red sandstone found all about Chester.

The cloister is perhaps the most beautiful part of the building to one who has never lived in a Catholic country. Its utter peacefulness in the afternoons I spent there, the Norman wall with its half-effaced designs on which the eyes of unfaith gaze in bland astonishment after a thousand years, the rain that fell so quietly or the sun that shone so remotely into the green court in the center, with its old, thick sod, its pear tree and its fleur-de-lis, they made the desirableness of the cloister in the stormy years seem not impossible. Without Norman and Saxon butchered each other, and poachers were flayed alive and forests planted over the ruins of free holders' homesteads, but within the cloister the garden court was green, the ale went to the abbot's cellar, and the venison to his table, and though kings were slain or communities wiped out the order of prayers and offices and penances was never broken.[4]

Among the hundred interesting features of the cathedral, there is an odd bit of English history built into the stone of the choir. In the thirteenth century, during the reign of Edward I, the monks were finishing the north side of the choir, and beautiful work they made of it, with their pointed arches of fluted stone beautifully toned by their own shadows. When King Edward came up to make war with the Welsh, he and his queen stopped at the monastery and appropriated its revenue for his campaign.

4. George N. Kates considered that "the meditation first evoked here in an English medieval cloister" would continue to the end of Willa Cather's life, coming to full expression in *Death Comes for the Archbishop* (1927) and *Shadows on the Rock* (1931). It was the inception of a line of development extending even to "her last, unfinished story," set in the Palace of the Popes at Avignon. Kates, ed., *Willa Cather in Europe*, pp. 14–15.

Consequently the south wall of the choir is of cheap and shallow workmanship and shabby finish, representing exactly the period of poverty the monastery endured because of the king's extremities. Further on the old rich style is resumed again. [July 20, 1902, p. 11]

"*Out of the Beaten Track*"

Willa Cather's discovery of A. E. Housman and her delight in his work already have been recorded (see "Old Books and New [October 1897]," The Home Monthly, *above, and "Yeats and Housman,"* Books and Authors *[IV], above), so it is not surprising that she and Miss McClung left the "beaten track" for Shropshire. Later on, in London, the two young ladies and Dorothy Canfield called on the poet in his lodgings in Highgate; but the visit was not a great success from anyone's point of view.*[5] *A more felicitous souvenir was Willa Cather's poem, "Poppies on Ludlow Castle," which appeared in* April Twilights.[6]

LUDLOW, Shropshire, July 11.—(Special Correspondence.)—The beaten track of the summer tourist in England, from Chester to Warwick, Warwick to Stratford on Avon, and Stratford to London, can be soon learned and, luckily soon avoided. Shropshire, one of the western shires which runs along the Welsh border, is the source of Mr. Housman's little volume of lyrics entitled, "A Shropshire Lad." Anyone who had ever read Housman's verse at all must certainly wish to live awhile among the hillside fields, the brooklands and villages which moved a modern singer to lyric expression of a simplicity, spontaneity and grace the like of which we have scarcely had in the last hundred years. The remoteness, the unchangedness and time-defying stillness of much of the Shropshire country perhaps explains Mr. Housman as well as its own singularly individual beauty. Shrewsbury is almost the only town in the shire which is ever visited at all by foreigners. The town is almost surrounded by a loop of the Severn, which is nowhere more green and cool and clear, and nowhere more indolent and inaudible in its flowing. The broad meadows across the stream from the town are those on which Housman says that boys played football in the days of his boyhood, and as we sat beside the Severn looking across to the fields, who should come racing out over the green but a company of lads with their pigskin ball. It was in these meadows, by the way, that the boy Darwin played football and did his first botanizing

5. For an account of the visit, see Brown, *Willa Cather*, pp. 105–109.
6. *AT(1903)*, pp. 41–42.

when he was a pupil at the old boys school founded in Shrewsbury by Edward VI. There is a large bronze statue of him standing now before the old school building, today used as a library. I went to Shrewsbury chiefly to get some information about Housman and saw the old files of the little country paper where many of his lyrics first appeared as free contributions and signed "A Shropshire Lad."[7] There was one copy of his book in the public library, but no one knew anything in particular about him. By doing some telegraphing to his London publishers, getting his London address, etc. we unintentionally created quite an excitement before we left the town, and several gentlemen, who have local reputations as being well read to sustain, called on us to ask for the name of his publisher, etc., and were greatly astonished to hear that the book had been selling in America for six years.

It is some twenty miles south of Shrewsbury, however, that one comes upon the real Housman country and enters the real rural Shropshire. Mr. Housman himself describes it as:

In valleys of springs of [and] rivers,
By Ony and Teme and Clun,
The country for easy livers,
The quietest under the sun.

We arrived in Ludlow about six o'clock one afternoon, and drove through noiseless streets to our hotel. The town is a place of some 3,500 inhabitants, somewhat smaller now than it was in Queen Elizabeth's time. High green hills rise to the north and west, all marked off into tiny pocket handkerchief fields bordered by green hedge rows and looking like the beds of a large hillside garden. To the south lies the valley of the Teme, with low, round hills on either side, none of them wood covered. The Teme is a narrow stream, even for an English river, not more than twenty feet wide anywhere, with the meadow lipping it on either side and the hay grass dipping into the water when the wind is high. There are no naked straggling clay banks; the river does not flow through the bottom of a ravine, but on a level with the fields, like a canal, and it runs deep and green and clear and quiet under its arched stone bridges. On either side of

7. "As far as I know, none of the poems in *A Shropshire Lad* ever appeared in any newspaper or periodical before being printed in the book in 1896. I know of none [Housman] ever wrote for a paper in Ludlow, or any ever signed 'A Shropshire Lad.'" William White, quoted in Bennett, p. 244. See also William White, "A Note on Scholarship: Willa Cather on A. E. Housman," *Victorian Newsletter*, No. 13 (Spring 1958), 26.

it are the pollard willows to which Mr. Abbey,[8] the painter, so utterly lost his heart when Harper Brothers sent him into rural England in his youth to make some drawings for them. They are never more than twelve feet high, with a trunk perhaps three feet thick and little round bushy tops that make them look very much like the painted trees of the antediluvian world that are always found in toy Noah's arks. Beside this river, on the top of a cliff over a hundred feet high, rise the magnificent remains of Ludlow castle, once one of the most important and always one of the hotly contested fortresses in the kingdom. This cliff side, from castle wall to river brink, is now sort of hanging, tipped endwise, and from rock to rock the ivy hangs powdered over with huge bouquets of blooming alder trees and climbing dog roses with stems and suckers of fabulous proportions.

There are very few modern homes at all in Ludlow. Many of the shops were shops in Queen Anne's time and many of the more impecunious people live in houses that have been patched up since Queen Elizabeth's day. The Feathers hotel at which we stopped was named for the Prince of Wales' crest and was a flourishing inn before Elizabeth came to the throne, and was used as a sort of overflow house for such guests as the castle could not accommodate. Almost the entire interior is of black oak with huge beams across the ceiling, and all the windows are the tiny diamond panes. The entire ceiling of the dining room is carved with the arms of various lords of the western border, and about the great fireplace is a mass of intricate wood carving culminating in the work above the mantel where [the] star of the order of the garter and its creditable motto are cut the size of a tea-table top. My sleeping room overhangs the street and I walk up an inclined plane from the dresser to my bed, but for all that I never expect to sleep again in a place so beautiful. The knocker on the spike studded outer-door alone would make a house desirable. No one comes here except the country gentlemen about, when they ride into town, or folk who bicycle over from the neighboring towns of a Sunday. The only other guests beside ourselves who seem established here are a theatrical couple from London, who are spending their honeymoon here, and, as they are desirous of solitude, we never encounter them except at meals or occasionally in some willow thicket along the river where they have embowered themselves. A bicycling pair from Chicago came in the other day, propped their

8. For Edwin A. Abbey, see note 9, The *Gazette*, above. For the singer David Bispham, mentioned below, see note 44, The Musical World (II), above.

Baedeker against the water bottle at dinner, read it madly aloud, then departed with a little whir and a little cloud of dust and into the quiet of the Teme and the misty hills that is never broken except by the chimes that ring the quarter hours so melodiously one is glad to have them pass, and, three times a day, play the whole of some old English air. I heard a chime, at Evesham, which played the whole of "Drink to Me Only With Thine Eyes," more rhythmically than anyone but Bispham can sing it, and played it always in the most unusual and uncanny hours when the whole performance seemed supernatural.

Mr. Housman is by no means the only singing Shropshire lad; Sir Philip Sidney courted the lyric muse there long before him. Ludlow Castle was magnificently renewed and enlarged by Sir Henry Sidney, his father, who was made governor of the border under Elizabeth, and Philip spent the formative part of his boyhood and youth in that country which is surely the country for the making of poets if ever one was. The ruins of the great hall built by Sir Henry for the council of the governing heads of Wales, and of the extensive chambers and banqueting halls built for the entertainment of his royal sovereign and her peers tax the imagination; they so far surpass modern notions of splendor. The most interesting part of the castle, however, is the keep itself, which was built by Joce de Dinan, a Norman knight, who also built the circular chapel, dedicated to St. Mary Magdalene, which is the only one of its kind left standing in England. The castle and its lords played an exceedingly prominent part in the wars of the roses, as it was the place of residence of Richard Plantagenet, Duke of York, and the two sons of Edward IV, who were afterward murdered in the tower, were reared and educated there. Their two adjoining rooms, with their little fire places, are still pointed out. There Prince Arthur, son of Henry VII, died, leaving his wife an inheritance to his brother, Henry VIII. But the prettiest chapter of the castle's long history is an early one, dating back to the day of its Norman founder, Joce de Dinan, which is beautifully told by a fourteenth century chronicler. Joce de Dinan had a mortal foe, Walter de Lacy, who was also a stalwart knight, and one morning in a combat which took place by the river below the castle, de Lacy and two of his companions were taken prisoner and confined in the keep. They were well treated and permitted to dine with the household and one of de Lacy's knights, an Arnold de Lisle, won the affection of a little French maiden, Marion de la Bruyere, who was being reared in Joce de Dinan's household. She effected his escape by tying sheets and towels together and his lord escaped with him. Some nine months afterward Joce de Dinan went away to marry his daughter to a young lord, and left the castle in charge of fifty knights, going himself secretly. Poor Marion, who had not seen her lover since the day of his escape and who was by this time well nigh desperate for loneliness, sent a message and a rope ladder to Arnold, telling him the weak state of the garrison in order to persuade him to come to her. He came and went with her to her apartments in the unguarded side of the castle that was protected by the precipice, but after him came a hundred armed knights up the ladder, and they slew the garrison in their beds and put to the sword every vassal of de Dinan, every man, woman and child in the town nestled below the castle. When Marion of the Heath arose next morning she opened her windows and saw the smoke of the burning village and dead men lying by the wall. She caught up her lover's sword and ran it through his breast and threw herself from her window down the side of the cliff that is now so white with dog roses and alder bloom. [July 27, 1902, p. 11]

"*The Canal Folk of England*"

From this letter, Willa Cather derived an article, "The Strangest Tribe of Darkest England," which appeared in the Pittsburgh Gazette *on August 31, 1902.*

LONDON, July 16.—(Special Correspondence.)—Every American traveling in England gets his own individual sport out of the toy passenger and freight trains and the tiny locomotives, with their faint, indignant, tiny whistle. Especially in western England one wonders how the business of a nation can possibly be carried on by means so insufficient. The one great canal in the west answers this question and largely takes the place of the freight car, affording a circuitous but continuous passage from Liverpool to London. From the Mersey river, which forms the Liverpool harbor, the canal runs west to Chester, a distance of about fifteen miles, then forty-five miles southwest to Shrewsbury, then east to Birmingham, and from there southeast to London.

This canal, which is owned by several companies and called by several names, is altogether different from an American canal; it is in every way smaller, quieter, less obtrusive, seemingly not to be greatly depended upon, but in reality quite as reliable as anything we have. It is nowhere more than thirty feet wide, and winds so obsequiously among the green meadows that but for the hedge beside the towpath one might lose it altogether. The boats are of two builds; the largest are about seventy-five feet long and fifteen wide and carry a cargo of about fifty tons. These are called barges or bachelor boats, and are manned by a crew of four men, no women being allowed in the crew. They carry grain, pig iron, wrought iron and heavy or bulky freight. I saw one loaded to the water edge with bridge frames from the United States Steel company. These boats are drawn by a single horse only, but always a draft horse of powerful build. These larger ones are the only boats on the canal that are taken to Liverpool to be loaded. They are taken into the great ship canal at Elsmere Port, and some fourteen of them are hitched to a tug, and dragged through the heavy swell of the Mersey, which almost buries them entirely, to the Liverpool harbor.

The larger are greatly out-numbered by the smaller and lighter "flats." These boats are as long as the barges but are of lighter build and nowhere more than five feet wide, their capacity being only thirty tons. They are loaded so heavily that they just avoid dipping water, though the canal is as still as only stagnant water can be. These boats receive their cargo at Elsmere Port, as they would immediately be overturned in the impetuous tides that sweep up the Mersey. Neither barges nor flats have even a pretense of a deck. The cabin is a sort of dugout, exactly five by six, and the remaining space in the boat is every inch of it given up to the freight, which is stowed in from the top, very much as it would be in a row boat. When the cargo is once in place, heavy sheets of oil cloth are drawn over it and tied down. While this method of stowing and protecting a cargo from the weather may look insecure to a landsman, every sort of merchandise from perfumes and fruit to upright pianos are shipped thus.

These narrow boats, of which there are nearly three thousand now running on the canal, are responsible for a peculiar sect of people, an element in the British working classes little heard of outside of England. If Darwin had wished to study further the part played by environment in the differentiation [of] species, he could have taken no better subjects than the canal people. Originally the boatmen were Englishmen, with all the earmarks of the British working man. They have become a solitary and peculiar people who have not their like in the world, an Englishman only in his speech. He is a sort of half-land, half-water gypsy, a vagabond who manages to keep within the trace of labor, a tramp of one road, the best paid and worst nourished manual laborer in the kingdom.

In the stern of each flat there is a cave-like cabin, five by six, and in this cabin live, winter and summer, the boatman, his wife, and anywhere from two to ten children. One of the managers of the Chester division of the canal told me that it had scarcely ever occurred in his time that the son of a boatman had followed any other than his father's calling. The shackles of caste were never more adamantine among the Hindoos than these people have made them for themselves. The men invariably wear the same cap and corduroy trousers, and the women are never seen without their peculiar headdress, which is seen nowhere else in England, but which closely resembles that of the women in some parts of Italy. These women are quite as good boatmen as their husbands, and take the more difficult of the two principal tasks, managing the tiller while their husbands follow the towpaths. She does this, too, with half a dozen children clinging to her skirts. In addition to managing the tiller and tending the children she does what housekeeping can be done in a box six feet by five and just high enough to stand in. In this cave there is a stove, a table on hinges, a berth which is let down from the wall and in which the boatman and his wife sleep. The berth is too short to admit of their lying straight, but the boatwomen assured us that it was quite comfortable to sleep doubled up when you got used to it. The boatwoman seldom carries a change of clothes, and neither she nor her husband undress when they go to bed at night, but kick off their shoes, wearing their clothing as faithfully as an animal does his fur. The managers of the company insist on a certain show of cleanliness, and the walls and floors of the cabin are usually scrubbed until they are white as wax. Both the men and women have a passion for brass; they stud the walls of the cabin with brass-headed tacks and collect brass cooking utensils and candlesticks greedily.

My interest in the canal was aroused the first night we spent in Chester. A number of flats were tied up at the lock house waiting to be lowered to the level, sandy plains about the river Dee. In the course of a walk we came accidentally upon that part of the canal which runs under the Northgate street bridge, at the bottom of a cut seventy-five feet deep in the solid rock. The cut is narrow and on either side the red sandstone walls rise sheer, loops of wild vines hanging from the crevices, yellow sweet clover growing here and there, and the tops of both cliffs overhung by that species of tall, bushy alder tree, white with bloom, that makes

English gardens so beautiful in early summer. At the foot of these red cliffs, in the green black water that reflected the walled gardens high above it, we saw these long gondolas of trade, with those brown, foreign looking men and women eating their dinner on top of the dug-out cabin. The lock-keeper afterward told me that the cut had often been painted and sold as "A Quiet Waterway, Venice." When the canal people had finished their dinner and rinsed the dishes off in the canal, the men struck off for the public house and their women began to dress to go into town to witness the coronation festivities which came off, coronation or no. They dressed in the open air, in the vestibule to their cabin, probably because it was cooler there than in the cabin itself. Our gaze disconcerted them not at all; their backs and breasts and arms were as brown as the darkest Neapolitan's. The woman nearest me, when she had made her toilet, dressed her little boy in his first trousers, which she had made on board for him, and when he whined to have his hands in his pockets she threatened to put his petticoats back on him, quite in the fashion of decent, land-staying mothers, though the lock-keeper said she would be as tipsy as a soldier when she got back. Like all the boat-women, this woman had been born in the cabin of a flat, had been a baby and had all her childish ailments and grown to maidenhood shut in a box 5 × 6, with half a dozen brothers and sisters. She had been courted and married somewhere between the tiller and the tow-path, tied up at Chester or Birmingham and spent the night at a public house by way of a honeymoon, and borne her children in the cabin where she herself was born. But the canal boat woman certainly does not consider herself unfortunate. She is fond of her children, but the fact that they clamber all over the top of the boat like monkeys and nimbly jump from stern ashore to gather buttercups, never alarms her. She had the same dangerous playground. "If they lose their holt, they kin ketch by their toes," she remarks. When the children are a little older they will do practically all the work, and she and "him" as she calls her husband, can lie all day on top of the hot oil cloth that covers the cargo and smoke their pipes or quarrel over their bottle, as they feel disposed. The boat-woman likes to get pleasantly tipsy and lie without any feeling of responsibility and watch the green fields and little towns go by, and she can do this as soon as the children are old enough to be pressed into service. That is her season of roses. But when her boys have learned to manage a boat well, that is to say, when they are about eighteen years of age, they marry some boatman's daughter and take the management of a boat of their own. There is never any question about a son's getting his own boat: no man who was not born on one of these frail, cramped crafts can ever manage or live on them, and the demand for boatmen grows every day. As soon as her daughters are fifteen some boatman's lad hurries them into marriage. When a boy gets a boat of his own he must have a wife to avoid wasting his earnings on a hired helper. Only a boatman's daughter can help him at his work and endure the hardships of his life. When he takes his wife to his new boat, a trail of boats follow him through the night singing and carrying lanterns hung on poles. This is his wedding march. When he dies they lay him out in his cabin, shut the door and tie a black rag on it, carry him to the end of his run, where they bury him. It is not exactly his native earth, for he was born in a cabin, but is the part of the earth with which he was most nearly connected; the place where he tied up at night, and where he found his favorite public house; in short, literally and metaphorically, it is the end of his run.

When the sons and daughters are all married the boatman and his wife must take up the management of the boat again, when they are old and stiff and given to drink. These old couples were the only discontented people I saw on the canal. They have neither the consolation of education nor religion. Not one in a hundred can read, and they are the most frank and unabashed of pagans. The old lock keeper at Chester had several long talks with me about the extent of his responsibility for their poor souls. To use his words spoken with the deepest and most sincere melancholy, "They won't listen to the Bible, howsoever I try 'em. They don't fear an awful God, much less trust a loving Savior." The lock keeper, a very thin, pale man and a covenanter, cannot speak of this aspect of the boatman's life without deep emotion. He spends a great deal of time silent in the sunshine on the lock house porch, his eyes closed, but not asleep, and I am inclined to believe that he is often praying. He has his worldly ambition as well, and it seems a queer one enough. One morning when he was clipping his hedge he told me that he saved a little money each year to one end: After he got his eight daughters married off, and his wife comfortably settled for old age, then his turn was to come, and he was going to imagine himself "a young lad, again, mayhap," and start off with reverential awe to see—Niagara Falls! "The mightiest revelation of the Almighty left us now-a-days, as I take it."

But, unlettered as they are, the boatmen are apt enough at getting what they want out of life. The finer aspects of their peculiar culture have puzzled the government detectives for years. The boats carry a great deal of liquor and the lock keeper explained to me that the boatman loads on his cargo at the bonded warehouse, takes with it a sample of the same liquor, the bottle shut in a glass case and sealed with a long inscription stamped into the wax. On the trip the boatman can take seven buckets full of whisky out of each barrel and yet deliver it stronger than the sample. The cleverest detectives have never yet found their means of adulteration.

The old lock keeper, being a man of conscience and reflection and "having daughters of his own," grieves a good deal over some of the uglier aspects of the life of the barge girls. He said he had got good places for them and prevailed upon them to go out to service time and again, but they can not endure either steady work or in-door life. The girl always runs away to marry the boatman's lad who beat her with his fist when she was a little girl and who will beat her with his fists again, and her children after her. No more will the boatman quit his boat. He has been a gypsy from his cradle. He follows his mule and smokes his pipe, winding through fields and woods, a pagan, letterless, lawless, godless, who tramps up and down through the heart of England, yet mingles not with Englishmen. "The road to perdition" the lock keeper called the tow path, but it is surely the fairest road that ever went there, though we hear tell that many of them are fair. It is a path that runs by shadowed woods and the sweetest hay fields in the world, that is sown with buttercups and scarlet poppies, that is skirted by hedges, and runs neighborly with full, quiet rivers. We began our acquaintance with the canal at Chester and tested the tow-path, we found it again at Shrewsbury, crossed and recrossed it on the way to Birmingham, followed it through the Avon country, slept near it at Evesham; and when we were running into London, a wilderness of bigness and newness and strangeness, between the bulk of warehouses, from the maze of streets, emerged the canal, a part of the country side lost in London, and we welcomed it like the homely and trustworthy face of an old friend, good to see in this glitter of things untried. [August 3, 1902, p. 11]

"*Seeing Things in London*"

Willa Cather and Isabelle McClung spent three weeks in London; they were joined there by Dorothy Canfield,[9] *and it was during this period that they paid the call on Housman referred to above.*

9. Willa Cather to Mariel Gere, August 28, 1902.

LONDON, July 22.—(Special Correspondence.)—When I came to London two weeks ago my first endeavor was to avoid that part of the city given over to pensions and lodging houses, and to make it possible to live in a part of the city that the folks quartered in, Russell and Mecklenberg squares or about the British museum. We managed to find a very comfortable and satisfactory little hotel patronized chiefly by folk from the country who come to town to do their modest shopping on King street, off Cheapside. That puts us within two squares of the Bank of England and the lord mayor's residence, almost under the dome of St. Paul's, and on the same street up which Lady Jane Grey daily went to meet her judges at the Guildhall. The lord mayor still goes up to the Guildhall by the same street, and he drives by our windows daily in scarlet and gold. This is rather the bargain counter end of London; by no means extreme, like the Whitechapel section, but the part of town where one is always among the common people; small tradesmen, shop girls, clerks, people who go a-shopping with slender purses, young men who aspire to be men of fashion on small salaries. We came here because we wished to be in the heart of the old City of London, within walking distance of the Tower, Old Bailey and the Temple, but the living city and not the dead one has kept us here and the hard garish, ugly mask of the immediate present drags one's attention quite away from the long past it covers. One starts out at 10 o'clock, before which hour of the day no shops or buildings are open, to make pilgrimages in the orthodox fashion, but one ends by merely watching the procession with perplexity. If the street life, not the Whitechapel street life, but that of the common but so-called respectable part of the town, is in any city more gloomy, more ugly, more grimy, more cruel than in London, I certainly don't care to see it. Sometimes it occurs to one that possibly all the failures of this generation, the world over, have been suddenly swept into London, for the streets are a restless, breathing, malodorous pageant of the seedy of all nations.

But of all the shoddy foreigners one encounters, there are none so depressing as the London shoddy. We have spent morning after morning on High Holborn or the Strand, watching this never-ending procession of men in top hats, shabby boots, ragged collars; they invariably have a flower in their button-hole, a briar pipe between their teeth, and an out-of-the-fight look in the eyes that ranges anywhere from utter listlessness to sullen defiance. Stop at any corner on the Strand at noon and you will see a bar, the street doors wide open, and a crowd of laboring men, red-faced and wet-eyed, pouring can after can of liquor down their throats.

Usually there are several old women whining and complaining and tugging at their man's arm, but if one gets her husband's pewter pot away from him she usually finishes it herself with evident satisfaction. One cannot come to realize at once what an absolutely gin soaked people these London working folk are. Time and again we have seen sturdy, bonny, well-dressed little children trying with the most touching seriousness and gentleness to steer home two parents, both of whom were so far gone in their cups that the little folk had great ado to keep them on their feet at all. A drunken man, fairly well clad and looking the prosperous workman, will walk down the street, his hands in his pockets, beside his wife who carries the baby, cursing her with a richness and variety of phrase leaving one breathless, and no one pays the least attention to him. When I am on the street at night in this part of the town I am always perfectly sure that men are mauling women with their fists or battering them up with furniture just around the corner anywhere. I am no voice of an oppressed sex crying aloud, however; the women drink their share. Yesterday, passing through St. James's Park in the rain, I counted the women lying shelterless, flat on the ground, in poses which passed belief, dead to the world. The park benches are always full of them. The beautiful river front on the east side of the Thames called the Albert Embankment, from which one gets the most satisfying and altogether happy view of the Houses of Parliament up the river, is night and day thronged with drunken, homeless men and women who alternately claw each other with their nails and give each other a chew of tobacco.

At night the high white globular lights which flank this marble terrace are beautifully reflected in the river, and by each light post hangs a life preserver to recall any tipsy wretch who may drop over the wall to [end] his useful activities. But very few of these night birds are fond of water and next to gin they are enamoured of life; of these muddy day skies and leaky night skies, of their own bench along the embankment, of the favorite neighbor they beat or chew or claw, of the sting of cheap gin in empty stomachs, and the exciting game of chess they play with the police back and forth across those marble squares.

About the London shop girls of the meaner sort no derogatory remarks can be too strong, just as no commendation can be too high of the courtesy, honesty and good nature of the girls who wait on you in the shops on Oxford and Bond streets. This court born, alley-nursed, street bred girl is everywhere. Sometimes she is sober, oftener she is not. She sells you flowers and fruit on every corner, serves in bars and cheap eating houses. We have nothing at all at home to correspond to her. Her voice is harder than her gin-sodden face, it cuts you like a whiplash as she shouts, "Rowses! rowses! penny a bunch,"[10] or "all the words of the hopry!" When she is sober she sleeps under cover somewhere; when she isn't she sleeps on the steps of the Nelson column in Trafalgar and likes that quite as well.

The shop girl, who rather prides herself on being respectable and sleeping under a roof and maybe going to church, is in a class of her own. Her round boy's straw hat, her wonderful coat, her lace and cheap jewelry, her stooped shoulders, untidy hair and "I-can-take-care-of-myself-sir" air make her easily recognizable. She has absolutely nothing of the neatness and trimness which characterizes our working girls at home. She would blush to wear a gingham shirt waist, preferring rather to feel elegant in a cotton satin one of unspeakable griminess. She wears flowers and paste jewels, but she seldom bathes, never has enough hair pins and considers tooth brushes necessary only for members of the royal family.

The most advantageous place to see her is in the gallery at Covent Garden or one of the better theatres, when she has come out with one of her chums with the purpose of being both elegant and intellectual. She has her hair curled all over her head, is always rouged and heavily powdered, and she scans the house with her glasses, pointing out to her friends the nobility in the boxes. She affirms that her second cousin is a friend of the chiropodist of this duchess, and the history she proceeds to paint for the very well-bred and often remarkably beautiful woman at whom she points is beyond the dreams of Edna [Emma] Southworth.[11] When she has finished with the dukes and duchesses she begins on the opera company. Her scandals have infinite variety and the detail of a past master in realism, and I must admit that I envy her her fecundity of invention. One of the favorite relaxations of the flower girl—that name that we have been taught to associate with idyllic innocence—is fisticuffing her friends and acquaintances. She is by turns fury and bacchante, and a cruel sight it is to behold her leaping through the streets in the impetus of her gin-fed joy. Whoever thinks that Kipling exaggerated conditions in his "Record of Badalia Herodsfoot,"[12] let him come and see. Since I have been in London

10. Cf. the poem "London Roses," in *April Twilights*, which begins: "'Rowses! Rowses! Penny a bunch!' they tell you—/ Slattern girls in Trafalgar, eager to sell you." *AT(1903)*, p. 35.

11. For Emma Southworth, see "Literature in the Capital," Washington Correspondent, above.

12. "The Record of Badalia Herodsfoot" (1890) is found in Kipling's *Many Inventions* (New York: D. Appleton & Co., 1893).

I have thought Kipling a greater man than I ever thought him before. Coming to the city fresh from the colonies he caught with admirable truth the coloring of the place, together with its greatness and griminess.

On Sunday last the Italians of London, who are both fewer and poorer than those of New York, celebrated the feast of Our Lady of Mount Carmel. As Miss Dorothy Canfield had joined us and is particularly interested in all phases of Italian life at home and abroad, we went into the Italian quarters to see the procession. It was a most unfortunate day for anything that required enthusiasm. The skies were an even, ashen grey, hopeless and changeless, the rain descended lightly but steadily. The streets were a thick, gritty paste of mud. Where the poor southerners found courage to erect and decorate the arch at the head of the street, I could not conjecture. There was scarcely a window that had not a little shrine before it with a tiny image and burning candles, carefully protected from the rain. The Italian quarter here is a poor place enough, and these attempts at ceremonial splendor in spite of time, absence, poverty and distance, in spite of the oppressive greyness, in spite of the oppressively ugly city, were not a little pathetic. The lace curtains were tacked to the brick walls outside the windows, and, poor as the people are, nearly every window had a garland or bunch of cut flowers. The approach of the festal procession was announced by a slow march played by drums and fifes that had, on this occasion, no military suggestion whatever. The air was intensely appealing and individual, though it recalled a little some parts of Cavalleria Rusticana. First came the guards, then the thurifer, cross-bearer and acolytes, glorious spots of color in the grey English drip. Then came men of various religious societies in costume, all with bowed heads, praying devoutly, never heeding that their gorgeous apparel was trailing in the mud. Then more thurifers and acolytes and clergy and holy images, then women, bareheaded and praying, then a body of Italian boys, all in red surplices, their little shiny black heads bowed and their hands clasped together.

Some of the older girls who marched in the line seemed quite pale from emotion. The old women were simply dignified and melancholy. So far from being a street show, the procession was a religious ceremony, even to me, who understood neither its origin nor significance. Before one realized it one was all clouded about with mysticism as with incense; fire of some sort burned in one, enthusiasm none the less real that one had little idea what it was for. These poor Latins, undauntedly trying to carry a little of the light and color and sweet devoutness of a Latin land into their grey, cold London had done with us what a great actor can sometimes do. I did not see one self-conscious looking figure in all the procession. Never did a little boy smile or poke his neighbor. The tiniest child was able to abandon itself wholly to this beautiful experience they made for themselves in the heathen heart of the London slums. The police stood in double file along the streets to protect the worshipers from what stood without, and what stood without I know, for I stood among them; Gomorrah stood without, and Sodom, Babylon shorn of both splendor and power. The howling, hooting heathen London mobs; men drunk, women drunk, unwashed and unregenerate. I stood next a man in a top hat with a frock coat buttoned up over his under shirt. Next him stood a girl with a straw hat and a heavy cloak under which she wore no dress waist. This cloak was finished in a piece of dirty cat fur. She had white lips and few teeth and her face was covered with eruptions. She could hardly have been twenty. There was Gin Moll and Barley Sally, their old bonnets tilted like horns over their bleary eyes, their skirts on wrong side first. They stared at the far distance and swore quietly. The thrifty coster boys sold standing room on top of their barrows. These people who have never been inside a church, this sodden heathendom, made the setting of the devout little procession as it moved slowly along. Said Kipling: "A city where the common people are without religion and without God, but are nightly drunken and howl in the streets like jackals, the men and the women together."[13] Of all the British painters, surely Hogarth was the only realist and the only man who knew his London. Lower London today is exactly what it was when he studied and hated it. Every day faces from "The Idle Apprentice," "Cruelty" and "The Harlot's Progress" pass one in the streets like the hideous distortions of a nightmare. [August 10, 1902, p. 11]

"*The Kensington Studio*"

Willa Cather's visit to the Kensington studio of Sir Edward Burne-Jones (1833–1898), as Mildred R. Bennett was the first to point out, provided "the setting and framework of the story 'The Marriage of Phaedra' in The

13. Cather obviously is quoting from memory from "One View of the Question," also in *Many Inventions* (see note 12, above). Apparently she telescoped two passages: "I see clearly that this town, London, . . . is accursed, being dark and unclean, devoid of sun, and full of low-born, who are perpetually drunk, and howl in the streets like jackals, men and women together" (p. 81); and "The common folk have no god" (p. 83).

Troll Garden."[14] *But the fictionalizing of the experience began even before the story, with this* Journal *letter. The body of the piece supposedly reports a conversation with the artist's valet, James, but according to Burne-Jones's granddaughter, the late Angela Thirkell, he "never [had] a valet and never one called James—either by Christian name or surname."*[15] *This was affirmed by the late Sir Sydney Cockerell, who stated: "Burne-Jones had neither valet nor butler. He was not that kind of man. There was no one called James in his household. He died in 1898 so Willa Cather's visit was four years after his death, when the studio had been cleared out." Other painters mentioned are George Frederic Watts (1817–1904), well-known portrait artist, who also treated allegorical and symbolical subjects, and Frederick Leighton (1830–1896), famed for his draughtsmanship and his use of classical subjects. This letter, which carried no date, clearly was a continuation of the July 16 letter.*

The beautiful surfaces and the beautiful life of London lie from Trafalgar square westward through St. James's park and Hyde park, along Piccadilly, through Kensington to Hammersmith. From Trafalgar westward the very color of the city changes; the grimy blackness of the smoke-laden town grows to a splendid grey about the National Gallery and St. Martin-in-the-Fields, and from there the color runs gradually into a higher and higher key, into the glorious green of the parks and the bold white of the club houses along Piccadilly, and finally into the broad asphalts of Kensington that are covered, or rather dusted, with a yellow sand that catches the sunlight like gold powder, lying bright between their lines of elm and plane trees.[16] On those rare occasions when there is sunshine in London, it seems all to be concentrated along the winding avenues of Kensington, where it plays bravely upon the endless rows of high, white, cement-faced houses, the high brick garden walls whose dull brick is crowned by iron lattice work through which one sees the beautiful sanded gardens, yellow and smooth, without a blade of grass, but with beds of scarlet and crimson geraniums and orange nasturtiums, gaudier than

14. Bennett, p. 163. "The Marriage of Phaedra" was first published in *The Troll Garden* (1905); *CSF*, pp. 219–234.

15. Quoted in Bennett, p. 249, as is the statement following from Sir Sydney Cockerell.

16. Cf. the descriptions of the golden London light in *Alexander's Bridge* (Boston: Houghton Mifflin Co., 1912). Two examples: "The slender towers were washed by a rain of golden light" (p. 45); ". . . all the thickness and shadow of London are changed to a kind of shining, pulsing, special atmosphere; . . . the smoky vapors become fluttering golden clouds; . . . all the roofs and spires, and one great dome, are floated in a golden haze" (p. 117).

Browning's "gaudy melon flower" set close together as though some one had spilled a pot of paint on the sand. About the edges of these little gay Saharas, grow tall hawthorn bushes, and the variegated laurel with brilliant white patches all over its glossy leaves, and lilacs that droop indolently over the wall, and stiff, hardy holly, green and variegated, and the polled locusts, cut round and thick into balls of yellow green, just the shape of the pollard willows. Behind these gardens are the dull brick houses, never painted and keeping the natural color of the brick, or cement-faced houses as white as those along the coast of Morocco are said to be. These white houses in their sand gardens are peculiarly effective; their white fronts are never relieved by porch or cornice or portico or column, and the level white surface is only relieved by those window boxes so common in England, filled with yellow or pink or crimson flowers that fairly scream at you in the lustiness of their color.

Whether brick or cement, these homes are built wall to wall, all exactly the same height and of the same plainness and solidity and decorousness and reserve and have the same non-communicative aspect. Here and there, among these miles and miles of houses whose similar faces are only varied by occasional loops of wisteria vine across the white or red, is a square or two of villas. These of course are built more variously, with larger gardens and high brick walls and iron gateways under ivy-grown brick archways. It was in one of these high brick walls, the red top set with broken, jagged green glass set in hard cement to exclude night intruders, that I found the door of Sir Edward Burne-Jones' studio, called here the Garden studio. The studio is built against the garden wall like a porter's lodge, with a street door, and another door into the garden beyond which stands the house in which the painter lived. Lady Burne-Jones lets the house now, having changed her place of residence to Prince's Gate, Hyde Park, but she keeps the studio unchanged as her husband requested. We were admitted first into the vestibule, a little square place with a brick floor and whitewashed brick walls, where James, valet to Sir Edward's person and to his art, kept guard and still keeps guard, sitting the day long with his pipe and a copy of "Sporting Life," watcher and warden still. The studio itself is a bare tank of a place, bare as a room could well be save for the beauty with which its walls are clad, long and narrow, so narrow that three standing abreast can reach from wall to wall, entirely windowless, with only the cold north light that streams in searchingly through the glass roof. There are perhaps a score of pictures in oil, finished and unfinished, and some hundreds of studies in crayon and black and white and sepia. To catalogue the names of pictures without accompanying reproductions is wearisome and profitless, and I will not attempt it. Among the finished pictures are the Venus Concordia and the companion Venus Discordia, a series of panels depicting the adventures of Perseus, and a Blind Love. To anyone who has ever come under the subtle and melancholy spell of Burne-Jones' work it is only necessary to say that all these things, from the slightest study of an arm to the finished pictures are most really and wholly and convincingly his and could be the conception or execution of no other man. Certainly there can be no question nowadays as to who was master of all English painters. It seems well established that he was the only painter the island has produced whose color-sense can not be challenged, and excepting Rossetti, he alone is unstained by that muck of sentimentality which has choked all truth and courage and vividness out of English art. There is something that speaks from every canvas or study on the studio wall, from the long-limbed languid women, the wide far-seeing eyes, the astonishingly bold, yet always delicate and tender, experiments in composition and color scheme, which speak from no other canvas stretched in English land. For this grace of curve and pregnant beauty of line, this harmony between figure and setting, this depth of atmosphere and truth of tone and subtle poetry of color, you can find no equal here.

It was James, the valet to the arts, who showed us the dozens of studies from which many of the well known pictures grew. James is wide and red of countenance, with diminutive mutton chops and a keen grey eye, a very typical English gentleman's gentleman who lived from his boyhood in Sir Edward's service.

"There," remarked James, "are the drawings Sir Edward made for Mr. Morris to illustrate the book of Chaucer. This set are for the Legend of Good Women, and there is Chaucer hisself lyin' asleep a-dreamin' of them. Here is a number of studies he made for the mermaid—everybody knows that paintin'. He had great trouble with the pose and done them over a good bit, and here's the study for the head of the dead man she was draggin' under the sea. Models? Oh no, he didn't often use the same one twice. He weren't particular, Sir Edward. Any model would do for him, and his studies was never like the models a bit when he'd done 'em. He knowed what he wanted his women to look like, he just used models for the pose merely, and the drapery. He never had no models for the face at all, just for crooks of the neck and shoulders and that. He knowed what he wanted. You won't find models lookin' like any of his heads, I fancy."

These are the words of James faithfully set down, and I put them down because I wish to remember them, for it has not often been my good fortune to pass a summer afternoon with such a valet of such a hero. In reading a transcription of James' dissertation, however, it is necessary to entirely eliminate the letter h wherever it occurs in order to get a correct idea of his speech. James' personal attitude I found interesting and perplexing, one could no more accuse him of having any sort of comprehension of painting than one could accuse him of an artistic temperament. Yet he is no fake of the sort who besets you at Stratford and chants, "Here died the immortal bard in 1616." James has no sepulchral tone and no speeches fast committed. It is not his business to talk and he is not a guide. Only friendly overtures and silver and a claim of mutual acquaintance drew him from his somber silence. Once started, his enthusiasm carried him on. The source of his enthusiasm baffled me. He knew the name of the most meagre study, into what picture it had gone at last, how many times it had been done and something of the technical difficulties it presented. He spoke of the vanquishing of these difficulties with a pride peculiar to the makers of things. He had somewhat to say of Watts and all the many and much gifted Rossettis, and of the Morrises and Ford Madox Brown, whose daughter married D. G. Rossetti's brother.[17] I would give James many bright sovereigns for his head full of recollections.

The picture Burne-Jones was working on when he died hangs in the studio. It is called "The Passing of Venus" and the realization of it seems to have caused him not a few low moments, for there are many impatient studies for it in chalk and crayon and three canvases which were nearly finished and then thrown aside as inadequate. "It was one of them as went bad from the beginning, as some will, you know," said James. "But them was often Sir Edward's best. He was workin' on it of nights when he died, only then it stood over there where the big picture always stood." By the big picture James seemed to mean the picture on which the strain of labor fell. Whatever it happened to be it was for James and Sir Edward "the big picture."

James planted his sturdy broad finger on one after another of the things of inspiration and told us when and where and how, and neither his air of certainty nor his English offended. There was about him the

17. Previously unidentified: William Morris (1834–1896), a sort of jack-of-all-arts, poet, prose-writer, furniture-maker, etc., prominently associated with the Pre-Raphaelites; Ford Madox Brown (1821–1893), English painter, specializing in historical, religious, and literary subjects, also a Pre-Raphaelite.

undisputable conviction of an authority. He knew in what collection all Sir Edward's pictures are held, how they were born and where and of the pain of their bearing. Yet he knew so little about art that he declared Sir Edward's son "a foin portrait pynter." Nevertheless I would wager that James knows more about Burne-Jones himself than any other person living knows, and more about the road he trod and what beset his soul by the way. I suspect too, that were all the Burne-Jones pictures in the world in danger of immediate and utter destruction that James would risk his neck a deal quicker than the painter's most soulful and penetrating and comprehensive lovers. There is a warmer note in James' admiration than in that of any enthusiast I have ever talked with. The pictures are, in a fashion, his life works, and certainly his life interest. I can only conjecture that, though his doors are shut and heaven gave him no windows, yet James has been valet to the arts so long, washed palettes and ground colors and stretched canvas as well as their painter's trousers, that some of the radiance in which the painter lived has got somehow in through the roof of James, doorless and windowless as he is. As he talked James fell after a time into the lingo of the studio, into the artist's way of measuring what part of the day was good for anything, into the painter's peculiar anatomical terms, and all this with never an "h" in his whole flow of speech. Certainly James knows what he knows and has food for reflection when he wearies of "Sporting Life." As he remarked with a smile and a shrug, "Livin' with artists all my life, I couldn't get on elsewhere, it's likely." Even though he never laid eyes on the high lady who in priceless moments was wont to come there, James may have felt something in the air and light and golden calm and the silence of swift work that told him she was there, and now that she keeps tryst no more, he sits with his paper and his briar pipe and mounts guard before the little cell where once she came and went, while he fended off the pagan world from the holy moments that were hers.

I have spent some time in Watts' studio and in Rossetti's and in that house beautiful of Egyptian woodwork and Moorish tiles and priceless stone work and glass work from the orient where Sir Frederick Leighton painted his pictures, but after these show studios Sir Edward's gloomy tank seems only the more richly clad with loveliness. Neither the high, clear tinkle of the fountain [which] sings incessantly in the stone faced, shadowy Arabian hall at Leighton house, nor the balconies that hang over a little province of high walled orchard, can altogether make one forget the pathetic ignominy of Leighton's canvases, where flesh of man, woman, and beast are of one texture with drapery, earth, and sky and where all are lost in muddy color and the rigidity and flatness of death. Rossetti's studio is now let to other hands and his sketches are scattered, though I have succeeded in finding one large collection. In Watts' studio only the portraits are worth serious study and it is probable that he will hold his place among painters only through them. It was only in his portraits that he was wholly and only a painter, that he entirely escaped that passion for seeing and making sermons in paint which has been the damnation of English artists. The great majority of his pictures are interesting only because of their literary associations or the story they tell, and photographic reproductions of them are more satisfying than the originals. Even in a nightmare, the humblest Italian painter of any of the early schools, could not have dreamed of such transgressions in color as some of them present. [August 17, 1902, p. 11]

"*Merry Wives of Windsor*"

This first installment of a letter sent from Paris concludes Willa Cather's reports on her stay in England. She had, of course, seen countless Shakespearean productions, and previously had commented on Ellen Terry, Mrs. Kendal, and Sir Herbert Beerbohm Tree (see, respectively, "Sir Henry Irving and Ellen Terry," The Star System [IV], "The Kendals," The Star System [I], and "That Old Twenty-third of April," The Theatre [II], above).

PARIS, Aug. 8.—Probably no play has been produced in London for some years which has proved so solid a financial success as Mr. Beerbohm Tree's revival of "The Merry Wives of Windsor." The production was planned as a feature of the coronation festivities, and though nearly all such ventures miscarried, Mr. Tree's was and is a marked exception. In the first place, people take pretty much whatever comes to His Majesty's theatre. In the second, this production was interesting as a means that at last brought about a truce between the two most popular women on the English stage—Mrs. Kendal and Ellen Terry. The breach between the two actresses was of some twenty years standing, and seemed likely to endure until the end of their working days, for Mrs. Kendal is relentlessness itself, and Miss Terry is not overly prone to sue for pardon. But the coronation being an occasion of no little importance, and the king's interest in Mr. Tree's venture being known, the two ladies were got together and the terms of the peace arranged, Miss Terry being cast for the better of the two principal female parts.

The mechanical appurtenances of the production were superb. The costuming and the scenic embellishments were quite as artistic as any other features of the performance. The scenes laid in the village of Windsor gained considerable verity by reason of the careful reproduction of just such streets and buildings as one finds in Chester and Ludlow today, left over from Elizabethan days. One device which added greatly to the finish of the stage picture was the covering of the floor of the stage with a carefully wrought imitation of the cobble-stone streets of old Windsor.

As an acting play, it is not easy to pass a verdict on "The Merry Wives of Windsor," or even venture an opinion. It is a farce pure and simple, and a good deal of its humor is of the sort that children delight to watch in the circus ring. There is so much beating of bodies and staggering of the drunken, that one wonders whether Voltaire were not bearing this particular comedy [in mind] when he describes Shakespeare as a "drunken savage with glimpses of genius." Certainly a comedy which presents three plots, no two of which have the remotest essential connection, could only seem a work of madness to any critic with a Latin feeling for form. What business Sir Hugh Evans and Dr. Caius have in the play at all is quite beyond the guessing of the ordinary play-goer. The only reasonable attitude of the spectator is to consider the play as one must consider certain English novels, without any reference to its form at all. The comedy seems to have been written merely as a farcical presentation of English village life, and the types were, as likely as not, taken from Stratford itself. This is not denying that the piece had its raison d'etre in Sir John Falstaff, for the versatile knight might have graced almost any plot or been at home in any setting. Originally the comedy must have appealed to the British stomach by reasons of its noise and cudgeling and broad jests, and largely because of the local color and the title, which caught the ear of the London public as "The Merry Wives of Yorkers" might that of New York today. Today people go to see it because it is lavishly staged in Mr. Tree's theater, because such a revival is not likely to occur again for many years, because Falstaff has everywhere penetrated the public comprehension, and because London loves to vigorously applaud whenever Mrs. Kendal and Miss Terry embrace each other. Certainly from "The Merry Wives of Windsor" as it is given now in London, no one could ever guess the author of "Twelfth Night" or "As You Like It."

About Mr. Tree's expurgation of the comedy, there may be several opinions. Certainly the lines of Sir John himself are pruned away until there is little left of the character and his aims and motives are alike unexplained. Mr. Tree argues that the knight's lines would necessarily offend a modern audience, so he presents a Falstaff whose resemblance to Shakespeare's goes little further than the paunch. Mr. Tree's argument recalls the story of the classic Mrs. Siddons' "Rosalind." She wished to play the character and she did not wish to incur the exposure of a page's costume, so she appeared in a sort of Highland kilt which was quite too much even for the gravity of a London audience. Neither Mrs. Siddons nor Mr. Tree were compelled to revive Shakespearean comedies if they did not wish to, but it would seem as though if they did present them they ought to do it honestly. If the English have a national poet who cannot be read in public, then they are the only nation so unfortunate. When you hear a play of Moliere's given at the Francais, or sit through five interminable acts of "Ruy Blas" in which every line is given its full value, you begin to realize what respect for tradition means.

Mr. Tree's presentation of the fat knight can scarcely be termed anything but unfortunate. He plays the character with an earnestness which quite robs it of its flavor. His Falstaff takes himself with the utmost seriousness and is quite [without] the one saving grace of a keen sense of humor, which his creator certainly meant he should have. He comments upon the graces of his person with the utmost seriousness, which even though it is most characteristically English, is tedious and absurd. When this Falstaff puts on the stag horns for his rendezvous in Windsor forest, he does it as seriously as though he were donning a new doublet. Poor Sir John had faults enough, surely, and it is quite superfluous that Mr. Tree should add to the catalogue the crowning sin of grave stupidity. The farce ends in a masque, a fairy pantomime. After the husbands have made mirth at Sir John's expense in the forest and the children have pinched and tweaked him the dance begins. In their revel the merry wives acquit [themselves] right well, and poor Sir John renders tribute to English sentiment by admirably dancing with the children. The curtain falls on a jovial can-can between the fat knight and a little girl of six or seven, a touching picture of amiable and domestic old age, a scene of the Victor-Hugo-among-his-grandchildren order, which the French people are so partial to.

If the production is at all justified, it is the two merry wives who do it. The amount of sport which Mrs. Kendal as "Mrs. Ford" and Miss Terry as "Mrs. Page" get out of the wild and incongruous situation of the play, well nigh makes one forget their absurdity. Both the ladies wear head-dresses with heavy drapery about the throat and chin, which effectually conceals any ravages of relentless time and renders them delightfully youthful. Mrs. Kendal, indeed never quite loses that dignity wherein she keeps her state, and it is fitting that Mrs. Ford should be the more reserved of these two honest, but merry, wives. But the spirit, the dash and gleam of the whole performance emanate from Ellen Terry. Neither a dull daughter nor a stolid Falstaff can daunt her. She plays as though she were seventeen yesterday; with an elasticity, a lightness and a relish that might well have captivated even so dull a Falstaff. It is not her grace, her spirited reading or her bounding step only that charm. She seemed the only player wholly in atmosphere, the only one who was imbued with the spirit of things Elizabethan. Now I believe I understand better that wildfire wit which has always baffled me. There is a bit of old England left in Ellen Terry. This play delights her as it delighted the spectators in the pit of the old playhouses. There is some of the strong old wine left in her, light of touch as she is, and under all her sweeping lines of grace, there is something of the naive, romping spirit which Shakespeare meant as the keynote of Mrs. Page and Mrs. Ford, those two very merry wives of Windsor. In her comedy there is just the faintest aroma of all that jumble of fisticuffing and jocular horseplay which for several centuries constituted English comedy. This is the warm, live heart of her harmonious and graceful art, and gives it the convincing and carrying power. [August 24, 1902, p. 16]

"*Dieppe and Rouen*"

The absence of a date indicates that this is a continuation of the letter sent from Paris on August 8, 1902.

We crossed from Newhaven to Dieppe on a night when the channel ran smoothly as glass and the stars stood clear in the midnight sky. Soon after the long lines of the coast-wise lights of England had quite died away, the sky clouded and, except where a pale star here and there struggled through there was nothing to break the common blackness of the sea and sky. If one stared hard enough and long enough it was possible to divine the horizon line rather than see it. The boat was crowded and the wind blew cold and the decks were peopled with miserable shivering Latins who had not secured state rooms and crouched under rubber blankets. When we quitted the decks at about 1 o'clock in the morning, they were scenes of chill and heaviness and discomfort. About 3 o'clock, however, I heard a rush of feet aft and tumbling into my ulster and mufflers hurried out to see what had occasioned the excitement. Above the roar of the wind and thrash of the water I heard a babble of voices, in which I could only distinguish the word "France" uttered over and over again with a fire and fervor that was in itself a panegyric. Far to the south there shone a little star of light out of the blackness, that burned from orange to yellow and then back to orange again; the first light of the coast of France. All the prone, dispirited figures we left two hours before were erect and animated, rhetorical and jubilant. They were French people from all over the world; women who had been teaching French in the United States; girls who had been governesses in England; journeymen tailors and workers at various handicrafts. They clutched and greeted each other indiscriminately, for it was the hour when all distinctions were obliterated and when the bond of brotherhood drew sweet and hard. Above all the ardent murmurings and the exclamations of felicity, there continually rose the voice of a little boy who had been born on a foreign soil and who had never been home. He sat on his father's shoulder with his arms locked tight about his neck and kept crying with small convulsions of excitement, "Is it France? Is it France?" No wonder a Parisian speaks so pityingly when he says of certain ones of the Bourbon family, "He died in exile."

By the time the first excitement was over a dozen lights outlined the coast, and then the dawn began to come up. The black water broke in long-lashed, regular waves toward the shore. The sky was black behind us and gray before, a yellow crescent of the old moon hung just over the red lighthouse top. The high chalk cliffs of Normandy were a pale purple in the dim light. Little fishing boats passed us continuously, their ragged sails patched with red and blue. When we touched the dock the sky, the gravel beach, the white town, were all wrapped in a pale pink mist and the narrow streets were canals of purple shadows. Certainly so small body of water as the English channel never separated two worlds so different. In the railway station here every poster was a thing of grace and beauty. The very porters spoke in smooth, clear voices that phrased the beautiful tongue they spoke almost as music is phrased. The cries of the street boys were musical. As we drove to our hotel we passed only work men and market folks and one old rag picker in wooden shoes and skirts almost up to her knees, who looked hungrily at us out from under her white cap as she fished with her stick in the gutter. Surely there is no other country where there are so many aged women, or where they retain their activity so long. When we arrived at our hotel we were too sleepy to notice anything except that the entire front of the building was glass, that the beach before it was very yellow and the sea very blue. When we awoke and revisited the world about 8 o'clock, everyone else seemed to feel as happy and as freshly created as ourselves. In the glass dining room where we breakfasted there were many flowers and a few smiling people. The children were running up and down the beach with their nurses. The sanded yards were splashed here and there with beds of red geraniums. The last of the fishing boats were dipping below the horizon. The purple chalk cliffs were dazzling white now, and our eyes, accustomed for some weeks to the blackness of London, ached with the glare of the sun on the white stone and yellow sand. A little boy on the stone terrace was flying a red and green kite, quite the most magnificent kite I have ever seen, and it went up famously, up and up until his string ran short, and of a truth one's heart went just as high.

Dieppe today subsists chiefly through marine industries. From time immemorial the men of the town have been famous seamen and have divided their energies between fishing and hating the English. Their boats go to Norway and Sweden for lumber and to Newfoundland and Iceland for fish. The shores are full of drying nets and fishing boats a-mending. Among the great navigators born and bred there were Jean Cousin and Jean de Ribault, who was massacred by the Spaniards in Florida. The town, because of its hardy seamen and venturesome spirit was peculiarly favored by most of the French kings, particularly by Francis I. Louis XIV was its worst enemy and nearly ruined the place through taxation because so many of the Huguenots escaped through their port. The chateau at Dieppe is not so interesting as that at Arques, a few miles distant. The chateau d'Arques is the ruins of a Norman structure of gigantic proportions which stands upon the top of a chalk hill beside the river Arques. In this chalk cliff there are cut tunnels which give egress to various points along the coast and were invaluable in the long sieges the castle often sustained. Some of these underground passages are twenty-five miles long. Only a little boy, however, or a Robert Louis Stevenson, could understand or set forth the romantic possibilities of these winding tunnels or the thrice-walled and moated structure from which they lead. One so happily gifted might lie of a sunny morning on the smooth decline of the grassy moat and hear the harness clank upon the knights riding, with William the Norman at their head, down the long white road that winds up to the castle on the hill. They keep William's portrait at the castle still, and the restless, scornful, unhappy face of him seems an impossible product for that kindly cheerful Norman country.

That afternoon we rode away through miles of brook-fed valleys and yellow wheat fields sown thick with poppies, and tall lombard poplars and pale willows and grey elms, such as Corot and Puvis de Chavannes so often painted. Late in the day we arrived at Rouen, the well fed, self-satisfied bourgeois town built upon the hills beside the Seine, the town where Gustave Flaubert was born and worked and which he so sharply satirized and bitterly cursed in his letters to his friends in Paris. In France it seems that a town will forgive the man who curses it if only he is great enough. One of the first things that greets your eye in Rouen is the beautiful monument erected to Flaubert in the very wall of the museum, which is Rouen's holy of holies. Just across the walk from him, in front of a dense cluster of sycamore trees, is his friend and pupil, Guy de Maupassant. The Maupassant statue at Rouen is, I think, quite as impressive as that in Paris—perhaps more so, and it is even more happily placed. Besides, there is something very fitting in the idea of commemorating together the master and the pupil who surpassed him.

It happened to be the afternoon when the children had been for their examination in catechism, and as we crossed tree lined squares we met troops of them, each wearing a wreath and each bearing a prize, for the happy feature of these catechism contests seems to be that everyone gets a share of the honor. I am unable to believe statistics as to the stationary population of France. I never saw so many children anywhere as I have seen in Paris and the northern towns; no, nor such pretty children nor such happy ones.

The most beautiful thing about Rouen is the stillness and whiteness and vastness of its cathedral. The exterior is by no means so fine as the beautiful church of St. Ouen, which stands near it, but the interior is vested with a peace that passes understanding. The columns and arches are beautifully fluted and of the most delicate and slender gothic, vault after vault rising high and effortless as flame. The uniform whiteness of the walls and arches and high slender columns is varied by the burning blue and crimson of two rose windows almost as beautiful as those of Notre Dame. The place is so vast that even the vesper service could be heard only near the altar, and so dusky that the lighted tapers cast dancing reflections on the white stone. All the light streams from windows so high that one seems to look up at them from the bottom of a well. Behind the choir is a reclining figure of Richard Coeur-de-Lion, and under it is the urn in which his heart was placed. On every side of him is dim, rich light and a very forest of white, slender, stone columns, with silence absolute and infinitely sweet. There could scarcely be a better place for so hot a heart to rest.[18] [August 31, 1902, p. 16]

"*Two Cemeteries in Paris*"

Willa Cather's preoccupation with cemeteries can be traced to her earliest Sunday columns for the Journal *(see "In the Midst of Life," The Local Scene [I], above), and it is not in the least surprising that she devoted a letter to two Parisian cemeteries, in particular Père-Lachaise, that "great harvest field of death," where there lay so many of those who, like Balzac, had won the "longed-for chrism, a grave marked by a single name" (see "Carvalho," The Musical World [I], above). In this letter occur many names familiar to the readers of her columns—Baudelaire, Verlaine, Dumas* fils, *Heine, Musset, Chopin, and Balzac. In Paris, Willa Cather and Isabelle McClung stayed at a pension at 11 rue de Cluny; Dorothy Canfield was with them for a time, then left to join her parents in Scotland.*[19]

PARIS, August 21.—(Special Correspondence.)—The cemetery of Montmartre has one of the most beautiful situations in Paris. The hill of Montmartre towers above the city like one of those cloud-topped volcanoes in children's geography books. On the very summit of the hill rises the church of Sacre-Coeur, largest of all modern churches, and a hill in itself. The church is all of white stone, with round Byzantine towers and dome. If one approaches Paris from the north the white gleam of Sacre-Coeur is the first thing that strikes the eye, and on a sunny day the rest of the city, below, lies bathed in a violet light, with here and there white towers. From the terrace at St. Germain, Montmartre, with the purple city below, looks like the city of St. John's vision, or the Heavenly City that Bunyan saw across the river. Montmartre is one of the most picturesque quarters of Paris and of late years has been much affected by painters and poets and political theorists, who have colonized there from the Latin quarter.

18. George N. Kates, in *Willa Cather in Europe*, pp. 92–93, has suggested that this paragraph be compared with the passage describing Claude Wheeler's feelings as he first visits an old Gothic church in Rouen (*One of Ours*, pp. 342–344). The description here is of the Cathedral and that in *One of Ours* is of the Church of St. Ouen, but there are striking similarities in tone and detail (for example, "a very forest of white, slender, stone columns" becomes "slender white columns in long rows, like the stems of silver poplars").

19. Willa Cather to Mariel Gere, August 28, 1902.

The Moulin Rouge is there,[20] and the narrow streets leading down from Sacre-Coeur were favorite haunts of Baudelaire and Paul Verlaine. The roadways and narrow streets are cobble-paved, built up on either side with ancient stucco houses, with here and there a walled garden. These garden walls are all overgrown with wisteria, and tall sunflowers nod over them. The effect of these high old houses with straight wall-like fronts, rising on either side of the narrow streets into the high pale blue Paris sky, is in itself very singular. The effect is heightened by the vines that trail over the white fronts of the houses, and the brilliant flowers that grow wherever there is a spot of earth to bear them. A little below these picturesque streets lies one of the two great burial grounds of Paris. A really appreciative attitude toward Paris cemeteries is well-nigh impossible to any one but a Frenchman. There is not a blade of grass anywhere in them, the entire enclosures being covered with gravel, which is occasionally raked to keep it loose. I heard an American girl remark that "it seemed exactly like burying people in a tennis court." The trees are very beautiful and carefully kept, but there is no low, green tent for the Paris dead. Their relatives heap over them great masses of stone, most of which are monstrosities of taste. These heavy, somber piles are decorated with the most objectionable artificial flowers and dozens of wreaths, anchors, cornucopias, etc., made of brilliantly colored glass beads strung on wire. Some of the tombs are decorated with immense wreaths of painted china roses, weighing a dozen pounds or so.

In their death as in their life the Latins are more socially disposed than we, and the graves in their cemeteries almost always touch each other, they are so closely crowded together. Occasionally flowers or shrubs are planted about the tombs, but for the most part they are mere unsightly masses of stone, decorated with glass and tin wreaths, with narrow gravel walks running about them. The general effect strongly suggests a tennis court converted into a grave yard.

Marked exceptions to the generally execrable taste exhibited in Paris cemeteries are the tombs of its great men, which are usually very impressive. One of the first of these tombs that I found in Montmartre was that to the brothers Goncourt,[21] a flat stone with bronze medallions. The

20. See also the poem and note, "Mills of Montmartre," in *April Twilights; AT(1903)*, pp. 9–10.

21. The Goncourt brothers, Edmond (1822–1896) and Jules (1830–1870), famed French men-of-letters, best known for their *Journal*. The Prix Goncourt was established in 1903 under the terms of Edmond's will.

tomb of Alexandre Dumas fils is by St. Marceaux and is one of the most beautiful in the cemetery. The dramatist lies full length on the top of the flat stone, under a marble canopy. He is clad in his dressing gown, his feet bare, his head noble and calm. On the stone above him are carved camellia flowers in low relief. On the canopy above him is an inscription from one of his works: "I am keenly interested in my life which pertains to time, but I am more interested in my death which pertains to eternity." On the other side of the cemetery is the grave of Alphonsine du Plessis, the original of "La Dame aux Camelias." She died in 1845, but there were [a] few flowers upon her grave a week ago, which speaks volumes for the inborn and unblushing sentimentality of Parisians. Far be it from them to miss such an opportunity! One of the tombs most often visited is that of Heinrich Heine and his wife, Mathilde. The tomb is surmounted by a bust of the poet, made from his later photograph, not the rotund, cynical face of the young Henry Heine but a man grave and wan, with the clutch of pain upon him, whom the "Aristophanes of the universe" was already outdoing in irony.[22] The head is a little bowed as though the weight of life had bent the proud neck of [the] poet of scorn. On the day I saw the grave it was almost covered with bunches of blue forget-me-nots. Heine died in 1856, but the youth of the world, seemingly, remembers him still. The flowers were probably from some young German sojourning in Paris; certainly they were a tribute from youth, for the melody of Heine's verse never rings quite so true as in the years that lie the other side of twenty. Probably the youth of countless generations to come will exultantly discover him, feverishly read him, and passionately proclaim him. Scarcely a schoolboy will ever stand for the first time before the Venus de Milo in the Louvre without remembering that a death struck Jew once sobbed his adieu to life there.

The cemetery of Pere-Lachaise is the largest in Paris. The great monument to the dead there is one of the noblest works of modern sculpture.[23] It is a great wall of white marble, set against a green hillside, representing a wall in the middle of which is a door. This door is literally the door to the tomb. On either side of this door are emaciated figures, life-sized or larger, who are being driven all unwillingly toward the dreaded portal. These figures are in every attitude of despair and opposition; one woman is bowed with her head upon the ground, one is kissing her hand in a

22. For this allusion, see "Philistines on the March," The Urban Scene, above.

23. This sculpture group has been identified by George N. Kates as the *Monument aux Morts* by Paul-Albert Bartholomé, dating from 1895. *Willa Cather in Europe*, p. 102.

despairing adieu to her friends in the world; another, a strong young man, is trying to hold back. The male figures are equally unwilling; young men, bowed with chagrin at their own physical weakness, old men who clutch the very stones with their toes in their pitiful effort to remain yet a little while in the happy world of living things. The realistic treatment of the sculptor has been now and then bitterly criticized, and people have found the horror of these struggling figures too poignant. It would seem, however, that they in reality only heighten the enviable repose of the central and emphatic figure of the work. There are two figures, a man and a woman, who have actually passed the portal, who are erect in the doorway, passing into the mystery that awaits them. No shrinking, no horror, no distortion or contraction there. They stand upright and calm: fearless, indifferent, and weary. Once inside the portal there is no fear, no longing for the backward path. Below this there is a crypt in which lie a nude man and woman, their stiffened hands feebly interlocked, and across their bodies lies that of a chubby little child. It is to all Adam's seed, this monument, to the human family and all its dead of the ages. Not to artist or statesman or warrior, but to man, out of dust fashioned, to woman, made to replenish the earth, and to the children she has borne. The simplicity and vastness of the conception cannot be described in words, and no pictorial reproduction gives one any adequate idea of it.

The tomb of Alfred de Musset is one of the most carefully kept in Pere-Lachaise, and will be so long as the Pantheon stands and ficklehearted youth awakens in the Latin quarter from dreams of glory. When the boy from the provinces first comes up to Paris, after quaking his way under the gold dome of the Invalides, he makes his pilgrimage to the tomb of the poet who sang all his ambitions, all his callow cynicism, all his self-inflicted torments. There are almost always fresh flowers lying before the bust of the poet, and below the bust runs an inscription in verse to this effect:

Friends of mine, when I shall die,
Plant a willow over me
In its sad shade would I lie
Its pallid leaf is dear to me.
Light its tender shade will weep
O'er the earth where I shall sleep.

This willow, requested by the poet, has become a subject of mirth even among Parisians, whose sense of the ridiculous is almost entirely lacking. Ever since 1857 gardener after gardener has tried to make a willow tree grow over the tearful singer's grave, but the soil of Pere-Lachaise is high and sandy, and the result of fifty years of effort is a spindling yellow seedling, five feet high, so nearly dead that its shade is as light as even so sensitive a gentleman could have wished it. De Musset certainly never got anything that he wanted in life, and it seems a sort of fine drawn irony that he should not have the one poor willow he wanted for his grave. On the other hand, no one ever quite so thoroughly enjoyed the idea of missing all he wanted, and the condition of this willow would certainly delight his artistic sense as a most effective instance of the relentlessness of a destiny of which he was never tired of complaining.

The monument to the late Felix Faure[24] by St. Marceaux, is a striking example of the dignity that modern realistic sculpture has attained. The president lies at full length, in bronze, his head slightly turned. He is in evening dress, with the broad ribbon of the Legion of Honor across his breast. The details of his costume are simply worked out, even the silk facing on his coat, yet it is absolutely free from any suspicion of triviality. The lower part of the body is draped in the flag of France. The tomb of Frederick Chopin is also carefully kept. Over a medallion of the composer, weeps a muse with her lyre. Balzac's monument is conspicuously ugly and deserted, but Balzac seems more a living fact than a dead man of letters. He lives in every street and quarter; one sees his people everywhere. The city of gray stone and stucco, interlaced by its clear green river and planted with sycamores and poplars, dominated by Notre Dame and the Invalides and the columns of victory, is no more real a thing than the great city of thought which Honore de Balzac piled and heaped together and left, a ruin of chaotic magnificence, beside the Seine.

He told the story, not only of the Paris of yesterday, but of the Paris of today and tomorrow. Whatever changes take place in one's scale of estimates in Paris, the figure of that barbarian of letters looms larger and larger, until he seems second only to Napoleon himself. It was Balzac himself who used to wander in the Pere-Lachaise in the days of his hard apprenticeship, reading the names on the tombs of the great. "Single names," he wrote his sister, "Racine, Moliere, etc.; names that make one dream." Surely none among all the names there calls up visions more vast. None better earned the right to lie among the dead whom, as a contemporary French writer puts it, "Paris loved so well; whom Paris forgets so soon."

24. François Félix Faure (1841–1899), president of France, 1895–1899.

The French people have a rather better way of commemorating their great men than building monuments to them—though there is a monument in every square and a dozen in every park—and that is naming their streets after them. This seems, someway, to keep the men still in the mouths of the living, to make their names still mean something in the big, stirring life of the common [people]. There is a rue Balzac and rue Racine and rue Moliere as well as a Place Wagram and a rue Arcola. Nearly every street in Paris bears the name of a victory—either of arms or intellect.[25] [September 14, 1902, p. 18]

"*One Sunday at Barbizon*"

Because she admired the painters of the Barbizon school, particularly Millet, Willa Cather made the pilgrimage to the village; but perhaps most interesting to her—and certainly most interesting to us—was her discovery of the resemblance of the landscape to the country around Bladen and Campbell, little towns on the Divide northwest of Red Cloud, a few miles from the homestead on which Willa Cather had lived when she first came to Nebraska. The date given below, September 10, is clearly a misprint for September 1, since the next letter, from Avignon, is dated September 3.

PARIS, Sept. 10.—As it is impossible to reach Barbizon by railway, we left the train at the town of Fontainebleau, which lies well in the forest of Fontainebleau. The palace of Fontainebleau is chiefly interesting through its souvenirs of Henry IV, Francis I, and Napoleon. There we saw Napoleon's bed, the table on which he signed his abdication, the grand portico from which he said adieu to the grand army, and his little throne, with the back round like a drum.[26] We lunched at a place called the Cordon Bleu, which was thronged with bicyclers. In Fontainebleau is the only monument I have yet seen in a French park which seemed in bad taste. The monument is to Rosa Bonheur,[27] and consists of an immense bronze bullock mounted on a pedestal. On the pedestal one finds, at length, a small bas-relief of the painter's virile face, but the first impression the monument gives is startling and somewhat shocking. From

25. See the poem "Paris," in *April Twilights; AT(1903)*, p. 49.

26. See the review of *L'Aiglon*, "Bernhardt and Maude Adams," Washington Correspondent, above.

27. Rosa Bonheur (1822–1899), popular for her animal paintings, particularly of horses.

Fontainebleau we drove some five or six miles through the forest to Barbizon.

The village of Barbizon is a little place of one street, which street begins in Fontainebleau forest and ends in a wheat field. It was originally a wretched little settlement of peasants who came to till the few acres of open land which happened to occur hereabout in the great forest. The tireless admiration of Millet, Rousseau and a few fellow artists made the place a rendezvous of artists from all over the world. Yet when you drive through the one crooked street of the town, between the two rows of low, straw-roofed stucco houses, and the garden wall covered with grapevine, it is hard to believe that for thirty years painters, litterateurs and musicians have lived and worked there for months together. The first care of all these people has been to leave intact the beauty that first drew them there. They have built no new and shining villas, introduced no tennis courts, or golf links, or electric lights. They have even heroically denied themselves any sewage system whatever, and the waste water from the kitchens and water tubs flows odorously along through the streets. The village at first sight, looks like any other little forest town; the home of hard-working folk, desperately poor, but never so greedy or so dead of soul that they will not take time to train the peach tree against the wall until it spreads like a hardy vine and to mass beautiful flowers of every hue in their little gardens. If you look closely you will presently see the skylight of little mud walled studios here and there, Millet's and Rousseau's the poorest and barest among them.

We had decided to stop at the Hotel des Artistes, which, though rather less interesting than Les Charmettes, is rather more reputable for women traveling alone. We entered the hotel through a stone-paved court, which led into the garden, completely enclosed by the various wings of the rambling home. This garden, and it was no small one, was almost entirely roofed by an enormous horse chestnut tree, under which several dozen small tables were placed. Our rooms faced upon this garden, and we were sheltered from the afternoon sun by the boughs of this mighty tree. In the late afternoon we walked to the end of the little street. The further we went from the hotel the more simple and primitive did the houses become; little huts of mud and stone, draped with vines and made [less?] gloomy by a clump of poppies or marigolds flaming upon the roof. Two-wheeled carts, grindstones, scythes, rakes and various implements of husbandry were strewn about the doors of the dwellings. The wheat fields beyond the town were quite as level as those of the Nebraska divides.

The long, even stretch of yellow stubble, broken here and there by a pile of Lombard poplars, recalled not a little the country about Campbell and Bladen, and is certainly more familiar than anything I have seen on this side the Atlantic. To complete the resemblance, there stood a reaper of a well known American make, very like the one on which I have acted as super-cargo many a time. There was a comfortable little place where a child might sit happily enough between its father's feet, and perhaps, if I had waited long enough, I might have seen a little French girl sitting in that happy, sheltered place, the delights of which I have known so well. The fields already cut were full of stackers; men in their long blue blouses that hang about their knees like skirts, and women bare-headed and brown faced and broad of shoulders. They all wore wooden shoes, their skirts were high above the ankle, and few of them wore stockings. After the rakers and stackers came the gleaners—usually women who looked old and battered, who were bent and slow and not good for much else. Such brave old faces as most of these field working women have, such blithe songs they hum and such good-humored remarks they bawl at a girl who sees too much of one particular reaper. There is something worth thinking about in these brown, merry old women, who have brought up fourteen children and can outstrip their own sons and grandsons in the harvest field, lay down their rake and write a traveler directions as to how he can reach the next town in a hand as neat as a bookkeeper's. As the sun dropped lower the merriment ceased; the women were tired and grew to look more and more as Millet painted them, warped and bowed and heavy. The horses strained in their harness, the ring dove began to call mournfully from the pine wood in the west and I found there was a touch of latent homesickness in the wide, empty, yellow fields and the reaper with the cozy seat which some little brown-skinned Barbizon girl would have tomorrow. Storm clouds were piling themselves up about the gorgeous sunset, and we tramped silently back to Barbizon, through the little winding street where tired women sat on the wooden door steps, singing tired children to sleep.

Dinner was being served when we reached the Hotel des Artistes, which hostelry derives its very attractive name from the fact that it has a studio to let and that the walls of the bar are decorated with oil sketches, furnished mostly by painters who were unable to pay their accounts. White cloths were laid on the little tables under the big horse-chestnut, and the six homely daughters of the proprietor were running about calling "red wine or white, monsieur?" Soon after we were seated a few drops of rain fell, and, although they did not penetrate the sheltering leaves of the great tree, such exclamations of woe and alarm arose from guests and servitors that you might have conjectured an earthquake was approaching, or that rain had never fallen in Barbizon before. The changing skies are one of the chief beauties of the forest, and in a few minutes the clouds had entirely disappeared. Then the gas lamps that hung from the boughs of the chestnut were lighted, and the dinner proceeded merrily.

Our fellow guests were an interesting lot of people. There were several French families who had come out to Barbizon to spend Sunday, and they were amused at everything and delighted with everything. There was a miserable, snakey little painter, with black hair and beard, whom we had often seen in the Latin quarter. He wore his usual black felt hat and long black necktie, with sash-like ends that fell almost to his waist. He had his sweetheart with him, a rather pretty girl who wore powder and a preposterously small waist. We had noticed them in Paris, strolling arm in arm through the Luxembourg gardens. Next day we saw him in the forest painting busily and leaving the sweetheart to her own devices. There were several other artists, older men and of a sturdier type, and an English bridal couple. The bride had visited the village before, we gathered, and had singled it out as the properest kind of a place for a honeymoon. The groom entertained her busily through dinner, breakfasted alone next morning, and was very much afraid that people might think that he was but recently married. The waitresses, who brought our order on the run from the first course, had reached a mad gallop by the time the coffee appeared. Everybody was particularly gay, and for no particular reason. Because the moon was soon to rise, forsooth, or because there were such fine green chestnut trees in the world and such good salads in that happy part of the world called France. The painter looked at his wasp-waist lady as though she were a goddess, and the mamma of the Fremont family smiled at her daughters, who were uttering feeble witticisms to the sons of the Picard family, and wondered however she came to have such clever daughters. Pere Picard and Pere Fremont were telling each other stories of their conscript days in the army and roaring, each at his own anecdotes. Oh, we were a motley, clever, self-appreciative lot of people at Barbizon that night, and it was a good world we lived in.

The conversation grew less animated, and we sat for a long time watching the glorious rising of the harvest moon before going for a walk through the moon-lit avenues of the forest. After sunset there is not a light in Barbizon, except here and there from a cottage window.

The next day we spent in the forest, walking all morning through the western section of it. Sometimes we kept to the white roads under the arching elms, and sometimes we went for miles over the blossoming heather, and again over glades of slippery pine needles or clambered over masses of tumbled rocks. It was at Barbizon and in the forest about, as all English-speaking people well remember, that Robert Louis Stevenson first met and became enamored of the woman whom he afterward married in California. Certainly if there is any spot in the world where a young man might be flung headlong into the most extravagant romance, it would be the forest of Fontainebleau. The old spell seems still to hold good, for we met occasionally a Columbine and her Pierrot. But much more often we encountered the one institution which you can never get away from in France—the family. Old men playing with their grandsons, young men walking with their mothers, sisters hand in hand, brothers arm in arm. They stopped to name every wild flower, they held hands and spanned the girth of all the big trees. What a fine tree to hide behind if a bear should come, said grandpa, and grandma and the young people laughed and called him a famous comedian, a regular Coquelin of a fellow. We were rather startled once at hearing a rollicking drinking song, by male and female voices, coming toward us through the wood, but it was only a bourgeois papa, his white waistcoat on; mamma stout and puffing as she plodded, her skirts held up under her elbow, and half a dozen sons and daughters, who were singing for joy of life and companionship.

That night we left Barbizon, unwillingly enough. When we drove away at about sunset, the harvesters were still working in the fields, and the chatter of the brave old peasant women who plodded across the stubble made the best kind of music in our ears. [September 21, 1902, p. 18]

"The Old City of the Popes"

Perhaps the high point of Willa Cather's first trip to Europe was the time spent in Provence, particularly in Avignon. Two of her closest friends have written of what this country and this city meant to her. Edith Lewis told of a letter from Willa Cather to a former teacher, Mrs. A. K. Goudy, in which she said how deeply the Provençal landscape moved her, that she found in it "something that in a hidden way linked itself with the American West."[28] *Miss Lewis added that "on this first visit to Provence one place fascinated her above all others—Avignon." Elizabeth Shepley Sergeant related that when she herself was in Provence some years later, Willa Cather wrote to her recalling "the yellow mustard in the tragic theatre at Arles and the little willows of Avignon resting their elbows in the flooded Rhone. Her most splendid memory was of the Rocher des Doms and its Virgin, golden above the great river, finest in the world, maybe. Did the same swirling mighty current rush past the old Pont d'Avignon? . . . Like the Southwest it was a land that made one mad with delight."*[29] *Again and again throughout her life Willa Cather revisited Provence; and Avignon in the time of the popes was the setting of her last, unfinished story.*[30]

AVIGNON, Sept. 3.—(Special Correspondence.)—We began our journey south without much enthusiasm, for Paris is a hard place to leave, even when it rains incessantly and one coughs continually from the dampness. We left from the Gare de Lyon at night, arriving at Lyon early in the morning. As we had come to Lyon second class, having an entire compartment to ourselves and sleeping quite as comfortably as in a Pullman sleeping car, my friend and I felt it our duty to be economical and to journey down to Avignon third class. It seemed, indeed, that all the world was going south, for there were eight women and one wretched infant in our compartment, most of them women of the people and of the soil. Those women of the soil are all very well in pictures by Millet or Bastien-Lepage, but they are not the most desirable traveling companions in a little compartment on a burning August day when the mistral is blowing and white dust hangs heavy on the olive and fig trees. The baby had not much more clothing on than an infant Bacchus, and its mother was so tired and hot and discouraged with life that she threw the infant upon me and my dress suitcase and left it to its own devices. Next to my friend sat a German girl who had been shipped from some town in Prussia and was booked through to Tarascon. She spoke no French, and was so warm and

28. This quotation and the one following from Lewis, *Willa Cather Living*, p. 56.

29. Sergeant, *Willa Cather*, pp. 96, 97.

30. For an account of the unfinished Avignon story, "Hard Punishments," see George N. Kates' essay in Willa Cather, *Five Stories: with an article . . . on Miss Cather's Last, Unfinished, and Unpublished Avignon Story* (New York: Vintage Books, 1956), pp. 177–214, esp. Miss Lewis's description of the story, 200–205.

stupid that she had much ado to speak German. She looked very much like a fat, pink pig that has been playing in the mud. She wore a heavy stuff dress and she had not bathed these many years, all the smelling salts we had brought with us could not hide that fact. She had a sort of leather porte-monnaie hung about her neck by a piece of twine. Promptly at one o'clock she took from this a fat bologna sausage, a lump of black bread and a bit of cheese that may have been fresh when she left her dear Deutschland a week before. After she had devoured the last of the cheese our troubles were somewhat easier to bear. After all no troubles of that sort could be really unbearable with [the] Rhone just outside your car window, the Cevennes on one side of you and the Alps on the other. It is a river indeed, the Rhone; none of your clear English streamlets that wind through rose-hedged meadows, but a great, green flood of water, sweeping swiftly and fiercely along between its banks of red clay. On every hillside were vineyards, a little red and brown now from the south wind, and above almost every vineyard the white ruin of one of the castles of the old lords of Dauphiny. Below Livron the scenery grows constantly more characteristically southern. The soil of the hills is red, the poplars are taller and more slender than in the north, and about all the level plains are the tall black plumes of the cypress, planted there to shield the wretched little patches of melons and Indian corn from the mistral. Everywhere is the glossy green of the fig and the dusty grey of the olive, everywhere the relentless glare of the fervid sun of the Midi. The farm houses are all low rambling structures built of cobble stone, with walls four and five feet thick to keep out the heat. The barns and dwellings are all under one roof, with a big open court between where the wagons and farm implements are kept. All the gardens are hedged with hollyhocks and sunflowers. The whole atmosphere is pervaded by the odor of drying sunflowers. The villages are white clusters of stucco and cobble stone houses with red tiled roofs, with grape vines trained above all the windows. Every street is a fine avenue of sycamores. But no matter how dusty the plains or how stunted the corn or how swart the olives, there were always and always the pine trees, the faithful sisters of the Rhone who have followed her down from her blue birthplace up in the cool Alps, and who never leave her, no matter how dwarfed or dusty they become in their southern grape land, until she flings her impetuous water into the Mediterranean at last.

At the end of four hours the guard called Avignon, the signal for our release from the German girl and her luncheon, and from the infant

Bacchus who was cutting his teeth and had by this time nearly eaten the straps off my suit case. Oh what a thing is a good hotel at the end of a weary journey, a journey full of heat and dust and hungry French fleas and people that are more distasteful than them all. I feel now that I could spend the rest of my life at this hostelry and ask for nothing better. It was only after we were comfortably installed in a room cheerfully papered in red, with three big gilt mirrors and a famous old writing table, the floor tiled in red stone, that I remembered how affectionately Henry James speaks for this particular hotel in one of his essays. It is primitive enough, too; one takes a bath in a washbasin and goes to bed by candle light, but people know how to live in this country. As we had carried no bologna with us, we were naturally interested in the dining room on the afternoon of our arrival. It happens to be the chapter-room of an ancient church which stood next the hotel several hundred years ago. It is a large hall, with a Gothic ceiling of arches that spring from columns on each side the wall, and very old stained glass windows that throw pools of color on the white stone floor. On the wall is a great chromo of Napoleon watching the burning of Moscow. Our companions at dinner were half a dozen bachelor merchants of Avignon, some people from Arles, a German professor studying the antiquities of southern France and several French officers. The dinner consisted of ten courses, each better than the last, with wines that made us sad because we knew we would never taste their like again. Little white fish, just caught in the Rhone and popped into the pan, calf's head with tomato sauce, lamb chops with a wonderful sauce of spinach, big yellow melons and figs and grapes, cream of carrot soup and patties of rice, broiled larks on toast and marvellous little cakes made of honey and spice and flour. Yet for all this luxury we pay something less than two dollars a day.

How to write of Avignon itself, the fine old city of the popes, I am sure I do not know. Though tourists frequent it so little that we are the only English-speaking people in the place, its history alone would make it one of the most interesting towns in France. When, in 1309, because of political complications Pope Clement V left Italy, he chose Avignon as his residence seat. Until 1377 the popes reigned here and Avignon was the center of the Catholic world. Today the papal arms are as much in evidence here as they were 600 years ago and everything centers about and is dominated by the papal palace. At the north end of the town there rises an enormous facade of smooth rock 300 feet above the Rhone. This sheer precipice, accessible from the river side only by winding stone stairways, is crowned by the great palace of the popes. The palace is a huge, rambling Gothic pile, flanked by six square Italian towers, with a beautiful little cathedral in front. The palace faces toward the town, and behind it, overhanging the Rhone, are the popes' gardens. Those popes were luxurious fellows, one would judge, and certainly they were men of taste. Whether they occasionally grew homesick for Italy is not told us, but they brought Italy with them. It must have been an undertaking of some magnitude to make an Italian garden on the top of a bald rock 300 feet above the Rhone, but there it lies today as beautiful as when Clement VI planted and watched over it. Four successive terraces rise one from another, each walled with white marble and connected with the terrace above and below it by winding avenues overhung with feathery fir trees, brown with cones. The garden is really a little terraced forest, cool in the hottest noontime and black with shadows. There are hundreds of oleanders as tall as chestnut trees and now heavy with pink and scarlet blossoms. There are almond trees and black cypresses and tall hedges of ilex and mulberry and lemon trees with thick, glossy leaves. There is a fountain, too, and a lake with white swans on it. But all this is as nothing when one has reached the topmost terrace and once looked upon the valley of the Rhone and what lies beyond it. Surely the holy fathers knew where to build their fine home. Immediately below one lies the white town, with its narrow streets and red roofs and the big, rushing, green river. Beyond that are interminable plains of figs and olives and mulberries, of poplars and willow hedgerows with here and there a wayside cross and its weather-wracked Christ. Then, to the south, the Cevennes mountains, and to the north and east Alps and Alps and forever Alps. The first unfolding of it as one mounts the terrace strikes awe to the most phlegmatic soul. It was late afternoon when we first saw it, and it seemed as though, besides Avignon and the Rhone, there was nothing else in the world but the Alps. The clouds hung about their flanks, but the bases and the peaks were clear, and the snow gleamed blindingly in the upper gorges. At that hour they were a pale, pinkish-purple, as though all the lilac blossoms that had ever been since the world began had been heaped up there against the hot, blue sky. The smell of them, even, seemed to blow to one across the plain. It must have been a fine place for those Italy-loving popes here where they could always watch the Alps with one eye, and with the other look down upon the Rhone, the great highway to Italy, where every day barges and galleys went leaping down the current to Naples.

At the foot of the cliff, four great stone arches of the famous old Avignon bridge still reach out into the Rhone. There were twenty arches once, when the bridge reached clear across the river to the tower of Philippe le Bel. It was upon this bridge that the young men and maids of Avignon used to dance the farandole on Sundays and at eventime, as Daudet tells in his fine story "The Pope's Mule." It was built by a fraternity of bridge-making friars, and in the third span of the bridge they made two beautiful little chapels of white stone. The clever and talkative old woman who has the bridge in charge now took us out to these chapels and told us many stories of the good old times when the people of Avignon used to dance on the bridge to the tambourine. In the hard stone of the pier there is a green fig tree growing with no morsel of earth to nourish it, and it clambers up the chapel wall. The seed which grew it was brought down the Rhone once in flood time, so the old woman said. It had begun to grow there, between the crevices of the stone when she was a girl, and she had lived to see it bear fruit. Ah the Rhone was a terrible thing in flood time! It entirely covered the island and only the tips of the Lombard poplars along the shore stuck out of the brown, roaring flood.

The people of Avignon are awake to the beauties of their town. In the afternoon the papal gardens are full of people, but when the cathedral bell rings half past six they disperse to drink a glass in the shady public square before dinner. The sun drops rapidly this far south, and darkness falls as suddenly as though a curtain were suddenly dropped from somewhere. Even while the last sun rays still rest on the high garden, one can see the darkness creeping swiftly over the plains below. It is as though you were looking down on the farms and vineyards through smoked glass. The Alps become a mere dark, irregular line against the horizon. The ilex and cypress trees of the garden of the popes are thick masses of blackness. The scent of the oleanders grows oppressively heavy. The stars come out fast in the blue night sky, and the only sound is from the Rhone, that with all its Alp-born impetus, rushes past one in the dark.

This, then, is how the days go by in the fine city of the popes. In the morning there is the soup bowl full of chocolate, the hard rolls and pats of fresh butter wrapped in green fig leaves. When we go into the dining room to get it, Jules arises and puts on a black coat over his suit of white duck, and serves us with ceremony. Then it is time to walk to some of the old feudal ruins perched about on the hills. Through the heat of the day we read in the ilex arbors of the garden above the river. In the late afternoon we watch the changing glories of the Alps until we go off to dine in our Gothic chapter house and night comes down with rest and healing over dusty, parched Provence. [September 28, 1902, p. 15]

"*Country of the Fabulous*"

From Avignon, Willa Cather and Isabelle McClung traveled to Marseilles and Hyères. Marseilles was forever inscribed in her imagination as the city of Edmond Dantès, hero of The Count of Monte Cristo, *which was so much a part of her childhood and which she had so warmly commended to young readers (see "Books Old and New [January 1897]," The* Home Monthly, *above).*

HYERES, Sept. 6.—(Special Correspondence.)—It was not until I saw the little white island of the Chateau d'If lying out in the sea before the old harbor at Marseilles that I awakened to the fact that we were at last in Monte Cristo's country, fairly into the country of the fabulous, where extravagance ceases to exist because everything is extravagant, and where the wildest dreams come true. The road down from Avignon had not been conducive to castle building, for the rain fell drearily and persistently, and, though this itself is a sort of fairy tale in Provence, it did not stimulate our imagination. But the clouds had broken by the time we looked out from the old harbor at Marseilles, and the sunlight played on the white cliffs of the little island, and the first shock produced by the color of the Mediterranean, coupled with the name of the Chateau d'If, were enough to heat fancies that all day had been as wet as the dripping olive trees. Even had the famous state prison not been there, I think the sailors who ran about the harbor would have recalled to me the story in which Dumas put the Arabian Nights to shame. The Chateau d'If was the beginning of a marked change in our feelings. In a moment one felt the kindling of something that had burned in one long ago, when one lived and suffered and triumphed with Edmond Dantes. This prison and its island, I found, were quite as important to me, quite as hallowed by tradition, quite as moving to contemplate, as Westminster or Notre Dame. Aside from the signal importance this island once had for me, I had to consider its attraction for a certain small brother of mine, and bear all his thrills upon me.

Eastward of Marseilles we passed for a long time through the olive country. The fields were small and stony, terraced along the hillsides, and the earth, which had been freely worked about the trees was as red as brick dust, exactly as a southern painter made it in his fine Provence landscape in the Luxembourg. The longer one stays in the south the more suggestive the olive tree becomes. It is such a gracious and humble tree; it struggles so hard and patiently against circumstances the most adverse, and yet, like the people who love it, manages always to preserve in its contour, no matter how stony the soil, or how heavy the white dust hangs on its leaves, something of grace and beauty. We journeyed on so through the olive country until evening, now close to the sea, now whirled back into the valleys behind the hills.

Through the complications of an excursion ticket, we were landed at the dock yards of La Seyne, a little shipping town out on the Mediterranean, late at night, with no train leaving for our destination for three hours. We would have spent the night there, but the only discoverable hotel in the place did not tempt us, tired as we were. We alighted from the station omnibus about six feet from the edge of the sea, in the heart of the sailors' quarters. On one side of the narrow, cobble paved street was a row of sailors' taverns and cafes. On the other side the Mediterranean itself. Lights of every color shone from the freight vessels in the harbor beside us. On each side of this harbor there were hills that stood out into the water, and beyond them the open sea. We stood for some moments in the middle of the street surrounded by a crowd of voluble sailors, all chattering gaily in the most perplexing dialect. Edmond Dantes was everywhere, dressed exactly as we have all seen him on the stage and as we have all imagined him in our childhood. Wide trousers of white duck, a navy blue woolen jacket, the wide braided collar of his light blue cotton shirt reaching outside of his jacket and over his broad shoulders. He wore military mustaches, sometimes earrings, a white cotton tam-o-shanter with a red tassel at the top, and a red sash about his waist. There were scores of him all about us. It occurred to us that some of our friends at home would be alarmed if they knew that we were standing in the middle of the sailors' quarter in a Mediterranean shipping town, quite alone, so late at night. But we saw about us only the most amiable brown faces, and when we asked where we could find a hotel, not one but a score replied. They spoke faster and faster and inserted dozens of perplexing expletives; they lined up and snatched off their caps and pointed out the direction for us, as the chorus of a light opera point and look expectantly when the strain that introduces the tenor sounds in the orchestra. A fine tableau they made, too, in the red lights from the cafe windows.

The dining room of the hotel hung over the sea, and was full of shippers and sailors, with one merchant from Paris who was the center of interest. We were served a very passable sort of dinner by a lightning transformation waiter who attended to twelve people and did it well. While the shippers were talking of the prices of things and the sailors recounting the adventures of the last voyage, and all were pressing each others' hands and patting each other on the shoulder, the weather took a turn. Very suddenly a boisterous storm broke over the sea. Blue lightning and wild gusts of rain, and metallic thunder that rattled rather than roared, with a great dashing and splashing of water. For a moment I was perplexed; I had seen just such a storm as that before somewhere, but where? Finally it burst upon me and I remembered well enough. It was on the stage of the Funke theatre, when Mr. James O'Neill used to be sewn up in a sack and flung by the supers from the Château d'If into the Mediterranean. This was exactly such a harmless, spectacular storm; a stage storm, a mere fit of Mediterranean temper that explodes in a stiletto flash, and then melts away into smiles and tears. About two hours later we got a train out for Hyeres, and I have left many a more attractive place with less regret than this rough little sea port where we were thrown by chance. Next morning we were awakened at 5 o'clock in our comfortable hotel chamber at Hyeres by the fierce glare of a tropical sun, rising over the tops of the date palms.

Hyeres is one of the oldest health resorts on the Mediterranean and in the winter is much frequented by English people. There is even an English bank here, which is open for two hours on two days in the week. So far, however, we have met no one who speaks English except a little black Provencal, who has a large sign "English Pharmacie; English Spoken," over the door of his shop. We went and addressed him in that tongue and the little man was covered with confusion. He blushed crimson and hung his head and muttered guiltily, "Un peu Anglaise je parle, Miss." Hyeres itself is a red-roofed town that hangs on the side of a steep pine clad hill above the sea. All the streets are shaded by date palms and giant eucalyptus trees, and the powdery mimosa trees of Algiers and the desert. The fields in the valley below grow all the roses and violets that Paris wears in the winter time. Not a night at the opera that the violets of Hyeres, grown here in this limpid air and warm sea wind, are not worn by the beautiful women of the capital. Then there are olive orchards, and about them all the blossoming hedges of oleander. Below Hyeres, the scented pine hills slope down to the sea, very high hills, covered with scrub pine and fir trees that grow with straight stems and no branches at all until they suddenly flare out wide at the top, like big green umbrellas. There is no beach at all: six feet from the pine trees is the sea, as still and motionless as a plaque of blue porcelain, with a sky of enamel above it. In the distance the hills are a pale violet. The still water is cut here and there by sail boats, sweeping along in their blue furrows with [the] swiftness of boats in a fairy tale. Some of them have white sails, others salmon pink, such as the boats of Venice that Zeim so often paints. All the sailors wear white caps and red sashes and they all sing. Everyone here sings and sings musically and tunefully. The young house painter at work on our hotel sings airs from "Rigoletto" all day as he works, the olive oil buyer across the way rumbles the choruses from "Trovatore" in a sonorous bass, like a big bumble bee, as he goes to the postoffice. Last night a beggar sang in the square one of the most beautiful minor airs I ever heard, and always and everywhere one hears the "L'Arlesienne" of Bizet. Bizet still lives in Provence, though they know his "Arlesienne" better even than Carmen.

The beach is almost deserted at this season of the year. We walk about four miles from town and have the world to ourselves, with nothing but the pines and the sea and a book of Provencal poetry. Far away, on the hilltops, is the white ruin of a castle that the Saracens held in the tenth and eleventh centuries, and which was later the stronghold of a band of pirates who ravaged the coast and terrorized the sea. But my purpose is not to tell here of the beauties of Hyeres, only to suggest the lightning transformations and magical changes that may occur in a land that is a sort of Christmas pantomime for scenery. What more of life could one wring out of twenty-four hours, if you please? At noon the wet olives of Arles; at nightfall a chorus of gay sailors, made up to the life, and the rattle of stage thunder, much blue lightning and a great tossing of blue water; at dawn a red sunrise over feathery date palms, with the sea at one's feet and a porcelain sky above. What more could one ask for, even in the country of Monte Cristo? [October 5, 1902, p. 15]

"*In a Principality of Pines*"

[LE] LAVANDOU, Sept. 10.—(Special Correspondence.)—We came to Lavandou chiefly because we could not find anyone who had ever been here, and because in Paris people seemed never to have heard of the place. It does not exist on the ordinary map of France, and Baedeker, in his "Southern France," merely mentions it. Lavandou is a fishing village of less than a hundred souls, that lies in a beautiful little bay of the Mediterranean. Its score or so of houses are built on the narrow strip of beach between the steep hillside and the sea. They are scarcely more than huts, built of mud and stone on either side of one narrow street. There is one cafe, and before it is a little square of sycamore trees where the sailors, always barefoot, with their corduroy trousers and tam o' shanter caps, play some primitive game of ball in the afternoon. There is one very fairly good hotel, built on the sea, and from the windows of our rooms we have the whole sweep of ocean before us. There is a long veranda running the full length of the house on the side facing the sea, straw-thatched and overgrown by gourd vines, where all our meals are served to us. The fare is very good for a semi-desert country, though the wine here is thin and sour and brackish, as though the seawash had got into the soil that grew it. The wine of the country just here is all red, for the white grapes which flourish about Avignon grow poorly here. We have good fish, however, excellent sauces, plenty of fresh figs and peaches, and the fine little French lobster called langouste. Every morning the one little train that rattles in over the narrow-gauge tracks from Hyeres, brings us our piece of ice, done up in a bit of sail cloth, and we watch for it eagerly enough. This little train constitutes our railroad service, and it comprises a toy engine, a coal car, a mail and baggage car and two coaches, one for first and one for second class.

The coast, for a hundred miles on either side of us, is quite as wild as it was when the Saracens held it. It is one endless succession of pine hills that terminate in cliffs jutting over the sea. There are no cattle or pigs raised here, and the people drink only goat's milk besides their own wines. The gardens are for the most part pitiful little hillside patches of failure. Potatoes, figs, olives and grapes are almost the only things that will grow at all in this dry, sandy soil. The sea is an even more uncertain harvest, as, with the exception of the lobsters, the fish of the Mediterranean are not particularly good, and bring a low price in the market. The water, indeed, is not cold enough to produce good fish. How the people live at all I am not able to discover. They burn pine knots and cones for fuel—the thermometer never goes down to freezing point—and they are able to make a savory dish of almost anything that grows. They are very fond of a salad they make of little sea-grass, dressed with the oil they get from their olives. But never imagine they are not happy, these poor fishermen of this smiling, niggardly sea. Every day we see them along the road as we walk back to the village; before every cottage the table set under an arbor or under an olive tree, with the family seated about eating their figs and sea-grass salad and drinking their sour wine and singing—always singing.

Out of every wandering in which people and places come and go in long successions, there is always one place remembered above the rest because there the external or internal conditions were such that they most nearly produced happiness. I am sure that for me that one place will always be Lavandou. Nothing else in England or France has given me anything like this sense of immeasurable possession and immeasurable content. I am sure I do not know why a wretched little fishing village with nothing but green pines and blue sea and a sky of porcelain, should mean more than a dozen places that I have wanted to see all my life. No books have ever been written about Lavandou, no music or pictures ever came from here, but I know well enough that I shall yearn for it long after I have forgotten London and Paris. One cannot divine nor forecast the conditions that will make happiness; one only stumbles upon them by chance in a lucky hour at the world's end somewhere, and holds fast to the days as to fortune or fame.

About a mile down the shore from the village, there is a little villa of white stucco, with a red tiled roof and a little stone porch, built in the pines. It is the winter studio of a painter who is in Paris now. He has managed to keep away from it all the disfiguring and wearisome accompaniments of houses made with hands. There is no well, no stable, no yard, no driveway. It is a mere lodge set on a little table of land between two cliffs that run out into the sea. All about it are the pines, and the little porch and plateau are covered with pine needles. You approach it by a winding path that runs down through the underbrush from the high-road. There, for the last week, we have taken up our abode. Nominally we stopped at the Hotel de la Mediterrane, but we only slept and ate there. For twelve hours out of the twenty-four we were the possessors of a villa on the Mediterranean and the potentates of a principality of pines. There is before the villa a little plateau on the flat top of a cliff extending out into the sea, brown with pine needles and shaded by one tall, straight pine tree that grows on the very tip of the little promontory. It is good for one's soul to sit there all the day through, wrapped in a steamer rug if the sea breeze blows strong, and to do nothing for hours together but stare at this great water that seems to trail its delft-blue mantle across the world. Then, as Daudet said, one becomes a part of the foam that drifts, of the wind that blows and of the pines that answer.

Besides having a manor, we have a demesne as well, a fair demesne of lavender tufts that grow thick over the hills; and their odorous blossoms, drying in the sun, mingle their fresh, salt perfume with the heavier odor of the pines. Our only labor is to gather these blossoms, but so regal is our idleness that we have much ado to accomplish it.

Going to and fro we have made the acquaintance of certain neighboring princes and princesses whose kingdoms lie round about.[31] There are, in the first place two little girls, whom we meet every day seeking pasture for their goat. As the goat supplies the milk and butter for the family, it is most necessary that she should have good grass and that, on this arid coast, is not easy to find in September. When they have found a green spot they carefully tether her, and with many parting injunctions to her not to run away, and to eat all she can and be a good little goat, they leave her. Then there is the old man who lives in a thatch on the hillside, from whom we buy figs, and the woman who goes about with scales and basket, selling lobsters. At the hotel there is an old Parisian who has exiled himself from the gaieties of the capital, and is living out the remainder of a misspent life in the solitudes of his native south. His eyes fairly devour anyone who comes from Paris, and he beams when a bicyclist or two pump into Lavandou to solace his loneliness. For several days he has been the only guest at the hotel besides ourselves, and he eats his lobster and sips his benedictine in sadness.

The other day we left our manor long enough to make a royal progress to Cavalaire, a village six miles down the coast. The road is a wild one; on one side the steep hillside, on the other the sea. If we had not tested the kindliness of these southerners before, we might have been rather intimidated by the loneliness of the road. We met nothing more terrible that a sailor boy sitting on the stone coping of a bridge trying to tie up a badly bruised foot in a piece of cloth torn from the sash about his waist. He had been put ashore that morning off a freight boat because his foot disabled him, and was limping along to St. Praid, twenty-five miles down the coast, where his people lived. He did not ask for charity, nor vouchsafe

31. For the mood of this letter, cf. "The Treasure of Far Island," *New England Magazine*, 27 (October 1902), 234–249; *CSF*, pp. 265–282.

his story until he was questioned. We gave him some money and a pin to keep the cloth on his foot, and, as we were returning late in the afternoon, we met him limping on his way. We met also a few fishermen, and several women walking beside little carts drawn by a donkey no bigger than a sheep, and every woman was knitting busily as she walked, stopping only long enough to greet us. The village of Cavalaire consists of a station house and a little tavern by the roadside. The station agent lay asleep on a bench beside his door, and his old mother and wife were knitting beside him. The place is not a little like certain lonely way stations in Wyoming and Colorado. Before we reached our own village that night the moon was already throwing her tracks of troubled light across the sea.

But always we come back to the principality of pines and decide there is nothing else quite so good. As I said before, there is nothing but a little cardboard house of stucco, and a plateau of brown pine needles, and green fir trees, the scent of dried lavender always in the air, and the sea reaching like a wide blue road into the sky. But what a thing it is to lie there all day in the fine breeze, with the pine needles dropping on one, only to return to the hotel at night so hungry that the dinner, however homely, is a fete, and the menu finer reading than the best poetry in the world! Yet we are to leave all this for the glare and blaze of Nice and Monte Carlo, which is proof enough that one cannot become really acclimated to happiness. [October 12, 1902, p. 15]

"*In the Country of Daudet*"

Willa Cather had often written admiringly and affectionately of Daudet (see, especially, "The Death of Daudet," Books and Authors [III], above), and it was fitting that the last of her European letters should celebrate his country. But the most impressive section of the piece looks back to her earlier comments on the conflict between the "fine, subtle, sensitive, beauty-loving Latin races" and the destroying and renewing barbarians from the north, and also points to one of the two major themes of The Troll Garden.[32]

ARLES, Sept. 16.—(Special Correspondence.)—It is with something like a sigh of relief that one quits the oppressive splendor of Monte Carlo to retrace our steps back into Daudet's country. I am sure I do not know why

32. For earlier comments on the Roman-Barbarian conflict, see "Romance," Books and Authors (II). For a discussion of its application to *The Troll Garden*, see *KA*, pp. 92 ff. and 442–444.

the beauty of Monte Carlo should not satisfy more than it does. The bluest of all seas is nowhere bluer than when you see it between the marble balustrades of the long white terrace before the casino, palms are nowhere greener than in that high garden which the mountains screen from every unkind breath, no colors could be more rich and various than those of the red and purple Alps that tower up behind the town, on whose summits such violent thunderstorms gather and break. But, for me, at least, there was not at all the pleasure I had anticipated in this dazzling white and blue, these feathery palms and ragged Alps. It is a common experience that, in pleasant dreams, where conditions are approaching to perfection, when the work long undone is done, or the friend who has so long been bitter grows kind, with this flood of exultation there comes the conviction "this is a dream." I had a continual restless feeling that there was nothing at all real about Monte Carlo; that the sea was too blue to be wet, the casino too white to be anything but pasteboard, and that from their very greenness the palms must be cotton. It may be that other things, as well as the superb stage settings of the place, go to produce this effect. Though all Europe goes to spend its money in this little kingdom not three miles long, there is nothing at all produced or manufactured there, and no life at all that takes hold upon the soil or grapples with the old conditions set for a people. In atmosphere and spirit the entire kingdom of Monaco is an extension of the casino.

A day's riding through red earth and olives and miles of vineyard lands where the grape-pickers are busy, brought us back to middle Provence, the heart of Daudet's country. The country of tambourines and Muscat wine, he calls it, and the phrase is more presentive than a volume of close description. It is a high, windy, dusty country, just anchored on the banks of the turbulent Rhone, where the mistral continually threatens to dislodge it and blow it away. The mistral is a fierce reality now, it buffets us like a gale at sea, more terrible than any wind that ever came up from Kansas. The fig trees are powdered with white dust until they are all but as grey as the olives, the vineyards are red as October oak leaves, the smell of drying fruit, of ripe things and of making wine is everywhere. Even in Arles the sycamore leaves are beginning to turn a little, and over her narrow streets in the evening there falls the chill of autumn, the strange homesick chill that always makes one want to be at home, where there are geraniums to be potted for winter and little children to be got ready for school. But in the daytime one forgets these things in the excitement of continual novelty, and who could be gloomy on a September morning at Arles? The town could never have retained its color and quaintness had it been in any touch with modern commerce, but Arles is the centre of a large pastoral district, a great country of shepherd kings, and farmer barons, of fat priests, of old customs and simple living. Every one of these known [brown?] stone farm houses, stable and dwelling together with the farm yard court between, is a sort of feudal manor. Usually three generations and many servants live there: the grandparents, the married son who has inherited the farm, his children, and the wagoners and shepherds. No farmer has a desire to be anything else, or to live in any better house than the one his father lived in, or to see a larger city than Arles. They keep carefully all their ancient festivals, the Noel and the feasts of their patron saints and name saints. They desire to live honorably and long, to marry their daughters well and to have strong sons to succeed them, to avoid innovation and change, to drink their Muscat wine and eat their boiled snails and tomatoes fried in oil to the end. The word of the master is the only law needed; the women sit down to meat only after the men are served. When a child is born, his godmother stands at the four corners of his bed holding salt, bread, eggs, and wine; if he have always enough of those, that is quite enough to wish for him. Simple ambitions, these seem for this century, but they express nearly the whole will and need of the people of Provence, who are a truly pastoral people still. Besides being shepherds and farmers, almost every Provencal is a poet. The gallery of the portraits of native poets at Arles represents several hundred poets, and the unpublished rhymesters are of course even more numerous. They make songs as they make wine down in this country; it grows up from this old red soil that bred the first troubadours ages since, it distills from the pines, it breaks from the red grapes. Boys come into some knack of song-making as they come into long trousers, as they come into the age when they go a-courting. It is natural, and makes no great stir unless it develops to a higher degree of perfection, as it did in Daudet. The shepherds make songs in the mountains as they watch their flocks at night, the grandfather sings by the fire on winter nights the songs he made in his youth, and the grandson sings to some Arlesienne the song he made yesterday.

The women of Arles alone might well account for the songful bent of their country. They are noted all over France for their beauty, which is of a rather Moorish type and now and then strangely Roman. Their clear cut features, olive skin, oval faces and fine, full eyes are well set off by their costume of velvet and lace, their fine fichus brought low about their bare brown throats, and their lace and ribbon caps on their blue-black hair. Their splendid, generous figures are an especial point of pride with them. Surely if poor little Mrs. Fiske had ever been to Arles and come and gone among these splendid brown creatures for a time, she would never have found the courage to produce Daudet's "L'Arlesienne."[33]

We are not fortunate enough to see a bull fight at Arles, as they occur only on Sunday and we cannot stay over. The bulls for the ring are reared in a desolate fever-stricken marshy land called the Camargue. The only intruders on this reedy wildness are the herdsmen, the duck-hunters and the mistral. The herdsmen live there from year's end to year's end, "and their existence is so solitary," Daudet remarks, "that when they come to town once or twice a year the little cafes of Arles seem to them more magnificent than the palaces of the Ptolemies." The bull fights still take place in the old Roman amphitheatre, built in this rich colonial town in the first Christian century. This amphitheatre is one of the most extensive Roman ruins in France, and is in a much better state of preservation than the coliseum at Rome. It is 500 yards in circumference, and contains forty-three tiers of seats. It originally held 26,000 people, but so numerous are the exits that the house could be emptied of this crowd in four minutes. The edifice at present looks as though it might last until the end of time, as long as the Latin tongue is echoed anywhere. The ravages of the years are but little apparent; it is still as huge and white under its blue porcelain sky as it was in the days of Constantine, and even the loftiest gothic seems small beside its stubborn, arrogant, defiant hugeness.

The tragic theatre, though ill preserved, is quite as impressive. The white ledge on which the auditors sat remains, though stained and broken. The stone box about the pit from which the curtain rose is intact, but only two remain of the twenty splendid marble columns which stood so slenderly against the sky and formed a noble back-ground for the toga-clad players. Why is it that neither Daudet nor Flaubert nor Gautier ever attempted to give us a study of the civilization of those proud old Roman colonies? In the south it seems quite as though the living tie between France and her mother country had never been cut. This ruined theatre,

33. For Minnie Maddern Fiske, see The Star System (III), and (IV), above.

its marble sunk in turf and overgrown with mild mustard and candytuft,[34] seems a legitimate part of Provence, a growth of its own soil. What an active and vigorous life the colonists must have lived here in their Arelate, as they called it, in the days when Constantine built his palace by the Rhone. The wreck of that palace is still here, wind-wracked and flood-wracked but unmistakable. A wonderful liking the Romans had for this gothic soil they had subdued; they liked the climate, the wines, the remoteness from the turbulent political strife of Italy. They made a continual effort to recall Italy in the architecture, dress and social life of their colony. They called Arelate the "Gallic Rome" and adorned her with theatres and baths and a forum, just as the cities of the French provinces today copy Paris. These colonists had a sort of Chicago like vehemence in adorning their city and making it ostentatiously rich. They sent their artists to Rome to be trained and gave them enough to do on their return. Every galley that came up the Rhone from Naples brought masterpieces of weaving, sculpture, painting or pottery, musicians and actors who came to the colonies to play in the summer season when the heat of southern Italy drove play-goers to the Apennines. The famous Venus of Arles in the Louvre at Paris was originally brought from Rome to grace the foyer of the theatre, and was found there in 1651. Before the theatre was a fountain, Silenus reclining on a fat wine-skin, from the open mouth of which the jet of water played. This fountain is now preserved in the museum at Arles. The theatre was begun in the reign of Augustus, and the head of the emperor which stood in the foyer is certainly the finest portrait I have ever seen of him, though they are in every museum in Europe. There is an equally fine head of Livia, which stood by that of her husband, and one of the little Marcellus, erected before his death, when he was still the hope and pride of the empire. There is an interesting head, too, of the infant Constantine, grave and devout as a little St. John. But of all the sculptures which have been found in this old town that the Latins made so fair, the most beautiful is a triplex bas-relief that was placed in the wall of their theatre. The middle section represents the triumph of the poet; laurel crowned, the muses behind him, calmness and dignity upon his brow, striking his lyre with all the confidence of mastery. At the left is a smaller scene, a single figure, Apollo, sharpening his knife on a stone. At the right is another picture with but one figure, Marsyas,

34. Cf. "Provençal Legend" in *April Twilights*, which begins: "On his little grave and wild, / Faustinus, the martyr child, / Candytuft and mustards grow" (*AT(1903)*, pp. 20–21).

the poet of the middle panel, hanging from an oak tree by his thonged hands, his skin hanging limp and wet about his flayed limbs, his broken lyre at his feet.[35] Surely it was a frank fashion these Romans had of encouraging their tragic poets!

After one spends a day or two among the Roman remains in the museums here, the portrait busts and mosaics and beautifully sculptured tombs, it seems almost as if there may be some truth in the old story that the women of Arles owe their beauty to the vows they used to make to their pagan Venus in secret, and that their children come into the world with the fine, clear profiles that are cut on the old Roman tombs. In Italy itself one could scarcely feel [more] the presence of Rome, of the empire and all it meant, of its self-devouring and suicidal vastness, than here in the land where the richest and proudest of its colonies flourished. One sunny afternoon we were examining some broken columns and fragments of capitals tumbled beside a wall of turf and overgrown with white candytuft which makes the air sweet and keeps the bees coming and going. The finest thing we found was a section of a cornice, perhaps six feet long, with a great eagle upon it, a garland in his beak. The eagle, the one and only eagle, here in the far corner of the earth where the shadow of his great wings fall, the one bird more terrible in history than all the rest of brute creatures put together. Above him was the inscription "Rome Eternal." Yet they say that even the most remote of his descendants are doomed, that all who echo his tongue and bear his blood must perish, and these fine, subtle, sensitive, beauty-making Latin races are rotten at heart and must wither before the cold wind from the north, as their mothers did long ago. Whoever is a reasonable being must believe it, and whoever believes it must regret it. A life so picturesque, an art so rich and so divine, an intelligence so keen and flexible—and yet one knows that this people face toward the setting, not the rising sun.

I was in London several months ago when Lord Kitchener and his troops returned from Africa. On the day of the commander's arrival, after the procession from Paddington, and while the reception at St. James's was in progress, there were several thousand cavalry horses picketed in Hyde Park. There was a tramping of red coats everywhere, and the trains of rajahs from the east were moving this way and that, glittering in gold and crimson, the nobles of a conquered race. But the spirit of that day lay

35. See "Lament for Marsyas" in *April Twilights; (AT(1903)*, pp. 27–28).

not in these things. Before those thousands of horses there were rows and rows of children, children who had clambered out of carriages, children who had clambered out of gutters, children who seemed to have sprung from a sowing of the dragon's teeth, and they were all petting and stroking the animals with a pride, an earnestness, a wistfulness touching to see. There they were; "Cook's son, duke's son, son of a hundred kings," each whispering a vow to the horses of the cavalry. One felt in a flash of conviction from what blood the world's masters were to come. The poet of the line said that "On the bones of the English, the English flag is stayed." From the time the Englishman's bones harden into bones at all, he makes his skeleton a flagstaff, and he early plants his feet like one who is to walk the world and the decks of all the seas. [October 19, 1902, p. 9]

APPENDICES
A NOTE ON THE EDITING
BIBLIOGRAPHY
ACKNOWLEDGMENTS
INDEX

❋ ❋ ❋

APPENDIX I

"Willa Cather Mourns Old Opera House"

This letter addressed to Harvey E. Newbranch, editor-in-chief of the Omaha World-Herald *and a friend of Willa Cather's since college days, appeared in the Diamond Jubilee edition of the paper, October 27, 1929, p. 9. The Red Cloud Opera House opened on October 26, 1885; it was located on Webster Street, above a hardware store, and seated about five hundred.*[1]

Dear Mr. Newbranch: It's a newspaper's business, is it not, to insist that everything is much better than it used to be? All the same, we never gain anything without losing something—not even in Nebraska. When I go about among little Nebraska towns (and the little towns, not the big cities, are the people), the thing I miss most is the opera house. No number of filling stations or moving picture theatres can console me for the loss of the opera house. To be sure, the opera house was dark for most of the year, but that made its events only the more exciting. Half a dozen times during each winter—in the larger towns much oftener—a traveling stock company settled down at the local hotel and thrilled and entertained us for a week.

That was a wonderful week for the children. The excitement began when the advance man came to town and posted the bills on the side of a barn, on the lumberyard fence, in the "plate glass" windows of drug stores and grocery stores. My playmates and I used to stand for an hour after school, studying every word on those posters; the names of the plays and the nights on which each would be given. After we had decided which were the most necessary to us, then there was always the question of how

1. Mildred R. Bennett, "The Incomparable Opera House," *Nebraska History* 49 (Winter 1968), 373–374.

far we could prevail upon our parents. Would they let us go every other night, or only on the opening and closing nights? None of us ever got to go every night, unless we had a father who owned stock in the opera house itself.

If the company arrived on the night train, when we were not at school, my chums and I always walked a good half mile to the depot (I believe you call it "station" now) to see that train come in. Sometimes we pulled younger brothers or sisters along on a sled. We found it delightful to watch a theatrical company alight, pace the platform while their baggage was being sorted, and then drive off—the men in the hotel bus, the women in the "hack." If by any chance one of the show ladies carried a little dog with a blanket on, that simply doubled our pleasure. Our next concern was to invent some plausible pretext, some errand that would take us to the hotel. Several of my dearest playmates had perpetual entry to the hotel because they were favorites of the very unusual and interesting woman who owned it. But I, alas, had no such useful connection; so I never saw the leading lady breakfasting languidly at nine. Indeed, I never dared go near the hotel while the theatrical people were there—I suppose because I wanted to go so much.

How good some of those old traveling companies were, and how honestly they did their work and tried to put on a creditable performance. There was the Andrews Opera Company, for example; they usually had a good voice or two among them, a small orchestra and a painstaking conductor, who was also the pianist. What good luck for a country child to hear those tuneful old operas sung by people who were doing their best: *The Bohemian Girl, The Chimes of Normandy, Martha, The Mikado.* Nothing takes hold of a child like living people. We got the old plays in the same day [way?], done by living people, and often by people who were quite in earnest. *My Partner, The Corsican Brothers, Ingomar, Damon and Pythias, The Count of Monte Cristo.*

I know that today I would rather hear James O'Neill, or even Frank Lindon, play *The Count of Monte Cristo* than see any moving picture, except three or four in which Charlie Chaplin is the whole thing. My preference would have been the same, though even stronger, when I was a child. Moving pictures may be very entertaining and amusing, and they may be, as they often claim to be, instructive; but what child ever cried at the movies, as we used to at *East Lynne* or *The Two Orphans?*

That is the heart of the matter; only living people can make us feel. Pictures of them, no matter how dazzling, do not make us feel anything more than interest or curiosity or astonishment. The "pity and terror" which the drama, even it its crudest form, can awaken in young people, is not to be found in the movies. Only a living human being, in some sort of rapport with us, speaking the lines, can make us forget who we are and where we are, can make us (especially children) actually live in the story that is going on before us, can make the dangers of that heroine and the desperation of that hero much more important to us, for the time much dearer to us, than our own lives.

That, after all, was the old glory of the drama in its great days; that is why its power was more searching than that of printed books or paintings because a story of human experience was given to us alive, given to us, not only by voice and attitude, but by all those unnamed ways in which an animal of any species makes known its terror or misery to other animals of its kind. And all the old-fashioned actors, even the poor ones, did "enter into the spirit" of their parts; it was the pleasure they got from this illusion that made them wish to be actors, despite the hardships of that profession. The extent to which they could enter into this illusion, much more than any physical attributes, measured their goodness or badness as actors. We hear the drama termed a thing in three dimensions; but it is really a thing in four dimensions, since it has two imaginative fires behind it, the playwright's and the actor's.

I am not lamenting the advent of the "screen drama" (there is a great deal to be said in its favor), but I do regret that it has put an end to the old-fashioned road companies which used to tour about in country towns and "cities of the second class." The "movie" and the play are two very different things; one is a play, and the other is a picture of a play. A movie, well done, may be very good indeed, may even appeal to what is called the artistic sense; but to the emotions, the deep feelings, never!

Never, that is, excepting Charlie Chaplin at his best—and his best—I have noticed, really gets through to very few people. Not to his enormous audience, but to actors and to people of great experience in the real drama. They admire and marvel.

I go to the picture shows in the little towns I know, and I watch the audience, especially the children. I see easy, careless attention, amusement, occasionally a curiosity that amounts to mild excitement; but never that breathless, rapt attention and deep feeling that the old barnstorming companies were able to command. It was not only the "sob stuff" that we took hard; it was everything. When old Frank Lindon in a frilled shirt and a velvet coat blazing with diamonds, stood in the drawing room of Mme. Danglars' and revealed his identity to Mme. de Morcerf, his faithless Mercedes, when she cowered and made excuses, and he took out a jeweled snuff box with a much powdered hand, raised his eyebrows, permitted his lip to curl, and said softly and bitterly, "A fidelity of six months!" then we children were not in the opera house in Red Cloud we were in Mme. Danglars' salon in Paris, in the middle of lives so very different from our own. Living people were making us feel things, and it is through the feelings, not at all through the eye, that one's imagination is fired.

Pictures of plots, unattended by the voice from the machine (which seems to me much worse than no voice), a rapid flow of scene and pageant, make a fine kind of "entertainment" and are an ideal diversion for the tired business man. But I am sorry that the old opera houses in the prairie towns are dark, because they really did give a deeper thrill, at least to children. It did us good to weep at *East Lynne*, even if the actress was fairly bad and the play absurd. Children have about a hundred years of unlived life wound up in them, and they want to be living some of it. Only real people speaking the lines can give us that feeling of living along with them, of participating in their existence. The poorest of the old road companies were at least made up of people who wanted to be actors and tried to be—that alone goes a long way. The very poorest of all were the *Uncle Tom's Cabin* companies, but even they had living bloodhounds. How the barking of these dogs behind the scenes used to make us catch our breath! That alone was worth the price of admission, as the star used to say, when he came before the curtain.

Very cordially yours,
WILLA CATHER

APPENDIX II

"A la Malibran"

Stanzas XX, XXI, XXII, and XXIII of Alfred de Musset's "À la Malibran," Oeuvres Complètes *(Paris: Editions du Seuil, 1963), pp. 163–164. For Willa Cather's translation,* *see page 451–452.*

XX

Que ne l'étouffais-tu, cette flamme brûlante
Que ton sein palpitant ne pouvait contenir!
Tu vivrais, tu verrais te suivre et t'applaudir
De ce public blasé la foule indifferente,
Qui prodigue aujourd'hui sa faveur inconstante,
A des gens dont pas un, certes, n'en doit mourir.

XXI

Connaissais-tu si peu l'ingratitude humaine?
Quel rêve as-tu donc fait de te tuer pour eux?
Quelques bouquets de fleurs te rendaient-ils si vaine,
Pour venir nous verse de vrais pleurs sur la scène,
Lorsque tant d'histrions et d'artistes fameux,
Couronnés mille fois, n'en ont pas dans les yeux?

XXII

Que ne détournais-tu la tête pour sourire,
Comme on en use ici quand on feint d'être ému?
Hélas! on t'aimait tant, qu'on n'en aurait rien vu.
Quand tu chantais *le Saule*, au lieu de ce délire,
Que ne t'occupais-tu de bien porter ta lyre?
La Pasta fait ainsi: que ne l'imitais-tu?

XXIII

Ne savais-tu donc pas, comédienne imprudente,
Que ces cris insensés qui te sortaient du coeur
De ta joue amaigrie augmentaient la paleur?
Ne savais-tu donc pas que, sur ta tempe ardente,
Ta main de jour en jour se posait plus tremblante,
Et que c'est tenter Dieu que d'aimer la douleur?

APPENDIX III

"The Hundred Worst Books and They That Wrote Them"

Although Willa Cather's first published book was a collection of poetry, between 1900 and the end of 1902 she had published nine signed short stories and one under the pseudonym of "Henry Nicklemann," five in the Library, *three in* New England Magazine, *and one each in* Cosmopolitan *and the* Saturday Evening Post.[1] *As 1903 opened, there appeared in* Scribner's "'*A Death in the Desert,*'" *which she regarded well enough to include in* The Troll Garden *(1905) and* Youth and the Bright Medusa *(1920), although it was omitted from her collected works (1937–1941).*[2] *Toward the end of 1903, Willa Cather summed up her feelings about the popular fiction that it had been her lot to review in "Books and Magazines" for the* Leader *and in "Old Books and New" for the* Home Monthly, *and which had evoked many a "meatax" comment along the way, in her early* Journal *Sunday columns and in "The Passing Show."*

As it has been found possible to tabulate, to the satisfaction of some people at least, the world's Hundred Best Books, so, twenty years ago, it might have been possible to enumerate and set down the hundred least worthy that had then appeared under the imprint of reputable publishers. The enormous output since that time, however, has made such a task impossible in a literal sense. Even the most patient and plodding student,

1. See *CSF*, pp. 586–588.

2. "'A Death in the Desert,'" *Scribner's*, 33 (January 1903), 109–121; *CSF*, pp. 199–217. Willa Cather made extensive revisions in this story before it was collected in *The Troll Garden* and revised it again before she reprinted it in *Youth and the Bright Medusa.*

tabulating for his doctorate degree, would sink appalled before the herculean task of selecting the hundred worst from the thousands sufficiently poor.

The causes for this unprecedented eruption of inferior literature have been several, and the invention of the American typewriting machine is surely not the least of them. When one of the first of these machines was shown to George Eliot by an Oxford professor, she exclaimed with prophetic fervor: "Ah, I can see that it will be responsible for many a bad book, and we have poor ones enough as it is." There can be no doubt, that the mere facilitating of the mechanical labor of authorship has induced many young people who were otherwise unemployed to try their hands at literature, and only too often they have produced what other idle youngsters like themselves found readable enough. A class of ephemeral fiction has resulted which might well be called that of the stenographers' school, consisting of novels made by the almost unassisted efforts of the machine.

The great increase of publishing firms, many of which are frankly and solely interested in satisfying the lowest element of the reading public, has had, no doubt, much to do with this plague of books which, rated at nothing, would be overestimated. But it seems probable that the public library, despite many a good turn it has done for culture, is even more guilty in this general debauching of public taste. People will read a great many more novels borrowed from a public library than they would ever buy, and the great majority of people, reading many, will happen upon more poor ones than good. In the old days, when there was no getting at a new book except by the outlay of $1 or $1.50, reading people thought awhile before they chose and were not likely to select a novel by a man never heard of before, even if the title was as alluring as the publisher could make it. The young man with the nimble typewriting machine found the road to fortune slower then. The public library has, with one class of readers, largely taken the place of the old Seaside Library of fiction; it supplies them with books that they read, but would never care to keep.[3] The sale of works of fiction to the public libraries alone is now almost large enough to justify the publisher in issuing them.

The hundred poorest authors would perhaps be easier to classify than the hundred poorest books, though they are, for the most part, a most respectable company, who stand well in the eyes of their readers and publishers. The day has quite passed for making sport of such unpretentious frauds as the "Duchess," Bertha M. Clay and Laura Jean Libbey.[4] These

3. The Seaside Library, founded by George P. Munro in 1877, made cheap reprints of popular novels.

4. Not previously mentioned: Laura Jean Libbey (1862–1924), a prolific sentimental novelist.

innocent purveyers of sentiment to loverless maids and husbandless spinsters have been superseded by a much cleverer generation of charlatans. The alarming peculiarity of the mountebank in fiction today is that he has learned something about his trade; that he is usually wily enough to keep clear of the flatly ridiculous and can trick out his sham with some garnish of wit or bravery. The very complexity of life today makes it possible that almost any shrewd fellow can make a novel that will interest someone, merely for the subject's sake, if for nothing else.

We have innumerable industrial novels, dealing with all sorts of trades, with every complexion of politics, and with geographical and sociological conditions. We have novels purporting to picture the conditions of almost every city and state in the union; novels of Washington, Chicago, San Francisco; of Kansas, Nebraska, Iowa, Missouri, Pennsylvania, etc., which doubtless command a considerable local sale, quite irrespective of their literary merits. We have copper, steel, lumber, tar, wheat and corn stories, the great majority of which treat very superficially of temporary conditions and present characters which are but the exponents of more or less abortive theories. The general run of these inventions, however, do not offend more seriously than by their dreary commonplaceness.

The most extreme and outrageous books, however bad they may be, are never the worst. The Mary MacLanes[5] of fiction are self-limited, like certain disease-bearing germs, and they exterminate each other, even in the regard of the most depraved public. The books which sell by such thousands as make one ashamed of his country are of another order. Probably the most glaring and inexplicable instance of successful fraud that we have to admire today is that of Ashtoreth of the pen, Marie Corelli. Miss Corelli is rather more picturesque than our own Ella Wheeler Wilcox and Amélie Rives[6] because, preposterous as that may seem, she takes herself even more seriously. Her residence at Stratford, her championship of "the bard" who sometime inhabited there, her fanciful portrayals of herself in several of her novels, all indicate that here we have a female genius of the good old school—rapt, ethereal, art-dedicated. Among all the estimable women who turn out their two novels a year and eat the bread of toil, there is no second to this inspired and raving sibyl, who could have been fitly described and adjectived only by Ouida in her vanished prime. It is this very high seriousness of Miss Corelli's that seems occasionally to hypnotize sensible people until they accept her ludicrous philosophy, distorted ethics and sophomoric pyrotechnics of

5. Mary MacLane (1881–1929) published *The Story of Mary MacLane* in 1901.

6. Amélie Rives (1863–1945), later Princess Troubetzkoy, made a great reputation with her best seller *The Quick or the Dead?* in 1888. For Cather's comments on the book and its author, see *Journal*, March 8, 1896, p. 13; *KA*, pp. 334–335.

style at very nearly her own estimate. In all the dull grind of contemporary literature we have nothing else so rare as this Stratford Sappho, unless it be the Hall Caine, trumpeting superlatives from his Manx castle, and if we lacked other evidence that the same brush had tarred and immortalized them, their recent exchange of hostilities would suggest it.

But Miss Corelli and her tribe, all their tempestuous passions and madness of adjectives, have never done so much to deprave the novel and the taste of its constant readers as has the ill-starred renaissance of the historical romance. The doublet and the dagger are calling us to account again, and the word "colonial" has as much to answer for in fiction as it has in architecture. Tricked out in knee breeches and identified with an historical period, anything will go. The mere costuming of such a romance seems to render it attractive, and the introduction of any colonial hero, however basely he may be used, gives it a certain authority with the average patriotic reader. However frequent the anachronisms, however grossly facts may be wilfully distorted, the tradition that historical novels are "instructive" remains unassailable.

If there are not more than a hundred of them in themselves I should surely put into the category of poor books most of these insincere historical romances, from sweet Janice[7] and *When Knighthood Was in Flower* down to the least successful and least convincing of the lot. Their gross distortion of facts, their barrenness of any true imaginative power, their false standards of beauty, together with their overwhelming sentimentality and their atrocious unreality make them formidable adversaries. Not the most repulsive product of realism can possibly tend to the general vitiating of public taste as does the mawkish idealism, the absurd sentimentality and the misinterpretation of life, in which many of these stories abound.

There can be but a narrow enough future for a mind brought up upon the priggish distortions of the "Elsie books," weaned upon translations from Mrs. Marlitt,[8] and finally graduated into the pseudo-historical novels with which our presses are groaning and of which our public libraries keep thirty copies in circulation at a time. The question critics are continually asking, why people, and especially young people, no longer read Dickens and Scott and Thackeray and George Eliot, why they never open the books in which their fathers delighted? this question Janice and her ilk must answer.

Gazette, November 29, 1903, pp. 11, 14.

7. A reference to *Janice Meredith* by Paul Leicester Ford (1865–1902), a best seller in 1899.

8. The Elsie books, which began with *Elsie Dinsmore* (1867), were the work of Martha Finley (1828–1909), writing under the name of Martha Farquharson. Mrs. Marlitt was the pseudonym of Eugenie John.

A Note on the Editing

It is with the utmost diffidence that one approaches the task of editing such a writer as Willa Cather, and it should be stated at the outset that the editorial handling of these volumes would have been far different had they included work that Willa Cather herself saw through the press. But there is no evidence that she supervised any of the selections; moreover, there is no way of determining to what extent these articles and reviews were edited after the copy left her hands, although it is a safe assumption that in the great majority of cases they were copyedited to conform to the house style of the newspaper or periodical in which they first appeared. (This is most readily seen by comparing the 1900–1901 Washington letters and columns which ran in both the *Nebraska State Journal* and the *Index of Pittsburg Life*.) "In a sense," as another editor in this series has written, "for newspaper writings of this kind there is no primary text, proofread by the author, and demanding exact reprinting."[1] Consequently, the selections have been edited to correct typographical errors and misspellings and erroneous proper names, place-names, and titles, and to eliminate obsolete usage and archaic printer's conventions. It should be emphasized, however, that there has been no attempt to correct syntax or revise wording, and that the original texts have been followed exactly except in the respects described below.[2]

Original punctuation has been retained—unorthodox though it frequently is—unless an alteration is necessary for clarity. Modern usage in capitalization has been preferred, and it has been made consistent within a selection or series of selections grouped under one title and within

1. *KA*, p. 453. Miss Slote points out that it is possible Willa Cather checked her articles in the *Courier* during the weeks in 1895 when she was associate editor. It also is possible that the *Ladies' Home Journal* sent her galley proofs of "The Man Who Wrote 'Narcissus.'"

2. In the case of a number of major pieces which appeared in the *Courier* between September 7 and November 30, 1895, and in the *Journal* between November 21, 1895, and May 17, 1896, I have depended in part on the texts established by Bernice Slote in *The Kingdom of Art* and on her annotation of these selections.

closely related sections. Misspelled proper names and place-names have been corrected and made consistent throughout. Book and play titles are given correctly. Certain words that occur repeatedly (e.g., *Shakespearean, theatre, mediaeval*) have been made consistent throughout. The name *Pittsburgh* presented a special problem because at the turn of the century the forms *Pittsburgh* and *Pittsburg* both were used. In these volumes *Pittsburgh* is used throughout except when the other form occurs in a title (e.g., *Pittsburg Leader, Index of Pittsburg Life*).

Misspelled words are silently corrected. Variant spellings are allowed to stand, but are made consistent within a selection or group of selections. Compounds are generally (though not invariably) treated according to present-day usage. Temporary compounds may be hyphenated when preceding a noun, and the solid (or closed) form is preferred for *today, hothouse, lukewarm, everyone, something, downstairs, lifetime, buttonhole, theatregoer*, etc. However, when there is evidence that an unorthodox usage was deliberate on the author's part it has been preserved (e.g., the hyphenation of *hotel-child* in "The Hotel Child").

Obvious misprints and garbled sentences are silently corrected, and when a misprint is suspected an alternate reading is provided in brackets with a question mark (e.g., *nurse* [*muse?*], *intensively* [*intensely?*]). In a few cases it was possible to clear up a confusion in the text by referring to another selection in which the same passage appeared. For example, *bluggy melodrama*, occurs in a *Courier* piece on Lizzie Hudson Collier (March 18, 1899). The same sentence reappears in the *Library*, June 2, 1900, from which it can be seen that *bluggy* is a misprint for *Bijou*. Corrections of this kind are made silently.

Original paragraphing has been retained except in a few cases where dialogue or poetry has been run on without indention. Play and book titles, titles of works of art and musical compositions, and foreign words and phrases are treated according to present-day usage. Numbers are spelled out where present-day usage calls for it. Diacritical marks have been supplied except in The European Scene (see below). Omissions are indicated by ellipses. If an ellipsis occurred in the original text, it has been so noted in brackets. As mentioned in the Editor's Preface, quotation marks enclosing the title of a selection indicate that the original title has been used; other titles were supplied by the editor.

The above editorial principles have been applied to all the selections except those in The European Scene. In this chapter, for the reason given in the introductory note (page 889), the editing has been restricted to a bare minimum. Because a prior edition of Willa Cather's 1902 letters from abroad, edited by George N. Kates, departs from the *Journal* text in respects other than those specified by Mr. Kates, we have been concerned to make available a more accurate text, avoiding all but essential changes and recording all emendations not shown on the page.

In the introduction to *Willa Cather in Europe*, p. x, Mr. Kates stated that "spellings and occasional punctuation have been standardized; and there also have been made a few occasional small changes necessary for sense. . . . No crudities were erased, no repetitious language improved upon." In standardizing the spelling Mr. Kates used the English forms (*labour, honour, splendour*, etc.) preferred by Willa Cather in her later work, but which are not characteristic of her early writing. More importantly, there were textual alterations beyond those which he described. Despite the statement to the contrary, so-called crudities were erased in a number of instances, as shown in the following examples:

	Kates	*Journal*
p. 15, ll. 15–16:	in the region where	in the region of where
p. 27, ll. 14–16:	The remoteness, the unchangedness, and time-defying stillness . . . perhaps explain	The remoteness, the unchangedness and time-defying stillness . . . perhaps explains
p. 54, ll. 19–21:	to make it possible to live in a part of the city near Russell and Mecklenberg squares	to make it possible to live in a part of the city that the folks quartered in [,] Russell and Micklenberg squares
p. 59, ll. 10–11:	nothing of the neatness and trimness which characterize	nothing of the neatness and trimness which characterizes
p. 84, ll. 21–22:	even to venture an opinion	even venture an opinion
p. 98, l. 16:	One of the first things that greet your eye	One of the first things that greets your eye
p. 99, ll. 12–14:	The exterior is by no means so fine as that of the beautiful church of St. Ouen	The exterior is by no means so fine as the beautiful church of St. Ouen
p. 168, ll. 8–9:	one quits the oppressive splendour of Monte Carlo to retrace one's steps	one quits the oppressive splendor of Monte Carlo to retrace our steps

And in at least one case a repetition was deleted:

p. 70, ll. 20–21:	high garden walls whose dull brick	high brick garden walls whose dull brick

Some twenty-four other alterations, which are not "necessary for sense" and which as often as not actually impair the text, are more difficult to understand. (Why flatten "the blue night sky" and "a red sunrise" to "the blue sky" and "a sunrise"? Why change "a mere fit of Mediterranean temper that explodes in a stiletto flash" to "explodes in a stiletto"?) Commenting on the *Journal* text, Mr. Kates observed that one "fancies the uninstructed local compositor, in Nebraska—no doubt reading hastily written copy—often has only added further error." Similarly, in the Kates text the most sensible explanation for the alterations shown below is that they resulted either from faultily transcribed copy or from the New York compositor's errors.

p. 5, ll. 20–22:	the silk draperies which bore the inscription "God Save the King" and been torn down	the silk draperies which bore the inscription "God Save the King" had been torn down
p. 6, ll. 17–18:	an equestrian statue, done in bronze	an equestrian statue of Queen Victoria, done in bronze
p. 8, ll. 7–8:	nothing in their trays half as brilliant	nothing in their trays half so brilliant
l. 11:	frauds of the sort	frauds of this sort
p. 10, l. 3:	the long file	the long line
p. 22, l. 2:	an old bit of English history	an odd bit of English history
p. 29, ll. 1–2:	Mr. Housman describes it	Mr. Houseman himself describes it
p. 42, l. 8:	The woman does this	She does this
p. 47, l. 21:	taking with it a sample	takes with it a sample
p. 55, l. 2:	That put us	That puts us
p. 75, l. 13:	accuse him of any artistic temperament	accuse him of an artistic temperament
p. 77, ll. 6–7:	[knows] more about the road he trod, and what beset his soul on the way.	[knows] more about the road he trod and what beset his soul by the way.
p. 78, l. 9:	sits with his paper and briar pipe	sits with his paper and his briar pipe
l. 22–23:	the little province of high-walled orchard	a little province of high-walled orchard
p. 123, l. 14:	the winding street	the little winding street
p. 133, l. 7:	had not bathed for many years	had not bathed these many years
p. 140, ll. 22–23:	The stars come out fast in the blue sky	The stars come out fast in the blue night sky
p. 145, l. 21:	The prison	This prison
p. 149, ll. 1–2:	a mere fit of Mediterranean temper that explodes in a stiletto	a mere fit of Mediterranean temper that explodes in a stiletto flash
p. 151, l. 20:	at dawn a sunrise	at dawn a red sunrise
p. 157, ll. 9–11:	one place remembered above the rest because the external or internal conditions	one place remembered above the rest because there the external or internal conditions
ll. 13–14:	Nothing else in England or France has given anything	Nothing else in England or France has given me anything
p. 169, l. 1:	when conditions	where conditions
p. 170, l. 11:	makes one want to be home	makes one want to be at home
p. 172, l. 18:	poor Mrs. Fiske	poor little Mrs. Fiske

Obvious misprints corrected both in the Kates text and the text in this volume include: *on'eself* (one's self), *workinb men* (working men), *never ore* (never more), *fariety* (variety), *girl-fed* (gin-fed), *grimly* (grimy), *top, hats* (top hats), *teenth* (teeth), *rigidly* (rigidity), *supect* (suspect), *rdesteuction* (destruction), *cancases* (canvases), *L'Auguste* (langouste), *appurtences* (appurtenances), *paly* (play), *fairly* (fairy), *secard* (secured), *evrying* (everything), *party* (part), *wreats* (wreaths), *cemtery* (cemetery), *altitude* (attitude), *of* (on), *anly* (only), *pooped* (popped), *spinage* (spinach), *pots* (pats), *is* (its), *in* (on), *plague* (plaque), *very* (every), *ad* (and), *herdsemen* (herdsmen), *quit* (quite), *month* (mouth), *three* (tree), *demense* (demesne), *neith-* (neither), *faucet* (faced), *heart* (beast), *slighthly* (slightly), *barer* (bases), *pleace* (place), *sland* (island), and, among proper names and place-names, *Treer* (Tree), *Mr. Siddons* (Mrs. Siddons), *Kenday* (Kendal), *Bastiers Lepage* (Bastien Lepage), *Merciur* (Mercians), *Lowvre* and *Louvere* (Louvre), *Venice* (Venus), *Heyeres* and *Heyers* (Hyeres).

In addition to the correction of obvious typographical errors and jumbled lines, the following emendations have been made in the text:

FIRST GLIMPSE OF ENGLAND. P. 890, l. 21: *Union* for *union*. P. 891, l. 26: semicolon for comma. P. 892, l. 24: period supplied; *When* for *when*.

A VISIT TO OLD CHESTER. P. 894, l. 8: *reigns* for *reign;* l. 31: *Catharine* for *Katharine*. P. 896, l. 16: *Hewletts* for *Hewlitts;* l. 31: *Herefordshire* for *Herfordshire;* l. 35: *Hereford* for *Herford*. P. 896, l. 4: *centuries* for *century;* l. 5: period for comma; *Two* for *two*.

OUT OF THE BEATEN TRACK. P. 897, ll. 15–16: *Warwick* for *Warick;* l. 18 and throughout: *Housman* for *Houseman*. P. 899, l. 6: *diluvian* for *deluvian; Beside* for *Besides;* l. 18: *Wales'* for *Wales;* l. 30: comma added after *about*. P. 900, l. 22: *Magdalene* for *Magdelene;* l. 37: *Bruyere* for *Bruere*. P. 901, l. 10: *vassal* for *vassel*.

THE CANAL FOLK OF ENGLAND. P. 903, l. 19: *boatman* for *boatmen*. P. 905, ll. 33–35: position of quotation marks corrected.

SEEING THINGS IN LONDON. P. 907, l. 4: comma added after *in; Mecklenberg* for *Micklenberg;* l. 5: period for comma; *We* for *we;* l. 10: *Grey* for *Gray;* l. 18: *Tower* for *tower;* l. 19: *Temple* for *temple;* l. 21: *past* for *part;* l. 33: *Holborn* for *Holborne*. P. 908, l. 17 and throughout: *St. James's* for *St. James;* l. 22: *Houses of Parliament* for *house of parliament*. P. 909, l. 5: *Trafalgar* for *Trafalger*.

THE KENSINGTON STUDIO. P. 912, l. 17 and throughout: *Piccadilly* for *Picadilly; Hammersmith* for *Hammarsmith;* l. 19: *National Gallery* for *national gallery;* ll. 19–20: *St. Martin-in-the-Fields* for *St. Martins-in-the-Field*. P. 914, l. 4: comma added after *Perseus;* l. 12 and throughout: *Rossetti* for *Rosetti*. P. 916, l. 10: *James'* for *James;* l. 14: *palettes* for *palets;* l. 22: comma added after *shrug*.

MERRY WIVES OF WINDSOR. P. 917, l. 23: 1902 omitted in dateline; l. 33: *days* for *day*.

DIEPPE AND ROUEN. P. 920, l. 27: *Newhaven* for *New Haven*. P. 921, l. 9: *dispirited* for *disspirited;* l. 21: comma for period. P. 923, l. 8: *bourgeois* for *burgoise;* l. 30: *church* for *churches*.

TWO CEMETERIES IN PARIS. P. 925, l. 5: comma added after *wisteria;* l. 34: *Goncourt* for *Gondcourt*. P. 926, l. 5: *camellia* for *camelia;* l. 8: *Alphonsine du Plessis* for *Alphonsin Duplesse;* l. 16: *Aristophanes* for *aristophanes*. P. 927, l. 24: period for comma; *When* for *when*. P. 928, l. 28: *one's* for *ones*.

ONE SUNDAY AT BARBIZON. P. 929, l. 20 and throughout: *Fontainebleau* for *Fontainbleu*. P. 930, l. 36: *marigolds* for *merrigolds*. P. 931, l. 17: *rakers* for *raker*. P. 932, l. 10: *lamps* for *lamp;* l. 35: comma for period. P. 933, l. 9: *clambered* for *clamored;* l. 26: *bourgeois* for *bourgoise*.

THE OLD CITY OF THE POPES. P. 934, l. 18 and throughout: *Lyon* for *Lyons*. P. 936, ll. 15–16: *side wall* for *side the wall;* l. 24: *calf's* for *calves'*. P. 937, l. 29: *besides* for *beside*. P. 938, l. 5: *eventime* for *even time;* l. 34: period for comma; *When* for *when*.

COUNTRY OF THE FABULOUS. P. 939, l. 14 and throughout: *Cristo* for *Christo*. P. 941, l. 7: comma added after *shoulder;* l. 13: *O'Neill* for *O'Neil*. P. 942, l. 12: *Rigoletto* for *Rigolletto;* l. 17: open quotes inserted.

IN A PRINCIPALITY OF PINES. P. 944, l. 30: *Mediterrane* for *Mediterranee*.

IN THE COUNTRY OF DAUDET. P. 947, l. 5: *colors* for *color;* l. 12: *grows* for *grow*. P. 948, l. 19: semicolon for comma; l. 37: comma deleted after *France*. P. 949, l. 14: comma added after *solitary*. P. 950, l. 18: *Apennines* for *Appenines;* l. 21: *Silenus* for *Seilenus*. P. 952, l. 4: comma added after *teeth*.

Bibliography

Bibliographical Note

This bibliography of Willa Cather's journalistic writing from 1893 to 1903 excludes from consideration poetry and fiction. (Bibliographies for Cather's poems and short stories of these years appear in two earlier volumes in this series: *April Twilights (1903)* and *Willa Cather's Collected Short Fiction, 1892–1912.*) Since my concern is with Cather's professional writing, I also have excluded her contributions to student publications, although one selection from the *Hesperian* appears in the text. (For comment on the extent of Cather's student writing and a list of attributions, see *KA*, pp. 461–462.)

Originally my research was based on the annotated bibliography compiled by Flora Bullock and completed in 1945, now in the Benjamin D. Hitz Collection at the Newberry Library, Chicago, Illinois, and on the bibliographies in "Willa Cather in Pittsburgh," an article by John P. Hinz in the *New Colophon* 3 (1950), and in "Willa Cather's Apprenticeship," an unpublished doctoral dissertation by Harry Finestone (University of Chicago, 1953). Subsequently I used Bernice Slote's "Checklist of Willa Cather's Critical and Personal Writing, 1891–1896" (*KA*, pp. 461–477), which revised and extended all previous bibliographies for the Lincoln years and for 1896–1897 in Pittsburgh. I have corrected some errors in the Hinz bibliography and added some new attributions of unsigned *Home Monthly* and *Leader* pieces, as well as two pieces signed "Sibert." Nonetheless the following bibliography does not claim to be complete. Undoubtedly Cather did a good deal of additional writing for both these publications; in fact, one is almost tempted to say that the unsigned *Home Monthly* editorials during her tenure are all her work and that she began to contribute to the *Leader*'s "Books and Magazines" as early as October 1896. Moreover, references in her letters indicate that she was doing free-lance work that has not yet been located. (For example, in a letter to Frances Gere, June 7, 1898, Cather stated that she had been in Washington covering the Wellman polar expedition for the Associated Press.) The researcher's difficulties are, of course, compounded not only by the anonymity of much newspaper writing but also by Cather's use of pseudonyms, and given her astonishing prolificacy it is quite possible that a definitive bibliography of her writing for these early years will be forever beyond our reach.

Seven unsigned *Home Monthly* articles and editorials dating from 1896 are identified in *The Kingdom of Art.* This bibliography adds two for that year—"La Pucelle Again" (August 1896) and "Nordica Has Returned" (October 1896). All twelve of the unsigned *Home Monthly* articles and editorials for 1897 are new. I also have added seven unsigned "Books and Magazines" columns which appeared in the *Leader* from October 15, 1897, through January 28, 1898, and the review of *The Romance of the House of Savoy*, which appeared in "Books and Magazines," November 4, 1898, p. 13, in the part of the column following the review signed "Sibert." Another unsigned *Leader* piece is "Miss Mould Talks," February 6, 1898, p. 5. The new *Leader* piece signed "Sibert" is: "With Nansen to the Pole," December 1, 1897, pp. 4–5.

In identifying the unsigned pieces I have tested them by the criteria proposed in *The Kingdom of Art* (pp. 457–459):

(1) *Circumstance*—the writer must be at hand, in a logical position to be doing the work;
(2) *Style;*
(3) *Reference*—the work must relate to other writing by direct statement, repetition, or a variation on the content.

All three of these elements are present in the newly attributed pieces. In the listing below I have either cited parallel passages, characteristic comment, or variations or referred the reader to the signed or proved piece relating to the item in question. ("Books and Magazines" pieces are not cross referenced unless the parallel passage comprises more than a sentence or two.) If most of a column has been shown to be written by Cather, I have assumed that the entire column may be attributed to her. There is usually additional comment in the textual notes on the newly identified pieces reprinted in these volumes; and, needless to say, the most convincing proof is gained from the reading of an entire piece. The style and swing are unmistakably Cather's

The arrangement of the listings is as follows: Lincoln newspapers in chronological order according to the date of the first entry; Pittsburgh periodicals and newspapers in chronological order according to the date of the first entry; miscellaneous items; and a selected bibliography of works consulted.

Bibliography of Articles and Reviews

NEBRASKA STATE JOURNAL

The titles of Willa Cather's Sunday columns in the *Journal* were as follows: "One Way of Putting It"—November 6, 1893 to January 21, 1894; "Plays and Players" and "With Plays and Players,"—February 11, 1894 to March 11, 1894; "Between the Acts"—March 25, 1894 to April 29, 1894; "Utterly Irrelevant" —September 16, 1894 to October 28, 1894; "As You Like It"—November 11, 1894 to June 20, 1895; "The Passing Show"—July 21, 1895 to June 14, 1896.

"One Way of Putting It." Vignettes. Unsigned. November 5, 1893, p. 13.

"One Way of Putting It." Vignettes. Unsigned. November 12, 1893, p. 13.

"One Way of Putting It." Vignettes. Unsigned. November 19, 1893, p. 9.

"Amusements." Review of Walker Whiteside in *Richelieu*. Unsigned. November 22, 1893, p. 6.

"Amusements." Review of Clara Morris in *Camille*. Unsigned. November 23, 1893, p. 5.

"One Way of Putting It." Vignettes, Clara Morris. Unsigned. November 26, 1893, p. 10.

"Amusements." Review of Robert Downing in *Virginius*. Unsigned. November 30, 1893, p. 6.

"One Way of Putting It." Vignettes, Robert Downing. Unsigned. December 3, 1893, p. 13.

"Amusements." Review of *Friends* (the second of two in the column) titled "'Friends' is Purely Ideal." Signed: W.C. December 14, 1893, p. 6.

"One Way of Putting It." Vignettes. Unsigned. December 17, 1893, p. 13.

"Amusements." Review of Emily Bancker in *Gloriana*. Signed: W.C. January 10, 1894, p. 6.

"Amusements." Review of Lewis Morrison's *Faust*. Unsigned. January 18, 1894, p. 5.

"Amusements." Review of Hoyt's *A Trip to Chinatown*. Unsigned. January 20, 1894, p. 3.

"One Way of Putting It." Comments on the theatre. Unsigned. January 21, 1894, p. 16.

"Amusements." Review of James O'Neill in *Monte Cristo*. Unsigned. January 26, 1894, p. 6.

"One Way of Putting It." Miscellaneous comments. Unsigned. January 28, 1894, p. 13.

"Amusements." On the Kendals in *The Ironmaster*. Unsigned. February 7, 1894, p. 3.

"Amusements." Review of *The Spider and the Fly*. Unsigned. February 11, 1894, p. 6.

"The Critic's Province." Editorial. Unsigned. February 11, 1894, p. 12.

"Plays and Players." On Lincoln theatregoers, the Kendals, the Gerry Society. Signed: Deus Gallery. February 11, 1894, p. 13.

"Amusements." Review of *Fantasma*. Unsigned. February 13, 1894, p. 5.

"The Curtain Falls." On the performance of Greek and Latin plays at the University of Nebraska. Unsigned. February 17, 1894, p. 5.

"Amusements." Review of Craigen and Paulding in *A Duel of Hearts*. Unsigned. February 20, 1894, p. 2.

"Amusements." Review of Craigen and Paulding in one-act plays, *The Setting Sun* and *The Dowager Countess*. Unsigned. February 21, 1894, p. 3.

"Amusements." Review of *In Old Kentucky*. Unsigned. February 22, 1894, p. 5.

"Amusements." Review of second performance of Greek and Latin plays. Unsigned. February 24, 1894, p. 6.

"With Plays and Players." On Greek tragedy, Lillian Lewis, Ostrovsky, Modjeska. Unsigned. February 25, 1894, p. 9.

"Amusements." Review of Julia Marlowe in *The Love Chase*. Unsigned. March 1, 1894, p. 3.

"Amusements." Review of *The Ensign*. Unsigned. March 2, 1894, p. 3.

"With Plays and Players." On Julia Marlowe, Steele MacKaye, Sarah Bernhardt, Olive May. Signed: Deus Gallerie. March 4, 1894, p. 13.

"With Plays and Players." On Modjeska, Maggie Mitchell, Warde and James, English taste. Unsigned. March 11, 1894, p. 13.

"Amusements." Review of Craigen and Paulding in *Romeo and Juliet*. Unsigned. March 13, 1894, p. 2.

"Amusements." Review of Craigen and Paulding in *A Duel of Hearts*. Unsigned. March 14, 1894, p. 2.

"Amusements." Review of *The White Squadron*. Unsigned. March 16, 1894, p. 3.

"Amusements." Review of *The Idea*. Unsigned. March 17, 1894, p. 3.

"Amusements." Review of *The Voodoo*. Unsigned. March 22, 1894, p. 6.

"Amusements." Review of Lewis Morrison in *Richelieu*. Unsigned. March 23, 1894, p. 3.

"Between the Acts." On criticism, Clara Morris, romance and realism, Lewis Morrison. Unsigned. March 25, 1894, p. 13.

"Amusements." Review of Hermann the Magician. Unsigned. March 30, 1894, p. 8.

"Between the Acts." On Lincoln theatres, Marie Tempest. Unsigned. April 1, 1894, p. 13.
Doubtful.

"Amusements." Review of *The Black Crook*. Unsigned. April 3, 1894, p. 5.

"Amusements." Review of Marie Tempest in *The Fencing Master*. Unsigned. April 4, 1894, p. 5.

"Amusements." Review of William Crane in *Brother John*. Unsigned. April 5, 1894, p. 6.

"Amusements." Review of *Police Patrol*. Unsigned. April 6, 1894, p. 6.

"Amusements." Review of Della Fox and DeWolf Hopper in *Panjandrum*. Unsigned. April 7, 1894, p. 2.

"Between the Acts." On plays of the week, Cora Tanner, Mounet-Sully, Marie Tempest. Unsigned. April 8, 1894, p. 13.

"Between the Acts." On Mrs. Kendal, Gilbert and Sullivan, Rider Haggard's *She*. Unsigned. April 15, 1894, p. 13.

"Amusements." Review of a minstrel show. Unsigned. April 18, 1894, p. 3.

"Amusements." Review of *She*. Unsigned. April 20, 1894, p. 6.

"Between the Acts." On dramatizing novels, Sousa, Richard Mansfield. Unsigned. April 22, 1894, p. 13.

"Amusements." Review of Richard Mansfield in *Beau Brummell*. Unsigned. April 24, 1894, p. 5.

"Amusements." Review of *The District Fair*. Unsigned. April 26, 1894, p. 5.

"Amusements." Review of vaudeville. Unsigned. April 27, 1894, p. 6.

"Between the Acts." On Richard Mansfield, Shakespeare's birthday. Unsigned. April 29, 1894, p. 13.

"Amusements." Review of Salvini in *The Three Guardsmen*. Unsigned. May 4, 1894, p. 6.

"Amusements." Review of Sousa band concert. Unsigned. May 5, 1894, p. 2.

"Amusements." Review of recital by California poet-humorist Fred Emerson Brooks. Unsigned. May 5, 1894, p. 2.

"Amusements." Review of Blind Tom, Negro pianist. Unsigned. May 18, 1894, p. 6.

"Under the White Tents." Backstage at the circus. Signed: Willa Cather. May 27, 1894, p. 13.

"The Competitive Drill." The annual competition of the University Cadet Corps. Signed: Willa Cather. May 28, 1894, p. 13.

"Amusements." Review of *Lady Windermere's Fan*. Signed: W.C. June 5, 1894, p. 1.

"Amusements." Review of *The Chimes of Normandy*. Signed: W.C. June 7, 1894, p. 2.

"An Old River Metropolis." Brownville, Nebraska. Signed: Willa Cather. August 12, 1894, p. 13.
See also "The Hottest Day I Ever Spent," signed "George Overing," *Library*, July 7, 1900, pp. 3–4.

"Amusements." Review of Cora Potter and Kyrle Bellew in *In Society*. Unsigned. August 29, 1894, p. 6.
Included by Bullock. Questioned by Slote.

"Amusements." Review of Roland Reed in *The Woman Hater*. Unsigned. September 13, 1894, p. 5.

"Amusements." Review of the Royal Entertainers in vaudeville. Unsigned. September 14, 1894, p. 6.

"Amusements." Review of *Underground*. Unsigned. September 16, 1894, p. 3.

"Utterly Irrelevant." On art exhibits at the State Fair, interview with a magician, *Trilby*. Unsigned. September 16, 1894, p. 13.

"Utterly Irrelevant." On the use of libraries, Annie Kenwick, Marion Manola, Sarah Grand's *The Superfluous Woman*, the duty of an author. Unsigned. September 23, 1894, p. 13.

"Amusements." Review of *The Devil's Auction*. Unsigned. September 28, 1894, p. 3.

"Amusements." Review of *Uncle Tom's Cabin*. Unsigned. September 30, 1894, p. 2.

"Utterly Irrelevant." On music and theatre. Unsigned. September 30, 1894, p. 13.

"Amusements." Review of Robert Downing in *The Gladiator*. Unsigned. October 2, 1894, p. 3.

"Amusements." Review of *The Derby Winner*. Unsigned. October 5, 1894, p. 6.

"Utterly Irrelevant." On William McKinley, Robert Downing, church hymns, theatre notes. Unsigned. October 7, 1894, p. 13.

"Amusements." Review of *Gloriana*. Unsigned. October 9, 1894, p. 2.

"Amusements." Review of *Charley's Aunt*. Unsigned. October 12, 1894, p. 5.

"Amusements." Review of *Rush City*. Unsigned. October 14, 1894, p. 6.

"Utterly Irrelevant." On Duse and Bernhardt, town and gown, Oliver Wendell Holmes, war in China, practical education. Unsigned. October 14, 1894, p. 13.

"Under the Golden Leaves of Autumn." A wedding. Unsigned. October 20, 1894, p. 6.

"Utterly Irrelevant." On the Lincoln concert season, Queen Victoria, the artist's role, standards of criticism. Unsigned. October 21, 1894, p. 13.

"Amusements." Review of *The Hustler*. Unsigned. October 25, 1894, p. 2.

"Utterly Irrelevant." On *Trilby*, theatre audiences, Sordello Clubs, interview with an actor in the penitentiary. Unsigned. October 28, 1894, p. 13.

"Amusements." Review of *A Wife's Honor*. Unsigned. October 30, 1894, p. 2.

"Amusements." Review of *Married for Money*. Unsigned. October 31, 1894, p. 6.

"Music and Drama." Review of Hoyt's *A Trip to Chinatown*. Unsigned. November 1, 1894, p. 2.

"More or Less Personal." On Hoyt, *The Green Carnation*, Bacon and Shakespeare, Duse. Unsigned. November 4, 1894, p. 12.

"Amusements." Review of Royle's *Friends*. Unsigned. November 6, 1894, p. 8.

"Amusements." Review of *Hot Tamales*. Unsigned. November 7, 1894, p. 5.

"Amusements." Review of *Oh, What a Night*. Unsigned. November 9, 1894, p. 6.

"Amusements." Review of *Pinafore*. Unsigned. November 10, 1894, p. 6.

"As You Like It." On Olga Nethersole, private libraries, Bliss Carman, Pauline Hall, the French. Unsigned. November 11, 1894, p. 13.

"Music and Drama." Review of "Gustave Frohman's Company No. 13" in *Jane* and *The Great Mogul*. Unsigned. November 14, 1894, p. 2.

"As You Like It." On criticism, Mrs. Kendal, Lillie Langtry, Bernhardt. Unsigned. November 18, 1894, p. 13.

"Amusements." Review of Pauline Hall in *Dorcas*. Unsigned. November 21, 1894, p. 2.

"Amusements." Review of the Wilber Entertainment Company. Unsigned. November 22, 1894, p. 6.

"As You Like It." On Pauline Hall and other operetta stars, death of Anton Rubinstein. Unsigned. November 25, 1894, p. 13.

"As You Like It." On football, stage marriages, Robert B. Mantell, and Maurice Barrymore. Unsigned. December 2, 1894, p. 13.

"Amusements." Review of Nat Goodwin in *A Gilded Fool*. Unsigned. December 4, 1894, p. 8.

"Music and Drama." Review of *A Summer Blizzard*. Unsigned. December 5, 1894, p. 3.

"Amusements." Review of *Killarney*. Unsigned. December 8, 1894, p. 2.

"Amusements." Review of the Tavary Grand Opera Company in *Il Trovatore*. Unsigned. December 9, 1894, p. 4.

"As You Like It." On the art of Nat Goodwin, William Crane in *Brother John*, Lillian Russell, living pictures. Unsigned. December 9, 1894, p. 13.

"Amusements." Review of Helena von Doenhoff in *Il Trovatore*. Unsigned. December 10, 1894, p. 8.

"Amusements." Review of Thomas Q. Seabrooke in *Isle of Champagne*. Unsigned. December 14, 1894, p. 6.

"Amusements." Review of *O'Neil, Washington, D.C.* Unsigned. December 15, 1894, p. 2.

"As You Like It." On playing Shakespearean comedy, stage realism, the artist's social role, Helena von Doenhoff. Unsigned. December 16, 1894, p. 13.

"Amusements." Review of *Lady Windermere's Fan*. Unsigned. December 18, 1894, p. 2.

"Amusements." Review of *In Old Kentucky*. Unsigned. December 20, 1894, p. 3.

"As You Like It." On Stevenson, Kipling, *Trilby*. Unsigned. December 23, 1894, p. 13.

See also "Death of George Du Maurier," unsigned, *Home Monthly*, November 1896, p. 9.

"As You Like It." On Zola and Bernhardt. Unsigned. December 30, 1894, p. 13.

"Amusements." Review of Sol Smith Russell in *The Heir at Law*. Unsigned. January 4, 1895, p. 6.

"Amusements." Review of Belasco's *The Charity Ball*. Unsigned. January 6, 1895, p. 6.

"As You Like It." On the exhibition of the Haydon Art Club, Belasco, criticism. January 6, 1895, p. 13.

"Amusements." Review of *Thro' the War*. Unsigned. January 8, 1895, p. 2.

"Amusements." Review of *A Jolly Good Fellow*. Unsigned. January 11, 1895, p. 8.

"Amusements." Review of *Yon Yonson*. Unsigned. January 12, 1895, p. 6.

"As You Like It." On Sappho, Elizabeth Barrett Browning, and Christina Rossetti. Unsigned. January 13, 1895, p. 13.

"Amusements." Review of Warde and James in *Henry IV*. Unsigned. January 18, 1895, p. 8.

"As You Like It." On Shakespeare's history plays, Julia Marlowe. Unsigned. January 20, 1895, p. 13.

"Amusements." Review of Belasco's *Men and Women*. Unsigned. January 22, 1895, p. 8.

"Amusements." Review of recital by elocutionist and violinist. Unsigned. January 23, 1895, p. 6.

"Amusements." Review of E. K. Emmett in *Fritz in a Madhouse*. Unsigned. January 26, 1895, p. 6.

"Amusements." Review of Belasco's *The Girl I Left Behind Me*. Unsigned. January 27, 1895, p. 6.

"As You Like It." On Belasco's plays, interview with Bernice Wheeler, marriage of Helena von Doenhoff, Dumas *fils*, Nat Goodwin. Unsigned. January 27, 1895, p. 13.

"Amusements." Review of *Hendrick Hudson*. Unsigned. February 1, 1895, p. 5.

"Amusements." Review of *Charley's Aunt*. Unsigned. February 2, 1895, p. 6.

"As You Like It." Interview with Gustave Frohman. Unsigned. February 3, 1895, p. 13.

"Amusements." Review of Hoyt's *Temperance Town*. Unsigned. February 7, 1895, p. 6.

"As You Like It." On a Mendelssohn concert, Charles Hoyt and American comedy, the Russian ballerina Ksheninka. Unsigned. February 10, 1895, p. 13.

"Amusements." Review of *The Passport*. Unsigned. February 14, 1895, p.2.

"As You Like It." On François Coppée. Unsigned. February 17, 1895, p. 9.

"Amusements." Review of Eddie Foy in *Off the Earth*. Unsigned. February 22, 1895, p. 8.

"As You Like It." On Browning as a playwright, Max O'Rell lecture, Katherine Kidder as Madame Sans Gêne. Unsigned. February 24, 1895, p. 13.

"Amusements." Review of *The New "Paul Kauvar"* by Steele MacKaye. Unsigned. February 26, 1895, p. 6.

"Amusements." Review of Clay Clement in *The New Dominion*. Unsigned. March 2, 1895, p. 6.

"Amusements." Review of Marie Tempest in *The Fencing Master*. Unsigned. March 3, 1895, p. 8.

"As You Like It." On Dorothy Morton, Clay Clement. Unsigned. March 3, 1895, p. 13.

"As You Like It." On Clay Clement, Modjeska, Hamlet, Mrs. James Potter. Unsigned. March 10, 1895, p. 13.

"As You Like It." On Verdi's *Falstaff*, Emma Eames in *Otello*. Unsigned. March 31, 1895, p. 13.

"Amusements." Review of Griffith's *Faust.* Unsigned. April 2, 1895, p. 8.

"As You Like It." On the dramatization of *Trilby*, actors' private lives. Unsigned. April 7, 1895, p. 13.

"As You Like It." On a play called *Nebraska*, Beerbohm Tree, Hamlin Garland. Unsigned. April 14, 1895, p. 13.

"Amusements." Review of Bronson Howard's *Shenandoah.* Unsigned. April 17, 1895, p. 5.

"Amusements." Review of *The Black Crook.* Unsigned. April 18, 1895, p. 3.

"As You Like It." On Shakespeare, Sardou, Madame Réjane. Unsigned. April 21, 1895, p. 13.

"Amusements." Review of the Spooners in *Inez.* Unsigned. April 23, 1895, p. 5.

"Amusements." Review of Effie Ellsler in *Doris.* Unsigned. April 25, 1895, p. 8.

"Amusements." Review of the Spooners in *The Buckeye.* Unsigned. April 26, 1895, p. 8.

"As You Like It." On Marie Wainwright in *The Daughters of Eve*, John L. Sullivan, Lillian Russell. Unsigned. April 28, 1895, p. 14.

"As You Like It." On Bernhardt, Salvini, Max O'Rell and Mark Twain. Unsigned. May 5, 1895, p. 14.

"As You Like It." On Clara Morris and other stars, Julia Magruder's serial *Princess Sonia.* Unsigned. May 12, 1895, p. 12.

"Amusements." Review of Emily Bancker in *Our Flat.* Unsigned. May 14, 1895, p. 6.

"As You Like It." On Lillian Russell, Ada Rehan, Nethersole, *Lady Windermere's Fan.* Unsigned. May 19, 1895, p. 12.

"As You Like It." On Marie Tempest, Chicago *Chap-Book*, Hobart Chatfield-Taylor. Unsigned. May 26, 1895, p. 12.

"As You Like It." On the Trilby fad, Warde and James in *Henry IV*, Sardou. Unsigned. June 2, 1895, p. 9.

"Amusements." Review of Oriole Opera Company. Unsigned. June 7, 1895, p. 6.

"As You Like It." On *Princess Sonia*, Melba, theatre notes. Unsigned. June 9, 1895, p. 12.

"As You Like It." On Marie Burroughs, Duse, French taste. Unsigned. June 16, 1895, p. 12.

"As You Like It." On Henry Irving, Beerbohm Tree, Rubinstein, Max O'Rell, French and American women. Unsigned. June 30, 1895, p. 12.

"As You Like It." On William Winter as critic, Lillian Russell, Otis Skinner, Katherine Fisk. Unsigned. July 7, 1895, p. 9.

"As You Like It." On *When Dreams Come True* by Edgar Saltus, William Dean Howells, Bernhardt's book. Unsigned. July 14, 1895, p. 9.

"The Passing Show." On Dumas *fils*, Bernhardt, Zola, Mary Anderson, Augustin Daly, Clara Morris. Unsigned. July 21, 1895, p. 9.

"The Passing Show." On Henry Guy Carleton and Belasco, Olive May interview, Howells, Henry James, Browning. Unsigned. August 4, 1895, p. 9.

"The Passing Show." On death of Madame Carvalho, Melba, America and Rome, Marlowe in *Henry IV*, Stanley Weyman. Unsigned. August 11, 1895, p. 9.

See also "Prodigal Salaries to Singers," unsigned, *Home Monthly*, October 1896, p. 14.

"Amusements." Review of exhibition of hypnotism. Unsigned. September 3, 1895, p. 6.

"Amusements." Review of Roland Reed in *The Politician*. Unsigned. September 5, 1895, p. 2.

"Amusements." Review of the Spooners in *The Buckeye*. Unsigned. September 10, 1895, p. 8.

"Amusements." Review of Griffith's *Faust*. Unsigned. September 11, 1895, p. 8.

"Amusements." Review of *The Hustler*. Unsigned. September 24, 1895, p. 8.

"Amusements." Review of Belasco's *The Wife*. Unsigned. September 25, 1895, p. 3.

"Amusements." Review of *Rush City*. Unsigned. September 27, 1895, p. 8.

"Amusements." Review of William Gillette in *Too Much Johnson*. Unsigned. October 2, 1895, p. 3.

"Amusements." Review of Hoyt's *A Contented Woman*. Unsigned. October 10, 1895, p. 5.

"Amusements." Review of *Human Hearts*. Unsigned. October 15, 1895, p. 6.

"Amusements." Review of the Dovey Sisters. Unsigned. October 17, 1895, p. 2.

"Amusements." Review of Lillian Lewis in *Cleopatra*. Unsigned. October 23, 1895, p. 6.

"Amusements." Review of DeWolf Hopper in *Wang*. Unsigned. October 25, 1895, p. 6.

See also review of Hopper in *El Capitan*, signed "Sibert," *Leader*, March 23, 1897, p. 4.

"Amusements." Review of *The Globe Trotter*. Unsigned. October 30, 1895, p. 6.

"Amusements." Review of *The Black Crook*. Unsigned. October 31, 1895, p. 6.

"Amusements." Review of *The Colonel's Wives*. Unsigned. November 7, 1895, p. 3.

"Amusements." Review of Walker Whiteside in *Hamlet*. Unsigned. November 21, 1895, p. 6.

"Amusements." Review of Robert Downing in Sardou's *Helena*. Unsigned. November 24, 1895, p. 3.

"Amusements." Review of Emily Bancker in *Our Flat*. Unsigned. November 26, 1895, p. 6.

"Amusements." Review of Effie Ellsler in *As You Like It*. Unsigned. December 6, 1895, p. 6.

"Amusements." Review of *Newest Devil's Auction*. Unsigned. December 13, 1895, p. 3.

"Amusements." Review of Louis James in *Othello*. Unsigned. December 14, 1895, p. 6.

"The Passing Show." On Dumas *fils*, Paderewski, Heine, the Intermezzo from *Cavalleria Rusticana*. Unsigned. December 15, 1895, p. 9.

"The Passing Show." On Louis James as Othello, Mansfield, a charity concert. Unsigned. December 22, 1895, p. 9.

"The Passing Show." On Stevenson's letters, Victor Maurel, Calvé, Clay Clement. Unsigned. January 5, 1896, p. 9.

"The Passing Show." On Hall Caine's *The Bondman*, Campanini, the divorce of Sadie Martinot, *Ladies' Home Journal*. Unsigned. January 12, 1896, p. 9.

See also review of *The Bondman*, signed "Helen Delay," *Home Monthly*, July 1897, p. 14; "Italo Campanini," unsigned, *Home Monthly*, January 1897, p. 11.

"The Passing Show." On Yvette Guilbert, Alfred Austin as Poet Laureate, monument to Stevenson, Lillie Langtry, Walt Whitman. Unsigned. January 19, 1896, p. 9.

See also "Stevenson's Monument," unsigned, *Home Monthly*, September 1896, p. 3.

"The Passing Show." On James Lane Allen, Bernhardt, death of Pearl Etynge. Unsigned. January 26, 1896, p. 9.

"Amusements." Review of *Wang*, with Albert Hart. Unsigned. January 31, 1896, p. 6.

"The Passing Show." On the death of Paul Verlaine, Thomas Hardy's *Jude the Obscure*. Unsigned. February 2, 1896, p. 9.

"Amusements." Review of the Holdens in *Roxy, the Waif*. Unsigned. February 4, 1896, p. 6.

"The Passing Show." On the English Poet Laureate, Dumas *fils*, Robert W. Ingersoll. Unsigned. February 9, 1896, p. 9.

"The Passing Show." On Zola's *The Fat and the Thin*, Bernhardt, Margaret Mather. Unsigned. February 16, 1896, p. 9.
See also review of *The French Market Girl*, signed "Sibert," *Leader*, May 27, 1898, p. 5.

"The Passing Show." On Eugene Field's *The Love Affairs of a Bibliomaniac*, Oscar Hammerstein, Marie Corelli. Unsigned. February 23, 1896, p. 9.
See also review of *Love Affairs*, signed "Sibert," *Leader*, December 16, 1899, p. 3.

"The Passing Show." On *Mary Magdalen* by Edgar Saltus, Richard Hovey, Ambroise Thomas and Père-Lachaise, Duse-Bernhardt duel. Unsigned. March 1, 1896, p. 9.

"The Passing Show." On Byron, Herbert Bates, Amélie Rives, summary of theatre season. Unsigned. March 8, 1896, p. 13.

"The Passing Show." On Conan Doyle, Dumas *père*, prodigies, Max Nordau, Anatole France. Unsigned. March 15, 1896, p. 9.

"The Passing Show." On Herbert Bates, the realism of *Anna Karenina*, mystery stories and Stevenson's *The Wrecker*, Duse. Unsigned. March 22, 1896, p. 9.
See also "Stevenson's Monument," unsigned, *Home Monthly*, September 1896, p. 3.

"Amusements." Review of *Fleur de Lis*. Unsigned. March 26, 1896, p. 2.

"Amusements." Review of Richard Mansfield in *A Parisian Romance*. Unsigned. March 29, 1896, p. 5.

"The Passing Show." On Henry James's *The Tragic Muse* as a novel of the stage, Sol Smith Russell in *Mr. Valentine's Christmas* and *An Everyday Man*. Unsigned. March 29, 1896, p. 9.

"The Passing Show." On Henri Murger's *Scènes de la vie de Bohème*, death of Jennie Kimball. Unsigned. April 15, 1896, p. 16.

"The Passing Show." On *The Crime of Sylvestre Bonnard, Tom Brown's Schooldays*, Mansfield, Minnie Maddern Fiske. Unsigned. April 12, 1896, p. 13.
See also review of *Sylvestre Bonnard*, signed "Helen Delay," *Home Monthly*, March 1897, p. 16.

"The Passing Show." On Anthony Hope's *Phroso*, Bernice Harraden, the Chicago *Chap-Book*, Sir Richard and Lady Burton, and the author of "Kathleen Mavourneen." Unsigned. April 19, 1896, p. 13.

"The Passing Show." On Hovey and Carman, Bernhardt, Lillian Russell. Unsigned. April 26, 1896, p. 13.

"The Passing Show." On Mary Anderson, Paderewski's prize for American composers. Unsigned. May 3, 1896, p. 13.

"The Passing Show." On *The Rivals*, prolific authors, notes on stars. Unsigned. May 10, 1896, p. 13.

"The Passing Show." On Ruskin, Tolstoi's new art. Unsigned. May 17, 1896, p. 13.

"The Passing Show." On Burns and Scottish writers, Kipling and the Balestiers. Unsigned. May 24, 1896, p. 13.
See also "The Burns Centenary," *Home Monthly*, September 1896, p. 12.

"The Passing Show." On Mrs. Humphry Ward and George Eliot, Nethersole and Daly, Henry Irving's stagecraft. Unsigned. May 31, 1896, p. 13.

"The Passing Show." On a personal letter from Clay Clement, Daudet and the *roman à clef*. Unsigned. June 7, 1896, p. 13.

"Amusements." Review of Boston Comic Opera Company in *Olivette*. Unsigned. June 12, 1896, p. 6.

"The Passing Show." On Frances Hodgson Burnett's *A Lady of Quality*, the failure of Abbey and Grau, death of Clara Wieck Schumann. Unsigned. June 14, 1896, p. 13.

"The Passing Show." Massenet's *Eve*, E. M. Holland in *A Social Highwayman*, Campanini. Signed: Willa Cather. From Pittsburgh. December 6, 1896, p. 13.
See also "Italo Campanini," unsigned, *Home Monthly*, December 1896, p. 11.

"The Passing Show." On Nordica and Jean de Reszke, Howells, *Princess Osra* dramatized. Signed: Willa Cather. From Pittsburgh. December 13, 1896, p. 13.
See also "Nordica Has Returned," unsigned, *Home Monthly*, October 1896, p. 14.

"The Passing Show." On Henry James's *The Other House*, Frank Daniels in *Wizard of the Nile*. Unsigned. December 20, 1896, p. 13.
See also review of *Wizard of the Nile*, signed "Sibert," *Leader*, December 15, 1896, p. 6.

"The Passing Show." On Anna Held. Signed: Willa Cather. From Pittsburgh. January 3, 1897, p. 13.
See also "Beautiful Anna Held," signed "Sibert," *Leader*, December 22, 1896, p. 6.

"The Passing Show." On Handel's *Messiah*, Anna Held and Henry C. Frick, Henry E. Abbey's career. Signed: Willa Cather. From Pittsburgh. January 10, 1897, p. 13.

"The Passing Show." On Jessie Bartlett Davis, Sunday music, Elia W. Peattie. Signed: Willa Cather. From Pittsburgh. January 17, 1897, p. 13.
See also review of Miss Davis in *Robin Hood*, signed "Sibert," *Leader*, January 5, 1897, p. 4.

"The Passing Show." On Fanny Davenport in Sardou's *Gismonda* and *La Tosca*. Signed: Willa Cather. From Pittsburgh. January 31, 1897, p. 13.
See also review of *Gismonda*, signed "Sibert," *Leader*, January 19, 1897, p. 10.

"The Passing Show." On Carreño in concert. Signed: Willa Cather. From Pittsburgh. February 7, 1897, p. 13.

"The Passing Show." On Julia Marlowe as Juliet, E. S. Willard. Signed: Willa Cather. From Pittsburgh. February 14, 1897, p. 13.
See also review of Marlowe, signed "Sibert," *Leader*, February 2, 1897, p. 5.

"The Passing Show." On Nordica in concert, Sothern in *An Enemy to the King*. Signed: Willa Cather. From Pittsburgh. February 28, 1897, p. 13.

"The Passing Show." On Margaret Mather in *Cymbeline*, *The Heart of Maryland*. Signed: Willa Cather. From Pittsburgh. March 7, 1897, p. 13.
See also review of Mather in *Cymbeline*, signed "Sibert," *Leader*, February 23, 1897, p. 4.

"The Passing Show." On *Lohengrin* and *Tannhäuser*. Signed: Willa Cather. From Pittsburgh. March 14, 1897, p. 13.
See also review of *Lohengrin*, signed "A Woman Lover of Music," *Leader*, March 4, 1897, p. 5; and review of *Tannhäuser* (by "a lady who wields a trenchant pen"), *Leader*, March 6, 1897, p. 6.

"The Passing Show." On Nethersole in *Carmen*, *Camille*, and *The Wife of Scarli*. Signed: Willa Cather. From Pittsburgh. March 28, 1897, p. 13.
See also review of Nethersole in *Carmen*, signed "Sibert," *Leader*, March 16, 1897, p. 4.

"The Passing Show." On Nat Goodwin in *An American Citizen*, DeWolf Hopper in *El Capitan*, Julia Marlowe. Signed: Willa Cather. From Pittsburgh. April 4, 1897, p. 13.
See also review of *An American Citizen*, signed "Sibert," *Leader*, March 9, 1897, p. 4; and review of *El Capitan*, signed "Sibert," *Leader*, March 23, 1897, p. 4.

"The Passing Show." On Maude Adams and John Drew in *Rosemary*, Mansfield in *The Merchant of Venice*. Signed: Willa Cather. From Pittsburgh. May 2, 1897, p. 13.
See also review of *Rosemary*, signed "Sibert," *Leader*, April 6, 1897, p. 2, and review of *The Merchant of Venice*, signed "Sibert," *Leader*, April 20, 1897, p. 9.

"The Passing Show." On Yvette Guilbert, Kipling as bard. Signed: Willa Cather. From Pittsburgh. May 16, 1897, p. 13.

"The Passing Show." On Calvé in concert. Signed: Willa Cather. From Pittsburgh. May 23, 1897, p. 13.

"The Passing Show." On Lizzie Hudson Collier in *Rosedale*, Mrs. Fiske in *Tess of the D'Urbervilles*. Signed: Willa Cather. From Pittsburgh. May 30, 1897, p. 13.
See also review of *Rosedale*, signed "Sibert," *Leader*, May 25, 1897, p. 9.

"A Statesman and Scholar." On death of Senator Cushman K. Davis, *Hedda Gabler*. Signed: Willa Sibert Cather. Dateline: "Washington, Dec. 7." December 9, 1900, p. 9.
See also *Index of Pittsburg Life*, December 22, 1900, p. 6, and December 29, 1900, p. 14.

"In Washington." On the opening session of the Senate, Carreño's concert. Signed: Willa Sibert Cather. Dateline: "Washington, Dec. 12." December 16, 1900, p. 19.
See also *Index*, December 22, 1900, p. 6.

"Washington in Olden Days." On English playwright Haddon Chambers, early life in Washington, Olga Nethersole, Christmas in Washington. Signed: Willa Sibert Cather. Dateline: "Washington, D.C., Dec. 12." December 30, 1900, p. 13.
See also *Index*, January 19, 1901, pp. 10–11.

"Jefferson, Painter Actor." On an exhibition of paintings by Joseph Jefferson. Signed: Willa Sibert Cather. Dateline: "Washington, D.C., Jan. 3." January 6, 1901, p. 14.
See also *Index*, January 12, 1901, p. 10.

"In the Corcoran Gallery." On racial studies by Hubert Vos, Daniel Frohman interview. Signed: Willa Sibert Cather. Dateline: "Washington, D.C., Jan. 8." January 13, 1901, p. 9.
See also *Index*, January 19, 1901, pp. 10–11.

"Claims Against Turkey." On settling of missionary claims in Turkey, members of the diplomatic corps. Signed: Willa Sibert Cather. Dateline: "Washington, Jan. 18." January 20, 1901, p. 9.
See also *Index*, January 26, 1901, pp. 10–11.

"Bernhardt in Washington." On Bernhardt and Maude Adams in *L'Aiglon*, Rostand. Signed: Willa Sibert Cather. Dateline: "Washington, D.C., Jan. 24." January 27, 1901, p. 9.
See also *Index*, February 2, 1901, pp. 10–11.

"Second View of Bernhardt." On *La Tosca* and *Camille*. Signed: Willa Sibert Cather. Dateline: "Washington, D.C., Feb. 1." February 4, 1901, p. 8.

"Seton-Thompson at Tea." On Ernest Seton-Thompson, Pittsburgh Symphony Orchestra, death of Queen Victoria. Signed: Willa Sibert Cather. Dateline: "Washington, D.C., Feb. 6." February 10, 1901, p. 9.
See also *Index*, February 16, 1901, p. 8.

"The Charm of Washington." On the inhabitants and sights, White House souvenirs. Signed: Willa Sibert Cather. Dateline: "Washington, D.C., Feb. 14." February 17, 1901, p. 9.

See also *Index*, February 9, 1901, pp. 8–9.

"Washington Gridiron Club." On annual Gridiron dinner, musical debut of Marquis Francesco de Sousa and Clara Clemens. Signed: Willa Sibert Cather. Dateline: "Washington, D.C., Feb. 17." February 24, 1901, p. 9.

See also *Index*, February 23, 1901, p. 12.

"In Washington." On the poetry of Helen Hay, the career of Mrs. E.D.E.N. Southworth. Signed: Willa Sibert Cather. Dateline: "Washington, D.C., Feb. 28." March 3, 1901, p. 12.

See also *Index*, March 16, 1901, pp. 8–9.

"In Washington." Review of Pinero's *The Gay Lord Quex*. Signed: Willa Sibert Cather. Dateline: "Washington, D.C., March 7." March 10, 1901, p. 13.

See also *Index*, March 9, 1901, pp. 8–9.

"Hunting the North Pole." On the Baldwin-Ziegler expedition, Count Cassini's collections. Signed: Willa Sibert Cather. Dateline: "Washington, D.C., March 16." March 17, 1901, p. 13.

"Music." Ethelbert Nevin obituary. Signed: Willa Sibert Cather. March 24, 1901, p. 13.

"First Glimpse of England." Arrival in Liverpool. Signed: Willa S. Cather. Dateline: "Liverpool, Eng., July 1." July 13, 1902, p. 4.

"A Visit to Old Chester." Signed: Willa S. Cather. Dateline: "Chester, July 1." July 20, 1902, p. 11.

"Out of the Beaten Track." On Shropshire and A. E. Housman. Signed: Willa S. Cather. Dateline: "Ludlow, Shropshire, July 11." July 27, 1902, p. 11.

"The Canal Folk of England." Signed: Willa Sibert Cather. Dateline: "London, July 16." August 3, 1902, p. 11.

See also "The Strangest Tribe of Darkest England," *Gazette*, August 31, 1902, Magazine section, p. 4.

"Seeing Things in London." Signed: Willa Sibert Cather. Dateline: "London, July 22." August 10, 1902, p. 11.

"The Kensington Studio." On Burne-Jones. Signed: Willa S. Cather. No dateline. August 17, 1902, p. 11.

"Merry Wives of Windsor." Beerbohm Tree's revival of *The Merry Wives of Windsor*. Dateline: "Paris, Aug. 8." August 24, 1902, p. 16.

"Dieppe and Rouen." Signed: Willa S. Cather. No dateline. August 31, 1902, p. 16.

"Two Cemeteries in Paris." Montmartre and Père-Lachaise. Signed: Willa S. Cather. Dateline: "Paris, August 21." September 14, 1902, p. 18.

"One Sunday at Barbizon." Signed: Willa S. Cather. Dateline: "Paris, Sept. 10." [Misprint for September 1.] September 21, 1902, p. 18.

"The Old City of the Popes." Signed: Willa S. Cather. Dateline: "Avignon, Sept. 3." September 28, 1902, p. 15.

"Country of the Fabulous." On Marseilles and Hyères. Signed: Willa S. Cather. Dateline: "Hyeres, Sept. 6." October 5, 1902, p. 15.

"In a Principality of Pines." On Le Lavandou. Signed: Willa S. Cather. Dateline: "Lavandou, Sept. 10." October 12, 1902, p. 15.

"In the Country of Daudet." Monte Carlo, the Provençal countryside, Arles. Signed: Willa S. Cather. Dateline: "Arles, Sept. 16." October 19, 1902, p. 9.

LINCOLN EVENING NEWS

Willa Cather reported the thirteenth annual Nebraska Chautauqua Assembly, held at Crete, Nebraska, July 3–14, 1894, for the Lincoln *Evening News*. A class in practical newspaper work was conducted at the assembly by Will Owen Jones, managing editor of the *Nebraska State Journal*, Miss Ray Manley, and Willa Cather.

"The Fourth at Crete." Description of the programs on July 3 and 4, including three lectures on modern French art, sculpture, and Dutch and German painters by Lorado Taft. Signed: Willa Cather. From Crete, July 5, 1894, p. 8.

"At the Chautauqua." Daily life at the assembly, lectures on "The Roman Empire" by Dr. Joseph T. Duryea and on the "Conscience of the State" by Bayard Holmes. Signed: Willa Cather. July 6, 1894, p. 1.

"Notable Concert." Lecture by Professor L. Fossler on Teutonic religion, song recital by Miss Electra Gifford. Signed: Willa Cather. From Crete. July 7, 1894, p. 5.

"Sunday at Crete." Description of a Chautauqua dinner, lecture on Biblical criticism by Professor Charles F. Kent. Signed: Willa Cather. July 9, 1894, p. 5.

"Life at Crete." Piano recital by Mrs. Will Owen Jones. Signed: Willa Cather. July 10, 1894, p. 4.

"In Dunning Hall." Description of the dormitory for the staff and performers, song recital by Mrs. Katherine Fisk. Signed: Willa Cather. July 11, 1894, p. 5.

"Crete Chautauqua." Anne L. Barr's class in physical education, dramatic impersonations by Charles F. Underwood, song recital by Mrs. Fisk. Signed: Willa Cather. July 12, 1894, p. 4.

"Mrs. Fisk's Concert." Awarding of diplomas to Chautauqua graduates, lectures by Dr. Duryea and Professor Holmes, concert by Mrs. Fisk and mixed chorus. Signed: Willa Cather. July 13, 1894, p. 5.

"Empty Cottages." The scene after the assembly has dispersed. Signed: Willa Cather. From Crete. July 14, 1894, p. 1.

COURIER

"The Passing Show." On Patti, Jean de Reszke and Calvé, Mansfield and Shaw, the third act of *Hamlet*, DeWolf Hopper, *Trilby*, the opening of the Creighton Theatre in Omaha. Unsigned. August 24, 1895, pp. 6–8.

"The Passing Show." On Felix Morris and Eddie Foy, Rubinstein's son, Royle's *Mexico*, the Bowery as home of talent. Unsigned. August 31, 1895, pp. 6–8.

"The Passing Show." On Julia Arthur and the training of actors, dramatizing *Romola*, Ella Wheeler Wilcox, Calvé, Mascagni. Unsigned. September 7, 1895, pp. 6–7.

"The Theatres." Review of Roland Reed in *The Politician*, the Flints' hypnotism act. Unsigned. September 7, 1895, p. 8.

"The Passing Show." On George Sand's *Consuelo*, Kipling and Anthony Hope Hawkins, the Dovey sisters. Unsigned. September 14, 1895, pp. 6–7.

"The Theatres." Review of Griffith's *Faust*, the Spooners. Unsigned. September 14, 1895, p. 8.

"The Passing Show." On Hall Caine, Duse, Sir Henry Irving, Marion Crawford. Unsigned. September 21, 1895, pp. 6–7.

"The Passing Show." On Oscar Wilde, Judith Gautier, Zélie de Lussan, Clara Morris. Unsigned. September 28, 1895, pp. 6–7.

"The Theatres." Review of Belasco's *The Wife*. Unsigned. September 28, 1895, p. 8.
See also "The Return of the Romantic Drama," unsigned, *Home Monthly*, November 1896, p. 12.

"Man and Woman / A Symposium." Contribution. Signed: Willa Cather. September 28, 1895, p. 10.

"The Passing Show." On Nell Gwyn, Maude Adams and Richard Harding Davis, Howells and *Harper's*, Paganini. Unsigned. October 5, 1895, pp. 6–7.

"The Theatres." Review of William Gillette in *Too Much Johnson*. Unsigned. October 5, 1895, p. 8.

"The Passing Show." On Poe. Unsigned. October 12, 1895, pp. 6–7.

"The Passing Show." On Richard Harding Davis and Anne Reeve Aldrich, Amélie Rives Chandler, Margaret Mather, Cora Potter. Unsigned. October 19, 1895, pp. 6–7.

"The Passing Show." On Lillian Lewis as Cleopatra, Josef Hofmann. Unsigned. October 26, 1895, pp. 6–7.

"The Passing Show." On DeWolf Hopper, Romance, Stevenson's letters, Nat Goodwin. Unsigned. November 2, 1895, pp. 6–7.

"The Theatres." Reviews of Mrs. Dion Boucicault in *The Globe Trotter, The Black Crook.* Unsigned. November 2, 1895, p. 8.

"The Passing Show." On Anthony Hope's Zenda stories, Pierre Loti's *The Romance of a Spahi*, Dumas' *Route de Thèbes*, death of Eugene Field, *The Colonel's Wives*. Unsigned. November 9, 1895, pp. 6–7.

"The Passing Show." On overproductive writers, Henry James. Unsigned. November 16, 1895, pp. 6–7.

"The Passing Show." On Ouida and women novelists, Walker Whiteside's Hamlet. Unsigned. November 23, 1895, pp. 7–8.

"The Passing Show." On Swinburne, Scottish writers—Ian Maclaren, Samuel Crockett, James M. Barrie. Unsigned. November 30, 1895, pp. 6–7.

See also "'Ian Maclaren' as a Minister," unsigned, *Home Monthly*, December 1896, p. 11.

"The Passing Show." On the horse show, Charles Stanley Reinhart. Signed: Willa Cather. From Pittsburgh. October 23, 1897, pp. 8–9.

"The Passing Show." On Sousa and Kipling, the Carnegie Prize committee, Will H. Low on Stevenson and Bouguereau. Signed: Willa Cather. From Pittsburgh. October 30, 1897, p. 3.

"The Passing Show." On Heine and Hugo, Evangelina Cisneros, Lillian Russell in *The Wedding Day*. Signed: Willa Cather. From Pittsburgh. November 6, 1897, p. 2.

See also review of *The Wedding Day*, signed "Sibert," *Leader*, October, 26, 1897, p. 6.

"The Passing Show." On Writers' Club dinner for Anthony Hope Hawkins and interview. Signed: Willa Cather. From Pittsburgh. November 13, 1897, pp. 2–3.

See also "Anthony Hope's Lecture," unsigned, *Leader*, October 30, 1897, p. 6.

"The Passing Show." On President McKinley in Pittsburgh, Campanari concert. Signed: Willa Cather. From Pittsburgh. November 20, 1897, pp. 2–3.

"The Passing Show." On Victor Herbert's *Serenade*, Anton Seidl and the

United Singers. Signed: Willa Cather. From Pittsburgh. December 4, 1897, p. 2.

"The Passing Show." On Minnie Maddern Fiske in *Tess of the D'Urbervilles.* Signed: Willa Cather. From Pittsburgh. December 11, 1897, pp. 2–3.

See also review signed "Sibert," *Leader,* November 16, 1897, p. 11.

"The Passing Show." On Writers' Club dinner for Fridtjof Nansen and interview. Signed: Willa Cather. From Pittsburgh. December 18, 1897, pp. 4–5.

See also "With Nansen to the Pole," signed "Sibert," *Leader,* December 1, 1897, p. 2.

"The Passing Show." On Nansen's views on literature, *New World* Symphony, musicians' stories. Signed: Willa Cather. From Pittsburgh. December 25, 1897, pp. 2–3.

"The Passing Show." On Olive May in *White Heather,* William Gillette's *Secret Service.* Signed: Willa Cather. From Pittsburgh. January 1, 1898, pp. 2–3.

"The Passing Show." On the death of Daudet. Signed: Willa Cather. From Pittsburgh. January 22, 1898, pp. 2–3.

See also "Phases of Daudet," signed "Sibert," *Leader,* December 26, 1897, p. 16, and "Old Books and New," signed "Helen Delay," *Home Monthly,* February 1898, p. 12.

"The Passing Show." On Melba in *The Barber of Seville,* Yone Noguchi. Signed: Willa Cather. From Pittsburgh. January 29, 1898, p. 2.

See also review of Melba signed "Sibert," *Leader,* January 4, 1898, p. 4.

"The Passing Show." On Ethelbert Nevin's Carnegie Hall recital. Unsigned. From Pittsburgh. February 5, 1898, pp. 3–4.

The omission of Willa Cather's name from the box at the head of the column was clearly a mechanical error. It was omitted again the following week, and on April 16 only "Cather" appeared in the head.

"The Passing Show." On interviewing Adelaide Mould [misspelled "Moned"], daughter of Marion Manola. Unsigned. From Pittsburgh. February 19, 1898, pp. 2–3.

See also "Miss Mould Talks," unsigned interview, *Leader,* February 6, 1898, p. 5.

"The Passing Show." On E. S. Willard. Signed: Willa Cather. From Pittsburgh. February 26, 1898, pp. 2–3.

See also review of Willard in *Garrick,* signed "Sibert," *Leader,* January 18, 1898, p. 4.

"The Passing Show." On New York productions of *The Lady of Lyons,*

Ada Rehan in *The Country Girl*, Modjeska in *Mary Stuart*. Signed: Willa Cather. From Pittsburgh. March 5, 1898, pp. 2–3.

"The Passing Show." On New York productions of *The Tree of Knowledge*, *The Conquerors*. Signed: Willa Cather. From Pittsburgh. March 12, 1898, pp. 2–3.

"The Passing Show." On Melba, Nat Goodwin, Vesta Tilley. Signed: Willa Cather. From Pittsburgh. March 19, 1898, pp. 2–3.
See also review of Vesta Tilley signed "Sibert," *Leader*, March 1, 1898, p. 10.

"The Passing Show." Letter to Nat Goodwin. Signed: Willa Cather. From Pittsburgh. April 9, 1898, p. 3.

"The Passing Show." On Mrs. Harcourt Williamson's *The Barn-Stormers*. Signed: Cather [error noted above]. April 16, 1898, p. 3.
See also "Books and Magazines," signed "Sibert," *Leader*, March 18, 1898, p. 8.

"The Passing Show." On Lieutenant Jenkins and the sinking of the *Maine*, Mansfield in *The Devil's Disciple*. Signed: Willa Cather. April 23, 1898, pp. 3–4.
See also review of Mansfield, signed "Sibert," *Leader*, March 29, 1898, p. 4.

"The Passing Show." On Charles Coghlan's *The Royal Box*. Signed: Willa Cather. April 30, 1898, pp. 3–4.
See also review of Coghlan, signed "Sibert," *Leader*, April 19, 1898, p. 10.

"The Passing Show." On Mrs. Fiske in *A Bit of Old Chelsea* and *Love Will Find a Way*. Signed: Willa Cather. December 24, 1898, p. 3.

"The Passing Show." On Israel Zangwill's lecture, "The Drama as a Fine Art." Signed: Willa Cather. From Pittsburgh. January 7, 1899, p. 11.

"The Passing Show." On interviewing Mrs. Fiske. Signed: Willa Cather. From Pittsburgh. January 14, 1899, p. 3.

"The Passing Show." On Nat Goodwin in Clyde Fitch's *Nathan Hale*. Signed: Willa Cather. From Pittsburgh. January 21, 1899, p. 4.
See also review of Goodwin, signed "Sibert," *Leader*, November 29, 1898, p. 5.

"The Passing Show." On Julia Marlowe in *As You Like It* and *The Countess Valeska*. Signed: Willa Cather. From Pittsburgh. January 28, 1899, pp. 2–3.
See also review of *The Countess Valeska*, signed "Sibert," January 10, 1899, p. 10.

"The Passing Show." On Johnstone Bennett, Rosenthal concert, Sothern in *The King's Musketeers*. Signed: Willa Cather. From Pittsburgh. February 4, 1899, p. 3.

See also review of Sothern, signed "Sibert," *Leader*, December 20, 1898, p. 8.

"The Passing Show." On Richard Realf. Signed: Willa Cather. February 25, 1899, pp. 3–4.

See also "Genius in Mire," *Leader*, February 12, 1899, p. 20; and "Richard Realf, Poet and Soldier," signed "Helen Delay," *Home Monthly*, May 1899, pp. 10–11.

"The Passing Show." On Kipling's *A Day's Work*. Signed: Willa Cather. March 4, 1899, pp. 2–3.

See also "Books and Magazines," signed "Sibert," *Leader*, February 18, 1899, p. 5.

"The Passing Show." On Lizzie Hudson Collier in *Jane*, Maude Adams in *The Little Minister*. Signed: Willa Cather. March 18, 1899, p. 5.

"The Passing Show." On Richard Realf, Frank Norris's *McTeague*. Signed: Willa Cather. April 8, 1899, pp. 2–3.

See also review of *McTeague* in "Books and Magazines," signed "Sibert," *Leader*, March 31, 1899, p. 7.

"The Passing Show." On Rostand's *Cyrano de Bergerac*. Signed: Willa Cather. April 15, 1899, pp. 2–3.

See also review, signed "Sibert," *Leader*, March 21, 1899, p. 7.

"The Passing Show." On Mansfield as Cyrano. Signed: Willa Cather. April 22, 1899, pp. 2–3.

See also review cited in preceding entry.

"The Passing Show." On the Metropolitan Opera Company in Pittsburgh—*Lohengrin*. Signed: Willa Cather. June 10, 1899, p. 3.

"The Passing Show." On the Metropolitan Opera Company in Pittsburgh—*Die Walküre*. Signed: Willa Cather. June 17, 1899, pp. 2–3.

"The Passing Show." On the death of Augustin Daly. Signed: Willa Cather. July 1, 1899, p. 3.

"The Passing Show." On Ethelbert Nevin, titled "An Evening at Vineacre." Signed: Willa Cather. July 15, 1899, pp. 4–5.

See also "The Man Who Wrote 'Narcissus,'" signed Willa Sibert Cather, *Ladies' Home Journal*, November 1900, p. 11.

"The Passing Show." On Nethersole in *The Second Mrs. Tanqueray*. Signed: Willa Cather. July 22, 1899, pp. 5, 9.

"The Passing Show." On John Buchan's *A Lost Lady of Old Years*, Arnold Bennett's *A Man from the North*. Signed: Willa Cather. July 29, 1899, pp. 3–4.

See also review of Buchan in "Books and Magazines," signed "Sibert," *Leader*, July 22, 1899, p. 6.

"The Passing Show." On Kate Chopin's *The Awakening*, Maurice Hewlett's *The Forest Lovers*. Signed: Willa Cather. August 26, 1899, pp. 3–4.

See also review of *The Awakening*, "Books and Magazines," signed, "Sibert," *Leader*, July 8, 1899, p. 6.

"The Passing Show." On Richard Whiteing's *No. 5 John Street*. Signed: Willa Cather. September 2, 1899, pp. 3–4.

See also "Books and Magazines," signed "Sibert," *Leader*, June 17, 1899, p. 5.

"The Passing Show." On Zola's *Germinal*, Eden Phillpotts' *Children of the Mist*. Signed: Willa Cather. September 16, 1899, pp. 3–4.

See also review of Zola in "Books and Magazines," signed "Sibert," *Leader*, November 18, 1899, p. 9.

"The Passing Show." On Isobel Strong's lecture on Stevenson. Signed: Willa Cather. October 21, 1899, p. 3.

"The Passing Show." On Elia W. Peattie, Maupassant's *Strong as Death*. Signed: Willa Cather. November 4, 1899, pp. 3–4.

See also review of Maupassant, "Books and Magazines," signed "Sibert," *Leader*, October 28, 1899, p. 9.

"The Passing Show." On Hall Caine's *The Christian*, dramatized. Signed: Willa Cather. November 25, 1899, pp. 2–3.

See also review signed "Sibert," *Leader*, November 1, 1899, p. 10.

"The Passing Show." Letter to Joseph Jefferson. Signed: Willa Cather. December 2, 1899, pp. 3–4.

"The Passing Show." Letter to Lillian Nordica. Signed: Willa Cather. December 16, 1899, p. 3.

"The Passing Show." On Pinero's *Trelawney of the Wells*, Olive May. Signed: Willa Cather. December 23, 1899, p. 2.

"The Passing Show." On Joseffy and Pachmann, titled "Two Pianists." Signed: Willa Cather. December 30, 1899, p. 2.

"The Passing Show." On Clara Butt. Signed: Willa Cather. January 6, 1900, pp. 2–3.

"The Passing Show." On Frank Norris's *Blix*. Signed: Willa Cather. January 13, 1900, pp. 2–3.

See also "Books and Magazines," signed "Sibert," *Leader*, November 4, 1899, p. 5.

"The Passing Show." On Booth Tarkington's *The Gentleman from Indiana*, titled "A Popular Western Novel." Signed: Willa Cather. January 20, 1900, pp. 2–3.

See also "Books and Magazines," signed "Sibert," *Leader*, December 9, 1899, p. 9.

"The Passing Show." On Mark Hambourg, titled "The Pianist of Pure Reason." Signed: Willa Cather. January 27, 1900, p. 3.

See also "A Talk with Hambourg," signed "Sibert," *Leader*, January 7, 1900, p. 8.

"The Passing Show." On Henry Irving and Ellen Terry in *The Merchant of Venice*. Signed: Willa Cather. February 17, 1900, pp. 2–3.

"The Passing Show." On Francis Lynde's *The Helpers*, titled "A Great Denver Novel," and on Stephen Phillips' *Paolo and Francesca*, titled "England's New Dramatic Poet." Signed: Willa Cather. March 3, 1900, pp. 2–3.
See also review of *The Helpers* in "Books and Magazines," signed "Sibert," *Leader*, December 2, 1899, p. 6.

"The Passing Show." On A. E. Housman, titled "A Lyric Poet." Signed: Willa Cather. March 10, 1900, pp. 2–3.

"The Passing Show." On Jane Addams' lecture on Tolstoi. Signed: Willa Cather. March 17, 1900, pp. 3–4.

"The Passing Show." On the Kendals in *The Elder Miss Blossom*, Mary Johnston's *To Have and to Hold*. Signed: Willa Cather. March 24, 1900, p. 3.
See also review of *The Elder Miss Blossom*, signed "Sibert," *Leader*, March 13, 1900, p. 10.

"The Passing Show." On Frank Norris, titled "An Heir Apparent." Signed: Willa Sibert Cather. April 7, 1900, p. 3.

"The Passing Show." On Mrs. Fiske in *Becky Sharp*. Signed: Willa Sibert Cather. April 21, 1900, p. 3.

"The Passing Show." On *The Barber of Seville, Cavalleria Rusticana, Don Giovanni*. May 12, 1900, p. 11.

"When I Knew Stephen Crane." Article. Signed: "By Willa Sibert Cather, in the Library." July 14, 1900, pp. 4–5.
See also the *Library*, June 23, 1900, pp. 17–18.

"Comment and Commentary." On Western railroads, Ernest Seton-Thompson. Signed: Willa Sibert Cather "for the Courier." July 20, 1901, p. 3.
See also "A Modern Man," unsigned, *Home Monthly*, February 1897, p. 12.

"Observations." Editorial comment on: "Real Strike Instigators" [on the incidence of steel strikes], "Lax Denver Law" [politics and municipal corruption], "A Dramatized Omar" [George Seibel's play intended for Richard Mansfield], "Constant's Victoria" [unpopularity of Benjamin Constant's portrait of the queen], "Edward MacDowell," "A New Drought Theory," "[William M.] Chase," "Chicago Art Institute," "The Deterioration of a Composer" [Victor Herbert]. Signed: Willa Sibert Cather. August 10, 1901, pp. 1–3.

Review of Eden Phillpotts' *Sons of the Morning*. Signed: Willa Sibert Cather. August 10, 1901, p. 7.

"Observations." Editorial comment on: "Schley's Accuser" [Admiral W. S. Schley accused of cowardice by Edgar S. McClay], "A Tragedy of Environment" [on the Dowager Empress Frederick of Germany], "Small Town Funerals," "Will White or Funston?," "A New Library Line." Signed: Willa Sibert Cather. August 17, 1901, pp. 1–3.

"Observations." Editorial comment on: "With David Nation" [supporting his suit for divorce from Carry Nation], "Henry of Orleans" [on the death of the Duc d'Orléans], "The Real Homestead," "Rodin's Victor Hugo," "Train News Boys," "Forms of Food Adulteration," "J. Pierpont Morgan," "A Fore Runner" [Kipling], "Warm Praise for [Charles] Dawes" [comptroller of the currency retiring to run for the Senate], "Duse and 'Il Fuoco.'" Signed: Willa Sibert Cather. August 24, 1901, pp. 1–3.

HOME MONTHLY

"La Pucelle Again." Editorial. Unsigned. August 1896, p. 12.

Includes a reference to "Mark Twain's *Personal Recollections* [of Jeanne d'Arc], with their inimitable savor of Mississippi steamboat life and studies of Yankee character." See also *Courier*, October 5, 1895, p. 7.

"Stevenson's Monument." Article. Unsigned. September 1896, p. 3.

See also *Journal*, January 19, 1896, p. 9, and March 22, 1896, p. 9.

"Two Women the World Is Watching." Article on Mrs. William McKinley and Mrs. William Jennings Bryan. Signed: "Mary K. Hawley." September 1896, pp. 4–5.

See also "The Personal Side of William Jennings Bryan," *Library*, July 14, 1900, pp. 13–15.

"The Burns Centenary." Editorial. Unsigned. September 1896, p. 12.

See also *Journal*, May 24, 1896, p. 13.

"Nordica Has Returned." Editorial (not listed in table of contents). Unsigned. October 1896, p. 14.

See also *Journal*, December 13, 1896, p. 13.

"Prodigal Salaries to Singers." Editorial. Unsigned. October 1896, p. 14.

See also *Journal*, August 11, 1895, p. 9.

"The Origin of Thanksgiving." Article. Signed: "Helen Delay." November 1896, p. 8.

"Death of George Du Maurier." Article. Unsigned. November 1896, p. 9.

See also *Journal*, December 23, 1894, p. 13.

"The Return of the Romantic Drama." Editorial. Unsigned. November 1896, p. 12.

See also *Courier*, September 28, 1895, p. 8.

"Italo Campanini." Article (not listed in table of contents). Unsigned. December 1896, p. 11.

See also *Journal*, December 6, 1896, p. 13.

"'Ian Maclaren' as a Minister." Article. Unsigned. December 1896, p. 12. See also *Courier*, November 30, 1895, p. 6.

"Books Old and New." (Listed in table of contents as "Old Books and New.") On romances, Edna Lyall, children's classics. Signed: "Helen Delay." January 1897, p. 23.

"A Modern Man." Editorial on Prince Michael Hilkoff. Unsigned. February 1897, p. 12.

See also *Courier*, July 20, 1901, p. 3.

"Old Books and New." (Listed in table of contents as "Books Old and New.") On romances, *The Prisoner of Zenda, Treasure Island.* Signed: "Helen Delay." February 1897, p. 19.

"The Carnegie Museum." Article. Signed: Willa Cather. March 1897, pp. 1–4.

"The Passing of 'The Duchess.'" Article. Unsigned. March 1897, p. 7. Characteristic comment: "Most people read trash at some period of their lives, and 'The Duchess' trash is as harmless as new milk and as sweet as honey and the honeycomb."

"The Sultan's Musical Taste." Editorial. Unsigned. March 1897, p. 12. Characteristic comment: "We are all a good deal alike after all; the villain has his soft spots and the saint his weaknesses. Someone should send the Sultan the intermezzo from *Cavalleria Rusticana*, as everyone who cannot play at all is sure to rank that among their favorite selections." See *Journal*, December 15, 1895, p. 9.

"'Mark Twain's' Poverty." Editorial. Unsigned. March 1897, p. 12. Characteristic comment: "Recently Mr. Clemens' work has been but an echo of his old self, and he has done nothing in his old vigorous style since he wrote Pudd'nhead Wilson." See also *Leader*, February 9, 1897, p. 4.

"Old Books and New." (Listed in table of contents as "Books Old and New.") On *Kings in Exile, The Crime of Sylvestre Bonnard, Phroso.* Signed: "Helen Delay." March 1897, p. 16.

See also comments on *Sylvestre Bonnard, Journal*, April 12, 1896, p. 13.

"'Little Greece.'" Editorial. Unsigned. April 1897, p. 12.

Characteristic comment: "What a history that little country has had! The very utterance of its name calls up slendid visions of its supremacy in art and its zeal for liberty—two things that will go hand in hand until the end of time." See also review of *Going to War in Greece, Leader*, March 4, 1898, p. 8; "King George of Greece," *Home Monthly*, May 1897, p. 12; and "The Paper Age," *Home Monthly*, June 1897, p. 12.

"The Byronic Renaissance." Editorial. Unsigned. April 1897, p. 12.

See also "Old Books and New," *Home Monthly*, June 1897, p. 14.

"German Opera in Pittsburgh." Editorial. Unsigned. April 1897, p. 12.
Characteristic comment: "Lohengrin sang his adieu to his swan with a frog in his throat, and poor Frau Venus coughed upon her couch until you wondered what business she had up in wintry Germany anyway." See also *Leader*, March 4, 1897, p. 2.

"Old Books and New." (Listed in table of contents as "Books Old and New.") On *Les Misérables, A Kentucky Cardinal*. Signed: "Helen Delay." April 1897, p. 16.

"Nursing as a Profession for Women." Article. Signed: "Elizabeth L. Seymour." May 1897, p. 3.

"King George of Greece." (Title misplaced in table of contents.) Editorial. Unsigned. May 1897, p. 12.
Characteristic comment: "One thing is sure, whatever the outcome of his policy, his action on the Cretan question has proved him a man and has given him for the first time the love and sympathy of his people. . . . The Greeks are a degenerate nation, but they still demand one attribute in a man, and that is courage." See also "'Little Greece,'" *Home Monthly*, April 1897, p. 12.

"Old Books and New." On *David Copperfield*, Mark Twain, Mrs. Humphry Ward and George Eliot, the imaginative boy. Signed: "Helen Delay." May 1897, p. 18.

"Victoria's Ancestors." Article. Signed: Willa Cather. June 1897, pp. 1–4.

"The Paper Age." Editorial. Unsigned. June 1897, p. 12.
Characteristic comment: "So the war in the East has drivelled out and come to nothing, and our war correspondents Stephen Crane and Richard Harding Davis will soon be coming home again. I would rather like to see one good-sized, full-grown war occur once again, just to be sure that somewhere in the world men have convictions worth fighting for and courage enough to fight for them. In some ways the world seems to be running down at an appalling rate. . . . And yet we certainly have a better civilization, a more intelligent society than we had twenty-five years ago. But the great physical forces seem to have died out somehow. . . ." See also "'Little Greece.'" *Home Monthly*, April 1897, p. 12.

"Emma Calvé." Article. Unsigned. June 1897, pp. 13–14.
See also *Courier*, May 23, 1897, p. 13.

"Old Books and New." On Moore and Byron; a filler paragraph from the *Hesperian* gives a "simple recipe for making a novel *à la* Ouida." Signed: "Helen Delay." June 1897, p. 14.
See also *Journal*, March 8, 1896, p. 14.

"The Great Woman Editor of Paris." Article on Mme. Juliette Adam, editor of *Nouvelle Revue*. Unsigned. July 1897, p. 8.

Characteristic references to George Sand and Pierre Loti.

"Not to the Queen's Taste." Editorial on Victoria's dislike of Melba. Unsigned. July 1897, p. 12.
See also *Journal*, August 11, 1895, p. 9.

"Old Books and New." On Emerson, Hall Caine's *The Bondman*. Signed: "Helen Delay." July 1897, p. 14.
See also *Journal*, January 12, 1896, p. 9.

"Old Books and New." On Gilbert Parker's *The Seats of the Mighty*, Dickens' *A Tale of Two Cities*. Signed: "Helen Delay." September 1897, p. 14.

"Old Books and New." On Housman, Frances Hodgson Burnett's *A Lady of Quality*, Thackeray, *Alice in Wonderland*. Signed: "Helen Delay." October 1897, p. 14.
On Housman, see also *Courier*, March 10, 1900, pp. 2–3; on Burnett, see also *Journal*, June 14, 1896, p. 13.

"Old Books and New." On George Eliot's *Mill on the Floss*. Signed: "Helen Delay." November 1897, p. 14.

"Old Books and New." On William Allen White, Kipling's *Captains Courageous*. Signed: "Helen Delay." December 1897, p. 12.
See also review of *Captains Courageous*, *Leader*, October 22, 1897, p. 2.

"*The Wandering Jew*." Review of Eugène Sue's novel. Signed: "Helen Delay." December 1897, p. 19.

"Old Books and New." On S. Weir Mitchell's *Hugh Wynne: Free Quaker*, Anthony Hope's *Rupert of Hentzau*, Charlotte Brontë's *Jane Eyre*. Signed: "Helen Delay." January 1898, p. 12.
See also review of *Hugh Wynne* in *Leader*, October 15, 1897, p. 2.

"Old Books and New." On the death of Daudet, *Quo Vadis?*. Signed: "Helen Delay." February 1898, p. 12.
On Daudet, see also *Leader*, December 26, 1897, p. 16, and *Courier*, January 22, 1898, pp. 2–3.

"Richard Realf, Poet and Soldier." Article. Signed: "Helen Delay." May 1899, pp. 10–11.
See also "Genius in Mire," *Leader*, February 12, 1899, p. 20; and "The Passing Show," *Courier*, February 25, 1899, pp. 3–4, and April 8, 1899, pp. 2–3.

"Some Pittsburgh Composers." Article. Signed: "Helen Delay." December 1899, pp. 6–7.

PITTSBURG LEADER

Review of Roland Reed in *The Wrong Mr. Wright*. Unsigned. September 22, 1896, p. 9.

Review of Sol Smith Russell in *A Bachelor's Romance*. Unsigned. October 13, 1896, p. 10.

Review of Joseph Jefferson in *Rip Van Winkle*. Unsigned. November 10, 1896, p. 5.

Review of the Hollands in *A Superfluous Husband* and *Colonel Carter of Cartersville*. Signed: Willa. November 24, 1896, p. 5.

Review of Hoyt's *A Milk White Flag*. Signed: "Sibert." December 1, 1896, p. 4.

Review of *Thoroughbred*. Signed: "Sibert." December 8, 1896, p. 2.

Review of Frank Daniels in *Wizard of the Nile* by Victor Herbert. Signed: "Sibert." December 15, 1896, p. 6.

See also "The Passing Show," *Journal*, December 20, 1896, p. 13.

"Beautiful Anna Held." Signed: "Sibert." December 22, 1896, p. 6.

See also "The Passing Show," *Journal*, January 3, 1897, p. 13.

Review of James Herne's *Shore Acres*. Signed: "Sibert." December 29, 1896, p. 6.

Review of Jessie Bartlett Davis and The Bostonians in *Robin Hood*. Signed: "Sibert." January 5, 1897, p. 4.

See also "The Passing Show," *Journal*, January 17, 1897, p. 13.

Review of Otis Skinner in *A Soldier of Fortune*. Signed: "Sibert." January 12, 1897, p. 10.

Review of Fanny Davenport in *Gismonda*. Signed: "Sibert." January 19, 1897, p. 10.

See also "The Passing Show," *Journal*, January 31, 1897, p. 13.

Review of *My Friend from India*. Signed: "Sibert." January 26, 1897, p. 8.

Review of Julia Marlowe in *Romeo and Juliet*. Unsigned. February 2, 1897, p. 5.

See also "The Passing Show," *Journal*, February 14, 1897, p. 13.

Review of *Pudd'nhead Wilson*. Signed: "Sibert." February 9, 1897, p. 4.

Review of Margaret Mather in *Cymbeline*. Signed: "Sibert." February 23, 1897, p. 4.

See also "The Passing Show," *Journal*, March 7, 1897, p. 13.

Review of *The Sporting Duchess*. Signed: "Sibert." March 2, 1897, p. 6.

Review of *Lohengrin*. Signed: "A Woman Lover of Music." March 4, 1897, p. 2.

See also "The Passing Show," *Journal*, March 14, 1897, p. 13.

Review of *Tannhäuser*. Unsigned (in a prefatory note author is described as "a lady who wields a trenchant pen"). March 6, 1897, p. 6.

See also "The Passing Show," *Journal*, March 14, 1897, p. 13.

Review of Nat Goodwin in *An American Citizen*. Signed: "Sibert." March 9, 1897, p. 4.

See also "The Passing Show," *Journal*, April 4, 1897, p. 13.

Review of Nethersole in *Carmen*. Signed: "Sibert." March 16, 1897, p. 4.
See also "The Passing Show," *Journal*, March 28, 1897, p. 13.

Review of DeWolf Hopper in *El Capitan* by John Philip Sousa. Signed: "Sibert." March 23, 1897, p. 4.
See also "The Passing Show," *Journal*, April 4, 1897, p. 13.

Review of Maude Adams and John Drew in *Rosemary*. Signed: "Sibert." April 6, 1897, p. 4.
See also "The Passing Show," *Journal*, May 2, 1897, p. 13.

Review of Richard Mansfield in *The Merchant of Venice*. Signed: "Sibert." April 20, 1897, p. 9.
See also "The Passing Show," *Journal*, May 2, 1897, p. 13.

Review of Lizzie Hudson Collier in *Rosedale*. Signed: "Sibert." May 25, 1897, p. 9.
See also "The Passing Show," *Journal*, May 30, 1897, p. 13.

Review of *The People's King*. Signed: "Sibert." June 1, 1897, p. 4.

Review of *Never Again*. Signed: "Sibert." September 28, 1897, p. 4.

Review of *Divorce* by Augustin Daly. Signed: "Sibert." October 5, 1897, p. 4.

"Books and Magazines."[1] Reviews of *Tales from McClure's: Tales of Humor*, *Edgar Allan Poe: Characteristic Short Stories*, *Old Ebenezer* by Opie Read, *Hugh Wynne, Free Quaker* by S. Weir Mitchell. Unsigned. October 15, 1897, p. 2.
Parallel sentences and passages in "Old Books and New," *Home Monthly*, December 1897, p. 12, and January 1898, p. 12, and in Poe essay, *Courier*, October 12, 1895, pp. 6–7.

Review of *The Prisoner of Zenda*. Signed: "Sibert." October 19, 1897, p. 4.

"Books and Magazines." Reviews of *Captains Courageous* by Rudyard Kipling, *The Days of Jeanne d'Arc* by Mary Hartwell Catherwood. Unsigned. October 22, 1897, p. 2.
Parallel passage in "Old Books and New," *Home Monthly*, December 1897, p. 12. Characteristic phrase: "Jeanne d'Arc has been for centuries a beautiful abstraction, a misty ideal"; also characteristic references to Mark Twain and Andrew Lang. Cf. "La Pucelle Again," *Home Monthly*, August 1896, p. 12.

Review of *The Wedding Day*. Signed: "Sibert." October 26, 1897, p. 4.
See also "The Passing Show," *Courier*, November 6, 1897, p. 2.

"Anthony Hope's Lecture." Signed: "Sibert." October 30, 1897, p. 6.
See also "The Passing Show," *Courier*, November 13, 1897, pp. 2–3.

"Books and Magazines." Reviews of *For the Cause* by Stanley Weyman and "How the Greeks Were Defeated" by Frederick Palmer, *Forum* (November 1897). November 5, 1897, p. 12.

1. Books and magazine pieces given brief notices are listed in the Supplement, below.

Characteristic comments: "Mr. Stanley Weyman's tales are almost as refreshing [as Stevenson's]"; and of his style: "straightforward simplicity, ... quaint brevity and lack of exaggerated feeling." Cf. *Journal*, August 11, 1895, p. 9. On Palmer see parallel sentence in "Books and Magazines," *Leader*, March 4, 1898, p. 8: "Mr. Palmer remarks that perhaps a 'great downfall' suited the Greek officers quite as well as a great victory would have done; it gave them something to talk about and in their recitals they lost none of its dramatic possibilities."

Review of Mrs. Fiske in *Tess of the D'Urbervilles*. Signed: "Sibert." November 16, 1897, p. 11.

See also "The Passing Show," *Courier*, December 11, 1897, pp. 2–3.

"Books and Magazines." Reviews of *The Charm and Other Drawing Room Farces* by Sir Walter Besant and Walter Pollock and *The Love Affairs of Some Famous Men*. Unsigned. November 19, 1897, p. 4.

See comments on "The Charm" in "The Passing Show," *Journal*, February 23, 1896, p. 9.

Review of Belasco's *The Wife*. Signed: "Sibert." November 23, 1897, p. 8.

"Books and Magazines." Reviews of *The Latimers* by Henry McCook, *A Fountain Sealed* by Walter Besant, *Blown Away* by Richard Mansfield, *Thro' Lattice Windows* by Dr. W. J. Davidson. Unsigned. November 26, 1897, p. 4.

Parallel passage on *The Latimers* in "Old Books and New," *Home Monthly*, January 1898, p. 12. See also review of Besant's *The Changeling* in "Books and Magazines," *Leader*, November 19, 1898, p. 5.

Review of *The Sporting Duchess*. Signed: "Sibert." November 30, 1897, p. 10.

"With Nansen to the Pole." Signed: "Sibert." December 1, 1897, p. 2.

See also "The Passing Show," *Courier*, December 18, 1897, pp. 4–5.

Review of "Salt of the Earth." Signed: "Sibert." December 14, 1897, p. 4.

"Phases of Alphonse Daudet." Signed: "Sibert." December 26, 1897, p. 16.

See also "The Passing Show," *Courier*, January 22, 1898, pp. 2–3, and "Old Books and New," signed "Helen Delay," *Home Monthly*, February 1898, p. 12.

Review of *The Lost Paradise*. Signed: "Sibert." December 28, 1897, p. 4.

Review of Melba in *The Barber of Seville*. Signed: "Sibert." January 4, 1898, p. 4.

See also "The Passing Show," *Courier*, January 29, 1898, p. 2.

"Books and Magazines." Reviews of *The School for Saints* by John Oliver Hobbes (Pearl Craigie), *The Habitant* by William H. Drummond. Unsigned. January 7, 1898, p. 13.

See also review of *Tales by John Oliver Hobbes*, "Books and Magazines," signed "Sibert," March 11, 1898, p. 4.

Review of William H. Crane in *A Virginia Courtship*. Signed: "Sibert." January 11, 1898, p. 6.

Review of E. S. Willard in *Garrick* by Augustin Daly. Signed: "Sibert." January 18, 1898, p. 4.

See also "The Passing Show," *Courier*, February 26, 1898, pp. 2–3.

"Books and Magazines." Reviews of *Reminiscences of William Wetmore Story* by Mary E. Phillips, *There Is No Devil* by Marius Jokal (Maurus Jokai). Unsigned. January 28, 1898, p. 5.

"In the kingdom of art there is no God, but one God"; cf. *Journal*, March 1, 1896, p. 9. Characteristic references to "our Lady of Art" and to Horace.

"Miss Mould Talks." Interview. Unsigned. February 6, 1898, p. 5.

See also "The Passing Show," *Courier*, February 19, 1898, pp. 2–3.

Review of Vesta Tilley in vaudeville. Signed: "Sibert." March 1, 1898, p. 10.

See also "The Passing Show," *Courier*, March 19, 1898, p. 3.

"Books and Magazines." Reviews of *Going to War in Greece* by Frederick Palmer and "English as Against French Literature" by Henry D. Sedgwick, *Atlantic* (March 1898). Signed: "Sibert." March 4, 1898, p. 8.

"Books and Magazines." Reviews of *The Tales of John Oliver Hobbes* (Pearl Craigie), *The Story of Evangelina Cisneros* by Evangelina Cisneros and Karl Decker. Signed: "Sibert." March 11, 1898, p. 4.

"Books and Magazines." Review of *The Barn-Stormers* by Mrs. Harcourt Williamson. Signed: "Sibert." March 18, 1898, p. 3.

See also "The Passing Show," *Courier*, April 16, 1898, p. 3.

"Books and Magazines." Reviews of *Across the Salt Sea* by John Bloundell-Burton, *In the Midst of Life: Tales of Soldiers and Civilians* by Ambrose Bierce. Signed: "Sibert." March 25, 1898, p. 9.

Review of Mansfield in *The Devil's Disciple*. Signed: "Sibert." March 29, 1898, p. 4.

See also "The Passing Show," *Courier*, April 23, 1898, pp. 3–4.

"Books and Magazines." Reviews of *The Romance of Zion Chapel* by Richard Le Gallienne, *Woman's Bible*, Volume II, by Elizabeth Cady Stanton. Signed: "Sibert." April 8, 1898, p. 9.

"Books and Magazines." Review of *Fantasia* by George Egerton. Signed: "Sibert." April 15, 1898, p. 14.

See also "The Passing Show," *Courier*, April 30, 1898, pp. 3–4.

Review of Charles Coghlan in *The Royal Box*. Signed: "Sibert." April 19, 1898, p. 10.

See also "The Passing Show," *Courier*, April 30, 1898, pp. 3–4.

"Books and Magazines." Reviews of *A Bride of Japan* by Carlton Dawe, *Here and There and Everywhere* by Mrs. M. E. W. Sherwood. Signed: "Sibert." May 6, 1898, p. 9.

"Books and Magazines." Review of *The French Market Girl* by Emile Zola. Signed: "Sibert." May 27, 1898, p. 5.

See also review of *The Fat and the Thin*, "The Passing Show," *Journal*, February 16, 1896, p. 9.

"Books and Magazines." Review of *The Brown-Laurel Marriage* by Landis Ayr. Signed: "Sibert." June 24, 1898, p. 5.

"Books and Magazines." Review of *The Aurelian Wall and Other Poems* by Bliss Carman. Signed: "Sibert." July 22, 1898, p. 6.

Review of *The Bride Elect* by John Philip Sousa. Signed: "Sibert." October 25, 1898, p. 2.

Review of *The Tree of Knowledge*. Signed: "Sibert." November 1, 1898, p. 11.

"Books and Magazines." Review of *The Romance of the House of Savoy* by Althea Wiel. Signed: "Sibert." November 4, 1898, p. 13.

Review of Modjeska in *Mary Stuart*. Signed: "Sibert." November 15, 1898, p. 6.

"Books and Magazines." Review of *A Yankee Boy's Success* by Harry S. Morrison, *The Changeling* by Sir Walter Besant. Signed: "Sibert." November 19, 1898, p. 5.

Review of Nat Goodwin in *Nathan Hale* by Clyde Fitch. Signed: "Sibert." November 29, 1898, p. 5.

See also "The Passing Show," *Courier*, January 21, 1899, p. 4.

"Books and Magazines." Reviews of *In the Cage* by Henry James, *Plays, Pleasant and Unpleasant* by G. Bernard Shaw. Signed: "Sibert." December 2, 1898, p. 14.

"Books and Magazines." Reviews of *Dream Days* by Kenneth Grahame, *The Money Captain* by William Howard Payne, *Ashes of Empire* by Robert W. Chambers. Signed: "Sibert." December 10, 1898, p. 9.

Review of E. A. Sothern in *The King's Musketeers*. Signed: "Sibert." December 20, 1898, p. 8.

See also "The Passing Show," *Courier*, February 4, 1899, p. 3.

Review of Julia Marlowe in *The Countess Valeska*. Signed: "Sibert." January 10, 1899, p. 10.

See also "The Passing Show," *Courier*, January 28, 1899, pp. 2–3.

"Books and Magazines." Reviews of *Omar the Tentmaker* by Nathan Haskell Doyle, *The Borderlands of Society* by Charles B. Davis. Signed: "Sibert." January 20, 1899, p. 13.

Review of *Mr. Barnes of New York*. Signed: "Sibert." January 24, 1899, p. 10.

"Genius in Mire." On Richard Realf. Signed: "Sibert." February 12, 1899, p. 20.

See also "The Passing Show," *Courier*, February 25, 1899, pp. 3–4; and "Richard Realf, Poet and Soldier," signed "Helen Delay," *Home Monthly*, May 1899, pp. 10–11.

"Books and Magazines." Review of *The Day's Work* by Rudyard Kipling. Signed: "Sibert." February 18, 1899, p. 5.

See also "The Passing Show," *Courier*, March 4, 1899, pp. 2–3.

"Books and Magazines." Reviews of *The Two Standards* by William Barry, *The Maine* by Captain Charles D. Sigbee. Signed: "Sibert." March 10, 1899, p. 12.

Review of Mansfield in Rostand's *Cyrano de Bergerac*. Signed: "Sibert." March 21, 1899, p. 4.

See also "The Passing Show," *Courier*, April 15, 1899, pp. 2–3 and April 22, 1899, pp. 2–3.

"Books and Magazines." Review of Frank Norris's *McTeague*. Signed: "Sibert." March 31, 1899, p. 7.

See also "The Passing Show," *Courier*, April 8, 1899, pp. 2–3.

"Books and Magazines." Reviews of *A Daughter of the Vine* by Gertrude Atherton, *Hickery Ann and Other Girls and Boys* by Elia W. Peattie. Signed: "Sibert." April 22, 1899, p. 5.

Review of Francis Wilson in *The Little Corporal*. Signed: "Sibert." May 2, 1899, p. 2.

"Books and Magazines." Reviews of *The Perfect Wagnerite: A Commentary on the Ring of the Nibelungs* by G. Bernard Shaw and *Holland as Seen by Americans* by James H. Gore. Signed: "Sibert." May 27, 1899, p. 5.

"Books and Magazines." Reviews of *The Professor's Daughter* by Anna Farquhar, *The Wind Among the Reeds* by William Butler Yeats, *War Is Kind* by Stephen Crane. Signed: "Sibert." June 3, 1899, p. 6.

"Books and Magazines." Reviews of *The Market Place* by Harold Frederic, *Oliver Cromwell: A History* by Samuel Harraden Church. Signed: "Sibert." June 10, 1899, p. 5.

"Books and Magazines." Reviews of *No. 5 John Street* by Richard Whiteing, *More* by Max Beerbohm. Signed: "Sibert." June 17, 1899, p. 5.

See also review of *No. 5 John Street* in "The Passing Show," *Courier*, September 2, 1899, pp. 3–4.

"Books and Magazines." Review of *The Vengeance of the Female* by Marion Wilcox. Signed: "Sibert." July 1, 1899, p. 5.

"Books and Magazines." Reviews of *The Awakening* by Kate Chopin,

What Women Can Earn, and *Outsiders: An Outline* by Robert W. Chambers. Signed: "Sibert." July 8, 1899, p. 6.

See also review of *The Awakening* in "The Passing Show," *Courier*, August 26, 1899, pp. 3–4.

"Books and Magazines." Reviews of *George Borrow: Life and Correspondence* (2 vols.) by William Knapp, *A Silent Singer* by Clara Morris. Signed: "Sibert." July 15, 1899, p. 5.

"Books and Magazines." Review of *A Lost Lady of Old Years* by John Buchan. Signed: "Sibert." July 22, 1899, p. 6.

See also "The Passing Show," *Courier*, July 29, 1899, pp. 3–4.

"Books and Magazines." Reviews of *Strong as Death* by Guy de Maupassant, *The Vizier of the Two-Horned Alexander* by Frank Stockton, *The Mormon Problem* by George Seibel. Signed: "Sibert." October 28, 1899, p. 9.

See also review of *Strong as Death* in "The Passing Show," *Courier* November 4, 1899, pp. 3–4.

"Books and Magazines." Reviews of *Blix* by Frank Norris, *La Princesse lointaine* by Edmond Rostand, *Where Angels Fear to Tread* by Morgan Robertson. Signed: "Sibert." November 4, 1899, p. 5.

See also review of *Blix* in "The Passing Show," *Courier*, January 13, 1900, pp. 2–3.

Review of *The Christian* by Hall Caine. Signed: "Sibert." November 7, 1899, p. 10.

See also "The Passing Show," *Courier*, November 25, 1899, pp. 2–3.

"Books and Magazines." Review of *Active Service* by Stephen Crane. Signed: "Sibert." November 11, 1899, p. 9.

"Books and Magazines." Review of *Germinal* by Emile Zola. Signed: "Sibert." November 18, 1899, p. 9.

See also "The Passing Show," *Courier*, September 16, 1899, pp. 3–4.

"Books and Magazines." Reviews of *Cashel Byron's Profession* by G. Bernard Shaw, *Don Cosme* by Troilus Hilgarde Tyndale, *The Rubáiyát of Omar Kháyyám* translated by Mrs. H. M. Cadell, *The Future of the American Negro* by Booker T. Washington. Signed: "Sibert." November 25, 1899, p. 6.

"Books and Magazines." Review of *The Helpers* by Francis Lynde. Signed: "Sibert." December 2, 1899, p. 6.

See also "The Passing Show," *Courier*, March 30, 1900, pp. 2–3.

"Books and Magazines." Review of *The Gentleman from Indiana* by Booth Tarkington. Signed: "Sibert." December 9, 1899, p. 9.

See also "The Passing Show," *Courier*, January 20, 1900, pp. 2–3.

"Books and Magazines." Review of *The Love Affairs of a Bibliomaniac* by Eugene Field. Signed: "Sibert." December 16, 1899, p. 3.

See also "The Passing Show," *Journal*, February 23, 1896, p. 3.

"A Talk with Hambourg." Signed: "Sibert." January 7, 1900, p. 8.
See also "The Passing Show," *Courier*, January 27, 1900, p. 3.

Review of Nethersole in *Sapho*. Signed: "Sibert." January 9, 1900, p. 4.

Review of the Kendals in *The Elder Miss Blossom*. Signed: "Sibert." March 13, 1900, p. 10.
See also "The Passing Show," *Courier*, March 20, 1900, p. 3.

Supplement to "Books and Magazines"

Listed here are books and magazine stories or articles given brief notices in the columns.

October 15, 1897.
Health of Mind and Body by T. W. Topham, M.D., *In the Days of the Pioneers* by Edward S. Ellis, *The Negro and the White Man* by Bishop John Wesley Gaines.

October 22, 1897.
An African Millionaire by Grant Allen, *Herrmann, The Magician: His Life, His Secrets* by H. J. Burlingame, *The Century Book of the American Revolution* by Elbridge S. Brooks, *How to Build a Home* by Francis C. Moore, *Tales of Romance Selected from McClure's Magazine*, *The Last Three Soldiers* by William Henry Shelton, *A New Baby World* edited by Mary Mapes Dodge.

November 5, 1897.
A Girl's Ordeal by Lucy C. Lillie, *The Man Invisible* by H. G. Wells, *The God Yutzo* by Lord Gilhooley, *Hours with the Ghost* by H. R. Evans. "Good Americans" by Mrs. Burton Harrison, "The Cherub among the Gods" by Chester Bailey Fernaid, "An Imperial Dream" by Sara Y. Stevenson, *Century* (November 1897). "How the Greeks Were Defeated" by Frederick Palmer, *Forum* (November 1897). Article on Walter Saterlee, *Art Amateur* (November 1897). "Struck by a Boomerang" by Frank Stockton, *Pocket Magazine* (November 1897). Other comments on *Harper's Round Table*, *Popular Science*, *Southern States Farm Magazine*, *Athenaeum* (student magazine from University of West Virginia).

November 19, 1897.
Bird Neighbors by Nellie Blanchan, *Cupid's Game with Hearts: As Told by Documents* illustrated by Stella Wittram, *This Country of Ours* by Benjamin Harrison.

November 26, 1897.
Tales of the Real Gypsy by Paul Kester, *The Living Christ* by Paul Tyne.

January 7, 1898.

The Sinner by "Rita," *Social Facts and Forces* by Washington Gladden.

January 28, 1898.

"My Valentine" (a drawing) by Charles Dana Gibson, "The Doctor" by Hamlin Garland, *Ladies' Home Journal* (February 1898).

March 11, 1898.

A Treasury of American Verse, ed., Walter Learned, *Bladys of Stewpony* by S. Baring Gould.

March 18, 1898.

The Building of the British Empire by Alfred Thomas Story, *How to Play Golf* by H. J. Wigham, *Orderly Book of George Washington.*

March 25, 1898.

Carita: A Cuban Romance by Louis Pendleton.

April 8, 1898.

Admirals and other verses by Henry Newbolt, *Who Findeth a Wife* by William LeQuex. "The King's Jackal" by Richard Harding Davis and "The Legend of Welley Legrave" by Duncan Campbell, *Scribner's* (April 1898).

April 15, 1898.

Priscilla's Love Story by Harriet Prescott Spofford, *Last Man's Love* by Katherine Green.

May 27, 1898.

The Londoners by Robert Hichens.

June 24, 1898.

Tales from McClure's: Tales of Camp and Battlefield.

November 4, 1898.

Charles Porterfield Krauth by Adolph Spaeth, *The Town Traveler* by George Gissing, *The Christian Teacher* by Leo Tolstoi, *Departmental Ditties, the Vampires, etc.* by Rudyard Kipling, *Tales from the Heroic Ages: Siegfried and Beowulf* by Zenaide A. Ragozin, *Rex Wayland's Fortune or the Secret of the Thunderbird* by H. A. Stanley. Comment on *The Youth's Companion* (November 1898), and *Ledger Monthly.*

November 19, 1898.

Friendship and Folly by Maria Louise Poole, *Tokla* by Robert Barr, *Along the Bosphorus* by Mrs. Lew Wallace.

December 2, 1898.

A Slave to Duty and Other Women by Octave Thanet, *Tennyson: His Homes, His Friends and His Work* by Elizabeth L. Cory, *John Burnet of Barnes* by John Buchanan, *Glimpses of England* by Moses Coit Tyler, *Little Journey to the Homes of American Statesmen* by Elbert Hubbard, *Where Ghosts Walk* by Marion Harland, *Historic Towns of New England*, ed. Rev. Lyman P. Powell, *Calendar of Social Life*, *The Archie Gunn Calendar*, *Cartoons of Our War with Spain* by Charles

Nelan, *The Young Bank Messenger* by Horatio Alger, *Cowmen and Rustlers* by Edward S. Ellis.

December 10, 1898.

The Depew Story Book by Will M. Clement, *Love in Art* by Mary Knight Potter, *Angels in Art* by Clara Erskine Clement, *Etiquette for Americans*, *The Rainbow's End: Alaska* by Alice Palmer Henderson, *Out of Mulberry Street: Stories of Tenement Life in New York City* by Jacob A. Riis.

January 20, 1899.

The Seven Voices by J. Hooker Hammersly.

April 22, 1899.

Hilda by Sarah Jeannette Duncan, *Love's Dilemma* by Robert Herrick.

May 27, 1899.

Pan and the Young Shepherd by Maurice Hewlitt, *Sand'n Bushes* by Maria Louise Poole, *Carpet Courtship* by Thomas Cobb, *Some Verses* by Helen Hay, *A Short History of the United States* by Justin H. McCarthy, *The Cougar Tamer* by F. W. Calkins.

June 3, 1899.

The Silence of Love by Edmond Holmes, *When Love is Lord* by Tom Hall, *Austria* by Sidney Whitman.

June 10, 1899.

Poems by Ernest Hartley Coleridge, *Unaddressed Letters* by Frank Athelstane Sweetenham.

June 17, 1899.

Young Lives by Richard LeGallienne.

July 1, 1899.

The Island Race by Henry Newbolt, *Oliver Iverson: His Adventures in the City of New York During Four Days and Nights in April, 1890* by Ann Devoree, *A Deliverance* by Allan Monkhouse.

July 8, 1899.

The Mutineers by Arthur E. J. Legge, *Professor Hieronimus* by Amelia Skram.

July 15, 1899.

The Paths of the Prudent by J. S. Fletcher.

July 22, 1899.

The Song of America and Columbia and *The War for the Union* by Kinahan Cornwallis, *Practical Confectionery Recipes* by Professor DuNiel.

October 28, 1899.

Shakespeare's Sonnets.

November 4, 1899.

Katalogue Und Goethe Souvenir.

November 11, 1899.

The Mandate by T. Barron Russell, *Lyrics of Brotherhood* by Richard

Burton, *Little Beasts of Field and Wood* by William Everett Cram, *Things as They Are* by Boulton Hall.

November 18, 1899.

One of Cleopatra's Nights by Théophile Gautier, *The Standard Operaglasses* by Charles Annesley.

December 2, 1899.

The Golden Age by Kenneth Grahame, *The Island* by Richard Whiteing, *The Lively City O'Ligg* by Gelett Burgess, *The Circle of a Century* by Mrs. Burton-Harrison, *Smith Brunt, U.S.N.* by Waldron K. Post, *Famous Actors of To-day* by L. C. Strang, *Famous Violinists of To-day and Yesterday* by Henry C. Luhee.

December 9, 1899.

The Crown of Life by George Gissing, *The Unchanging East* by Robert Barr, *Northland Lyrics* by W. C. Roberts, Theodore Roberts and Elizabeth Roberts Macdonald.

December 16, 1899.

Gray Weather: Moorland Tales of My Own People by John Buchan, *Gulliver's Travels* by Jonathan Swift, *His Defense* by Harry Sitwell Edwards, *Father Goose: His Book*, *The Four-masted Catboat* by Charles Battell Loomis, *Little Jim Crow* by Clara Morris, *Pax Spheros* by Caroline Brooks, *Her Sailor* by Marshall Saunders, *The Loom of Destiny* by Arthur J. Stringer.

LIBRARY

"Some Personages of the Opera." Article. Signed: Willa Sibert Cather. March 24, 1900, pp. 18–20.

"Our of Their Pulpits." Article on Pittsburgh clergy. Signed: "Helen Delay." April 14, 1900, pp. 7–8.

"A Philistine in the Gallery." Article. Signed: "Goliath." April 21, 1900, pp. 8–9.

See also "The Philistine in the Art Gallery," *Gazette*, November 17, 1900, p. 6.

"One of Our Conquerors." Article. Signed: "Henry Nicklemann." June 2, 1900, pp. 3–4.

"Letters to a Playwright." Article. Signed: Willa Sibert Cather. June 9, 1900, p. 7.

"Pittsburgh Matinee Driving Club." Article on horse racing. Signed: "Henry Nicklemann." June 16, 1900, pp. 12–13.

"When I Knew Stephen Crane." Article. Signed: "Henry Nicklemann." June 23, 1900, pp. 17–18.

See also *Courier*, July 14, 1900, pp. 4–5.

"The Hottest Day I Ever Spent." Article. Signed: "George Overing." July 7, 1900, pp. 3–4.
See also "An Old River Metropolis," *Journal*, August 12, 1894, p. 13.
"The Children's Part in a Great Library." Article on Pittsburgh's Carnegie Library. Signed: "Henry Nicklemann." July 7, 1900, pp. 16–17.
"The Personal Side of William Jennings Bryan." Signed: "Henry Nicklemann." July 14, 1900, pp. 13–15.
See also "Two Women the World Is Watching," *Home Monthly*, September 1896, pp. 4–5.
"A Chinese View of the Chinese Situation." Interview. Signed: "Henry Nicklemann." July 28, 1900, pp. 16–17.
See also "Pittsburgh's Richest Chinaman," *Gazette*, June 15, 1902, Magazine section, p. 5.
"A Houseboat on Land." Article. Signed: "Henry Nicklemann." August 4, 1900, pp. 17–18.
See also "Lives in a Streetcar All Year Round," *Gazette*, August 24, 1902, Section IV, p. 2.

INDEX OF PITTSBURG LIFE

"Winter Sketches in the Capital." On the opening session of the Senate, Carreño concert, death of Senator Davis. Signed: Willa Sibert Cather. Dateline: Washington, D.C., December 20, 1900. December 22, 1900, p. 6.
See also *Journal*, December 9, 1900, p. 9, and December 16, 1900, p.19.
"Winter Sketches in the Capital." On *Hedda Gabler*. Signed: Willa Sibert Cather. Dateline: Washington, D.C., December 27, 1900. December 29, 1900, p. 14.
See also *Journal*, December 9, 1900, p. 9.
"Winter Sketches in the Capital." On the Chinese minister to the United States, Wu T'ing-fang. Signed: Willa Sibert Cather. Dateline: Washington, D.C., January 3, 1901. January 5, 1901, p. 22.
"Winter Sketches in the Capital." On Joseph Jefferson. Signed: Willa Sibert Cather. Dateline: Washington, D.C., January 10, 1901. January 12, 1901, p. 10.
See also *Journal*, January 6, 1901, p. 14.
"Winter Sketches in the Capital." On early days in Washington and Hubert Vos's racial studies. Signed: Willa Sibert Cather. Dateline: Washington, D.C., January 17, 1901. January 19, 1901, pp. 10–11.
See also *Journal*, December 30, 1900, p. 19, and January 13, 1901, p. 9.
"Winter Sketches in the Capital." On the diplomatic corps. Signed:

Willa Sibert Cather. Dateline: Washington, D.C., January 24, 1901. January 26, 1901, pp. 10–11.
See also *Journal*, January 20, 1901, p. 9.

"Winter Sketches in the Capital." On Sarah Bernhardt and Maude Adams in the title-role of Rostand's *L'Aiglon*. Dateline: Washington, D.C., January 31, 1901. February 2, 1901, pp. 10–11.
See also *Journal*, January 27, 1901, p. 9.

"Winter Sketches in the Capital." On various aspects of Washington and the White House. Signed: Willa Sibert Cather. Dateline: Washington, D.C., February 7, 1901. February 9, 1901, pp. 8–9.
See also *Journal*, February 17, 1901, p. 9.

"Winter Sketches in the Capital." On Ernest Seton-Thompson, Victor Herbert and the Pittsburgh Symphony Orchestra. Signed: Willa Sibert Cather. Dateline: Washington, D.C., February 14, 1901. February 16, 1901, p. 8.
See also *Journal*, February 10, 1901, p. 9.

"The Gridiron Club Dinner." Article. Signed: Willa Sibert Cather. Dateline: Washington, D.C., February 21, 1901. February 23, 1901, p. 12.
See also *Journal*, February 24, 1901, p. 9.

"*The Gay Lord Quex*." Review of Pinero's play. Signed: Willa Sibert Cather. Dateline: Washington, D.C., March 7, 1901. March 9, 1901, pp. 8–9.
See also *Journal*, March 10, 1901, p. 13.

"Literature in the Capital." On Helen Hay's poetry, Edna [Emma] Southworth. Signed: Willa Sibert Cather. Dateline: Washington, D.C., March 14, 1901. March 16, 1901, pp. 8–9.
See also *Journal*, March 3, 1901, p. 12.

PITTSBURGH GAZETTE

"The Philistine in the Art Gallery." Article. Signed: "Henry Nicklemann." November 17, 1901, p. 6.
See also "A Philistine in the Gallery," *Library*, April 21, 1900, pp. 8–9.

"Popular Pictures." Article. Signed: "Henry Nicklemann." November 24, 1901, p. 6.

"Pittsburgh's Mulberry Street." Article. Signed: "Henry Nicklemann." December 8, 1901, Section V, p. 5.

"The Christmas Side." Article. Signed: "Henry Nicklemann." December 22, 1901, Section IV, p. 1.

"Stage Celebrities Who Call Pittsburgh Home." Article. Signed: "Henry Nicklemann." March 2, 1902, p. 8.

"A School for Servants." Article. Signed: "Henry Nicklemann." April 13, 1902, Section IV, p. 6.

"Pittsburgh's Richest Chinaman." Article. Signed: "Henry Nicklemann." June 15, 1902, Magazine section, p. 5.
See also "A Chinese View of the Chinese Situation," *Library*, July 28, 1900, pp. 16–17.

"The Hotel Child." Article. Signed: Willa Sibert Cather. August 10, 1902, Magazine section, p. 4.

"Lives in a Streetcar All Year Round." Article. Signed: "Henry Nicklemann." August 24, 1902, Section IV, p. 2.
See also "A Houseboat on Land," *Library*, August 4, 1900, pp. 17–18.

"The Strangest Tribe of Darkest England." Article. Signed: Willa Sibert Cather. August 31, 1902, Magazine section, p. 4.
See also *Journal*, August 3, 1902, p. 11.

"Pittsburgh Authors Known to Fame." Article. Signed: "Henry Nicklemann." November 30, 1902, Literary section, pp. 20–21.

"Poets of Our Younger Generation." Article. Signed: Willa Sibert Cather. November 30, 1902, Literary section, p 24.

"The 100 Worst Books and They That Read Them." Article. Signed: Willa Sibert Cather. November 29, 1903, Literary section, pp. 11, 14.

MISCELLANEOUS

Review of *Ash Wednesday*, a farce. Unsigned. New York *Sun*, February 9, 1898, p. 7.
Probable. See text, p. 421.

Reviews of Modjeska in *Mary Stuart* and of *Way Down East*. Unsigned. New York *Sun*, February 11, 1898, p. 7.
Probable. See text, pp. 421/457–459, and note 31, The Star System (III).

"The Man Who Wrote 'Narcissus.'" Article on Ethelbert Nevin. Signed: Willa Sibert Cather. *Ladies' Home Journal*, November 1900, p. 11.
See also *Courier*, July 15, 1899, pp. 4–5.

Selected Bibliography of Works Consulted

WORKS BY WILLA CATHER

Willa Cather's Collected Short Fiction, 1892–1912. [Edited by Virginia Faulkner]. Introduction by Mildred R. Bennett. Lincoln: University of Nebraska Press, 1965.

The Kingdom of Art: Willa Cather's First Principles and Critical Statements, 1893–1896. Selected and edited with two essays and a commentary by Bernice Slote. Lincoln: University of Nebraska Press, 1967.

April Twilights (1903). Edited with an introduction by Bernice Slote. Lincoln: University of Nebraska Press, 1962; rev. ed., 1968.

The Troll Garden. New York: McClure, Phillips & Co., 1905. Reprinted in *Collected Short Fiction*.

Alexander's Bridge. Boston: Houghton Mifflin Co., 1912; new edition with a preface, 1922.
Paperback edition published by Bantam Books, 1966.

O Pioneers! Boston: Houghton Mifflin Co., 1913.
Sentinel Edition published by Houghton Mifflin, 1962.

The Song of the Lark. Boston: Houghton Mifflin Co., 1915; rev. ed., 1937.
Sentinel Edition, 1963.

My Ántonia. Boston: Houghton Mifflin Co., 1918; rev. ed., 1926.
Sentinel Edition, 1961.

Youth and the Bright Medusa. New York: Alfred A. Knopf, Inc., 1920.

One of Ours. New York: Alfred A. Knopf, Inc., 1922.

A Lost Lady. New York: Alfred A Knopf, Inc., 1923.

April Twilights and Other Poems. New York: Alfred A. Knopf, Inc., 1923.

The Professor's House. New York: Alfred A. Knopf, Inc., 1925.

My Mortal Enemy. New York: Alfred A. Knopf, Inc., 1926.
Vintage Book edition published by Knopf, 1961.

Death Comes for the Archbishop. New York: Alfred A. Knopf, Inc., 1927.

Shadows on the Rock. New York: Alfred A. Knopf, Inc., 1931.

Obscure Destinies. New York: Alfred A. Knopf, Inc., 1932.

Lucy Gayheart, New York: Alfred A. Knopf, Inc., 1935.

Not Under Forty. New York: Alfred A. Knopf, Inc., 1936.

Sapphira and the Slave Girl. New York: Alfred A. Knopf, Inc., 1940.

The Old Beauty and Others. New York: Alfred A. Knopf, Inc., 1948.

Willa Cather on Writing. New York: Alfred A. Knopf, Inc., 1949.

"Plays of Real Life." *McClure's* 40 (March 1913), 70–72.

"Three American Singers." *McClure's* 42 (December 1913), 33–48.

"New Types of Acting." *McClure's* 42 (March 1914), 51.

"Uncle Valentine." *Woman's Home Companion* 52 (February, March 1925), 7–9, 86, 89–90; 15–16, 75–76, 79–80.

(*Manuscript materials*)

Letters at the Nebraska State Historical Society, Lincoln, Nebraska

Letters at the Willa Cather Pioneer Memorial and Educational Foundation, Red Cloud, Nebraska

Letters in the possession of Mrs. George Seibel, Capitola, California

BIBLIOGRAPHY

WRITINGS ABOUT WILLA CATHER

Bennett, Mildred R. *The World of Willa Cather*. New edition with notes and index. Lincoln: University of Nebraska Press, 1961.

Brown, E. K. *Willa Cather: A Critical Biography*. Completed by Leon Edel. New York: Alfred A. Knopf, Inc., 1953.

Giannone, Richard. *Music in Willa Cather's Fiction*. Lincoln: University of Nebraska Press, 1968.

Kates, George N. Introduction and commentary in *Willa Cather in Europe: Her Own Story of the First Journey*. New York: Alfred A. Knopf, Inc., 1956.

Lewis, Edith. *Willa Cather Living: A Personal Record*. New York: Alfred A. Knopf, Inc., 1953.

Moorhead, Elizabeth. *These Two Were Here: Louise Homer and Willa Cather*. Pittsburgh: University of Pittsburgh Press, 1950.

Sergeant, Elizabeth Shepley. *Willa Cather: A Memoir*. Lincoln: University of Nebraska Press, 1963.

Shively, James R. Introduction to *Writings from Willa Cather's Campus Years*. Lincoln: University of Nebraska Press, 1950.

Adams, Frederic B., Jr. "Willa Cather." *Colophon* 3 (September 1939), 90.

Bennett, Mildred R. "Willa Cather in Pittsburgh." *Prairie Schooner* 33 (Spring 1959), 64–76.

Hinz, John P. "Willa Cather in Pittsburgh." *New Colophon* 3 (1950), 198–207.

Kates, George N. "Willa Cather's Unfinished Avignon Story." In *Five Stories: with an article . . . on Miss Cather's Last, Unfinished, and Unpublished Avignon Story*, pp. 177–214. New York: Vintage Books, 1952.

Seibel, George. "Miss Willa Cather from Nebraska." *New Colophon* 2, Part 7 (1949), 195–208.

Slote, Bernice. "Stephen Crane and Willa Cather." *The Serif* 6 (December 1969), 3–15.

———. "Willa Cather." In *Fifteen Modern American Authors: A Survey of Research and Criticism*, edited by Jackson R. Bryher, pp. 23–62. Durham, N.C.: Duke University Press, 1969.

———. "Willa Cather Reports Chautauqua." *Prairie Schooner* 43 (Spring 1969), 117–128.

OTHER WORKS CONSULTED

Archer, William. *The Theatrical 'World' of 1897*. London: William Scott, Ltd., 1898.

Baldwin, Leland D. *Pittsburgh: The Story of a City*. Pittsburgh: University of Pittsburgh Press, 1937.

Brooks, Van Wyck. *The Confident Years: 1885–1915*. New York: E. P. Dutton & Co., 1952.

Burroughs, Marie. *The Marie Burroughs Art Portfolio of Stage Celebrities*. Chicago: A. N. Marquis Co., 1894.

Chapman, John and Garrison P. Sherwood, eds. *The Best Plays of 1894–1899*. New York: Dodd, Mead & Co., 1955.

Cordell, Richard A. *Henry Arthur Jones and the Modern Drama*. New York: Ray Long and Richard R. Smith, Inc., 1932.

Duffey, Bernard. *The Chicago Renaissance in American Letters*. East Lansing: Michigan State College Press, 1934.

Eaton, Quaintance. *Opera Caravan: Adventures of the Metropolitan on Tour, 1883–1956*. New York: Farrar, Straus & Co., 1957.

Felheim, Marvin. *Theater of Augustin Daly: An Account of the Late Nineteenth Century American Stage*. Cambridge: Harvard University Press, 1956.

Grosvenor, Gilbert. *The National Geographic Society and Its Magazines*. 3rd ed. Washington, D.C.: National Geographic Society, 1948. Reprinted from Cumulative Index to the *National Geographic Magazine*, 1899–1946.

Hapgood, Norman. *The Stage in America, 1897–1900*. New York: Macmillan Co., 1901.

Hart, James D. *The Popular Book: A History of America's Literary Taste*. New York: Oxford University Press, 1950.

Hartnoll, Phyllis, ed. *The Oxford Companion to the Theatre*. London: Oxford University Press, 1950.

Hewitt, Bernard Wolcott, *Theatre U.S.A., 1668–1957*. New York: McGraw-Hill Book Co., 1959.

Hibbert, Henry George. *The Theatrical World of 1896*. London: Walter Scott, Ltd., 1897.

Hornblow, Arthur. *A History of the Theatre in America*. 2 vols. Philadelphia: J. B. Lippincott Co., 1919.

Hughes, Glenn. *A History of the American Theatre, 1700–1950*. New York: Samuel French, Inc., 1951.

Huneker, James. *Steeplejack*, 2 vols. New York: Charles Scribner's Sons, 1922.

Kolodin, Irving. *The Story of the Metropolitan Opera, 1883–1950*. New York: Alfred A. Knopf, Inc., 1953.

Mantle, Burns and Garrison P. Sherwood, eds. *The Best Plays of 1899–1909*. New York: Dodd, Mead & Co., 1944.

McKay, Frederic Edward, ed. *Famous American Actors of Today*. New York: Crowell, 1896.

Morris, Lloyd R. *Curtain Time: History of the American Theatre*. New York: Random House, 1953.

Mott, Frank Luther. *Golden Multitudes.* New York: Macmillan Co., 1947.

———. *A History of American Magazines.* 4 vols. Cambridge: Harvard University Press, 1957.

Nicoll, Allardyce. *A History of English Drama, 1660–1900.* Vol. VI *Alphabetical Catalogue of the Plays.* 6 vols. Cambridge: Cambridge University Press, 1959.

Odell, George C. D. *Annals of the New York Stage to 1894.* Vol. XV (1891–1894). 15 vols. New York: Columbia University Press, 1927–1949.

Quinn, Arthur Hobson. *American Fiction: An Historical and Critical Survey.* New York: D. Appleton-Century Co., 1936.

———. *A History of the American Drama.* Vol. II *From the Civil War to the Present Day.* 2 vols. 2nd ed. New York: Appleton-Century-Crofts, 1945.

Russell, Charles E. *Julia Marlowe: Her Life and Art.* New York: D. Appleton & Co., 1927.

Smith, Cecil. *Musical Comedy in America.* New York: Theatre Art Books, 1950.

Spiller, Robert E., Willard Thorp, Thomas H. Johnson, and Henry Seidel Canby, eds. *Literary History of the United States.* New York: Macmillan Co., 1953.

Strang, Lewis C. *Famous Actors of the Day in America.* 2nd series. Boston: L. C. Page & Co., 1902.

———. *Famous Actresses of the Day.* Boston: L. C. Page & Co., 1899.

———. *Players and Plays of the Last Quarter Century.* 2 vols. Boston: L. C. Page & Co., 1902.

Thompson, Vance. *Life of Ethelbert Nevin.* Boston: Boston Music Co., 1913.

Towse, John Ranken. *Sixty Years of the Theater: An Old Critic's Memories.* New York: Funk & Wagnalls Co., 1916.

Winter, William. *The Wallet of Time.* 2 vols. New York: Moffat, Yard & Co., 1913.

Acknowledgments

During my years of work on these volumes I have accumulated debts to a number of persons. My first thanks go to the late Frederick J. Hoffman, who directed my attention to the journalistic writings of Willa Cather. The late Elsie M. Cather, in a memorable conversation, gave me much valuable information, and Mrs. George Seibel has graciously permitted me to read and cite Willa Cather's letters to her and to her husband. Like all Cather scholars, I am indebted to Mildred R. Bennett and Bernice Slote for their research and publications bearing on Willa Cather's early life, and I have enjoyed the stimulus of discussions with them. I am further indebted to Professor Slote and to Professor James Woodress for reading The World and the Parish in manuscript and calling my attention to a number of errors. I wish also to thank my assistants, Frank Larose, who helped gather biographical detail on many of the persons mentioned, and Judith Opacki, who aided me in editorial details.

For their assistance in many ways, I am indebted to the staffs of the University of Wisconsin Library, the University of Illinois Library, especially to Helen Welch and Eva Fay Benton, the University of Nebraska Libraries, the Nebraska State Historical Society Library, the Henry E. Huntington Library and Art Gallery, the Carnegie Library of Pittsburgh, and the Willa Cather Pioneer Memorial and Educational Foundation.

This study was facilitated by a grant from the Penrose Fund of the American Philosophical Society in 1963. My work was immeasurably aided by two Faculty Summer Fellowships granted to me in 1960 and 1966 by the University of Illinois Research Board and by assistance in preparation of the manuscript afforded by these grants and by the English Department of the University of Illinois. In addition, I am indebted to the English Department and to Robert W. Rogers, F. Leonard Dean, and A. Lynn Altenbernd for funds for research and travel.

I want to acknowledge also a special debt to the publishers, whose care and guidance helped me to make this work a better one than I could have made alone. The index was prepared by Kathleen Mary Dillon Brennan, and most of the manuscript was typed, patiently and well, by Martha Baxter, Beverly Johnson, Alva Bishop, and Viola Kaufman. My most important debt is to my wife: researcher, typist, editor, critic. I am solely responsible, however, for any errors these volumes may contain.

W. M. C.

Index

❈ ❈ ❈